TOOLS & TECHNIQUES

Brought to you by the publisher of Tax Facts

8TH EDITION

FINANCIAL PLANNING

LEIMBERG
SATINSKY
DOYLE
JACKSON

ISBN: 978-0-87218-932-4
Library of Congress Control Number: 2007931585

This publication is designed to provide accurate and authoritative information in regard to the subject matter covered. It is sold with the understanding that the publisher is not engaged in rendering legal, accounting or other professional service. If legal advice or other expert assistance is required, the services of a competent professional person-should be sought. – From a Declaration of Principles jointly adapted by a Committee of The American Bar Association and a Committee of Publishers and Associations.

Circular 230 Notice – The content in this publication is not intended or written to be used, and it cannot be used, for the purposes of avoiding U.S. tax penalties.

published by

THE NATIONAL UNDERWRITER COMPANY

The National Underwriter Company
P.O. Box 14367
Cincinnati, Ohio 45250-0367

Eighth Edition

Printed in the United States of America

DEDICATIONS

Stephan R. Leimberg

To my wife, Jo-Ann Leimberg, my daughters, Charlee and Lara,
my sons-in-law, Rob and Oded,
and to my grandsons, Max and Aaron
I love you all so very much!

Martin J. Satinsky

To Marcia

Robert J. Doyle, Jr.

To Kathy, my loving and understanding wife,
and to my three principal inspirations,
Erin, Stevie, and Bob

Michael Jackson

To my wife Maria, for her unwavering support.
To my son Jared, for his continuing
inspiration. I love you both!

ABOUT THE AUTHORS

Stephan R. Leimberg

Stephan R. Leimberg is CEO of LISI, Leimberg Information Services, Inc., a provider of e-mail/internet news and commentary for professionals on recent cases, rulings, and legislation; CEO of Leimberg and LeClair, Inc., an estate and financial planning software company; and President of Leimberg Associates, Inc., a publishing and software company in Bryn Mawr, Pennsylvania.

Leimberg is the author of numerous books on estate, financial, and employee benefit and retirement planning and a nationally known speaker. Leimberg is the creator and principal author of the entire nine book *Tools and Techniques* series including *The Tools and Techniques of Estate Planning, The Tools and Techniques of Financial Planning, The Tools and Techniques of Employee Benefit and Retirement Planning, The Tools and Techniques of Life Insurance Planning, The Tools and Techniques of Charitable Planning, The Tools and Techniques of Income Tax Planning, The Tools and Techniques of Investment Planning, The Tools and Techniques of Risk Management, and The Tools and Techniques of Practice Management*. Leimberg is co-author, with noted attorney Howard Zaritsky, *Tax Planning with Life Insurance, The Book of Trusts, 4th Edition* with attorneys Charles K. Plotnick and Daniel Evans, and *How to Settle an Estate* with Charles K. Plotnick.

Leimberg is creator or co-creator of many software packages for the financial services professional including *NumberCruncher* (estate planning), DeCoupleCruncher (estate planning in decoupled estates), *IRS Factors Calculator* (actuarial computations), *Financial Analyzer II, Estate Planning Quickview* (Estate Planning Flow Charts), *Toward a Zero Estate Tax* (PowerPoint Estate Planning Client Seminar), *Gifts That Give, Gifts That Give Back* (PowerPoint Client Charitable Planning Seminar), and Long-Term Care (PowerPoint Client Seminar).

A nationally known speaker, Professor Leimberg has addressed the Miami (Heckerling) Estate Planning Institute, the NYU Tax Institute, the Notre Dame Law School and Duke University Law School's Estate Planning Conference, The American Bar Association Planning Techniques for Large Estate and Sophisticated Planning Techniques courses of study, the National Association of Estate Planners and Councils, and the AICPA's National Estate Planning Forum. Leimberg has also spoken to the Federal Bureau of Investigation, and the National Aeronautics and Space Administration.

Leimberg was named 1998 Edward N. Polisher Lecturer of the Dickinson School of Law, and was awarded the Excellence in Writing Award of the American Bar Association's Probate and Property Section. He has been honored as Estate Planner of the Year by the Montgomery County Estate Planning Council and as Distinguished Estate Planner by the Philadelphia Estate Planning Council. He is also a recipient of the President's Cup of the Philadelphia Life Underwriters, a two time Boris Todorovitch Lecturer, and the first Ben Feldman Lecturer.

Martin J. Satinsky

Marty Satinsky, CPA/PFS, J.D., LL.M., AEP, has been providing tax and financial planning services to individuals and businesses for over thirty years. He has worked with regional and international accounting firms, including seven years as a tax partner with Coopers & Lybrand. Mr. Satinsky currently practices in his own accounting firm.

As a partner in the accounting firm of Smart and Associates, LLP, Mr. Satinsky specialized in tax consulting for high net worth individuals and closely-held businesses. As Director of Professional Development, he was also responsible for the Firm's training and Continuing Professional Education (CPE) program through Smart University.

An accomplished author on personal financial matters, he has co-authored seven books on income and estate taxes and personal financial planning, including the popular "Tools and Techniques of Income Tax Planning".

Mr. Satinsky was also a founding shareholder of Second Opinion Financial Services, Inc. (SOFS) a company with a focus on educating professionals on the use and mechanics of life insurance. SOFS developed a software program that dynamically illustrated the impact of the variables affecting the performance of life insurance products.

A frequent lecturer, Mr. Satinsky has also been an instructor at the American College, Temple University Law

School, Georgetown University Law School, Syracuse University Law School, the University of Pennsylvania, and Philadelphia University.

A graduate of the Pennsylvania State University and the Law School of the University of Pennsylvania, he also received his Master of Law degree in Taxation from Temple University Law School.

He is a Certified Public Accountant in Pennsylvania and has been admitted to the Pennsylvania Bar. He is a member of the American Institute of Certified Public Accountants, and the Pennsylvania Institute of Certified Public Accountants, as well as the American Bar Association and the Philadelphia Bar Association. He has served as an officer of the Philadelphia Estate Planning Council and as a member of the AICPA Personal Financial Planning Executive Committee and the PICPA Personal Financial Planning Committee.

Mr. Satinsky has conducted numerous seminars on tax, estate planning and financial planning topics, including many presentations on life insurance issues, for such organizations, as the Pennsylvania Bar Institute, the AICPA, PICPA, FPA NAPFA, Accountants' Continuing Education Network, CLE Options, and several Estate Planning Councils. In 2000, he was honored with the Distinguished Estate Planner Award by the Philadelphia Estate Planning Council and in 2006 he received the Distinguished Accredited Estate Planner Award from the National Association of Estate Planners and Councils.

Mr. Satinsky is a past Chairman of the Jewish Community Centers of Greater Philadelphia and is an emeritus member of its Board. He has also served as the Treasurer of Hillel of Greater Philadelphia and a member of the Board of Jewish Community Center Association and the Maccabi Continental Games Board. He has been active with the Federation of Jewish Agencies in Philadelphia, Washington, D.C. and Syracuse, N.Y., and is now serving on the Board of Directors of the Gordon Jewish Community Center of Nashville and Temple Sherith Israel.

Robert J. Doyle, Jr.

Robert J. Doyle, Jr. is an independent financial consultant, writer and speaker, and software developer specializing in executive compensation, retirement planning, investment and insurance tax planning, business valuation, and business continuation planning. He is currently affiliated with Surgent McCoy CPE in Devon, Pennsylvania, as a writer and speaker. Surgent McCoy CPE is a publisher of continuing professional education courses for CPAs. It is the largest vendor in the United States of continuing professional CPA education courses in the topic areas of taxation and advisory services.

Prior to his affiliation with Surgent McCoy CPE, Mr. Doyle was Senior Vice President of Mandeville Financial Services, Inc., a diversified insurance, real estate, employee benefits, and executive compensation consulting firm and life insurance agency. Before joining Mandeville Financial Services, Mr. Doyle spent 15 years as Associate Professor of Finance and Insurance at The American College where he was responsible for courses in retirement and wealth accumulation planning in the College's CLU and ChFC professional designation programs. Mr. Doyle also has served as Adjunct Professor of Taxation in the graduate tax program of Widener University Graduate School of Management where he has taught courses in taxation of investments and taxation for financial planning and Adjunct Professor of Finance in the Haub School of Business at St. Josephs' University where he has taught courses on pensions and benefits and personal financial planning.

He is an author or co-author of over a dozen books and monographs including *The Tools & Techniques of Investment Planning*, *The Tools & Techniques of Life Insurance Planning*, *Can You Afford to Retire?* and *Solutions Handbook for Personal Financial Planning, Business Planning, Employee Benefits, Estate Planning*. He has written and presented numerous professional education courses for CPAs for Surgent McCoy CPE on tax, retirement, investment, business, and other financial planning topics. Beyond his book and education courses, Mr. Doyle has published nearly fifty articles in the academic, professional, and trade press and he has appeared as a financial planning expert on radio and television talk shows around the country.

In addition to speaking at dozens of conferences sponsored by The American College and at several hundred CPA continuing education seminars, Mr. Doyle has addressed audiences in regional and national conferences sponsored by The Widener Tax Institute, The International Association of Financial Planners, The Institute of Certified Financial Planners, Commerce Clearing House, The American Society of CLU & ChFC, TIAA-CREF, and a number of state CPA Institutes. He has spoken before dozens of chapters of The American

Society of CLU & ChFC and numerous regional Estate Planning Councils as well as various community groups and charitable organizations.

Mr. Doyle did his graduate study as a Huebner Fellow at the Wharton School of the University of Pennsylvania. He holds the MA and MBA degrees from Wharton, a BA from Macalester College, is a CLU and a Chartered Financial Consultant (ChFC).

Mr. Doyle resides in Wayne, Pennsylvania with his wife, Kathryn, and their three children.

Michael S. Jackson

Michael S. Jackson, CPA/PFS, M.T., has provided tax compliance and consulting services to closely held business and high net worth individual clients for over 15 years. Mr. Jackson is currently a Senior Manager in the tax department of Smart and Associates, LLP in Devon, Pennsylvania. Over the last ten years, he expanded his services into fee-based personal financial planning and is certified as a Personal Financial Specialist by the American Institute of Certified Public Accountants.

Prior to joining Smart and Associates, Mr. Jackson moved to Martin J. Satinsky & Associates, P.C in 1993 to serve as a tax and financial planning manager after spending three years as a senior accountant in the Philadelphia tax department of Ernst & Young, LLP. He joined Isdaner & Company in 1999 as part of its merger with Martin J. Satinsky & Associates. At Isdaner & Company, Mr. Jackson worked as a manager in the firm's tax department and provided a diverse range of professional tax and financial planning services to his clients. While at Ernst & Young, he spent the majority of his time with the Entrepreneurial Services Group specializing in S corporation, partnership and individual tax consulting and compliance.

Mr. Jackson received his Masters Degree in Taxation from Villanova University School of Law. He graduated Magna Cum Laude from Drexel University with a Bachelor of Science in Business Administration, majoring in accounting and finance. As a student, he participated in internships in the tax departments of Fishbein & Company and Arthur Young.

Mr. Jackson is a Certified Public Accountant in Pennsylvania and a member of the American Institute of Certified Public Accountants and Pennsylvania Institute of Certified Public Accountants. He has been a frequent lecturer of tax and financial planning topics for various organizations, written for a number of publications and has been a monthly columnist for the Suburban and Wayne Times.

Case Writers

Michael E. Kitces, MSFS, CFP®, CLU, ChFC is Director of Financial Planning for Pinnacle Advisory Group, a private wealth management firm located in Columbia, Maryland. He graduated Magna Cum Laude and Phi Beta Kappa from Bates College with a Bachelor of Science in Psychology with Honors, earned a Master of Science in Financial Services from the American College, and holds numerous designations and certificates. Michael has written on and been quoted regarding numerous topics in the Financial Planning and Financial Services fields. He is a Moderator for the professional discussion boards on Financial Planning Interactive, and is an active member of the Financial Planning Association of Maryland. In his spare time, Michael studies (in addition to his textbooks) Hapkido and Ju-Jitsu, Ballroom Dancing, is an active bridge player and is the Managing Director of Washington Improv Theater (WIT).

Angie Herbers is founder of Financial Advisor Resource Inc., a practice management and consulting firm that helps financial planners and corporations develop career development tracks to attract and retain the next generation of financial planning talent. Throughout her career, Angie has worked with over 200 financial professionals. She uses her entrepreneurial spirit and business ownership experience to help others make proactive and strategic business decisions. Angie's work has appeared in the *NAPFA Advisor*, *Investment Advisor*, *Solutions*, *Ticker*, *Journal of Financial Planning*, *Advisor Today*, the *Journal of Personal Finance*, *Bloomberg Wealth Manager* and *Financial Planning*. Angie has a Bachelor of Science in Personal Financial Planning and a minor in Business Administration from Kansas State University, a CFP-registered university program. Angie is an active member of the Financial Planning Association and serves on the National Career Development task force. Angie can be contacted at www.FinancialAdvisorResource.com.

PREFACE TO THE EIGHTH EDITION

In the few short years since the Seventh Edition was published much of the world as we knew it has irrevocably changed – and yet much has remained the same.

The tax law has changed – and we have continued to expand and update TOOLS AND TECHNIQUES OF FINANCIAL PLANNING for all those tax law changes affecting it.

The book was carefully edited for tax law changes by these exceptionally competent tax attorneys on the staff of The National Underwriter Company's Professional Publishing Division: John H. Fenton, J.D., M.S.B.A., Sonya E. King, J.D., LL.M.; Deborah A. Miner, J.D., CLU, ChFC; Joseph F. Stenken, J.D., CLU, ChFC; and William J. Wagner, J.D., LL.M., CLU.

More importantly, the tools and techniques of financial planning have changed. There are now many new ways to help clients prepare for the costs of their children's education and for their own retirement. Segmented planning, a concentration on specific, immediate, and intermediate goals such as education funding, retirement funding, disability funding, and post death liquidity funding, is now the term of preference in the profession.

Economics have changed. Economic upturns, a recession, relatively low – and currently stable - interest rates, and the mergers, acquisitions and bankruptcies (and even re-bankruptcies) of many major financial institutions since the last edition have alerted clients as well as planners of the importance of investment management, diversification, and constant asset appropriateness checks.

Computers and computer graphics have become more useful as communications and persuasions tools; a simple pie or bar chart conveys in a millisecond what columns of numbers take minutes, hours, or never succeed in transmitting. This edition contains dozens of such graphs to make the point to planners who in turn can learn by experiencing that "seeing is believing," that graphics "quicken" understanding, and share that illumination with others.

Our sister books have changed. At one time, there was only THE TOOLS AND TECHNIQUES OF ESTATE PLANNING. Now there are many other sibling texts, the newest of which will be THE TOOLS AND TECHNIQUES OF RETIREMENT INCOME PLANNING and THE TOOLS AND TECHNIQUES OF DIVORCE PLANNING. There are also substantial revisions and updates to our books, THE TOOLS AND TECHNIQUES OF EMPLOYEE BENEFIT AND RETIREMENT PLANNING, THE TOOLS AND TECHNIQUES OF LIFE INSURANCE PLANNING, THE TOOLS AND TECHNIQUES OF CHARITABLE PLANNING, and THE TOOLS AND TECHNIQUES OF PRACTICE MANAGMENT. Financial planners seeking easily accessible information in those areas will find a familiar chapter format and writing style with all the essential information on a topic in one place.

The concentration of wealth has changed; more wealth than imaginable in past periods has been amassed in a relatively few hands—and the gap between the ultra wealthy and the merely affluent is widening almost as much as the vast divide between the average American and those in the top two percent of the income and asset ranges. This convergence will have many implications.

So many things have changed. Therefore the need for this Eighth edition of TOOLS AND TECHNIQUES OF FINANCIAL PLANNING.

Yet so many things have remained the same.

The need for a planner to continue to study and learn new concepts remains. And the challenge of keeping current with respect to new products and the tax laws that affect them has changed only in that it is more difficult than ever.

The need for a planner to understand the person – as well as the statement of financial condition, as Dr. Jerald W. Mason, then education director for the International Association for Financial Planning, called it – is more important than ever.

As we learned so painfully from the Wall Street scandals, Enron, Worldcom, and Global Crossing and others, and the tax shelter scandals involving the accounting and legal professions, the need for honesty and objectivity and ethics and competence is greater than ever. Ethical backbone and intellectual integrity will prove to be one of the most important attributes of the planner in the coming decade.

The need to seek out and solve other people's problems remains—as does the need to impress clients with the significance and urgency of action; what we call the "money value of time."

Our goals in writing this book have not changed. We want to help professionals help individuals and businesses obtain and retain financial dignity and achieve their economic dreams.

My co-authors and I invite you to share in our knowledge and experience—and to feel free to give us more feedback so that we can make the ninth edition more useful to you.

STEPHAN R. LEIMBERG

ABOUT THE TOOLS AND TECHNIQUES OF FINANCIAL PLANNING

Financial planning is fascinating and challenging (not only to the novice – but also to the seasoned professional) because it involves the interplay between clients, those they love, their personal and financial goals, the myriad of barriers to reaching those goals, and the tools and techniques and other resources available to meet those objectives.

No two people, or set of problems, are ever the same. There are no perfect solutions either. Clients must understand that there are no "cost free" or "instant" ways to become—or stay—rich. Every transaction has costs or downsides, and each suggestion the planner makes must be measured against that cost. Long-term holistic goals must be weighed against much easier to see and much more simplistic and obvious short-term results.

In other words, financial planning is much more than merely accumulating as much property or income as possible; it is far more complex because people and their relationship to each other, to their property, and to their objectives are involved.

Nor is there a "quick fix" route to learning financial planning. The field is constantly changing, vast, and affected directly and indirectly (and sometimes in uncertain ways) by a multiplicity of factors.

THE OBJECTIVES OF TOOLS AND TECHNIQUES

The objectives of this book are to provide the reader with accurate, up-to-date, highly practical, lucid, comprehensive, and holistic information on a wide range of financial planning tools and techniques.

Through our unique format (one concept at a time – with all aspects of that subject explained in one place), we have striven to accomplish these objectives in a succinct yet creative manner useful to the layman or novice. *The Tools and Techniques of Financial Planning* is a "briefcase essential" for even the most sophisticated and seasoned planner who wishes to review and update knowledge of basic investment products and concepts and the impact of tax law on these. It can also be an invaluable aid to any planner who needs a well-organized approach for explaining financial planning tools and techniques to individual clients (or to potential clients in seminars) and who is concerned with client-suitability of the products and services he offers.

The *NumberCruncher* Estate and Financial Planning software (610-924-0515 or http://www.leimberg.com) were used to produce some of the illustrations in this book. Readers will find LISI, Leimberg Information Services at http://www.leimbergservices.com, a highly useful tool for keeping current and obtaining nationally recognized experts' commentary on recent tax law cases and rules involving financial planning. Each week, nationally recognized financial guru and Tools and Techniques author, Dr. Robert T. LeClair, provides a unique insight into developments in finance and the world's markets.

WHO WILL FIND THE BOOK USEFUL

Every present and aspiring member of the financial planning team will find *The Tools and Techniques of Financial Planning* useful, including bankers, stockbrokers, accountants, attorneys, instructors and students of financial planning courses at colleges and universities, instructors and students of adult education and personal finance courses, law schools, CPA firms, insurance agents, paraprofessionals, and even sophisticated clients.

CONTENTS

Part 1: Principles and Processes

Part 2: Financial Planning Concepts

Part 3: Fundamentals

Part 4: Legal

Part 5: Major Disciplines

Case Studies

Appendices

Part 1:

PRINCIPLES AND PROCESSES

Chapter 1

WHAT IS FINANCIAL PLANNING?

In the purest sense, financial planning is, quite simply, *cash flow planning*. It is planning to have available the amount of cash needed at the time it is needed (or in the hands of the desired person) to accomplish an individual's financial goals.

The steps taken to implement a financial plan will be in response to these cash flow goals. For example, if a couple is currently retired and their only source of cash to maintain their lifestyle is the limited investments in their Individual Retirement Accounts (IRAs), those investments will need to be structured more for current income and less for appreciation. On the other hand, if the couple is comfortable that they have more than enough assets to handle their personal financial needs for the rest of their lives, they may allocate more of their investments for growth in order to enhance their ultimate bequests to their children or to charity.

Financial planning can also be defined as

1. creating order out of chaos
2. a deliberate and continuing process by which a sufficient amount of capital is accumulated and conserved and adequate levels of income are attained to accomplish the financial and personal objectives of the client
3. the development and implementation of coordinated plans for the achievement of a client's overall financial objectives
4. income tax planning, retirement planning, estate planning, investment and asset allocation planning, and risk management planning

Select one of the above, or select all. There seems to be no one universally accepted definition of what financial planning is. That's understandable since the planner's role must be as different as the needs of clients and their ability or willingness to pay for advice. No two people or problems will ever be exactly the same.

For many clients, the creation of a simple and workable system that will help them control their cash and pay their bills on time will be highly successful financial planning. For others, successful financial planning will involve the full time efforts of a planner, staff, and sophisticated computer and administrative support. Most planners will be working with clients whose needs fall somewhere between these two extremes.

The financial problems our clients face in their lives can be categorized by the letters L-I-V-E-S.

L. LACK OF LIQUIDITY – Liquidity is the possession of sufficient cash and/or income to pay bills, debts, taxes, and other expenses on time. A lack of liquidity is the inability to quickly turn invested capital into spendable cash without incurring unreasonable cost. This problem can result in a forced sale of assets at pennies on the dollar. For instance, if a client must sell stocks or mutual fund shares in a "down market," or if an executor must sell a valuable real estate portfolio to pay federal or state death taxes and administrative expenses, the buyer will offer to pay the lowest possible price for the most precious asset. This forced sale often becomes a "fire sale," a loss of prime growth or income producing assets at a fraction of their real value.

I. INADEQUATE RESOURCES – Insufficient capital or income in the event of death, disability, at retirement, or for special needs such as college or preparatory school or to provide needed services for a handicapped child.

I. INFLATION – Not enough has been done to "inflation proof" the client's portfolio. Figure 1.1 emphasizes the crippling impact of inflation on each dollar's ability to buy goods and services.

I. IMPROPER DISPOSITION OF ASSETS – The client is leaving the wrong asset to the wrong person at the wrong time and in the wrong manner. Picture, for instance, a client leaving a sports car to a 10-year old child or $100,000 cash outright to a 21 year old college student.

Figure 1.1

EROSION OF PURCHASING POWER

Amount $100,000

After Years	Annual Rate of Inflation 1%	2%	3%	4%	5%
1	99,010	98,039	97,087	96,154	95,238
2	98,030	96,117	94,260	92,456	90,703
3	97,059	94,232	91,514	88,900	86,384
4	96,098	92,385	88,849	85,480	82,270
5	95,147	90,573	86,261	82,193	78,353
6	94,205	88,797	83,748	79,031	74,622
7	93,272	87,056	81,309	75,992	71,068
8	92,348	85,349	78,941	73,069	67,684
9	91,434	83,676	76,642	70,259	64,461
10	90,529	82,035	74,409	67,556	61,391

Reprinted courtesy *NumberCruncher* Software.

V. VALUE – Not enough has been done to stabilize and maximize the financial security value of the client's business and other assets.

E. EXCESSIVE TAXES – Excessive taxes add to the cost of an investment and retard progress toward a client's objectives.

S. SPECIAL NEEDS – Clients have desires that go beyond mere quantifiable goals. Psychological assurance and comfort should be part of the financial planning process. For example, a client may want to provide additional levels of financial care for a spouse or children who are disabled or emotionally troubled.

No matter how you define financial planning, all clients are confronted with the need to determine whether their available resources are adequate to accomplish their financial goals and objectives.

The financial planning resources are

1. earned income (salary, wages, business income) while still working (full time or part time)

2. accumulated investment assets

3. employer pension plans and Social Security benefits

The usual financial planning goals and objectives can be broadly categorized as

1. current lifestyle

2. children's education

3. retirement funding

4. parental issues

5. estate planning

6. other special needs (such as a disabled child)

In addressing these goals, the client's charitable desires often come into play. Some clients want to maximize the charitable giving during their lifetime while other clients prefer to give less while they are living but are desirous to leave much of their estate to charities.

When focusing on parental issues, keep in mind that there are two distinct sides to this coin. While it is most common for clients to consider the needs of their parents as a use for their resources, many clients look to their parent's assets as a resource to fund their own retirement. But, as people are living longer, and are often afraid to let go of their assets while living, it has become common for clients counting on inheritances to fund their retirement to find that they are well beyond retirement age before they see a penny of their parent's money. The clients' planning for their own retirement has been, to put it simply, poor.

One critical point in looking at what financial planning is and what it is not – most clients are in the position where their resources are not adequate to attain all of their goals and objectives. Sometimes compromises need to be made, but, more commonly, and more accurately, the clients must engage in a process of *prioritization*. The financial resources must be focused on whichever goal or goals the client determines is most important.

For example, when a client wants to determine whether he will be able to retire at a certain age, the process usually involves comparing the expected accumulated resources at the desired retirement date to the remaining lifetime financial needs from the retirement date on. If it is determined that the resources are not adequate to cover those needs, the client must evaluate three options (or combinations thereof):

1. reduce lifestyle, currently and/or during retirement
2. modify his investment strategy to yield a higher return, knowing that there will be a commensurately higher risk; and/or
3. retire later.

It is very difficult for most individuals approaching retirement date to significantly reduce their lifestyle. It is also foolhardy for someone nearing retirement, with limited resources, to take the risk of investing for a significantly higher rate of return. There simply is no time to recover from a negative result. Consequently, the alternative that typically takes priority is extending the retirement date. There is very little room to compromise. In addition, any desire to leave a significant estate for the next generation will usually take a back seat to the priority of maintaining current lifestyle.

WHAT A FINANCIAL PLANNING REPORT SHOULD COVER

Many clients look to the formal Financial Planning Report as THE PLAN. This, of course is an over-simplification. In any event, the report is the "product" of the financial planning professional's analysis, and should be a carefully prepared document that summarizes for the client, the client's family, and the client's advisers, the following:

1. Analysis – WHERE YOU ARE NOW
2. Objectives – WHERE YOU WANT TO BE
3. Strategy – HOW TO GET TO WHERE YOU WANT TO BE

The actual presentation can (and in many cases should) be brief, or it can be long. The length of the report must be determined by the task set by the client (does the client want you to do a full analysis or just solve one or two problems?), by time and cost considerations, by your style as a professional, and by your feelings as to how much the client needs to know to have confidence in and take action on your suggestions.

A good rule of thumb is, "Overstate and bore, understate and score." Most clients prefer to have their problems and potential solutions stated as succinctly (and as graphically) as possible. We suggest liberal use of graphs and checklists.

See Figure 1.2 for a table of contents for a full-blown analysis.

However, the financial plan is a dynamic expression of ever changing circumstances. Clients' goals change, as do their resources. These changes often occur without warning and require an immediate response. Obviously, in those situations, there is no time for a formal planning document.

Figure 1.2

Where You Are Now

1. balance sheet
2. cash flow analysis
   a) normal situation—current
   b) normal situation—projected
   c) death of "breadwinner"
   d) disability of "breadwinner"
   e) retirement
3. asset liquidity analysis
4. employee benefits
5. risk assessment
6. risk tolerance

Where You Want to Be

Quantification of goals
1. increasing investable income
2. improving liquidity
3. reducing risk
4. increasing income or meeting capital needs at death, disability, retirement, or for special situations
5. increasing financial security for heirs and satisfying charitable objectives

How to Get to Where You Want to Be

1. tax strategy
   - income
   - estate and gift
2. investment strategy
   - selection
   - portfolio balancing and asset allocation
   - diversification
3. risk management strategy
   - life
   - health & long-term care
   - disability
   - asset preservation & protection
   - property & liability
4. wealth transfer strategy
   - estate planning
   - trusts
   - retirement plan beneficiary elections
   - business succession
   - titling
   - charity

Summary and Assignment of Responsibilities

1. summary
2. priorities
3. who must take action
4. what must be done
5. timetable for implementation
6. date of next review
7. contingencies that accelerate review & revision of plans

Chapter 2

WHO IS A FINANCIAL PLANNER?

Every individual's finances are planned, some by inaction, lack of concern, or failure to appreciate the multitude of problems standing between the individual and his or her goals. ("No Plan is a Plan!") These individuals allow fate to do their planning. The results are often disappointing and sometimes tragic and disastrous. Others take a careful, calculated, and systematic approach to financial security. Their peace of mind is justified by the existence of a judicious mix of assets producing both adequate income and sufficient capital to safely meet their goals.

In this most general sense, anyone who earns, spends, saves, invests, owns, manages, marries, shares ownership, buys, sells, gives, protects what is theirs, inherits, or retires can be said to be a financial planner. This book, however, is designed for use by the planner who earns the right, by the acquisition of knowledge and dedication to the financial security of others (rather than merely by charging a fee or commission) to call himself or herself a *professional*.

It is foolhardy, even negligent in some cases, to expect that any adviser, no matter how bright or knowledgeable will know everything necessary to properly execute a comprehensive financial plan. For this reason, a financial planning team should include several other advisors: a CPA (for tax matters), a tax attorney (for legal matters and drafting), a CFP®, ChFC, or CPA•PFS (for specific financial advice), a CLU (for life insurance), and a CPCU (for property and casualty insurance advice). The term "team" implies more than the sum of its parts and requires constant interaction and cooperation among the members to the extent necessary to achieve the client's goals.

Who should lead the financial planning process? In practice, financial planning typically will be initiated by one member of the team. Others will contribute in varying degrees. The extent to which each will participate will be determined by the circumstances of the particular case, the experience, skills, and personalities of the parties, and their relationship with the client.

Since the client is the ultimate planner, he or she should always be considered the single most important member of the financial planning team. The professional must

1. uncover and describe the nature and extent of the client's problems and professionally impress the client with the urgency and significance of action

2. discuss the viable alternatives

3. explain what should be done and why

4. match the plan to what the client really needs and wants (and can understand and is likely to accomplish)

5. match the plan to the client's risk taking propensity, investment philosophy, and order of priorities

6. explain in understandable terms why present arrangements fail to accomplish the client's objectives or maximize the utility of his resources

Absent any one or more of these, it is likely that the client's present "plan" will continue.

The College for Financial Planning performed an extensive study of the professional responsibilities and knowledge requirements of financial planners. The survey, conducted by Dr. Larry Skurnik, a Measurement Research Specialist, covered a large number of CFPs and ChFCs as well as others in the field. The broad categories of inquiry are instructive as to what you must do and know as a practicing financial services professional.

What you must do is

1. evaluate client needs

2. explain financial planning concepts

3. clarify client goals

4. analyze information

5. prepare comprehensive financial plans

6. implement comprehensive financial plans

7. monitor comprehensive financial plans

8. establish and maintain accurate records and perform other professional functions.

What you must know are

1. communications skills

2. risk management

3. investment planning

4. tax planning

5. retirement planning

6. estate planning

The College for Financial Planning Study indicates that aside from a necessary "must know" common core of skills and information, what you, as a planner, must be able to do or know depends on

1. your background

2. personal characteristics

3. whether you are a sole practitioner, a member of a firm of planners, or an employee with a narrower range of responsibilities

4. the major tasks, duties, and scope of your client engagement

5. the market in which you work

In short, the planner must have competence in many areas and compassion and concern for the financial and emotional well-being of others.

THE "CO-OP" APPROACH TO FINANCIAL PLANNING

As noted above, no single financial planner can possibly know all that needs to be known or do all that needs to be done for every client. Nevertheless, no transaction should ever be recommended to a client until the planner acquires a working knowledge of how that recommendation will affect and be affected by

1. taxes (income, gift, estate, and generation-skipping) at both the federal and state level

2. retirement and education planning (including a practical understanding of Social Security, inflation, and the psychological dynamics of retirement planning)

3. estate planning (which encompasses property law, domestic relations law, and other state laws as well as tax law)

4. wealth and asset management (which requires, aside from knowledge of various products and their alternatives, an understanding of cash flow implications and present and future value and rate of return computations)

5. risk-reward principles (both economic and psychological)

Since no one person can know all these things in great depth, a truly professional financial planner must view himself or herself as part of a financial planning "cooperative" with the client and with other professionals, with each professional adding to the efficiency and effectiveness of the plan.

The first step in working as a member of this cooperative is to become aware of

1. the client's long, intermediate, and short range goals

2. the problems faced by and opportunities available to the client in the quest to achieve those goals

3. what each of the other professional advisers has already done for the client

4. what each of the other professional advisers may be able to contribute to the improvement of the client's plan to achieve his goals.

It is extremely important that, no matter who is the coordinator of this cooperative effort, each member of the cooperative be offered the opportunity to participate in the process.

Most importantly, the client, the principal member of the cooperative, must never be forgotten. Clients who are not given an opportunity to express their desires or thoughts or who do not understand a suggestion or the rationale for it will not implement or continue the plan and will resent paying what the planner feels is a reasonable price for the service rendered.

Chapter 3

STEPS IN THE FINANCIAL PLANNING PROCESS

"People don't plan to fail; they fail because they don't plan."

It is important to understand the concept of financial planning as a process, not a product or a service. It is a series of interrelated activities that a client engages in on a continuing basis. It is not something that the client completes, even successfully, and then puts away or forgets. Financial planning must be done regularly and continually in order to take into account changes in the client's personal circumstances, the availability of new products, and varying conditions in the financial markets.

The professional chosen by a client to guide him or her through the financial planning process can be as crucial as the plan itself. Finding someone with the appropriate professional credentials is important. However, a planner with whom the client feels comfortable as well as one who has been recommended by satisfied clients is just as important. Personal financial planners, including Certified Financial Planners (CFP), Chartered Financial Consultants (ChFC), Chartered Life Underwriters (CLU), Personal Financial Specialists (CPA•PFS) and stockbrokers, are each trained in different areas of financial planning and consulting, so it is in the client's best interest to research the background of the planner chosen to make sure the planner's training is best suited to the client's needs. The best financial planner will take all relevant information into consideration and offer advice and implementation techniques that are reasonable to meet the client's goals and objectives.

As new products appear, as market conditions and personal circumstances change, even the best-prepared financial plan will tend to become obsolete and out of date. Births, deaths, marriage, divorce, or a new business can have a great impact on personal planning.

The following activities in the process of financial planning should be carried out and, where necessary, may involve qualified professional advisers:

1. establish and define the relationship
2. gathering background information
3. establishing financial objectives
4. developing financial plans
5. executing and controlling plans
6. measuring performance

The flowchart shown in Figure 3.1 provides a summary of the individual activities involved in the process and shows the relationships between them.

ESTABLISH THE RELATIONSHIP[1]

The first step is that the client has agreed to meet with the planner, either through the planner's marketing efforts, or because the client sought out the planner on his own. The relationship should start by outlining the responsibilities of *both* the planner and the client. Conflicts of interest, compensation arrangements, length of the agreement period, and the products or services to be provided should be fully disclosed and agreed upon. Certain professional practice standards (e.g., the CFP Board Practice Standard 100-1) and regulatory agencies outline the expectations of this step. For example, the Securities and Exchange Commission requires that all Registered Investment Advisors (RIAs) distribute part two of Form ADV (the Uniform Application for Investment Advisor Registration) to clients and prospective clients. In short, step one considers the regulatory, legal, contractual, and professional expectations of the planner-client relationship.

GATHERING BACKGROUND INFORMATION

Effective planning requires comprehensive information on all aspects of the client's financial program. Such information includes a record of income and expenditures as well as the client's individual or family financial position.

In setting his or her objectives, the client will need to take into account the sex, health, age, lifestyle, tastes, and preferences of individual family members. Much

Figure 3.1

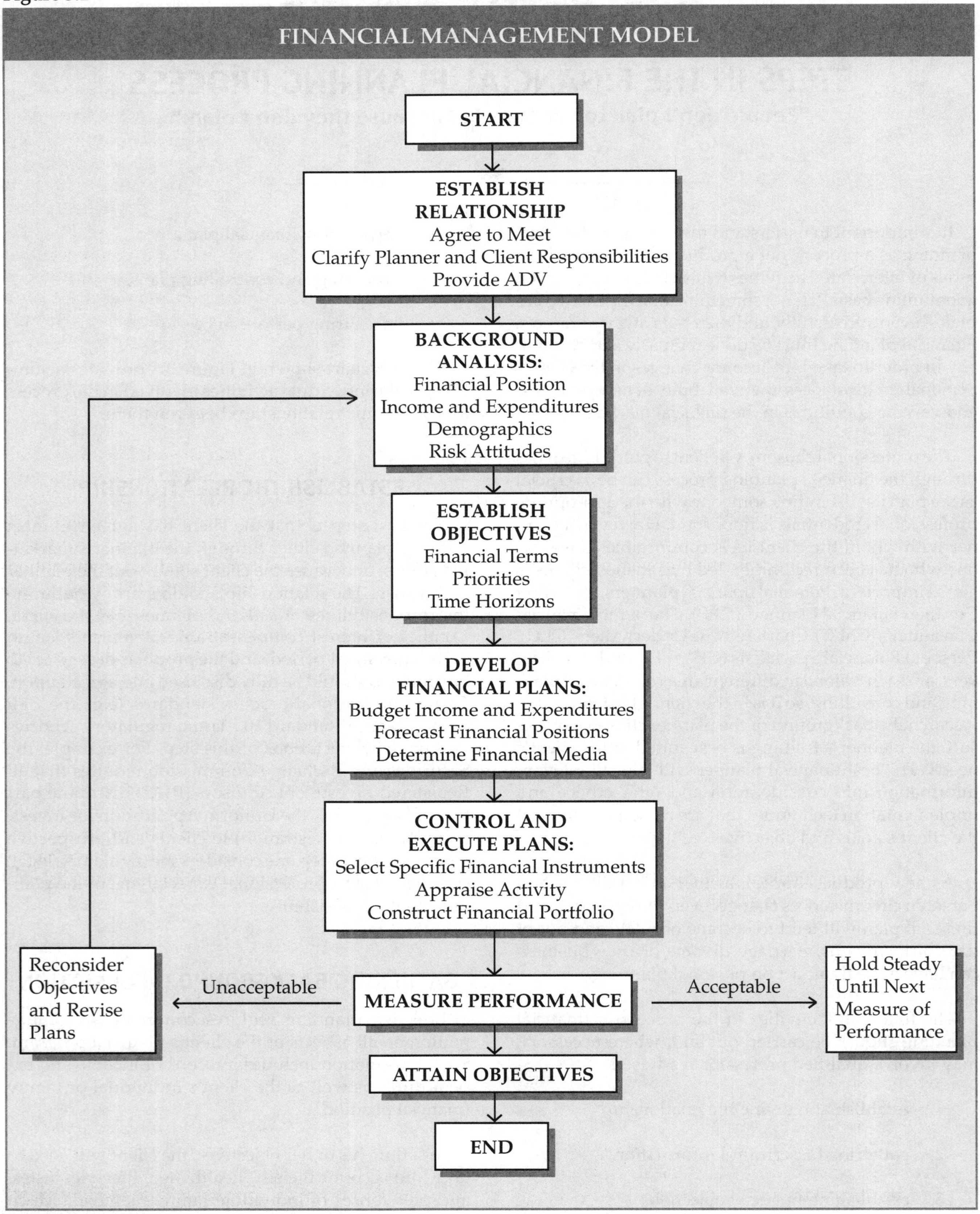

FINANCIAL MANAGEMENT MODEL
START
ESTABLISH RELATIONSHIP
Agree to Meet
Clarify Planner and Client Responsibilities
Provide ADV
BACKGROUND ANALYSIS:
Financial Position
Income and Expenditures
Demographics
Risk Attitudes
ESTABLISH OBJECTIVES
Financial Terms
Priorities
Time Horizons
DEVELOP FINANCIAL PLANS:
Budget Income and Expenditures
Forecast Financial Positions
Determine Financial Media
CONTROL AND EXECUTE PLANS:
Select Specific Financial Instruments
Appraise Activity
Construct Financial Portfolio
Reconsider Objectives and Revise Plans
Unacceptable
MEASURE PERFORMANCE
Acceptable
Hold Steady Until Next Measure of Performance
ATTAIN OBJECTIVES
END

of this information is subjective, and attitudes may shift considerably over the years. Such changes make it important that the client (generally prompted by the financial planner) update his or her plan regularly. Keeping the client's records on a personal computer will enable you to revise your data and add new information whenever necessary.

Another important area of background analysis has to do with the client's attitudes toward the degree of risk he or she is willing to accept in the financial plan. Feelings about investment risk, personal financial security, and independence are just as important as their income statement or net worth. An awareness of these feelings enables the client and planner to establish realistic, acceptable objectives. By ignoring these feelings you may develop a "good plan" that is simply out of touch with your client's personality. Such plans are not likely to be implemented, and a great deal of time and effort will have been wasted.

Unfortunately, attitudes toward risk are very difficult to measure for a number of reasons. First, defining the nature of risk is highly subjective and will vary considerably from one person to another. Second, attitudes about risk are likely to change dramatically over an individual or family's life cycle. What seemed perfectly reasonable to the 25-year-old bachelor may be totally unacceptable to the 40-year-old father of four high school age children. Finally, risk attitudes are a function of many personal psychological factors that may be difficult to deal with. Yet you, as the planning professional, should try, through discussions with family members and other advisers, to determine their feelings about risk and be alert to significant changes that may occur over time.

ESTABLISHING FINANCIAL OBJECTIVES

The process of articulating the client's financial objectives in a concrete way is a difficult but essential part of the planning process. One reason many plans fail is that financial goals are not described in operational terms. Objectives often are presented in vague language that is difficult to translate into action.

Each of the objective statements should have the following characteristics. First, it should be well-defined and clearly understood by everyone involved. Unless you and the client really know and understand what you are trying to accomplish, the plan probably will not succeed.

Asking the client to write down his or her objectives is one way of working toward a set of clear and useful statements. Comments such as "I want a safe and secure retirement income" do not provide much guidance for financial planning. They merely express a wish that may be very real to them, but is hard to put into effective terms and plans. In contrast, a statement such as "I want sufficient savings to produce a retirement income level equal to 70% of my pre-retirement income, invested at no more than a moderate risk level that produces an average return of 6% per year," is a measurable, concrete goal that can be quantified.

In other words, good financial objectives are generally stated in quantitative terms. Only by attaching numbers to the client's plans can both you and the client know when the objective has been accomplished. This is a particularly important factor in regard to long-term objectives, such as those concerning education funds or retirement. It is desirable to measure progress toward your goals at various points along the way.

The goal of having a particular sum for retirement in 20 years can be reviewed each year to see if the necessary progress has been made. If earnings have been lower than anticipated, you may have to encourage the client to make larger contributions in future years. If a higher rate of return has actually been realized, contributions can be reduced (or you can consider the "excess" as a safety cushion against years when returns are not as high as anticipated). Such fine tuning is impossible unless numbers are associated with plan objectives. Adding numbers to objectives will also help to make them easier to understand by all members of the family.

Finally, each of the client's goals or objectives should have a time dimension attached to it. When will a particular goal be accomplished? How much progress has been made since the last review? How much time remains until the goal is to be accomplished? These questions and similar ones can be answered only if you have helped the client establish a schedule with objectives listed at particular points in time.

Some parts of the plan, such as retirement objectives, will have very long time lines. Others, such as a change in savings, may be accomplished in a few months or a year. Whether long-term or short-term, the timing aspect of objectives is very important. Even long-term goals can be broken down into shorter time periods, which can be included in an annual review of the plan.

After the objectives have been identified, they should be ranked in order of priority. This ranking process is necessary since many objectives normally will compete for limited resources. It's not likely that the client will be able to satisfy all of his or her wishes at the same time. Some goals will be more important, more urgent, than others. Critical short-term needs may have to be satisfied ahead of long-range plans.

Once certain goals have been reached, funds may be channeled to other areas. An example would be education funding for the client's children. After this goal has been met, you may allocate money the client previously spent on education costs to building a retirement fund or some other long-range objective. Unless you have assigned specific priorities to these and other goals, it will be difficult for you and the client to organize and carry out an effective plan. Conversely, a set of well-integrated financial objectives can make the actual planning process a relatively easy task.

Individuals and families should have workable objectives in each of the following areas:

1. *Standard of living* – Maintaining a particular lifestyle generally takes most of a person's resources. Setting an objective in this area calls for you to analyze required spending (such as food and housing costs) as well as optional spending (travel, vacations, and entertainment). If almost all of the client's income is being spent in this area, it will be very difficult to accomplish his other objectives.

   One widely used rule of thumb states that no more than 80% of gross income should be spent on maintaining a given standard of living. The remaining 20% of income should be allocated to the other financial objectives. Obviously, this guideline will vary from one person or family to another. But unless a significant portion of the client's income can be directed toward the remaining objectives, you are not likely to be successful in helping him reach his other goals.

2. *Savings* – Everyone recognizes the need for money that can be used to meet an emergency or other special need. However, determining the ideal level of savings can be a complicated problem. It will depend on the nature of the client's income, personal risk attitudes, stability of employment, and other factors such as the type of health and dental insurance coverage he has.

   Many experts recommend maintaining savings equal to at least three months' disposable income. These funds should be kept in a safe and highly liquid form where the rate of return is a secondary consideration. A money market mutual fund or a bank money market account offers a good vehicle for emergency type savings. These investments offer a high degree of safety, and ready access to emergency money, as well as a reasonable rate of return.

3. *Protection* – This objective covers life, health, disability, property, and liability insurance coverage. It should be designed to provide protection against insurable risks and related losses. Objectives in this area should take into account any coverage that is provided through public programs such as Social Security as well as group insurance offered as an employee benefit.

4. *Accumulation* (investment) – This is the most complex objective in a number of ways. It relates to the future buildup of capital for significant financial needs. These needs can be as diverse as a child's college education, a wedding, or a vacation home. The sheer number and variety of such goals makes it difficult to define this objective and to set priorities.

   Adding to the difficult nature of this planning area is the generally long time involved, which may extend for 20 years or more. Finally, the wide variety of potential investments adds to the overall complexity. Regardless of the reason for building capital, the critical ingredients in this objective are the ability to quantify needed amounts and to state target dates for accumulation. An annual review in this area is essential.

5. *Financial independence (retirement)* – This objective is typically the most important example of the accumulation objective, and usually requires the building of assets over a long time. Financial independence may be desired at a particular age and may or may not actually correspond with retirement from work. Instead, the client may wish to have security and financial independence while continuing to work at an enjoyable occupation or profession.

   More than most others, this area will be affected by changes in government programs such as Social Security and benefits paid by employers. Also, since the planning period is such a long one, this objective should be broken down into subgoals that can be evaluated, analyzed, and reworked over the years.

6. *Estate planning* – Objectives in this area are typically concerned with the preservation and distribution of wealth after the estate owner's death. However, accomplishing such goals usually requires a number of actions well before that time. Having a will prepared is the most fundamental act in estate planning, and yet thousands of persons die each year without having done so. These people die intestate, leaving the distribution of their assets to be determined by state laws and the courts.

   For larger estates, avoidance or minimization of estate taxes is an important consideration. These objectives can be accomplished, but they call for careful planning and implementation prior to the owner's death. The use of various trust instruments, distribution of assets through gifts, and proper titling of property can all result in a smaller taxable estate. However, carrying out such a program will take time and should be an ongoing process as various assets are acquired. This is also an area in which professional guidance is generally necessary. An attorney should be included on the planning team, to draft a will or prepare any needed trust documents.

DEVELOPING FINANCIAL PLANS

Once realistic, well-defined objectives have been established, you can begin to develop the client's actual plans. This planning stage includes the budgeting of income and expenditures for the near term along with a forecast of future activity. You should also make a projection of the client's expected financial position for the next several years. This will give you an idea of the future growth and returns that will be necessary for the client to reach his or her overall net worth objective.

Your plans should identify the financial instruments that will be included in programs to meet the client's specific objectives. For example, you should identify specific savings media if the client needs more emergency funds. You may consider recommending regular savings accounts, money market certificates, or shares in a money market fund. If an investment program is called for, you should recommend appropriate types of investments such as securities, real estate, or mutual funds.

CONTROLLING AND EXECUTING PLANS

The next stage of the financial planning model calls for you to set the plan in motion. This may involve the purchase or sale of various assets, changes in the client's life insurance protection, additional liability coverage, and other changes. All of these activities should be closely monitored and appraised to see that they are effective in accomplishing the client's objectives. The outcome of some actions will be apparent quickly, while others may take a long time to produce results.

MEASURING PERFORMANCE

Measuring performance is an important step; it helps you determine the progress the client is making toward the attainment of his or her objectives. If performance to date is acceptable, you may not need to take any particular corrective action until the next scheduled review. However, if you determine that progress to date is not satisfactory, action will be necessary. This may include a review of the client's plans to see if they are still valid and an analysis of the financial environment to take note of unexpected changes.

If the original objectives are no longer realistic and desirable, you will want to review and recommend that the client alter them. In that case, the entire plan may have to be recycled through each of the stages described above. This model of financial planning is a dynamic one that is continually repeated as personal, financial, and environmental factors change.

CHAPTER ENDNOTES

1. See Lytton, Grable, & Klock, *The Process of Financial Planning: Developing a Financial Plan*, Chapter 6 (Cincinnati, OH: National Underwriter, 2006).

Chapter 4

TOOLS IN THE FINANCIAL PLANNING PROCESS

WHAT ARE THEY?

Three critical aspects of the financial planning process require different types of financial planning tools. The roles of the professionals in the financial planning team will also vary during each stage. The three important segments are

1. *Planning* – Establishing goals and objectives, gathering data, creating "the plan" and identifying the steps for implementation

2. *Implementation and product* – Execution of wills, trust agreements and other estate and financial planning documents, allocation of investments, acquisition of appropriate investment and insurance products

3. *Management* – Monitoring cash flow (budget-to-actual analysis), realigning investment allocation, updating documents, as needed, re-evaluating goals and objectives, acknowledging the need and be willing to change as circumstances dictate.

Planning

The tools for the planning phase include basic counseling skills, including the ability to listen to what the client has to say. It is nearly impossible to provide a client with an effective plan without a clear understanding of where he is coming from, his attitudes and priorities. Of equal importance is the talent to communicate to the client your understanding of these attitudes and confirming that you are on the same page. (Chapter 5 is devoted to the issues of client attitudes).

Gathering data is a more mechanical function, but still requires strong communication skills. Clients will invariably forget some resource or responsibility that may have a significant impact on the plan. While many clients have "their affairs in order" so that data gathering can be accomplished efficiently, numerous, if not most clients have no idea what they spend, what their income is, where their funds are invested, or what debts they have. Obviously, such clients need help to accumulate the information necessary to prepare the plan. Data gathering forms and checklists are helpful, but it is typically the clients who most need these aids who "don't have the time" or are simply less inclined to use them. In such cases, the planner should use checklists and forms to facilitate guiding the client through the process.

Implementation

Implementing the financial plan requires the effective interaction of all the members of the financial planning team, all of whom may participate in the planning but also fulfill other functions:

1. the tax accountant, responsible for projections and quantitative analysis

2. the estate attorney who drafts the appropriate documents

3. the insurance and investment advisors who recommend any necessary products and investments

As with most teams, there is usually only one quarterback, one person in charge of coordinating the team's efforts and marshalling the resources, as needed. That person may be any member of the team, depending on the client's individual circumstances. He may be a family member, an old fraternity brother, or simply the first of the advisory group the client needed.

For clients who are professionals, such as doctors, engineers, accountants, etc, that first person is often an insurance advisor, since insurance is often the first financial product needed. For a sole-proprietor or owner of a closely-held business, the accountant handling the financial statements and tax returns of the business will be looked to as the one to fill the leadership role.

Whoever is the team quarterback must take the role seriously. He is the person the client counts on to create the plan and carry out its implementation. The other members of the team may often struggle to keep their egos in check when not "in charge," but their roles, for that client, are supportive, using their special skills to assist the client in accomplishing his goals.

Management

The management of the plan and its implementation will frequently fall to the quarterback of the implementation team. In many cases, the role will shift to some other team member, or will often be assumed by the client himself. When the client takes control of the plan's management, there is a higher probability that something will be forgotten or overlooked. The client is not a financial management professional. In addition, he will tend to focus his energies on his family and career priorities, consequently reducing the effort expended on maintaining the integrity of the financial plan. In such circumstances, each professional advisor must evaluate the strength of his relationship with the client and ask himself such questions as:

- How good a job is the client doing in managing his financial plan?
- Will the client allow me to question his performance?
- How can I communicate to the client that he is not doing as good a job as he thinks he is?
- Am I willing to risk my relationship with the client to get him back on track?

GOLDEN PRINCIPLES OF FINANCIAL PLANNING

The following golden principles of financial planning are basic to all the tools of the financial planning process. There is nothing new (including this maxim) under the sun. Yet, there is a very good reason why certain sayings, rules of thumb, or guidelines have been around so long: they work! The rate of change in the tax law affecting financial planning has been surpassed only by the rapid change in the investment and insurance products and services designed to meet clients' needs.

1. *Cover your assets before taking greater risk* – Never suggest that a client proceed to the next level of risk before the gains already made have been protected. This is the basic principle behind risk management as well as the proper assessment of life and disability income needs.

2. *Seek first a return **of** principal before a return **on** principal* – Put safety of principal and certainty of income before gain on capital or growth of income. This "safety first" caveat is really another way of saying, "Don't be greedy or you may lose it all." An adviser must always remind a client of the balance between risk and reward, but protection of principal must always come first.

3. *No risk, no reward* – Strong profits are not gained by faint hearts. Money is made and taxes are saved by taking prudent (defined on a client-by-client basis) risk. It is important for clients to recognize that there are three types of risk: financial risk, purchasing power risk, and lost opportunity risk.

   Doing nothing is the greatest risk of all. At only 3% inflation, $100,000 loses more than 25% of its purchasing power in just ten years, as the *NumberCruncher* printout shown in Figure 4.1 illustrates. And the average rate of inflation during the past 15 years (even considering the very low rates of the last few years) has been significantly more than that 3% rate! Clients ignore inflation – even low rates of inflation – at great peril.

4. *Without both liquidity and marketability, there is no flexibility* – Liquidity is a measure of the investor's ability to quickly turn all or most of an investment back into cash, with little or no loss. Marketability is a measure of the probability that, and the speed and ease at which, a buyer (through sale, trade, or otherwise) can dispose of an investment.

   If a client does not have enough cash or assets that can quickly, inexpensively, and easily be turned into cash, how will he or she meet an emergency or take advantage of an opportunity? Inadequate cash often translates into either a forced sale or a lost opportunity. This problem becomes especially acute when an investor dies and large and often unexpected cash drains (payable according to the IRS's timetable) occur and too often a fire sale results.

5. *A successful investor has to be right three times* – To profit from any investment, it is not good enough to merely select the right investment; it is also necessary that the asset be purchased and sold at the right time and also in the right manner. Selection, timing, and titling (i.e., the right decision concerning who should hold legal title to property) are all keys to success (as is keeping the spread or commission and loading charges paid on an investment as low as reasonably possible).

Figure 4.1

EROSION OF PURCHASING POWER

Amount $100,000

After Years	Annual Rate of Inflation 1%	2%	3%	4%	5%
1	99,010	98,039	97,087	96,154	95,238
2	98,030	96,117	94,260	92,456	90,703
3	97,059	94,232	91,514	88,900	86,384
4	96,098	92,385	88,849	85,480	82,270
5	95,147	90,573	86,261	82,193	78,353
6	94,205	88,797	83,748	79,031	74,622
7	93,272	87,056	81,309	75,992	71,068
8	92,348	85,349	78,941	73,069	67,684
9	91,434	83,676	76,642	70,259	64,461
10	90,529	82,035	74,409	67,556	61,391

Reprinted courtesy *NumberCruncher*.

6. *An investor should never put all his eggs into one basket* – But if they are put in one basket, the basket must be watched carefully. Diversification is one of the most important principles of financial planning. It is the driving force behind the success of the mutual fund. Although it is conceivable that a person could diversify into mediocrity, this result is not likely if diversification is combined with the other golden principles.

Diversification should be not only "horizontal" and "vertical" but, if feasible, "multidimensional." That means an investor should, if economically possible, diversify in terms of investment vehicles (for instance, divide capital between stocks, bonds, real estate, and money markets), within a class or type of investment, by geographic location, and through timing (e.g., bonds with different maturities within the same type of investment, and dollar cost averaging as explained in number 20 below).

The letters R-B-R will help you to remember the goals and advantages of diversification.

R – Return: Diversify to achieve the *highest after-tax return* consistent with asset growth and income needs.

B – Balance: Diversify to acquire the proper balance of liquidity and marketability.

R – Risk: Diversify to match a client's risk-taking propensity and temperament.

It is the authors' opinion that few people should invest significantly in individual stocks until they have first built up sizable mutual fund portfolios.

7. *Put yourself on your own payroll* – at the top of the payroll.

If a client doesn't know where to start, he probably won't (start). The place to start is on top. The point is that most people pay their bills and end with little, if anything, for themselves. Reverse that chaos with order, the right order, and help the client to use the budgetary process to take care of himself first. Clients should budget for savings and investment, just as they budget for the payment of monthly debt.

8. *Capitalize on the miracle of the "forgotten" automatic investment* –

By far, the greatest financial security most individuals have results from having put aside money on a regular automatic basis before they see it or consider it "spendable." This includes salary savings plans, employer sponsored pension and profit sharing and 401(k) plans, as well as what must be the most common example of all, the month after month reminder that life insurance premiums are due. That "forgotten" money compounds year after year (putting into play the power of compound interest) so that when you need it the most, it's there in the amount needed.

9. *It is as important to increase the rate of investing as it is to increase the rate of return –*

It is far easier and safer to find or create small incremental increases of discretionary cash to invest each month over a long period of time than to uncover or create large lumps of assets at one time or dramatically increase investment return. In fact, a small increase in input of regular investment is equal to a dramatic increase in the rate of return on current investment.

We suggest that clients increase the amount they invest each week or month until they reach the "ouch" point. The "ouch" point is reached when the level of investment begins to have an adverse impact on their standard of living. By constantly raising the "ouch" point, more and more is being invested on a regular basis, putting less pressure on the assets already saved to meet objectives. This is another way of saying that by increasing investment input, the return (spelled R-I-S-K) that must be obtained by current investments to meet a given goal is reduced.

Increasing the level of investments also provides an additional hedge against inflation as well as a "luxury level" in excess of merely meeting the "bare bones" financial objective.

Master planner Harold Gourgues, in his *Financial Planning Handbook* (Simon & Schuster, 1983) describes the use of a "rate of return matrix" to properly align assets. The principles behind this system are these two questions

- How "fast" do assets have to "move" to get to their goal on time? (In other words, "What internal rate of return must be realized on the current income producing assets and current stream of investable income to meet the quantified financial goals of the client?")
- What risks must be taken to move assets faster toward their goal of reaching the desired amount?

In the event the current mix of assets and the current level of investment result in a projected shortage of college or retirement funds, solutions include

a) trying a new mix of assets (increasing risk) to increase average rate of return

b) increasing capital

c) increasing annual contributions

d) taking down capital at retirement

e) retiring at a later date to buy more time, or

f) using a combination of these solutions

Discretionary cash flow (investable cash) can be increased by

a) reducing income or other taxes imposed during the client's lifetime, and by

b) programming and controlling moderate to major expenses (Two techniques, simple budgeting and controlling of inflows and outflows of cash and the use of financial management accounts, will help to create or improve discretionary cash flow.)

10. *Let purpose help define the level of risk taken –*

If the client's need to satisfy a given objective is great (for example, he has two children and anticipates a minimum need of $60,000 for college education funds in six years), he may not be willing to risk significant capital to obtain 2% or 3% higher return. On the other hand, if a client has allocated a given amount of money as a crapshoot and has no special purpose for the money, he or she will probably be willing to take much higher risks more often.

Be sure the client understands not only the level (or degree) of risk the client is taking but also the *types of* hidden risks the client may be assuming (e.g., the tradeoffs between one risk versus another). For instance, it may appear that a 4% return in a savings account with a major bank is a riskless investment. Likewise, a fully secured loan of $100,000 to a major financial institution seems risk free. Yet in both cases the purchasing power of the investor's capital is invisibly eroded by inflation. This is just one of the hidden risks that must be understood by clients. Another risk is that the institution will become insolvent. Still another risk is "alternative risk." Had the money been placed in an alternative investment, to what level would it have grown?

11. *Assets and income maintain their utility only to the extent they maintain or increase their purchasing power –*

Figure 4.2

INFLATION-ADJUSTED INCOME & ASSET ANALYSIS

Desired Income From Investments $100,000

Income Producing Assets $1,000,000

Assumed Return on Investments 0.060

Assumed Inflation Rate 0.030

Year	Inflation Adjusted Income	Value of Assets	Income From Assets	Use of Capital	Assets at End of Year
1	$100,000	$1,000,000	$60,000	$40,000	$960,000
2	$103,000	$960,000	$57,600	$45,400	$914,600
3	$106,090	$914,600	$54,876	$51,214	$863,386
4	$109,273	$863,386	$51,803	$57,470	$805,916
5	$112,551	$805,916	$48,355	$64,196	$741,720
6	$115,927	$741,720	$44,503	$71,424	$670,296
7	$119,405	$670,296	$40,218	$79,187	$591,109
8	$122,987	$591,109	$35,467	$87,520	$503,589
9	$126,677	$503,589	$30,215	$96,462	$407,127
10	$130,477	$407,127	$24,428	$106,049	$301,078
11	$134,392	$301,078	$18,065	$116,327	$184,751
12	$138,423	$184,751	$11,085	$127,338	$57,413
13	$142,576	$57,413	$3,445	$139,131	$0
14	$146,853	$0	$0	$146,853	$0
15	$151,259	$0	$0	$151,259	$0
16	$155,797	$0	$0	$155,797	$0
17	$160,471	$0	$0	$160,471	$0
18	$165,285	$0	$0	$165,285	$0
19	$170,243	$0	$0	$170,243	$0
20	$175,351	$0	$0	$175,351	$0

Reprinted courtesy *NumberCruncher*.

As Figure 4.2 illustrates, it will be difficult for an investor to maintain a $100,000 a year purchasing power even if he has $1,000,000 of income producing assets earning 6% if inflation erodes that buying power at only a 3% rate.

By the tenth year, it will take $130,477 to buy what $100,000 would have purchased in the first year. Invasion of the fund producing the income is necessary from the beginning, since even in the first year there is a $40,000 gap between what is produced and what is needed. By the thirteenth year, the fund will be sufficiently depleted that the income will no longer be maintainable. (Consider as you ponder this harsh reality that a 65-year-old female has a life expectancy of about 17 years.)

12. *Increase expenditures (especially nondeductible ones) at a lower rate than you increase your income –*

Controlling inefficient spending and debt acquisition is the lowest risk way to increase dollars available for investment. Although budgeting is often considered the least sophisticated aspect of financial planning, in a surprising number of cases monetary waste and uncontrolled cash flow are not only major impediments to financial success but also to financial stability or survival.

Figure 4.3

TRUE RETURN TABLE THE TRUE RETURN ON MONEY IS:						
TAXABLE RATE OF RETURN	**COMBINED FEDERAL & STATE TAX BRACKET**					
	0.15	**0.30**	**0.35**	**0.40**	**0.45**	**0.50**
0.02	0.017	0.014	0.013	0.012	0.011	0.010
0.03	0.026	0.021	0.020	0.018	0.017	0.015
0.04	0.034	0.028	0.026	0.024	0.022	0.020
0.05	0.043	0.035	0.033	0.030	0.028	0.025
0.06	0.051	0.042	0.039	0.036	0.033	0.030
0.07	0.060	0.049	0.046	0.042	0.039	0.035
0.08	0.068	0.056	0.052	0.048	0.044	0.040
0.09	0.077	0.063	0.058	0.054	0.049	0.045
0.10	0.085	0.070	0.065	0.060	0.055	0.050
0.11	0.093	0.077	0.072	0.066	0.060	0.055
0.12	0.102	0.084	0.078	0.072	0.066	0.060
0.13	0.110	0.091	0.084	0.078	0.071	0.065
0.14	0.119	0.098	0.091	0.084	0.077	0.070
0.15	0.128	0.105	0.098	0.090	0.082	0.075
0.16	0.136	0.112	0.104	0.096	0.088	0.080
0.17	0.145	0.119	0.111	0.102	0.094	0.085
0.18	0.153	0.126	0.117	0.108	0.099	0.090
0.19	0.162	0.133	0.124	0.114	0.105	0.095
0.20	0.170	0.140	0.130	0.120	0.110	0.100
0.21	0.179	0.147	0.137	0.126	0.116	0.105
0.22	0.187	0.154	0.143	0.132	0.121	0.110
0.23	0.196	0.161	0.150	0.138	0.127	0.115
0.24	0.204	0.168	0.156	0.144	0.132	0.120
0.25	0.213	0.175	0.163	0.150	0.138	0.125

13. *Think of financial security only in terms of the bottom line –*

It's not what you earn that counts; it's what you get to keep.

Too many clients judge the health of their wealth at the top line. But getting ahead in terms of absolute wealth or absolute income is a false security. Many planners use the analogy of a funnel; wealth and income are diverted from a straight path down the funnel to the client and his or her family because of (a) taxes, and (b) slippage.

Consider that state and federal taxes, expenses of producing income, inflation, and transfer costs will significantly diminish the purchasing power of what's left on the bottom line. Remember that it's only what makes it to the bottom line that generates purchasing power. For instance, Figure 4.3 shows that after taxes, the true return on a taxable investment is far less than it otherwise appears.

This bottom line philosophy must be extended to all phases of financial and estate planning. For example, if a 60 year old executive dies and leaves $9,000,000 in his pension plan to his granddaughter, the transfer is subject to a federal estate tax, a generation-skipping transfer tax (assuming he had already utilized his exemption), an income tax, probably a state inheritance or estate tax, and in many states, a state income tax. If the pension plan is fully subject to tax at the maximum federal tax rates, the grandchild may receive less than 20 cents on the dollar.

14. *He is wise who can turn top tax dollars into assets or spendable income without undue risk –*

Marginal income tax rates are what eat into the last dollar of income, if permitted. High tax brackets indicate planning opportunities. A good planner will search for opportunities to accomplish the following key objectives of financial and estate planning:

a) *Create estate tax free wealth* – For instance, it is possible to transfer wealth from one generation to another through a death benefit only plan or an irrevocable life insurance trust.

b) *Divide and conquer the tax systems* – The progressive nature of the income, estate, and gift tax systems can be used against each other by creating more taxpayers, each at lower brackets. Using the annual gift tax exclusion and unified credit equivalent to shift income to lower tax brackets, thereby lowering the resulting income tax is an example.

c) *Deduct* – It is obvious that deductions reduce tax liability. The benefit of a deduction is directly related to the marginal tax bracket you are in; the higher the bracket, the greater the benefit from the deduction. The formula for computing the tax saving from a deduction is

(Amount of deduction) x
(investor's marginal tax rate).

So the tax saving to an investor in a 28% bracket with a $1,000 deduction appears to be $280. We say, "appears to be" since a planner must take into consideration state as well as federal taxes and the interplay between them.

The *NumberCruncher* illustration in Figure 4.4 shows that an individual's combined income tax bracket is much higher than the federal bracket alone, even though a deduction from the federal bracket may be allowed for the state tax paid. The illustration also points out that the return on the individual's investments is substantially lowered, but the net cost of borrowing is also significantly lowered by the leverage of the tax deduction.

For more information on the estate planning process, see our companion text, *The Tools and Techniques of Estate Planning*.

d) *Defer* – Deferring income from one tax year to another or over many years has multiple advantages. First, deferral of receipt translates into a deferral of taxation. Money that otherwise would have taken a one way trip to Washington, D.C., on April 15th can be used year after year to earn income for the client. Deferral of tax is, temporarily at least, like a no or low cost loan from the IRS.

Second, in some cases it may be possible to defer long enough so that the tax on the deferred income need never be paid. For instance, the internal build up within a life insurance contract is never taxed if the policy is held by the owner until the death of the insured. Money inside a Roth IRA or an IRC Section 529 educational plan not only can accumulate tax-free for many years, but also can be received income tax free.

Third, income that may be taxed in a high bracket year can be deferred to a lower bracket year. For example, a 40% combined federal and state bracket reduces the after-tax return of a 10% investment yield to 6%. (See True Return Table, Figure 4.3.) The same investment yields 7% if the investor is in a 30% bracket when the income becomes taxable.

Figure 4.4

AFTER-TAX RETURN/COST CALCULATOR	
Federal Tax Bracket	0.280
State Tax Bracket	0.070
Combined Marginal Tax Bracket	0.330
Before-Tax Return on Investment	0.080
After-Tax Return on Investment	0.054
Before-Deduction Borrowing Rate	0.120
Net Cost of Borrowing	0.080

Reprinted courtesy *NumberCruncher.*

Figure 4.5

DISCOUNTING THE FEDERAL ESTATE TAX

End Yr.	Amount Payable	Cumulative Premiums	Cost Per $	Tax Free Proceeds Above Premiums	Cash Value	Cash Value as % of Premium
1	$1,000,000	$27,430	$0.03	$972,570	$410	1.5%
5	$1,034,000	$137,150	$0.13	$896,850	$11,094	8.1%
10	$1,132,400	$246,870	$0.22	$885,530	$294,567	119.3%
20	$1,214,900	$246,870	$0.20	$968,030	$601,135	243.5%

Reprinted courtesy *NumberCruncher*.

Of course, it is important to consider nontax factors such as the possibility that the creditor who is able to pay in the year of deferral may not be able to pay in the later year.

Deferral is accomplished through a variety of mechanisms, such as (i) deferring interest income by, for example, purchasing T-bills maturing in a later tax year or by purchasing U.S. Savings bonds; (ii) contracting with an employer for a nonqualified deferred compensation plan; (iii) sending out bills late in December with the expectation that they will not be paid until January (i.e., the following tax year for cash basis taxpayers); and (iv) postponing the due date of interest a debtor is liable to pay you from this year to a future tax year.

e) *Discount* – Pay real estate and other local taxes early where the taxing entity provides an advantageous discount. This technique will increase cash flow but requires cash flow control (budgeting) to work.

Another "discount" device that should not be overlooked by planners is the ability to pay federal estate tax at a "discount" through properly arranged (out of the estate but available for the estate) life insurance. The *NumberCruncher* illustration in Figure 4.5 shows how a substantial estate tax payment can be made for literally pennies on the dollar.

f) *Eliminate the tax on wealth* – Through devices such as a private annuity, it is possible to transfer wealth through one or more generations free of federal estate tax.

g) *Freeze the growth on wealth and shift it to another generation* – Private annuities, installment sales, self-canceling installment notes, and certain recapitalizations are all techniques that can stop or slow down the buildup of assets and assist in the "intentional defunding" of a client's estate and the shift of assets (and therefore income) from the client to younger generations.

h) *Gelt (Yiddish for "money") trip through time* – Among the most valuable of the financial planner's tools is the ability to use time value of money concepts (see Chapter 20, "Time Value of Money and Quantitative Analysis") by literally "turning the actuarial tables" against the IRS. Techniques such as GRITs (grantor retained income trusts), GRATs (grantor retained annuity trusts), and GRUTs (grantor retained unitrusts) can result in hundreds of thousands and even millions of dollars of estate transfer cost savings as well as significant income tax advantages. (These estate planning devices are covered in detail in our sister book, *The Tools and Techniques of Estate Planning*.)

15. *The essence of risk management is protecting the ground that's already been gained without losing more in the process* –

Consider the effect on discretionary cash flow of dollars misdirected toward unnecessary insurance premiums or the potential damage to a client's financial security caused by underinsurance. Insure only what is of measurable value or need and cannot be easily or economically replaced without insurance.

There are three key categories of risk management that must be considered by the financial planner:

a) property (fire, storm, loss, theft, shipwreck)

b) income (death, accident, sickness)

c) liability

16. *It's not enough just to make money; an investor has to create automatic mechanisms to make money with the money he's made –*

To reach any financial goal first requires (a) better positioning of what the client already has and then (b) automatic and cost-effective channeling of the return on investments. For example, most mutual funds and many stocks provide automatic (and low or no commission) dividend reinvestment plans.

17. *Always use the lowest risk solution that satisfies the need –*

The planner must

a) measure the client's needs

b) establish an order of needs

c) give first preference to what the client most wants to accomplish

If each level of need is satisfied before moving to the next higher level, needs and risk should typically match. For instance, one of the most primary and "first level" needs is for an emergency fund. (The term "first level" refers to the analogy that financial planning builds security from a firm foundation at the ground level and then moves up floor by floor to the roof, or from the base to the apex of a pyramid, with each new level representing a higher risk.) When many of the foundation and first floor level needs have been satisfied, the client can afford to take greater risk and therefore attempt to achieve a greater return.

Stated in different terms, risk, like income taxes, should increase progressively but only after lower bracket financial needs have been satisfied. This can be called the "hierarchy of financial needs and risks" equation.

18. *At a certain point, action must replace cogitation and articulation –*

The finest plan is worthless until executed. It is extremely important to establish a timetable that lists not only the action to be taken but also the party who is responsible for each phase of the plan. This should be broken down into segments small enough to be accomplished but large enough so that everyone in the financial planning cooperative retains perspective and can see and appreciate the role played by others.

The creation of a full blown financial planning timetable is an extremely valuable exercise because it will force you to consider not only what must be done, but also the capacity of those involved to accomplish the plan according to a schedule which will be distributed to all concerned parties. This changes concepts into commitments.

19. *No tool or technique is without cost –*

Perhaps the most insidious trap a planner can fall into is giving too much attention to one problem area without giving enough attention to the others that may be affected by a suggested move. Do not create more problems for the future than you solve in the present by ignoring or failing to consider other problems you may be creating. Saving estate taxes on a small amount of estate taxable at a 37% bracket sounds good, but not if the saving is at the expense of a much higher income tax on a large taxable base not far down the road.

Before you suggest any transaction, use this checklist to consider each of the following and its implications for all parties concerned:

a) the federal income tax

b) the federal gift tax

c) the federal estate tax

d) the federal generation-skipping transfer tax

e) state taxes of all four of the above varieties

f) the alternative minimum tax (AMT)

g) cash flow at both the business and personal level

h) property law, domestic law, and other state laws

i) psychological and emotional implications including issues of control, flexibility, and certainty

j) legal, ethical, and moral implications

k) implementation problems, aggravation, and cost

l) the relation of all these to each other and to the client's personal goals

20. *Patience and discipline are the parents of financial success –*

Clients who lack either the patience or the discipline to follow through on a long-range plan will end up, if with anything other than broken dreams, with a number of uncoordinated products or hastily conceived packages.

Financial success depends upon

a) the ability and willingness to suppress greed

b) efficiency (low tax, low load)

c) willingness to take risk

d) discipline (and patience)

e) education

f) wisdom – knowing when to start and when enough is enough

Discipline is the principle behind "dollar cost averaging," a long-recognized and respected strategy for successful investing.

Combining dollar cost averaging with diversification can be accomplished through regular monthly mutual fund purchases. The investor buys the same dollar amount of the fund (the same concept will work with any type of investment) each month, regardless of the current share price of the fund. That means the investor buys more shares when the market price is low and fewer shares when the market price is high. Mathematically, dollar cost averaging will result in an average cost lower than the average price over the acquisition period.

Risk is reduced by diversification over time. Of course, so is the potential for gain.

Three points should be made about this "patience and discipline" technique. First, it works only if the investor does in fact stay with the system for an extended period of time. This is particularly important as the market price per share is dropping. Second, the benefit of dollar cost averaging will be leveraged if the client increases the dollar amount of his or her investment during the time of declining prices and decreases the dollar amount invested as prices go up. Third, this system does not maximize profit potential. In fact, it guarantees that potential return is not maximized. If an investor is sure that the market has bottomed out and will be rising, a much greater profit may be obtained by investing all available funds at that point. The problem, of course, is that no one really knows when the bottom – or top – will be reached.

21. *Whether it is better to "own" or "loan" depends on one's own situation –*

An investor "loans" when he or she provides capital and in exchange receives a fixed or guaranteed rate of return. At a specified time or event, the investor recovers the original capital placed into the investment. Loan-type investments include bonds, money markets, savings accounts, and C.D.s.

Own-type investments are made when an investor buys an asset or an interest in property with the hope and expectation that the asset will increase in value over time but with no fixed or guaranteed assurance of the rate or amount. This category of investment includes common stocks, mutual funds, real estate, precious metals, and collectibles.

Loaning or owning are the only two choices an investor has when deciding what category of investment to make. Both have advantages and disadvantages.

Loan-type investment advantages –

a) The interest is predictable.

b) The amount of capital to be received is predictable.

c) The time capital will be recovered is predictable.

d) The investment is always liquid.

Loan-type investment disadvantages –

a) In an inflationary economy, the investor's principal will lose purchasing power if the investor does not accumulate and reinvest his earnings since what is recovered is exactly what was in existence at the beginning of the investment in absolute dollars but greatly diminished in terms of purchasing power. For instance, at only a 4% inflation rate, $100,000 loaned out today will have the purchasing power of only $67,566 ten years from now.

b) Interest payments will typically remain level and not increase.

c) After taxes, it may be difficult, or even impossible for interest rates to keep up with inflation rates over an extended period of time.

Own-type investment advantages –

a) There is an opportunity for growth of capital.

b) There is an opportunity for growth of income.

Own-type investment disadvantages –

a) It is impossible to predict the value at any given time in the future.

b) Both income and capital may drop or even be lost.

c) Often, this type of property is illiquid. An emergency creating the necessity for a forced sale will result in much less received than the original investment. A lack of liquidity may also result in the loss of opportunity to achieve even higher return.

Financial risk tends to increase as an investor adds more own-type investments to his "rate of return matrix" (portfolio), but purchasing power risk tends to decrease (assuming the potential return is in fact realized). On the other hand, financial risk tends to decrease as an investor adds more loan-type investments to his "rate of return matrix," but purchasing power risk tends to increase.

Diversification to reduce both financial and purchasing power risk is the obvious answer; the investor must mix the investments in his portfolio to defend against these two risks, or risk the consequences in return for the potential rewards.

22. *Debt, like spending, should be at the discretion of and fully controlled by the investor –*

When a client has no choice about debt and must borrow, two rules should always be followed. First, find the lowest true rate of interest available under favorable terms. Second, never borrow more than can be paid back under the schedule agreed upon.

Better yet, position your client's budget so that borrowing, as investing, is discretionary. This means the planner's goal should be to make the decision to borrow a matter of the client's choice. Aside from the emotional and psychological constraints and the very important principle that no investment decision can be made in a vacuum, the decision can be made on an analytical formula basis:

> Borrow only when it is probable that the return on the investment will exceed (after taxes are considered) the cost of the borrowed funds.

For instance, assume a client could invest $10,000 at 12%. His after-tax return, as shown by the example in Figure 4.6, would be $720 if his combined tax bracket was 40%. If the investment was financed by a loan that required a 9% payment, the after-tax cost of the loan would be $540, assuming the interest was fully deductible. The $180 spread ($720-$540) would be the true net advantage of the investment.

This is an example of the important financial concept known as "leveraging." Whenever part or all of the investment is made with borrowed money, leveraging is at work; for the client if things go well, against the client if things don't go well. In this example, even though the return to the client seems small in terms of absolute dollars, if the investment is considered in terms of the percentage return on the investor's own equity, the return is infinite since none of his money was involved.

Figure 4.6

COMPUTING THE AFTER TAX COST OF AN INVESTMENT AFTER TAX RETURN	
AMOUNT OF INVESTMENT	$10,000
RATE OF RETURN	0.120
INCOME	$1,200
COMBINED FEDERAL AND STATE TAX RATE	0.40
AFTER-TAX RETURN	$720
AFTER TAX COST OF INVESTMENT	
AMOUNT BORROWED	$10,000
INTEREST RATE	0.090
INTEREST EXPENSE	$900
AFTER-TAX COST (IF DEDUCTIBLE)	$540
AFTER-TAX RETURN	$720
AFTER-TAX COST	$540
ADVANTAGE	$180

Few investments use the 100% leverage found in the example above. In most cases of leveraging, a portion of the investment is borrowed and a portion of the investment is made with the investor's own assets. There is therefore both leverage (debt) and equity (ownership) in most leveraged investments.

Where there will be both debt and equity and the goal is to maximize the return on the investor's capital, use this rule of thumb:

> Maximize leverage where the reasonably predictable after-tax return will exceed the reasonably predictable after-tax cost of the debt.

A financial planner should assist a client with the question of the debt to equity mix by doing a debt to equity analysis.

Where the rate of return on an investment is higher than the cost to borrow money, an investor increases the after-tax return on his equity by increasing the leveraging, that is, by increasing the ratio of debt to equity in the investment. In other words, it is better to borrow than to own.

Where the rate of return is lower than the cost to borrow, an investor increases after-tax return by increasing the ratio of equity to debt. In other words, it is better to own than to borrow.

Keep in mind that these maxims must be themselves tempered by the concept of "opportunity costs." Opportunity costs are the costs of missing an alternative (and better) use of the investor's money (whether the money is owned or borrowed) and the after-tax income the investor's money could have earned in the alternative investment. An investor must always ask whether he is making the best use of his money (whether that money is owned or borrowed).

Opportunity costs are not a relevant consideration if any after-tax alternative return (after considering any borrowing costs) is the same as the after-tax return (after considering any borrowing costs) on the chosen investment.

But if the after-tax return (after considering any costs of borrowing) on any alternative investment is greater than the after-tax return (after considering any costs of borrowing) on the chosen investment (if you could have made more on any equity and received a greater differential on any borrowed money in another investment), then your overall return on equity effectively decreases as you increase equity in the chosen investment.

Financial leverage can be further enhanced by "tax leverage" (see item 23, below), the favorable condition that occurs when a deduction is allowed against taxable income or a tax credit is allowed against a tax because a client has purchased a "Code blessed" investment. The tax benefit either lowers investment cost or increases investment return.

"Double leverage," where both financial leverage and tax leverage are present in the same investment, accelerates the result. If the result is positive and the investor makes a profit, that profit will be dramatically higher than it would have been without leverage. Conversely, the double leverage significantly increases the investor's risk.

Borrowing to finance all or a part of the purchase price of an asset will meet or beat inflation if (a) the asset's value appreciates in price at or above the inflation rate, and (b) the after-tax cost of the interest payable is equal to or less than the difference between appreciation and inflation.

Keep in mind the limitation on the deduction of investment interest. (See Chapter 27, "Income Tax Planning.")

23. *Tax leverage is a concept similar to financial leverage and can provide similar advantages* – Tax leverage occurs when an investment provides tax benefits that allow an investor to defer taxes that would otherwise have been paid currently if the investment had not been made or had been made in some other form. Tax leverage allows an investor to use money that would otherwise be paid to Uncle Sam in taxes to earn additional returns on investment. What's even better, the "loan" from the government is interest free. There is, of course, a risk in using tax leverage: there is the chance that tax law changes will eliminate the tax benefits of the investment – and an investment that is a winner with tax advantages might not be a winner without those advantages.

Tax leverage is created in essentially two ways. What have been called tax-advantaged investments typically use special provisions in the Internal Revenue Code that provide up-front deductions or credits to encourage certain types of investments. As a result, although an investor must put up, say, $10,000, the actual cost to him is $10,000 less the taxes saved because of the deductions or credits. There is no free lunch, though, and taxes that are saved up front typically must be paid at some later date. But in the meantime the investor has enjoyed the use of the tax money at zero interest.

Tax leverage is also created when taxes on investment earnings are deferred. For example, the earnings in life insurance policies and annuities and series EE savings bonds typically accumulate on a tax-deferred basis. However, the most common example of this type of tax leverage is the tax deferral on capital appreciation. The tax on gains on stocks, real estate, and other capital assets is generally deferred until the asset is sold. Each year that investors enjoy tax-deferral on their earnings, they receive additional interest-free "loans" from the government that leverage future earnings just as if they had borrowed money at zero interest.

Many investments provide both types of tax leverage. For example, contributions to qualified retirement plans and IRAs are often tax deductible and taxes on the earnings within the plans are deferred until the funds are distributed.

One feature that makes tax leverage different from financial leverage is that the amount of the "loan" that must be repaid (the deferred taxes) depends on the tax rate at the time proceeds from the investment are received in a taxable transaction. If an investor is in a lower tax bracket when the taxes must ultimately be paid, part of the loan is in essence "forgiven." In contrast, if the investor is in a higher tax bracket when the deferred taxes must be paid, the amount of the "loan" is increased. However, in many cases even if an investor is in a higher tax bracket when the deferred taxes must be paid, the benefit of the tax deferral will outweigh the cost of the additional taxes.

24. *The after-tax return on the repayment of debt is essentially risk free* –

Sooner or later, an investor must repay debt incurred to finance an investment. In essence, this repayment is an important alternative to other investments. Repayment offers almost certain savings of the after-tax interest cost that would have been paid had the debt not been paid off. These savings can be thought of as "earnings" on the money used to pay the debt. With the lower tax brackets, the cost of interest (and the savings that can be realized by paying off debt) has increased. In many cases the after-tax return from the elimination of debt will be as good if not better than many investment alternatives.

25. *When planning for retirement, the wise planner and client will assume a lower than hoped for rate of return on investments, a higher than anticipated level of inflation and cost of living, and put less reliance on what Social Security or a pension will provide* –

In some cases, it is best to show a "worst case," "best case," and "probable case" scenario rather than just one set of figures. Clients often put undue reliance on figures that are mathematically accurate but are built on dubious long-range assumptions. In the authors' opinion, few clients can realize, net after taxes, a long term steady and loss free growth in excess of 5 or 6%. Likewise, the authors suggest inflation planning be based on at least a 3 to 5% assumption.

26. *When doing estate planning, the wise planner will assume the highest reasonable liquidity demands and the lowest reasonable cash to meet those needs –*

Few executors or widows have complained of having too much cash. Few trust beneficiaries have sued because they received more income than they expected or needed.

The above comments regarding the wisdom of presenting a range of possibilities to clients, and the false reliance that clients tend to place on overly optimistic numbers in a report (especially those done by computer) apply here, too.

27. *The best investment, bar none, is education –*

Clients should not rely solely on any planner. Good planners will encourage clients to read the business and financial reports in the newspapers and keep up with the impact of politics and world economic and social events on their financial security. The difference between financial dignity and financial despair may be an awareness of what's coming.

28. *Before making any suggestion to a client regarding any investment or any tool or technique, the planner should ask and answer these questions –*

a) What are the advantages – and disadvantages – of the viable alternatives?

b) Which of the viable alternatives provides the highest return at the least cost with the greatest certainty?

c) What happens if the client takes no action?

Chapter 5

ATTITUDES AND BEHAVIORAL CHARACTERISTICS OF CLIENTS

The initial emphasis in personal financial planning is, and should be on the first word, *personal*. Every client you deal with is a unique individual and needs and deserves to be treated that way.

What makes each person unique, and how does that impact your role as a financial planner? Obviously, each client's distinctive financial circumstances make him unique, as do his personal goals and priorities. In addition, everyone has his own tolerance for different types of risks (investment, debt, personal activity, property and liability) that contributes to a person's individualization.

INFLUENTIAL FACTORS

What factors or events lead to an individual's choice of goals, objectives and priorities? Put another way, what makes each of us who we are? The most obvious environmental attributes (as distinguished from inherited or genetic factors) include:

1. *Cultural background* – Religious, country of origin, urban or rural home life, economic surroundings, etc.

2. *Family experiences* – Two parent or single parent families, divorce, siblings (many or few) or only child, living grandparents nearby, large or small extended family (cousins, aunts and uncles), etc.

3. *Emotional and medical factors* – Always or never sick as a child, parents or siblings with chronic illness, depressive disorders in the family, etc.

4. *Life cycle stage and age* – Is your client at the peak of his or her career, or getting ready to retire? Does he feel older or younger than his years would suggest? Is he or she emotionally and physically, but not financially, ready to retire?

5. *Knowledge* – Education, expertise, and personal experiences – The stimulus of intellectual challenge, the client's experience in managing his own investments, street-wise experience – knowing what he can manage personally and when he needs professional assistance, etc.

Each of these influencers affects all of us to varying degrees and often in surprisingly different ways. For example, two old friends and business partners, Sam and Abe, are "Children of the Depression." Both of them saw how their parents dealt with similar hardships during the 1930s, and as a result, the two friends have very different perspectives on dealing with their own financial good fortune. On the one hand, Sam lives as if everyday will be his last and there is nothing that he can do to materially affect his future. Accordingly, he lives well, spending his earnings and not worrying about how he'll meet his future financial needs. To the other extreme, Abe believes he will live forever, be sick every day the rest of his life, and will need to save every penny he can.

While Sam is not worried about his own needs, he is concerned about his children, as his parents were concerned for him and his siblings. Accordingly, part of Sam's current spending has been regular gifting to his children as well as significant premiums on life insurance to fund an identified amount of inheritance for them. At the other extreme, Abe lives on less than one-third of his income, gives nothing to his children and doesn't believe in life insurance. He is afraid he will personally need every cent he has earned (even though his lifestyle is far below what his assets can provide), and the kids will get whatever may be left (if anything) when he is gone. Abe doesn't care that he may live to be 95 and his children would be in their 70's when they finally receive what in all likelihood will be a substantial inheritance. He simply can't bear to part with the "safety blanket" of his life savings.

It is important to highlight that neither Sam nor Abe is absolutely right or wrong in his basic financial philosophy. Again, the key to each person's financial plan is his *personal financial and emotional goals* based on his own personal experiences and priorities. It is inappropriate to criticize someone for acting in a manner consistent with his personality. At the same time, it is a critical error for a financial planner not to advise each client of the financial consequences of his spending, saving, gifting, and investing decisions. Let the client make his own decisions based on all available information, not purely from emotion and ignorance of the potential results of his choices.

STEREOTYPICAL BEHAVIOR

Even though people will react differently to similar circumstances and influences, certain actions and responses will typically fall within ranges of predictability. Such probable behavior is typically referred to as stereotypical. Stereotypes are based on patterns of reality. And, although not all responses of all people will be predictable, established stereotypes do provide a starting point in understanding how clients with certain traits and characteristics will react to their circumstances and your recommendations.

Take the attitude of Abe in the above example. It is typical for someone influenced by the hard times his parents experienced during the Depression, experiences of which he was continuously reminded, to follow the lead of his parents and to become, in the kindest term, "frugal." Sam's reaction would be considered less conventional.

What are some examples of stereotypical behavior a financial planner can expect to deal with in advising a client? Consider the following examples:

1. *Retirees* –

   As an individual approaches retirement, or if he is already retired, the realization sets in that the assets he has accumulated, plus anticipated Social Security and pension benefits, is all he has available to meet his financial goals for the rest of his life. These assets and benefits may be all he needs to fulfill all of his objectives. Most likely, the retiree will demonstrate a certain level of trepidation that he no longer has the ability to replenish his reserves now that he is no longer working. Only a small number of individuals have assets that clearly exceed their needs. Most clients have "enough," but are extremely sensitive to the following "uncontrollable" factors that may irreplaceably deplete their funds:

   a) inflation

   b) stock market volatility

   c) major medical expenses

   d) needs of their children and grandchildren that they may have to cover

   e) simply living too long (out-living their money)

   The stereotypical fears realized by the retirees often lead to irrational behavior; not eating properly, wearing old clothes, not caring for their homes, keeping the heat and air conditioning too low, leaving lights off, reducing telephone services, and not traveling anywhere. In summary, their tendency is to spend less than they can afford and, more importantly, less than they need to maintain their well-being.

   Getting retirees comfortable with the assurance that they do have enough, or that they can manage with limited adjustments to their spending habits, is not easy. All the quantitative analyses and projections in the world won't ease the emotional concerns they have as they realize they are in their final years.

2. *Divorced people* –

   Newly divorced clients are subject to many of the same fears as are retirees since, in many cases, these people must face a future with a much lower income than the amount necessary to maintain the life style to which they have become accustomed. Accordingly, they too are looking to an identified pool of resources to meet their financial needs and goals for the rest of their lives. In this case the resources typically include the assets received in the property settlement, occasionally alimony (for as long as it lasts, and it typically is not for life), pension benefits (their own and whatever share of their ex-spouse's they are entitled to under the divorce settlement – often paid in lump sum and rolled over to an IRA), and Social Security retirement benefits (their own or spousal benefits).

   The fears of the divorced individual are often exacerbated by two non-financial worries:

   a) *The fear of being alone for the rest of their lives* – This is particularly a concern for individuals who divorce in their 40's and 50's, who see many lonely years ahead of them. They may fear having no chance to remarry, and may be faced with replacing friendships and relationships that were predominantly derived from their former marriage. Even their older friends, from college and high school, are probably married, making the newly divorced individual feel like a third wheel in many situations.

b) *The fear of managing money for the first time* – Some divorced individuals who did not manage their own finances, or participate in the management of the family's finances during the marriage, may feel lost, if not in total fear of managing monthly bills and checkbooks. The idea of a budget may be foreign to them.

Imagine how the divorced person in this situation feels about managing the investment of the funds received in a property settlement. How does he or she know whom to turn to? Who can be trusted? How do you build trust? Many divorced individuals compound the personal crisis by making poor choices of investment managers. The risks of such errors are devastating since the client may have no opportunity to financially recover.

In the case of women the change of life may compound these traumas, leading to irrational behavior and a poor decision making process. Patience and sensitivity to this fragility are critical to providing meaningful advice and counsel to these clients.

3. *Widows* –

Similar to retirees and divorcees, widows are confronted with the realization that the assets left to them by their late spouses represent all they have to manage their financial needs for the balance of their lives. They are subject to all of the emotional issues previously discussed. If they are young widows, they may be concerned with being alone and raising children alone for a very long time. Older or younger, they are all particularly vulnerable to an acute loneliness because of how they arrived at this status – the death of a loved one.

Older widows sometimes find that the adjustment to new responsibilities, such as the management of money and investments, is beyond them. The fact that the family assets might have been more than adequate to fulfill the needs of both spouses during retirement, even if the assets are supplemented by life insurance on the deceased spouse, is irrelevant. They simply never had to cope with matters relating to money. They may be fearful that it is beyond them *and* there will not be enough.

The emotional issues associated with the loss of a spouse cannot be overstated. Perceptions of dependency on the lost spouse, particularly as relates to financial matters, are often illogically intensified.

4. *Young singles* –

The number one financial priority of young singles is typically spending, particularly if they have lived a financially limited life during their college years. Having money of their own, not being on an allowance, is a new experience for them. Some can handle this; they'll live at home for a while, maximize contributions to 401(k) plans, and just generally be "financially responsible." Others will go to the other extreme, buy an expensive car, rent an unnecessary large apartment that they're never in, and even incur significant credit card debt while still trying to manage to pay off education loans. It's only after their credit is cut off, or in the extreme they are facing personal bankruptcy that they wake up.

5. *Young married couples/ no children* –

These clients are often like young singles, except that a double appetite for the "good life" compounds the problem. What may be perceived as a double income of two working spouses is often reduced by the marriage tax penalty of progressive tax rates and double FICA taxes.

In many cases, one of the two young spouses will be more fiscally responsible and strong enough to influence the joint spending and saving habits. The drive to buy a first home and have a family can be powerful. It is not uncommon, however, for these differences in attitudes toward money matters to lead to stress in the early years of a marriage that can even become fatal to the relationship.

6. *Couples with young children (or soon to be parents)* –

Here's when things get serious. The responsibilities of a family become an often-frightening reality, and a priority. The first (or larger) house, the loss or reduction in one spouse's income, the possible need for private schools are examples of the financial stressors the young couple must now deal with.

Interestingly, what has emerged as a common characteristic of young parents is the desire, and often obsession, to pre-fund the college education of their youngsters. Many couples are willing to defer the funding of their retirement and reduce their current lifestyles in order to put aside as much as possible for their children's future. Many of these parents want to pre-fund both college and graduate school at the most expensive universities. More typically, depending on the income potential of the couple, four years of college is the identified goal. The availability of tax-favored investment vehicles, such as 529 plans, makes these goals more realistic. But, since college costs have, at least in recent years, been rising at speeds that often exceed twice the rate of inflation, even tax advantaged spending doesn't adequately relieve this financial burden.

Habits are often hard to break, so it is not uncommon for young couples who have reduced their lifestyles to save for the college needs of their children to simply shift to saving for retirement, leaving their lifestyles at the same basic level. These couples will often retire with assets far beyond their needs for the balance of their lives, having never spent up to what they could afford.

Life insurance plays a key role in managing the education funding aspirations of the young parents. With an identifiable number of years that creation of an instant pool of funds is needed, term life insurance is usually the appropriate tool.

Two final thoughts – firstly, stereotypical behavior is just that, typical behavior, not everyone's manner or reaction to particular circumstances. As stated in the beginning of this chapter, every person is unique and should be treated as special and distinctive. Not everyone will react as you might expect. As a simple example, not every widow was dependent on the deceased spouse to manage the day-to-day finances. Who pays the bills in your family?

Secondly, there is a clear, recurrent relationship between stress and money. When someone is dealing with financial issues and concerns, these problems pour over to every aspect of his life. Similarly, if someone is dealing with a monumental emotional or stressful event, whether perceived or actual, money and financial concerns are often given an unrealistic and irrational priority. In many cases, only time will soothe these concerns. In some cases, they will linger forever.

WHERE CAN I FIND OUT MORE ABOUT IT?

Eugene Kennedy and Sara C. Charles, M.D., *On Becoming a Counselor Revised Edition: A Basic Guide for Nonprofessional Counselors and Other Helper* (New York, NY: Crossroad Publishing Company, 2001).

Chapter 6

FINANCIAL SERVICES INDUSTRY REGULATIONS

INTRODUCTION

The Securities and Exchange Commission (SEC) regulates investment advisers and their activities under the Investment Advisers Act of 1940. One of the central elements of the regulatory program is the requirement that, unless you are exempt under specific provisions of the Act, you must register with the SEC as an investment adviser. Part I of this chapter describes the regulatory process and Part II provides detailed information on how to register as an investment adviser.

Investment advisers that have less than $25 million of assets under management and are subject to state securities regulation are generally prohibited from registering with the SEC. Assets under management are defined as securities portfolios with respect to which an investment adviser provides continuous and regular supervisory or management services. Investment advisers with $25 million of assets under management or in those states that do not regulate investment advisers must register with the SEC as described below. In addition, many states have investment adviser laws that are patterned after the federal investment adviser law, described below.

PART I – REGULATION

Definition of an Investment Adviser

The Investment Advisers Act of 1940 (the Act) provides a three-part definition for determining who is an investment adviser. An investment adviser is a person who (1) provides advice, or issues reports or analyses, regarding securities; (2) is in the business of providing such services; and (3) provides such services for compensation.[1] All three prongs of this test must be met for the definition to apply.

It is important to note that the SEC defines compensation as "the receipt of any economic benefit," which includes commissions on the sale of products.

Exclusions from the Definition

The Act excludes certain organizations and individuals from the definition of an investment adviser. These include

1. banks and bank holding companies
2. lawyers, accountants, engineers, or teachers, if their performance of advisory services is solely incidental to their professions
3. brokers or dealers if their performance of advisory services is solely incidental to the conduct of their business as brokers or dealers, and they do not receive any special compensation for their advisory services
4. publishers of bona fide newspapers, news magazines, or business or financial publications of general and regular circulation
5. those persons whose advice is related only to securities that are direct obligations of or guaranteed by the United States

Caution must be exercised by practitioners relying on the exclusions provided under (2) and (3), above. The SEC has taken the position that the "incidental practice" exception provided by these sections is not available to individuals who hold themselves out to the public as providing financial planning, pension consulting, or other financial advisory services. It is the view of the SEC that if persons are promoting or advertising themselves as providing such services, it is unlikely that these services are merely incidental to their businesses.

In addition to these exclusions, the Act allows some advisers to be exempt from registration if they meet certain limited criteria discussed in the next section.

Exemptions from Registration

The Act provides limited exemptions from registration. Particularly important is the exemption for investment advisers who, during the course of the preceding 12 months, had fewer than 15 clients and who do not hold themselves out generally to the public as investment advisers.[2]

This is a very limited exemption and applies only if both conditions are met. Even if an investment adviser has fewer than fifteen clients, he is not exempt if he holds himself out to the public as an investment adviser in any manner. Examples of this public notice include

1. maintaining a listing as an investment adviser in a telephone, business, building, or other directory

2. expressing willingness to existing clients or others to accept new clients

3. using a letterhead indicating any investment adviser activity

This exemption also is not available to an investment adviser who advises an investment company (mutual fund) registered under the Investment Company Act of 1940, or a business development company that has elected to be treated as such under that Act.

Another exemption provides that any investment adviser, all of whose clients are residents of the same state as the principal office and place of business, is exempt if he does not furnish advice or analysis concerning any security listed or traded on any national securities exchange.[3]

Are Financial Planners Investment Advisers?

Financial planning as such or the provision of investment advice in connection with non-financial planning services triggers the issue of whether there is an investment adviser for purposes of the Act. As described above, the Act defines an investment adviser as "any person who, for compensation, engages in the business of advising others, either directly or through publications or writings, as to the value of securities or as to the advisability of investing in, purchasing, or selling securities, or who, for compensation and as part of a regular business, issues or promulgates analyses or reports concerning securities."[4]

1. A person includes a natural person as well as a company, irrespective of the form of its organization.[5]

2. A security includes any note, stock, bond, debenture, evidence of indebtedness, certificate of interest or participation in any profit-sharing agreement, collateral-trust agreement, pre-organization certificate or subscription, transferable share, or investment contract (including variable annuities).[6]

However, financial planning may encompass a wide variety of services, principally advisory in nature, which may, or may not, trigger the registration requirement. These services may be broadly segmented in three service categories.

Generally, financial planning services involve preparing a financial program for a client based on the client's financial circumstances and objectives. This information normally covers present and anticipated assets and liabilities, including insurance, savings, investments, and anticipated retirement or other employee benefits. The program developed for the client usually includes general recommendations for a course of activity, or specific actions to be taken by the client. Recommendations may be made, for example, that the client obtain insurance or revise existing coverage, establish an individual retirement account, increase or decrease funds held in savings accounts, or invest funds in securities. A financial planner may develop tax or estate plans for clients or refer clients to an accountant or attorney for these services. The provider of these services in most cases assists the client in implementing the recommended program by, among other things, making specific recommendations to carry out the general recommendations of the program, or by selling the client insurance products, securities, or other investments. The financial planner may also review the client's program periodically and recommend revisions. People who provide financial planning services use various compensation arrangements. Some financial planners charge clients an overall fee for developing an individual client program while others charge clients an hourly fee. In some instances financial planners are compensated, in whole or in part, by commissions on the sale to the client of insurance products, interests in real estate, securities (such as common stocks, bonds, limited partnership interests, and mutual funds), or other investments.

A second common form of service relating to financial matters is provided by pension consultants who typically offer, in addition to administrative services, a variety of advisory services to employee benefit plans and their fiduciaries based upon an analysis of the needs of the plan. These advisory services may include advice as to the types of funding media available to provide plan benefits, general recommendations as to what portion of plan assets should be invested in various investment media, including securities, and in some cases, recommendations regarding investment in specific securities or other investments. Pension consultants may also assist plan fiduciaries in determining plan investment objectives and policies and in designing funding media for the plan. They may also provide general or specific advice to plan fiduciaries as to the selection or retention of persons to manage the assets of the plan. Persons providing these services to plans are customarily compensated for their services through fees paid by the plan, its sponsor, or others, by means of sales commissions on the sale of insurance products or investments to the plan, or through a combination of fees and commissions.

A rarer form of financial advisory service is provided by persons offering a variety of financially related services to entertainers or athletes based upon the needs of the individual client. Such persons, who often use the designation "sports representative" or "entertainment representative," offer a number of services to clients, including the negotiation of employment contracts and development of promotional opportunities for the client, as well as advisory services related to investments, tax planning, or budget and money management. Such persons providing these services to clients may assume discretion over all or a portion of a client's funds by collecting income, paying bills, and making investments for the client. Such representatives are customarily compensated for their services primarily through fees charged for negotiation of employment contracts but may also receive compensation in the form of fixed charges or hourly fees for other services provided, including investment advisory services.

The SEC has issued guidance concerning the application of the Act in Investment Advisers Act Release No. 1092 (IA 1092). According to IA 1092, all of the facts and circumstances must be examined in determining whether a person providing integrated advisory services meets the definition of an investment adviser.

1. A person who provides advice, or issues or promulgates reports or analyses, which concern securities, generally is an investment adviser.

   This includes analysis of rate of return on current portfolio and opinions concerning the efficacy of the asset allocation to achieve the financial goals.

   This also includes giving advice as to the selection or retention of an investment manager if the advice is based on the client's investment objectives.

   Providing a list of investment mangers without recommendation in conjunction with a financial planning business is considered investment advice, while the providing of a list of money managers is not considered investment advice.

2. A person who advises clients concerning the relative advantages and disadvantages of investing in securities in general as compared to other investments is an investment adviser.

In general, therefore, any person engaging in any of the types of financial planning services described above is considered an investment adviser unless otherwise qualifying under one of the exclusions or exemptions described above.

The clearest instance of an investment adviser being in the business of giving advice is where the person clearly holds himself to others as an adviser or as one who gives advice.

In a case where the person's principal business is the giving of financial services other than investment advice the person is still considered to be in the business if there are discussions concerning investments that go beyond a discussion of the advisability of investing in securities in general terms[7] or if the giving of investment advice is regularly a part of the business activities.[8] The giving of advice need not be the principal business activity for the person to be in the business of giving investment advice.

Example. A CPA is reviewing the tax return with a client. In response to the client's question about reducing taxes, the CPA indicates that municipal bonds would reduce such taxes. If similar statements are regularly made in the course of reviewing clients' tax returns or assets, the CPA is in the business of giving investment advice.

According to the SEC, a person is considered to be in the business of giving advice with respect to securities if that person

1. holds himself out as an investment adviser or as a provider of investment advice

2. receives separate or additional compensation that is a clearly definable charge for the provision of advice about securities, regardless of whether the compensation is separate or included in overall compensation

3. provides specific investment advice other than in rare, isolated, or non-periodic instances[9]

The SEC will also consider other financial services activities offered to clients. For example, if a financial planner structures his planning so as to give only generic, non-specific investment advice as a financial planner, but then gives specific securities advice in his capacity as a registered representative of a dealer or as an agent of an insurance company, the person would not be able to assert that he was not "in the business" of giving investment advice.

Compensation Element

The compensation element of being an investment adviser is satisfied by the receipt of any economic benefit, whether in the form of an advisory fee or some other fee relating to the total services rendered, commissions, or some combination of the foregoing. It is not necessary that the person who provides investment advisory and other services to a client charge a separate fee for the investment advisory portion of the total services. The compensation element is satisfied if a single fee is charged for a number of different services, including investment advice or the issuing of reports or analyses concerning securities. But the fact that no separate fee is charged for the investment advisory portion of the service could be relevant to whether the person is "in the business" of giving investment advice.

It is not necessary that an adviser's compensation be paid directly by the person receiving investment advisory services, only that the investment adviser receive compensation from some source for his services. A person providing a variety of services to a client, including investment advisory services, for which the person receives any economic benefit, for example, by receipt of a single fee or commissions upon the sale to the client of insurance products or investments, is providing advisory services for compensation.

Subsidiaries and Affiliates

The controlling entity of a registered investment adviser may likewise have to register unless the controlled entity has a separate, independent existence evidenced by

1. being adequately capitalized

2. having a buffer between the subsidiary's personnel and the parent's

3. having employees, officers, and directors who are not otherwise engaged in an investment advisory business of the parent

4. determining the investment advice given to clients and not limiting sources of investment information to its parent

5. keeping its investment advice confidential until communicated to its clients[10]

The Exception for Accountants

Even if an accountant is considered to be an investment adviser in the business of providing investment advice, an accountant may be specifically excluded from the definition of an investment adviser for purposes of the Act. The issue is whether the investment advice is given solely incidental to the practice of accounting.[11] There are no specific regulatory or judicial announcements to guide accountants on the meaning of the incidental rule; however, the SEC has issued a "No-Action" letter in which it enumerated three factors to be considered:[12]

1. whether the accountant (or firm) holds himself out to the public as an investment adviser

2. whether the services rendered are in connection with and reasonably related to accounting services

3. whether the fee charged for advisory services is based on the same factors as those used to determine the accounting fee

The No-Action letter provides that the exception is not available to an accountant who holds himself out, or a firm that holds itself out, to the public as providing financial planning, pension consulting, or other financial advisory services. In that case, the performance of investment advisory services by that person is deemed to be incidental to the practice of financial planning or pension consulting profession and not incidental to the practice of accounting. In this respect, financial planning appears to be considered as something outside the practice of accounting for purposes of this exception.

Even if an accountant is an investment adviser and cannot rely on the accountants exemption, there are exemptions from registration which may be available. However, those individuals remain liable under the Act's anti-fraud provisions.

Brochure Rule

Investment advisers are generally required to deliver a written disclosure statement (brochure) on their background and business practices upon entering into an advisory contract with a client.[13] The brochure rule is designed to assure that clients are provided with pertinent information useful in the selection or retention of an investment adviser.

The rule also requires investment advisers, on an annual basis, to deliver (or to offer in writing to deliver) to clients a free brochure. Advisory contracts with investment companies and contracts for impersonal advisory services of less than $200 per year are exempt from the brochure rule. An adviser entering into a contract for impersonal advisory services of more than $200 per year need only offer to deliver a brochure.

The information required by the brochure rule is included in Part II of Form ADV, the registration form for investment advisers. To comply with the brochure rule, an investment adviser may deliver either: (1) Part II of Form ADV, or (2) another document containing at least that information.

Books and Records – Inspections

The 1940 Adviser's Act and the SEC's rules require that advisers maintain and preserve specified books and records and make them available to Commission examiners for inspection. This rule allows computer and microfilm record-keeping under certain conditions.[14]

Prohibited Contractual and Fee Provisions

The Act requires advisory contracts to provide that the contract may not be assigned without the client's consent. If the investment adviser is a partnership, the contract must provide that the adviser will notify the client of a change in its membership.

The Act also prohibits any type of fee arrangement contingent on capital gains or appreciation in the client's account. There is a statutory exception from the performance fee prohibition for contracts with a registered investment company or certain clients with more than $1 million in managed assets if specific conditions are met.[15] In addition, performance fee contracts are permitted with clients with $750,000 under the adviser's management or a net worth in excess of $1.5 million under certain conditions.[16]

Restrictions on Use of the Term "Investment Counsel"

A registered investment adviser may not use the term "investment counsel" unless its principal business is acting as an investment adviser and a substantial portion of its business is providing "investment supervisory services." Investment supervisory services are the giving of continuous advice on the investment of funds on the basis of the individual needs of each client.[17]

Anti-Fraud Provisions and Disclosure Requirements

Fraudulent activities by investment advisers are prohibited. This applies to all investment advisers, registered or not.[18] SEC regulations establish restrictions on advertising by investment advisers, custody or possession of a client's funds or securities, and when advisers may pay cash referral fees.[19]

Misstatements or misleading omissions of material facts and fraudulent acts and practices in connection with the purchase or sale of securities, or the conduct of an investment advisory business, are prohibited.[20] As a fiduciary, an investment adviser owes his clients undivided loyalty and may not engage in activity in conflict with a client's interest. U. S. Supreme Court rulings have also held that advisers have an affirmative obligation "of utmost good faith and full and fair disclosure of all material facts" to their clients, as well as a duty to avoid misleading them.

Three rules are particularly important:

1. All investment advisers are prohibited from using any advertisement that contains any untrue statement of material fact or which is otherwise misleading. Specific prohibitions apply to the use of testimonials, past specific recommendations, and charts, graphs, formulas, and similar devices.[21]

2. Regulations detail how client funds and securities in the custody of the adviser must be held and require the adviser to provide specified information to clients. Under these rules, advisers with custody must have an annual, unannounced examination of the funds and securities by an independent public accountant and file that report with the SEC.[22]

3. An investment adviser is prohibited from paying cash fees for soliciting clients, on a direct or indirect basis, except under specific conditions.[23]

Fiduciary Duty

The SEC has stated that an investment adviser has a fiduciary obligation to render disinterested and impartial advice; to make suitable recommendations to clients in light of their needs, financial circumstances, and investment objectives; to exercise a high degree of care to insure that adequate and accurate representations and other information about securities are presented to clients; and to have an adequate basis in fact for its recommendations, representations, and projections.[24]

Responsibility for Compliance – SEC Assistance

This chapter merely highlights selected provisions of the 1940 Investment Advisers Act and its rules. It does not state all applicable regulatory provisions. You should consult the Act (15 U.S.C. 80b-1 et. seq.) and its regulations, which are found in Title 17, Part 275 of the Code of Federal Regulations.

We recommend that advisers obtain these regulations (Title 17, CFR, Part 240 through the end). They are available online from the Superintendent of Documents at http://bookstore.gpo.gov, or by calling toll free 866-512-1800.

The rules and regulations can also be accessed through the Government Printing Office's website, www.access.gpo.gov.

State Requirements

Most states have securities laws requiring registration of investment advisers. In the majority of the states with these laws, the laws are patterned on the Act and the same three-pronged definition determines who is and who is not an investment adviser. Some states have amended their securities laws in recent years to bring financial planners within the definition of investment adviser.

Most of the states require completion of the ADV form or their own version of the ADV form; most also have an exam requirement and a filing fee. In some states a bond must be posted, with amounts varying from state to state. Requests for information about the requirements of any particular state should be addressed to that state's officials. The name and address of those officials can be obtained by contacting:

North American Securities
Administrators Association
750 First Street NE, Suite 1140
Washington, DC 20002
(202) 737-0900
http://www.nasaa.org/

Compliance Requirements of CFP Certificants

In addition to complying with federal and state regulations, CFP certificants also must satisfy CFP Board requirements and standards. The CFP Board was instituted in an attempt to uphold high standards of competence and ethical practice in the absence of uniform government regulation of the profession. To accomplish this objective, the CFP Board requires all its certificants to adhere to the CFP Board Code of Ethics and Professional Responsibility and Financial Planning Practice Standards. Failure to do so can result in the loss of the CFP certification mark. The CFP certification mark is now available in all 50 states and in more than 10 countries.

To hold the CFP designation, an individual is "required to know the four 'Es': education, examination, experience, and ethics." An applicant must have three years of relevant experience if he or she has an appropriate college degree or five years without one. The CFP Board, however, recently determined that by 2007, all new certificants will be required to hold a bachelor's degree. In addition, the applicant must pass an examination on the various topics relevant to financial planning profession and sign a Declaration and Agreement form disclosing information about whether the individual has been involved in any type of litigation or inquiry. Moreover, the applicant is required to adhere to the previously mentioned code of ethics and practice standards, and acknowledge the Board's right to enforce them. The Board also conducts background checks of its applicants. An applicant must then pay an initial fee and during the time that the individual is certified, complete continuing education credits.

The CFP Board Code of Ethics and Professional Responsibility is currently being updated by a Disclosure Task Force composed of twelve individuals with different jobs related to the financial planning profession. In order to enhance public trust in the financial planning profession, the Task Force's goal is to encourage greater disclosure, primarily of compensation methods hitherto not required under federal or state regulation, to allow consumers to make informed decisions as to their own financial planning needs while not unduly burdening the practitioner. A principle of fairness also underlies the responsibility of a CFP certificant. A CFP certificant must perform all services to the client in a manner that is fair and reasonable and in addition must disclose any conflicts of interest affecting the relationship.

PART II – REGISTRATION

Introduction

A person subject to SEC registration as an investment adviser must file Form ADV, keep it current by filing periodic amendments, and file a brief report annually. These requirements are discussed below.

A person subject to registration also must comply with the "brochure rule," (described above) which requires most advisers to provide clients and prospective clients with information about the adviser's business practices and educational and business background. For more information about the brochure rule, consult the document "General Information on the Regulation of Investment Advisers" (contact the nearest regional office of the Securities and Exchange Commission for a copy) or Rule 204-3.[25]

General Filing Requirements

Forms – Copies of Forms ADV and ADV-W can be obtained from the SEC's Office of Consumer Affairs and Information Services in Washington, DC, or from a local Commission office.

Copies – All adviser filings must be submitted in triplicate and typewritten. Copies can be filed, but each must be signed manually. If an applicant fails to submit three copies, the filing will be returned and may be declared delinquent when it is resubmitted. An applicant should keep a fourth copy of all filings for his own records.

Name and signatures – Full names are required. Initials may not be used, unless an individual legally has only an initial. Each copy of an execution page must contain an original manual signature. If the registration application is filed by a sole proprietor, it should be signed by the proprietor; if filed by a partnership, it should be signed in the name of the partnership by a general partner; if filed by a corporation, it should be signed in the corporation's name by an authorized principal officer.

The changes in technology have demanded the need for a more convenient way for investment advisers to file the required forms to register. In response to this growth in technology, the SEC adopted Rule 203-1 under the Advisers Act requiring that all investment advisers registered with the SEC after January 1, 2001, submit registration forms to the SEC electronically. This rule allows investment advisers to electronically file all forms needed to meet the requirements of both federal and state laws conveniently over the Internet. This established the goal of a one-stop electronic filing system for investors.

Investment Adviser Public Disclosure

On September 25, 2001, the SEC and NASAA launched the Investment Adviser Pubic Disclosure (IAPD) website that allows investors, free of charge, to access the system and access information about any investment advisers registered on IAPD. People searching for an investment adviser can access those investment advisers' Form ADVs who have registered electronically and in turn get information about the adviser's business operations as well as disciplinary proceedings in which the adviser and its employees have been involved. Until recently, the site only displayed registered investment adviser firms and not individual advisers. This changed on March 18, 2002, when the system began accepting individual filings. The website does not warn investors that the adviser's Form ADV accessed on the website is not approved by the SEC or state security authority, and therefore may not be completely accurate. This site will not only aid investors and financial planners (interested in their competitors), but the SEC as well, since this system allows the SEC to more closely monitor advisers and focus on possible areas that may need special attention.

Form ADV

Form ADV is the application for registration with the SEC as an investment adviser. Part I asks for information that is used to review the application and in the SEC's investment advisory program. Part II requires information on the background and business practices of the investment adviser, and can be given to clients to comply with the "brochure rule." Both parts must be filed with the SEC.

Within 45 days after a registration application is filed, the SEC must grant registration or begin proceedings to deny it. The only grounds for denial are if the Commission finds that the adviser has committed prohibited acts and the public interest requires denial.

Make sure that all items on the form and accompanying schedules are properly completed in full. If the registration application filed is incomplete, it will be returned and the 45 day period will not begin again until a complete application is submitted.

Amending Form ADV

Form ADV must be amended to be updated. Rule 204-1 governs which information must be corrected promptly and which must be corrected within 90 days of the end of the fiscal year.

Amending the form requires completing the execution page (page one) and the entire page containing the updated items. Circle the items being amended. Rule 204-1(a) and (b) and the instructions to Form ADV give more complete information on amendments.

Balance Sheets

All registrants must maintain "true, accurate, and current books and records" as specified in Rule 204-2.[26] However, not all registrants are required to submit financial statements to the Commission. Registrants who must file a balance sheet are those with custody or possession of client funds or securities, or those requiring prepayment of advisory fees six months or more in advance and in excess of $500 per client.

If an adviser is required to submit a balance sheet, it must be audited by an independent public accountant. It is filed annually on Schedule G as an amendment to Form ADV.

Withdrawal from Registration – Form ADV-W

If an adviser is no longer engaged in business as an investment adviser, he may apply to withdraw his registration by filing Form ADV-W (Notice of Withdrawal from Registration as an Investment Adviser) in accordance with the instructions on the form. He must file Form ADV-W to withdraw his registration voluntarily.

SECURITIES REGULATION OF BROKER-DEALERS AND ASSOCIATED PERSONS

Federal Regulation

Many financial planners are also subject to federal regulation of broker-dealers under the Securities Exchange Act of 1934 (the 1934 Act). Section 15 of the 1934 Act requires securities brokers or dealers to register with the SEC. Brokers act as agents and are defined broadly by the 1934 Act as "any person engaged in the business of effecting transaction in securities for the account of others." In addition to the obvious case of an individuals (or businesses) executing securities transactions, financial planners may fall under the SEC's definition depending on the extent of their participation in soliciting or negotiating a transaction or if they receive transaction-based compensation. The 1934 Act defines dealers, who (or which) act as principals, as "any person engaged in the business of buying and selling securities for such person's own account through a broker or otherwise."

Federal regulation of securities sales includes broad antifraud provisions such as section 10(b) of the 1934 Act: It is unlawful for any person "[t]o use or employ, in connection with the purchase or sale of any security ... any manipulative or deceptive device ... in contravention of such rules and regulations as the Commission may prescribe as necessary or appropriate in the public interest or for the protection of investors." Broker-dealers are also subject to the "shingle theory," which holds that when a broker-dealer hangs out a shingle, "he impliedly represents that he will deal fairly and competently with his customers." In addition to registering with the SEC and being subject to the Act's antifraud provisions, a broker or dealer must also become a member of the National Association of Securities Dealers (NASD).

Individuals who work for a registered broker-dealer, referred to as "associated persons," are not required to register with the SEC, but must register with, and satisfy the qualification standards of, the broker-dealer's applicable SRO (typically the NASD). An "associated person" is "any partner, officer, director, or branch manager of such broker or dealer . . . , any person directly or indirectly controlling, controlled by, or under common control with such broker or dealer, or any employee of such broker or dealer," unless the associated person's functions are "solely clerical or ministerial." The services provided by many financial planners qualify them as "associated persons" and, thus, they are subject to federal oversight, though indirectly through the NASD. Typically, financial planners associated with a registered broker-dealer are sales personnel, and they are therefore required to register and qualify as NASD "registered representatives."

Other important components of NASD regulation are its examination requirements, which affect many financial planners. Since 1956, the NASD has required individuals associated with member firms to pass a written examination. The NASD offers more than 30 types of examinations, and individuals selling certain products or acting in certain supervisory capacities are required to pass one or more exams based on their specific roles within the broker-dealer or as associated persons. Financial planners subject to broker-dealer regulation typically must pass the Series 7, *General Securities Registered Representative Examination*, and are subject to continuing education requirements. Branch offices of broker-dealers are also the focus of regulatory scrutiny by the NASDR, including heightened supervision of the sale of certain products such as variable annuities. State-imposed tests such as the Series 63 Exam for registered representatives add to the panoply of brokerage oversight.

State Regulation

Those financial planners who earn commissions on the sale of securities must also concern themselves with state regulation of broker-dealers, which is very similar to federal regulation. Most states regulate broker-dealers through statutory schemes based on a version of the Uniform Securities Act or regulations adopted by the NASAA. Typically, states require a broker-dealer to register annually. Most states also require passage of an examination on securities laws and principles by persons associated with a broker-dealer.

In many states, NASD tests satisfy the requirement. Other common features include bonding and net capital requirements and a provision for service of process.

INSURANCE REGULATION

Financial planning often includes an analysis of a client's insurance needs. Financial planners, therefore, may find themselves subject to government regulation of insurance, which primarily means state regulation. In some states, financial planners are even subject to regulation if they recommend a generic insurance product or a specific amount of insurance without referring the client to an insurance agent or acting as insurance agents themselves.

Financial planners who actually sell insurance products, that is, who are insurance agents, are typically required to obtain a license from the insurance department in their home state. Licensing requirements also typically apply to insurance brokers, individuals who are not agents but who act as intermediaries for parties seeking insurance and insurers. Many states define brokers broadly to include anyone who, for compensation, "aids in any manner in negotiating contracts for insurance or placing risks or effecting insurance for another." A financial planner who receives referral fees from an insurance agent would likely satisfy such a definition. Finally, some states license insurance "advisers," "analysts," or "consultants," terms that clearly apply to financial planners who render insurance advice for a fee. Some states, however, make insurance licensing easier for accredited financial planners by exempting individuals holding the CFP or other designations from insurance testing requirements.

State licensing provisions typically require passage of an examination as well as educational requirements. A number of states require insurance advisers to have had three or more years of experience as a licensed insurance agent. This creates a licensing "Catch 22" for fee-only planners entering the business without an insurance background because they cannot become licensed to meet the experience requirement since insurance companies would only hire commission-based agents or producers. In addition, many states prohibit financial planners who are insurance agents, brokers, or advisers from receiving both insurance commissions and financial planning fees unless a written agreement is signed before providing the services.

CHAPTER ENDNOTES

1. 15 USC §80b-2(a)(11).
2. 15 USC §80b-3(b)(3).
3. 15 USC §80b-3(b)(1).
4. 15 USC §80b-2(a)(11).
5. 15 USC §80b-2(a)(16).
6. 15 USC §80b-2(a)(18).
7. IA 770.
8. IA 1092.
9. IA 1092 indicates that asset allocation advice concerning the percentages of various assets that should be held is considered equivalent to giving advice with respect to specific securities.
10. Richard E. Ellis/R.E. Holdings Limited, SEC No-Action Letter (Sept. 17, 1981).
11. 15 USC §80b-2(a)(11)(B).
12. Hauk, Soule, & Fasani, P.C., SEC No-Action Letter (May 2, 1986).
13. 17 CFR 275.204-3.
14. 15 USC §80b-4; 17 CFR 275.204-2.
15. 15 USC §80b-5.
16. 17 CFR 275.205-3.
17. 15 USC §§80b-2(a)(13), 80b-8(c).
18. 15 USC §80b-6.
19. 17 CFR 275.206(4)-1, 275.206(4)-2, 275.206(4)-3.
20. 15 USC §§77q, 78j(b), 80b-6; 17 C.F.R. 240.10b-5.
21. 17 CFR 275.206(4)-1.
22. 17 CFR 275.206(4)-2.
23. 17 CFR 275.206(4)-3.
24. SEC, Investment Adviser Examination Manual (1980).
25. 17 CFR 275.204-3.
26. 17 CFR 275.204-2.

individuals agree to be bound by CFP Board's Code of Ethics and Practice Standards. This demonstrates to the public that certificants have agreed to provide personal financial planning in the client's best interest and to act in accordance with the highest ethical and professional standards for the practice of financial planning.

Before being authorized to use the CFP certification marks, and each time certificants renew their certification, they must disclose whether they have ever been involved in any criminal, civil, self-regulatory organization, or governmental agency inquiry, investigation, or proceeding. They must also acknowledge the right of CFP Board to enforce its Code of Ethics and Practice Standards through its Disciplinary Rules and Procedures.

The CFP Board may verify employment records, qualifications and disciplinary history through the NASD®'s Central Registration Depository (CRD), the National Association of Insurance Commissioners' (NAIC) depository, and other regulatory authorities. The CFP Board will review all disciplinary information so obtained. The length of the review process varies depending on the circumstances being investigated and may take anywhere from several weeks to one year. In general, certificants will not be authorized to use the CFP marks during the CFP Board's review process.

This chapter covers the Code of Ethics and Professional Responsibility and the Disciplinary Rules and Procedures. Chapter 8 will discuss the Financial Planning Practice Standards.

Code of Ethics And Professional Responsibility

The code of ethics and professional responsibility includes the following sections:

- Ethics Overview
- Part I – PRINCIPLES
- Part II – RULES
- Advisory Opinion 2000-1
- Advisory Opinion 2003-1
- Sample Disclosure Forms

Overview

Preamble and Applicability

The *Code of Ethics and Professional Responsibility (Code of Ethics)* has been adopted by Certified Financial Planner Board of Standards Inc. (CFP Board) to provide principles and rules to all persons whom it has recognized and certified to use the CFP®, CERTIFIED FINANCIAL PLANNER™ and certification marks (collectively "the marks"). CFP Board determines who is certified and thus authorized to use the marks. Implicit in the acceptance of this authorization is an obligation not only to comply with the mandates and requirements of all applicable laws and regulations but also to take responsibility to act in an ethical and professionally responsible manner in all professional services and activities.

For purposes of this *Code of Ethics*, a person recognized and certified by CFP Board to use the marks is called a CFP Board designee. This *Code of Ethics* applies to CFP Board designees actively involved in the practice of personal financial planning, in other areas of financial services, in industry, in related professions, in government, in education or in any other professional activity in which the marks are used in the performance of professional responsibilities. This *Code of Ethics* also applies to candidates for the CFP® certification who are registered as such with CFP Board. For purposes of this *Code of Ethics*, the term CFP Board designee shall be deemed to include current certificants, candidates and individuals who have been certified in the past and retain the right to reinstate their CFP certification without passing the current CFP® Certification Examination.

Composition and Scope

The *Code Of Ethics* consists of two parts: Part I – Principles and Part II – Rules. The Principles are statements expressing in general terms the ethical and professional ideals that CFP Board designees are expected to display in their professional activities. As such, the Principles are aspirational in character but are intended to provide a source of guidance for CFP Board designees. The comments following each Principle further explain the meaning of the Principle. The Rules in Part II provide practical guidelines derived from the tenets embodied in the Principles. As such, the Rules describe the standards of ethical and professionally responsible conduct expected of CFP Board designees in particular situations. This *Code Of Ethics* does not undertake to define standards of professional conduct of CFP Board designees for purposes of civil liability.

Due to the nature of a CFP Board designee's particular field of endeavor, certain Rules may not be applicable to that CFP Board designee's activities. For example, a CFP Board designee who is engaged solely in the sale of securities as a registered representative is not subject to the written disclosure requirements of Rule 402 (applicable to CFP Board designees engaged in personal financial planning) although he or she may have disclosure responsibilities under Rule 401. A CFP Board designee is obligated to determine what responsibilities he or she has in each professional relationship including, for example, duties that arise in particular circumstances from a position of trust or confidence that a CFP Board designee may have. The CFP Board designee is obligated to meet those responsibilities.

The *Code Of Ethics* is structured so that the presentation of the Rules parallels the presentation of the Principles. For example, the Rules which relate to Principle 1 – Integrity are numbered in the 100 to 199 series, while those Rules relating to Principle 2 – Objectivity are numbered in the 200 to 299 series.

Compliance

CFP Board requires adherence to this *Code Of Ethics* by all CFP Board designees. Compliance with the *Code Of Ethics*, individually and by the profession as a whole, depends on each CFP Board designee's knowledge of and voluntary compliance with the Principles and applicable Rules, on the influence of fellow professionals and public opinion, and on disciplinary proceedings, when necessary, involving CFP Board designees who fail to comply with the applicable provisions of the *Code Of Ethics*.

These *Code Of Ethics'* Principles express the profession's recognition of its responsibilities to the public, to clients, to colleagues and to employers. They apply to all CFP Board designees and provide guidance to them in the performance of their professional services.

Principles

Principle 1 – Integrity

A CFP Board designee shall offer and provide professional services with integrity.

As discussed in "Composition and Scope," CFP Board designees may be placed by clients in positions of trust and confidence. The ultimate source of such public trust is the CFP Board designee's personal integrity. In deciding what is right and just, a CFP Board designee should rely on his or her integrity as the appropriate touchstone. Integrity demands honesty and candor which must not be subordinated to personal gain and advantage. Within the characteristic of integrity, allowance can be made for innocent error and legitimate difference of opinion; but integrity cannot co-exist with deceit or subordination of one's principles. Integrity requires a CFP Board designee to observe not only the letter but also the spirit of this *Code Of Ethics*.

Principle 2 - Objectivity

A CFP Board designee shall be objective in providing professional services to clients.

Objectivity requires intellectual honesty and impartiality. It is an essential quality for any professional. Regardless of the particular service rendered or the capacity in which a CFP Board designee functions, a CFP Board designee should protect the integrity of his or her work, maintain objectivity, and avoid subordination of his or her judgment that would be in violation of this *Code Of Ethics.*

Principle 3 - Competence

A CFP Board designee shall provide services to clients competently and maintain the necessary knowledge and skill to continue to do so in those areas in which the CFP Board designee is engaged.

One is competent only when he or she has attained and maintained an adequate level of knowledge and skill, and applies that knowledge effectively in providing services to clients. Competence also includes the wisdom to recognize the limitations of that knowledge and when consultation or client referral is appropriate. A CFP Board designee, by virtue of having earned the CFP® certification, is deemed to be qualified to practice financial planning. However, in addition to assimilating the common body of knowledge required and acquiring the necessary experience for certification, a CFP Board designee shall make a continuing commitment to learning and professional improvement.

Principle 4 - Fairness

A CFP Board designee shall perform professional services in a manner that is fair and reasonable to clients, principals, partners and employers, and shall disclose conflict(s) of interest in providing such services.

Fairness requires impartiality, intellectual honesty and disclosure of conflict(s) of interest. It involves a subordination of one's own feelings, prejudices and desires so as to achieve a proper balance of conflicting interests. Fairness is treating others in the same fashion that you would want to be treated and is an essential trait of any professional.

Principle 5 - Confidentiality

A CFP Board designee shall not disclose any confidential client information without the specific consent of the client unless in response to proper legal process, to defend against charges of wrongdoing by the CFP Board designee or in connection with a civil dispute between the CFP Board designee and client.

A client, by seeking the services of a CFP Board designee, may be interested in creating a relationship of personal trust and confidence with the CFP Board designee. This type of relationship can only be built upon the understanding that information supplied to the CFP Board designee will be confidential. In order to provide the contemplated services effectively and to protect the client's privacy, the CFP Board designee shall safeguard the confidentiality of such information.

Principle 6 - Professionalism

A CFP Board designee's conduct in all matters shall reflect credit upon the profession.

Because of the importance of the professional services rendered by CFP Board designees, there are attendant responsibilities to behave with dignity and courtesy to all those who use those services, fellow professionals, and those in related professions. A CFP Board designee also has an obligation to cooperate with fellow CFP Board designees to enhance and maintain the profession's public image and to work jointly with other CFP

Board designees to improve the quality of services. It is only through the combined efforts of all CFP Board designees, in cooperation with other professionals, that this vision can be realized.

Principle 7 - Diligence

A CFP Board designee shall act diligently in providing professional services.

Diligence is the provision of services in a reasonably prompt and thorough manner. Diligence also includes proper planning for, and supervision of, the rendering of professional services.

Rules

As stated in Part I – Principles, the Principles apply to all CFP Board designees. However, due to the nature of a CFP Board designee's particular field of endeavor, certain Rules may not be applicable to that CFP Board designee's activities. The universe of activities engaged in by a CFP Board designee is indeed diverse and a particular CFP Board designee may be performing all, some or none of the typical services provided by financial planning professionals. As a result, in considering the following Rules, a CFP Board designee must first recognize what specific services he or she is rendering and then determine whether or not a specific Rule is applicable to those services. To assist the CFP Board designee in making these determinations, this *Standards of Professional Conduct* includes a series of definitions of terminology used throughout the *Code Of Ethics*. Based upon these definitions, a CFP Board designee should be able to determine which services he or she provides and, therefore, which Rules are applicable to those services.

Rules that Relate to the Principle of Integrity

Rule 101

A CFP Board designee shall not solicit clients through false or misleading communications or advertisements:

A. *Misleading Advertising:* A CFP Board designee shall not make a false or misleading communication about the size, scope or areas of competence of the CFP Board designee's practice or of any organization with which the CFP Board designee is associated; and

B. *Promotional Activities:* In promotional activities, a CFP Board designee shall not make materially false or misleading communications to the public or create unjustified expectations regarding matters relating to financial planning or the professional activities and competence of the CFP Board designee. The term "promotional activities" includes, but is not limited to, speeches, interviews, books and/or printed publications, seminars, radio and television shows, and video cassettes; and

C. *Representation of Authority:* A CFP Board designee shall not give the impression that a CFP Board designee is representing the views of CFP Board or any other group unless the CFP Board designee has been authorized to do so. Personal opinions shall be clearly identified as such.

Rule 102

In the course of professional activities, a CFP Board designee shall not engage in conduct involving dishonesty, fraud, deceit or misrepresentation, or knowingly make a false or misleading statement to a client, employer, employee, professional colleague, governmental or other regulatory body or official, or any other person or entity.

Rule 103

A CFP Board designee has the following responsibilities regarding funds and/or other property of clients:

A. In exercising custody of, or discretionary authority over, client funds or other property, a CFP Board designee shall act only in accordance with the authority set forth in the governing legal instrument (e.g., special power of attorney, trust, letters testamentary, etc.); and

B. A CFP Board designee shall identify and keep complete records of all funds or other property of a client in the custody, or under the discretionary authority, of the CFP Board designee; and

C. Upon receiving funds or other property of a client, a CFP Board designee shall promptly or as otherwise permitted by law or provided by agreement with the client, deliver to the client or third party any funds or other property which the client or third party is entitled to receive and, upon request by the client, render a full accounting regarding such funds or other property; and

D. A CFP Board designee shall not commingle client funds or other property with a CFP Board designee's personal funds and/or other property or the funds and/or other property of a CFP Board designee's firm. Commingling one or more clients' funds or other property together is permitted, subject to compliance with applicable legal requirements and provided accurate records are maintained for each client's funds or other property; and

E. A CFP Board designee who takes custody of all or any part of a client's assets for investment purposes, shall do so with the care required of a fiduciary.

Rules that Relate to the Principle of Objectivity

Rule 201

A CFP Board designee shall exercise reasonable and prudent professional judgment in providing professional services.

Rule 202

A financial planning practitioner shall act in the interest of the client.

Rules that Relate to the Principle of Competence

Rule 301

A CFP Board designee shall keep informed of developments in the field of financial planning and participate in continuing education throughout the CFP Board designee's professional career in order to improve professional competence in all areas in which the CFP Board designee is engaged. As a distinct part of this requirement, a CFP Board designee shall satisfy all minimum continuing education requirements established for CFP Board designees by CFP Board.

Rule 302

A CFP Board designee shall offer advice only in those areas in which the CFP Board designee has competence. In areas where the CFP Board designee is not professionally competent, the CFP Board designee shall seek the counsel of qualified individuals and/or refer clients to such parties.

Rules that Relate to the Principle of Fairness

Rule 401

In rendering professional services, a CFP Board designee shall disclose to the client:

a. Material information relevant to the professional relationship, including, conflict(s) of interest, the CFP Board designee's business affiliation, address, telephone number, credentials, qualifications, licenses, compensation structure and any agency relationships, and the scope of the CFP Board designee's authority in that capacity; and

b. The information required by all laws applicable to the relationship in a manner complying with such laws.

Rule 402

A CFP Board designee in a financial planning engagement shall make timely written disclosure of all material information relative to the professional relationship. In all circumstances and prior to the engagement, a CFP Board designee shall, in writing:

a. Disclose conflict(s) of interest and sources of compensation; and

b. Inform the client or prospective client of his/her right to ask at any time for information about the compensation of the CFP Board designee.

c. As a guideline, a CFP Board designee who provides a client or prospective client with the following written disclosures, using Form ADV, a CFP Board Disclosure Form or an equivalent document, will be considered to be in compliance with this Rule:

- The basic philosophy of the CFP Board designee (or firm) in working with clients. This includes the philosophy, theory and/or principles of financial planning which will be utilized by the CFP Board designee; and

- Résumés of principals and employees of a firm who are expected to provide financial planning services to the client and a description of those services. Such disclosures shall include educational background, professional/employment history, professional designations and licenses held; and

- A statement that in reasonable detail discloses (as applicable) conflict(s) of interest and source(s) of, and any contingencies or other aspects material to, the CFP Board designee's compensation; and

- A statement describing material agency or employment relationships a CFP Board designee (or firm) has with third parties and the nature of compensation resulting from such relationships; and

- A statement informing the client or prospective client of his/her right to ask at any time for information about the compensation of the CFP Board designee.

Rule 403

Upon request by a client or prospective client, the CFP Board designee in a financial planning engagement shall communicate in reasonable detail the requested compensation information related to the financial planning engagement, including compensation derived from implementation. The disclosure may express compensation as an approximate dollar amount or percentage or as a range of dollar amounts or percentages. The disclosure shall be made at a time and to the extent that the requested compensation information can be reasonably ascertained. Any estimates shall be clearly identified as such and based on reasonable assumptions. If a CFP Board designee becomes aware that a compensation disclosure provided pursuant to this rule has become significantly inaccurate, he/she shall provide the client with corrected information in a timely manner.

Rule 404

The disclosures required of a CFP Board designee in a financial planning engagement described under Rule 402 shall be offered at least annually for current clients, and provided if requested.

Rule 405

A CFP Board designee's compensation shall be fair and reasonable.

Rule 406

A CFP Board designee who is an employee shall perform professional services with dedication to the lawful objectives of the employer and in accordance with this Code of Ethics.

Rule 407

A CFP Board designee shall:

a. Advise his/her employer of outside affiliations which reasonably may compromise service to an employer;

b. Provide timely notice to his/her employer and clients about change of CFP® certification status; and

c. Provide timely notice to clients, unless precluded by contractual obligations, about change of employment.

Rule 408

A CFP Board designee shall inform his/her employer, partners or co-owners of compensation or other benefit arrangements in connection with his or her services to clients, which are in addition to compensation from the employer, partners or co-owners for such services.

Rule 409

If a CFP Board designee enters into a personal business transaction with a client, separate from regular professional services provided to that client, the transaction shall be on terms which are fair and reasonable to the client and the CFP Board designee shall disclose, in writing, the risks of the transaction, conflict(s) of interest of the CFP Board designee, and other relevant information, if any, necessary to make the transaction fair to the client.

Rules that Relate to the Principle of Confidentiality

Rule 501

A CFP Board designee shall not reveal — or use for his or her own benefit — without the client's consent, any personally identifiable information relating to the client relationship or the affairs of the client, except and to the extent disclosure or use is reasonably necessary:

A. To establish an advisory or brokerage account, to effect a transaction for the client, or as otherwise impliedly authorized in order to carry out the client engagement; or

B. To comply with legal requirements or legal process; or

C. To defend the CFP Board designee against charges of wrongdoing; or

D. In connection with a civil dispute between the CFP Board designee and the client.

For purposes of this rule, the proscribed use of client information is improper whether or not it actually causes harm to the client.

Rule 502

A CFP Board designee shall maintain the same standards of confidentiality to employers as to clients.

Rule 503

A CFP Board designee doing business as a partner or principal of a financial services firm owes the CFP Board designee's partners or co-owners a responsibility to act in good faith. This includes, but is not limited to, adherence to reasonable expectations of confidentiality both while in business together and thereafter.

Rules that Relate to the Principle of Professionalism

Rule 601

A CFP Board designee shall use the marks in compliance with the rules and regulations of CFP Board, as established and amended from time to time.

Rule 602

A CFP Board designee shall show respect for other financial planning professionals, and related occupational groups, by engaging in fair and honorable competitive practices. Collegiality among CFP Board designees shall not, however, impede enforcement of this *Code Of Ethics*.

Rule 603

A CFP Board designee who has knowledge, which is not required to be kept confidential under this *Code Of Ethics*, that another CFP Board designee has committed a violation of this *Code Of Ethics* which raises substantial questions as to the designee's honesty, trustworthiness or fitness as a CFP Board designee in other respects, shall promptly inform CFP Board. This rule does not require disclosure of information or reporting based on knowledge gained as a consultant or expert witness in anticipation of, or related to, litigation or other dispute resolution mechanisms. For purposes of this rule, knowledge means no substantial doubt.

Rule 604

A CFP Board designee who has knowledge, which is not required under this *Code Of Ethics* to be kept confidential, and which raises a substantial question of unprofessional, fraudulent or illegal conduct by a CFP Board designee or other financial professional, shall promptly inform the appropriate regulatory and/or professional disciplinary body. This rule does not require disclosure or reporting of information gained as a consultant or expert witness in anticipation of, or related to, litigation or other dispute resolution mechanisms. For purposes of this Rule, knowledge means no substantial doubt.

Rule 605

A CFP Board designee who has reason to suspect illegal conduct within the CFP Board designee's organization shall make timely disclosure of the available evidence to the CFP Board designee's immediate supervisor and/or partners or co-owners. If the CFP Board designee is convinced that illegal conduct exists within the CFP Board designee's organization, and that appropriate measures are not taken to remedy the situation, the CFP Board designee shall, where appropriate, alert the appropriate regulatory authorities, including CFP Board, in a timely manner.

Rule 606

In all professional activities a CFP Board designee shall perform services in accordance with:

A. Applicable laws, rules and regulations of governmental agencies and other applicable authorities; and

B. Applicable rules, regulations and other established policies of CFP Board.

Rule 607

A CFP Board designee shall not engage in any conduct which reflects adversely on his or her integrity or fitness as a CFP Board designee, upon the marks, or upon the profession.

Rule 608

The Investment Advisers Act of 1940 requires registration of investment advisers with the U.S. Securities and Exchange Commission and similar state statutes may require registration with state securities agencies. CFP Board designees shall disclose to clients their firms' status as registered investment advisers. Under present standards of acceptable business conduct, it is proper to use registered investment adviser if the CFP Board designee is registered individually. If the CFP Board designee is registered through his or her firm, then the CFP Board designee is not a registered investment adviser but a person associated with an investment adviser. The firm is the registered investment adviser. Moreover, RIA or R.I.A. following a CFP Board designee's name in advertising, letterhead stationery, and business cards may be misleading and is not permitted either by this *Code Of Ethics* or by SEC regulations.

Rule 609

A CFP Board designee shall not practice any other profession or offer to provide such services unless the CFP Board designee is qualified to practice in those fields and is licensed as required by state law.

Rule 610

A CFP Board designee shall return the client's original records in a timely manner after their return has been requested by a client.

Rule 611

A CFP Board designee shall not bring or threaten to bring a disciplinary proceeding under this *Code Of Ethics*, or report or threaten to report information to CFP Board pursuant to Rules 603 and/or 604, or make or threaten to make use of this *Code Of Ethics* for no substantial purpose other than to harass, maliciously injure, embarrass and/or unfairly burden another CFP Board designee.

Rule 612

A CFP Board designee shall comply with all applicable renewal requirements established by CFP Board including, but not limited to, payment of the biennial CFP Board designee fee as well as signing and returning the Terms and Conditions of Certification in connection with the certification renewal process.

Rules that Relate to the Principle of Diligence

Rule 701

A CFP Board designee shall provide services diligently.

Rule 702

A financial planning practitioner shall enter into an engagement only after securing sufficient information to satisfy the CFP Board designee that:

A. The relationship is warranted by the individual's needs and objectives; and

B. The CFP Board designee has the ability to either provide requisite competent services or to involve other professionals who can provide such services.

Rule 703

A financial planning practitioner shall make and/or implement only recommendations which are suitable for the client.

Rule 704

Consistent with the nature and scope of the engagement, a CFP Board designee shall make a reasonable investigation regarding the financial products recommended to clients. Such an investigation may be made by the CFP Board designee or by others provided the CFP Board designee acts reasonably in relying upon such investigation.

Rule 705

A CFP Board designee shall properly supervise subordinates with regard to their delivery of financial planning services, and shall not accept or condone conduct in violation of this *Code Of Ethics*.

Advisory Opinion 2000-1

Loans between CFP Board designees and their clients should be avoided in the client-planner relationship.

Background

The Board of Professional Review (the "BOPR") has generally viewed loans between CFP Board designees and their clients unfavorably and, in the majority of cases, to be a violation of the *Code Of Ethics and Professional Responsibility (Code Of Ethics)*. Since the *Code Of Ethics* does not have a rule that specifically prohibits such transactions, however, the BOPR has addressed the issue under various rules, depending upon the facts and circumstances of the case being examined.

Due to an increase in the number of disciplinary cases that involve the issue of loans between a CFP Board designee and his or her client, the BOPR is issuing this advisory opinion to clarify its position and to serve as a guide to both CFP Board designees and their clients.

Issue

Whether a loan between a CFP Board designee and his or her client(s) violates the *Code Of Ethics*.

Analysis

Cases involving a loan between a CFP Board designee and a client involve an investigation of whether that CFP Board designee has violated the *Code Of Ethics*. The BOPR has evaluated these cases under a number of rules, including, but not limited to, Rules 201, 202, 401, 402, 606, 607 and 703. To determine which, if any, rules have been violated, the BOPR considers:

- Whether the designee is a financial planning practitioner (as defined by the Code Of Ethics).
- Whether the client is a family member or a financial institution. The degree to which the CFP Board designee is related to the client is relevant. (The rationale for considering the type of relationship is discussed later in this opinion.)
- Whether the terms and conditions of the loan are fair and reasonable to the client.

While any and/or all of the rules mentioned above, and others, may apply in a particular case, this advisory opinion focuses on two rules which are implicated in the majority of "loan" cases and are, therefore, most frequently cited by the BOPR: Rules 202 and 607.

Rule 202

Rule 202 of the *Code Of Ethics* requires financial planning practitioners to act in the best interest of their clients. Accordingly, this rule applies to CFP Board designees who are acting as financial planning practitioners, defined in the *Code Of Ethics* as:

> "[A] person who is capable and qualified to offer objective, integrated and comprehensive financial advice to or for the benefit of clients to help them achieve their financial objectives and who engages in financial planning using the financial planning process in working with clients."

Borrowing from a Client

In cases involving a loan between a financial planning practitioner and a client, where the client is the lender and the practitioner is the borrower, the BOPR presumes that the practitioner is not acting in the best interest of the client.

Exceptions

There are two exceptions to this presumption:

1. When the client is a family member; or

2. When the client is a financial institution acting in its normal course of business activity.

The Board recognizes that borrowing and/or lending of funds between family members is a common, generally accepted, practice. Likewise, financial institutions are in the business of borrowing and lending funds and, as such, often provide loans to individuals, regardless of whether they are CFP Board designees. In both instances, loans between these groups can fall outside the scope of the planner-client relationship.

In either of the two situations described above, while the Board does not presume that the planner's borrowing of funds is a violation of Rule 202, it may still find that the transaction was not in the client's best interests if the financial planning practitioner is unable to establish that:

- The terms and conditions of the loan were clearly and objectively disclosed to the client, taking into consideration the client's level of sophistication;

- The terms and conditions of the transaction were fair and reasonable under the circumstances; and

- The client fully understood (a) the terms and conditions of the transaction and (b) the impact of the transaction on his/her financial situation.

Lending to a Client

In the more rare case where a financial planning practitioner lends funds to a client, the BOPR will presume that the practitioner is not acting in the best interest of the client, as a client who borrows funds from his or her planner is likely to be inhibited from ending the planner-client relationship, regardless of whether the client's financial planning needs are being met. Even if the financial planning practitioner can demonstrate that a particular loan to a client did not inhibit the client from ending the relationship, the transaction will still be presumed to be a violation of Rule 202 if (a) the loan was used as an enticement for the client to make a financial decision, including, but not limited to, purchasing a financial product, or (b) the loan had a below market interest rate and could be considered a form of rebate.

The exception to this presumption is when the client is a family member. Even if the client is a family member, however, the BOPR may still find that the transaction was not in the client's best interest if the financial planning practitioner is unable to establish that (a) the terms and conditions of the loan were clearly and objectively disclosed to the client, taking into consideration the client's level of sophistication, (b) the terms and conditions of the transaction were fair and reasonable under the circumstances, and (c) the client fully understood the terms and conditions of the transaction and the impact the transaction may have on his/her financial situation.

Rule 607

Rule 607 prohibits a CFP Board designee from engaging "in any conduct which reflects adversely on his or her integrity or fitness as a CFP Board designee, upon the marks, or upon the profession."

As defined in the *Code Of Ethics*, CFP Board designees include individuals who are currently certified, candidates for certification, and individuals who have any entitlement, either direct or indirect, to use the CFP certification marks. Accordingly, this rule has been interpreted to apply to all CFP Board designees regardless of whether they are practitioners, including candidates for certification, and individuals who have the right to renew their CFP® certification without re-taking CFP Board's CFP® Certification Examination.

Whether the Client is the Borrower or Lender

The BOPR interprets Rule 607 broadly, finding conduct which gives the "appearance of impropriety" to be a violation of the rule. Accordingly, the BOPR has taken the position that most loans between a CFP Board designee and a client give the appearance of impropriety and, therefore, reflect negatively on the integrity of the designee, the CFP marks and the financial planning profession.

Exceptions

The same two exceptions discussed under Rule 202 (i.e., loans between a planner and a family member or loans between a planner and a financial institution) apply under Rule 607 when the planner is the borrower. In cases where the client is the borrower, only the family member exception applies. Even if one of the exceptions applies, the BOPR may still find that the transaction violates Rule 607 if the CFP Board designee fails to establish that:

- The terms and conditions of the loan were clearly and objectively disclosed to the client;
- The terms and conditions of the transaction were fair and reasonable under the circumstances; and
- The client fully understood (a) the terms and conditions of the transaction and (b) the impact of the transaction on his/her financial situation.

Summary

The BOPR urges all CFP Board designees to avoid the practice of borrowing from or lending to clients. This advisory opinion focuses on the two most frequently cited rules (Rules 202 and 607) in cases involving loans between CFP Board designees and their clients. CFP Board designees should remember, however, that the BOPR may find such transactions to be in violation of other rules in the *Code Of Ethics*, as well.

Advisory Opinion 2003-1

CFP Board designees must avoid possible misrepresentation when using the term "fee-only."

Background

The Board of Professional Review ("BOPR") views misrepresentation of compensation arrangements to be a violation of the *Code of Ethics and Professional Responsibility (Code of Ethics)*. The *Code of Ethics* defines the term "fee-only" as denoting "a method of compensation in which compensation is received solely from a client with neither the personal financial planning practitioner nor any related party receiving compensation which is contingent upon the purchase or sale of any financial product." BOPR Advisory Opinions 97-1 and 97-2 allowed for a designee to use the term "fee-only" to describe the compensation received from a specific client, even if other methods of compensation were used with other clients, and could offer "fee-only" services to a client, even if the designee also received commissions from the same client or other clients for other services. In light of recent regulatory trends regarding the misrepresentation of methods of compensation, media focus on the issue, and the perceptions of the general public, the BOPR has redefined the appropriate use of the term "fee-only."

The purpose of this Advisory Opinion is to reduce confusion on the part of CFP Board designees, their clients, and the public, and to maintain consistency with other organizations' use of the term "fee-only." Thus, the Board of Governors withdrew Advisory Opinions 97-1 and 97-2 in January 2002 and the *Code of Ethics* definition can no longer be considered an accurate reflection of the BOPR's position on this issue.

Issue

When may a CFP Board designee use the term "fee-only" to describe the designee as an individual, the designee's practice or the designee's services?

Analysis

A fee arrangement exists when the CFP Board designee is compensated solely by the client, or another party operating exclusively on behalf of the client, for professional services provided. The BOPR has defined types of compensation arrangements. The following qualify as fees:

- *Hourly, fixed or flat fees;*
- *Percentage fees*, which are based on some aspect of the client's financial profile, such as assets under management or earned income; and
- *Performance-based fees*, which are tied to the profitability of the client's invested assets.

Use of the Term "Fee-Only"

In order for a CFP Board designee to describe his or her compensation as "fee-only", all compensation from all clients must be derived solely from fees. Minimal exceptions may be allowed provided the compensation is inconsequential and independent of the purchase of any product or service. Likewise, when using terms including, but not limited to, "fee-only services" and "fee-only firm," the same requirements apply.

Potential Rule Violations

Cases involving misrepresentation of compensation arrangements or failure to disclose compensation arrangements warrant investigation of whether that CFP Board designee has violated the Code of Ethics. The rules implicated in this analysis include, but are not limited to, Rules 101(a) and (b), 102, 201, 202, 401, 402, 606, 607 and 702. The BOPR must consider whether the CFP Board designee is a financial planning practitioner (as defined by the Code of Ethics) in determining which, if any, rules have been violated. While any and/or all of the rules mentioned above may apply in a particular case, this advisory opinion focuses on three rules that would most often be implicated in a case involving misrepresentation of and/or failure to disclose compensation arrangements: Rules 101(a) and (b), 401 and 402.

Rule 401

Rule 401 of the Code of Ethics requires CFP Board designees to disclose to the client material information relative to the professional relationship, including compensation structure. The BOPR urges that disclosures under Rule 401 be clear, straightforward and unambiguous so as to be easily understood by all parties. In cases involving CFP Board designees who represent themselves as "fee-only" to a client but accept compensation not defined as fees by the BOPR from that relationship or other client relationships, the BOPR presumes that the CFP Board designee has failed to disclose material information relative to the professional relationship.

Rule 402

Rule 402 requires CFP Board designees in a financial planning engagement to make timely written disclosure of all material information relative to the professional relationship, in all circumstances and prior to the relationship, including sources of compensation. Adherence to the provisions of Rule 402 by CFP Board designees in financial planning engagements allows the public to make informed decisions about whether to use the professional services of the CFP Board designee. Rule 402(a) is violated when the CFP Board designee in a financial planning engagement, in the disclosure provided to the client, represents himself or herself as "fee-only" when, in fact, that designee accepts compensation not defined as fees by the BOPR in that relationship or other client relationships.

Rule 101(a) and (b)

Rule 101(a) and (b) prohibit CFP Board designees from soliciting clients through false or misleading advertisements and/or promotional activities. The use of the term "fee-only" must be used carefully and only when the CFP Board designee derives all compensation from all clients solely from fees. The BOPR presumes advertisements and/or promotional activities to be false or misleading when they contain the term "fee-only" and the CFP Board designee advertising or promoting his or her services accepts compensation not defined as fees from that client relationship or any other client relationships.

Summary

The public regards compensation structure as important information when choosing a financial planning professional. The Code of Ethics requires CFP Board designees to act with integrity and fairness toward the public in all activities. The appropriate use of the term "fee-only" in all public discourse provides a key opportunity for CFP Board designees to demonstrate professionalism by avoiding casual use of the term. The BOPR advises CFP Board designees to avoid using the term "fee-only" except when all compensation from all clients is derived solely from fees. CFP Board designees should also avoid the use of other terms designed to induce the public into a distorted belief that the designee receives "fee-only" compensation when in fact the designee receives commissions, referral compensation, or any other form of compensation not defined as fees by the BOPR.

Sample Disclosure Forms

Following are two sample disclosure forms for use by CFP® certificants in complying with CFP Board's *Code Of Ethics and Professional Responsibility* disclosure requirements. The first form (Form FPE) may be used when providing personal financial planning services. The second form (Form OPS) is for use when providing other professional services.

These forms provide for certain disclosures to clients (or potential clients) as required by CFP Board's *Code of Ethics*, with corresponding Rules in the *Code of Ethics* referenced in parentheses. The client acknowledgments at the end of each disclosure form are not required by CFP Board's *Code of Ethics*, but CFP certificants may wish to use them for their own purposes. Please note in Part II, section E of Form FPE, a CFP certificant shall not hold out as a fee-only financial planning practitioner if the CFP certificant receives commissions or other forms of economic benefit form related parties. (Refer also to Advisory Opinion 2003-1.) Also note that the disclosure of Part II, section B of Form OPS, is not required if the services contemplated by the client relationship have been completed. CFP certificants may use these forms, SEC Form ADV Part II, or a form of their own design or choosing as long as the required *Code of Ethics* disclosures are included in whatever form is used by the CFP certificant.

Compliance with the client disclosure requirements of the *Code of Ethics* is accomplished only when all material information relevant to the professional relationship (which includes everything required, pertinent and appropriate to the given client relationship) has been disclosed to the client or prospective client. Such disclosure should include, if material, (1) information about the financial condition of the CFP certificant and/or his or her firm which is reasonably likely to impair the ability of the CFP certificant to meet contractual commitments to the client and (2) any legal or disciplinary event relative to the CFP certificant that is material to a client's or potential client's evaluation of the CFP certificant's integrity or ability to meet contractual commitments to the client. Mere completion of a suggested disclosure form does not, in and of itself, constitute full compliance with the *Code of Ethics* disclosure requirements.

Figure 7.1

CFP® CERTIFICANT DISCLOSURE FORM (FORM FPE)

For Use In Financial Planning Engagements

This disclosure form gives information about the CFP® certificant(s) and his/her/their business. This information has not been reviewed, approved or verified by CFP Board or by any governmental or self-regulatory authority. CFP Board does not warrant the specific qualifications of individuals certified to use its marks, nor does it warrant the correctness of advice or opinions provided.

PART I. General Information (Code reference - Rule 401)

A. Business affiliation:

B. Address:

C. Telephone number:

D. Information required by all laws applicable to the relationship (e.g., if the CFP® certificant is a registered investment adviser, the disclosure document required by laws applicable to such registration):

PART II. Material Information Relevant to the Professional Relationship
(Written disclosures required to be provided **prior to** the engagement) (Code reference – Rule 402)

A. Basic philosophy of the CFP certificant (or firm) in working with clients:

B. Philosophy, theory and/or principles of financial planning which will be utilized:

C. Attached to this disclosure form, or summarized in the space provided below, are résumés of principals and employees of the CFP certificant's firm who are expected to provide financial planning services:

1. Educational background:

2. Professional/employment history:

3. Professional certifications and licenses held:

D. Description of the financial planning services to be provided by the CFP certificant:

Figure 7.1 (cont'd)

E. Conflict(s) of interest and source(s) of compensation:

1. Conflict(s) of interest:

2. Source(s) of compensation:

F. Contingencies or other aspects material to the certificant's compensation:

G. Agency or employment relationships:

1. Material agency or employment relationships with third parties:

2. Compensation resulting from such agency or employment relationships:

H. Other material information relevant to the professional relationship:

PART III. Additional Notification

A. As a client or prospective client, you have the right to ask me, as a CFP certificant, at any time for information about my compensation related to the services I provide you. I will communicate the requested information in reasonable detail as it relates to our financial planning engagement, including compensation derived from implementation. This disclosure of compensation:

1. May be expressed as an approximate dollar amount or percentage or as a range of dollar amounts or percentages;
2. Shall be made at a time and to the extent that the requested information can be reasonably ascertained;
3. Will be based on reasonable assumptions, with estimates clearly identified, and;
4. Will be updated in a timely manner if actual compensation significantly differs from any estimates.
(Code reference - Rules 402 and 403)

B. As a CFP certificant's personal financial planning client, you have the right to receive annually my current SEC Form ADV Part II or the current revision of the disclosure you received when our relationship began. (Code reference - Rule 404)

I hereby acknowledge receipt of this required disclosure.

____________________ / ________
Client's Signature Date

____________________ / ________
Client's Signature Date

Figure 7.2

CFP® CERTIFICANT DISCLOSURE FORM (FORM OPS)

For Use When Providing Other Professional Services

This disclosure form gives information about the CFP® certificant(s) and his/her/their business. This information has not been reviewed, approved or verified by CFP Board or by any governmental or self-regulatory authority. CFP Board does not warrant the specific qualifications of individuals certified to use its marks, nor does it warrant the correctness of advice or opinions provided.

PART I. Material Information Relevant to the Professional Relationship (Disclosures required to be provided at the time of entering into a client relationship) (Code reference - Rule 401)

A. Material information relevant to the professional relationship:

B. Conflict(s) of interest:

C. Information required by all laws applicable to the relationship (e.g., if the CFP certificant is a registered investment adviser, the disclosure document required by laws applicable to such registration):

PART II. Subsequent Disclosures (Disclosures required to be provided subsequent to entering into a client relationship)

A. Changes in any of the following information since entering into a client relationship:
(Code reference - Rule 401)

1. Business affiliation:
2. Address:
3. Telephone number:
4. Credentials:
5. Qualifications:
6. Licenses:
7. Compensation structure:
8. Agency relationships:
9. Scope of the CFP certificant's authority in any agency relationship:

I hereby acknowledge receipt of this required disclosure.

____________________ / ________ Client's Signature Date

____________________ / ________ Client's Signature Date

Disciplinary Procedures

Disciplinary Process and Procedures

The disciplinary procedures of CFP Board have been devised to ensure a fair and reasonable process for a CERTIFIED FINANCIAL PLANNER™ professional against whom allegations of Code of Ethics' violations are brought.

1. *Request for Investigation* – Upon receipt of a written complaint, staff counsel reviews the allegations to determine if further investigation is warranted.

2. *Investigation* – If staff counsel determines to proceed with an investigation a CERTIFIED FINANCIAL PLANNER™ professional is given written notice of the investigation, which contains the general nature of the allegations. The CERTIFIED FINANCIAL PLANNER™ professional is given 30 days within which to file a written response. If no response is received within the allotted 30 days a formal complaint is issued and the case is presented to a hearing panel.

3. *Probable Cause Determination* – CFP Board Staff Counsel determines if there is probable cause to believe grounds for discipline exist. If so, staff will issue a formal complaint against the CERTIFIED FINANCIAL PLANNER™ professional and a notice of hearing. The complaint contains the specific allegations of misconduct and the potential Code of Ethics and/or Practice Standards violations. The CERTIFIED FINANCIAL PLANNER™ professional has 20 days from the date of receipt of the complaint to file a written answer. If no answer is received, the allegations in the complaint are deemed admitted and the CERTIFIED FINANCIAL PLANNER™ professional's right to use the CFP certification marks is administratively revoked.

4. *Hearing Panel* – When a formal complaint is filed a hearing takes place before a panel of a minimum of three individuals. At least one member of every hearing panel is a member of the Board of Professional Review and at least two members must be CERTIFIED FINANCIAL PLANNER™ professionals. The respondent is entitled to appear in person or telephonically, to be represented by counsel at the hearing, to cross-examine witnesses and to present evidence on his or her behalf.

5. *Board of Professional Review* – The hearing panel submits its findings for review to the full Board of Professional Review which, after considering all the facts and recommendations, renders a final decision.

6. *Board of Appeals* – If a CERTIFIED FINANCIAL PLANNER™ professional is aggrieved by the decision of the Board of Professional Review a CERTIFIED FINANCIAL PLANNER™ professional has the right to petition the decision to the Board of Appeals. The Board of Appeals is composed of up to four members of the Board of Governors, at least two of whom are first year members of the Board. Members of the Board of Appeals may not be members of the Board of Professional Review.

Forms of Discipline

If grounds for discipline have been established, the Board of Professional Review may impose any of the forms of discipline below. All disciplinary actions, except private written censure, may be publicly disseminated.

- a private written censure
- a public letter of admonition

- suspension of the right to use the CFP marks for a specified period of time, not to exceed five years
- permanent revocation of the right to use the CFP marks.

Grounds for Discipline

Misconduct by a CERTIFIED FINANCIAL PLANNER™ professional, including the following acts or omissions, constitutes grounds for discipline, whether or not the misconduct occurred in the course of a client relationship:

- any act or omission which violates the provisions of CFP Board's Code of Ethics and Professional Responsibility (Code of Ethics)
- any act or omission which violates the criminal laws of any state or of the U.S.
- any act which is the proper basis for suspension of a professional license
- any act or omission which violates CFP Board's Disciplinary Rules & Procedures
- failure to respond to a request by the Board of Professional Review without good cause
- obstruction of the Board of Professional Review's performance of its duties
- any false or misleading statement made to CFP Board

This list is not exclusive, and there may be other acts or omissions amounting to unprofessional conduct, which may also constitute grounds for discipline.

SOCIETY OF FINANCIAL SERVICE PROFESSIONALS

Introduction

The Society of Financial Service Professionals was founded in 1928 and has over 22,000 members in nearly 200 Chapters in all 50 states, Puerto Rico, Canada, and Singapore. The Society's mission is to promote professionalism among its members through the highest quality continuing education and the maintenance of high ethical standards and conduct.

Society members are credentialed financial service professionals who provide financial planning, estate planning, retirement counseling, asset management and other financial services and products to their clients. Members work in a variety of contexts, and include fee-only financial planners, estate planning attorneys, accountants, asset managers, employee benefits specialists, and life insurance agents.

Code of Professional Responsibility

The Code of Professional Responsibility of the Society of Financial Service Professionals is divided into five components, as follows:

- Preamble – a brief introduction to the Code of Professional Responsibility, including its history and purpose.
- Canons – aspirational model standards of exemplary professional conduct.
- Rules – specific standards of a mandatory and enforceable nature.
- Applications – practical examples of how the canons and rules apply in given situations.
- Disciplinary Procedures – the mechanisms for enforcement of the Code of Professional Responsibility.

Preamble

The Society of Financial Service Professionals is dedicated to setting and promoting standards of excellence for professionals in financial services. In fulfillment of this mission, the Society's Board of Directors has adopted this Code of Professional Responsibility. All Society members are automatically bound by its provisions.

The ultimate goal of enacting the Code is to serve the public interest. The path to fulfilling the goal is the fostering of professionalism in financial services. A profession has been defined in the writings of Solomon S. Huebner as possessing four essential traits:

- knowledge or expertise
- service to others
- working with other professionals to enhance the practice and reputation of one who is a member
- self-regulation

Through its Code of Professional Responsibility, the Society strives to improve the level of ethical behavior among its members by articulating standards that are aspirational in nature, that is, by identifying the lofty, altruistic ideals that define a true profession, and by delineating and enforcing minimum standards of ethical conduct.

This Code of Professional Responsibility has its origin in the code of ethics of the American Society of CLU & ChFC, the predecessor organization of the Society of Financial Service Professionals. The members of the Society created and adopted a code of ethics in 1961. With a name change in the fall of 1998, and a broadened membership constituency, it became appropriate to create this new Code of Professional Responsibility.

The Society acknowledges the diversity of its membership…from those that serve the public directly, as advisers, to those that serve indirectly through companies, educational organizations, and the like. Whatever role he or she plays within the financial services industry, it is the responsibility of each Society member to understand and adhere to the Code of Professional Responsibility.

From time to time, a Society member may be unclear about the ethical implications of a given course of action. In such cases, a Society member may request an advisory opinion from the Society; or may seek confidential advice through the Society's Ethics Information Line. Advisory opinions will be unpublished and specific to the inquiring member. However, there may be instances in which the subject matter of the advisory opinion has broad, general application and in such cases, at its discretion, the Society may chose to publish a given opinion for the benefit of all members, preserving the anonymity of those involved.

An alleged violation of the Society's Code of Professional Responsibility will result in an enforcement action, carried out in accordance with the Disciplinary Procedures. The procedures ensure that any member charged with ethical misconduct is afforded appropriate due process. The procedures also provide for appropriate sanctions, such as reprimand, censure, and revocation of membership, should a member be found to have acted in violation of the Code.

True enforcement of ethical behavior must come from the personal conscience of each individual, rather than external forces. Nevertheless, as an organization that promotes its members' education and expertise to the consumer, the Society believes it is essential that it act in an enforcement capacity.

Canons

CANON 1 Fairness

A member shall perform services in a manner that respects the interests of all those he/she serves, including clients, principals, partners, employees, and employers. A member shall disclose conflicts of interests in providing such services.

Fairness requires that a professional treat others as he/she would wish to be treated if in the other's position. A professional also strives to avoid unfairness by inflicting no unnecessary harm on others and, when possible, shielding others from harm.

Rule 1.1

A member shall not engage in behavior involving concealment or misrepresentation of material facts.

Applications for Rule 1.1:

A1.1a. In the sale of financial products, the use of product projections that are more aggressive than the company's current assumptions – without offering alternate illustrations/projections using more conservative assumptions – is a form of misrepresentation. It is best to show a range of assumptions for each product to illustrate the impact of changes on the rate of return and other expenses.

A1.1b. To avoid misrepresentation, the financial services professional is advised to use unbiased historical illustrations, show past performance, and to educate the consumer on the difference between past results and projections, and actual future results.

A1.1c. Improper replacement is a form of misrepresentation. When considering the replacement of one insurance, annuity, or other financial product for another, a thorough comparison of both products, including surrender charges, incontestable clauses, expenses, fees, and tax consequences, should be completed. The Society's Replacement Questionnaire (RQ) provides a tool for the thorough analysis of replacement issues.

A1.1d. Failing to note a preexisting medical condition on an insurance application is a form of concealment.

Rule 1.2

A member shall respect the rights of others.

Rule 1.3

A member shall disclose to the client all information material to the professional relationship, including, but not limited to, all actual or potential conflicts of interest. In a conflict of interest situation, the interest of the client must be paramount.

Applications for Rule 1.3

A1.3a. A potential conflict of interest is inherent in the relationship between the client and the financial service professional when the professional is compensated by commissions on the sale of financial products. In such circumstances, if asked by the client or prospect, the professional should disclose, to the best of his/her knowledge, all forms of compensation, including commissions, expense allowances, bonuses, and any other relevant items.

A1.3b. The potential for a conflict of interest exists when a financial service professional receives fees for referring business to another practitioner. The referring professional should disclose this information.

A1.3c. A member who serves as a director or trustee of an organization/business faces a conflict of interest when competing to provide product or services to this organization for compensation. For example, Jackie Jones, ChFC, a professional money manager, is on the board of XNet Corporation. XNet is currently interviewing candidates to manage its $10 million investment portfolio. If Jackie decides to seek XNet's account, she is in a conflict of interest situation. Under these circumstances, Jackie should disclose the conflict to all relevant parties and have the parties acknowledge and accept the conflict. Additionally, Jackie should consider recusing herself from all discussions and decision-making regarding the selection of XNet's money manager. She may also consider resigning from the board or taking her name out of consideration for the money manager position.

Rule 1.4

A member shall give proper respect to any relationship that may exist between the member and the companies he or she represents.

Application for Rule 1.4

A1.4a. Society members frequently have contractual relationships with the company whose products they sell. Honoring the terms of these contracts and refraining from negative statements about such companies are examples of giving proper respect to the relationship. Note, however, the need to balance the requirements of Rule 1.4 with the duty to act in the best interest of the client.

Rule 1.5

A member shall make and/or implement only recommendations that are appropriate for the client and consistent with the client's goals.

Applications for Rule 1.5

A1.5a. Compliance with Rule 1.5 requires the financial service professional to use his/her best efforts to (1) understand the client's/prospect's personal and financial background and experience; (2) understand the client's/prospect's risk tolerance; and (3) educate the client about the various options available to meet identified needs and goals. This may include utilizing a fact-finding and/or risk assessment tool, one-on-one educational/counseling sessions, sharing newspaper or magazine articles, etc. In these circumstances, the financial service professional is cautioned against providing advice if he or she is not properly licensed or authorized to do so. See also Rule 2.2 and the Application A2.2a.

A1.5b. Appropriateness of the recommendation to the client's needs must take precedence over any sales incentives available to the financial service professional, such as conventions, trips, bonuses, etc. For example, Bob Bucks needs to sell just one more policy to qualify for MDRT. He knows he can convince his best client to purchase additional insurance coverage even though Bob knows the current coverage is more than adequate. If Bob makes this sale, he has violated Rule 1.5.

Rule 1.6

In the rendering of professional services to a client, a member has the duty to maintain the type and degree of professional independence that (a) is required of practitioners in the member's occupation, or (b) is otherwise in the public interest, given the specific nature of the service being rendered.

Application for Rule 1.6

A1.6a. The requirement of professional independence mandated by Rule 1.6 presents a special challenge for Society members who are contractually bound to sell the products of only one company, or a select group of companies. In such cases, the member must keep paramount his/her ethical duty to act in the best interest of the client, even if this means forgoing a sale.

CANON 2 Competence

A member shall continually improve his/her professional knowledge, skill, and competence.

Professionalism starts with technical competence. The knowledge and skills held by a professional are of a high level, difficult to attain, and, therefore, not held by the general public. Competence not only includes the initial acquisition of this specialized knowledge and skill, but also requires continued learning and practice.

Rule 2.1

A member shall maintain and advance his/her knowledge in all areas of financial service in which he/she is engaged and shall participate in continuing education programs throughout his/her career.

Application for Rule 2.1

A2.1a. Compliance with Rule 2.1 requires, at a minimum, meeting the applicable continuing education standards set by state licensing authorities, the Society of Financial Service Professionals, the American College, the CFP Board of Standards, and any other entity with appropriate authority over the member's license(s) or other credentials. For example PACE, the joint CE program of the Society of and the American College requires 30 hours of CE every 2 years. The CFP Board of Standards also requires 30 hours of continuing education every 2 years for CFP® licensees.

Rule 2.2

A member shall refrain from giving advice in areas beyond the member's own expertise.

Applications for Rule 2.2

A2.2a. A member shall not give tax, legal, insurance, accounting, actuarial, investment, or other advice unless the member has professional training and is properly licensed in these areas. For example, to avoid the unauthorized practice of law, the financial service professional will clearly mark specimen documents, such as living or testamentary trusts or buy-sell agreements, as samples and inform the client that the documents must be reviewed by a licensed attorney.

A2.2b. Billy Burke, CFP®, has a specialized financial planning practice that focuses on assisting clients with funding college for their children. When Billy's long-time client and friend, Margaret Hamilton, asks for help in managing the distribution of funds from her defined benefit plan, Billy knows this is beyond his area of expertise, but he doesn't want to let his friend down. Billy proceeds to recommend several investment options to Margaret, but neglects to mention the early withdrawal taxes and penalties. Billy has violated Rule 2.2.

CANON 3 Confidentiality

A member shall respect the confidentiality of any information entrusted to, or obtained in the course of, the member's business or professional activities.

A financial service professional often gains access to client records and company information of a sensitive nature. Each Society member must maintain the highest level of confidentiality with regard to this information.

Rule 3.1

A member shall respect and safeguard the confidentiality of sensitive client information obtained in the course of professional activities. A member shall not divulge such information without specific consent of the client, unless disclosure of such information is required by law or necessary in order to discharge legitimate professional duties.

Application for Rule 3.1

A3.1a. Examples of sensitive client information include, but are not limited to, medical data, information about financial status, Social Security or credit card numbers, information about personal relationships, etc. In determining whether information is sensitive, the Society member should take a cautious approach, and if in doubt, discuss the issue with the client.

Rule 3.2

A member shall respect and safeguard the confidentiality of sensitive company/employer information obtained in the course of professional activities. A member shall not divulge such information without specific consent, unless disclosure of such information is required by law or necessary in order to discharge legitimate professional duties.

Rule 3.3

A member must ensure that confidentiality practices are established and maintained by staff members so that breaches of confidence are not the result of intentional or unintentional acts or omissions.

Application for Rule 3.3

A3.3a. A member who employs others who work with sensitive, confidential client information has the responsibility to train these employees in the handling of such information. These employees must be instructed that they will be held responsible for unauthorized disclosure of confidential data. For example, Judy Parker has set up detailed procedures for her staff to follow in safeguarding confidential client information. On three separate occasions, Judy overhead her office manager gossiping with friends about the size of Client X's investment portfolio. Judy has not taken any action in regard to the office manager's behavior. Judy has violated Rule 3.3.

CANON 4 Integrity

A member shall provide professional services with integrity and shall place the client's interest above his/her own.

Integrity involves honesty and trust. A professional's honesty and candor should not be subordinate to personal gain or advantage. To be dishonest with others is to use them for one's own purposes.

Rule 4.1

A member shall avoid any conduct or activity that would cause unnecessary harm to others by:

- Any act or omission of a dishonest, deceitful, or fraudulent nature.
- Pursuit of financial gain or other personal benefits that would interfere with the exercise of sound professional judgments and skills.

Rule 4.2

A member shall establish and maintain dignified and honorable relationships with those he/she serves, with fellow practitioners, and with members of other professions.

Application for Rule 4.2

A4.2a. A member needs to be respectful in all dealings with another financial service professional in competitive engagements and avoid at all costs defamatory remarks to the client or other professionals. This does not mean a member cannot provide impartial factual information about a competitor. For example, in trying to help a friend make a decision about which long-term care policy to purchase, Joe Carter, CLU, reviews the features of each contract and accurately notes that his competitor's policy fails to provide coverage for Home care. Joe recommends that his friend review this information with his agent.

Rule 4.3

A member shall embrace and adhere to the spirit and letter of laws and regulations governing his/her business and professional activities. See also Rule 6.1.

Rule 4.4

A member shall be truthful and candid in his/her professional communications with existing and prospective clients, and with the general public.

Applications for Rule 4.4

A4.4a. Financial service professionals will not use words or make statements in brochures or advertising materials or in any client communication that create false impressions or have the potential to mislead. For example, product salespersons should not refer to themselves as financial/estate planners/consultants, if they do not provide these services. Words such as deposits or contributions should not be used to describe life insurance premiums. Life insurance policies should not be referred to as retirement plans. Discussion of vanishing premiums and guaranteed performance should be avoided. Financial service professionals must avoid creating the impression that they represent a number of companies when they place business with only a few companies. (See also Rule 1.6.)

A4.4b. Candid communication is required when a client is acting or intends to act outside the law. In such cases, the member should terminate the professional relationship and seek the advice of appropriate advisers. For example, Lisa Long, CLU, CFP®, an investment adviser, has been asked by her client to effect a transaction based on insider information. Lisa must immediately advise her client that insider trading is a violation of SEC rules and could result in criminal charges. Lisa should also document what has happened; and if, the client plans to proceed with the transaction, Lisa should terminate the relationship. Lisa should also consult her own legal and ethical advisers as to whether she has additional legal obligations under these circumstances. Lisa's legal obligations will impact her ethical obligations.

Rule 4.5.

A member shall refrain from using an approved Society designation, degree, or credential in a false or misleading manner.

CANON 5 Diligence

A member shall act with patience, timeliness, and consistency in the fulfillment of his/her professional duties.

A professional works diligently. Knowledge and skill alone are not adequate. A professional must apply these attributes in a prompt and thorough manner in the service of others.

Rule 5.1

A member shall act with competence and consistency in promptly discharging his/her responsibilities to clients, employers, principals, purchasers, and other users of the member's services.

Rule 5.2

A member shall make recommendations to clients, whether in writing or orally, only after sufficient professional evaluation and understanding of the client's needs and goals. A member shall support any such recommendations with appropriate research and documentation.

Rule 5.3

A member shall properly supervise subordinates with regard to their role in the delivery of financial services, and shall not condone conduct in violation of the ethical standards set forth in this Code of Professional Responsibility.

CANON 6 Professionalism

A member shall assist in raising professional standards in the financial services industry.

A member's conduct in all matters shall reflect credit upon the financial services profession. A member has an obligation to cooperate with Society members, and other financial service professionals, to enhance and maintain the profession's public image and to work together to improve the quality of services rendered.

Rule 6.1

A member has the duty to know and abide by the local, state, and national laws and regulations and all legal limitations pertaining to the member's professional activities.

Applications for Rule 6.1

A6.1a. The financial service profession is subject to state and federal laws and regulation in the areas of securities, insurance, banking, and unfair trade practices, among others. Society members must understand these laws and regulations and their applicability to their practices. For example, Susan Short, CLU, just earned her CFP® license, and is planning on expanding her practice to include comprehensive financial planning services. Does Susan need to register as an investment adviser? Must she be licensed with the National Association of Securities Dealers? What about state insurance laws? Susan must answer these questions and comply with the appropriate requirements for her business activities.

A6.1b. Jon Planner receives equity commissions throughout the year. As part of a prearranged agreement, he transfers these commissions to the corporation for whom he works. Jon later learns that this is a violation of NASD rules and that commissions cannot be split with corporations. Jon is ethically obligated to correct this situation and to further educate himself on the rules and regulations applying to his business.

Rule 6.2

A member shall support the development, improvement, and enforcement of such laws, regulations, and codes of ethical conduct that foster respect for the financial service professional and benefit the public.

Application for Rule 6.2

A6.2a. Suppose Congress is contemplating a measure that would increase the regulatory burden on financial service professionals by requiring increased documentation of specific client transactions. There is firm evidence that enactment of this measure would substantially reduce the likelihood of client's being misled or confused about such transactions. Rule 6.2 would require Society members to support such a measure.

Rule 6.3

A member shall show respect for other financial service professionals and related occupational groups by engaging in fair and honorable competitive practices; collegiality among members shall not impede enforcement of this Code.

Rule 6.4

A member shall cooperate with regulatory authorities regarding investigations of any alleged violation of laws or regulations by a financial service professional.

CANON 7 Self-Regulation

A member shall assist in maintaining the integrity of the Society's Code of Professional Responsibility and of the professional credentials held by all Society members.

Every professional has a responsibility to regulate itself. As such, every Society member holds a duty of abiding by his/her professional code of ethics. In addition, Society members have a duty to facilitate the enforcement of this Code of Professional Responsibility.

Rule 7.1

A member has the duty to know and abide by all rules of ethical and professional conduct prescribed in this Code of Professional Responsibility.

Application for Rule 7.1

A7.1a. Society members are advised to review the Code of Professional Responsibility at least annually.

Rule 7.2

A member shall not sponsor as a candidate for Society membership any person known by the member to engage in business or professional practices that violate the rules of this Code of Professional Responsibility.

Rule 7.3

A member shall not directly or indirectly condone any act by another member prohibited by this Code of Professional Responsibility.

Application for Rule 7.3

A7.3a. If requested, a Society member should serve on such committees, boards, or hearing panels as are prescribed by the Society for administration or enforcement of the Code of Professional Responsibility. A Society member is obligated to disqualify him/herself from such service if he/she cannot not serve in a fair and impartial manner.

Rule 7.4

A member shall immediately notify the Society if he/she is found in violation of any code of ethics to which he or she is subject and shall forward details to the Society.

Rule 7.5

A member shall immediately notify the Society of any revocation or suspension of his/her license by a state or federal licensing or regulatory agency and forward details to the Society.

Application for Rule 7.5

A7.5a. If, after due process, a Society member is judged to have violated the code of ethics of another organization, he/she should notify the Society and provide such detail as may be necessary.

Rule 7.6

A member possessing unprivileged information concerning an alleged violation of this Code of Professional Responsibility shall report such information to the appropriate enforcement authority empowered by the Society to investigate or act upon the alleged violation.

Applications for Rule 7.6

A7.6a. If a member believes that another member of the Society may have violated the Code of Professional Responsibility, the Society recommends, where feasible, that direct communication between the two members be the first step in addressing the problem.

A7.6b. The Society's Code of Professional Responsibility places responsibility upon all members to report violations of this Code. (See also Rule 7.6.)

Rule 7.7

A member shall report promptly to the Society any information concerning the unauthorized use of an approved Society designation, degree, or credential.

Application for Rule 7.7

A7.7a. The Society logo may be imprinted on business cards and stationery used exclusively by the person who is a Society member. (See also Rule 4.6.)

NATIONAL ASSOCIATION OF PERSONAL FINANCIAL ADVISORS

History and Mission

NAPFA is the largest professional association of *fee-only* comprehensive financial planners in the United States. Its approximately 1,000 members and affiliates nationwide provide consumers and institutions with objective financial advice on a fee-only basis. NAPFA's members believe that to keep the best interests of clients in mind, neither the advisor nor any related party should receive compensation contingent on the purchase or sale of a financial product.

Core Values

NAPFA outlines the following as its Core Values:

- **Competency:** Requiring the highest standards of proficiency in the industry.
- **Comprehensive:** Practicing a holistic approach to financial planning.
- **Compensation:** Using a Fee-Only model that facilitates objective advice.
- **Client-centered:** Committing to a fiduciary relationship that ensures the client's interest is always first.
- **Complete Disclosure:** Providing an explanation of fees and potential conflicts of interest.

NAPFA Code of Ethics

Objectivity: NAPFA members strive to be as unbiased as possible in providing advice to clients and NAPFA members practice on a fee-only basis.

Confidentiality: NAPFA members shall keep all client data private unless authorization is received from the client to share it. NAPFA members shall treat all documents with care and take care when disposing of them. Relations with clients shall be kept private.

Competence: NAPFA members shall strive to maintain a high level of knowledge and ability. Members shall attain continuing education at least at the minimum level required by NAPFA. Members shall not provide advice in areas where they are not capable.

Fairness & Suitability: Dealings and recommendation with clients will always be in the client's best interests. NAPFA members put their clients first.

Integrity & Honesty: NAPFA members will endeavor to always take the high road and to be ever mindful of the potential for misunderstanding that can accrue in normal human interactions. NAPFA members will be diligent to keep actions and reactions so far above board that a thinking client, or other professional, would not doubt intentions. In all actions, NAPFA members should be mindful that in addition to serving our clients, we are about the business of building a profession and our actions should reflect this.

Regulatory Compliance: NAPFA members will strive to maintain conformity with legal regulations.

Full Disclosure: NAPFA members shall fully describe method of compensation and potential conflicts of interest to clients and also specify the total cost of investments.

Professionalism: NAPFA members shall conduct themselves in a way that would be a credit to NAPFA at all times. NAPFA membership involves integrity, honest treatment of clients, and treating people with respect.

NAPFA Fiduciary Oath

The advisor shall exercise his/her best efforts to act in good faith and in the best interests of the client. The advisor shall provide written disclosure to the client prior to the engagement of the advisor, and thereafter throughout the term of the engagement, of any conflicts of interest, which will or reasonably may compromise the impartiality or independence of the advisor.

The advisor, or any party in which the advisor has a financial interest, does not receive any compensation or other remuneration that is contingent on any client's purchase or sale of a financial product. The advisor does not receive a fee or other compensation from another party based on the referral of a client or the client's business.

What the Fiduciary Oath means to you – the client

- I shall always act in good faith and with candor.
- I shall be proactive in my disclosure of any conflicts of interest that may impact you.
- I shall not accept any referral fees or compensation that is contingent upon the purchase or sale of a financial product.

Standards of Membership and Affiliation

Applicants for any category of membership (Members) or affiliation (Affiliates) with NAPFA must meet the certain standards to be considered for admission, and must continue to abide by such standards in order to maintain eligibility and good standing in NAPFA.

NAPFA's definition of a Fee-Only financial planner

NAPFA defines a Fee-Only financial advisor as one who, in all circumstances, is compensated solely by the client, with neither the advisor or any related party receiving compensation that is contingent on the purchase or sale of a financial product. Neither Members nor Affiliates may receive commissions, rebates, awards, finder's fees, bonuses or other forms of compensation from others as a result of a client's implementation of the individual's planning recommendations. "Fee-offset" arrangements, 12b-1 fees, insurance rebates or renewals and wrap fee arrangements that are transaction based are examples of compensation arrangements that do not meet the NAPFA definition of Fee-Only practice.

Prohibition of certain ownership interests and employment relationships

Neither a member nor an affiliate may own more than a 2% interest in, or be employed by, a financial services industry firm (see definition below) that receives transaction based compensation as prohibited by the NAPFA Standards of Membership and Affiliation.

A related party (see definition below) to a member or an affiliate may not own more than a 2% interest in a financial services industry firm that receives transaction based compensation as prohibited by NAPFA; and to whom the member or affiliate makes referrals or otherwise directs business.

Financial services industry firm includes any entity or individual that offers any type of financial service, e.g., securities broker or dealer, investment adviser, asset manager, investment company, banking institution, savings institution, trust company, mortgage bank, credit union, savings and loan association, insurance broker or dealer or agent, real estate broker or agent, commodities broker or dealer or agent. Related party means a household member with whom a member or affiliate shares income or economic benefits.

Compliance with NAPFA standards and industry regulations

Members must comply with all NAPFA standards and with all industry laws and regulations.

All members and affiliates

- must abide by the NAPFA Code of Ethics, Standards of Membership and Affiliation, Bylaws, resolutions adopted by the Board and all rules set forth in the NAPFA Policies and Procedures Manual.
- agree to comply with all federal and state statutes, rules, regulations, administrative and judicial rulings, and other authorities applicable to the provision of financial planning or advisory related services.
- agree that they will make all appropriate filings, amendments and renewals as appropriate to required filings with regulatory authorities. This shall include, but is not limited to, Form ADV. As a condition of NAPFA membership, any and all Form ADV filings may be reviewed by the Membership Task Force.

Prompt notification of certain disciplinary and legal events

Members and Affiliates have a continuing obligation to inform the NAPFA National Office, in a prompt manner and in writing, of significant disciplinary and legal events. These events include, but are not limited to, the following:

- any disciplinary inquiry or proceeding initiated by any federal, state or local civil or criminal authority or regulatory body, including any inquiry or proceeding relating to the firm with which the individual is associated;
- any disciplinary inquiry or proceeding initiated by a credentialing or membership organization or authority to which the individual is subject, e.g., Certified Financial Planner Board of Standards, State Board of Public Accountancy;
- any bankruptcy, receivership, or other type of assignment or arrangement for the benefit or protection of creditors of the individual or any entity in which the individual holds an interest of 5% or more.

NAPFA reserves the right to decline membership if the applicant has failed to comply with statutes or regulations governing the profession, or has been unsuccessful in the defense of civil claims arising from professional services, unless such violations or claims are not material.

CHAPTER ENDNOTES

1. Adapted from *The Tools & Techniques of Estate Planning*, 14th Ed., by Stephan R. Leimberg, et al., Copyright 2006, The National Underwriter Company, Cincinnati, OH, p. 79.

Chapter 8

FINANCIAL PLANNING PRACTICE STANDARDS

WHAT ARE PRACTICE STANDARDS?

Practice standards draw from ethics and disciplinary rules to describe the process a financial planner should use in working with a client. Because practice standards are related to ethics and disciplinary rules, they provide strong guidance on how to conduct a financial planning practice in accordance with those principles. Unlike ethical standards and disciplinary rules, however, a planner who deviates from a specific practice standard will not be subject to discipline on that basis alone.

CFP Board Financial Planning Practice Standards

Overview

The Board of Governors approved the first three Practice Standards in 1998, after solicitation and consideration of comments from CFP certificants. These standards, in the 100 and 200 series, became effective for all CFP certificants on January 1, 1999. The 300 series went into effect in 2000, the 400 series in 2001, and the 500 and 600 series on January 1, 2002. All six series were updated effective January 1, 2002. The topic areas covered by the six series comprising the Financial Planning Practice Standards are listed below:

- 100 Series: Establishing and Defining the Relationship with the Client
- 200 Series: Gathering Client Data
- 300 Series: Analyzing and Evaluating the Client's Financial Status
- 400 Series: Developing and Presenting the Financial Planning Recommendation
- 500 Series: Implementing the Financial Planning Recommendation(s)
- 600 Series: Monitoring

Statement of Purpose for Financial Planning Practice Standards

Financial Planning Practice Standards are developed and promulgated by the CFP Board for the ultimate benefit of consumers of financial planning services.

These *Practice Standards* are intended to:

1. Assure that the practice of financial planning by CERTIFIED FINANCIAL PLANNER™ professionals is based on established norms of practice;
2. Advance professionalism in financial planning; and
3. Enhance the value of the financial planning process.

Description of Practice Standards

A *Practice Standard* establishes the level of professional practice that is expected of CFP Board designees engaged in financial planning.

This material is derived from the Certified Financial Planners Board of Standards, Inc. web site: http://www.cfp.net.

Practice Standards apply to CFP Board designees in performing the tasks of financial planning regardless of the person's title, job position, type of employment or method of compensation. Compliance with the Practice Standards is mandatory for CFP Board designees, but all financial planning professionals are encouraged to use the *Practice Standards* when performing financial planning tasks or activities addressed by a *Practice Standard*.

Conduct inconsistent with a *Practice Standard* in and of itself is neither intended to give rise to a cause of action nor to create any presumption that a legal duty has been breached. The *Practice Standards* are designed to provide CFP Board designees a framework for the professional practice of financial planning. They are not designed to be a basis for legal liability.

Practice Standards are not intended to prescribe the services to be provided or step-by-step procedures for providing any particular service. Such procedures may be provided in practice aids developed by various financial planning organizations and other sources.

Practice Standards were developed for selected financial planning activities identified in a financial planner job analysis first conducted by CFP Board in 1987, updated in 1994 by CTB/McGraw-Hill, an independent consulting firm, and again in 1999 by the Chauncey Group. The financial planning process is defined as follows:

Financial Planning Process	**Related Practice Standard**
1. Establishing and defining the relationship with a client	100-1 Defining the Scope of the Engagement
2. Gathering client data	200-1 Determining a Client's Personal and Financial Goals, Needs and Priorities 200-2 Obtaining Quantitative Information and Documents
3. Analyzing and evaluating the client's financial status	300-1 Analyzing and Evaluating the Client's Information
4. Developing and presenting financial planning recommendations	400-1 Identifying and Evaluating Financial Planning Alternative(s) 400-2 Developing the Financial Planning Recommendation(s) 400-3 Presenting the Financial Planning Recommendation(s)
5. Implementing the financial planning recommendations	500-1 Agreeing on Implementation Responsibilities 500-2 Selecting Products and Services for Implementation
6. Monitoring	600-1 Defining Monitoring Responsibilities

Format of Practice Standards

Each *Practice Standard* is a statement regarding an element of the financial planning process. It is followed by an explanation of the Standard, its relationship to the *Code of Ethics*, and its expected impact on the public, the profession and the practitioner.

The Explanation accompanying each *Practice Standard* explains and illustrates the meaning and purpose of the *Practice Standard*. The text of each *Practice Standard* is authoritative and directive. The related Explanation is a guide to interpretation and application of the *Practice Standard* based, where indicated, on a standard of reasonableness, a recurring theme throughout the *Practice Standards*. The Explanation is not intended to establish a professional standard or duty beyond what is contained in the *Practice Standard* itself.

Compliance with Practice Standards

The practice of financial planning consistent with these *Practice Standards* is required for CFP Board designees. Enforcement is based on the disciplinary rules and procedures established by CFP Board and administered by CFP Board's Board of Professional Review and Board of Appeals.

PRACTICE STANDARD 100 SERIES: ESTABLISHING AND DEFINING THE RELATIONSHIP WITH THE CLIENT

100-1: Defining the Scope of the Engagement

The financial planning practitioner and the client shall mutually define the scope of the engagement before any financial planning service is provided.

Explanation of this Practice Standard

Prior to providing any financial planning service, the financial planning practitioner and the client shall mutually define the scope of the engagement. The process of "mutually-defining" is essential in determining what activities may be necessary to proceed with the engagement.

This process is accomplished in financial planning engagements by:

1. Identifying the service(s) to be provided;
2. Disclosing the practitioner's material conflict(s) of interest;
3. Disclosing the practitioner's compensation arrangement(s);
4. Determining the client's and the practitioner's responsibilities;
5. Establishing the duration of the engagement; and
6. Providing any additional information necessary to define or limit the scope.

The scope of the engagement may include one or more financial planning subject areas. It is acceptable to mutually define engagements in which the scope is limited to specific activities. Mutually defining the scope of the engagement serves to establish realistic expectations for both the client and the practitioner.

This *Practice Standard* does not require the scope of the engagement to be in writing. However, as noted in the "Relationship" section, which follows, there may be certain disclosures that are required to be in writing.

This material is derived from the Certified Financial Planners Board of Standards, Inc. web site: http://www.cfp.net.

As the relationship proceeds, the scope may change by mutual agreement.

This *Practice Standard* shall not be considered alone, but in conjunction with all other *Practice Standards*.

Effective Date

Original version, January 1, 1999. Updated version, January 1, 2002.

Relationship of this Practice Standard to CFP Board's Code of Ethics and Professional Responsibility

This *Practice Standard* relates to CFP Board's *Code of Ethics and Professional Responsibility (Code of Ethics)* through the *Code of Ethics'* Principle 4 – Fairness and Rule 402; and Principle 7 – Diligence and Rule 702.

Principle 4 states "A CFP Board designee shall perform professional services in a manner that is fair and reasonable to clients.... "Although, as stated earlier, there is no requirement that the scope of the engagement be in writing, Rule 402 in the Code of Ethics requires a financial planning practitioner to make "timely written disclosure of all material information relative to the professional relationship. In all circumstances and prior to the engagement, a CFP Board designee shall, in writing: (a) Disclose conflict(s) of interest and sources of compensation; and (b) Inform the client or prospective client of his/her right to ask at any time for information about the compensation of the CFP Board designee."

Principle 7 states "A CFP Board designee shall act diligently in providing professional services." Rule 702 requires that financial planning practitioners enter into an engagement only after obtaining sufficient information to satisfy that "the relationship is warranted by the individual's needs and objectives; and the CFP Board designee has the ability to either provide requisite competent services or to involve other professionals who can provide such services."

Anticipated Impact of this Practice Standard

Upon the Public

The public is served when the relationship is based upon a mutual understanding of the engagement. Clarity of the scope of the engagement enhances the likelihood of achieving client expectations.

Upon the Financial Planning Profession

The profession benefits when clients are satisfied. This is more likely to take place when clients have expectations of the process, which are both realistic and clear, before services are provided.

Upon the Financial Planning Practitioner

A mutually defined scope of the engagement provides a framework for the financial planning process by focusing both the client and the practitioner on the agreed upon tasks. This enhances the potential for positive results.

PRACTICE STANDARDS 200 SERIES: GATHERING CLIENT DATA

200-1: Determining a Client's Personal and Financial Goals, Needs and Priorities

The financial planning practitioner and the client shall mutually define the client's personal and financial goals, needs and priorities that are relevant to the scope of the engagement before any recommendation is made and/or implemented.

Explanation of this Practice Standard

Prior to making recommendations to the client, the financial planning practitioner and the client shall mutually define the client's personal and financial goals, needs and priorities. In order to arrive at such a definition, the practitioner will need to explore the client's values, attitudes, expectations, and time horizons as they affect the client's goals, needs and priorities. The process of "mutually-defining" is essential in determining what activities may be necessary to proceed with the client engagement.

Personal values and attitudes shape the client's goals and objectives and the priority placed on them. Accordingly, these goals and objectives must be consistent with the client's values and attitudes in order for the client to make the commitment necessary to accomplish them.

Goals and objectives provide focus, purpose, vision and direction for the financial planning process. It is important to determine clear, and measurable objectives that are relevant to the scope of the engagement. The role of the practitioner is to facilitate the goal-setting process in order to clarify, with the client, goals and objectives. When appropriate, the practitioner shall try to assist clients in recognizing the implications of unrealistic goals and objectives.

This *Practice Standard* addresses only the tasks of determining the client's personal and financial goals, needs and priorities; assessing the client's values, attitudes and expectations; and determining the client's time horizons. These areas are subjective and the practitioner's interpretation is limited by what the client reveals.

This *Practice Standard* shall not be considered alone, but in conjunction with all other Practice Standards.

Effective Date

Original version, January 1, 1999. Updated version, January 1, 2002.

Relationship of this Practice Standard to CFP Board's Code of Ethics and Professional Responsibility

This *Practice Standard* relates to CFP Board's *Code of Ethics and Professional Responsibility (Code of Ethics)* through the *Code of Ethics'* Principle 7 – Diligence, and Rules 701 through 703. Rule 701 states that "A CFP Board designee shall provide services diligently." Rule 702 requires a financial planning practitioner to "enter into an engagement only after securing sufficient information to satisfy the CFP Board designee that ... the relationship is warranted by the individual's needs and objectives...." In addition, Rule 703 requires a financial planning practitioner to "make and/or implement only recommendations which are suitable for the client."

This material is derived from the Certified Financial Planners Board of Standards, Inc. web site: http://www.cfp.net.

Anticipated Impact of this Practice Standard

Upon the Public

The public is served when the relationship is based upon mutually defined goals, needs and priorities. This Practice Standard reinforces the practice of putting the client's interests first which is intended to increase the likelihood of achieving the client's goals and objectives.

Upon the Financial Planning Profession

Compliance with this Practice Standard emphasizes to the public that the client's goals, needs and priorities are the focus of the financial planning process. This encourages the public to seek out the services of a financial planning practitioner who uses such an approach.

Upon the Financial Planning Practitioner

The client's goals, needs and priorities help determine the direction of the financial planning process. This focuses the practitioner on the specific tasks that need to be accomplished. Ultimately, this will facilitate the development of appropriate recommendations.

200-2: Obtaining Quantitative Information and Documents

The financial planning practitioner shall obtain sufficient quantitative information and documents about a client relevant to the scope of the engagement before any recommendation is made and/or implemented.

Explanation of this Practice Standard

Prior to making recommendations to the client and depending on the scope of the engagement, the financial planning practitioner shall determine what quantitative information and documents are sufficient and relevant.

The practitioner shall obtain sufficient and relevant quantitative information and documents pertaining to the client's financial resources, obligations and personal situation. This information may be obtained directly from the client or other sources such as interview(s), questionnaire(s), client records and documents.

The practitioner shall communicate to the client a reliance on the completeness and accuracy of the information provided and that incomplete or inaccurate information will impact conclusions and recommendations.

If the practitioner is unable to obtain sufficient and relevant quantitative information and documents to form a basis for recommendations, the practitioner shall either:

A. Restrict the scope of the engagement to those matters for which sufficient and relevant information is available; or

B. Terminate the engagement.

The practitioner shall communicate to the client any limitations on the scope of the engagement, as well as the fact that this limitation could affect the conclusions and recommendations.

This *Practice Standard* shall not be considered alone, but in conjunction with all other *Practice Standards*.

Effective Date

Original version, January 1, 1999. Updated version, January 1, 2002.

Relationship of this Practice Standard to CFP Board's Code of Ethics and Professional Responsibility

This *Practice Standard* relates to *CFP Board's Code of Ethics and Professional Responsibility (Code of Ethics)* through the *Code of Ethics'* Principle 7 – Diligence and Rules 701 through 703. Rule 701 states "A CFP Board designee shall provide services diligently." Rule 702 requires a financial planning practitioner to "enter into an engagement only after securing sufficient information to satisfy the CFP Board designee that ... the relationship is warranted by the individual's needs and objectives...." In addition, Rule 703 requires a financial planning practitioner to "make and/or implement only recommendations which are suitable for the client."

Anticipated Impact of this Practice Standard

Upon the Public

The public is served when financial planning recommendations are based upon sufficient and relevant quantitative information and documents. This Practice Standard is intended to increase the likelihood of achieving the client's goals and objectives.

Upon the Financial Planning Profession

The financial planning process requires that recommendations be made based on sufficient and relevant quantitative data. Therefore, compliance with this Practice Standard encourages the public to seek financial planning practitioners who use the financial planning process.

Upon the Financial Planning Practitioner

Sufficient and relevant quantitative information and documents provide the foundation for analysis. Ultimately, this will facilitate the development of appropriate recommendations.

This material is derived from the Certified Financial Planners Board of Standards, Inc. web site: http://www.cfp.net.

PRACTICE STANDARDS 300 SERIES: ANALYZING AND EVALUATING THE CLIENT'S FINANCIAL STATUS

300-1: Analyzing and Evaluating the Client's Information

A financial planning practitioner shall analyze the information to gain an understanding of the client's financial situation and then evaluate to what extent the client's goals, needs and priorities can be met by the client's resources and current course of action.

Explanation of this Practice Standard

Prior to making recommendations to a client, it is necessary for the financial planning practitioner to assess the client's financial situation and to determine the likelihood of reaching the stated objectives by continuing present activities.

The practitioner will utilize client-specified, mutually agreed upon, and/or other reasonable assumptions. Both personal and economic assumptions must be considered in this step of the process. These assumptions may include, but are not limited to, the following:

- Personal assumptions, such as: retirement age(s), life expectancy(ies), income needs, risk factors, time horizon and special needs; and
- Economic assumptions, such as: inflation rates, tax rates and investment returns.

Analysis and evaluation are critical to the financial planning process. These activities form the foundation for determining strengths and weaknesses of the client's financial situation and current course of action. These activities may also identify other issues that should be addressed. As a result, it may be appropriate to amend the scope of the engagement and/or to obtain additional information.

Effective Date

Original version, January 1, 2000. Updated version, January 1, 2002.

Relationship of this Practice Standard to CFP Board's Code of Ethics and Professional Responsibility

This *Practice Standard* relates to *CFP Board's Code of Ethics and Professional Responsibility (Code of Ethics)* through the *Code of Ethics'* Principle 2 - Objectivity and Rules 201 and 202; Principle 3 - Competence and Rule 302, and Principle 7 - Diligence and Rule 701.

Principle 2 states "A CFP Board designee shall be objective in providing professional services to clients." Rule 201 states "A CFP Board designee shall exercise reasonable and prudent professional judgment in providing professional services" and Rule 202 states "A financial planning practitioner shall act in the interest of the client."

Principle 3 states "A CFP Board designee shall provide services to clients competently and maintain the necessary knowledge and skill to continue to do so in those areas in which the designee is engaged." Rule 302 states "A CFP Board designee shall offer advice only in those areas in which the CFP Board designee has competence. In areas where the CFP Board designee is not professionally competent, the CFP Board designee shall seek the counsel of qualified individuals and/or refer clients to such parties."

Under Principle 7, Rule 701 states "A CFP Board designee shall provide services diligently."

Anticipated Impact of this Practice Standard

Upon the Public

The public is served when objective analysis and evaluation by a financial planning practitioner results in the client's heightened awareness of specific financial planning issues. This Practice Standard is intended to increase the likelihood of achieving the client's goals and objectives.

Upon the Financial Planning Profession

Objective analysis and evaluation enhances the public's recognition of and appreciation for the financial planning process and increases the confidence in financial planning practitioners who provide this service.

Upon the Financial Planning Practitioner

Analysis and evaluation helps the practitioner establish the foundation from which recommendations can be made that are specific to the client's financial planning goals, needs and priorities.

PRACTICE STANDARDS 400 SERIES: DEVELOPING AND PRESENTING THE FINANCIAL PLANNING RECOMMENDATION(S)

Preface to the 400 Series

The 400 Series, "Developing and Presenting the Financial Planning Recommendation(s)," represents the very heart of the financial planning process. It is at this point that the financial planning practitioner, using both science and art, formulates the recommendations designed to achieve the client's goals, needs and priorities. Experienced financial planning practitioners may view this process as one action or task. However, in reality, it is a series of distinct but interrelated tasks.

These three *Practice Standards* emphasize the distinction among the several tasks which are part of this process. These *Practice Standards* can be described as, "What is Possible?," "What is Recommended?" and "How is it Presented?" The first two *Practice Standards* involve the creative thought, the analysis, and the professional judgment of the practitioner, which are often performed outside the presence of the client. First, the practitioner identifies and considers the various alternatives, including continuing the present course of action (*Practice Standard* 400-1). Second, the practitioner develops the recommendation(s) from among the selected alternatives (*Practice Standard* 400-2). Once the practitioner has determined what to recommend, the final task is to communicate the recommendation(s) to the client (*Practice Standard* 400-3).

The three *Practice Standards* that comprise the 400 series should not be considered alone, but in conjunction with all other *Practice Standards*.

400-1: Identifying and Evaluating Financial Planning Alternative(s)

The financial planning practitioner shall consider sufficient and relevant alternatives to the client's current course of action in an effort to reasonably meet the client's goals, needs and priorities.

This material is derived from the Certified Financial Planners Board of Standards, Inc. web site: http://www.cfp.net.

Explanation of this Practice Standard

After analyzing the client's current situation (*Practice Standard* 300-1) and prior to developing and presenting the recommendation(s) (*Practice Standards* 400-2 and 400-3) the financial planning practitioner shall identify alternative actions. The practitioner shall evaluate the effectiveness of such actions in reasonably meeting the client's goals, needs and priorities.

This evaluation may involve, but is not limited to, considering multiple assumptions, conducting research or consulting with other professionals. This process may result in a single alternative, multiple alternatives or no alternative to the client's current course of action.

In considering alternative actions, the practitioner shall recognize and, as appropriate, take into account his or her legal and/or regulatory limitations and level of competency in properly addressing each of the client's financial planning issues.

More than one alternative may reasonably meet the client's goals, needs and priorities. Alternatives identified by the practitioner may differ from those of other practitioners or advisers, illustrating the subjective nature of exercising professional judgment.

Effective Date

Original version, January 1, 2001. Updated version, January 1, 2002.

Relationship of this Practice Standard to CFP Board's Code of Ethics and Professional Responsibility

This *Practice Standard* relates to CFP Board's *Code of Ethics and Professional Responsibility (Code of Ethics)* through the *Code of Ethics'* Principle 2 – Objectivity and Rules 201 and 202; Principle 3 – Competence and Rule 302; Principle 6 – Professionalism and Rule 609; and Principle 7 – Diligence and Rules 701 and 703.

Principle 2 states "A CFP Board designee shall be objective in providing professional services to clients." Rule 201 states "A CFP Board designee shall exercise reasonable and prudent professional judgment in providing professional services." Rule 202 states "A financial planning practitioner shall act in the interest of the client."

Principle 3 states "A CFP Board designee shall provide services to clients competently and maintain the necessary knowledge and skill to continue to do so in those areas in which the designee is engaged." Rule 302 states "A CFP Board designee shall offer advice only in those areas in which the CFP Board designee has competence. In areas where the CFP Board designee is not professionally competent, the CFP Board designee shall seek the counsel of qualified individuals and/or refer clients to such parties."

Principle 6 states "A CFP Board designee's conduct in all matters shall reflect credit upon the profession." Rule 609 states "A CFP Board designee shall not practice any other profession or offer to provide such services unless the CFP Board designee is qualified ... and is licensed as required by state law."

Principle 7 states "A CFP Board designee shall act diligently in providing professional services." Rule 701 states "A CFP Board designee shall provide services diligently." Rule 703 states "A financial planner practitioner shall make and/or implement only recommendations which are suitable for the client."

400-2: Developing the Financial Planning Recommendation(s)

The financial planning practitioner shall develop the recommendation(s) based on the selected alternative(s) and the current course of action in an effort to reasonably meet the client's goals, needs and priorities.

Explanation of this Practice Standard

After identifying and evaluating the alternative(s) and the client's current course of action, the practitioner shall develop the recommendation(s) expected to reasonably meet the client's goals, needs and priorities. A recommendation may be an independent action or a combination of actions which may need to be implemented collectively.

The recommendation(s) shall be consistent with and will be directly affected by the following:

- Mutually defined scope of the engagement;
- Mutually defined client goals, needs and priorities;
- Quantitative data provided by the client;
- Personal and economic assumptions;
- Practitioner's analysis and evaluation of client's current situation; and
- Alternative(s) selected by the practitioner.

A recommendation may be to continue the current course of action. If a change is recommended, it may be specific and/or detailed or provide a general direction. In some instances, it may be necessary for the practitioner to recommend that the client modify a goal.

The recommendations developed by the practitioner may differ from those of other practitioners or advisers, yet each may reasonably meet the client's goals, needs and priorities.

Effective Date

Original version, January 1, 2001. Updated version, January 1, 2002.

Relationship of this Practice Standard to CFP Board's Code of Ethics and Professional Responsibility

This *Practice Standard* relates to *CFP Board's Code of Ethics and Professional Responsibility (Code of Ethics)* through the *Code of Ethics'* Principle 2 – Objectivity and Rules 201 and 202; Principle 3 – Competence and Rule 302; Principle 6 – Professionalism and Rule 609; and Principle 7 – Diligence and Rules 701, 703 and 704.

Principle 2 states "A CFP Board designee shall be objective in providing professional services to clients." Rule 201 states "A CFP Board designee shall exercise reasonable and prudent professional judgment in providing professional services." Rule 202 states "A financial planning practitioner shall act in the interest of the client."

This material is derived from the Certified Financial Planners Board of Standards, Inc. web site: http://www.cfp.net.

Principle 3 states "A CFP Board designee shall provide services to clients competently and maintain the necessary knowledge and skill to continue to do so in those areas in which the designee is engaged." Rule 302 states "A CFP Board designee shall offer advice only in those areas in which the CFP Board designee has competence. In areas where the CFP Board designee is not professionally competent, the CFP Board designee shall seek the counsel of qualified individuals and/or refer clients to such parties."

Principle 6 states "A CFP Board designee's conduct in all matters shall reflect credit upon the profession." Rule 609 states "A CFP Board designee shall not practice any other profession or offer to provide such services unless the CFP Board designee is qualified ... and is licensed as required by state law."

Principle 7 states "A CFP Board designee shall act diligently in providing professional services." Rule 701 states "A CFP Board designee shall provide services diligently." Rule 703 states "A financial planner practitioner shall make and/or implement only recommendations which are suitable for the client." Rule 704 states "... a CFP Board designee shall make a reasonable investigation regarding the financial products recommended to clients. Such an investigation may be made by the CFP Board designee or by others provided the CFP Board designee acts reasonably in relying upon such investigation."

400-3: Presenting the Financial Planning Recommendation(s)

The financial planning practitioner shall communicate the recommendation(s) in a manner and to an extent reasonably necessary to assist the client in making an informed decision.

Explanation of this Practice Standard

When presenting a recommendation, the practitioner shall make a reasonable effort to assist the client in understanding the client's current situation, the recommendation itself, and its impact on the ability to meet the client's goals, needs and priorities. In doing so, the practitioner shall avoid presenting the practitioner's opinion as fact.

The practitioner shall communicate the factors critical to the client's understanding of the recommendations. These factors may include but are not limited to material:

- Personal and economic assumptions;
- Interdependence of recommendations;
- Advantages and disadvantages;
- Risks; and/or
- Time sensitivity.

The practitioner should indicate that even though the recommendations may meet the client's goals, needs and priorities, changes in personal and economic conditions could alter the intended outcome. Changes may include, but are not limited to: legislative, family status, career, investment performance and/or health.

If there are conflicts of interest that have not been previously disclosed, such conflicts and how they may impact the recommendations should be addressed at this time.

Presenting recommendations provides the practitioner an opportunity to further assess whether the recommendations meet client expectations, whether the client is willing to act on the recommendations, and whether modifications are necessary.

Effective Date

Original version, January 1, 2001. Updated version, January 1, 2002.

Relationship of this Practice Standard to CFP Board's Code of Ethics and Professional Responsibility

This *Practice Standard* relates to *CFP Board's Code of Ethics and Professional Responsibility (Code of Ethics)* through the *Code of Ethics'* Principle 1 – Integrity and Rule 102; Principle 2 – Objectivity and Rule 201; and Principle 6 – Professionalism and Rule 607.

Principle 1 states "A CFP Board designee shall offer and provide professional services with integrity." Rule 102 states "... a CFP Board designee shall not ... knowingly make a false or misleading statement to a client...."

Principle 2 states "A CFP Board designee shall be objective in providing professional services to clients." Rule 201 states "A CFP Board designee shall exercise reasonable and prudent professional judgment in providing professional services."

Principle 6 states "A CFP Board designee's conduct in all matters shall reflect credit upon the profession." Rule 607 states "A CFP Board designee shall not engage in any conduct which reflects adversely on his or her integrity or fitness as a CFP Board designee...."

Anticipated Impact of these *Practice Standards*

Upon the Public

The public is served when strategies and objective recommendations are developed and are communicated clearly to specifically meet each client's individual financial planning goals, needs and priorities.

Upon the Financial Planning Profession

A commitment to a systematic process for the development and presentation of the financial planning recommendations advances the financial planning profession. Development of customized strategies and recommendations enhances the public's perception of the objectivity and value of the financial planning process. The public will seek out those professionals who embrace these *Practice Standards.*

Upon the Financial Planning Practitioner

Customizing strategies and recommendations forms a foundation to communicate meaningful and responsive solutions. This increases the likelihood that a client will accept the recommendations and act upon them. These actions will contribute to client satisfaction.

This material is derived from the Certified Financial Planners Board of Standards, Inc. web site: http://www.cfp.net.

PRACTICE STANDARDS 500 SERIES: IMPLEMENTING THE FINANCIAL PLANNING RECOMMENDATION(S)

500-1: Agreeing on Implementation Responsibilities

The financial planning practitioner and the client shall mutually agree on the implementation responsibilities consistent with the scope of the engagement.

Explanation of this *Practice Standard*

The client is responsible for accepting or rejecting recommendations and for retaining and/or delegating implementation responsibilities. The financial planning practitioner and the client shall mutually agree on the services, if any, to be provided by the practitioner. The scope of the engagement, as originally defined, may need to be modified.

The practitioner's responsibilities may include, but are not limited to the following:

- Identifying activities necessary for implementation;
- Determining division of activities between the practitioner and the client;
- Referring to other professionals;
- Coordinating with other professionals;
- Sharing of information as authorized; and
- Selecting and securing products and/or services.

If there are conflicts of interest, sources of compensation or material relationships with other professionals or advisers that have not been previously disclosed, such conflicts, sources or relationships shall be disclosed at this time.

When referring the client to other professionals or advisers, the financial planning practitioner shall indicate the basis on which the practitioner believes the other professional or adviser may be qualified.

If the practitioner is engaged by the client to provide only implementation activities, the scope of the engagement shall be mutually defined, orally or in writing, in accordance with Practice Standard 100-1. This scope may include such matters as the extent to which the practitioner will rely on information, analysis or recommendations provided by others.

Effective Date

January 1, 2002.

Relationship of this Practice Standard to CFP Board's Code of Ethics and Professional Responsibility

This *Practice Standard* relates to *CFP Board's Code of Ethics and Professional Responsibility (Code of Ethics)* through the *Code of Ethics'* Principle 3 – Competence and Rule 302; Principle 4 – Fairness and Rules 402; Principle 6 – Professionalism and Rules 606 and 609; and Principle 7 – Diligence and Rule 701.

Principle 3 states "A CFP Board designee shall provide services to clients competently and maintain the necessary knowledge and skill to continue to do so in those areas in which the designee is engaged." Rule 302 states "A CFP Board designee shall offer advice only in those areas in which the CFP Board designee has competence. In areas where the CFP Board designee is not professionally competent, the CFP Board designee shall seek the counsel of qualified individuals and/or refer clients to such parties."

Principle 4 states "A CFP Board designee shall perform professional services in a manner that is fair and reasonable to clients.... "Although, as stated earlier, there is no requirement that the scope of the engagement be in writing, Rule 402 in the Code of Ethics requires a financial planning practitioner to make "timely written disclosure of all material information relative to the professional relationship. In all circumstances and prior to the engagement, a CFP Board designee shall, in writing: (a) Disclose conflict(s) of interest and sources of compensation; and (b) Inform the client or prospective client of his/her right to ask at any time for information about the compensation of the CFP Board designee."

Principle 6 states "A CFP Board designee's conduct in all matters shall reflect credit upon the profession." Rule 606 states "... a CFP Board designee shall perform services in accordance with: (a) Applicable laws, rules, and regulations of governmental agencies and other applicable authorities...." Rule 609 states "A CFP Board designee shall not practice any other profession or offer to provide such services unless the CFP Board designee is qualified ... and is licensed as required by state law."

Under Principle 7, Rule 701 states "A CFP Board designee shall provide services diligently."

500-2: Selecting Products and Services for Implementation

The financial planning practitioner shall select appropriate products and services that are consistent with the client's goals, needs and priorities.

Explanation of this Practice Standard

The financial planning practitioner shall investigate products or services that reasonably address the client's needs. The products or services selected to implement the recommendation(s) must be suitable to the client's financial situation and consistent with the client's goals, needs and priorities.

The financial planning practitioner uses professional judgment in selecting the products and services that are in the client's interest. Professional judgment incorporates both qualitative and quantitative information.

Products and services selected by the practitioner may differ from those of other practitioners or advisers.

More than one product or service may exist that can reasonably meet the client's goals, needs and priorities.

The practitioner shall make all disclosures required by applicable regulations.

Effective Date

January 1, 2002.

This material is derived from the Certified Financial Planners Board of Standards, Inc. web site: http://www.cfp.net.

Relationship of this Practice Standard to CFP Board's Code of Ethics and Professional Responsibility

This *Practice Standard* relates to *CFP Board's Code of Ethics and Professional Responsibility (Code of Ethics)* through the *Code of Ethics'* Principle 2 – Objectivity and Rule 202; Principle 4 – Fairness and Rules 402 and 409; Principle 6 – Professionalism and Rule 606; and Principle 7 – Diligence and Rules 701, 703 and 704.

Principle 2 states "A CFP Board designee shall be objective in providing professional services to clients." Rule 202 states "A financial planning practitioner shall act in the interest of the client."

Principle 4 states "A CFP Board designee shall perform professional services in a manner that is fair and reasonable to clients … and shall disclose conflict(s) of interest in providing such services." Rule 402 states "A CFP Board designee in a financial planning engagement shall make timely written disclosure of all material information relative to the professional relationship. In all circumstances and prior to the engagement, a CFP Board designee shall, in writing: (a) Disclose conflict(s) of interest and sources of compensation; and (b) Inform the client or prospective client of his/her right to ask at any time for information about the compensation of the CFP Board designee." Rule 409 states "If a CFP Board designee enters into a personal business transaction with a client, separate from regular professional services provided to that client ... the CFP Board designee shall disclose, in writing, the risks of the transaction, conflict(s) of interest of the CFP Board designee, and other relevant information ... necessary to make the transaction fair to the client."

Principle 6 states "A CFP Board designee's conduct in all matters shall reflect credit upon the profession." Rule 606 states "In all professional activities a CFP Board designee shall perform services in accordance with: (a) Applicable laws, rules and regulations of govern-mental agencies and other applicable authorities; and (b) Applicable rules, regulations and other established policies of CFP Board."

Principle 7 states "A CFP Board designee shall act diligently in providing professional services." Rule 701 states "A CFP Board designee shall provide services diligently." Rule 703 states "A financial planning practitioner shall make and/or implement only recommendations which are suitable for the client." Rule 704 states "… a CFP Board designee shall make a reasonable investigation regarding the financial products recommended to clients."

Anticipated Impact of these *Practice Standards*

Upon the Public

The public is served when the appropriate products and services are used to implement recommendations; thus increasing the likelihood that the client's goals will be achieved.

Upon the Financial Planning Profession

Over time, implementing recommendations using appropriate products and services for the client increases the credibility of the profession in the eyes of the public.

Upon the Financial Planning Practitioner

It is for the long-term benefit of the practitioner to put the interest of the client before that of others in the selection of products and services.

PRACTICE STANDARDS 600 SERIES: MONITORING

600-1: Defining Monitoring Responsibilities

The financial planning practitioner and client shall mutually define monitoring responsibilities.

Explanation of this Practice Standard

The purpose of this *Practice Standard* is to clarify the role, if any, of the practitioner in the monitoring process. By clarifying this responsibility, the client's expectations are more likely to be in alignment with the level of monitoring services which the practitioner intends to provide.

If engaged for monitoring services, the practitioner shall make a reasonable effort to define and communicate to the client those monitoring activities the practitioner is able and willing to provide. By explaining what is to be monitored, the frequency of monitoring and the communication method, the client is more likely to understand the monitoring service to be provided by the practitioner.

The monitoring process may reveal the need to reinitiate steps of the financial planning process. The current scope of the engagement may need to be modified.

Effective Date

January 1, 2002.

Relationship of this Practice Standard to CFP Board's Code of Ethics and Professional Responsibility

This *Practice Standard* relates to *CFP Board's Code of Ethics and Professional Responsibility (Code of Ethics) through the Code of Ethics'* Principle 7 – Diligence and Rule 702.

Principle 7 states "A CFP Board designee shall act diligently in providing professional services." Rule 702 requires that financial planning practitioners enter into an engagement only after obtaining sufficient information to satisfy that "the relationship is warranted by the individual's goals and objectives; and the CFP Board designee has the ability to either provide requisite competent services or to involve other professionals who can provide such services."

Anticipated Impact of this Practice Standard

Upon the Public

The public is served when the practitioner and client have similar perceptions and a mutual understanding about the responsibilities for monitoring the recommendation(s).

This material is derived from the Certified Financial Planners Board of Standards, Inc. web site: http://www.cfp.net.

Upon the Financial Planning Profession

The profession benefits when clients are satisfied. Clients are more likely to be satisfied when expectations of the monitoring process are both realistic and clear. This *Practice Standard* promotes awareness that financial planning is a dynamic process rather than a single action.

Upon the Financial Planning Practitioner

A mutually defined agreement of the monitoring responsibilities increases the potential for client satisfaction and clarifies the practitioner's responsibilities.

Part 2:

FINANCIAL PLANNING CONCEPTS

Chapter 9

FINANCIAL GOALS – CURRENT LIFESTYLE

How important is it to you to have one car, or two cars, or even three cars? Do you believe you need an SUV, a Lexus, or a Jaguar?

Is eating dinner out seven nights a week a part of your normal life style that you clearly cannot do without?

Do you need to get away on two week luxury vacations two times or three times a year, or is a one week modest road trip and a few days at home around holiday times enough?

These and numerous similar questions define an individual's lifestyle. There is no right or wrong, no excess or excessive sacrifice that is or should be viewed as the appropriate norm. The financial aspects of your *personal* lifestyle are quite simply determined by

1. how much you want to spend to maintain your desired lifestyle
2. where current lifestyle fits into your personal financial priority spectrum
3. what resources do you have available to fund your desired lifestyle and your other financial goals

For example, if a retired client has accumulated investment and retirement assets totaling $5,000,000 and is happy (comfortable?) with an after-tax lifestyle of $200,000 a year, leaving aside issues of inflation, a 4% after-tax current yield covers his cost of living. Even if the $5,000,000 never earned a penny, the funds would last 25 years with withdrawals of $200,000 a year.

If the client wanted to ultimately leave his heirs the full $5,000,000 accumulated during his lifetime, the funds would need to earn the 4% a year. If the client were concerned with the effects of inflation on his spending and the value of his heirs' inheritance, the investments would require a higher yield:

Assume the client expects to live for another 20 years, with annual inflation of 3%:

- To leave his heirs the future value of the $5,000,000 at the end of the 20 years, the value of the assets at that time would need to grow to approximately $9,030,000. In order to maintain an inflation-adjusted lifestyle of $200,000 a year for all 20 years, and accumulate the desired $9,030,000, the client's investments would be required to earn an average of approximately 7.14% a year for the entire 20 years.
- If his lifestyle were to remain flat at $200,000, in order to accumulate the $9,030,000 planned, 3% inflation-adjusted inheritance, the assets would be required to earn an average of approximately 6.25% per year.

All of the alternatives discussed in this example can be summarized as follows:

Current Lifestyle	Inflation Rate for Lifestyle	Inflation Rate for End Value Growth	Asset Value in 20 Years	Required Earnings Rate
$ 200,000	0%	0%	$ 1,000,000	0%
$ 200,000	0%	0%	$ 5,000,000	4%
$ 200,000	0%	3%	$ 9.030,000	6.25%
$ 200,000	3%	3%	$ 9,030,000	7.15%

This example provides a simple reminder of the basic investment adage: in order to attain a higher rate of return, you will be facing a higher level of risk. Although 7.15% does not appear to be much more than 6.25% (only 90 basis points), it is a 14.4% higher rate of return. If you could be certain that the investment you choose will yield at least the lower target of 6.25%, then you really have no downside risk. But, it is unrealistic to expect such guarantees, and the true downside or worst-case risk may be less security than you are willing to accept.

The lesson to be learned here is only partially related to rates of returns and expected returns. The real message concerns the importance of the information derived from effective analysis. Decisions should be made with the highest degree of understanding of the resulting consequences. Most mistakes are made due to ignorance of the range and probability of results and the lack of planning for the contingencies of the underperformance of chosen strategies.

LIFESTYLE AND PRIORITIES

Where does lifestyle fit in among a client's priorities? There are two levels of analysis to consider:

1. How high a priority is lifestyle among the following basic goals of financial planning?
   a) current lifestyle
   b) children's education
   c) retirement funding
   d) parental issues
   e) estate planning
   f) other special needs (such as a disabled child)
2. What elements of current lifestyle are most important to the client? (Refer to Chapter 16, "Budgeting and Cash Management," for a more detailed analysis of personal budget planning and the components of individual spending.)

Figure 9.1 provides a simple pie chart illustration of the allocation of financial resources among the basic goals of financial planning, while Figure 9.2 provides a similar illustration of the allocation of the resources devoted to current lifestyle among various non-discretionary (fixed) and discretionary components.

The chart in Figure 9.1 demonstrates a resource allocation of an individual who views current lifestyle as

Figure 9.1

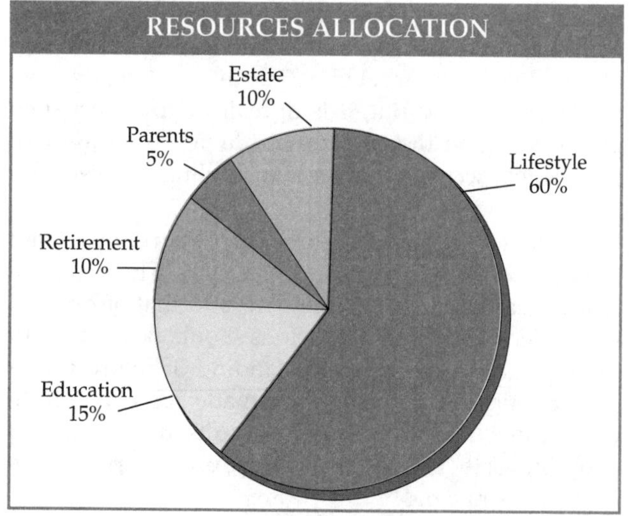

Figure 9.2

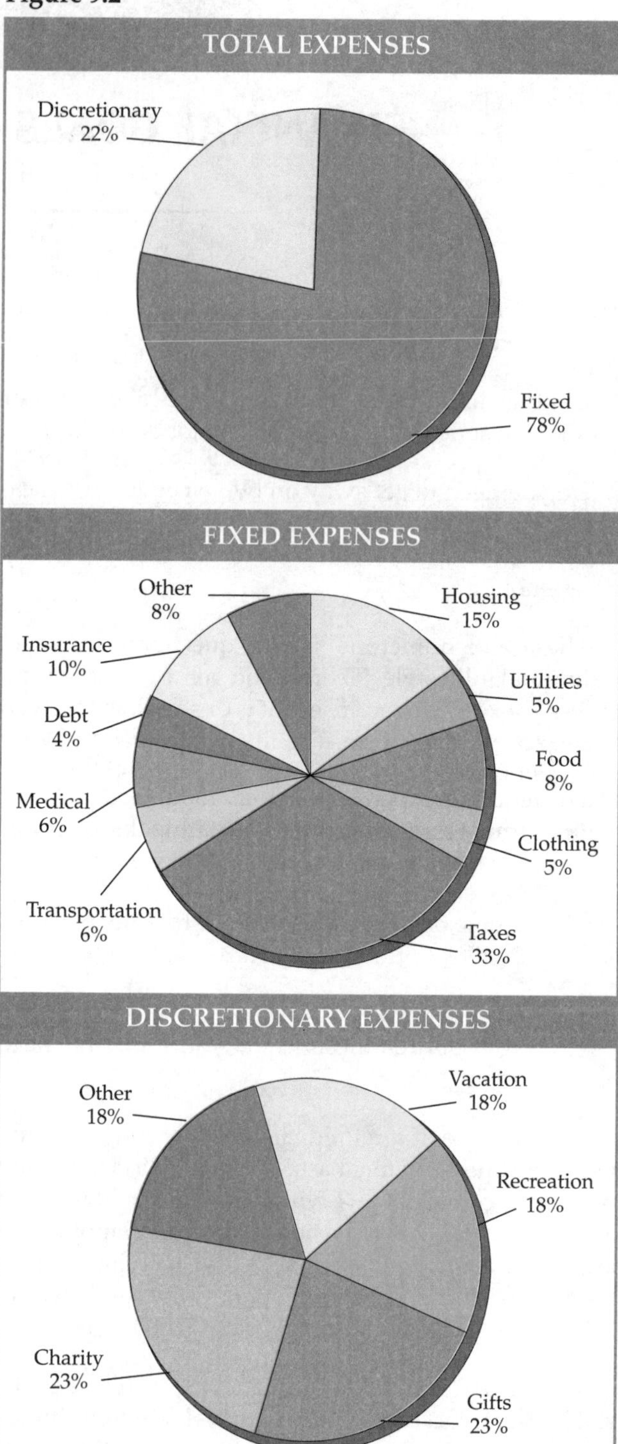

a relatively low priority. Allocations of 90% or 95% are not unusual. Two reasons for only 60% of resources being used for common lifestyle are easily identified: (1) the person is very (overly?) concerned about the other priorities of his funds, limited though they may be, or (2) the individual has far more assets than are necessary to maintain current lifestyle so that the "excess" funds can easily be saved and invested for other, future needs.

Most of our clients have goals and financial objectives that exceed the available resources, making the choice of prioritizing current lifestyle well above other needs a more difficult choice. Sometimes the allocation choices are eased by outside factors, such as

- not having any children
- children receiving college scholarships
- exceptional employer-funded pension plans
- trust funds and anticipated inheritances to fund retirement needs, children's education or inheritances for children.

Knowing and understanding all of the outside funding factors that may be available makes it easier to determine how much will be available to spend now for a greater lifestyle.

The basic allocation between fixed and discretionary expenses is obviously influenced by available resources. Fixed, required expenses, such as food, housing and clothing, must come first. But, even within this category of expenditures, there are options. How big a house do you need, or want? How often do you eat at home or eat out? Do you serve more steak or hamburger?

Among discretionary expenses, vacations tend to be a major expenditure, as do general recreational expenses. Season tickets to the local professional baseball, football, ice hockey, and basketball teams can be a huge expense, but for some people is more important than eating hamburger every night.

Chapter 5, discussing "Attitudes and Behavioral Characteristics of Financial Planning Clients," is worth mentioning at this point. As that chapter explains, there are many non-financial factors that influence basic financial planning decisions. These factors, which include (1) cultural background, (2) family experiences, (3) emotional and medical issues, (4) life cycle stage and age, and (5) education, expertise, and personal experiences, are usually as important as the resources available to a client when making important allocation decisions. These influencers are less obvious and consequently more difficult to assimilate and understand their impact on the decision-making process.

A simple example, as discussed in Chapter 5, is the effect of being raised in a household with parents who were scarred by the "Great Depression." Such children will tend to be either very conservative in their own spending, constantly worried about the future, or they will be so "turned-off" by their parent's stinginess that they will become big spenders or even spendthrifts, heavily in debt.

Chapter 10

EDUCATION FUNDING

OVERVIEW

The expense of educating children has become today's greatest financial burden facing parents because of the large, and constantly escalating, annual costs, the increasing number of years of college for undergraduates, and the graduate and/or professional school education required for many careers. Except for the purchase of a home and the accumulation of a retirement fund, paying for school is one of the highest priorities—and one of the most expensive decisions—that parents will ever make.

Although this discussion will focus on college education expenses, financial planners need to also consider that many clients will provide secondary—and even primary—school education for their children at private institutions with costs approaching, and in some cases even exceeding, college tuition costs. Ironically, attendance at a fine private high school may increase the probability of admission to one of the better (spelled expensive) colleges.

How much financing is actually needed will depend upon many factors, including the family's educational goals and the time remaining until the goals have to be met. Families often have some combination of the following goals:

1. to provide private school education at the elementary and secondary levels;

2. to provide funding of all or a portion of the college costs of one or more children at private institutions;

3. to provide all or a portion of the college costs of one or more children at public institutions;

4. to provide funding for all or a portion of the other educational programs (e.g., graduate or professional school education) for one or more children; or

5. to provide an educational fund for grandchildren or others.

As with other financial goals, parents must determine education funding goals for their children and set priorities. Many parents will not be able to achieve all their goals and must weigh potential tradeoffs among them. For instance, parents who send their children to private elementary and secondary schools are using resources they could be applying to a college education fund. However, if the private elementary and secondary schooling provides a child with a sufficiently advanced education, the child may qualify for the more elite and well-endowed private college institutions that typically have more financial resources for aid and scholarships. Consequently, resources spent on elementary and secondary school education may be an investment that pays off in lower absolute dollar expenditures for college education at what are considered the more prestigious and elite colleges or universities.

The balance of this chapter is divided into two major sections. Part I is a procedure and worksheet section to show you how to compute how much funding is necessary. Part II deals with the tools and techniques available for funding educational expenses.

PART I: COMPUTING THE REQUIRED EDUCATION FUNDING NEED

Estimating college education costs and funding requirements involves essentially four steps:

1. estimating education costs in current dollars;

2. projecting future education costs in inflated dollars;

3. determining the required current lump-sum investment; and

4. calculating the required periodic investment.

Each of these steps is discussed in turn below followed by a simplified college cost worksheet.

Estimating Expenses

For more and more children, college is becoming a normal stop in the road to a career and adulthood. About half of the nation's high school graduates enrolled in college in 1980, but by the late 1990's, two-thirds were college bound. As a result of these continuing trends, financing college has become one of the largest costs that many families face.

College costs also continue to increase. If recent annual increases were to continue at the same pace, the total expenses of one year in a 4-year private college would balloon from an average of about $33,000 for the 2007-2008 school year to about $65,000 in 10 years and over $127,000 in 20 years.

Despite these trends, paying for a child's college education is more within reach than many people think. For one thing, tax legislation enacted over the past decade has included provisions intended to make college more affordable. Still the costs of higher education can be expected to put a strain on the finances of most families, especially when more than one child is in college. Scholarships and financial aid may be insufficient or unavailable for many students. Also, the use of loans can stretch college financing for parents well beyond graduation day and saddle graduates with a heavy load of debt.

Understanding College Costs

What are parents paying for when their child attends college? There are several components to college costs, but for simplicity we will divide the components into three categories:

1. tuition;
2. room and board; and
3. everything else.

Tuition costs vary widely, as Figure 10.1 shows.

Private 4-year colleges and universities, which teach about 20 percent of students in the U.S., charge the highest tuition. Their average tuition, fees, and room and board of about $33,000 for the 2007-2008 school year for 4-year private institutions is almost 2.4 times the $14,000 average tuition, fees, and room and board charged by 4-year public colleges and universities.

The wide disparity between tuition levels arises because, unlike their public counterparts, private institutions cannot rely on tax revenues for support. (Note that many students may not be charged full tuition, especially the higher amounts listed by private schools, because colleges sometimes "discount" their published tuition as part of a financial aid offer.)

Room and board expenses typically constitute the next highest costs after tuition and fees. As you would expect, these costs take up a greater portion of total college costs—about twice as much—for resident students than for commuters. Everything else (i.e., books and supplies, transportation, laundry money, football tickets, pizza, activity fees, and so forth) makes up the rest of the costs.

When all of the costs of attending college are added up, one year of school in 2007-2008 might cost an average of well more than $14,000 for a four-year public institution, $33,000 for a private four-year school, and

Figure 10.1

AVERAGE UNDERGRADUATE TUITION, FEES, AND ROOM AND BOARD (R+B)

	2004-2005*	2007-2008**
2-Year Institution (no R+B)	$2,323	$2,919
2-Year Institution (w/ R+B)	$7,020	$8,821
4-Year Public Institution (no R+B)	$5,038	$6,331
4-Year Public Institution (w/ R+B)	$11,441	$14,376
4-Year Private Institution (w/ R+B)	$26,489	$33,285
4-Year All Institutions (w/ R+B)	$16,465	$20,689

* *Source:* U.S. Department of Education, National Center for Education Statistics. Public institution costs are for in-state.

** Projected at 7.91% college inflation rate.

even exceeding $50,000 for the most prestigious and expensive private colleges and universities!

Is a College Education Worth the Cost?

One important question arises: Is the time, money, and effort of attending college worthwhile? When looked at strictly from an earnings point of view, the answer is a resounding yes (see Figure 10.2). United States Census data show that college graduates earn an average of 80% more than high school graduates—an income advantage that has increased significantly over the years.

The President's Council of Economic Advisors also offers a rough estimate of the worth of a college degree. They have estimated that the return on an "investment" in a college education is between 11% and 13% a year for life.

Adjusting for Inflation

Recently, college costs at private institutions have been climbing at an annual rate from 4% to 10%. Inflation rates for college costs through 2006 (the most recent year for which data was available) and dating back to 1982 have compared to the overall inflation rates as follows:

Year	Tuition Inflation Rate** Private 4-Yr	Tuition Inflation Rate** Public 4-Yr	Overall Inflation Rate*
Last 5 years (2002 – 2006)	5.1%	9.2%	2.7%
Last 10 years (1997 – 2006)	5.5%	7.0%	2.4%
Last 15 years (1992 – 2006)	5.6%	7.0%	2.6%
Last 20 years (1987 – 2006)	6.2%	7.4%	3.1%
Last 25 years (1982 – 2006)	7.0%	7.7%	3.1%

* Source: *SBBI: Stocks, Bonds, Bills, and Inflation, 2007 Yearbook*, Morningstar, Chicago, IL

** Source: *Trends in College Pricing 2006*, College Board, www.colldgeboard.com.

Although the annual rate of increase for college education costs has slowed, the increases continue to be two or three times the rate of inflation. Figure 10.3 shows current and projected college costs for selected colleges.

If costs do grow at the 7% annual rate that many financial advisers suggest using as a reasonably conservative, high-end inflation rate for planning purposes, future college costs will quickly grow to incredible numbers. As Figure 10.4 shows, the parents of a child born in 2007 who expect their child to start college in about the year 2026 should anticipate average total 4-year college education costs to range from about $208,000 as a resident

Figure 10.2

HOW EDUCATION PAYS OFF

	Full and Part Time Workers				Full Time Workers Only			
Level of education*	Median Income	% of HSG	Mean Income	% of HSG	Median Income	% of HSG	Mean Income	% of HSG
Less than ninth grade	$17,422	65.7%	$20,308	64.1%	$20,826	66.0%	$24,078	65.0%
High school dropout	20,321	76.7%	23,612	74.6%	25,039	79.4%	28,663	77.4%
High school graduate	**26,505**	**100.0%**	**31,664**	**100.0%**	**31,539**	**100.0%**	**37,030**	**100.0%**
Some college	31,054	117.2%	37,089	117.1%	37,135	117.7%	44,634	120.5%
All education levels	32,140	121.3%	43,362	136.9%	39,336	124.7%	51,203	138.3%
Associate's degree	35,009	132.1%	39,662	125.3%	40,588	128.7%	46,146	124.6%
Bachelor's degree	43,143	162.8%	56,740	179.2%	50,944	161.5%	65,281	176.3%
Bachelor's degree or higher	49,303	186.0%	65,042	205.4%	56,078	177.8%	75,116	202.9%
Master's degree	52,390	197.7%	68,302	215.7%	61,273	194.3%	79,423	214.5%
Doctorate degree	70,853	267.3%	93,593	295.6%	79,401	251.8%	107,386	290.0%
Professional degree	82,473	311.2%	119,343	376.9%	100,000	317.1%	135,674	366.4%

More years of school correlate with higher incomes, according to U.S. Census Bureau data.

* *Source:* U.S. Census Bureau, Current Population Survey, 2006 Annual Social and Economic Supplement. People 25 years old and over as of March of the following year. Last revised: August 29, 2006. Educational Attainment—All people (all races and both sexes) 25 years old and over by total money earnings in 2005, work experience in 2005. (http://pubdb3.census.gov/macro/032006/perinc/new03_000.htm)

Figure 10.3

COLLEGE COSTS PROJECTED
Yearly Tuition, Fees, Supplies, Room & Board

NAME OF INSTITUTION	LOCATION	2007	Assuming Increases of 5% Per Year 2012	2017	2022
Auburn University	Auburn, Ala.	14,172	18,087	23,085	29,463
Bowdoin College	Brunswick, Maine	44.750	57,114	72,893	93,032
Brigham Young University	Provo, Utah	10,640	13,580	17,331	22,120
Bucknell University	Lewisburg, Pa.	43,368	55,350	70,642	90,159
The Citadel	Charleston, S.C.	18,458	23,558	30,066	38,373
Colorado State University	Ft. Collins, Colo.	12,706	16,216	20,697	26,415
Columbia College	New York, N.Y.	44,814	57,195	72,997	93,165
Dartmouth College	Hanover, N.H.	43,341	55,315	70,598	90,103
De Paul University	Chicago, Ill.	33,085	42,226	53,892	68,781
Drake University	Des Moines, Iowa	29,182	37,244	47,534	60,667
Duke University	Durham, N.C.	46,050	58,773	75,011	95,735
Emory University	Atlanta, Ga.	43,444	55,447	70,766	90,317
Florida State University	Tallahassee, Fla.	11,385	14,530	18,545	23,669
George Washington Univ.	Washington, D.C.	50,420	64,350	82,129	104,820
Hamline University	St. Paul, Minn.	33,312	42,515	54,262	69,253
Harvard College	Cambridge, Mass.	43,655	55,716	71,109	90,756
Jackson State University	Jackson, Miss.	8,976	11,456	14,621	18,660
Kansas State University	Manhattan, Kans.	12,246	15,629	19,947	25,459
Loyola College in Maryland	Baltimore, Md.	41,825	53,380	68,129	86,951
Marquette University	Milwaukee, Wis.	34,094	43,514	55,536	70,879
Michigan State University	E. Lansing, Mich.	15,784	20,145	25,710	32,814
Middlebury College	Middlebury, Vt.	45,570	58,160	74,229	94,737
Ohio State University	Columbus, Ohio	15,903	20,297	25,904	33,061
Oral Roberts University	Tulsa, Okla.	24,930	31,818	40,608	51,828
Purdue University	W. Lafayette, Ind.	14,268	18,210	23,241	29,662
Rutgers College	New Brunswick, N.J.	19,000	24,249	30,949	39,500
St. Lawrence University	Canton, N.Y.	42,530	54,280	69,277	88,417
Salem International Univ.	Salem, W.Va.	18,920	24,147	30,819	39,333
Seattle University	Seattle, Washington	32,598	41,604	53,099	67,769
Southern Methodist Univ.	Dallas, Tex.	41,705	53,227	67,933	86,702
Stanford University	Stanford, Calif.	45,046	57,491	73,375	93,647
Texas A & M University	College Sta., Tex.	15,905	20,299	25,908	33,065
Tulane University	New Orleans, La.	44,093	56,275	71,823	91,666
University of Arkansas	Fayetteville, Ark.	13,286	16,957	21,641	27,621
University of California	Berkley, Calif.	22,200	28,333	36,161	46,152
University of Louisville	Louisville, Ky.	12,148	15,504	19,788	25,255
University of New Mexico	Albuquerque, N.Mex.	12,236	15,617	19,931	25,438
University of Rhode Island	Kingston, R.I.	18,092	23,090	29,470	37,612
University of Virginia	Charlottesville, Va.	15,944	20,349	25,971	33,146
Vanderbilt University	Nashville, Tenn.	45,434	57,987	74,007	94,454
Yale University	New Haven, Conn.	45,850	58,518	74,685	95,319
Yeshiva University	New York, N.Y.	37,370	47,695	60,872	77,690
Average Cost		**29,018**	**37,035**	**47,266**	**60,325**

Explanation of Table. Costs for public schools assume the student is a resident of the state. Costs (i.e., tuition) for out-of-state students are generally substantially more then shown. Costs for supplies are included when available. Costs for transportation are not included. Since over the past decade college costs have more than kept pace with the rate of inflation, it seems highly likely that costs will continue to escalate in the years to come. In this regard, see the Consumer Price Index on page 330. Source of 2006-2007 college education costs: Author research of college internet sites during the month of January, 2007, supplemented by direct inquiry when required.

Source: Cady, *2007 Field Guide to Estate Planning, Business Planning, & Employee Benefits*, page 112 (Cincinnati, OH: The National Underwriter Company, 2007).

Figure 10.4

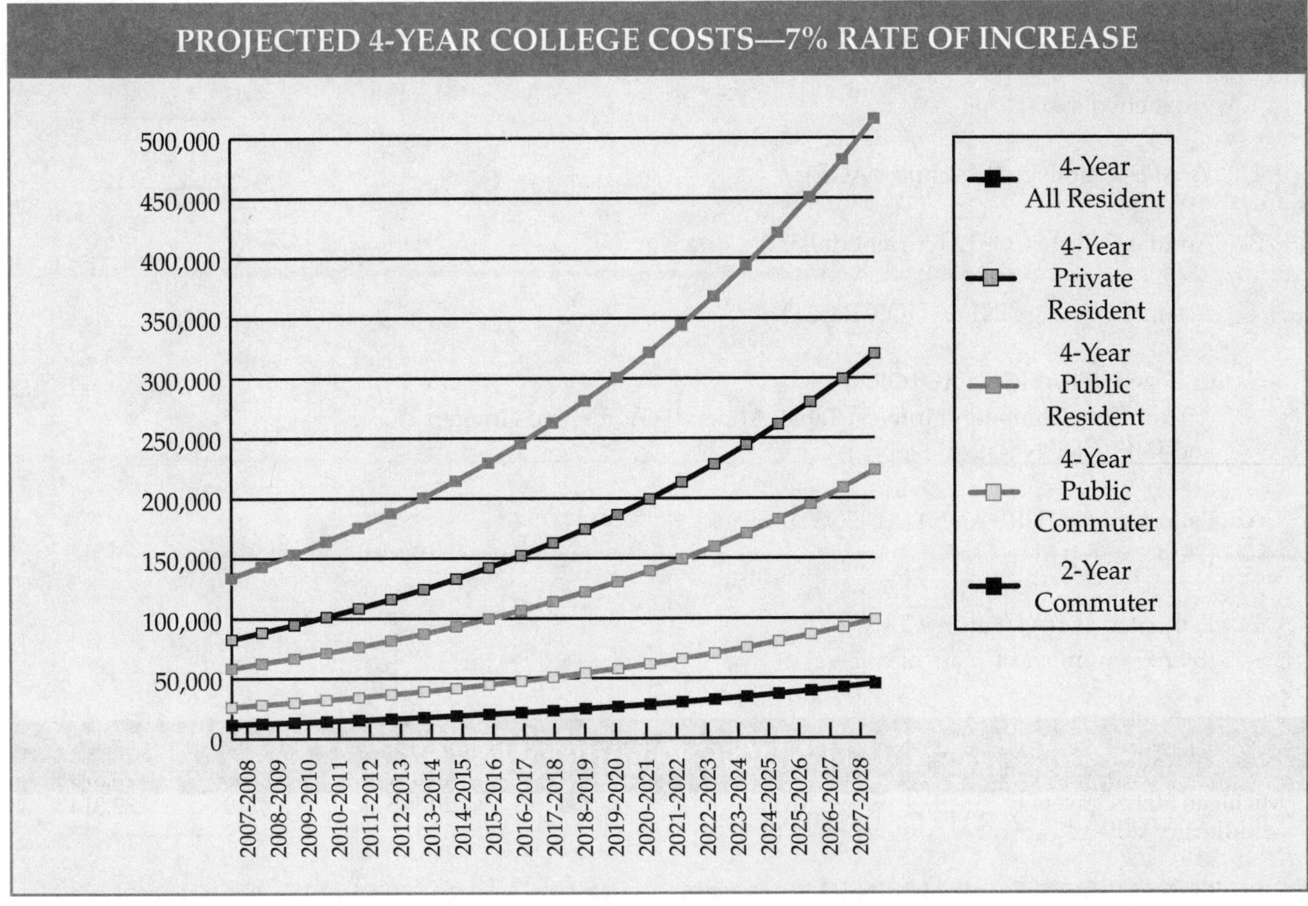

student at a public 4-year college to over $481,000 as a resident student at a private 4-year college). Moreover, surveys indicate that most people are not saving enough for college and that they also tend to underestimate how much college will cost.

If your clients can identify some particular college or university that they favor and to which they plan to send their children, up-to-date and accurate information about current and projected costs can be obtained by calling the placement director or financial aid officer of that school. Keep in mind, though, that in addition to tuition and room and board, students will also need funds for books, fees, clothes, and miscellaneous entertainment expenses and, if they are away from home, travel. Costs for books and lab fees in the sciences, for example, can run as high as $1,000 per semester.

Planners can estimate future college costs by using the formula for computing the future value of a lump-sum value:

FORMULA 1

$FV = PV \times (1 + I)^n$

Where FV is the Future Value (future costs) of one-year's college education;

PV is the Present Value (current cost) of one-year's college education;

I is the assumed inflation rate; and

n is the number of years until the payment must be made.

Most planners, however, prefer to use financial tables, financial calculators, or computer programs such as *The Financial and Estate Planner's NumberCruncher* to perform this computation. The Compound Interest Table in Appendix A has the necessary factors to compute future education costs using the following formula:

FORMULA 2

FV = PV x FV factor

Where FV and PV are defined as above; and

FV is the factor from the Compound Interest Table of Appendix A for the selected values of I (the assumed

Figure 10.5

SIMPLIFIED COLLEGE COST WORKSHEET	
1. Enter child's AGE	________
2. YEARS to College (18 - child's AGE)	________
3. Annual College COSTS (current dollars)	________
4. Assumed College INFLATION Rate (%)	________%
5. College INFLATION FACTOR (Factor from Compound Interest Table, Appendix A, for Years In Step 2 and INFLATION Rate in Step 4.)	________
6. Estimated FUTURE ANNUAL COSTS (Step 3 x Step 5)	________
7. Estimated TOTAL Future Costs (Step 6 x number of years of college)	________
FUNDING REQUIREMENTS	
8. Assumed After-tax RATE OF RETURN (%)	________%
9. Present Value of Future LUMP-SUM Factor (Factor from Present Value Table, Appendix B, for YEARS in Step 2 and RATE OF RETURN in Step 8.)	________
10. Total LUMP-SUM INVESTMENT Currently Required (Step 7 - Step 9)	________
11. AMOUNT ALREADY EARMARKED for Education	________
12. Additional LUMP-SUM Funding Required (Step 10 - Step 11)	________
13. YEARS OF FUNDING	________
14. Present Value of an Annuity Due Factor (Factor from Present Value of an Annuity Due Table, Appendix F, for YEARS in Step 13 and RATE OF RETURN in Step 8.)	________
15. ANNUAL TARGET AMOUNT to Invest (Step 12 ÷ Step 14)	________
16. Approximate MONTHLY TARGET AMOUNT to Invest (Step 15 ÷ 12)	________

inflation rate) and n (the number of years until the child begins college).

For example, assume that

1. The current annual costs (PV) for your client's choice of college are $21,420 per year.

2. Your client's child is now four years old (which means n = 14 years assuming the child will be age 18 when beginning college).

3. The assumed college cost inflation rate (I) is 7%. (very conservative).

The future value factor from the Table in Appendix D when I = 7% and n = 14 years is 2.5785. Applying Formula 2, the estimated first-year cost after adjustment for inflation is $55,231.

FV = $21,420 x 2.5785 = $55,231

For each successive year of college, the cost could be estimated in a similar manner using the FV factors from the table for n = 15, 16, 17, etc., until the end of the projected college term. In most cases, a suitable estimate of the total cost can be determined by multiplying the first-year cost by the number of years of college (generally four). In this case the total estimated cost is $220,924 ($55,231 x 4) for four years of college.

Determining the Required Current Lump-Sum Investment

According to a government survey, 70% of families with annual incomes of $30,000 or more are managing to set aside money for future college bills. But the median amount being set aside is obviously inadequate (i.e., $904 a year). As described above, assuming annual costs rise 7% per year from our assumed cost of $21,420, parents with a four year-old child in 2007 will confront college bills that could total over $220,000. To be ready to handle bills of that magnitude, the parents would have to set aside in 2007 a lump-sum investment of about $97,715 in an account earning 6% net after tax, or about $825 a month net after tax, every year until the child is age 18. Even if the parents could earn 10% net after tax on their money, they would still need a lump-sum investment of about $58,200 in 2007, or would have to save almost $600 a month until their child is age 18. (Examples of how to compute these amounts follow.) Few investments can provide such returns over such a long period of time—especially after taxes are considered. Those few investments that might provide such returns do so with significant risk to capital, and income may be lost. Clearly, many parents may find themselves grossly underfunded when it comes time to pay college bills for their children.

To estimate the current lump-sum investment required to fund future education expenses the following time value formula may be applied:

FORMULA 3

$$PV = FV \times \frac{1}{(1 + r)^n}$$

Where FV is the total estimated future education cost as determined above;

PV is the present value (required investment) of the future costs;

r is the assumed after-tax rate of return; and

n is the number of years until the child begins college.

The critical assumption when determining the required current investment is r, the assumed after-tax rate of return. The after-tax rate of return depends both on the type of assets in which the funds will be invested and on the tax that will apply to the earnings on those assets. Later in this chapter, the tax aspects of various accumulation strategies are discussed. A reasonable conservative estimate of the long-term after-tax rate of return should be used when projecting accumulations. If more aggressive investments and/or tax-deferring strategies are contemplated, a higher effective after-tax rate may be reasonable.

The Present Value Table in Appendix B may be used with the following formula to derive the same result as Formula 3:

FORMULA 4

PV = FV x PV factor

Where PV and FV are defined as above, and

PV factor is the factor from the Present Value Table of Appendix B for the selected values of r (the assumed rate of return) and n (the number of years until the child begins college).

For example, assume that

1. the total future costs are calculated (from above) to be $220,924;

2. the child will begin college in 14 years; and

3. the assumed after-tax rate of return is 6%.

In this case the PV factor from the Present Value Table of Appendix B is 0.4423. Applying Formula 4, the estimated current lump-sum investment required to fund the child's education is $97,715:

PV = $220,924 x 0.4423 = $97,715

If the parents have already earmarked assets for the child's education, the current value of these assets should be subtracted from the present value amount derived using Formula 4, to determine their current deficit. For example, if in the case described above the parents have already earmarked $22,500 for their child's education, their current deficit would be $75,215 ($97,715 – $22,500).

Determining the Required Periodic Investment

Most clients will not have sufficient assets to fully fund their children's education without some additional periodic investing. The amount they must save each year (or each month) depends principally on how long they have to accumulate the necessary funds—the earlier they start their funding, the less they will have to save each period. The level of required periodic investment necessary to fund their current deficit is determined using the following time value formula:

FORMULA 5

$$\text{Pmt} = \text{Current Deficit} \div \left[\left(\frac{1 - (1 + r)^{-nf}}{r}\right) \times (1 + r)\right]$$

To compute the *annual* payments that are necessary to fund the deficit, use r, the assumed after-tax rate of return used when determining the current funding deficit (as described above), and nf, which equals the number of years over which the funding will take place.

To compute the *monthly* payments that would be required, divide the annual rate of return (r) by 12 to determine the monthly rate of return and multiply the number of years (nf) by 12 and use these values in Formula 5 for r and n, respectively.

Note: The rate of return (r) assumed when using Formula 5 must be equal to the rate of return used in Formula 3. However, the number of years for funding (nf) *do not* have to equal the number of years until the child begins college (n). For example, a client may wish to determine the amount required each year to fund the deficit in five years, even though the child will not begin college for 10 years. More commonly, clients will want to know how much they will have to invest each year until the child's last year of school, which is typically three years longer than the number of years until the child begins college; however, this could result in underfunding because as principal is removed each year, the rate of return is received on an increasingly smaller amount. For purposes of the calculations below, the number of years for funding will equal the number of years until the child begins college.

The Present Value of an Annuity Due Table in Appendix F can be used with the following formula to compute the same result as in Formula 5:

FORMULA 6

Pmt = Current Deficit ÷ PVAD factor

Where Pmt is defined as above; and

PVAD factor is the Present Value of an Annuity Due factor from Table F for the selected values of r and nf.

For example, assume that

1. The current deficit is $75,215 (as determined above).

2. The number of years of annual funding (nf) is 14 years (until the child who is currently age four begins her first year of college at age 18).

3. The assumed after-tax annual rate of return (r) is 6%.

The PVAD factor from Appendix F when r equals 6% and nf equals 14 years is 9.8527. Therefore, the required annual funding is:

Pmt = $75,215 ÷ 9.8527 = $7,634

The required monthly funding can be approximated by dividing the required annual funding by 12. In the case presented, your client would need to invest about $636 per month at a 6% after-tax rate of return for the next

14 years to fully fund the current deficit in the estimated amount required for the child's education.

Assuming that the rate of return on the assets already earmarked for the child's education equals that assumed in Formula 6, the combined amounts will equal the FV amount in Formula 4.

Simplified College Cost Worksheet

For many clients the Simplified College Cost Worksheet (Figure 10.5) will provide adequate estimates to get them started on a savings program to meet their college funding requirements. The Simplified College Cost Worksheet incorporates the four steps discussed above in one simple planning tool. In Figure 10.6 the numbers from the example above are illustrated.

In cases where your clients must fund the education of several children, planning to "smooth out" the required funding schedule, so that the required payments are not too burdensome in any given year, involves additional complexity. However, a "unified" funding schedule can be devised in the following manner:

1. Using steps 1 through 10 of the Simplified College Cost Worksheet, determine the current required lump-sum investment for each child.

2. Add together the amounts derived in step (1) for all children to find the aggregate current required lump-sum investment. Place this value in step 10 of the Simplified College Cost Worksheet.

3. Use the remaining steps in the Simplified College Cost Worksheet to derive a level funding schedule over the desired funding period.

For example, assume that your clients

1. have an annual before-tax family income of $100,000;

2. have three children, ages 4, 6, and 10;

3. plan to fund 75% of the cost of their children's education at a private institution whose current tuition, fees, and room and board are about $21,420 per year (your clients believe the children should assume responsibility for 25% of the cost of their schooling);

4. believe they can invest at about a 6% after-tax rate of return;

5. have $30,000 currently earmarked to pay for their children's education;

6. estimate college costs will rise at 7% per year; and

7. want to fund their current deficit over the period until their youngest child begins his senior year in college.

Figure 10.7 shows the analysis for this case. Based on these assumptions, your clients would have to invest about $18,725 per year, or about $1,560 a month, for the next 14 years to pay 75% of their children's estimated college expenses. The annual payment represents more than 18% of the family's current before-tax income. As this example demonstrates, funding college education can be a substantial burden for most families, even for those with considerable incomes.

Clearly, if a family can raise its effective after-tax rate of return through the use of income-shifting, tax-reducing, and tax-deferring techniques, they can substantially reduce their required funding. For example, Figure 10.8 shows the analysis for the client described above assuming that the effective after-tax rate of return is raised to 8%. In this case, the required annual funding is $16,122 (monthly, $1,343), or about 14% less than that required when the after-tax rate of return is assumed to be 6%. The following sections of this chapter discuss various income-shifting, tax-reducing, and tax-deferring strategies and techniques that can help your clients increase their effective after-tax rate of return on their education funds.

PART II: TOOLS AND TECHNIQUES FOR FUNDING EDUCATION EXPENSES

There are seven methods of financing a child's education:

1. on a pay-as-you go basis out of current assets and income;

2. through government tax incentives;

3. through scholarships and loans;

4. working your way through school;

5. the parents engage in a systematic plan of early savings and investment;

Figure 10.6

COMPLETED COLLEGE COST WORKSHEET	
1. Enter child's AGE	4 years
2. YEARS to College (18 - child's AGE)	14 yrs.
3. Annual College COSTS (current dollars)	21,420
4. Assumed College INFLATION Rate (%)	7%
5. College INFLATION FACTOR (Factor from Compound Interest Table, Appendix A, for Years in Step 2 and INFLATION Rate in Step 4.)	2.5785
6. Estimated TOTAL Future Cost (Step 3 x Step 5)	55,231
7. Estimated TOTAL Future Cost (Step 6 x number of years of college)	x 4 $220,924
FUNDING REQUIREMENTS	
8. Assumed After-tax RATE OF RETURN (%)	6%
9. Present Value of Future LUMP-SUM Factor (Factor from Present Value Table, Appendix B, for YEARS in Step 2 and RATE OF RETURN in Step 8.)	0.4423
10. Total LUMP-SUM INVESTMENT Currently Required (Step 7 x Step 9)	97,715
11. AMOUNT ALREADY EARMARKED for Education	$ 22,500
12. Additional LUMP-SUM Funding Required (Step 10 - Step 11)	75,215
13. YEARS OF FUNDING	14
14. Present Value of an Annuity Due Factor (Factor from Present Value of an Annuity Due Table, Appendix F, for YEARS in Step 13 and RATE OF RETURN in Step 8.)	9.8527
15. ANNUAL TARGET AMOUNT to Invest (Step ÷ Step 14)	$ 7,634
16. Approximate MONTHLY TARGET AMOUNT to Invest (Step 15 ÷ 12)	$ 636

Figure 10.7

	COLLEGE COST ANALYSIS ASSUMING 6 PERCENT RETURN	4-yr. Old	6-yr. Old	10-yr. Old
1.	Enter child's AGE	4	6	10
2.	YEARS to College (18 - child's AGE)	14	12	8
3.	Annual College COSTS (current dollars)	16,065*	16,065*	16,065*
4.	Assumed College INFLATION Rate (%)	7%	7%	7%
5.	College INFLATION FACTOR (Factor from Compound Interest Table, Appendix A, for Years in Step 2 and INFLATION Rate in Step 4.)	2.5785	2.2522	1.7182
6.	Estimated FUTURE ANNUAL COSTS (Step 3 x Step 5)	$41,424	$36,182	$27,603
7.	Estimated TOTAL Future cost (Step 6 x number of years of college)	$165,696	$144,728	$110,412
	FUNDING REQUIREMENTS			
8.	Assumed After-tax RATE OF RETURN (%)	6%	6%	6%
9.	Present Value of Future LUMP-SUM Factor (Factor from present Value Table, Appendix B, for YEARS in Step 2 and RATE OF RETURN in Step 8.)	0.4423	0.4970	0.6274
10.	Total LUMP-SUM INVESTMENT Currently Required	$73,287	$71,930	$69,272
10a.	SUM of Line 10, all columns		$214,489	
11.	AMOUNT ALREADY EARMARKED for Education		$30,000	
12.	Additional LUMP-SUM Funding Required (Step 10a - Step 11)		$184,489	
13.	YEARS OF FUNDING		14**	
14.	Present Value of an Annuity Due Factor (Factor from Present Value of an Annuity Due Table, Appendix F, for YEARS in Step 13 and the RATE OF RETURN in Step 8.)		9.8527	
15.	ANNUAL TARGET AMOUNT to Invest (Step 12 ÷ Step 14)		$18,725	
16.	Approximate MONTHLY TARGET AMOUNT to Invest (Step 15 ÷ 12)		$1,560	

* 21,420 total current cost x 75 percent that parent plans to fund
** Years until youngest child starts first year of college

Figure 10.8

COLLEGE COST ANALYSIS ASSUMING 8 PERCENT RETURN		4-yr. Old	6-yr. Old	10-yr. Old
1.	Enter child's age	4	6	10
2.	YEARS to College (18 - child's AGE)	14	12	8
3.	Annual College COSTS (current dollar)	$16,065*	$16,065*	$16,065*
4.	Assumed College INFLATION Rate (%)	7%	7%	7%
5.	College INFLATION FACTOR (Factor from Compound Interest Table, Appendix A, for Years in Step 2 and INFLATION Rate in Step 4.)	2.5785	2.2522	1.7182
6.	Estimated FUTURE ANNUAL COSTS (Step 3 x Step 5)	$41,424	$36,182	$27,603
7.	Estimated TOTAL Future Cost (Step 6 x number of years of college)	$165,696	$144,728	$110,412
	FUNDING REQUIREMENTS			
8.	Assumed After-tax RATE OF RETURN (%)	8%	8%	8%
9.	Present Value of Future LUMP-SUM Factor (Factor from Present Value Table, Appendix B, for YEARS in Step 2 and RATE OF RETURN in Step 8.)	0.3405	0.3971	0.5403
10.	Total LUMP-SUM INVESTMENT Currently Required (Step 7 x Step 9)	$56,419	$57,471	$59,656
10a.	SUM of Line 10, all columns		$173,546	
11.	AMOUNT ALREADY EARMARKED for Education		$ 30,000	
12.	Additional LUMP-SUM Funding Required (Step 10a - Step 11)		$143,546	
13.	YEARS OF FUNDING		14**	
14.	Present Value of an Annuity Due Factor (Factor from Present Value of an Annuity Due Table, Appendix F, for YEARS in Step 13 and RATE OF RETURN in Step 8.)		8.9038	
15.	ANNUAL TARGET AMOUNT to Invest (Step 12 ÷ Step 14)		$ 16,122	
16.	Approximate MONTHLY TARGET AMOUNT to Invest (Step 15 ÷ 12)		$1,343	

* 21,420 total current cost x 75 percent that parent plans to fund
** Years until youngest child starts first year of college

6. the parents give gifts to children set aside sufficiently early to compound over a long period of time; and

7. through a combination of these techniques.

Most parents will use some combination of these techniques.

Pay-As-You-Go

From a planning perspective, the least favorable methods for financing education expenses are (1) using current assets and income on a pay-as-you-go system, and (2) depending on scholarships and loans. Financing an education out of current income or assets is the most expensive alternative because it takes the least advantage of the time value of money and the favorable tax treatment available for funds that might have been set aside for this purpose. In addition, this method places the greatest strain on current disposable income.

Government Provided Tax Credits and Other College Financing Tax Incentives

Hope Scholarship and Lifetime Learning Credits for Higher Education Expenses

Some taxpayers will be able to take advantage of the Hope Scholarship Credit and the Lifetime Learning Credit.

Hope Scholarship Credit

Individual taxpayers are allowed to claim a non-refundable Hope Scholarship Credit against federal income taxes *for each student, per year* in an amount equal to the sum of (1) 100% on the first $1,100 (as indexed)[1] of "qualified tuition and related expenses," and (2) 50% on the next $1,100 (as indexed) of qualified tuition and related expenses. Thus, for 2007, the maximum credit available is $1,650 ($1,100 + (50% x $1,100)). The credit may be claimed only with respect to expenses of a student for two taxable years and only with respect to expenses for a student who has not completed the first two years of post-secondary education before the beginning of the taxable year in which the credit is claimed.

This credit can only be used if the student is an "eligible student" for at least one academic period that begins during the taxable year. An "eligible student" is one who: (1) is enrolled in a degree, certificate, or other program (including a program of study abroad approved for credit by the institution at which such student is enrolled) leading to a recognized educational credential at an eligible educational institution; (2) carries at least one-half the normal full-time work load for the course of study the student is pursuing; and (3) has not been convicted of a felony (under state or federal law) relating to the possession or distribution of a controlled substance by the end of the taxable year with or within which the academic period ends.

Furthermore, only the tax filer who claims the student as a dependent (or the student, if independent) can claim the credit; married taxpayers who file separately are not eligible for the credit.

In addition, the Hope Scholarship Credit is limited by the amount of the claimer's income. Starting in 2007, the income limits increase. If the claimer is married and filing a joint return, the amount of the Hope Scholarship Credit for 2007 is gradually reduced (phased out in a pro-rata fashion) if modified adjusted gross income (MAGI) is between $94,000 and $107,000. Therefore, no Hope Scholarship Credit is permitted for married taxpayers filing jointly with MAGI above $107,000. For single filers, the phase-out range is between $47,000 and $53,000. These phase-out ranges are indexed for inflation for future years.

Planning Point–If qualified tuition and related expenses are paid during the taxable year for an academic period that begins during the first three months of the following year, the academic period is treated as beginning during the current year. This permits, for example, the payment in December of 2007 for the college term beginning on February 1, 2008 to qualify for the tax credit in 2007. It has other implications as well. Most post-secondary education is administered on a fall through spring term. For moderate-level expenses, the operation of the above rules may require not electing a credit for the fall semester freshman year but electing the spring freshman-fall sophomore year and spring sophomore-fall junior year as the time to elect to use the Hope Scholarship Credit. Alternatively, prepayment of the spring semester during the fall semester of the freshman year may allow the taxpayer to take full advantage of the credit in the earlier tax year. For example, suppose the *annual* qualified tuition and related expenses are $3,000 ($1,500 each term). Payment of the freshman fall term $1,500 expenses in 2007 results in a 2007 credit of $1,300 (100% x $1,100 + 50% x $400). In 2008, payment of $1,500 for the freshman spring term and another $1,500 for the sophomore term results in a credit of $1,650 (100% x $1,100 + 50% x $1,100). Because the credit has now been claimed in two taxable years, no further expenses would qualify for the credit and the taxpayer's Hope Scholarship Credits for the two years would total $2,950. If, instead, the taxpayer had prepaid the $1,500 spring freshman (2008) semester fees in 2007 and, again in 2008, prepaid the $1,500 for the sophomore 2009) spring semester, the taxpayer would be entitled to a $1,650 credit in both years, for a total of $3,300. This represents a $350 tax savings by properly planning for the use of the Hope Scholarship Credit.

Lifetime Learning Credit

The taxpayer may also claim a nonrefundable Lifetime Learning Credit against federal income taxes in an amount equal to 20% of "qualified tuition and related expenses" incurred during the taxable year that do not exceed $10,000. In contrast with the Hope Scholarship Credit, the Lifetime Learning Credit is applied on a per taxpayer basis rather than on a per student basis for the taxable year.

The "qualified tuition and related expenses" to which the Lifetime Learning Credit applies do not include those expenses with respect to an individual for whom a Hope Scholarship Credit is allowed for the taxable year. Expenses related to educational programs leading to a degree or certificate programs and, in certain cases, those that do not lead to a degree or certificate, may qualify for the Lifetime Learning Credit. Expenses incurred at either the undergraduate or graduate level (or professional degree program) may qualify for the credit. In addition to allowing a credit for the tuition and fees of a student who attends classes on at least a half-time basis as part of a degree or certificate program, the Lifetime Learning Credit is also available with respect to expenses related to any course of instruction at an "eligible education institution" (whether enrolled in by the student on a full-time, half-time, or less than half-time basis) to acquire or improve the student's job skills. In contrast to the Hope Scholarship Credit, the maximum amount of the Lifetime Learning Credit that may be claimed on a taxpayer's return will not vary based on the number of students in the taxpayer's family.

Qualified tuition and fees paid with the proceeds of a loan generally are eligible for the Lifetime Learning Credit (rather than the loan itself).

The Hope Scholarship Credit and the Lifetime Learning Credit share certain common features (See Figure 10.9):

- "Qualified tuition and related expenses" are those expenses (1) for the enrollment or attendance of (2) the taxpayer, the taxpayer's spouse or any dependent for whom the taxpayer is allowed a personal exemption (3) at an eligible education institution for courses of instruction of such individual at the institution.

Planning Point – In the case of divorced or divorcing parents, consideration of projected levels of adjusted gross income is a factor to be considered in determining who is entitled to the dependency exemption, since only a spouse who can claim the exemption and meets the AGI limits can take full advantage of the credits. This can, in appropriate circumstances, suggest that the divorce or separation agreement be structured so that the credits are available to one of the spouses.

- Expenses involving sports, games, or hobbies are not qualified tuition and related expenses unless this education is part of the student's degree program. Charges and fees associated with meals, lodging, student activities, athletics, insurance, transportation, and similar personal, living or family expenses are also not included. Neither credit is available for expenses incurred to purchase books. Qualified tuition and related expenses do not include expenses covered by educational assistance that are not required to be included in the gross income of either the student or the taxpayer claiming the credit. Thus, total qualified tuition and related expenses are reduced by any scholarship or fellowship grants excludable from gross income under IRC Section 117 and any other tax-free educational benefits received by the student during the taxable year (such as employer provided educational assistance excludable under IRC Section 127 or payments received from educational savings accounts or qualified tuition plans). In addition, such qualified tuition and related expenses and fees are also reduced by any payment (other than a gift, bequest, devise, or inheritance within the meaning of IRC Section 102(a)) that is excludable under any United States law. Moreover, a Lifetime Learning Credit is not allowed with respect to any education expense for which a deduction is claimed under IRC Section 162, or any other section of the Code.

- If a student is claimed as a dependent by the parent (or other taxpayer), the student is not entitled to claim either credit for that taxable year on the student's own tax return. If a parent (or other taxpayer) claims a student as a dependent, any qualified tuition and related expenses paid by the student are treated as paid by the parent (or other taxpayer) for purposes of the credits. On the other hand, if a child is not claimed as a dependent by the parent (or by any other taxpayer) for the taxable year, then the child has the option of electing either the Hope Scholarship or Lifetime Learning Credit for qualified higher education expenses paid during that year.

Planning Point – Because a parent (or other taxpayer) who claims a student as a dependent may treat qualified tuition and related expenses paid by the student as paid by the parent (or other taxpayer) for purposes of the credit, income-shifting to the eligible student becomes attractive because the source of the funds for payment is taxed at presumably no more than a 15% rate, yet it applies as an offset against the perhaps 25% tax rate of the taxpayer (based on tax rates in 2007).[2]

- "Eligible educational institutions" are defined by reference to Section 481 of the Higher Education Act of 1965. Such institutions generally are accredited post-secondary educational institutions offering credit toward a bachelor's degree, associate's degree, or another recognized post-secondary credential. Certain proprietary institutions and post-secondary vocational institutions also are eligible educational institutions. The institution must be eligible to participate in United Stated Department of Education student aid programs.

- Neither credit is allowed unless the taxpayer includes the name and taxpayer identification number on the taxpayer's tax return.

Caution – Neither credit is available to married taxpayers who file separate returns. This is particularly a problem in the context of a divorcing couple. In determining whether a couple is married, their legal relationship is generally examined as of the end of the taxable year. If they are legally separated under a divorce decree (or separate maintenance), they are not considered married. In a typical scenario, there will be at least one taxable year in which the couple is separated or estranged to the point that (assuming good advice) one of them will not subject themselves to the joint and several liability of the tax return. Should this occur at the time the couple's children are going to college (or one of the estranged couple is taking graduate work or other courses), the credits are threatened. It is another issue that must be negotiated in the divorce process.

- The Hope Scholarship Credit and Lifetime Learning Credit amount that a taxpayer may otherwise claim is phased out ratably for taxpayers with "modified adjusted gross income" (AGI) between $40,000 and $50,000 ($80,000 and $100,000 for joint returns) as indexed. For 2007, the phaseout ranges are $47,000 to $57,000 for single or head of household returns and $94,000 to $114,000 for joint returns. "Modified AGI" includes amounts otherwise excluded with respect to income earned abroad (or income from Puerto Rico or United States possessions).

Planning Point – The phaseout suggests tax strategies to reduce the taxpayer's adjusted gross income, which might include increasing the amount of the employee's IRC Section 401(k) elective deferrals, increasing the level of contribution to a self-employed individual's Keogh plan, and shifting investment income to another family member, including the student. Each of these strategies can be justified independent of the credit, but under certain circumstances—especially for taxpayers on or near the cusp—the available credit together with other new features makes each of these more attractive.

Example: A sole proprietor whose filing status is married filing jointly has an AGI of $99,000 in 2007 and a child about to enter college, which will incur $10,000 of annual qualified tuition expenses. How should he handle this?

Strategy One – Pay expenses out of current income. Assuming the sole proprietor does not have a large amount of itemized deductions and personal exemptions, this will be paid out of 25% income (i.e., income taxable at about 25%, based on 2007 rates). Grossing up, the proprietor is (with respect to the tuition) out-of-pocket $13,333.33 [$10,000 ÷ (1 - 0.25)]. If the Hope Scholarship Credit is used, there is a $1,650 credit "phased down" to $1,237.50 – that is, the $1,650 credit is reduced by $412.50 ($1,650 - [$1,650 x {$99,000 - $94,000}/$20,000]). Thus, net cost is, on an after-tax basis, $12,095.83 ($13,333.33 after-tax cost of tuition - $1,237.50 tax savings by credit).

Strategy Two – Reduce AGI to $94,000 by setting up a Keogh profit-sharing plan and contributing the $5,000 from Strategy One to the Keogh plan. This may well require borrowing the $5,000 to pay the tuition—but more on that later. This frees up from "phase out" the $412.50 credit reduction in Strategy One. Now, the net after-tax cost of college is $11,683.33 ($13,333.33 after-tax cost of tuition - $1,650 tax savings by credit).

Note: The application of the Hope Scholarship or Lifetime Learning Credit is elective. For tax years beginning before 2002, neither credit was available in a year in which an individual had excluded a distribution from what was then called an education IRA unless the individual elected to waive the exclusion with respect to such distribution. For tax years beginning after 2001, a taxpayer can claim either credit *and* exclude a distribution from a Coverdell Education Savings Account (ESA) on behalf of the same student *if* the distribution is not used to pay the same educational expenses for which the credit was claimed.

Planning Point – Taxpayers may not allocate qualified tuition and related expenses to the Hope Scholarship and Lifetime Learning Credits for the same student in the same tax year. For example, the payment of $7,200 tuition for one individual cannot be broken down into a $2,200 Hope Scholarship segment and a $5,000 Lifetime Learning segment. On the other hand, tuition and related expenses can be allocated to different credits on a per student basis. Thus, a taxpayer may claim the Lifetime Learning Credit for a taxable year with respect to one or more students, even though the taxpayer also claims a Hope Scholarship Credit (or claims an exclusion from gross income for certain distributions from qualified tuition programs or Coverdell ESA) for that same taxable year with respect to other students. If, for a taxable year, a taxpayer claims a Hope Scholarship Credit with respect to a student, then the Lifetime Learning Credit will not be available with respect to that same student for that year (although the Lifetime Learning Credit may be available with respect to that same student for other taxable years).

Withdrawals from IRAs for Educational Purposes

An individual generally is not subject to income tax on amounts held in an IRA, including earnings on contributions, until the amounts are withdrawn from the IRA. Amounts withdrawn from an IRA are includable in gross income (except to the extent of nondeductible contributions). In addition, a 10% additional tax generally applies to distributions from IRAs made before age 59½, unless the distribution is made: (1) on account of death or disability; (2) in the form of annuity payments; (3) for medical expenses of the individual and his spouse and dependents that exceed 7.5% of AGI; or (4) for medical insurance of the individuals and his spouse and dependents (without regard to the 7.5% AGI floor) if the individual has received unemployment compensation for at least 12 weeks, and the withdrawal is made in the year such unemployment compensation is received or the following year.

An important exception to the 10% additional tax is available for distributions from an IRA to the extent such distributions (other than those already excluded from the penalty) do not exceed the "qualified higher education expenses" of the taxpayer for the taxable year. For these purposes, "qualified higher education expenses" are those furnished to (1) the taxpayer, (2) the taxpayer's spouse, or (3) any child or grandchild of the taxpayer or the taxpayer's spouse, at an eligible educational institution. A child includes a son, daughter, stepson, or stepdaughter, an adopted child and, in certain circumstances, a foster child. Qualified higher education expenses are reduced by any amount excludable from gross income relating to the redemption of a qualified United States savings bond and certain scholarships and veterans benefits.

Note – The amount of qualified higher deduction expenses for any taxable year is reduced by (1) the amount of scholarships or fellowship grants excludable from gross income under IRC Section 117, (2) any other tax-free educational benefits received by the student during the taxable year (such as employer provided educational assistance excludable under IRC Section 127), and (3) any payment (other than a gift bequest, devise or inheritance within the meaning of IRC Section 102(a)) that is excludable under any United States law.

Coverdell Education Savings Accounts (ESAs)

Coverdell Education Savings Accounts (ESAs) were originally called "Education IRAs" (they were first introduced in 1997, and the name was changed in 2001). Coverdell ESAs allow for tax-free savings for certain educational expenses. An ESA is a trust or custodial account created or organized in the United States exclusively for the purpose of paying the "qualified education expenses" (see below) of the designated beneficiary of the account. The account must be designated as a Coverdell ESA when it is created, in order to be treated as such for tax purposes.[3]

Taxpayers may deposit cash of up to $2,000 per year into an ESA for a child younger than 18. Anyone may contribute to the child's ESA provided the total contributions (on behalf of a particular beneficiary) for a taxable year do not exceed the $2,000 limit. Any contribution to an ESA on behalf of a designated beneficiary is a completed gift. Therefore, the gift qualifies for the annual exclusion. An ESA may be considered an asset of the designated beneficiary (i.e., the child's asset) under the financial aid formulas. As discussed more fully in the section covering the college financial aid formula, this could reduce the amount of financial aid the family receives.

Amounts deposited in the ESA grow tax-free until distributed (like a Roth IRA). Once distributed, the child will not owe tax on the amount withdrawn from the account *if* the child's "qualified education expenses" at an eligible educational institution for the year equal or exceed the amount of the withdrawal.

The $2,000 contribution limit is subject to phaseout provisions for taxpayers (i.e., contributors) with modified adjusted gross income (MAGI) in excess of specified limits. The phaseout range begins at $190,000 for joint filers and $95,000 for single filers. The contribution limit is reduced proportionately for MAGI over these amounts, and is effectively eliminated once a taxpayer's MAGI reaches $220,000 for joint filers and $110,000 for single filers. Like IRAs, contributions to ESAs for a given year must be made by April 15 of the following year.

Example: T, a joint return filer, has MAGI of $195,000 in 2007. Therefore, T is $5,000 into the $30,000 phase out range. The maximum amount T may contribute to an ESA is $1,666.67 ($5,000 / $30,000 x $2,000 = $333.33 phase out). T must make the contribution by April 15, 2005.

Planning Point: The phaseout rules could prompt some taxpayers to indirectly fund an ESA by making a cash gift to a relative whose income is less than the threshold amount of the phaseout rules. The relative would then make the contribution into the ESA of the taxpayer's child. While this may still be attempted, this method is subject to attack by the IRS. In fact, a 2000 Tax Court case (not related to ESAs) held in favor of the Service where there was a pre-arranged plan of gifting. Taxpayers should be cautious because there is a 6% annual excise tax applied to excess contributions to an ESA. If the phaseout rules are an issue, EGTRRA 2001 made it clear that the rules applied only to individuals. Therefore, interpreters of the law have taken this to mean that corporations and other entities could be contributors, regardless of their income levels.

Distributions from an ESA are not included in the gross income of the distributee to the extent of the beneficiary's (1) qualified *higher* education expenses or (2) qualified *elementary and secondary school* expenses during the taxable year (together referred to as "qualified education expenses"). "Qualified higher education expenses" are defined as tuition, fees, books, supplies, and equipment required for the enrollment or attendance at a college or university (or certain vocational schools). In addition, reasonable costs for room and board are qualified expenses provided the student is taking at least one-half the normal load for the particular program. However, the amount cannot exceed the minimum amount included for room and board for such period in the cost of attendance (as defined in Section 472 of the Higher Education Act of 1965, 20 U.S.C. 1087II, as in effect on August 5, 1997) for the eligible educational institution for such period. For students who live in housing owned or operated by the eligible educational institution, the actual invoice amount charged for room and board will be includable in qualified higher education expenses if that is greater than the standard allowance.

"Qualified elementary and secondary school expenses" are defined as expenses for tuition, fees, academic tutoring, special needs services, books, supplies, and other equipment incurred in connection with the enrollment or attendance of the beneficiary at a public, private, or religious school providing elementary or secondary education (kindergarten through grade 12) as determined under state law. Also included in the definition is (1) room and board, uniforms, transportation, and supplementary items or services (including extended day programs) required or provided by such a school in connection with such enrollment or attendance of the beneficiary; and (2) the purchase of any computer technology, equipment, or Internet access and related services, if such technology, equipment, or services are to be used by the beneficiary and the beneficiary's family during any of the years the beneficiary is in school. Computer software primarily involving sports, games, or hobbies is not considered a qualified elementary and secondary school expense unless the software is educational in nature.

If the qualified expenses of the beneficiary for the year are less than the total amount of the distribution from an ESA, then the qualified expenses are deemed to be paid from a pro rata share of both the principal and earnings components of the distribution. An otherwise taxable distribution may be rolled over within 60 days into another ESA for the benefit of the same beneficiary, or a "member of the family," which means:

1. a spouse of the taxpayer;
2. a son or daughter of the taxpayer (or a descendant of either);
3. a stepson or stepdaughter of the taxpayer;

4. a brother, sister, stepbrother, or stepsister of the taxpayer;

5. the father or mother of the taxpayer (or an ancestor of either);

6. a stepfather or stepmother of the taxpayer;

7. a son or daughter of a brother or sister of the taxpayer;

8. a brother or sister of the father or mother of the taxpayer;

9. a son-in-law, daughter-in-law, father-in-law, mother-in-law, brother-in-law, or sister-in-law of the taxpayer;

10. any spouse of an individual named in (2) through (9); or

11. any first cousin of the taxpayer.

Rollovers of account balances may be made from an ESA benefiting one beneficiary to an ESA benefiting a different beneficiary (as well as redesignations of the named beneficiary), provided that the new beneficiary is a member of the family of the old beneficiary and is under age 30. Any balance remaining in a Coverdell ESA is deemed distributed within 30 days after the date that the beneficiary reaches age 30 (or, if earlier, within 30 days of the date that the beneficiary dies). The age limitations with respect to rollovers and required distributions do not apply in the case of a *special needs beneficiary*. Thus, a deemed distribution of any balance in a Coverdell ESA does not occur when a special needs beneficiary reaches age 30. Finally, the age 30 limitation does not apply in the case of a rollover contribution for the benefit of a special needs beneficiary or a change in beneficiaries to a special needs beneficiary.

Distributions from an ESA that are not offset by any qualified expenses are included in the distributee's gross income to the extent of the earnings on the accumulated contributions. In other words, the distributions are taxed under IRC Section 72 in the same manner as distributions from IRAs that include nondeductible contributions. The taxpayer recovers the nondeductible contributions in essentially a pro rata fashion. To the extent a payment or distribution from an ESA is includable in gross income, the recipient is subject to an additional penalty tax of 10% of the amount that is so includable. This 10% additional penalty tax can be avoided in the following circumstances:

1. The payment or distribution is made to a beneficiary (or his estate) on or after the death of the designated beneficiary.

2. The payment or distribution is attributable to the designated beneficiary's being disabled.

3. The payment or distribution is made on account of a scholarship, allowance, or payment described in IRC Section 25A(g)(2) received by the account holder to the extent the amount of the payment or distribution does not exceed the amount of the scholarship, allowance, or payment.

4. The distribution of any excess contribution to an ESA made during the taxable year on behalf of a designated beneficiary, which is received on or before the day prescribed by law (including extensions of time) for filing the contributor's return for that taxable year and is accompanied by the amount of net income attributable to the excess contribution. For these purposes, the net income attributable to the excess contribution is included in gross income for the taxable year in which such excess contribution was made. The additional 10% penalty does not apply to the distribution of a contribution if such distribution is made before the first day of the sixth month (i.e., June 1) of the taxable year following the taxable year in which the contribution was made.

Planning Point: A taxpayer may claim a Hope Scholarship or Lifetime Learning Credit for a taxable year and exclude from gross income amounts distributed (both the contributions and the earnings portions) from an ESA on behalf of the same student so long as the distribution is *not* used for the same educational expenses for which a credit was claimed.

Contributions may be made to an ESA and a qualified tuition program (QTP also known as a 529 plan) in the same year for a designated beneficiary. Prior to 2002, any amount contributed to an ESA and a QTP for a designated beneficiary in the same year subjected the ESA contribution to the excess contribution excise tax.

For estate tax purposes, the value in an ESA is generally not included in the gross estate of the donor or beneficiary. The exceptions are as follows:

- Amounts distributed on account of the death of the beneficiary are included in the gross estate of the designated beneficiary.

- If the donor made an election to treat certain excess contributions as made ratably over a 5-year period and dies before the close of such 5-year period, the gross estate of the donor includes the portion of such contributions properly allocable to periods after the date of death of the donor.

If the account holder's surviving spouse or family member acquires such holder's interest in an ESA by reason of being the designated beneficiary of such account at the death of the account holder, the ESA will be treated as if the spouse or family member were the account holder (provided the surviving spouse or family member has not yet attained age 30).

If anyone other than the account holder's surviving spouse acquires such holder's interest in an ESA, by reason of being the designated beneficiary of such account at the death of the account holder, it ceases being an ESA as of the date of death. If that is the case, an amount equal to the fair market value of the assets in the ESA on that date will be includable (if such person is not the estate of such holder), in the person's gross income for the taxable year which includes the date of death; or if the person acquiring it is the estate of such holder, in the gross income for the last taxable year of the estate. An appropriate deduction is allowed under IRC Section 691(c) (for income in respect of a decedent) to any person (other than the decedent or the decedent's spouse) with respect to amounts included in gross income by the person.

Any balance remaining in an ESA at the end of the 30-day period following the designated beneficiary's death will be deemed distributed.

An ESA will be tax-exempt in the event of a prohibited transaction, and any pledge of the account is treated as a distribution to the extent of the amount pledged. For these purposes, an individual for whose benefit an ESA is established and any contributor to the account are not considered engaged in a prohibited transaction with respect to any transaction concerning the account (which would otherwise be taxable) if IRC Section 503(d) applies with respect to the transaction.

Exclusion for Employer Provided Educational Assistance

An employee's gross income and wages do not include amounts paid or incurred by the employer for educational assistance provided to the employee if such amounts are paid or incurred pursuant to an educational assistance program that meets certain requirements. This exclusion is limited to $5,250 of educational assistance with respect to an individual during a calendar year. The exclusion applies to both undergraduate and graduate-level courses. In the absence of the exclusion, educational assistance is excludable from income only if it is related to the employee's current job.

Section 529 Plans

Section 529 plans, as the name implies, are governed by IRC Section 529, which deals with qualified tuition programs (QTPs). For simplicity purposes, we will refer to these programs as "529 plans" or "QTPs."

Under current law, a QTP is a program established and maintained by a state, state agency or an eligible education institution. The basic thrust of the program is to permit persons to: (1) purchase tuition credits or certificates on behalf of a designated beneficiary that entitle the beneficiary to a waiver or payment of qualified higher education expenses of the beneficiary; or (2) make contributions to an account that is established for the purpose of meeting qualified higher education expenses of the designated beneficiary of the account (a "savings account plan"). The terms and conditions of these programs vary from plan to plan.[4] However, there are some standard federal income tax rules that apply to these programs.[5]

There are two different types of 529 plans: (1) prepaid tuition plans; and (2) college savings plans or savings account plans. With a *prepaid tuition plan*, the account owner (e.g., a parent) contributes cash to a plan account for a beneficiary (typically a child), and the contribution purchases tuition credits (i.e., credit hours) based on then-current tuition rates. The account owner's contribution qualifies for the annual gift tax exclusion. When the beneficiary attends a college participating in the program, the beneficiary's tuition credits may be used to pay for all or a portion of the beneficiary's tuition and certain other college expenses, regardless of tuition rates at that time. If the beneficiary does not go to college, or goes to a nonparticipating college, the tuition credits will be refunded in cash (based on a set formula or index), which may then be used to pay tuition and other college expenses at a nonparticipating college.

Generally, any difference between (1) the value of the tuition and other expenses covered by the plan and (2) the total amount of the account owner's contributions to the plan is recovered tax-free.

With a *college savings plan*, the account owner contributes cash to a plan account for a beneficiary, and the contribution is invested according to the terms of the

Figure 10.9

HOPE SCHOLARSHIP CREDIT AND LIFETIME LEARING CREDIT SUMMARY AND COMPARISON		
	HOPE Scholarship Credit	**Lifetime Learing Credit**
Credit amount	Up to $1,500 per student per year. Indexed for inflation beginning in 2002 ($1,650 in 2007).	Up to $2,000 per taxpayer per year.
Concurrent use	Same taxpayer may elect both credits in the same year provided credits are not used for the same student's expenses.	
Application of expense limit	Per-student basis	Per-taxpayer basis
Phaseout	Married filing jointly: phase-out range between 94,000 and $114,000. Single: phase-out range is between $47,000 and $57,000. (2007 levels indexed for inflation each year).	
Qualified expenses	Qualified tuition and related expenses for the attendance by the taxpayer, taxpayer's spouse, or taxpayer's dependents at a post-secondary educational institution offering credit toward a degree or other recognized post-secondary educational credential.	Also includes qualified tuition and related expenses for course that is part of a nondegree program that is taken by the student to acquire or improve job skills.
Eligibility limitations	First two years of post-secondary education for any one student. Degree requirement Felony drug conviction restriction At least half-time attendance	All years of post-secondary education, graduate, and professional school. No degree requirement No felony drug conviction restriction No workload requirement
Credit available	For payments covering an academic period beginning in the same calendar year as the payment is made. Exception: for payments made during the calendar year to cover academic period that begins in January, February, or March of the following taxable year.	
Coordination with other tax provisions	Expenses excluded from gross income under **employer-provided educational assistance plan** cannot be used in credit base. Expenses claimed for the credits will reduce the amount of expenses eligible for **Section 135 exclusion (U.S. savings bond interest** used to pay for higher education). No credit if tax-free distribution from **Education Savings Account (ESA)** or **Qualified Tuition Plan (QTP)** in tax year unless student waives the tax-free treatment of the ESA or QTP and pays tax on ESA or QTP distribution.	
Payments included	Includes payments made with student's earnings, loan, gift, inheritance, savings (including savings from **qualified tuition program (QTP)**. Does **not** include payments made with **Pell Grant** or other tax-free scholarship, tax-free distribution from an **ESA**, or tax-free **employer-provided educational assistance**.	

plan. The account owner's contribution qualifies for the annual gift tax exclusion. When the beneficiary attends virtually any college, the funds in the account (i.e., the account owner's contributions plus all of the investment earnings thereon) may be used to pay for the beneficiary's tuition and certain other college expenses.

A specified individual must generally be designated as the beneficiary at the commencement of participation in a 529 plan (i.e., when contributions are first made to purchase an interest in such a program) *unless* interests in such a program are purchased by a state or local government or a tax-exempt IRC Section 501(c)(3) charity as part of a scholarship program operated by such government or charity under which beneficiaries to be named in the future will receive such interests as scholarships.

QTPs are themselves exempt from income tax. Cash distributions from QTPs are excluded from gross income to the extent that the distribution is used to pay for "qualified higher education expenses" (as reduced by any in-kind distributions). This exclusion from gross income also applies to distributions from QTPs established and maintained by an entity other than a state (or agency or instrumentality thereof).

The funds in the plan can be used for tuition, fees, books, and supplies needed for higher education. Room and board are also eligible expenses for such plans for beneficiaries who are at least "half-time" students. If the funds are not used for such expenses, the beneficiary will be taxed on the excess of the funds received over the amounts contributed.

For room and board expenses, QTPs may be used up to a specified level (generally the school's posted room and board charge).[6]

QTPs may be used to pay expenses not only at public and nonprofit institutions but also at "proprietary schools" (i.e., any school that is an eligible educational institution for purposes of the Hope Scholarship or Lifetime Learning Credits).

Contributions by donors are eligible for the $12,000 (in 2007) gift tax annual exclusion ($24,000 for "split" gifts by married couples). Therefore, for transfer tax purposes, such contributions are treated as a completed gift to the beneficiary. If the contribution is larger than the amount of the gift tax annual exclusion, the donor may prorate the contribution to the QTP over five years for purposes of claiming the gift tax annual exclusion. This allows a contribution of up to five times the amount of the annual exclusion (up to $60,000 for an individual in 2007 and up to $120,000 for split gifts) to be made without gift tax consequences. Note that the gift tax annual exclusion is indexed for inflation.

A QTP is controlled by the account owner, not the beneficiary. The account owner retains all the rights of ownership, including the right to name a new beneficiary, roll over assets from one plan to another, and receive distributions (albeit with possibly taxable results). Despite these facts, a QTP is generally not includable in the owner's estate for estate tax or generation-skipping transfer tax purposes, even though the owner retains the same degree of control over a QTP that, with respect to any other transfer of property, would cause inclusion for estate tax purposes.

The limits on the amount of contributions imposed by plans vary. Some, however, have limits high enough to take advantage of the full amount allowed under the election.

Example: In 2007, John (age 70) wants to put $120,000 into a college savings plan for his granddaughter. By using the gift-splitting technique, allowing John and his wife, Mary, (age 65) a $24,000 annual exclusion, and by electing to prorate the gift over a 5-year period, John can transfer the entire $120,000 in 2007 without using any of his or his spouse's unified credit or generation-skipping transfer tax exemption (i.e., there would be no gift tax or generation-skipping transfer tax consequences). If John dies during the next five years, his gross estate would include only that portion of the contributions allocable to periods after his death.[7] With that in mind, John makes the gifts in his wife's name, using the gift-splitting technique, since she is five years younger and has a longer life expectancy.

Prior to the 2001 tax law changes, a state tuition program was required to impose a penalty on any refund of earnings from the account (1) not used for "qualified higher education expenses" of the designated beneficiary, (2) made on account of the death or disability of the designated beneficiary, or (3) made on account of a scholarship received by the designated beneficiary to the extent that the amount of the refund did not exceed the amount of the scholarship.[8] The IRS had allowed states to set the penalty as low as 10%, and several had. For taxable years beginning after December 31, 2003, a 10% additional tax is imposed on any QTP earnings that are includable in taxable income because they are not used for "qualified higher education expenses." Note that QTPs are not precluded from continuing to impose their own penalties. However, it is anticipated that both states and educational institutions will welcome the administrative convenience, and would not receive sufficient revenues to warrant the competitive disadvantage they might suffer by imposing penalties.

The additional tax for nonqualifying distributions does not apply to distributions that are rolled over to a new QTP for the *same* beneficiary, or to a QTP for a *new* beneficiary who is a family member of the old beneficiary; nor does it apply to distributions made on account of (1) the death or disability of the beneficiary, or (2) the beneficiary receiving a scholarship equal to or greater than the amount of the distribution.

A change in the designated beneficiary of an interest in a QTP is generally not treated as a distribution *if* the new beneficiary is a "member of the family" (see below) of the old beneficiary. Thus, in the above example, if John and Mary's granddaughter decides not to go to college, they can change the beneficiary to their grandson without an adverse effect.

A transfer of credits (or other amounts) from an account benefiting one designated beneficiary to another account benefiting a *different* beneficiary is considered a distribution *unless* the beneficiaries are members of the same family. For this purpose, the term "member of the family" is defined as

1. a spouse of the beneficiary;
2. a son or daughter of the beneficiary (or a descendant of either);
3. a stepson or stepdaughter of the beneficiary;
4. a brother, sister, stepbrother, or stepsister of the beneficiary;
5. the father or mother of the beneficiary (or an ancestor of either);
6. a stepfather or stepmother of the beneficiary;
7. a son or daughter of a brother or sister of the beneficiary;
8. a brother or sister of the father or mother of the beneficiary;
9. a son-in-law, daughter-in-law, father-in-law, mother-in-law, brother-in-law, or sister-in-law of the beneficiary;
10. any spouse of an individual named in (2) through (9);
11. any first cousin of the beneficiary.

A transfer of credits (or other amounts) from one QTP for the benefit of a designated beneficiary to another QTP for the benefit of the *same* beneficiary is not considered a distribution. However, this "rollover" treatment does not apply to more than one transfer within any 12-month period with respect to the same beneficiary. This is intended to permit, for example, transfers between a prepaid tuition program and a savings program maintained by the same state, and between a state plan and a private prepaid tuition program.

One of the disadvantages of a QTP (at least in the eyes of some) is the prohibition against the owner or beneficiary from "directing the investment" of the contributions. Accordingly, choosing a QTP involves consideration of the program's investment strategy. The addition of rollover provisions may permit dissatisfied investors to monitor account performances, and where appropriate, change to programs employing investment methods that are more effective. Because the QTP sponsor no longer has captive funds, much more competitive investment programs have emerged from many of the more conservative programs previously in place.

Changes in many existing programs are bound to occur and one should never assume that any two or more plans are substantially identical in their terms or operation, or even that the terms of a plan are the same as they were previously. In this dynamic situation, individuals exploring their college funding options will require, in many cases, consultation with an attorney, accountant, or other financial advisor to assist in the review of all of the new particulars provided by a specific plan.

Many states have provided state tax advantages that mirrored to some extent the federal tax potential of tax deferral and the shifting of income to the presumptively lower tax bracket beneficiary. How states will treat educational institution sponsored trusts is not clear.

Taxpayers may claim a Hope Scholarship or Lifetime Learning Credit for a taxable year *and* exclude from gross income amounts distributed (both the principal and the earnings portions) from a QTP on behalf of the same student as long as the distribution is not used for the same expenses for which a credit was claimed (assuming that the other requirements for claiming the Hope Scholarship or Lifetime Learning Credit are satisfied and the modified AGI phase-out for those credits does not apply).

If, following a rollover or a change of beneficiary, the new beneficiary is in a generation lower than that of the old beneficiary (determined under the generation-assignment rules), the old beneficiary may be subject to gift tax on the amount rolled over, or, in the case of a change of beneficiary, on the entire QTP. If the new beneficiary is two or more generations lower than the old beneficiary, the old beneficiary may also be subject to a generation skipping transfer tax on such amount. In either case, the relevant amount should qualify for the annual gift tax exclusion and, if greater than the annual exclusion, such amount should be eligible for 5-year proration as discussed above, Any such amounts not thus covered by annual exclusions would either consume some of the unified gift and estate tax credit (and perhaps generation-skipping transfer tax exemption), or cause gift tax (and perhaps generation-skipping transfer tax) to be payable by the old beneficiary.

Recent letter rulings by the Department of Education regarding college savings plans indicate that a plan account will be treated as an asset of the owner for federal financial aid purposes. This is much more favorable than having the account treated as an asset of the beneficiary. Moreover, because the earnings portion of a distribution used for the beneficiary's qualified higher education expenses is not generally included in the beneficiary's income, it should not affect the beneficiary's federal financial aid calculation in subsequent years.

Prepaid tuition plans are treated neither as an asset of the owner or the beneficiary, but are considered to reduce the beneficiary's cost of attendance on a dollar-for-dollar basis, depending on the amount of tuition credits available to the beneficiary.

Grants, Scholarships, and Loans

Reliance on scholarships or special student loans is quite questionable, especially given the present financial aid trend away from outright grants and favorable loans. Even if favorable student loans are available, a client may not wish to saddle a child with large loans that must be paid off at a time when the child begins a career. Loans to parents are generally made at market interest rates and repayment commences shortly after the loans are taken out.

Most college aid packages include a combination of grants, loans, and work-study programs.

Federal Grants

Four federal grants are available: Pell Grants, Supplemental Educational Opportunity Grants (FSEOG), Academic Competitiveness Grants (ACG), and Nation Science and Mathematics Access to Retain Talent Grant (National Smart Grant). Unlike loans, grant recipients do not have to repay the grants unless, for example, the recipient is awarded funds incorrectly or withdraws from school.

Pell Grants are limited. The maximum award for the 2007-2008 award year is $4,310. Due to federal funding limits, the actual maximum grants may be less than this amount. Students who are eligible for Pell Grants receive the full amount they qualify for—each school participating in the program receives enough funds to pay the Pell amounts for all its eligible students. The amount of other student aid students might qualify for does not affect the amount of their Pell Grants.

Supplemental Educational Opportunity Grants (FSEOGs) are limited to a maximum of $4,000 per year. Both the Pell and Supplemental federal grants are awarded only to academically promising students who also qualify under the financial needs formulas. Unlike Pell Grants, the FSEOG amounts received depend not only on their financial need, but also on the amount of other aid the students gets. Therefore, receiving other aid might reduce the amount of a student's FSEOG award. In addition, not all schools participate in the FSEOG program and the funds available to those that do is limited. Each school participating in the FSEOG Program receives a certain amount of FSEOG funds each year from the United States Department of Education. When all of those funds have been disbursed for that award year, no more FSEOG awards can be made for that year. This is one reason why it is so important to apply early to be considered for these funds. Not everyone who qualifies for an FSEOG will necessarily get one.

Academic Competitiveness Grants (ACGs) began in the 2006–07 award year for full-time undergraduate students enrolled in an eligible program, who receive Federal Pell Grants, and are United States citizens. Students also must have completed a rigorous secondary school program of study and be enrolled in at least a two-year academic program acceptable for full credit toward a bachelor's degree or enrolled in a graduate degree program that includes three academic years of undergraduate education.

A rigorous secondary school program of study includes one of the following:

- Programs proposed by a state in response to the United States Department of Education's request.[9]

- An advanced or honors diploma program.

- A required set of courses similar to the State Scholars Initiative.[10]

- Advanced Placement (AP) courses or International Baccalaureate (IB) courses.

- Completion of two or more AP courses and a score of 3 or better on at least two AP exams for the courses completed or completion of two or more IB courses and a score of 4 or better on at least two IB exams for the courses completed.

In addition, first academic year undergraduate students must:

- be enrolled in an eligible program;

- have completed a rigorous secondary school program of study;

- not have been previously enrolled as a regular student in an undergraduate education program; and

- have graduated from high school after Jan. 1, 2006.

The award is up to $750 for first academic year undergraduate students.

Also, second academic year undergraduate students must:

- be enrolled in an eligible program;

- have completed a rigorous secondary school program of study;

- have graduated from high school after Jan. 1, 2005 and;

- have at least a 3.0 GPA for the first academic year for their eligible program.

The award is up to $1,300 for second academic year undergraduate students.

National Science and Mathematics Access to Retain Talent Grants (National SMART Grants) were first offered in the 2006-07 award year and are designed for full-time undergraduate students who are enrolled in the third or fourth academic year of an eligible program, who receive Federal Pell Grants, and are U.S. citizens. An eligible program in the National SMART Grant is one that leads to a bachelor's degree in an eligible major or a graduate degree program in an eligible major that includes at least three academic years of undergraduate education. The award is up to $4,000 for each of the third and fourth academic years.

To qualify, students must:

- be pursuing an eligible major in physical, life, or computer sciences, engineering, technology, mathematics or a critical need foreign language; and

- have at least a 3.0 cumulative GPA.

Non-Federal Grants and Scholarships

Most states have programs similar to the Supplemental Educational Opportunity Grants program for students who are residents of and attend school within the state. These grants generally provide amounts less than $4,000 per year and are available only to students who demonstrate need.

Most colleges and universities also offer their own grants or scholarships. These funds are predominantly given to students who demonstrate financial need and superior academic potential. Many schools offer some scholarships to the most gifted students, regardless of need, but competition for these grants is especially intense.

Loans

Low interest federal loans are still available and some high income families may qualify.

Perkins Loans (formerly called National Direct Student Loans) are awarded by colleges on a first-come, first-served basis. The college decides whether the applicant needs the loan. Students from families with lower incomes are typically given preference, but gifted students with solid academic credentials may also qualify under this program. Depending on when a student applies, the level of need, and the funding level of the school, a student can borrow up to (1) $4,000 for each year of undergraduate study up to a total of $20,000, and (2) $6,000 for each year of graduate or professional study up to a total of $40,000, including any Federal Perkins Loans borrowed as an undergraduate. Interest is only 5% and payments on these loans do not begin until after graduation. The loans are repaid over 10 years.

Stafford Student Loans are generally available to students who have financial need remaining after their Expected Family Contribution (EFC), Federal Pell Grant eligibility, and aid from other sources are subtracted from the cost of their attendance. There are two kinds of Stafford loans. The ***Direct Stafford loan*** is a direct government loan. The ***Federal Family Education Loan*** (FFEL) is a government-guaranteed bank loan. While the terms and conditions of these loans are similar, they differ in the source of the loan funds, the application process, and the available repayment plans. The government will pay the interest on the loan while the student is in school, for the first six months after the student leaves school, and when the student qualifies to have payments deferred. This type of loan is called a "subsidized loan."

Students who do not have financial need remaining may still utilize the Stafford Loan program for the amount of their EFC, or the annual Stafford Loan borrowing limit for their grade level, whichever is less. Because an unsubsidized loan is not awarded on the basis of need, the Student's EFC is not taken into account. In this case the loan is "unsubsidized" (i.e., interest is charged from the time the loan is disbursed until it is paid in full). However, the borrower may elect either to pay the interest as it accrues, or allow the interest to accumulate and be added to the principal amount of the loan. Students may receive a subsidized Stafford Loan and an unsubsidized Stafford Loan for the same enrollment period.

The maximum amounts students can be permitted to borrow under this program can vary year to year. The borrowing limits for the 2007-2008 academic year are discussed below.

Dependent undergraduate students can borrow up to the following amounts:

- $3,500 if they are first-year students enrolled in a program of study that is at least a full academic year;
- $4,500 if they have completed their first year of study and the remainder of their program is at least a full academic year;
- $5,500 a year if they have completed two years of study and the remainder of their program is at least a full academic year; and
- $23,000 total until they graduate.

Independent undergraduate students, or dependent students whose parents are unable to get a PLUS Loan (i.e., a parental loan) can borrow up to the following amounts:

- $7,500 if they are first-year students enrolled in a program of study that is at least a full academic year (no more than $3,500 of this amount may be in subsidized loans)
- $8,500 if they have completed their first year of study and the remainder of their program is at least a full academic year (no more than $4,500 of this amount may be in subsidized loans)
- $10,500 a year if they have completed two years of study and the remainder of their program is at least a full academic year (no more than $5,500 of this amount may be in subsidized loans)
- $46,000 total with no more than $23,000 of this amount being subsidized loans.

Graduate students can borrow up to $20,500 for each academic year, only $8,500 of which may consist of subsidized Stafford loans. In total, graduate students may borrow up to $138,500 with no more than $65,500 of this amount being in subsidized loans. This graduate student limit includes Stafford Loans received for undergraduate study.

The amounts described here are the maximum annual amounts students can borrow in both subsidized and unsubsidized Stafford Loans (individually or in combination). Because students cannot borrow more than the cost of attendance minus the amount of any Pell Grant they are eligible for and/or any other financial aid they will get, the amount they actually receive may be less than the annual maximum amounts.

The interest rate on Stafford Loans is variable (adjusted annually) but will never exceed 8.25%. The rate is determined based on the 91-day T-bill rate plus 1.7% during the time the student is in school. A 0.6%

increase is added upon graduation. Students who have loans outstanding are notified any time there is a rate change.

After students graduate, leave school, or drop below half-time enrollment, they have a six-month grace period before they must begin repayment. During this period, borrowers will receive information about repayment and will be notified of the date repayment begins. However, borrowers are responsible for beginning repayment on time, even if they do not receive this information. Payments are usually due monthly.

Most states also have ***subsidized state loan programs*** similar to the federal loan programs. To qualify, students typically must (1) demonstrate need, (2) be a resident of the state, and (3) attend a state college or university.

Parental Loans for Undergraduate Students (PLUS) to meet students' education costs are available through both the FFEL and Direct Loan programs. Parents who have a good credit history can borrow a PLUS Loan to pay the education expenses of a child who is a dependent student enrolled at least half-time in an eligible program at an eligible school. These loans are available from most banks.

To be eligible to receive a PLUS Loan, parents generally will be required to pass a credit check. A parent cannot be turned down for having no credit history —only for having an adverse one. If parents do not pass the credit check, they might still be able to receive a loan if someone, such as a relative or friend who is able to pass the credit check, agrees to endorse the loan. An endorser promises to repay the loan if a student's parents fail to do so. Parents might also qualify for a loan even if they do not pass the credit check as long as they can demonstrate that extenuating circumstances exist. The student and the parents must also meet other general eligibility requirements for federal student financial aid.

The annual limit on a PLUS Loan is equal to the student's cost of attendance minus any other financial aid the student gets. If the cost of attendance is $10,000, for example, and a student receives $6,000 in other financial aid, the parents can borrow up to $4,000.

The student's school will receive the money in at least two installments. No single payment may exceed 50% of the loan amount. The school may require the parents to endorse a disbursement check and send it back to the school. The school will then apply the money to the student's tuition and fees, room and board, and other school charges. If any loan money remains, the parents will receive the amount as a check or in cash, unless they authorize that it be released to the student. Any remaining loan money must be used for education expenses.

The interest rate is variable, but will never exceed 9%. The rate is tied to the 52-week T-bill rate plus 3.1% and is adjusted each year of repayment.

Parents will be notified of interest rate changes throughout the life of the loan. Interest is charged on the loan from the date the first disbursement is made until the loan is paid off. Generally, the first payment is due within 50 days after the final loan disbursement for the year. There is no grace period on these loans. Interest begins to accumulate at the time the first disbursement is made, and parents will begin repaying both principal and interest while their child is in school.

A Stafford Loan or PLUS Loan *may* be canceled under any of the following conditions:

- The borrower dies (or the student on whose behalf a parent borrowed dies).
- The borrower becomes totally or permanently disabled.
- The loan is discharged in bankruptcy.
- The school closes before the student completes the program of study.
- The school falsely certifies the loan.

Even if a student does not complete the program of study at the school, does not like the school or the program of study, or does not obtain employment after completing the program of study, these loans must nonetheless be repaid. Neither type of loan (Stafford or PLUS) can be canceled for these reasons.

Repayment assistance (i.e., not a cancellation, but another way to repay) may be available if a student serves in the military. For more information, contact a recruiting officer.

Most colleges and universities have their own loan funds as well. The qualifying criteria are generally similar to those used for loans, although most schools use the funds to help attract top students as well, regardless of the family's financial need. For example, the Consortium on Financing Higher Education, which encompasses the Ivy League and other schools, provides annual loans of up to $15,000 for 15 years at a variable rate that floats 200 basis points (2%) above the prime rate.

Students who qualify as "independents" are rated for college aid without considering parents' income or assets and, therefore, are much more likely to qualify for subsidized loans. However, qualifying for independent status is not an easy affair. (See "Independent Student Status" below.)

If parents incur unexpected expenses or if their accumulated savings are less than anticipated, student loans combined with loans to parents may be good planning supplements. However, relying solely upon the future availability of loan programs as the centerpiece of a plan for financing education is risky. Careful consideration of alternative (or at least supplementary) planning vehicles will help insure a client's ability to finance a child's education.

See Figure 10.10 for a comparison of the federal loan programs.

Figure 10.10

FEDERAL LOAN PROGRAMS (as of 2007)					
	Subsidized/ unsubsidized	**Eligibility**	**Limits**	**Interest rate**	**Payback**
Direct and FFEL Stafford Loan	Subsidized	Financially needy student	• Dependent: Frsh: $3,500 Soph: $4,500 Jr/Sr: $5,500 • Independent: Frsh: $7,500 (max $3,500 subsidized) Soph: $8,500 (max $4,500 subsidized) Jr/Sr: $10,500 (max $5,500 subsidized) • Grad student: $20,500/year (only $8,500 subsidized)	91-day T-bill + 2.3 points; Cap: 8.25%	Six mos. after graduation, leaving school, or dropping below half-time enrollment
Direct and FFEL Stafford Loan	Unsubsidized	Student — Not awarded on basis of financial need	Same as subsidized Stafford loan	Same as subsidized Stafford loan	Same as subsidized Stafford loan
Direct and FFEL PLUS Loan	Unsubsidized	Creditworthy parent, co-signed, or extenuating circumstances	Up to the full cost of attendance less other financial aid	91-day T-bill + 3.1 points; Cap: 9%	Repayment begins 60 days after payment to college; interest-only option during college years
Federal Perkins Loan	Subsidized	Undergraduate and graduate students — with financial need	Undergrads: up to $4,000/yr.; $20,000 total Grads: up to $6,000/yr.; $40,000 total	5%	Nine months after graduation, leaving school, or dropping below half-time status $40,000 total

Deductions for Educational Expenses

Student Loan Interest Deduction

In an effort to promote higher education, Congress passed a number of education incentives in 1997. Among these were provisions that permit the deduction of student loan interest in certain circumstances. An individual who has paid interest on a "qualified education loan" may claim a deduction for such interest expenses under IRC Section 221. A "qualified education loan" is any indebtedness incurred by the taxpayer solely to pay "qualified higher education expenses" that are incurred on behalf of the taxpayer, the taxpayer's spouse or a dependent (as of the time the debt was incurred), that are paid or incurred within a reasonable period of time before or after the debt was incurred, and that are attributable to education furnished during a period during which the recipient was an "eligible student." However, a debt owed to a related person cannot be a qualified education loan. In contrast, a refinancing of a qualified education loan is treated as a qualified education loan.

"Qualified higher education" expenses are the cost of attendance at an "eligible education institution," reduced by the amount excluded under an educational assistance plan, qualified education bonds, or qualified tuition program distributions, and the amount of any scholarship, allowance, or payment excluded with respect to the Hope Scholarship and Lifetime Learning Credits. An "eligible education institution" is the same as for the Hope Scholarship and Lifetime Learning Credits, (above), but the term also includes an institution conducting an internship or residency program leading to a degree or certificate awarded by an institution of higher education, a hospital, or a health care facility that offers postgraduate training.

An "eligible student" is defined the same as for the Hope Scholarship and Lifetime Learning credits above. In addition, the following requirements apply:

- The deduction is taken "above-the-line" in computing adjusted gross income (AGI).
- All student loan interest including voluntary payments are now potentially deductible, without limitation as to the length of time the payments are required. (Under earlier law, the deduction was allowed only with respect to interest paid on a qualified education loan during *the first 60 months* in which interest payments were required.)
- No deduction is allowed to an individual if that individual is claimed as a dependent on another taxpayer's return for the taxable year.

The amount of the deduction is limited in two ways:

- First, the amount allowable cannot exceed $2,500.
- Second, for 2007, the maximum amount otherwise allowable as a deduction is reduced by the maximum amount deductible (according to the limits above) multiplied by the ratio that the excess of the taxpayer's "modified adjusted gross income" (MAGI) over $50,000 ($105,000 for married taxpayers filing jointly) bears to $15,000 ($30,000 for married taxpayers filing jointly). For these purposes, "modified adjusted gross income" is computed after applying the Social Security inclusion, moving expenses, and passive loss rules, but without regard to either the student loan interest deduction, the exclusion for amounts received in redemption of qualified education savings bonds, the exclusion for certain adoption expenses, the foreign earned income exclusion and foreign housing exclusion, and amounts excluded from certain United States possessions or Puerto Rico.
- The maximum deduction amount is *not* indexed for inflation; however the phaseout amounts listed above are indexed for inflation (rounded down to the next closest multiple of $5,000). As a result of this reduction based on MAGI, in 2007, for single taxpayers no deduction may be taken if MAGI exceeds $65,000 and the amount that may be deducted is reduced proportionately if MAGI is between $50,000 and $65,000. For married taxpayers filing a joint return in 2007, no deduction may be taken if MAGI exceeds $135,000, and the amount that may be deducted is reduced proportionately if MAGI is between $100,000 and $130,000. Married taxpayers filing separately may not take the deduction.

Certain eligible education institutions, or any person in a trade or business, or any governmental agency, that receives $600 or more in qualified education loan interest from an individual during a calendar year must provide an information report on such interest to the IRS and to the payor.

Given the limitations on deductibility, many parents may not qualify to deduct interest on educational loans or may not be able to deduct all of the interest they pay on such loans. One possible alternative is to use home equity loans to help finance college education expenses. Interest on home equity loans of up to $100,000 may be deductible regardless of how the proceeds are used. In many cases, this may be a more tax-effective and less costly means to finance college education expenses than various educational loan programs.

Higher Education Expense Deduction

For tax years 2004 through 2007, taxpayers can deduct up to $4,000 of college tuition and fees paid for them, their spouses, or any other persons claimed as a dependent on their returns. This is an "above-the-line" deduction, which means taxpayers do not have to itemize in order to take advantage of the break. However, the $4,000 amount is the annual maximum, regardless of how many students taxpayers may have in their families. The other ground rules are as follows:

- Taxpayers do not get the full deduction if they are unmarried with modified adjusted gross income above $65,000, or are joint filers with modified AGI above $130,000. However, if their modified AGI is between $65,001 and $80,000 for singles or between $130,001 and $160,000 for joint filers, they are entitled to a reduced deduction of up to $2,000. (The deduction is reduced ratably over the phase-out range).

- Taxpayers are completely ineligible if they are married and file separately from their spouses.

- Any taxpayer who can be claimed as a dependent on another taxpayer's returns is ineligible for the deduction. Thus, taxpayers' dependent college-age children cannot claim the deduction when the parents' own AGI is too high to qualify.

- Taxpayers may not claim a deduction for expenses paid with earnings from a Section 529 plan or withdrawals from a Coverdell Education Savings Account. Also, taxpayers cannot claim the deduction in the same year they claim the Hope Scholarship or Lifetime Learning tax credit for the same student.

- Unless extended once again by an act of Congress, the Higher Education Expense Deduction expires after 2007.

Deduction for Employment Related Education Expenses

A deduction for certain education expenses is generally allowed under IRC Section 162 if the education or training (1) maintains or improves a skill required in a trade or business currently engaged in by the taxpayer, or (2) meets the express requirement of the taxpayer's employer (or requirements of applicable law or regulations) imposed as a condition of continued employment. As a general rule, education expenses are not deductible if they relate to certain *minimum* educational requirements or to education or training that enables a taxpayer to begin working in a *new trade or business*. In the case of an employee, education expenses (if not reimbursed by the employer) may be claimed as an itemized deduction only if such expenses relate to the employee's current job, and only to the extent that the expenses, along with other miscellaneous deductions, exceed 2% of the taxpayer's adjusted gross income (AGI).

Cancellation of Certain Student Loans

In the case of an individual, gross income subject to federal income tax does not include any amount from the forgiveness (in whole or in part) of certain student loans, provided that the forgiveness is contingent on the student's working for a certain period of time in certain professions for a broad class of employers.

Student loans eligible for this special rule must be made to an individual to assist the individual in attending an educational institution that normally maintains a regular faculty and curriculum and normally has a regularly enrolled body of students in attendance at the place where its education and activities are regularly carried on. Loan proceeds may be used not only for tuition and required fees, but also to cover room and board expenses (in contrast to tax free scholarships under IRC Section 117, which are limited to tuition and required fees). In addition, the loan must be made by (1) the United States (or an instrumentality or agency thereof), (2) a state (or any political subdivision thereof), (3) certain tax-exempt public benefit corporations that control a state, county, or municipal hospital and whose employees have been deemed to be public employees under state law, or (4) an educational organization that originally received the funds from which the loan was made from the United States, a state, or a tax-exempt public benefit corporation. Thus, loans made with private, non-governmental funds are not qualifying student loans for purposes of the IRC Section 108(f) exclusion.

The exclusion is also available with respect to forgiveness of loans made by tax-exempt charitable organizations (e.g., educational organizations or private foundations) if the proceeds of such loans are used to pay costs of attendance at an educational institution or to refinance outstanding student loans and the student is not employed by the lender organization. Again, the exclusion applies only if the forgiveness is contingent on the student's working for a certain period of time in certain professions for any of a broad class of employers. In addition, in the case of loans made by tax-exempt charitable organizations, the student's work must fulfill a public service requirement. The student must work in an occupation or area with unmet needs and such work must be performed for or under the direction of a tax-exempt charitable organization or a governmental entity.

Children Working

Parents are widely divided on whether children should help to pay for their college education by working during the school year. Some parents believe that their children will appreciate their college education more and apply themselves more diligently to their college studies if they have to work to pay for part of their education. Other parents are concerned that work during the school year may distract children from their studies and adversely affect their performance. Should the parents favor children working during the college months? Some studies indicate that students who work up to 20 hours per week during the school year perform no worse, and in some cases perform better, than their colleagues who do not work during the school year.

Students who decide that their financial situation requires them to work during the school year to make ends meet may qualify for the Federal Work-Study (FWS) Program. The FWS Program provides part-time jobs for undergraduate and graduate students with financial need, allowing them to earn money to help pay education expenses. The program encourages community service work and work related to the recipient's course of study. FWS can help students get a foot in the door by allowing them to gain valuable experience in their chosen field before they leave school.

Students in the FWS Program are paid by the hour. No FWS student may be paid by commission or fee. The school must pay students directly at least once a month. Wages for the FWS program must equal at least the current federal minimum wage, but may be higher depending on the type of work the student does and the skills required. The total FWS award depends on when the student applies, financial need, and the funding level at the student's school. The amount FWS students can earn cannot exceed their total FWS award. When assigning work hours, the employer or financial aid administrator will consider the award amount, the student's class schedule, and the student's academic progress.

The jobs available under the FWS program are usually provided by the student's school or by private nonprofit organization or public agencies, and the work performed must be in the public interest. In some cases, a FWS student's school may also have agreements with private for-profit employers for FWS jobs. This type of job must be relevant to the student's course of study.

Parents are more likely to favor their children working during the summer months. The planner should advise the parents that the college aid formula used when awarding aid to students presumes that students will work during their summer vacations and will contribute that money to the payment of their college expenses.

Systematic Saving and Gifts

For most parents, careful and early planning is essential to financing their children's education. Tax benefits can be used to increase the efficiency of long-term savings. In addition to the value of long-term compounding over time, the client may find that shifting the ownership of dollars saved to the child (or to an entity taxed at the child's tax bracket) may increase the after-tax yield on the fund. The earlier the client implements a long-term savings plan, and the younger the child is at the time the savings program is undertaken, the longer the interest and dividends produced by the fund will be compounding. These factors in turn enhance the efficiency of the savings effort. Although tax law offers only minimal opportunities for income-shifting to lower tax bracket children, some very limited opportunities are available. For example, with the reduced rates (e.g., 5% in 2007 – see Chapter 27) on most long-term capital gains for taxpayers in the 15% or 10% income tax brackets, gifts of appreciated property to children may result in tax savings.[11] For details, see "Taxation of Children" and "Gifts of Appreciated Assets to Minors" later in this chapter.

The College Aid Formula

Unfortunately, shifting assets from a client to a child may have adverse consequences with respect to the child's eligibility for financial aid. As will be discussed in more detail below, a standard formula is used for all applicants for financial aid to determine what is called the "expected family contribution (EFC)." The federal formula approved by Congress to calculate the EFC is called the Federal Methodology (FM). The federal methodology is used to determine eligibility for federal funds. If a college or university relies on a different formula for awarding its own funds, that formula is called the Institutional Methodology (IM). Different colleges and universities may use different institutional methodologies.

The EFC is the sum of the expected student contribution (ESC) and the expected parental contribution (EPC):

EFC = ESC + EPC

The calculation of the expected student contribution may differ from school to school if they use the institutional methodology, but is generally 20% to 35% of the student's assets and 50% of the student's income above an income protection allowance of about $2,500 to $4,000. (For the 2007-2008 academic year, the federal methodology contribution formula is 50% of income above a $3,000 income protection allowance and 20% of the student's reported assets.)[12]

For example, a student who has $4,500 of income in 2006 and qualifying assets of $10,000 is applying for aid in the 2007-2008 academic year. According to the federal methodology, fifty percent of the student's income of $976 (the amount in excess of the student's adjustments of $3,524, including a $3,000 income protection allowance), or $488, and $2,000 of the student's assets (20% of $10,000), or $2,488 total, will be treated as available to pay college education expenses when computing the student's aid package for the 2007-2008 academic year.

The federal methodology computes the expected parental contribution (EPC) in essentially the same way as the ESC with some addition adjustments to account for the number of parents with earned income, their income and assets, the age of the older parent, the family size, and the number of family members enrolled in post-secondary education. Income for this purpose includes not just the taxable income from the parents' tax return, but also nontaxable income such as Social Security benefits and child support. Home equity is not included in calculating the expected family contribution (EFC) under the federal methodology, but many private schools and universities include the parents' home equity when computing the aid formula using the institutional methodology as a way of rationing their school's own grant and scholarship funds. Money set aside in retirement plans such as a 401(k)s, IRAs, Keoghs, or 403(b)s are usually not counted as an asset. However, the funds contributed to a tax-deferred retirement program during the previous year must be included on the official financial aid form (FAFSA) as "other untaxed income." In addition, an asset protection allowance shelters a portion of the assets from the calculation of the parental contribution. The asset protection allowance increases with the age of the parents to allow for emergencies and retirement needs.

To illustrate using the federal methodology, assume the value of the parents' qualifying assets is $75,000, their income for this purpose is $50,000, they have three children, two of which are currently students in college, the oldest parent is age 55, and they are residents of Ohio. In this case, for the 2007-2008 award year, the parents' education savings and asset protection allowance is $55,900, so $19,100 ($75,000 - $55,900) of their assets enter the formula. At their ages and in their family circumstances, their total adjustments to income are $26,835, so $23,165 ($50,000 - $26,835) of income enters the formula. The amount of their expected contribution is computed by first adding 12% of their asset contribution, or $2,292 ($19,100 x 0.12), to their $23,165 income contribution, to derive an "adjusted available income" amount (AAI) of $25,457. Then they look up their AAI in a table, similar to a tax table, to determine the expected parental contribution. In this case, the parents' total expected contribution is $6,677.

Assuming both of the colleges that the two children attend employ the federal methodology, the parents would be expected to contribute $3,338 ($6,677 / 2) for each child.

Low-income families are most likely to qualify for aid, but even families with incomes in excess of $70,000 or even $100,000 may qualify, depending on circumstances. Do not arbitrarily assume children will not qualify for aid if a client's income is substantial—a family's income is only one factor in determining who receives aid. The parents' real estate assets, investments, and savings (and, in some cases, home equity, if the college employs the institutional methodology) are all counted when determining the parents' contribution.

The family financial burdens, such as medical bills, the size of the family, the number of children in private schools or colleges, and the years until the parents expect to retire may all reduce the required parental contribution amount. In addition, the larger is a student's income and savings, the smaller is the aid award—all else being equal.

Planning Tips for Reducing the EFC

There are several consequences of the structure of the needs analysis formula that are worth noting.

If a child is unlikely to qualify for aid, the family may be able to successfully employ income-shifting techniques to help accumulate funds for education (but see the discussion below regarding "Taxation of Children"). However, if a child would otherwise qualify for aid in the absence of income shifting and asset shifting to the child, employing income-shifting techniques may be counter-productive and parents would often do better accumulating funds themselves.

The obvious disincentives of the formulas for computing the expected family contribution put parents in a "Catch-22" position. Lower-income parents who are conscientious and thrifty may be less likely to receive aid than higher income, but more profligate parents. In addition, the assets and income of parents are "taxed" by the federal methodology need analysis formula at a much lower rate than those of the student. This means that it may not be to the advantage of the parties to shift income and assets to their children, despite potential income tax savings.

For example, parents who have managed to save $50,000 might be expected to contribute about $2,400 of it to help pay for a child's college expenses when the college works out the aid package for the child. If these assets had been transferred to the child, in general, at least $10,000 (20%), or $7,600 more than if the parents owned the assets, would be used when computing the child's aid award. Although a family's financial status is equal in either case, the aid award from the college will be considerably smaller when the assets are owned by the child.

Generally, after application of the federal methodology aid formulas, the practical effect is that no more than about 5.6% of a parent's assets (above an educational savings and asset allowance and excluding their home equity and retirement programs) are expected to be used for the child's educational costs. For virtually all parents, the first $40,000 to $50,000 of their assets (depending on their age and family size) will be ignored completely (sheltered by the asset protection allowance) in the federal methodology needs analysis formula.

Since the student's assets are "taxed" at a much higher rate than the parents' assets, the family should spend down the student's assets before using any of the parents' assets to pay for the student's education. Otherwise, the student's assets will again be subject to the high "tax" rate during the next year's needs analysis. Just because the formulas assumes that students contribute at least 20% of their assets and parents only about 5.6% does not mean that a client must treat those percentages as targets.

The federal aid methodology divides the parents' contribution by the number of children in college to determine the parents' contribution for each child. Changes in the number of family members in college can significantly affect the amount of aid received. For example, even families that are well off may become eligible for financial aid when two or more children are enrolled in college at the same time. So parents should not assume that they are ineligible for aid just because they earn a sizeable income.

The financial aid award or "package" for a given academic year is based on the assets and earnings for the calendar year *before* the academic year. For example, the financial aid award for the 2007-2008 academic year is based on the parents and student assets and earnings in 2006. So parents should be careful about their financial activity the year before their children enter college. For example, parents who avoid creating or recognizing capital gains during the child's senior year in high school will be at an advantage in the federal methodology need analysis system.

If the parents' income varies substantially from year to year, they should try to rearrange income fluctuations in their favor. For example they should try to defer income from the base year for determining aid to the next year. Also they should try to defer deductions from the year prior to the base year, or accelerate deductions from the year after the base year to the base year.

Business property is not treated in the same manner as the primary residence (which is only considered, in some instances, when schools use the institutional methodology, not the federal methodology) or any other real estate holdings in the needs analysis. If part of the primary residence is used for business purposes, be sure to indicate it on the financial statement.

Consumer debt (e.g., car payments, credit card payments, payments on personal notes, and so on) is not counted in the federal methodology needs analysis formula, but may or may not count in part, for exceptional items, in the institutional methodology However, home equity loans do reduce the home equity reported in the needs analysis when colleges use the institutional methodology. Therefore, using home equity loans to replace other consumer debt will sometimes lower the family assets in the institutional needs analysis formula and increase the potential aid award.

Parents should consider making any large, planned purchases in cash to reduce liquid assets immediately before filling out the financial aid forms. For example, if your client has been planning on buying a new car or making home improvements, he should be advised to pay for it using up liquid assets (savings) prior to filling out the form. The decreased savings reduce the family asset value and, thus, the expected parental contribution.

Clients should maximize elective deferrals to company-sponsored savings plans such as 401(k) plans or tax-deferred annuity plans (for clients who are employees of non-profit institutions). These retirement assets do not count as available assets on the needs analysis forms.

Additionally, tax-deferred investments such as single-pay life, whole life, variable life, and universal life insurance and annuities do not count as available assets in the needs analysis formula. This makes these instruments especially attractive investment vehicles if one is trying to maximize the potential financial aid award.

Independent Student Status

As noted earlier, students who qualify as independents are rated for college aid without including their parent's income or assets. This status may benefit some students who would otherwise not qualify to receive aid.

Students are considered independent if they meet any of the following criteria:

1. They will be 24 years old by December 31 of the award year, even if they are still living at home.
2. They are orphans or wards of the state.
3. They are armed forces veterans.
4. They have legal dependents other than a spouse.
5. They are graduate students or students at professional schools and will not be claimed as a dependent by their parents for the first calendar year of the award year.
6. They are married and will not be claimed as a dependent by their parents for the first calendar year of the award year.

The school may ask students who claim to be independent to submit proof before they can receive any federal student aid. Students who think they have unusual circumstances (other than one of those conditions listed above) that would qualify them as independent students may talk to their school's aid administrator. Aid administrators can change a student's status if they think a student's circumstances warrant it based on the documentation provided. But remember, aid administrators will not automatically do this. The decisions are based on the aid administrators' judgments, and they are final—students cannot appeal the aid administrators' decisions to the U.S. Department of Education.

Income-Shifting Techniques

Before the reach of the "kiddie tax" was broadened to include 18-year olds and students under age 24, parents and their student/children could often optimize their education funding by shifting income and assets and accumulating funds in a tax-advantaged way. Under the expanded kiddie tax rules, most of these opportunities are now all but extinct.

Taxation of Children

The Small Business and Work Opportunity Tax Act of 2007 (SBWOTA 2007) broadens the scope of the kiddie tax. This following discussion explains the broadened kiddie tax and the planning parents and students can undertake to blunt its impact.

Pre-SBWOTA 2007 "kiddie tax" rules. A child subject to the kiddie tax pays tax at his or her parents' highest marginal rate on the child's unearned income over $1,700 (for 2007) if that tax is higher than the tax the child would otherwise pay on it.[13] The parents can instead elect to include on their own return the child's gross income in excess of $1,700 (for 2007).[14]

A child is subject to the kiddie if he or she has not attained age 18 before the close of the tax year; either parent of the child is alive at the end of the tax year; and the child does not file a joint return for the tax year.[15]

"Kiddie tax" broadened under SBWOTA 2007. For tax years beginning after May 25, 2007, SBWOTA 2007 expands the "kiddie tax" rules to apply to children age 18, and children over age 18 but under age 24 who are full-time students—*if* their earned income does not exceed one-half of the amount of their support.[16]

Therefore, SBWOTA 2007 does not change the kiddie tax rules for children who are under age 18. Rather, it expands the kiddie tax to apply where the child:

- turns age 18, or turns age 19-23 if a full-time student, before the close of the tax year;

- has earned income for the tax year that does not exceed one-half of his or her support;

- has more than the inflation-adjusted prescribed amount of unearned income (i.e., $1,700, as further adjusted for inflation for the applicable tax year);

The other factors still apply—that is, the child has at least one living parent at the close of the tax year, and the child does not file a joint return for the tax year.

The expansion of the kiddie tax rules is an attempt by Congress to curtail a strategy some wealthy (and some moderate-income) parents were previously advised to use to take advantage of a beneficial feature of the long-term capital gains rates—a feature that is scheduled to become even more beneficial in 2008.

Specifically, this year (2007) the top tax rate on "adjusted net capital gain"—i.e., most long-term capital gains and corporate dividends—is 15%. But to the extent a taxpayer's adjusted net capital gain would otherwise be taxed in the two lowest income tax brackets—i.e., the 10% and 15% brackets—it's taxed at 5% for 2007, and 0% for 2008 through 2010. Some families sought to benefit from these rates by giving appreciated stock, mutual-fund shares, and other securities to their low-income, young-adult children who (if no longer subject to the kiddie tax rules and if in one of the two lowest tax brackets) could then sell the securities tax-free in 2008, 2009, and 2010. The new law changes will eliminate the opportunity to do this in many cases. However, if the earned incomes of children over age 18, or age 19-23 if a full-time students, exceeds one-half their support, the kiddie tax rules will not apply and he or she may be able to take advantage of the 0% capital gains rate in years 2008 through 2010.

The kiddie tax changes also can have a negative impact on families that did not engage in transfers of capital assets to children. Because earned income is always taxed at the child's tax rates, one way of providing a child with income without triggering increased tax liability under the kiddie tax rules is to employ the child (at reasonable compensation) in, for example, a trade or business owned by the parent. Computer literate children, for example, could help with a variety of tasks. As a result, the child's earnings will not be subject to the kiddie tax and will generate a deduction for the family business (assuming the wages are reasonable for the work actually performed). As an added bonus, this could help to avoid the kiddie tax on unearned income of a child age 18 or age 19 through age 23 if a full-time student.

For purposes of the kiddie tax, support is defined the same as it is for the dependency deduction requirement that a qualifying child not provide more than one-half of his or her own support for the tax year. However, any scholarships received by a student for study at an educational organization[17] are excluded in determining the total support paid for the student for the tax year.[18]

Consequently, because of the changes under SBWOTA 2007, any planned transfers of income-generating stocks, bonds, and other investments to children age 18, or those age 19-23 who are full-time students, must be reconsidered or postponed to eliminate or decrease the child's unearned income.

Although the opportunity to lower taxes by transferring income-producing assets to children age 18, or children age 19-23 who are full-time students, is curtailed by the kiddie tax rules, investing a child's funds in investments that produce little or no current taxable income, can help avoid the kiddie tax. These investments include, for example, stocks and mutual funds oriented toward capital growth that produce little or no current income; vacant land expected to appreciate in value; stock in a closely-held family business that pays little or no cash dividends; tax-exempt municipal bonds and bond funds; and United States series EE savings bonds for which interest reporting may be deferred.

Investments that produce no taxable income, and that are therefore not subject to the kiddie tax, also include tax-advantaged savings vehicles, such as, traditional and Roth IRAs (which the child, or the parents acting for the benefit of the child, can establish or contribute to if the child has earned income); qualified tuition programs ("529 plans"); and Coverdell education savings accounts ("CESAs").

Under the kiddie tax rules, a parent can elect (on Form 8814) to include in the parent's gross income for the tax year the child's gross income in excess of $1,700 (for 2007) if certain requirements are met. Doing so avoids the need to file a separate return for the child, and except where the child can claim certain deductions the electing parent cannot (see below), the tax on the child's income will generally be the same whether the parent elects to report the income or the child files a separate return. However, whenever parents make the election, they should consider that the addition of the child's income to the parents' adjusted gross income (AGI) may affect the various floors and ceilings for, and thus the amount of, the parents' deductions.

In addition, an electing parent cannot take certain deductions that the children could take on their own returns absent the parents' election—for example, the children's itemized deductions such as the children's investment expenses or charitable contributions. Therefore, whenever a child can claim any of these deductions, the parents should evaluate whether they may save taxes overall if the child files a separate return.

Taxation of Trusts

Trusts are required to use a calendar year for tax purposes; however, tax-exempt and charitable trusts are exceptions to this rule.

For tax years beginning in 2007, the indexed tax rate brackets for trusts are: 15% on the first $2,150 of taxable income; 25% on taxable income between $2,150 and $5,000; 28% on taxable income between $5,000 and $7,650; 33% on taxable income between $7,650 and $10,450; and 35% on taxable income over $10,450.[19]

The 2% floor on miscellaneous itemized deductions applies to trusts and estates as well as to individuals.

Quarterly payments of estimated tax are required of trusts in the same manner as they are of individual taxpayers.

The combination of the compressed trust tax rate schedule for undistributed trust income, the kiddie tax rules for distributions of trust income to children under the age of 19 (or under age 24, if a full-time student), and the college aid formulas that apply a "tax" (contribution) rate on assets held by children at a minimum rate of 20% as compared to an effective average parental asset "tax" (contribution) rate of about 5.6% has essentially eliminated the opportunity for the effective use of trusts for income and asset shifting to children for college funding purposes. Parents may still use trusts effectively for other financial planning purposes or special cases (such as in the case of divorce, special needs for children, and the like) that may include funding for a child's education among their other support objectives, but these are uses beyond the scope of this discussion of college education funding.

Taxation of Fellowships and Scholarships

Scholarships and fellowship grants of degree candidates are excludable from gross income only to the extent spent on tuition and course-related expenses. Any portion of the money that pays for room and board and other non-education costs is taxable. Also, IRS rulings require scholarships that are awarded to students who have teaching, research, or other responsibilities associated with the grant to be allocated between the "service" portion and the scholarship portion. The portion of a grant or scholarship allocated to service is considered taxable income to the student. Non-degree candidates receive no exclusion.

Income-Shifting and Parents' Support Obligation

Advisers should not recommend the use of income shifting techniques to help fund a child's education without some consideration of the tax impact such techniques may have as a result of a parent's support obligations. As a general rule, if resources are used to satisfy the parent's legal obligation to support a child, the parent, not the child, is subject to tax on the income. While the basic concept is easily understood, this issue has long been a subject with unknown boundaries. The principal question is whether or not a parent's legal obligation to support a child includes the obligation to pay for a child's college education.

The implication of the applicable case law is generally that in states where a college education is considered a normal support obligation of the parents, funds that parents have transferred to a child are the child's money. Therefore, the child does not have to use those assets to pay college expenses even though the parents gave the child the money with the express purpose of having the child use it to fund the child's college education! In other words, using non-parental funds to pay the normal support obligations of the parents (including paying college education expenses) in states that extend the support obligation to college education is a breach of parents' fiduciary duty. Such breaches could result in fines and penalties and would normally require that the parents make complete restitution. In addition, custodial funds used to pay college expenses would be taxable to the parents in a state where the parents have an obligation of support that extends to college education.

In general, the courts have considered a number of factors (e.g., the parents' means, ability to pay, and station in life) in determining whether a college education is a normal support obligation. If, after assessing a client's financial status, college financing needs, and their parental support obligation in their state, it appears that income and asset shifting may serve their purposes, advisers and parents should consider the tools and techniques that are still available in light of the expanded kiddie tax rules described in this chapter.

Gifts to Minors

The most direct method of giving funds to children is making gifts under the Uniform Gifts to Minors Act (UGMA) or under the Uniform Transfers to Minors Act (UTMA).

A gift to an UGMA or UTMA account (generally called a "custodial account") usually qualifies for the annual gift tax exclusion. The gift is completed by opening an account and transferring property to a custodian for the benefit of the minor child. Specially drafted legal documents are usually not required. The types of assets that can be transferred to a custodial account are defined by state law. In some states, the asset categories are limited to money, securities, and insurance policies. Other states have expanded the list to include real estate, partnership interests, and other investment properties. The trend has been toward a broader definition of eligible investments for custodial accounts.

The custodian of the custodial account has general investment powers over the account and has discretion to apply the principal and income in the account for the benefit of the minor. The property placed in a custodial account vests immediately and irrevocably in the minor at the time of transfer. Also, the entire principal and income of the custodial account must be delivered to the minor when the custodianship ends (typically at age 18 or 21). If the minor dies during the custodianship, the balance in the account must be delivered to the minor's estate.

The income from a custodial account is taxed to the minor *unless*, and to the extent that, the income is used to discharge a legal obligation of another person, in which case the income is taxed to that other person. If, for example, the funds are used to meet the parent's legal obligation to support the minor, the income will be taxed to the parent.

The major advantages of the custodial account are its

1. simplicity;
2. low cost; and
3. ease of administration.

The possible disadvantages include

1. loss of parental control over assets;
2. inflexible distribution requirements at termination of custodianship;
3. questions about education as a "support" item;
4. the prospect of the child receiving more money than he is capable of managing (or willing to apply toward the intended purposes); and
5. the revised "kiddie tax" rules, which reduce or eliminate tax savings.

In light of the kiddie tax rules being expanded to include full-time students under age 24, the benefits of this asset and income-shifting technique for education funding purposes are now significantly reduced. The parents can shelter from their higher tax rates only the first $1,700 (in 2007) of unearned income per year transferred to each child through the gifting of income-producing assets. Assuming the assets can earn 5% interest, this means that parents could transfer up to about $34,000 worth of assets to each child before the earnings would become subject to tax at the parents' rather than the child's rates.

However, for the families that might consider shifting assets to children for education funding—that is, those who are well-enough off that they would not expect to qualify for financial aid—the effort hardly seems worth the trouble. The maximum tax savings the family would enjoy by shifting the assets to a child is only $595 per year if the parents are in the 35% bracket and the child is effectively in the 0% percent bracket. Furthermore, once money is given to an UGMA or UTMA account, the money technically belongs to the child and so parents have no assurance that these monies will, in fact, be used for education funding.

However, if parents decide it is still advisable to use a custodial account, the types of assets that are placed in a custodial account can have a significant effect on the tax benefits. If a child is a full-time student under age 24 and, therefore, subject to the kiddie-tax rules, the parents could at least partially fund the custodial account with tax-free, tax-deferred, or low-income/high-appreciation investments in order to postpone realization of excess taxable income until the child attains age 24. Such investments include:

- Series EE savings bonds;
- zero-coupon municipal bonds;
- tax-deferred annuities;
- single-premium life insurance;
- growth stocks;
- stocks in a closely held business;
- land; and
- other growth-oriented assets that do not produce significant current income.

Gifts of Appreciated Assets to Minors

Gifts of appreciated assets to minor children have limited use for tax-favored college education funding because of the expanded kiddie tax rules.

However, in some circumstances such gifts might be a means to provide tax savings on the recognition of gains, but only if the (dependent) children recognize the gains after they become age 19, or, if students, the earlier of when they are no longer students or they become age 24. The one planning opportunity still available for such gifts in the college funding context is as a means to pay off debt incurred to pay college expenses. For example, assume that the parents, instead of liquidating appreciated assets to pay a child's college expenses, transfer appreciated assets to the child which the child then uses, in part, as collateral for loans to pay the college expenses. Assume the student incurs secured and unsecured debt of $20,000 for college expenses by the time the child graduates from college. Assume, for illustration, that the value of the gifted assets is $20,745 after the child finishes school and that the transferred assets had a basis of $5,000 when transferred. Under current (2007) tax rules, the gain would be taxed at a 15% rate if owned by the parents but, at most, at a 5% rate if owned by the child (assuming the child is in the 10% or 15% federal income tax bracket). The tax savings is computed as follows:

Taxable Gain Transferred from Parent to Child

Market Value	$ 20,745
Less Cost	(5,000)
Gain	$ 15,745
Parents' capital gain tax rate	x 0.15
Parents tax	$ 2,362
Child's tax cost	
Taxable gain	$ 15,745
Less dependent's deduction	(850)
Taxable income	$ 14,895
Child's tax rate	x 0.05
Child's tax	$ 745
Family Tax Savings	$ 1,617

So the tax savings in this case is about $1,617 and the actual economic savings are these tax savings less whatever interest was paid to carry the loans until the assets were liquidated to pay off the debt. The gift of appreciated property qualifies for the $12,000 (in 2007, $24,000 for split-gifts) gift tax annual exclusion and the parent's holding period and basis carries over to the child.

Interest-Free Loans and Below-Market Interest Loans

Below-market loans, interest-free or low-interest "demand" loans (i.e., loans that may be called at any time by the lender) are treated as follows: the lender (parent) is deemed to have made a loan to the borrower (child) at the "applicable federal rate" (a rate that is established and published monthly by the IRS). At the end of the calendar year, the child is deemed to have paid the parent interest at a rate equal to the applicable federal rate; therefore, the parent has interest income as if the imputed interest had been paid. The parent is then deemed to have made a gift to the child in the amount of that interest. The interest deemed to have been paid by the child will be subject to the general limitations on deductions of interest.

The imputed interest rules were devised to prevent income-splitting, but there are certain limited exceptions. The first exception to the general rule applies if the total amount of outstanding loans to a child does not exceed $10,000. However, if the loan is directly attributable to the purchase or carrying of income-producing assets, the rules do apply. What this means is that if the loan proceeds are invested in income-producing assets or placed in a savings account, the $10,000 exception will not apply.

The second exception allows a loan of up to $100,000 to escape the rules as long as the child's net investment income (from all sources) for the year does not exceed $1,000. If the child's net investment income does exceed $1,000, the amount of interest treated as being transferred is limited to the amount of the child's net investment income.

The application of the $10,000 exception depends on how the specific funds are spent; in contrast, the application of the $100,000 exception depends on how much investment income the child has. The following examples illustrate these rules:

Example 1: Assume that a father makes a loan of $10,000 to his son who has net investment income of $2,000. The son uses the loan to pay tuition. Assuming the principal purpose of the loan is not tax avoidance, the imputed interest rules do not apply because the loan qualifies under the $10,000 de minimis exception. However, if the son had placed the $10,000 in a savings account, the interest would have to be imputed.

Example 2: Assume that a mother makes a $100,000 loan to her son who has no investment income. The son uses the money to buy a house. The imputed interest rules do not apply and the loan qualifies under the $100,000 exception. But, if the son had $5,000 of investment income that year, the imputed interest rules would apply. However, the imputed interest would be limited to the amount of net investment income, $5,000.

The Family Partnership

A gift to children of an interest in a family partnership can also be an income-splitting device. The tax savings are limited, however, by the kiddie tax rules for children under age 19, or age 24, if they are students. If the child is age 19 or older and not a student, or age 24 or older, the income will be taxed at the child's tax rate.

In addition to the limitations imposed by the kiddie tax rules, several other potential pitfalls may arise when using family partnerships for family income shifting:

1. In most cases, children will not be recognized as partners unless it can be shown that the children are competent to manage their own affairs. Consequently, partnership interests owned by minors should generally be held in trust or in an UGMA account with an independent custodian.

2. Many states recognize a trust as a legal partner, but there are some that do not.

3. If the partnership interest is given to the trust by the parent, an independent trustee relationship should be established.

4. Control by the parent in any form can jeopardize recognition of the partnership interest.

5. If the trust for the children receives its partnership interest by gift and does not contribute any services, capital must be a significant factor in producing the income of the partnership in order for the Internal Revenue Service to recognize the children's partnership interest.

6. A child's interest in a personal service partnership (i.e., one in which most of the income is generated by commissions and fees) is generally not recognized by the Internal Revenue Service. This is because the partnership would be unable to satisfy the IRS requirement that capital be a significant income-producing factor.

S Corporations

A family-owned S corporation can be used to shift income to children in much the same way that a family partnership can. In contrast with the family partnership, S corporation stock can be owned even if capital is not a significant income-producing factor. However, this is not true in the case of a professional corporation electing S corporation treatment; shares cannot be transferred to a family member who is not licensed if the shareholders must be professionally licensed under state law to hold shares. For example, a doctor's stock in her medical S corporation cannot be transferred to her minor daughter or to a trust for her benefit, even if it were a trust that could otherwise hold S corporation stock.

Income-shifting and income-splitting may be accomplished by transferring S corporation shares to children because the tax treatment of S corporations resembles that of a partnership. Income, losses, deductions, and credits are passed through to the shareholders and are reported on the shareholder's individual returns. However, note that the "kiddie tax" rules apply to S corporation income. Therefore, the benefits of income-splitting will be limited unless the child has attained age 19, or is a student, age 24. (But planners should keep in mind estate tax and other advantages).

In most cases, children will not be providing significant services to the corporation. However, children may be employed by the corporation to perform services commensurate with their age and abilities. Consequently, an S corporation can be used to shift income in two ways: (1) through payment for services performed for the corporation; and (2) through distributions of profits to children who are shareholders. Given the limitations imposed by the kiddie tax on unearned income, payments for services provide the best income shifting opportunity by far.

In some cases it may be wise to use a custodial account or trust to hold the minor's stock. The use of a custodial account may be less complicated and less expensive, but does not provide for as much flexibility as a trust. In most states, the custodial arrangement ends at age 18, at which time the children take possession of the stock. At that point, the children may use the proceeds for any purpose they desire (which may or may not include paying for their college education).

If a trust is used to hold minor children's stock, the trust must be a Qualified Subchapter S Trust (QSST) or an Electing Small Business Trust (ESBT). What constitutes a QSST or ESBT is beyond this discussion. Generally, however, there are complex restrictions (e.g., how the trust can be structured, who can be a beneficiary, and how income can be distributed).

A QSST or ESBT is indicated when:

1. A parent does not want to give stock to a child outright.

2. A parent does not want the child to have ownership of the stock until he or she reaches a certain age.

3. Parents wish to distribute income on the stock to one beneficiary and later distribute the income and stock outright to another beneficiary when the trust terminates. (For example, the trust instrument could state that the income from the trust would go to the parent's child throughout his or her lifetime, and the remainder of the trust would go to a grandchild upon the child's death.)

Using the S corporation form for a family business, and transferring shares to children is especially suitable when the family may desire to transfer ownership of the business outright to the children at some later date, as well as providing income for a college education.

Employing Children

One of the best methods for shifting income to children is to employ them in a family-owned business. Employing children has a double tax benefit. First, income is shifted to the lower tax-bracket children and, second, the parent-employer receives a deduction for the amount paid in wages. The salary paid must be reasonable in relation to the services rendered, but the work performed need not be either significant or regular. For example, a child may be employed to clean the office, cut the grass, clear sidewalks of snow, perform maintenance or janitorial services, open the mail, make deliveries, or other similar tasks.

If the business is not incorporated, the services performed by a child under the age of 18 are excluded from Social Security coverage. The business may deduct the salary or wage payment, but avoid the added expense of Social Security taxes that would be required if the compensation were paid to unrelated employees.

A parent/business owner employing a child in the business may generally claim a dependency exemption for the child if (1) the parent/business owner furnishes more than one-half the child's support, and (2) the child is under 19 years of age, or is a full-time student under age 24. If the child is 24 years of age or older and a full-time student, the parent is not entitled to the dependency exemption unless the child earns less than the exemption amount ($3,300 in 2007).

A child who is a dependent may not claim any personal exemption, but is allowed to claim a standard deduction equal to the greater of (1) $850 (in 2007, as indexed) or (2) the sum of $300 and the dependent's earned income (up to the appropriate standard deduction limit, e.g., $5,350 for single taxpayers for 2007; thereafter, indexed for inflation). In other words, in 2007, a child with earned income pays zero tax on the first $5,350 of earned income. Therefore, by employing a child, the business owner in the 25% bracket (in 2007) will save $1,337.50 in taxes for the first $5,350 in wages paid to each child. On any compensation in excess of $5,350 paid, the business owner will save the difference in taxes between the child's low bracket amount and the parent's 25% bracket amount.

Children over 17 years of age can work any job, whether hazardous or not, for an unlimited number of hours. Under the Federal Fair Labor Standards Act, children aged 16 and 17 are restricted to nonhazardous jobs. They may work any type of nonhazardous job for an unlimited number of hours. If children are age 14 or

15, they may work no more than 3 hours on a school day and 18 hours in a school week, and are restricted to nonhazardous jobs. Fourteen is the minimum age for most non-farm work unless the child works for the parent in a nonhazardous job in a non-manufacturing business owned by the parent. In that situation there is no minimum age. Planners must also check state and city laws regarding employment of minors.

The Gift-Leaseback Technique

The Tax Court has approved the gift-leaseback technique as a legitimate means of reducing tax liability and shifting income. In the typical situation the taxpayer, such as a professional or perhaps a shareholder in a closely held corporation, establishes a trust for the children. Business property such as office buildings, furniture, equipment, autos, trucks, or machinery, is transferred to the trust, which agrees to lease it back to the taxpayer. The lease payments are then deductible by the high-bracket taxpayer and reported as income to the low-bracket trust beneficiaries (or to the trust if the income is accumulated).

If the children (the trust beneficiaries) have no other income, the first $850 (in 2007, as indexed) of the shifted income to each child is exempt from tax (because of the dependent's exemption). The next $850, regardless of age, is taxed at the child's tax rates. If the child is under age 19, or the child is a full-time student and under age 24, distributed income in excess of $1,700 is taxed at the parent's rates. This can be avoided by having the trust retain the income. If the child is 19 or over and not a student the distributed income is taxed at the child's rate. When the property is ultimately transferred to the income beneficiary (or the residual beneficiary, if different), gains on sales of assets are taxable to the beneficiary, not the grantor. The parent taxpayer will also continue to be entitled to a personal exemption for each dependent child who is at least 50% supported, so long as the dependency tests are met.

Investment Vehicles

The selection of an appropriate investment vehicle for college education funds depends on many factors, including the time until the funds are needed, whether the parent or child will be the owner of the asset, the client's attitudes towards risk and return, tax rates, and the like. Many clients are especially interested in investments that are particularly suitable for their children who are under age 19, or under age 24 and full-time students (and thus subject to the kiddie tax rules), and that provide tax advantages or certainty of value when college costs must be paid. The following sections briefly describe some of the investments that can meet these objectives.

Investments for Children Subject to the Kiddie Tax Rules; Investments for Tax Deferral

If funds are being transferred to a child subject to the kiddie tax rules, investments that minimize taxable income while providing relatively certain growth potential would be most suitable, since they will minimize the effect of the kiddie tax. Among those that the financial planner should consider are

1. *Variable and universal life insurance* – Inside buildup is tax-deferred or tax-free; a child may borrow cash value without paying tax on gains to pay college costs; secure.

2. *Zero coupon bonds* – Prior to JGTRRA 2003, some financial advisors favored zero coupon bonds (or "deep discount bonds") as a college savings vehicle because of their low cost, simplicity, and relative safety, despite the fact that taxes on the phantom income thrown off by these bonds is due and payable annually as the deemed interest accrues. Before JGTRRA was enacted, the rates on long-term capital gains (28%) were generally higher than the generally applicable ordinary income tax rate for children (15%) so bonds were viewed as being preferable to stocks.

   Under JGTRRA, "qualified" dividends and most long-term capital gains are generally taxed at 5% for children through the end of 2007 (and 0% in 2008 through 2010). On the other hand, ordinary interest income (including the "phantom" income thrown off by zero coupon bonds) is taxable at higher rates (i.e., 10% or 15% for most children). Because the tax rates "flip-flopped" when JGTRRA 2003 was enacted, zero coupon bonds are now generally less attractive as a college savings vehicle than they were prior to JGTRRA.

   In another JGTRRA-related development, some advisors now recommend shifting appreciated assets to children to take advantage of the existing capital gain rate differential between children (5% or 0%) and their parents (15%).

3. *Municipal bonds* – Interest is free of federal income tax and, in many cases, state income tax.

4. *High-growth, low-dividend stocks* – Tax on gain is deferred until recognized upon disposition. If leveraged, interest expense offsets dividend income (note that dividend income may be subject to lower income tax rates) and increases growth potential. In this way, leveraged growth stocks are similar to deep-discount bonds, except that there is much less certainty of value when the funds are needed for college. However, if there is at least 10 years until college begins, the risk/return potential is favorable as compared with bonds.

5. *High-growth, low-dividend stock mutual funds* – These funds are similar to high-growth, low-dividend stocks except that the leveraging possibilities are more limited and some capital gains must be recognized. The gains are subject to tax when the fund declares capital gains dividends each year.

6. *Series EE savings bonds* – Tax on accruing interest is deferred on savings bonds; high certainty of value. Some taxpayers may be able to exclude income used for college expenses, as described below.

Special Income Exclusion for Series EE and Series I Bonds

For Series EE bonds purchased after 1989 (and Series I bonds purchased after 1998), a parent who redeems these bonds—and pays certain education expenses of his child in the same year—may be entitled to exclude the accrued interest on the bonds. This exclusion is subject to the following limitations:

1. *Bond ownership requirement* – In order to qualify for the exclusion, the owner must have purchased the bonds after having attained the age of 24, and must be the sole owner of the bonds or own the bonds jointly with a spouse. The exclusion is not available to an individual who is the owner of a Series EE bond that was purchased by another individual, other than a spouse. For example, the exclusion is not available if a parent purchases a Series EE bond and puts the bond in the name of a child or another dependent. Also, the exclusion is not available for married taxpayers who do not file jointly. Furthermore, the exclusion is not available for any bonds that might be obtained as part of a tax-free rollover of matured Series E savings bonds into Series EE savings bonds.

2. *Qualified educational expenses* – Qualifying educational expenses include tuition and required fees for a taxpayer, or the taxpayer's spouse or dependents, net of scholarships, fellowships, employer provided educational assistance, and other tuition reduction amounts at an eligible educational institution. Such expenses do not include expenses with respect to any course or other education involving sports, games, hobbies, other than as part of a degree or certificate granting program.

3. *Limitation where redemption amount exceeds qualified expenses* – If the aggregate redemption amount (i.e., principal plus interest) of all Series EE and Series I bonds redeemed by the taxpayer during the taxable year does not exceed the amount of the student's qualified educational expenses, all interest for the year on the bonds is potentially excludable. For example, if the redemption amount is $10,000 ($5,000 each of principal and interest), and qualified educational expenses are $12,000, the entire $5,000 of interest may be excluded from income (subject to the phaseout described below). However, where the redemption amount exceeds the qualified educational expenses, the amount of excludable interest is reduced on a pro rata basis. For example, if the redemption amount is $10,000 ($5,000 each of principal and interest), and qualified educational expenses are $8,000, then the ratio of expenses to redemption amount is 80% ($8,000/$10,000) and $4,000 (5,000 x 0.80) of the interest may thus be excluded from income.

4. *Phaseout of exclusion where income exceeds certain amounts* – The exclusion is phased out for taxpayers with what is called "modified adjusted gross income" (MAGI) of $65,600 (in 2007; $98,400 for joint filers) or more for the taxable year. No amount is excludable for taxpayers whose MAGI exceeds $80,600 (in 2007; $128,400 for joint filers).[20]

Modified adjusted gross income (MAGI) is defined as the taxpayer's adjusted gross income for the taxable year including what would otherwise be excluded foreign earned income (or certain income of residents of Puerto Rico, Guam, American Samoa, or the Northern Mariana Islands), the partial inclusion of Social Security and Tier 1 Railroad Retirement benefits, the adjustments for contributions of retirement savings, and the adjustments with respect to limitations of passive activity losses and credits.

The amount that may be excluded when a taxpayer's MAGI falls within the phaseout range may be determined using the following formulas.

For singles and heads of households whose MAGI exceeds $65,600:

Adjusted Exclusion = Unadjusted Exclusion x [1 – (MAGI – $65,600) / $15,000]

For married taxpayers whose MAGI exceeds $ 98,400:

Adjusted Exclusion = Unadjusted Exclusion x [1 – (MAGI – $98,400) / $30,000]

Example 1: Assume a married taxpayer filing jointly who has a MAGI of $108,400 redeems bonds worth $12,000 ($6,000 principal and $6,000 interest) and pays qualified educational expenses of $13,000. The unadjusted exclusion is $6,000 because the qualified expenses exceed the redemption amount. Therefore, the adjusted exclusion computed using the formula shown above for married taxpayers is $4,000 [$6,000 x (1 - ($108,400 - $98,400) / $30,000)].

Example 2: Assume a single taxpayer who has a MAGI of $75,600 redeems bonds worth $12,000 ($6,000 each of principal and interest) and pays qualified educational expenses of $9,000. The unadjusted exclusion is 75% ($9,000 / $12,000) of $6,000, or $4,500. (Remember, if the redemption amount exceeds the qualified expenses, the amount of interest that is excludable is determined by multiplying the interest by the ratio of the total expenses to the total redemption amount.) Therefore, the adjusted exclusion using the formula shown above for single taxpayers is $1,500 [$4,500 x (1 - ($75,600 - $65,600) / $15,000)].

The phaseout levels are indexed annually for inflation; consequently, the phaseout will begin at higher nominal (but essentially the same real) level of income in future years.

Investments with Certainty in Reinvestment Rate or Return

One problem facing any accumulation program is the uncertainty regarding the rate that can be earned on reinvested income and, consequently, the uncertainty regarding the amount that will ultimately be accumulated by the target date. If your client wants certainty of value when the funds are needed to pay college expenses, the following investments should be considered:

1. *Zero-coupon bonds* – Zeros sell at a discount from face value and pay no cash interest. At maturity zeros pay their face value. Consequently, investors who hold the bonds to maturity are guaranteed that they will receive a rate of return equal to the original yield to maturity regardless of what happens to reinvestment rates over the term until the bond matures. However, most zero-coupon bonds are callable. Therefore, investors bear some risk. If the bonds are called before maturity, investors will not be able to reinvest the proceeds at a rate comparable to their original yield on the bonds.

2. *"Stripped "bonds* – "Stripped" bonds are artificially created zero-coupon bonds. These bonds are created by investment bankers who "strip" the coupons from the bond and sell the principal portion at a discount from face value. Strips are sometimes issued with "call protection," a guarantee against early redemption of the bonds that would force investors to reinvest the proceeds at potentially lower yields. The call protection feature is especially attractive on municipal bond strips since municipal bonds are generally much more likely to be called than taxable bonds.

3. *"Bunny" bonds* – These are bonds issued with rights to purchase additional bonds with the same coupon and terms as the original bond. Bunny bondholders may direct their coupon payments on the bonds to be used to purchase additional bonds, thus guaranteeing their reinvestment rate of return.

WHERE CAN I FIND OUT MORE?

1. *Applying for Financial Aid: A Guide for Students and Parents* (Iowa City, IA: American College Testing Program, Education Services Division, published annually).

2. Proia and Di Gaspari, *Barron's Handbook of American College Financial Aid* (Woodbury, NY: Barron's Educational Series, Inc., published annually).

3. Leider and Leider, *Don't Miss Out: the Ambitious Student's Guide to Financial Aid* (Alexandria, VA: Octameron Associates, updated annually).

4. Leider, *A's and B's of Academic Scholarships: 100,000 Scholarships for Top Students* (Alexandria, VA: Octameron Associates, updated annually).

5. Leider, *College Loans from Uncle Sam* (Alexandria, VA: Octameron Associates, updated annually).

6. Lyons, *How to Pay Your Way through College the Smart Way* (Putnam Pub. Group, 1984.)

7. *The Student Guide* – The Student Guide is published by the United States Department of Education and provides definitive information about federal aid programs, including Pell Grants, Federal Direct Loans, Federal Family Education Loans (FFEL), Federal Supplemental Educational Opportunity Grants (FSEOG), Federal Work-Study (FWS), and Federal Perkins Loans (Federal Student Aid Information Center, Washington D.C., annual). This publication can be viewed online at: www.ed.gov.

8. *Cash for College* and *Financial Aid: You Can Afford It* – The public page of the National Association of Student Financial Aid Administrators (NASFAA) includes the complete text of two publications for students and their families. The *Cash for College* (2001) pamphlet summarizes basic information about getting financial aid for college. The pamphlet *Financial Aid: You Can Afford It* (2002) provides an in depth overview of student financial aid. NASFAA, 1129 20th Street, NW, Washington, D.C., 20046; 202-785-0453; www.nasfaa.org.

9. *A Guide to Student Aid Programs and Application Procedures*: Published by the National Association of Student Financial Aid Administrators (NASFAA), 1129 20th Street, NW, Washington, D.C., 20046; 202-785-0453; www.nasfaa.org.

10. *Preparing Your Child for College: A Resource Book for Parents*: This is an online version of the publication by the United States Department of Education (www.ed.gov/pubs/Prepare). The publication talks about the benefits of a college education and how to prepare children for college educationally and financially. The topics include choosing a college, how much college will cost, how the parent will be able to afford it, the most common sources of financial aid, some ways to keep college costs down, setting up a long-range plan, and sources of further information. In addition, this booklet is available as a ZIP file for anonymous FTP, and also from the Consumer Information Center on their gopher. A paper copy may be ordered by calling 1-800-USA-LEARN (Washington D.C., 2002-2003).

11. *Websites* – A helpful list of websites that can assist in college planning can be found on The Vanguard Group website at: www.vanguard.com. An excellent website devoted to Section 529 plans may be found at www.savingforcollege.com.

CHAPTER ENDNOTES

1. The maximum Hope Scholarship Credit amount began at $1,500, but was indexed for inflation by adjusting the $1,000 amounts used to calculate the maximum credit, rounded to the next lowest multiple of $100. Thus, in the year in which the inflation adjustment reaches $1,100 (2007), the maximum credit rose to $1,650 ((100% x $1,100) + (50% x $1,100)).
2. Note, however, that transfers of income to children under age 18 (and older in certain cases) are now subject to the kiddie tax rules and so such income may continue to be taxed at the parents' higher tax rate.
3. Notice 97-60, 1997-2 CB 310, Sec. 3 Q&A-1.
4. Notice 97-60, 1997-2 CB 310, Sec. 6.
5. IRC Sec. 529.
6. Generally, the rules went into effect on January 1, 1998. However, the provision permitting QSTPs to be used to save for room and board expenses took effect August 20, 1996. Notice 97-60, 1997-2 CB 310, Sec. 6, Q&A-3.
7. IRC Sec. 529(c)(4)(C).
8. IRC Sec. 529(b)(3).
9. See list at www.ed.gov/admins/finaid/about/ac-smart/ state-programs06.html.
10. This program of study includes four years of English, three years of mathematics (including Algebra I and higher-level courses such as Algebra II, Geometry, or Data Analysis and Statistics), three years of science (including at least one year each of two of the following: biology, chemistry or physics), three years of social studies, and one year of a foreign language other than English.
11. Raising the age from under 14 to under 18 (and older in certain circumstances) with respect to the application of the "kiddie tax" greatly reduces any opportunities to save taxes by shifting investment income or capital gains from parents to children.
12. The federal methodology computes the student's contribution from income by starting with the student's taxable income; then (1) adding most other untaxed income and benefits received by the student; and (2) further adding to that any education credits claimed by the student, any child support paid, and any taxable earnings from need based employment programs, such as Federal

Work-Study and need based employment portions of fellowships and assistantships received by the student to derive the student's "Total Income" for aid purposes. Next, the federal methodology subtracts certain adjustments against income including any federal income tax the student paid on income, a state and other tax allowance, a Social Security tax allowance, an income protection allowance of $3,000, and an allowance if the parents' have a negative adjusted available income from the computation of their expected contribution under the federal methodology. The student's contribution from income is then equal to 50% of the difference between the student's total income and the student's total allowances.

The federal methodology computes the student's contribution from assets by starting with the student's cash, savings, and checking account balances and adding the net worth of the student's investments and the net worth of the student's business and/or investment farm, if any, and then multiplying this total net worth by 20%.

13. IRC Sec. 1(g).
14. IRC Sec. 1(g)(7).
15. IRC Sec. 1(g)(2)(A).
16. IRC Sec. 1(g)(2)(A), as amended by SBWOTA 2007.
17. As described in IRC Sec. 170(b)(1)(A)(ii).
18. IRC Sec. 1(g)(2)(A)(ii)(II).
19. IRC Sec. 1(i); Rev. Proc. 2006-53, 2006-48 IRB 996.
20. Rev. Proc. 2006-53, 2006-48 IRB 996.

Chapter 11

RETIREMENT ISSUES

WHAT IS IT?

Most workers have a dream – and that dream often involves not working anymore. Of course, they realize that not working comes at a cost. That check that magically appears in their bank account or mailbox every so often will suddenly stop.

Retirement planning, therefore, is essentially the process of making sure there will be enough assets accumulated that workers can afford to stop working at a given age and still live their desired lifestyle for the rest of their lives. The process should begin long before the anticipated retirement. Hopefully, you will never have a client come in and say, "I am retiring on Friday and I want to make sure that I have enough saved…"

At its core, retirement planning is nothing more than cash flow planning. Cash flow planning is making sure the money will be there when it is needed. Before retirement, decisions are made to spend or to save. Every dollar spent reduces the amount that will be available for retirement. After retirement, every dollar that is spent reduces the amount of time the nest egg will last. Of course, the goal of planning is not to stash the funds away, never to see the light of day again. It involves an understanding, or even an education, that decisions made now can have a dramatic impact on resources later.

Typically, retirement planning should begin at least 15 to 20 years before retirement. This will normally place the clients solidly in their most valuable years with the maximum potential for savings. Starting earlier is difficult beyond encouraging the contributions into the company retirement plan since you are dealing with workers who are seeing money for the first time, developing their personal lifestyle, and starting families.

Of course, by starting so far in advance of retirement, assumptions are going to be necessary. Anything planned will need to be reviewed and updated. Inflation, expected investment returns, salary, bonuses, job changes, college costs, etc. may all change during the years before retirement. Some of the factors that should be considered when making these assumptions are explained below, under "Sensitivity of Assumptions."

For more information on retirement planning, please consult Chapter 29 of this book, and our sister publication, *The Tools and Techniques of Employee Benefit and Retirement Planning.*

KEY STATISTICS

1. Retirees are living longer than ever. The average retiree can expect to live 20 to 25 years after retirement.

2. Fewer businesses are offering company-funded pensions. Therefore, most of the funds needed for retirement will need to come from the worker. This is putting a heavier emphasis on savings in advance of retirement – and most workers do not start the savings process until they are in their late-30's.

3. Despite the fact that Social Security benefits do not begin until age 62, at the earliest, most workers will have retired before they reach that age. However, with the recent economic uncertainties and fall in the stock markets, many retirees have headed back to the workforce.

4. The average savings rate in the U.S. is under 3% of disposable personal inocme.

HOW DOES THE RETIREMENT PLANNING PROCESS WORK?

Step 1: Evaluate the current situation – The planner needs to obtain accurate information about the client's current assets and liabilities, cash flow needs, and major expenditures or inflows expected in the future.

Be sure to understand everything about the client's employment benefits. What retirement plans exist? Are they permitted to contribute the maximum allowed under the law? Does the company match any contributions? Are there any benefits available for retirees? See Chapter 29 regarding how to obtain this information with respect to employer-funded plans.

Step 2: Determine retirement needs – It is impossible to predict what a client's spending level is going to be at retirement. The best approach for planning purposes is to ask the client, if they were to retire now, would their spending go up, down or stay the same. From there, you can apply an appropriate estimate of inflation to arrive at the projected retirement lifestyle. Figure 11.1 (found at the end of this chapter) can be used to accumulate client information and estimate the retirement need.

Example: A client needs $60,000 annually (in current dollars) in order to retire. If the client is 10 years from retirement, that need will grow to $88,814 assuming a 4% inflation rate. If inflation continues at 4%, and the client is able to earn an investment return of 7% (after-tax), the client will need $1,374,059 at his retirement date.

If the client has absolutely nothing saved when you are brought into the picture, he would need to save nearly $7,900 per month assuming he can achieve that same 7% return. Hopefully, that situation will not come up too often!

Step 3: Getting to retirement – The capital requirements needed for retirement will often seem daunting, if not downright unattainable. This is where the planner's strategy is developed and implemented.

It is hoped that the client will have hired you well in advance of retirement. This will allow for the periodic review of goals, needs, and resources to determine if the plan is still on track. Keep in mind that the overall plan should be reviewed whenever there is a life-changing event or major change in the tax law.

SENSITIVITY OF ASSUMPTIONS

As mentioned previously, financial planning is based in large part on assumptions that will be made about the future. Spending, inflation, and expected investment returns are only some of the factors that planners need to address when constructing a financial plan for a client.

How good are your assumptions? Time will tell, of course. Understanding how small changes in your assumptions affect long-range planning is an important aspect in explaining a plan to a client.

Let's consider inflation for a minute. A popular theme is that advances in technology are making things more affordable. But this isn't always the case. While it is true that a DVD player that was over $300 only a couple of years ago can be purchased for under $100 now, there is always a newer breed of technology that is commanding consumers' dollars. Look at the cost of televisions. You can spend as much or as little as you like. Technology has advanced to such a point that the older versions are being replaced by more expensive, powerful, and fancy models. Does that mean that your client needs to spend more? Not necessarily – but the lure of buying the bigger, better TV, for example is difficult to overcome. So, while advances in technology may bring down current prices of current models, those current models may become more difficult to find, own, and service as newer, more expensive models are continually being introduced to the public.

For retirees, inflation often doesn't have the same impact as it did when they were working. Most of their costs are more fixed, with the obvious exception of health insurance. The items that retirees tend to buy are not as impacted by inflation. Also, retirees tend to live further away from the big cities with the more inflated prices.

For example, Jack, a 65-year-old new retiree walks into your office with $2,000,000 of assets to support his retirement. He wants to know whether his assets will last for 20 years if he earns 6% after taxes. You look at him squarely in his eyes and say – "It depends…"

If you assume that inflation over the next 20 years will rise at 3% annually, Jack could spend $129,300 and have his money last. Jack breathes a sigh of relief and says – "That's good, I only spend $125,000 per year." However, if inflation rises to 5% per year, his annual lifestyle can be only $106,900 or else he will run out of money well in advance of his 20-year goal.

When dealing with expected returns on investments, most planners use a flat average annual rate of return. While this can work for simplicity's sake, do not overestimate this number – volatility, which is not considered in an assumed investment return, has a dramatic impact on the actual average rate of return.

Although the public has been educated by the media that volatility kills investment returns, it is rarely shown numerically. Consider the following. A planner uses a 10% average return in a client's financial plan. In five years, $100 grows to $161.05. Instead of assuming a flat 10% year-over-year return, what if the portfolio earned 20% in each of the first three years, then 5% in the fourth, but loses 15% in the fifth year. The "average" of those returns is still 10%, but the $100 only grows to $154.22.

Figure 11.2 shows other 10% average returns and the impact on the portfolio after 5 years. Obviously, if you extend the time period further, the impact is that much more dramatic.

The sensitivity of assumptions is clearly something that should be discussed with clients in order to allow for as complete an understanding of their financial plan as possible. Be conservative with your assumptions – that way, if things turn out better, you have other opportunities to plan in the future with more resources at your client's disposal. If you are too aggressive, the client may end up without the resources he expected and you will be unlikely to get a second chance to plan for your client's future.

THE NEAR-TERM OR TROUBLED RETIREMENT

As retirement approaches, many clients will have a sense or know that they do not have the funds to achieve their goals. This is where the tough decisions often need to be recommended to the clients.

Housing – Should the client consider downsizing his or her home in order to lower housing costs (real estate taxes, mortgage, utilities, etc.)?

Health care – What provisions have been made or can be made for health care during retirement? Does the client understand exactly what and how much is not covered by Medicare? How much does supplemental health insurance (Medigap) coverage cost? Have the clients made provisions for long-term care?

Pensions and Social Security – What options are available for pension payouts? Should Social Security benefits be started before "normal" retirement age?

Many workers under age 40 are not even counting on Social Security existing in its current form when they become eligible to collect. For many, the benefits received do not even begin to put a dent in their overall retirement need. However, for too large a percentage of the population, Social Security is the only method of forced savings they have – and, ultimately count on that check arriving each and every month.

Keep in mind that the younger you are, the older you need to be to collect your full Social Security benefit. For those who were born after 1938, normal retirement age is greater than age 65. If you were born after 1959, normal retirement age is age 67 (see Chapter 29 for details).

Figure 11.1

RETIREMENT PLANNING ASSET WORKSHEET

Date: ______________________________

Client's Name: ______________________________

Address: ______________________________

Telephone: (home) ____________________ (office) ____________________

Business Address: ______________________________

Spouse's Name: ______________________________

Business Address: ____________________ Telephone: ____________________

Figure 11.1 (cont'd)

RETIREMENT PLANNING ASSET WORKSHEET

ASSETS

Valuation as of date prepared unless otherwise indicated.

1. Cash and cash equivalents

	Value	Current Return (pretax)
a. checking accounts	______	______
b. saving accounts	______	______
c. money market accounts	______	______
d. life insurance cash values	______	______
Total Cash/Cash Equivalents	______	______

2. Retirement Plans
(Do not include defined benefit plans)

	Current Balance	Current Return (pretax)
a. IRA	______	______
b. Keogh	______	______
c. Section 401(k)	______	______
d. Section 403(b)	______	______
e. Other defined contribution	______	______
Total Retirement Plans	______	______

Figure 11.1 (cont'd)

3. Investments

(Do not include amounts included in 2 above)

	Fair Market Value	Adjusted Basis	Current Return (pretax)
a. Portfolio Investments			
(1) money market instruments			
certificate of deposit	______	______	______
T bills	______	______	______
commercial paper	______	______	______
(2) fixed-income securities			
U.S. government	______	______	______
U.S. agencies	______	______	______
municipal bonds	______	______	______
preferred stock	______	______	______
corporate bonds	______	______	______
notes receivable	______	______	______
(3) common stocks			
listed	______	______	______
OTC	______	______	______
restricted stock	______	______	______
(4) other portfolio Investments			
options	______	______	______
mutual funds	______	______	______
physical assets (collectibles)	______	______	______
b. Passsive Investments			
(1) direct participation investments	______	______	______
(2) real estate (passive)	______	______	______
c. Active Businesses			
(1) value of business owned and operated	______	______	______
(2) real estate (active participation)	______	______	______
Total Investments	______	______	______

Figure 11.1 (cont'd)

4. Personal Assets

	Fair Market Value	Adjusted Basis
a. primary residence		
b. other real estate		
c. household contents		
d. automobiles		
e. other		
Total Personal Assets		

LIABILITIES

1. Short-Term Liabilities

(12 months or less)

	Balance Outstanding	Interest Rate	Monthly Payment	Maturity Date
Consumer credit (credit card & open charge accounts)				
Personal notes payable				
Loans from life insurance policies				
Notes guaranteed				
Other				
Total				

2. Long-Term Liabilities

	Balance Outstanding	Interest Rate	Monthly Payment	Maturity Date
Mortgages on personal residences				
Loans against investment assets				
Loans against personal residences				
Total				

Figure 11.1 (cont'd)

3. Other

Deferred taxes	______	______	______	______
Alimony, child support, etc..	______	______	______	______
Judgements, etc..	______	______	______	______
Total	______			

SUMMARY

Assets (fair market value)

Total cash and cash equivalents	______	
Total retirement plans	______	
Total investments	______	
Total personal assets	______	
Total Assets		______

Liabilities (outstanding balances)

Short-term	______	
Long-term	______	
Other	______	
Total Liabilities		______

Figure 11.1 (cont'd)

RETIREMENT NEEDS WORKSHEET

Estimated Retirement Living Expenses and Required Capital (in current dollars)

	Per Month x 12 =	Per Year
1. Food	________	________
2. Housing:		
a. Rent/mortgage payment	________	________
b. Insurance (if not included in a.)	________	________
c. Property taxes (if not included in a.)	________	________
d. Utilities	________	________
e. Maintenance (if you own)	________	________
f. Management fee (if a condominium)	________	________
3. Clothing and Personal Care:		
a. Wife	________	________
b. Husband	________	________
c. Dependents	________	________
4. Medical Expenses:		
a. Doctor	________	________
b. Dentist	________	________
c. Medicines	________	________
d. Medical insurance to supplement Medicare	________	________
5. Transportation:		
a. Car payments	________	________
b. Gas	________	________
c. Insurance	________	________
d. License	________	________
e. Car maintenance (tires and repairs)	________	________
f. Other transportation	________	________
6. Recurring Expenses:		
a. Entertainment	________	________
b. Travel	________	________
c. Hobbies	________	________
d. Club fees and dues	________	________
e. Other	________	________
7. Insurance	________	________
8. Gifts and Contributions	________	________
9. Income Taxes (if any)	________	________

Figure 11.1 (cont'd)

10. Total Annual Expenses (current dollars)	________	$	________
11. Inflation Rate until Retirement (I)	________		
12. Total Years until Retirement (N)	________		
13. Inflation Adjustment Factor $(1 + I)^N$		x	________
14. Total Annual Expenses (future dollars)		=	________
15. Inflation Rate Postretirement (i)	________		
16. Aftertax Rate of Return (r)	________		
17. Anticipated Duration of Retirement (n)	________		
18. Inflation-Adjusted Discount Factor $a = \frac{1+i}{1+r}$			________
19. Capital Required at Retirement to Fund Retirement Living Expenses Amt line 14 x $\frac{1-a^n}{1-a}$		$	________
20. One-Time Expenses		+$	________
21. Total Capital Need at Retirement			=$ ________

Source: Robert J. Doyle, Jr., *Retirement Planning Handbook*, The American College, Bryn Mawr, PA.

Figure 11.2

Rate	Index	Rate	Index	Rate	Index	Rate	Index
	100.00		100.00		100.00		100.00
10%	110.00	20%	120.00	20%	120.00	-30%	70.00
10%	121.00	-20%	96.00	20%	144.00	-30%	49.00
10%	133.10	10%	105.60	20%	172.80	50%	73.50
10%	146.41	-5%	100.32	5%	181.44	50%	110.25
10%	161.05	45%	145.46	-15%	154.22	10%	121.28

Chapter 12

SPECIAL CIRCUMSTANCES

WHAT IS IT?

Because no two people are alike, it is safe to assume that no two financial planning situations are alike. We all handle our finances differently, even if we have the same job, make the same money, and have the same number of children. Financial planning is an inherently personal process and planners must make sure that they communicate this to the person or people sitting at the table. Every situation is unique.

Of course, some situations are "more" unique than others. Not every financial plan will be constructed around a husband, a wife, and two and a half children. According to the 2000 U.S. Census, only 52% of all American households consisted of married, opposite-sex partners. That leaves a great deal of households that are not "typical." Consider the following types of atypical households:

- one person households, such as widows or divorcees
- unmarried partner households
- same-sex households

Each type of household comes with very different issues. The planner must be prepared to elicit (with a great deal of poise and tact) the information needed to complete an accurate financial picture and be able to create the necessary projections. This is often a very complicated task. Some clients will be more than willing to divulge every nugget about their life, financial and otherwise. Others will play it close to the vest and may not be willing to discuss matters that do not have a dollar sign attached to them.

DIVORCE PLANNING

Nothing stirs up a financially stable marriage more than divorce. Too often the financial aspects of a divorce are worked out between the soon-to-be ex-spouses or, worse yet, themselves and their attorneys! Financial planners are often brought in after the fact even though they can play a valuable role in

1. structuring property settlements
2. negotiating the "proper" amount of alimony or child support
3. ensuring that the right assets are transferred in the most tax efficient manner
4. helping the client deal with financial burdens that he may never have handled before

Like widows, divorcees are often on their own for the first time in their adult life. The financial pressures often seem overwhelming, especially if your client feels like their "ex" got the better end of the deal.

If a divorce is inevitable, there are certain financial actions that should be started immediately. The following should be done in consultation with an attorney if one will be retained:

- establish bank, brokerage, and other financial accounts in a client's own name
- obtain new credit cards and establish a client's own credit rating (especially if the ex was not too good with money)
- change the beneficiary designations for retirement plans and life insurance
- make any necessary adjustments to estate planning documents such as wills and powers of attorney

One of the biggest decisions that needs to be made in a divorce is what happens with the house. Obviously, one of the two spouses will be out the door. In certain cases, it may make sense for both to leave.

The first factor to consider when deciding whether or not to stay in the home is likely to be emotional. However, the financial considerations need to follow quickly thereafter. Can the client afford to stay in the marital home? Planners may need to deal with feelings of entitlement or unwillingness to "trade-down." Too often after a divorce the former marital house becomes a burden instead of a home.

Starting with a new budget for the newly or soon-to-be divorced client, a cash flow projection should reveal whether the house is affordable or not. Be sure to consider all sources of income and expenditures and tactfully challenge the client's estimates. If this is not the first time through the budgeting process for the client, it is likely to be the first time going through a divorce.

Close attention needs to be paid to the division of retirement assets. Next to the house, retirement assets typically hold the most value, but also come with a cost – a potentially large tax cost. Even if assets are divided "equally," one spouse may end up in a much better financial situation than the other.

Example: Al and Dorothy Palmer are divorcing after 15 years of marriage. They are both 40 years old and have amassed $500,000 in a joint savings account and $500,000 in Al's IRA. They do not own any other assets, see no need to hire an attorney, and agree to divide their assets in half. For simplicity, Al suggests that Dorothy takes the savings account and he will keep the IRA. Although Al's suggestion does divide the assets in half in total, he is leaving himself without any current assets. Since he is under age 59½, he is unable to tap his IRA without penalty – and he would need to pay income taxes on top of that.

Many divorces are settled with regular payments being required from one of the former spouses. The structure of these payments will determine whether they are classified as alimony or not. Alimony is deductible by the payer and taxable to the recipient. On the other hand, property settlements and child support are not deductible by the payer and are not taxable to the recipient.

Payments will qualify as alimony only if all of the following requirements are met:

1. Payments must be made in cash.
2. Payments must be received by or on behalf of a spouse under a divorce or separation agreement.
3. The spouses must not be members of the same household at the time payments are made.
4. The parties must not identify the payments in the agreement as not being alimony for federal tax purposes.
5. Payments must terminate no later than at the death of the recipient and there must be no liability to make any payment (in cash or property) as a substitute for such payments.
6. The spouses must not file a joint return with each other.[1]

Child support is not treated like alimony. Payments which otherwise qualify as alimony but are reduced upon the happening of an event involving a child will not be treated as alimony for federal income tax purposes.[2]

In order to allow for the transfer of one spouse's defined contribution retirement plan (e.g., 401(k)) to the other spouse in a divorce, a court may issue a "qualified domestic relations order" or QDRO, for short.

It is more difficult to split employer-sponsored defined benefit plans (usually known as company pension plans), since these type of plans typically pay only in the future. If this asset is being evaluated as part of a property settlement, a present value is usually calculated and paid in a lump sum to the other spouse from other assets. Less frequently, it is paid out only when (and if) the employee receives the benefit in the future.

One very important consideration is health insurance, especially if the planner is dealing with the non-working ex-spouse. Once the spouses are no longer married, there is no requirement for the ex to continue carrying coverage for the former spouse unless the divorce decree says otherwise. If the ex does cut off the other spouse, all is not lost. Divorce is a qualifying event for COBRA purposes and up to 36 months of coverage may be purchased by the other spouse. Obviously, the kids' health insurance must be considered as well.

An ex-spouse may qualify for higher social security benefits after a divorce. Provided the marriage lasted at least ten years and the divorce occurred more than two years ago, a divorced spouse may claim benefits based upon her ex-spouse's earnings record. This does not impact the benefits the other ex-spouse will receive. When filing for benefits, an astute worker from the Social Security Administration should ask about prior marriages and check to see how benefits may change if this rule applies.

NONTRADITIONAL RELATIONSHIPS

More households than ever fall outside the traditional opposite-sex, married couple relationship. The most commonly encountered nontraditional relationships are opposite-sex unmarried couples and same-sex partners.

According to the 2000 U.S. Census, over nine percent of American households are led by unmarried partners. Approximately one in nine of these (1% of all American households) are same sex partner households. At some point in time, a planner will likely have a potential client that is involved in a nontraditional relationship.

There are a number of financial planning points to consider when dealing with nontraditional relationships:

- *Income taxes* – Under current rules, unmarried couples are not permitted to file a joint income tax return. However, as a result of the much-discussed "marriage penalty," taxpayers who use the married filing joint status typically will pay more in income taxes than two working taxpayers who each file using a single filing status. Married couples cannot elect to file single; if they do not file using a joint status, they are required to file separately – which often produces the worst tax result. So there is at least one positive financial outcome to a nontraditional relationship.

- *Gift taxes* – A marital deduction is only available to married couples.[3] Gifts to anyone other than a spouse are subject to the annual gift tax exclusion and lifetime unified credit.

- *Estate taxes* – A marital deduction is only available to married couples. Therefore, a married person dying with a taxable estate will pay less estate tax than an unmarried person with the same taxable estate. In fact, a married person will pay no estate tax upon death if the entire estate is left to the spouse.

- *Intestacy rights* – The surviving partner of a nontraditional relationship will often have no rights to a decedent's property if a will is not in place. When dealing with nontraditional relationships, it is crucial that proper and careful estate planning be performed.

- *Titling of assets* – One common way to protect both parties in a nontraditional relationship is to carefully title assets to ensure that lifetime wishes are carried out. Consider the following:

    - Joint Tenancy with Right of Survivorship

    - "Pay on Death" or "Transfer on Death" account designations

- *Beneficiary designations* – Partners in nontraditional relationships should review their retirement plan accounts and life insurance to make certain that their partners are named as the primary beneficiaries.

- *Power of attorney* – In order to make sure the world knows the true intentions, have it put it in writing. A power of attorney may cover all financial or medical aspects of a person's life or may be task-specific. It may be written so it could be used immediately or only so it could be used in the event of incapacitation or other defined event (a "springing" power of attorney). Since many families have difficulties understanding or accepting nontraditional relationships, this is an important step in making sure that the person the client wants making crucial decisions will be permitted to do so.

- *Social Security* – Couples in nontraditional relationships will not be able to rely on Social Security benefits like married couples do. Married spouses are entitled to claim the higher of the benefit determined under their own earnings record or one-half of their spouse's. Provisions are also in place for higher benefits for surviving spouses. Unmarried individuals must claim benefits on their earnings record alone.

- *Company pensions* – Although company sponsored pensions are becoming increasingly rare to find, they do still exist. Some companies have made adjustments to be more accepting of alternative life arrangements. However, in many cases, a pension is paid for the life of an unmarried employee. Upon the employee's death, the pension payments cease.

CHANGE OF EMPLOYMENT

No one seems to stay employed in one place very long. Gone are the days when everyone got his first job and stayed with the same company until he retired or died. People now change jobs almost as frequently as they change shoes. Company loyalty does not exist in the same fashion it did decades ago.

The companies share a large portion of the blame. Financial planners will rarely see a client who has a pension that is funded solely by the company. Some portion of the cost of benefits is more frequently passed on to the employee, making it more important for employees to "shop around" for the best deal for their services.

Financial planners will often be called upon to evaluate:

- the cost or benefit of changing jobs, especially where there is a change in location
- early retirement packages offered by a company
- severance and job assistance packages

Changing Jobs

The decision to accept a new job with a new employer must be made on several different levels. So much consideration needs to be given to how a job change is going to affect the employee, his or her family, and the potential for advancement, that the financial considerations may not be fully examined. Even worse, only one aspect of the finances – the salary – may be looked at, instead of the entire package.

In order to fully evaluate the financial part of the equation, a planner can assist in reviewing the value of the old job versus the value of the new. Often, this independent look can make the decision that much easier.

In addition to cash compensation or salary, a total compensation package will include some or all of the following:

- overtime
- vacation time
- retirement plan offerings including eligibility for matching
- health benefits, including dental and flexible spending arrangements
- life insurance
- dependent care assistance
- relocation assistance
- company car(s)
- stock bonuses, options, or other ownership programs
- club dues
- educational assistance
- business expense reimbursements

Obviously, this is by no means an all-inclusive list. Each company will have its own summary of benefits – be sure to get the whole picture.

If there is a change in job location, it is imperative to review the state and local tax impact. More municipalities are assessing taxes on their workers which could eat away at some of the perceived benefit of making a move to a new job.

Early Retirement

Instead of using layoffs to cut the workforce, many companies use an option of early retirement to entice workers to voluntarily leave. These types of package are often offered with little advance notice and decisions must be made within a month or two of the offer.

These types of packages must be reviewed very carefully before a recommendation to accept is provided. For example

- Are medical benefits provided in the package?
- Is the worker in any way barred from seeking employment in the same field with a competitor?
- How much of the employee's pension is lost (or increased) if the package is accepted?
- If the package is not accepted, does the employee risk being laid off or involuntarily relocated?

Severance Packages

Severance payments are commonly provided to employees who are laid off. Occasionally, such packages are provided with outplacement assistance services. These services may include job training, placement, or financial planning.

CHAPTER ENDNOTES

1. IRC Sec. 71(b).
2. IRC Sec. 71(c).
3. Couples who are considered married under common law may be eligible to use the marital deduction.

Chapter 13

SPECIAL NEEDS

WHAT IS IT?

Planners will often need to consider financial options for their clients that may have special needs, such as people with disabilities or terminal illnesses. Since planners will typically only deal with such situations on an infrequent basis, care should be taken before making recommendations that may not create the desired effect.

Consideration needs to be given to the myriad of government programs that are available for special situations such as those discussed in this chapter. Eligibility requirements are strict and may be violated even though the best intentions exist.

This chapter contains a discussion of the following special needs situations that a planner may encounter:

- clients with disabilities
- clients with terminal illnesses
- clients with special needs children

DISABILITIES

Financial planning for individuals with disabilities can be almost as important as the medical, psychological, and physiological needs they may have. This may seem to overemphasize the financial aspect of a disability, but maintaining, protecting, and properly utilizing accumulated assets could actually help improve the quality of care or life of the individual. If you consider the alternative, it is relatively easy to understand how critical financial planning is when dealing with disabled individuals.

Individuals with disabilities may receive benefits to help defray the costs from a number of different sources.

Disability Insurance

Benefits are provided in the form of periodic payments as a result of sustaining a sickness or injury that leaves one unable to work. Disability insurance may be even more important than life insurance for younger workers since the financial burden to the family is greater if a work-preventing injury or sickness occurs and the wage earner is not only unable to bring in his normal compensation, but also incurs additional living expenses.

Disability insurance is available either as part of a group policy or as an individual policy. The taxation of the disability benefits is contingent upon who pays the premiums. If a person's company pays the disability insurance premiums as a nontaxable fringe benefit, benefit payments will be taxable. If an individual pays for a disability policy himself, the premiums will be paid out of after-tax funds and will not be deductible, but the benefit payments will not be taxable. This is an important factor to consider when evaluating whether there is a disability insurance need for an individual.

Disability insurance contracts typically have the following components:

1. *Definition of disability* – There are several definitions of disability that insurance companies tend to use in their policies. There are many others, but most are some combination of the following:

    a) *Own occupation* – The insured is unable to perform the work required of his own occupation. Since this is the most liberal definition of a disability, it is the most expensive to purchase – and often the most difficult to find.

    b) *Modified own occupation* – The insured is unable to perform any reasonable occupation for which he may qualify based upon his education, experience, or training.

    c) *Any occupation* – The insured is unable to work in any occupation. This is the most restrictive type of definition and is the one followed by the Social Security Administration.

2. *Elimination period* – The time period an individual must wait after the occurrence of the disability before payments under the policy may begin.

3. *Benefit amount or percentage of compensation* – Insurance companies will normally offer a percentage of wages as the benefit amount. Adequate policies will pay around 60% to 70% of the regular wages as a benefit. This may seem low, but, if the individual is paying for the policy, the benefits will be paid free of federal income taxes. Many policies will also reduce the benefits should the insured qualify for and receive Social Security disability benefits.

4. *Benefit term* – The policy term usually covers a period of years up until a theoretical retirement age of somewhere between 62 and 65. Other policies may pay benefits for life or only a term of years.

Social Security Benefits

Disability benefits are available to workers under the Social Security program in limited circumstances. In order to receive benefits, an individual must be a qualified worker who becomes totally and permanently disabled. The generally accepted definition is an inability to perform any type of work. This disability must be expected to last for at least 12 months or be expected to result in death.

The determination of a qualified worker is dependent upon the individual's age when the disability occurred. An individual under age 24 needs to have worked only six quarters to receive benefits. Between ages 24 and 31, an individual must have worked for at least one half of the quarters available since age 21. Once an individual reaches age 31, he must be fully insured under the Social Security system (40 quarters) and have worked 20 of the last 40 quarters.

There is a five-month waiting period before the benefits may begin. If a worker qualifies, the spouse and any unmarried children who are under age 18 may also be eligible for benefits.

Medicare/Medicaid Benefits

If an individual receives disability benefits under the Social Security program, they are also eligible for Medicare regardless of age. Medicare is divided into Part A and Part B. Part A covers certain levels of hospital, skilled nursing, hospice, and home health care. Part B covers physicians' fees and outpatient services.

Medicaid benefits are not automatically received simply because an individual is disabled. Individuals are eligible for Medicaid based on their needs and resources. Each state determines the indigence level that one must be under in order to receive assistance. The state also determines the health services to be covered under the program.

It is important for a financial planner to understand how government programs for individuals with disabilities interact with their recommendations. The worst possible result would be the loss of the government benefits due to poor asset planning. Medicaid planning must be done with a professional who specializes in the area.

TERMINAL ILLNESSES

Just because someone is diagnosed with a terminal illness does not mean that there may not be an extended period that needs to be covered with existing financial resources. However, regardless of the number of months or years the doctors project, time is of the essence and planning should start immediately.

Obviously, the first financial step is to determine what the cost of living with the illness is going to be. Key questions that must be addressed include:

- How much will be covered by insurance?
- Are there lifetime maximums under the insurance policy that may be reached?
- What happens to the medical coverage if the employee decides to leave work?
- Are experimental treatments covered?
- Can the individual qualify for disability benefits under an existing policy, Social Security, or both?

The planner should consider life insurance policies that have been in place for a number of years as a potential source of cash to help defray the costs of living with a terminal illness. Insureds may be able to tap the cash value of a whole or universal life insurance policy. Alternatively, the insured can investigate the possibility of receiving accelerated benefits under the policy or selling the policy to a third party, also known as a "viatical settlement." These "living benefits" usually pay a percentage of the policy's normal death benefit.

Along with the financial issues, consideration should be given to existing (or nonexisting, as the case may be) estate documents. For terminally ill patients, the most important documents will be

- an advance medical directive (living will), which states what medical treatments will and will not be accepted
- a health care proxy (health care power of attorney), which names another person to make medical decisions in the event that the client is not able to do so
- a power of attorney, which will allow another person to act on the client's behalf in any legal, financial, business, investment, or other matters stipulated in the document

Of course, a will should be drafted to ensure that the client's wishes are carried out after his death. Guardians, executors, and trustees should be updated, if necessary. Beneficiaries of retirement plans and life insurance policies should also be reviewed and updated.

From an estate tax planning perspective, there may be certain transfers that can be made in contemplation of death. However, certain transfers require that the client survive for a certain period of time in order for the transfer to achieve the desired result. For example, the transfer of a life insurance policy into an irrevocable life insurance trust must be made more than three years before the policy owner's date of death. Otherwise, the insurance is treated as part of the decedent's estate.

Trying to take advantage of the positive aspects of the estate tax rules is also difficult. Gifts of appreciated property made to an individual within one year of the donor's death will not receive a step-up in basis if the donor reacquires the property through the estate.

DEPENDENTS WITH SPECIAL NEEDS

When clients have children or other dependents with special needs, the focus instantly turns to what would happen if the clients should die prematurely. Often, the discussions turn to estate planning and naming responsible guardians.

Of course there is more to it than that. The costs associated with a special needs child will often extend well into their adulthood. For this reason, many parents will set up trusts for their children. However, if not properly drafted, these trusts may do as much harm as good.

After the parents' death, special needs children may qualify for certain government program benefits such as Supplemental Security Income (SSI).[1] By qualifying for SSI, the child will automatically be eligible for Medicaid. SSI is a program that pays up to $623 per month (2007 federal benefit) for disabled individuals with less than $2,000 in assets and an inability to earn more than the income need standard ($623 per month for 2007).

Many experts who deal with special needs situation will recommend establishing a special needs trust (SNT). These special needs trust are typically funded by life insurance, real estate, or retirement plans and cover the needs of a child over and above what may be provided by a government program. Again, this is an area where an expert will be a valued addition to the financial planning team to ensure that the government program benefits will not be inadvertently lost by improper trust agreements.

CHAPTER ENDNOTES

1. See the "Supplemental Security Income (SSI)" page at "Social Security Online," http://www.ssa.gov/notices/supplemental-security-income/.

Chapter 14

ESTATE PLANNING

Many financial planners view the accumulation of wealth as the primary objective of most clients and, indeed, for most clients, building wealth is a primary goal. But wealth may fail to accomplish many of the client's most important goals and needs if, at the client's death or disability, it is lost or poorly used. Thus, planning for these events is an important part of the financial planner's art.

The purpose of this chapter is to provide an overview of estate planning and to alert planners to common problems and classic opportunities of estate planning. Because it is an overview, it does not cover all the tools or techniques of estate planning nor does it treat any in depth. (We wrote the *Tools & Techniques of Estate Planning* for those who want a solid foundation in estate planning and recommend the latest edition to all financial planners.)

The following topics will be covered:

1. the definition and objectives of estate planning
2. why client control is so important
3. people planning
4. why estate planning is not only for the wealthy
5. problems clients face
6. steps in the planning process
7. estate planning legal documents
8. events triggering a need for a review
9. the will as the cornerstone of the process
10. intestacy
11. letter of instructions
12. picking the executor
13. power of attorney
14. medical and health-related documents
15. administration of an estate
16. gift giving
17. computing the federal estate tax
18. the generation-skipping transfer tax
19. state death taxes

ESTATE PLANNING DEFINED

In the broadest sense, estate planning is the accumulation, conservation, and distribution of wealth in the manner that most efficiently and effectively accomplishes the client's objectives. An alternative definition, emphasizing the "planning" aspect, is that estate planning is a goal-oriented activity that uses tax minimization tools and techniques to provide the greatest possible financial security for an individual and his beneficiaries. Regardless of which definition is used, it is obvious that estate planning is a key element of overall financial planning.

THE IMPORTANCE OF CONTROL

Every estate is planned. Some estates are planned by default: by inaction some people allow their estate plan to be dictated by the federal and state governments. The person who dies without a valid will (that is, dies "intestate") allows the state in which he lived to draw one for him and determine who his heirs will be and how and when they will receive their inheritance. Those heirs must live with what is left by the system of income and death taxation structured by the federal and state governments even though those costs could have been significantly reduced by thoughtful planning. Few clients would agree to purchase a "one size fits all" wardrobe, yet that is exactly what happens when, by default, they allow the state government to decide who will receive their property, when and in what manner their property will be received, and even who will be the guardians of their children's assets or persons.

The best estate planning is controlled by the estate owner and the financial services professionals he enlists. Such people use a variety of methods for reducing taxes and the other causes of estate erosion, and they employ numerous tax and nontax tools and techniques to accomplish the client's objectives.

PEOPLE PLANNING

There are only two reasons for a client to engage in estate planning. The most obvious incentive is to build, conserve, and distribute assets. The less obvious, but more important, reason is the need for "people planning." In fact, from the financial planner's perspective, people planning should be the first and foremost consideration. People planning is the anticipation of the financial and psychological needs of those people and organizations the client loves or feels a duty towards. It involves providing adequate financial security in terms of absolute dollars and providing emotional assurance that loved ones will be able to continue their way of life. A great deal of what estate planning is designed to do is give people peace of mind.

Consider the extent of needs of the client who has minor children. "Would you leave young children at home without a babysitter?" "Would you allow a stranger to choose a babysitter for your children?" Few clients would answer affirmatively to either question, yet it is incredible how many clients haven't named a guardian for their children in their wills. Think about the client with the exceptionally artistic or intellectually gifted child. Will the child have the financial means to fully develop that talent if the client doesn't prepare now? If the client dies or becomes disabled, who will care for a retarded, emotionally disturbed, or physically handicapped child or other dependent who is not self-sufficient? What provision has been made for the spouse or child who is not intellectually or emotionally equipped or lacks experience (or just does not want) to manage large sums of money, a portfolio of securities, or an active business? Who will take care of aging parents and other relatives who depend on the client if the client does not or cannot care for them? Who cares for the client if the client cannot? (If the client does not prepare future care for himself in the event of a disability or prepare for his retirement, who will?)

IS ESTATE PLANNING ONLY FOR THE RICH?

At this point, it should be obvious that wealth should not be the planner's sole focus, although money is an essential part of the estate planning equation. It is a common misconception among most clients that estate planning is only for the wealthy. Although it is essential for those who have accumulated substantial wealth, estate planning may be even more important for those of modest or moderate wealth. Every dollar lost unnecessarily to taxes or administrative costs hurts survivors more when the estate is small. (The rich man's family can afford his mistakes better than the family of the man of modest or moderate wealth). Money saved and income provided by a well thought out tax savings device, even if it's only putting the right title on a bank savings account, will have the greatest significance where the potential tax threatens to wipe out a proportionately larger part of the client's assets.

PROBLEMS CLIENTS FACE

An estate often breaks up when the estate owner dies (or becomes disabled) – not because that person has done anything wrong – but because that person hasn't done anything. It is impossible to solve problems until one knows what they are. What are the problems that clients need to address?

There are six major estate planning problems that the financial planner should consider in addressing the needs of clients:

1. *Lack of liquidity* – This means insufficient cash. Test to see if there are enough assets in the client's estate that can quickly and inexpensively be turned into cash to meet tax demands and other estate settlement costs. Identify the specific source(s) from which the estate will pay last illness and funeral expenses, current and long term bills and debts, unpaid income taxes, attorney's, accountant's, and appraiser's fees, federal and state death taxes, and the additional costs of estate administration. A lack of liquidity is extremely serious because it often results in a forced sale at pennies on the dollar of the most valuable or important assets the client has (such as the family business, farm, vacation home, or a precious heirloom). Sacrifice sales of assets with substantial income producing power, or the family business or farm, not only results in a disproportionately large loss of income but sometimes results in a devastating psychological trauma that emotionally cripples survivors.

2. *Improper disposition of assets* – Check various dispositive instruments such as life insurance

policies, wills, trusts, joint bank accounts, pension plans, and other employee benefit plans to see if assets are going to the wrong person at the wrong time or in the wrong manner. For instance, it would be inappropriate to put a high powered sports car in the hands of a child. Yet hundreds of thousands of dollars worth of assets are often left outright to beneficiaries who are unwilling or who are legally and/or intellectually or emotionally unable to manage them properly. An incompetent and his money are soon parted.

3. *Inadequate income or capital* – It is essential that the financial planner quantify and verify that the client has adequate income sources or sufficient capital to provide for

   a) retirement

   b) the "special needs" discussed below

   c) the family at the client's death

   d) the client if he becomes disabled (A long term disability is a "living death." The loss of income due to the disability is often coupled with a massive financial drain caused by the illness itself. Both problems are compounded by the inadequate management of currently owned assets. Together, these forces tend to diminish the client's net worth with frightening speed.)

4. *Asset values destabilized and not maximized* – Compare the value and marketability of assets "before and after" the various types of changes that occur over the life cycle of a client. For instance, will a client's business be worth the same (in terms of income producing ability or financial net worth) after his death, disability, or divorce as it was worth before such an event? The lack of a backup management team, the failure of heirs to note a change in consumer preferences, or product or equipment obsolescence may result in a rapid decline in the value of a decedent's business. Does the client have a buy-sell agreement? Is it in writing? Does the price in that agreement reflect the current worth of that business? Is the agreement funded adequately so that his family's fortune is not dependent on the business? Is a life insurance policy worth as much to a client's family if it is paid to his estate, rather than to a named beneficiary (perhaps because the primary beneficiary died and there was no secondary beneficiary named)? Are assets needlessly exposed to the claims of creditors? Check to see what must be done to stabilize and maximize the value of the client's business and other assets.

5. *Excessive taxes and transfer costs* – Is the client paying unreasonably high income taxes? Is there an opportunity to reduce or defer income tax? Run a hypothetical probate. (See "Computing the Federal Estate Tax" below.) See if the client will be paying more in death taxes and other estate settlement costs than necessary. Often, through various commonly used estate planning tools or techniques, many thousands of dollars of income and transfer taxes can be saved within a family unit.

6. *Special needs* – Uncover and address what may be the most important and difficult of all the estate planning problems the typical client has – his "special" problems. Special problems include a spouse who cannot or will not handle money, property, or a family business. Such problems may also include the care of a dependent who is physically, emotionally, or intellectually handicapped, or mentally disturbed. Consider the importance of providing the proper financial support for exceptionally gifted children. Special needs also include the desire to provide meaningful financial support to schools, churches, synagogues, mosques, or other institutions and charities.

STEPS IN THE ESTATE PLANNING PROCESS

There are seven major steps in the estate planning process designed (a) to measure the client's needs, (b) to establish an order of priority in addressing these needs, and (c) to give first preference to those needs or problems which the client feels are most important. These seven steps are

1. Gather comprehensive and accurate data on all aspects of the client and the client's family including goals and desires.

2. Categorize the data into general problem areas such as the six major areas described above.

3. Estimate estate transfer costs and other liquidity needs. This amount is generally the sum of cash bequests in the client's will plus

a) funeral and administrative expenses

b) debts and taxes

c) the state death tax payable

d) the net federal estate tax payable

4. Set priorities for problems and prepare alternative solutions to each.

5. With the client and other advisers, formulate the overall plan (decide what can and should be done and the order in which things should be done) and determine the implementation procedure (decide which parties are responsible for each task and establish a timetable for action).

6. Test and implement the plan.

7. Review the plan.

ESTATE PLANNING LEGAL DOCUMENTS

An estate plan is a treasure map directing how wealth will be assembled and disposed of during life or upon death. The plan itself is useless, unless the documents that implement the plan have been drafted appropriately. The documents should direct personal representatives, fiduciaries, and beneficiaries through a maze of hidden traps along the journey to the successful distribution of wealth. These directions must comply with the laws of the state where they will be carried out and, most importantly, should unambiguously state one's intentions. A person should read all these documents carefully and understand every component before executing (the process of signing and giving validity to) the documents. An attorney should explain anything that is not understood before a person signs any documents.

Since these documents necessarily involve compliance with state law, they should be prepared by an attorney who specializes in estate planning in the local jurisdiction. Quite often, mail-order kits and software packages are available at tempting prices for the "do-it-yourselfer." In fact, a will-drafting software product has been on the top ten list for business software. Only in simple estate plans will these products be adequate (unless the consumer is an effective self-taught estate planner). Moreover, if the simple plan is all that is required, an attorney can be found for a minimal fee in any event.

The documents that should (or might) be necessary for an estate plan include the following:

1. *An asset and personal records inventory* – Perhaps the most important document the family will need after a person's death or incapacity is a written record listing the significant pieces of personal property the person owns and the location of the important documents (e.g., deeds, wills, trusts, insurance policies, employment records, tax records, etc.).

2. *A letter briefing the executor* – Although a will should be clear and effectively dispose of one's property, it is sometimes recommended that a person also leave a letter instructing the executor. This letter should include instructions as to the location of records and preferences for disposing of property. Quite often, the will provides general language as to beneficiaries' shares with no specific instructions on how the shares will be funded or as to which specific properties are to be given to which beneficiaries.

3. *A will* – Despite the obvious importance of a will, a recent *Consumer Reports* survey revealed that more than seven out of 10 American adults do not have a valid will. Do not let yourself or your clients be among the procrastinators.

4. *Trusts* – Not everyone will find the need to create trusts. However, those people who wish to make relatively sophisticated lifetime gifts or reduce probate will find living (inter vivos) trusts to be an essential part of their plan. Those people who need marital deduction tax planning in their wills or who must protect minor children will probably want to include testamentary trusts in their wills.

5. *Power of attorney* – If a person desires to have another individual take some specified actions (such as the management of a securities portfolio) for the person in certain circumstances (such as while one is out of the country or in the event of incapacity), a power of attorney should be considered.

6. *Living will* – If a person wants to give advance notice to medical care providers of the person's wishes in the event the person should become terminally ill or permanently comatose, a living will is recommended.

REVIEWING THE ESTATE PLAN

As is the case with financial planning, an estate plan is good for only as long as it fits the needs, desires, and circumstances of the parties involved. As these factors change, so must the plan. Among the events that should trigger a review are

1. marriage or remarriage, separation or divorce
2. birth or death
3. change of job
4. move to a new state
5. significant change in income, wealth, or living standard
6. change in health
7. major change in tax law

Automatic in-depth estate analysis reviews should be scheduled at least every three years in addition to normal annual financial security checkups. (We call these "Financial Fire Drills.") These reviews are particularly important when a family business is involved.

THE WILL: CORNERSTONE OF THE ESTATE PLANNING PROCESS

Defined

A will is a legal expression or testament of a "testator's" wishes that (1) provides for disposition of the probate estate; and (2) leaves instructions for the care of dependents and the settlement of the estate after the testator's death. Without a will a person will not be able to

- determine the beneficiaries of the probate assets; state law will determine the beneficiaries
- give specific assets to selected heirs
- name an executor
- make gifts from the estate in trust
- name the guardians of any minor beneficiaries
- give directions as to the payment of debts
- make charitable bequests
- take advantage of optimum marital-deduction tax planning

A will does not and cannot direct the disposition of assets that pass outside of probate. Among these non-probate assets are assets that pass at death by contract or by operation of law such as

1. life insurance payable to a named beneficiary other than the estate or its executor (as executor)
2. qualified retirement plan proceeds
3. IRA death benefits
4. jointly-owned property (real or personal) with right of survivorship
5. nonqualified deferred compensation death benefits
6. assets in a revocable or irrevocable living trust

A will can be changed or revoked at any time prior to the testator's death. It becomes operative only upon the testator's death and applies only to the probate assets and situation that exist at that time. Although many individuals do not have significant probate assets and their wills do not really dispose of the lion's share of their wealth, this should not dissuade anyone from having a valid will. A will has many benefits and is inexpensive relative to the tasks it accomplishes.

Requirements for a Valid Will

Anyone can draft his own will. But only an attorney should. The knowledge of tax, corporate, domestic relations, property, trust, real estate, and securities laws that must be considered and integrated into the will-writing process makes the "do-it-yourself" will dangerous and potentially expensive. The costs, unfortunately, of an error of omission or commission must be paid by those least able to afford the expense, the testator's survivors. Wills, like any other tool or technique in estate planning, must be part of the entire process and must consider assets passing outside the probate estate.

Although it is usually best to have an attorney draft the will, a person may draft the person's own valid will. In any event, everyone should be aware of the following important issues, regardless of whether one is drafting one's own will or is simply reviewing a will drafted by an attorney.

- A will must be written (handwritten or typed).
- A will should unambiguously state that it is intended to be a will.
- The will must be signed and dated at its logical end by the person for whom it is written (the testator).
- A number of witnesses (generally two or three depending on state law) must sign the will after the testator's signature attesting to the validity of the signature. Many states require that the witnesses not be beneficiaries under the will.
- The testator must have attained a threshold age (generally 18).

Components of a Valid Will

A well-drafted will should provide a plan for distributing probate assets according to the testator's desires and the beneficiaries' needs, giving due consideration to federal and state and other tax laws. It should consider the potential for change in all these factors after the will is originally drawn. A will should be complete and unambiguous with respect to the testator's desires.

There is no standard format that every will must follow and every state has its own laws regarding the requirements for a valid will. Most wills should contain at least the following provisions:

1. introduction (a clear statement of the intent to make a will, identification of the testator and of all heirs, and other relevant information)
2. direction to pay debts and expenses
3. tax apportionment and expense apportionment clauses (explaining how estate tax and expenses are to be paid or apportioned among beneficiaries of the estate)
4. specific bequests or devises of real and personal property to the targeted beneficiaries
5. disposition of residuary estate (the remaining property after all specific bequests, legacies, devises, and payment of the taxes and expenses of the estate)
6. nomination of the executor and all trustees of trusts created by the testator in the will
7. powers clause enumerating the powers granted to the executor
8. provisions for the disposition of property to minor beneficiaries and appointment of fiduciary (responsible for managing and safeguarding the financial assets of the estate until disposition)
9. common disaster or simultaneous death clause (to specify which actions to take in the event of the simultaneous or near simultaneous deaths of both husband and wife)
10. execution clause
11. signature, witness, and attestation clause
12. self-proving notarization

An attorney familiar with state law as well as tax law must carefully tailor each of these provisions to the client's individual needs and circumstances.

Grounds for Contesting A Will

Every state imposes its own requirements that must be met if a will is to be considered valid. Generally, the requirements of a valid will are

1. The testator must have "capacity"– both legal and mental. This means the testator must have been the statutory age (18 or 21 in most states) or older, and must have
   a) a full knowledge of the act in which he is involved
   b) an understanding of the property he owns
   c) a knowledge of the disposition he wants to make, and
   d) an appreciation of the parties who are the natural objects of his bounty

(Typically, if there is legal capacity, the courts will presume there is mental capacity. A contestant to the validity of a will on the ground of "incapacity" has the burden of proving a lack of capacity with clear and convincing evidence.)

2. The testator must have freedom of choice. A will is considered invalid if by clear and convincing evidence, it can be shown that the testator was subject to the undue influence of some other person at the time the will was drawn and executed. The types of undue influence that can prove a lack of freedom of choice include threats, misrepresentations, inordinate flattery, or a physical or mental or emotional coercion.

3. The will must be properly executed. Every state has a specific statute that spells out the form a will must take (usually in writing), where it must be signed (typically at its logical conclusion), how it must be signed (usually in ink), and the requirements for the signature of witnesses (three witnesses is the maximum any state requires). Some states allow a will to be "self proving." This means if a testator's signing of the will is witnessed by at least three individuals who sign in the presence of each other and of a notary, those witnesses do not have to appear at the probate of the will. This can save time, money, and aggravation. It is suggested that professionals consider that clients often move to a new state after signing a will. Therefore, the document should routinely comply with the most stringent requirements of any state rather than meet the least demanding state's rules. It is suggested, whenever possible, use of three witnesses (preferably unrelated to, and not beneficiaries of, the testator) who all sign in the presence of each other and a notary and attest to the testator's execution of the will.

Codicils

A will can be changed through a "codicil." Because the will does not become effective until the testator's death, it can be changed at any time until then. The codicil is a simple and convenient way to make minor changes in a will. Usually it is a very short document that states the change desired, but reaffirms all the existing provisions in the will except for that change.

The codicil must be executed in accordance with the same formalities as a will. It should be typed, signed, and witnessed in the same manner as the will.

There are situations in which a new will, rather than a codicil, is indicated. The old will should be destroyed and a new will, rather than a codicil, should be used when

1. Significant changes are to be made.

2. The size of the gift in the will is to be reduced or where a beneficiary is to be deleted. (In such a case, it may offend the beneficiary or even encourage a will contest if the change is made by codicil because, if a codicil is used, the original will must nonetheless be probated.)

Conversely, the old will should be retained and a codicil or a new will should be used when

1. The testator is older or in poor health and there is a strong potential that the will may be contested. (If for any reason the new will fails, the prior will may qualify and protect most of the testator's intended gift.)

2. A charitable gift was made in the first will and now a larger charitable gift is contemplated, but there is a high probability that the new will may be contested. (The original will can be used to show that the larger gift to charity is not merely an afterthought or the result of a mind unduly influenced by the charity).

Revocation and Modification

Wills, of course, can be revoked. Actually, both the testator and the law can revoke or modify a will. A testator can revoke a will by

1. making a later will which revokes a prior will

2. making a codicil expressly revoking a will

3. making a later will inconsistent with a former will, or

4. physically mutilating, burning, tearing, or defacing the will with the intention of revoking it

State law can revoke or modify a will automatically under circumstances that vary from state to state, but often include

1. divorce of the testator (In some states, if the testator divorces after making a will, all the provisions in the will relating to the former spouse are invalid.)

2. marriage of the testator (If the testator marries after making a will, the spouse receives the portion of the probate estate he would have received had the testator died without a valid will–unless the will provides for a larger share.)

3. birth or adoption (If the testator did not provide for a child born or adopted after the will was made and did not clearly state in the will that the omission was intentional, the child receives that share of the estate that the child would have received after a surviving spouse's share is taken out, had there been no will. See the discussion of intestacy below.)

4. murder (Many states have "slayers bounty" statutes that prohibit a person who participated in a willful and unlawful murder from acquiring property as a result of the deed.)

Right of Election

Aside from providing for contesting the validity of a will and for its revocation, many states provide another way by which the dispositive result can be changed: this is known as a "right of election." A right of election, typically given only to a surviving spouse, is a right to choose to "take against the will," that is, to take a specified portion of the probate estate regardless of what the will provides. One state, for instance, allows a surviving spouse to take that share the spouse would have been allowed had the deceased died without a valid will. This right is generally forfeited by a spouse who deserted the testator or who participated in the testator's willful and unlawful murder.

Safeguarding the Will

Safeguarding the will is extremely important. Usually, the original of a will should be kept together with all a client's important documents in a safe deposit box. (Check first on your state's rules that take effect when a safe deposit box owner dies. Although some states "freeze" the contents of the box and require that it remain sealed until state tax authorities can inventory the contents of the box, in most states a surviving spouse can quickly gain access to the will.) Although some authorities recommend leaving the original of a will with the attorney who wrote it, this may make it awkward for the executor to exercise his right to choose the estate's attorney, a right provided by many states' laws regardless of who drew the will. We suggest that, in most cases, the client should keep the original document in a safe deposit box. Some states provide for the "lodging" of a will; a mechanism for filing and safekeeping it in the office of the probate court (sometimes called orphans' or surrogate's court).

INTESTACY

The absence of a valid will at death is called "intestacy." State intestacy laws provide a will for the person who did not draw his own. State law, therefore, determines (1) who is entitled to receive an intestate decedent's probate property, (2) how such individuals will receive their shares (typically outright in a lump sum), and (3) when those shares will be paid out (usually, at the conclusion of the probate process or, if later, when the beneficiary reaches legal majority).

Generally, intestacy statutes enumerate certain preferred classes of survivors:

- decedent's spouse
- decedent's children and other descendants
- decedent's parents
- decedent's brothers and sisters

The distribution of a typical intestate estate is shown in Figure 14.1.

LETTER OF INSTRUCTIONS

A "letter of instructions" is an informal nonlegal way to convey highly personal thoughts and directions that cannot or should not be included in a will. A letter of instructions might provide the following information:

1. location of the will and other key documents

2. funeral and burial instructions (remember that a will is often not opened until long after the funeral)

3. suggestions or recommendations as to the continuation, sale, or liquidation of a business (it is easier to speak frankly and freely in the letter than in the will)

4. personal matters the client might prefer not to be made public (such as statements that might seem

Figure 14.1

TYPICAL DISTRIBUTION OF AN INTESTATE ESTATE		
	Decedent Dies Leaving	**Distribution**
Spouse and children or their descendants	Spouse receives one third	Children receive two thirds divided equally
Spouse and one child or child's descendants	Spouse receives one half	Child receives one half
Spouse but no children or their descendants, and decedent's mother or father survives	Spouse receives $10,000 plus one half of balance	Father and mother or surviving parent (if one is already deceased) receive one half of balance
Spouse but no children or their descendants, and no parent survives	Spouse receives $10,000 plus one half of balance	Brothers and sisters receive other half of balance divided equally
Spouse but no children or their descendants, and no parent, brother, sister, niece, nephew, grandparent, uncle, or aunt survives	Spouse receives all	
Child or children but no spouse		Child or children receive all divided equally
No spouse and no children or their descendants, and decedent's mother or father survives		Mother and father receive all
No spouse and no children or their descendants, and no parent of the decedent survives		Brothers and sisters receive all divided equally

unkind, harsh, or inconsiderate, but that would prove of value to the executor; for instance, a letter of instructions could provide guidance as to who could or could not be trusted or how to handle a spendthrift spouse or child addicted to drugs)

5. legal and accounting services (remember that because of the high personal liability that "comes with the job," executors typically have the legal right to their own choice of counsel – regardless of who may be named in the will)

6. an explanation of why certain actions were taken in the will (which may help avoid litigation) (For instance, "I left only $1,000 for my son, Bouillabaisse, because...")

PICKING THE EXECUTOR

It is the executor's principal duty to faithfully execute the wishes of the testator as directed by the will. It is often recommended that an attorney or a bank trust officer be named as an executor. Many experts recommend, however, that the executor should normally be a competent close member, or trusted friend, of the family, if one is available. A professional/and or an institution, such a bank trust department could be named as co-executor or hired by the family executor for advice. Naming a co-executor or contingent executors avoids problems and maintains continuity in the event the executor dies or becomes incapacitated during the administration of the estate.

Frequently, a surviving spouse is named as executor, or when there is no surviving spouse, one or more of the adult children is chosen. The reason for this is both psychological and financial. Who better than a close family member would know what a person's assets and liabilities are, where those assets and liabilities can be found, and what the deceased intended if any ambiguities or unsettled issues arise?

The individual selected to be executor should have: (1) competence; (2) the understanding and personal skills to deal with other heirs; (3) knowledge of the special needs of the testator's heirs; (4) knowledge of the testator's property; (5) the willingness to do a time-consuming and often thankless task; (6) honesty; (7) geographic proximity to the probate court, assets, and other heirs, to the greatest extent possible; and (8) the lack of any insurmountable conflicts of interest with the estate and other beneficiaries.

POWER OF ATTORNEY

A power of attorney is a legal instrument that gives another person or entity the right to legally perform specified acts for a person. The power of attorney can be limited or extensive. The person granting the powers decides what powers and rights the person is going to delegate to the other person.

Immediate or springing powers – A power of attorney can be immediate or springing. An immediate power of attorney takes effect upon its execution (when it is appropriately signed and notarized). A springing power of attorney will only "spring" into being upon a certain occurrence or a certain act. For example, a person can have a power of attorney that will only take effect when the grantor is out of the country, or, alternatively, a power of attorney that only takes effect upon the grantor's incompetence or disability. Such a power of attorney should have within it a definition of incompetency or disability.

Durable power –An immediate power of attorney can be granted as "durable." A durable power of attorney is one that is not revoked in the case of disability or incompetency. To meet this goal, the instrument granting the power of attorney must expressly state that it is granting a durable power, since any other powers are automatically revoked if the person granting the powers becomes disabled or incompetent.

Scope – A power of attorney can meet several estate-planning needs. It can grant broad powers to a person's attorney-in-fact to perform any task or transaction the person could normally perform for himself. For example, a broad-form durable power of attorney would permit the attorney-in-fact to make gifts of property to family members if the person granting the power became incompetent. This could reduce the eventual probate and taxable estate.

A power of attorney may also be limited to specific tasks. For example, a person could grant a power of attorney to a family member merely to make health-care decisions for the person if the person becomes disabled or loses capacity. Or, a person can grant a power of attorney to someone to sign contracts for him. In any event, the power of attorney should be carefully worded to specify its scope and instruct the individuals or entities that one hopes will honor the agreement. It is always a good idea to give copies of the power to individuals that will be expected to deal with the attorney-in-fact. For example, a person's banker and broker should have a copy of the power if the attorney-in-fact has the power to handle the person's finances.

MEDICAL AND HEALTH-RELATED DOCUMENTS

The Supreme Court decision in *Cruzan vs. Director, Missouri Department of Health,*[1] held that the U.S. Constitution does not prohibit states from requiring that evidence of an incompetent patient's wishes to have life-sustaining treatment withdrawn must be established by clear and convincing evidence. In Justice Scalia's concurring opinion, he stated that there is no federal constitutional basis whatsoever for preventing states from prohibiting patients (or their families) to refuse unwanted life-sustaining treatment.

Although the states and medical providers will vary on the degree of compliance with a patient's (or a patient's family's) wishes when extraordinary life-sustaining measures are required, the *Cruzan* decision means that a person can improve his chances that his wishes will be carried out through advance planning. If a person becomes legally incapacitated, terminally ill, or in a permanent vegetative state, medical decisions made by hospitals and physicians to prolong the person's life by artificial means could be imposed against the wishes of the patient's immediate family. More importantly, the decisions may not be what the person would have desired if the person could have made the choice before losing capacity. Such prolonged medical treatment and related family disputes are often an unwarranted emotional and financial drain on the family.

Two mechanisms are available for a person to indicate his wishes regarding life-sustaining measures if a person should become so disabled, so incompetent, that there is no reasonable hope or expectation of recovery. The two methods to indicate intent are the "Living Will" (also called Advanced Directive for Medical Care) and the "Durable Power for Health Care" (also known as Health Care Proxy). The laws of the state where a person is located will determine the validity of such documents and competent local counsel will provide the best assurance that the wishes expressed in the documents will be carried out.

Living Wills

A living will is a document indicating a person's intentions in the event the person becomes disabled and lacks the legal capacity to make medical decisions. A living will deals with the health-care measures desired in the event of disability and incapacity. The living will should carefully spell out whether or not heroic measures should be taken in the event of a terminal accident or illness or a permanent coma.

Legal environment – Living wills require a specific statute to be legally binding and are not valid in all states. However, many states recognize them and others currently have statutes pending. Most practitioners feel that the document provides clear and convincing evidence of a person's wishes and, even absent a statute, may cause health care providers to respond in accordance with a person's wishes (or will convince a court to force the doctors to comply).

Elements – A living will should contain the following:

- provisions conforming to the domicile state's living will statute, if any.
- the specific wishes with respect to various life-sustaining measures (Some specimen documents contain an actual list of the type of measures that one can either choose or avoid.)
- a proxy for someone to interpret its terms (A trusted family member or friend should be selected to make decisions if the interpretation is unclear.)
- language exonerating those medical-care providers and proxy-holders acting in reasonable compliance with the living will (This will help alleviate the liability concerns of those taking action.)

Durable Power of Attorney for Health Care

A durable power of attorney gives a selected agent the power to make health-care decisions for a person if the person becomes legally incompetent. The durable power for health care is more widely recognized and more flexible than a living will, since the designated agent may be able to act before a person's permanent incapacity. Of course, while a person is still competent, the person is still free to continue to make the person's own decisions and can revoke the power at any time the person still has the legal capacity to do so.

Suggested elements – The following are suggestions for durable powers for health care and should be discussed with counsel:

- The document should comply with state law and be broad enough to cover other jurisdictions where a person is likely to spend extended vacation or retirement time.
- The document should carefully enumerate the types of decisions the attorney-in-fact is granted the power to make.

Naming the attorney-in-fact – The decisions concerning medical care are best left to the person himself or his immediate family. To ensure this result, a person must take pro-active measures. Either a living will or a durable power for health care could accomplish the desired intentions. Quite often, a combination of the two is suggested to cover the broadest range of choices for medical decisions. In any event, the documents should be drafted in accordance with the laws of the domicile state and duplicate originals should be given to a person's doctor(s) and any family members who will be granted the power to act in the person's behalf.

HOW AN ESTATE IS ADMINISTERED

The administration of an estate can be a short and relatively simple process or it can be drawn out over many years and become a complex nightmare involving thousands of hours of work and dozens or even hundreds of difficult choices. Essentially, however, there are three main stages common to all administrations:

1. safeguarding and collecting the decedent's assets

2. paying of debts and taxes

3. distribution of any remainder to the heirs specified in the will or under state intestacy law

In other words, when a person dies, a process similar to a business liquidation occurs. Money owed to the decedent is collected, creditors (including all taxing authorities) must be notified and satisfied, and what is left is distributed to the appropriate individuals and organizations.

This process–also called probate–is generally supervised through a local court called a probate court (although sometimes called an orphans' or surrogate's court). The person who represents the decedent and in many ways "stands in the shoes of the decedent" with respect to legal matters is generally called the "personal representative." Male personal representatives, serving in situations where the decedent died "testate," i.e., with a valid will, are called executors; the term sometimes used for a female is "executrix." More than one executor can serve at a time and can be one or more individuals, corporate fiduciaries, or a combination of one or more persons and one or more corporations.

When there is no valid will, the court will appoint an administrator (or administratrix). This person has much the same responsibility and same powers as an executor (although an executor's power and responsibility can be expanded by the will beyond those permitted under state law).

Why is the administrative process important? There are three major reasons. The first is that bank accounts could not be collected and contracts could not be enforced if there were no one legally charged with that responsibility and given that authority. The second reason is that, without the probate process, title to property would be forever clouded with uncertainty. Real estate could not be made marketable because there would be no "chain of title" and no mechanism for proving that claims against the real estate had been satisfied. The third reason the administration process is important is the assurance to both the testator and heirs that the court will see that the decedent's wishes are carried out and that the appropriate heirs receive the property to which they are entitled. The probate process is therefore a device to safeguard the interests of the estate's beneficiaries (as well as to assure state taxes are paid, which they would in most states whether or not an asset "avoids probate").

GIFT GIVING

Why does good financial planning often include gift giving? Clients are often encouraged to make gifts for many reasons. Some of these are

1. Giving gifts, especially gifts of income producing assets, is a way to reduce probate costs and substantially reduce or eliminate income taxes and the death tax on wealth. If the client's annual exclusion is systematically used, as explained below, millions in dollars of estate tax savings is possible.

2. A gift creates certainty and avoids the unknown. For instance, a client who wants to be sure a gift goes to a child (rather than a former spouse or a creditor) will not wait to leave it by will. Wills can be broken or elected against and creditors' claims are an ever present danger, but a gift is a sure thing.

3. Giving affords the client the pleasure of seeing the recipient enjoy the gift and the opportunity to see how that gift and the income it produces are handled. Lifetime gifts help the client decide whether, when, and how to make additional gifts during lifetime or at death.

4. A lifetime gift is private. Only the donee (and perhaps tax authorities) has the right to any of the details. This makes it less likely that beneficiaries will fall prey to the advice of those people who always seem to know how to invest other people's money.

Reducing or Eliminating the Gift Tax

Federal tax law imposes a gift tax on taxable gifts made during lifetime. There are four ways the gift tax can be reduced or, in most cases, eliminated, even in the case of substantial gifts. These four are:

1. the gift tax annual exclusion

2. split gifts

3. the gift tax marital deduction

4. the unified credit

The gift tax annual exclusion allows anyone, married or single, to give up to $12,000 (as indexed in 2007) in cash or other property each year to each of any number of donees (whether or not they are related to the donor) entirely gift tax free.

Gifts made by a husband or wife to a third party such as a child can be "split," that is, treated as if half was made by each of the spouses. The gift will be treated as if each spouse gave half even if one contributed the entire amount. Gift splitting effectively doubles the annual exclusion amount to $24,000 (in 2007) per donee. A further advantage of gift splitting is that, because gift tax rates are "progressive" (the tax grows disproportionately higher the more a person gives), making two smaller gifts creates a lower total tax than one larger gift. For example, a taxable gift (the amount over and above any allowable annual exclusion) of $100,000 results in a tax of $23,800. If the same gift were split so that each spouse was considered to have given a taxable gift of $50,000, the tax on each gift would be only $10,600, a total of $21,200 (a saving of $2,600).

The gift tax marital deduction eliminates the tax entirely on gifts between spouses. Federal gift tax law allows one spouse to give another an unlimited amount free of gift tax (over and above the amount allowed as an annual exclusion). There is generally no upper limit on how much a client can give gift tax free to his or her spouse during lifetime. However, gifts to a spouse who is not a U.S. citizen generally qualify for a $125,000 (as indexed in 2007) "super annual exclusion" rather than the marital deduction.

There may be no tax payable even on that portion of a gift that, after any allowable annual exclusion, is still taxable. This is because a large dollar for dollar reduction in the gift tax payable is allowed to every taxpayer. This is called the "unified credit" because it can be allocated in any manner desired against gifts made during lifetime or at death to offset the taxes generated by the federal unified gift and estate transfer tax system. The unified credit is $345,800 for gift tax purposes. This offsets the tax on taxable property worth up to $1,000,000. So, during lifetime, any client, married or not, could give up to $1,000,000 to anyone, whether or not related, and pay no federal gift tax. Any unified credit that is not used during lifetime is available at death to offset estate taxes. The unified credit for estate tax purposes (but not for gift tax purposes) is scheduled to increase, as described later.

Helping the Client Select the Right Property

Planners should give a great deal of consideration to what property a client should–or should not–give, as well as the timing of that gift. These are some guidelines:

1. Give income producing property if the client is in a high income tax bracket and the donee is in a lower bracket.

2. Give assets likely to appreciate substantially in value. Make the gift when the gift tax value (and therefore the gift tax cost) is lowest. Life insurance, given away while the insured is alive, is a good example. Another example of good property to give away is the stock of a business; give it to a family member before a lucrative contract is signed.

3. Give away property owned in a state other than the one in which the client lives. This prevents "ancillary administration," a costly process involving probate in the state where the property is located as well as probate in the state of the decedent's domicile. For instance, clients who live in Florida and who own a home in Maryland, but no longer use it, might give away the home in Maryland to avoid the additional probate.

The wise planner knows not only "what to give," but just as important, "when" and "how" to make that gift. A gift should never be made if, for financial security or psychological reasons, the client is depending on it or the income it produces or may have such a need at any time in the future. Tax savings should never be achieved at the cost of even one night's lost sleep. But if the client can – in every respect – afford to make the gift, then the time to do it is now. Get it out of the client's estate as quickly as possible to save income taxes, avoid the claims of the client's creditors, and compound the potential estate tax savings.

If an asset fluctuates in value, it should be given away when its market value is low. If sale of the property by the client would result in a loss, it should be sold by the client rather than given away. The loss, if allowable, could be taken by the client (but could not be taken by the donee). The net proceeds could then be given away.

Discourage an older or ill client from giving away highly appreciated property. Although the gift may save some probate costs and inheritance taxes, the beneficiaries will end up paying more income taxes when the property is later sold. Why? Because appreciated property generally gets a "step-up in basis" (cost for purposes of calculating taxable gain) if it is held until death, but will not get that step-up if it is given away even a moment before death. (Basis step-up may be limited for decedents dying in 2010). Instead, its basis in the hands of the beneficiaries is the client's basis regardless of how low that was. For instance, if stock was purchased 40 years ago for $10 a share and it's now worth $1,000, the $990 built in gain is never subjected to income tax, either to the client or to his heirs, if it is held to the client's death. If the property is given away, the donee must carry over the donor's $10 a share basis.

HOW TO COMPUTE THE FEDERAL ESTATE TAX

The federal estate tax system was designed to "redistribute" wealth and is often, by intent and in result, "confiscatory." Financial planners who want to help clients keep more of their wealth within the family unit must understand how the federal estate tax system works and how the tax is computed. [EGTRRA 2001 repeals the estate tax for one year in 2010.] Study the form below, Figure 14.2, as you read the following explanations of how the tax is computed. A more comprehensive explanation can be found in our companion text, the *Tools & Techniques of Estate Planning*.

An Overview

The first step is the computation of the gross estate. This is the total of all property the client owns in his own name at death. It also includes some property that is not technically owned by the client but which the tax law requires the executor to include.

After the gross estate is computed, certain adjustments are allowed. These adjustments include deductions for

Figure 14.2

FEDERAL ESTATE TAX WORKSHEET			
1	Year of Death		______
2	Gross Estate (before exclusions)		$______
3	- Conservation Easement Exclusion		($______)
4	Gross Estate		$______
5	- Funeral and Administration Expenses Deduction	$______	
6	- Debts and Taxes Deduction	$______	
7	- Losses Deduction	$______	
8	- Subtotal: 5 to 7		($______)
9	Adjusted Gross Estate		$______
10	- Marital Deduction	$______	
11	- Charitable Deduction	$______	
12	- Other Deductions [State Death Taxes]	$______	
13	- Subtotal: 10 to 12		($______)
14	Taxable Estate		$______
15	+ Adjusted Taxable Gifts		$______
16	Computation Base		$______
17	Tax on Computation Base		$______
18	- Gift Tax on Adjusted Taxable Gifts		($______)
19	Tentative Tax		$______
20	- Unified Credit	$______	
21	- State Death Tax Credit	$______	
22	- Pre-1977 Gift Tax Credit	$______	
23	- Previously Taxed Property Credit	$______	
24	- Foreign Death Tax Credit	$______	
25	- Total Credits		($______)
26	Federal Estate Tax		$______

Source: *Advanced Sales Reference Service* (a National Underwriter Company publication).

funeral and administrative expenses, as well as for certain debts and taxes. The result is appropriately called the "adjusted gross estate."

One or more deductions can be taken from the adjusted gross estate. Major deductions are for (1) property passing in a qualifying manner to a surviving spouse (the "marital deduction"), and (2) property passing to a charity (the "charitable deduction"). The result of subtracting the allowable deductions is the taxable estate.

The term, "taxable estate" is a somewhat misleading term since the tax is not based on this amount but upon the "contribution base." The contribution base is the sum of the taxable estate and "adjusted taxable gifts," the taxable portion of lifetime gifts that weren't already included in the gross estate. For instance, if a divorced client had given his daughter $102,000 in cash in 2006, the taxable gift would be $90,000 ($102,000 less the $12,000 annual exclusion). That $90,000 would be added to the client's taxable estate.

The federal estate tax rates are applied to the total of the taxable estate and the adjusted taxable gifts. However, this tax on the contribution base is reduced by the gift tax that would be payable on the adjusted taxable gifts. This ensures the cumulative and progressive nature of the gift and estate tax rates (additional transfers are taxed at higher rates).

Once the tentative tax is computed, it may be reduced by one or more credits. These credits, which provide a dollar for dollar reduction of the tax, are

1. the unified credit
2. the credit for state death taxes
3. the credit for foreign death taxes
4. the credit for tax on prior transfers

It is important for the financial planner to note that total liquidity costs (demands on the executor for cash) include the following:

1. funeral and administration costs;
2. debts and unpaid income, gift, and real estate taxes;
3. state death tax;
4. the net federal estate tax(es); and
5. total cash bequests.

Figure 14.3 shows an example of an actual computation.

A Detailed Examination

Run what estate planners call a "hypothetical probate," a financial guesstimate of how much, in taxes and other expenses, would be incurred by the estate if the client died today. This exercise will give the client a good idea of how much liquidity is needed to avoid a forced sale of assets to raise needed cash. It also provides a "base line" for measuring the progress and tax saving realized through planning.

STEP 1: COMPUTE THE GROSS ESTATE. Make a list of the property owned by the client in each of the following eight categories and state the estimated value:

Category 1 – Property in client's name only.

Include all property the client owned in his own name at death such as

1 cash, stocks, bonds, notes, real estate, or mortgages payable to the client

2 tangible (touchable) personal (movable) property such as watches, rings, and other personal effects

3 bank accounts (checking and savings) in the client's own name

4 the right to future income such as the right to partnership profits, dividends, interest payments, or bonuses earned but not actually received at death.

Category 2 – Gifts in which income or control over the property or the income was retained.

This category encompasses property ostensibly given away before death, but in which the donor retained certain rights, such as the right to income produced by the property or the right to use, possess, or enjoy the property itself. Giving away property but keeping the right to enjoy or control it or determine who will receive the property or its income

Figure 14.3

	FEDERAL ESTATE TAX WORKSHEET		
1	Year of Death		2007
2	Gross Estate (before exclusions)		$2,500,000
3	- Conservation Easement Exclusion		$0
4	Gross Estate		$2,500,000
5	- Funeral and Administration Expenses Deduction	$35,000	
6	- Debts and Taxes Deduction	$45,000	
7	- Losses Deduction	$0	
8	- Subtotal: 5 to 7		($80,000)
9	Adjusted Gross Estate		$2,420,000
10	- Marital Deduction	$0	
11	- Charitable Deduction	$0	
12	- Other Deductions [State Death Taxes]	$132,400	
13	- Subtotal: 10 to 12		($132,400)
14	Taxable Estate		$2,287,600
15	+ Adjusted Taxable Gifts		$100,000
16	Computation Base		$2,387,600
17	Tax on Computation Base		$955,220
18	- Gift Tax on Adjusted Taxable Gifts		$0
19	Tentative Tax		$955,220
20	- Unified Credit	$780,800	
21	- State Death Tax Credit	N/A	
22	- Pre-1977 Gift Tax Credit	$0	
23	- Previously Taxed Property Credit	$0	
24	- Foreign Death Tax Credit	$0	
25	- Total Credits		($780,800)
26	Federal Estate Tax		$174,420

Source: *Advanced Sales Reference Service* (a National Underwriter Company publication).

is an incomplete disposition. The donee's full and complete possession and enjoyment doesn't start (and therefore the decedent's ownership doesn't end) until the decedent dies. That retained right will cause the entire value of the property–measured as of the date of the client's death–to be includable in his estate.

Category 3 – Gifts made conditional on surviving the decedent.

Where a client gives away property during lifetime but conditions the recipient's right to it upon surviving the client and there is a meaningful probability that the property will return to the client's estate (or be subject to disposition under the client's will or by intestacy), the value of the transferred property will be included in the client's estate.

For instance, suppose a client gave real estate worth $100,000 in trust to his son. Assume the trust provides, "the real estate is to go to my son but if he does not survive me, it is to go to the person I name in my will." The client's right to recover the property if the condition (survivorship) is not met is called a "reversionary interest." This reversionary interest is created by an incomplete disposition. Because the transfer of the reversionary interest will take effect at death, the value of the interest may be included in the client's estate.

Category 4 – Gifts with respect to which the client retained the right to alter, amend, revoke, or terminate the gift.

If a client makes a gift but retains the right to change the gift, i.e., to alter the size or amend the conditions of the gift or revoke or terminate the gift at whim, the value of the property subject to that power (measured at the time of death, rather than at the time of the gift) will be in his estate. This provision is broadly construed by the IRS. The mere power to control the date a beneficiary will receive an interest is enough to cause inclusion. In fact, even if the client retains any of the forbidden powers as trustee, the IRS will include the property in his estate.

Category 5 – Annuities or similar arrangements purchased by the client or on his behalf that are payable to the client for life and then to the client's designated heir.

If the client purchased an annuity (a systematic liquidation of principal and interest) which he is receiving or has the right to receive at the time of his death, and payments are to last for the client's life and will continue for the lifetime of his chosen survivor, the present value of the survivor's interest will be in the client's estate at his death. For instance, suppose a client (or the client's employer on behalf of the client as an employee benefit) purchased an annuity that would provide payments of $30,000 per year for the client's life and would then continue payments to the client's daughter. The amount includable in the client's estate would be the amount the same insurance company would charge for an annuity for the daughter's life.

There are limitations. First, if the annuity payments end at the client's death, there is nothing that can be transferred and nothing is includable in the estate. Second, to the extent the survivor can prove contribution of a portion of the cost of the annuity, that percentage of the value of the survivor annuity will not be includable in the client's estate. For instance, if the client's daughter paid for 25% of the annuity, only 75% of the discounted value of payments to be made to the daughter will be includable in the client's estate. (Payments made by an employer are treated as if made by the employee for this purpose).

Category 6 – Jointly held property where a person automatically receives the client's property merely by surviving.

Where property is owned as "joint tenants with right of survivorship" or as "tenants by the entireties," upon the death of either joint tenant, the survivor automatically becomes owner. There are two rules that generally apply to such jointly held property: (1) the "50-50" rule and (2) the "percentage of contribution" rule.

The 50-50 rule applies only to property held solely between spouses (furthermore, the interest must have been created after 1976); it cannot be used where anyone other than the husband and wife is a joint tenant. The rule provides that only half of property held jointly with right of survivorship will be in the estate of the first to die, regardless of which spouse paid (or how much either spouse contributed toward) the purchase price. For instance, assume a $200,000 home was purchased entirely from the wife's income. Assume the house appreciated to $800,000 by the date of the husband's death. Under the 50-50 rule, $400,000 would be includable in the husband's estate even though he actually made no contribution. Since this portion will pass to the husband's surviving spouse, it will qualify for the estate tax marital deduction and therefore will not generate any federal estate tax.

All property held jointly with right of survivorship that does not fall under the 50-50 rule is generally subject to the "percentage of contribution" rule (also known as the "consideration furnished" rule). This rule provides that such property is taxed in the estate of the first joint tenant to die except to the extent the survivor can prove contribution to the original purchase price from funds other than any acquired as a gift from the decedent. For instance, two brothers purchased property worth $300,000 and the younger contributed $100,000. At the death of the older brother, when the property was worth $900,000, only $600,000 would be includable in the older brother's estate. Because the survivor must be able to prove the amount of his contribution to the property, regardless of how long a period passes between purchase and the death of the first joint tenant, it is essential that the financial planner point out the importance of meticulous long term record keeping.

Where the property was acquired by the joint owners through gift or inheritance, only the decedent joint tenant's fractional interest is includable.

Category 7 – General powers of appointment (the unlimited right to specify who receives someone else's property).

A client may be given by someone else, such as a parent, the right to say who will receive that person's assets (which may be currently held in trust). This power to appoint (choose the ultimate recipient of the property) will cause the assets subject to the power to be included in the estate of the person who holds that power, if it is so broad that it is considered a "general" power. A power will be considered "general" if the holder can name himself (or his estate or his creditors) recipient of the assets. Thus, if a father creates a trust with $1,000,000 of assets and gives his son the right to specify who will receive those assets and the son has the right to have the trustee pay them to the son, the value of the assets in the trust will be included in the son's estate at the son's death.

Category 8 – Life insurance owned by the client or over which the client has certain rights, or which is payable to the client's estate.

Life insurance proceeds are included in a client's estate if (1) the client owns the policy at death or has any "incidents of ownership" (significant property rights) in the policy, or (2) the proceeds are payable to the client's estate (regardless of who owned the policy or who held the incidents of ownership).

If a client, at the time of death, owns life insurance on his life or had given it away within three years of his death, it will be included in his estate regardless of who was named as beneficiary. Any right to benefit from the policy in a meaningful way or to determine who can benefit from the policy in an economic sense will cause inclusion. Some of these incidents of ownership that cause estate tax inclusion are the right to

1) cash the policy in, or surrender it

2) change the beneficiaries

3) veto an owner's change of beneficiaries

4) borrow policy cash values

5) use the policy as collateral for loans

Life insurance owned by a corporation that the client controlled (that is, he owned more than 50% of the voting stock of the corporation) is also includable in a client's estate to the extent it is payable to a party other than the corporation or its creditors. The entire proceeds (to the extent so payable), not merely the client's ownership percentage, is includable. Planners should remember that these proceeds may also be considered a dividend for income tax purposes. This means that the potential taxes on the proceeds could approach 80% in 2007 (45% estate tax maximum plus 35% income tax).

The second rule that applies to life insurance proceeds is that the payment will be in the client's estate no matter who owned the policy or held incidents of ownership in it if it is payable to the client's estate or for the estate's benefit. For example, even if the policy was purchased and owned by the client's son, it would still be includable in the client's estate if the estate's executor (as executor) was named as beneficiary or if a creditor of the client received the proceeds.

These are the eight main categories of interests that cause inclusion of assets in the gross estate of a client. When doing a hypothetical estate probate, total the values of all the assets that fall under these categories. Don't worry that the figures are not exact. In the planning stage the goal should be a "guesstimation" of the estate's greatest potential need for cash. Err on the conservative side. A planner will never be sued by a surviving spouse who received "too much" cash.

STEP 2: ADJUST THE GROSS ESTATE.

The next step is to adjust the gross estate. An executor can deduct from the gross estate funeral expenses including interment, burial lot or vault, grave marker, and perpetual care costs. Administrative costs are also deductible. These include

1. expenses incurred in the collection and preservation of assets passing under the will

2. costs incurred in paying off debts

3. expenses incurred in distributing what's left to the appropriate beneficiaries

Administrative expenses include court costs, accounting fees, appraiser's fees, brokerage costs, executor's commissions, and attorney's fees. These costs will vary widely and be affected by (1) location, (2) size of the estate, and (3) complexity of the administrative problems. For instance, bank accounts, money market certificates, and life insurance are all good examples of "low probate cost," highly liquid assets. Where the estate has little cash and many assets or properties that must be appraised, the estate settlement expenses will be higher. Many planners, as a rule of thumb, estimate 5% to 7% of the probate estate for administrative expenses in a small to moderate sized estate (under $1,200,000) and 3% to 5% in a larger estate.

Figure 14.4

GIFT AND ESTATE TAX RATE SCHEDULES

2006 GIFT AND ESTATE TAX TABLE

Taxable Gift/Estate From	To	Tax on Col. 1	Rate on Excess
$0	$10,000	$0	18%
10,000	20,000	1,800	20%
20,000	40,000	3,800	22%
40,000	60,000	8,200	24%
60,000	80,000	13,000	26%
80,000	10,0000	18,200	28%
100,000	150,000	23,800	30%
150,000	250,000	38,800	32%
250,000	500,000	70,800	34%
500,000	750,000	155,800	37%
750,000	1,000,000	248,300	39%
1,000,000	1,250,000	345,800	41%
1,250,000	1,500,000	448,300	43%
1,500,000	2,000,000	555,800	45%
2,000,000	………	780,800	46%

2007 – 2009 GIFT AND ESTATE TAX TABLE

Taxable Gift/Estate From	To	Tax on Col. 1	Rate on Excess
$0	$10,000	$0	18%
10,000	20,000	1,800	20%
20,000	40,000	3,800	22%
40,000	60,000	8,200	24%
60,000	80,000	13,000	26%
80,000	10,0000	18,200	28%
100,000	150,000	23,800	30%
150,000	250,000	38,800	32%
250,000	500,000	70,800	34%
500,000	750,000	155,800	37%
750,000	1,000,000	248,300	39%
1,000,000	1,250,000	345,800	41%
1,250,000	1,500,000	448,300	43%
1,500,000	………	555,800	45%

2010 GIFT TAX ONLY TABLE

Taxable Gift/Estate From	To	Tax on Col. 1	Rate on Excess
$0	$10,000	$0	18%
10,000	20,000	1,800	20%
20,000	40,000	3,800	22%
40,000	60,000	8,200	24%
60,000	80,000	13,000	26%
80,000	10,0000	18,200	28%
100,000	150,000	23,800	30%
150,000	250,000	38,800	32%
250,000	500,000	70,800	34%
500,000	750,000	155,800	37%

2011 GIFT AND ESTATE TAX TABLE

Taxable Gift/Estate From	To	Tax on Col. 1	Rate on Excess
$0	$10,000	$0	18%
10,000	20,000	1,800	20%
20,000	40,000	3,800	22%
40,000	60,000	8,200	24%
60,000	80,000	13,000	26%
80,000	10,0000	18,200	28%
100,000	150,000	23,800	30%
150,000	250,000	38,800	32%
250,000	500,000	70,800	34%
500,000	750,000	155,800	37%
750,000	1,000,000	248,300	39%
1,000,000	1,250,000	345,800	41%
1,250,000	1,500,000	448,300	43%
1,500,000	2,000,000	555,800	45%
2,500,000	3,000,000	1,025,800	53%
3,000,000	10,000,000	1,290,800	55%
10,000,000	17,184,000	5,140,800	60%
17,184,000	………	9,451,200	55%

Debts and taxes are also deductible. The executor can deduct all the client's bona fide debts, including mortgages owed at death. Deductible taxes include income, gift, and property taxes owed but not paid at death. Casualty losses incurred during the administration of the estate are deductible, but most financial planners ignore this area unless assisting in an actual estate probate.

The sum of these deductions is taken from the gross estate. The result is appropriately called the "adjusted gross estate."

STEP 3: COMPUTE THE TAXABLE ESTATE.

Deductions may be taken to reduce the adjusted gross estate still further: (1) the marital deduction for certain transfers to a surviving spouse, (2) the charitable deduction for certain transfers to a qualified charity, (3) the deduction for qualified family-owned business interests (EGTRRA 2001 repeals this deduction after 2003), and (4) a deduction for state death taxes (replaces state death tax credit for 2005 to 2010).

The marital deduction is the most important deduction in most estates of married couples. This is because it is the largest deduction most estates receive. It's allowed for property passing outright, or in a manner that's tantamount to outright, to a surviving spouse. This deduction is virtually unlimited. A client can leave his entire estate to his surviving spouse and, regardless of its size, the deduction could wipe out the federal estate tax entirely. Use of a qualified domestic trust is generally required if the surviving spouse is not a U.S. citizen.

The charitable deduction, like the marital deduction, is virtually unlimited. Conceivably, a client could leave his entire estate to charity and no matter how large the bequest it would all be deductible.

The result of subtracting these deductions is the "taxable estate."

STEP 4: COMPUTE THE COMPUTATION BASE AND TENTATIVE TAX.

The term "taxable estate" is a misnomer because the tax is not calculated on the taxable estate. "Adjusted taxable gifts," that is, the taxable portion of certain lifetime gifts (post 1976 taxable gifts that were not already includable in the gross estate), are added back at this point in the computation.

When adjusted taxable gifts are added to the taxable estate, the sum is called the "computation base." This is the base upon which the estate tax rates (see Figure 14.4) are applied. The tax that would be payable on adjusted taxable gifts is also calculated (using the same tax rates, see Figure 14.4).

The tax on the computation base minus the tax on adjusted taxable gifts equals the tentative tax. The words, "tentative tax" are used because the tax computed by applying the rates to the base is not yet the final amount: it is next lowered by one or more credits.

STEP 5: COMPUTE THE NET ESTATE TAX PAYABLE.

Certain credits may be allowed. The two most important of these credits are the unified credit and the credit for state death taxes. The unified credit is a dollar for dollar reduction against the federal estate tax otherwise payable.

Year	Exclusion Equivalent	Unified Credit
2006-2008	$2,000,000	$780,800
2009	$3,500,000	$1,455,800
2010	NA	NA
2011-	$1,000,000	$345,800

The second major credit is the one allowed for state death taxes. The table in Figure 14.5 illustrates the amount of this credit. The credit is limited to the lower of (a) the state death tax actually paid or (b) the amount of credit from the government's table. EGTRRA 2001 phased out this credit and replaced it with a deduction for 2005 to 2010.

The third credit is for death taxes paid to a foreign country. This credit is designed to eliminate double taxation on property taxable both by the United States and by a foreign government.

The fourth credit is called the credit for tax on prior transfers. The purpose of this credit is to minimize the impact of estate taxation where the same property is includable in the estates of two or more persons who die within a short time (ten years or less) of each other. The closer the two deaths occur, the greater the credit allowed in the estate of the second decedent.

Figure 14.5

CREDIT FOR STATE DEATH TAXES

If the adjusted taxable estate is:	The maximum tax credit shall be:
Not over $90,000	8/10ths of 1% of the amount by which the adjusted taxable estate exceeds $40,000.
Over $90,000 but not over $140,000	$400 plus 1.6% of the excess over $90,000.
Over $140,000 but not over $240,000	$1,200 plus 2.4% of the excess over $140,000.
Over $240,000 but not over $440,000	$3,600 plus 3.2% of the excess over $240,000.
Over $440,000 but not over $640,000	$10,000 plus 4% of the excess over $440,000.
Over $640,000 but not over $840,000	$18,000 plus 4.8% of the excess over $640,000.
Over $840,000 but not over $1,040,000	$27,600 plus 5.6% of the excess over $840,000.
Over $1,040,000 but not over $1,540,000	$38,800 plus 6.4% of the excess over $1,040,000.
Over $1,540,000 but not over $2,040,000	$70,800 plus 7.2% of the excess over $1,540,000.
Over $2,040,000 but not over $2,540,000	$106,800 plus 8% of the excess over $2,040,000.
Over $2,540,000 but not over $3,040,000	$146,800 plus 8.8% of the excess over $2,540,000.
Over $3,040,000 but not over $3,540,000	$190,800 plus 9.6% of the excess over $3,040,000.
Over $3,540,000 but not over $4,040,000	$238,800 plus 10.4% of the excess over $3,540,000.
Over $4,040,000 but not over $5,040,000	$290,800 plus 11.2% of the excess over $4,040,000.
Over $5,040,000 but not over $6,040,000	$402,800 plus 12% of the excess over $5,040,000.
Over $6,040,000 but not over $7,040,000	$522,800 plus 12.8% of the excess over $6,040,000.
Over $7,040,000 but not over $8,040,000	$650,800 plus 13.6% of the excess over $7,040,000.
Over $8,040,000 but not over $9,040,000	$786,800 plus 14.4% of the excess over $8,040,000.
Over $9,040,000 but not over $10,040,000	$930,800 plus 15.2% of the excess over $9,040,000.
Over $10,040,000	$1,082,800 plus 16% of the excess over $10,040,000.

The term "adjusted taxable estate" means the taxable estate reduced by $60,000.

EGTRRA 2001 reduces the credit by 25% in 2002, 50% in 2003, 75% in 2004, and replaces it with a deduction in 2005.

COMPUTING THE TAX ON GENERATION-SKIPPING TRANSFERS

There is yet another level of potential federal tax – the tax on transfers which skip a generation. This generation-skipping transfer (GST) tax is imposed at the top estate tax rate (45% in 2007, see Figure 14.4), on transfers to grandchildren or others of that generation or younger. Although it is of concern to only wealthy clients, inflation coupled with long term growth of assets puts a surprising number of people into situations where planning for the tax can result in significant savings. [EGTRRA 2001 repeals the GST tax for one year in 2010.]

Three examples of how the GST tax works follow and illustrate how harsh the tax can be. The examples assume none of the GST tax exceptions described below is applicable:

1. *The "direct skip"* – The client makes a lifetime gift of cash or other property to her grandson in 2007. If the taxable gift was worth $1,000,000, the grandparent would be liable for a 45% tax on the $1,000,000 transfer. Here, the $450,000 tax is paid by the grandparent and is not paid from the gift itself. So the grandson nets the full $1,000,000.

2. *The "taxable distribution"* – The client sets up a trust that provides income or principal distributions to her daughter or granddaughter at the trustee's discretion. At the time the trustee distributes either income or principal to the granddaughter (while the daughter is still alive), the result is a taxable distribution. If the trustee distributed $100,000 of trust income in 2007, the result would be a 45% tax, $45,000. The granddaughter would net only $55,000.

3. *The "taxable termination"* – The client sets up a trust that provides income to her son for life. At the son's death, assets in the trust pass to the son's son, the client's grandchild. At the son's death in 2007, the amount passing to the

grandson becomes taxable. If $1,000,000 was placed into the trust, there would be a tax of $450,000 (45% of $1,000,000). The grandson would receive only $550,000.

Planners should recognize that it is possible that the cost of making a generation-skipping transfer can be greater than the value of the entire gift. For example, assume a client who is already in the 45% gift tax bracket writes a check to his granddaughter for $2,000,000 in 2007. The generation-skipping transfer tax will be 45% of the $2,000,000, or $900,000. In addition, since the transfer was a gift, the client must pay a gift tax at the rate of 45% on the gift, another $900,000. To make it even worse, the client is deemed to be making a second gift, a gift of the generation-skipping transfer tax ($900,000) upon which must be paid an additional 45% gift tax (or $405,000). The total tax is therefore $2,205,000.

An important exception to the GST tax is that each donor can transfer up to $2,000,000 (in 2007; this GST exemption equals the estate tax exclusion equivalent, see above, after 2003) before becoming subject to the tax. This exemption can be increased to $4,000,000 (in 2007) by "splitting" the exemption with a spouse (i.e., treating each spouse as if he or she made half the transfer). Also, gifts of up to $12,000 (as indexed in 2007) a year ($24,000 if the gift is split) can be made to an unlimited number of donees without being subjected to the GST tax (although a gift in trust requires a separate share for each exclusion).

STATE DEATH TAXES

Many clients have to pay state death taxes. Clients of modest to moderate wealth may lose far more to state death taxation than to the federal estate tax system. Given the changeover from the state death tax credit arrangement prior to 2005 to the state death tax deduction arrangement after 2004, many states have changed their state death tax systems in response to the change in federal method. Some states continue to impose a tax equal to the maximum amount for which a state death tax credit was available prior to EGTRRA 2001. Some states use a unified credit amount which is less than the federal amount. Other states have (re)imposed a separate state estate or inheritance tax. Planning can lower state death taxes considerably.

CONCLUSION

Estate planning is an essential part of the overall financial planning process. It is possible for most clients to efficiently and effectively conserve and distribute an estate in a manner that both minimizes taxes and accomplishes personal objectives. These results can be achieved only if the client can be helped to become aware of the scope and urgency of the problems and overcome a natural unwillingness to address difficult and sometimes distasteful issues (such as his own mortality). Above all, the planner must

1. show compassion and care for reasons beyond possible compensation

2. become competent in estate planning and/or work with other advisers who are

3. learn the goals, circumstances, and needs of all the people involved

4. bring the client and the client's family into the planning process as much as possible

CHAPTER ENDNOTES

1. 110 S.Ct. 111.

Part 3:

FUNDAMENTALS

Chapter 15

BUDGETING AND CASH MANAGEMENT

WHAT IS IT?

Budgeting can be defined as the ability to estimate the amount of money to be received and spent for various purposes within a given time frame. For purposes of this text, however, budgeting should be thought of as a deliberate plan for spending and investing the resources available to the investor. It ultimately serves as a yardstick against which to measure actual investment results.

HOW DOES IT WORK?

In simplest terms, the budgeting process works as a result of the establishment of a working budget model by an investor, followed by the comparative analysis of actual investment results with the expected results used to create the planning budget. It is the comparison of budget results with expectations that yields the benefits of the process to the user.

WHEN IS THE USE OF THIS TECHNIQUE INDICATED?

1. When there is a need to measure periodic progress towards the achievement of specific goals (a) within a defined time frame and (b) within the confines of limited resources.

2. When the elements of economic activity are of sufficient complexity to warrant continuous monitoring of the details.

3. When there is a need to provide guidelines for evaluating the economic performance of various elements or individuals.

4. When there is a need to communicate a planning strategy to those affected by the budget.

5. When there is a need to provide incentives (goals) for the performance of individuals involved.

6. Budgeting may be indicated for the following specific purposes:

   a) controlling household expenses

   b) accomplishing desired wealth accumulation/savings goals, such as

      (1) saving for retirement

      (2) funding the children's education

      (3) saving for vacation

   c) Monitoring the performance of a specific investment, such as

      (1) a securities portfolio

      (2) rental property

      (3) a closely-held business

ADVANTAGES

1. Budgeting helps coordinate activity of the investor and financial counseling team in developing objectives.

2. Budgeting reveals inefficient, ineffective, or unusual utilization of resources.

3. Budgeting makes family members aware of the need to conserve resources and helps to allocate roles in achieving overall financial objectives to various individuals.

4. Budgeting provides a means of financial self-evaluation and a guideline to measure actual performance.

5. Budgeting allows the recognition and forces the anticipation of problems before they occur and, thus, permits corrective action or preparation to be taken.

6. Budgeting highlights the possibility of, and the need for, alternative courses of action.

7. Budgeting provides a motivation for performance.

DISADVANTAGES

1. To the extent the data utilized are inaccurate, the conclusions drawn from the budget may be misleading.

2. Many individuals have a psychological aversion to the record keeping required and may not maintain sufficient information for the budget to be of use.

3. A rote dependence on budgeted numbers inhibits creativity, tends to stifle "risk taking," and encourages mechanical thinking. Such an investor may forfeit opportunities or fail to minimize losses.

HOW IS IT IMPLEMENTED?

The principal purpose of an investor's budget is to control and evaluate performance. Therefore, the basic sources of information in developing a budget are personal financial statements, prior years' tax returns, canceled checks, and projections of income and expenditures for the target period. Once initial estimates have been made, they must be adjusted in light of special circumstances or considerations.

Here are some guidelines to use when establishing a budget:

1. Make the budget flexible enough so that it will work even if there are emergencies, unexpected opportunities, or other unforeseen circumstances.

2. Keep the budget period short enough so that the estimates you make will involve the minimum amount of guesswork.

3. Establish a budget period long enough to utilize an investment strategy and a workable series of investment procedures. A typical family budget will cover twelve months and coincide with a calendar year.

4. Make the budget simple, short, and understandable.

5. Follow the form and content of the budget consistently.

6. Eliminate any extraneous information.

7. Do not attempt to obtain absolute accuracy, especially with insignificant items.

8. Tailor the budget to specific goals and objectives.

9. Remember that a budget is also a guideline against which actual results are to be measured. Unexpected results, highlighted by comparison with the budget, should be analyzed. It may be that the unexpected variance is in fact the norm, and should therefore be incorporated in a revised budget.

10. Determine, in advance, all the variables that may influence the amounts of specific items of income and expenditures. Income items include expected annual raises and increases or decreases in interest or dividend rates. Expenditures include increased costs, changing tastes or preferences, or changes in family circumstances.

Here is how to construct an income-expenditure budget:

STEP 1 – Estimate the family's annual income. Identify fixed amounts of income expected from the following:

a) salary

b) bonus

c) self-employment (business)

d) real estate

e) dividends – close corporations

f) dividends – publicly traded corporations

g) interest – savings accounts

h) interest – taxable bonds

i) interest – tax free bonds

j) trust income

k) other fixed payment income

l) variable sources of income

If a family experiences an irregular income flow, or because of extreme variations of income finds it difficult to predict, two income estimates should be developed. One estimate should be based on the lowest amount of income that might be received, while the other should show a higher, but still reasonable figure.

STEP 2 – Develop expenditure estimates broken down between fixed and discretionary expenses. Canceled checks and charge account receipts serve as a good basis for developing the following expenditure estimates:

FIXED

a) housing (mortgage or rental payments)

b) utilities

c) food, groceries, etc.

d) clothing and cleaning

e) income taxes

f) social security

g) property taxes

h) transportation

i) medical and dental

j) debt repayment

k) household supplies and maintenance

l) life and disability insurance

m) property and liability insurance,

n) current school expenses

DISCRETIONARY

a) vacations, travel, etc.

b) recreation and entertainment

c) gifts and contributions

d) household furnishings

e) education fund

f) savings

g) investments

h) other

STEP 3 – Determine the excess or shortfall of income within the budget period.

STEP 4 – Consider available methods of increasing income or decreasing expenses.

STEP 5 – Calculate both income and expenses as a percentage of the total and determine if there is a better or preferable allocation of resources.

Figure 15.3 (at the end of this chapter) is an illustration of the Sample family's 2007 personal budget using *NumberCruncher* computer software. This example reflects a $5,800 excess of budgeted income over expenditures for the year. With this estimate of the year's expected financial results available early in the year, the Sample family can plan their investment or spending of the projected excess.

However, as the illustration in Figure 15.4 (at the end of this chapter) indicates, if Mr. Sample does not receive his expected bonus of $15,000, the family will have a budgeted shortfall of $4,500. This is so even after a projected reduction in income taxes of $4,500 (from $28,000 to $23,500) and in Social Security taxes of $200 (from $7,700 to $7,500) as a result of not receiving the bonus. On this basis, the Sample family must modify their spending and investing plans for the year. This example illustrates the importance of preparing budgets reflecting conservative as well as optimistic results.

Figure 15.5 (at the end of this chapter) is a printout of a blank budget form from *NumberCruncher* that you may find helpful in preparing your personal budget.

WHERE CAN I FIND OUT MORE ABOUT IT?

1. Lawrence Gitman, *Personal Financial Planning with Financial Planning Software and Worksheets* (South-Western College Publishing, 2001).

2. *NumberCruncher* (Leimberg & LeClair, Inc.).

3. David L. Scott, *The Guide to Personal Budgeting* (Globe Pequot Press, 1995).

4. *Basic Budgeting* (Credit Union Nat'l Assoc., 1990).

5. *Armed Forces Guide to Personal Financial Planning: Strategies for Managing Your Budget, Savings, Insurance, Taxes, and Investments* (Stackpole Books, 1998).

QUESTIONS AND ANSWERS

Question – How long a period should the typical family budget cover?

Answer – A family budget should project income and expenditure activity for any planning period an investor feels is convenient or appropriate for a specific purpose. Most planners budget for 12 months at a time. This typically coincides with a calendar year, but may also be a fiscal period, such as a school year. Generally, the budget is calculated on a month-by-month basis.

It is often appropriate to budget for longer periods of time, such as the four-year costs of funding a college education. However, for any long-range budgeting, it is important to keep in mind that the accuracy of the budget will decrease as the length of the period covered increases.

Question – Are there special techniques that should be used by clients with highly irregular income flows or expenditures?

Answer – Families that experience difficulty in predicting income or who may have highly variable cash outflows should consider two budgets – one based on the lowest income and highest expenditures expected ("worst case" budget), and the second based on the client's reasonable expectations of income and expenses ("most probable" budget).

In some cases, it may also make sense to prepare a budget based on the highest possible income and lowest possible expenditures ("best case" budget). This third alternative budget is often used where a client wants to see whether the cost of a "hoped for" expenditure, such as an expensive new car, is within reach if everything falls into place.

Question – What variables should be considered in establishing a budget?

Answer – It is important to identify all major variables that can influence both income and expenses. The client's income can be affected by salary increases, bonuses, dividend or interest rate changes, proceeds from the sale of stocks or other assets, inheritances, etc. A client's expenditures can vary as a result of increased costs of living, unexpected business expenses, financial catastrophes, such as uninsured theft or fire losses, changes in tastes or preferences, and large-scale expenses, such as college or retirement.

Question – Why is it often helpful to divide a budget between fixed and variable components?

Answer – Many planners divide an income statement into income that is (a) fixed and certain and (b) variable or uncertain. Expenditures should be divided between those that are (a) fixed and (b) discretionary.

A budget based on only fixed and certain income would be considered conservative. Limiting expenditures to this conservative estimate of income will assure the client that fixed and expected costs can be covered. Any "excess" income can then be used for investments or discretionary spending.

Alternatively, excess income can be placed in a "contingency" fund, which every family should have for emergencies or opportunities. Some families, rather than building contingency funds, have emergency lines of credit through various banks or credit cards. This enables them to invest any excess income, or use it to increase their standard of living. There are two drawbacks to using this technique. First, the interest charged on such credit card borrowing is usually quite high. Second, the client must have sufficient income to repay the loan.

Annual expenditures can be classified as fixed or discretionary. But the term "fixed" applies only in the short run and can often be changed without imposing a radical shift in the client's lifestyle. Even the most "fixed" of all expenditures, housing, can be changed if necessary to meet financial requirements or objectives.

Discretionary expenditures, by definition, can be foregone or timed through proper budgeting so that they are incurred when sufficient income is available.

Question – How much should be allocated in a family's budget for "emergencies" and where should that money be kept?

Answer – Budgeting should allocate cash reserves for (a) emergencies, (b) scheduled forthcoming purchases, (c) investment opportunities and retirement savings, and (d) liquidity needs.

How much a family needs in cash emergency reserves depends upon several factors including (a) the size of the family, (b) the amount and stability of the family income, (c) the number of wage earners in the family, (d) the extent of property, life, disability, medical, and liability insurance coverage as well as the levels of deductibles and co-pays associated with the coverage, (e) other ready or liquid sources of cash such as personal or home lines of credit, unborrowed credit card balances, life insurance cash values, or other reliable sources of borrowing such as well-heeled parents, grandparents, or other relatives who would be willing to lend support in times of need, (f) the level and amount of the family's non-cash investments, as well as (g) any other factors increasing a family's financial risk or uncertainty such as occupational and recreational risk levels and other habits and behaviors.

In general, families need greater cash emergency reserves when the family is larger, the family income is greater (ironically, but they have to maintain a higher standard of living in the event of disruptions to their regular income), the family's income is less stable and predictable, there are fewer wage-earners in the family, the family has less complete insurance coverages or greater deductibles and co-pays, the family has relatively smaller non-cash investment balances, and the family has no or few lines or sources of ready credit.

As a general rule of thumb, families should place very short-term reserves to meet day-to-day needs in an interest-bearing checking account. Some advisers suggest that families keep no more than about $5,000 (or 5 percent of total cash reserves, if lower) in such accounts. However, the amount depends upon the family's typical short-term transactions levels and may need to be higher in rare cases. With the nearly ubiquitous use of credit cards for many day-to-day cash transactions, many families get by quite nicely with average checking account balances considerably below $5,000.

Another long-standing rule of thumb is that families should have between three to six months of family income in liquid reserves for family emergencies. These reserves can be held in money market funds that typically pay higher interest than checking accounts, but have the necessary liquidity if the need arises to tap these resources. However, the amount families hold in money market accounts can be lower if they have other sources of ready cash, such as personal lines of credit, unused credit card limits, home equity lines of credit, or other quick and ready sources of borrowing, such as life insurance cash values or untapped borrowing capacity from qualified retirement plans such as 401(k) plans. To the extent families have ready access to these sources of funds in emergency situations, they can redirect some of their cash reserve money from relatively low-interest money market funds into higher-yielding investments.

Another factor affecting the amount families should put into liquid cash reserves is the amounts they already have invested in other less-liquid non-cash investments such as stocks and bonds. Although stocks and bonds are generally very marketable (investors can usually sell these assets within one day), they are not liquid. Liquid assets not only can be converted to cash quickly, but they also can be converted to cash at a relatively fixed and known value. In the case of stocks and bonds, one can convert them to cash quickly, but there is no assurance at what price.

Despite this fact, the greater is the family's level of investment assets, the less is their need for liquid cash reserves because they can relatively quickly put their investment assets up as collateral and borrow necessary funds. In the case of stocks, the margin requirement is about 50% – meaning an investor can borrow up to 50% of the stock's value. For bonds, the margin requirement may be as low as 10%, so investors can often borrow up to 90% of a bond's value.

Question – If I can increase my investment contributions each year, what impact will this have on my ability to accumulate a stated amount of future capital?

Answer – The ability to increase future contributions to an investment program means that you could start with smaller amounts for the first several years than would otherwise be required. For example, suppose that you wanted to accumulate a retirement fund of $100,000 over the next twenty years. If you make uniform annual contributions, you will have to pay $2,718 a year for twenty years, assuming a 6% after-tax return on invested funds. However, if you could increase your contributions by 5% each year, the amount of your annual payment would be lower than this figure for the first nine years. The first year payment would be only $1,806. Payments would be higher during the final eleven years, but your income is likely to be greater as well. See Figure 15.1 for a listing of the entire payment schedule for this accumulation program.

Figure 15.1

CONTRIBUTIONS REQUIRED TO REACH A GOAL
IF CONTRIBUTIONS INCREASE ANNUALLY

Desired Future Value (Financial Goal) $100,000
Accumulation Period (Years) 20
After-Tax Return on Invested Capital.......... 0.060
Annual Percentage Increase in Contributions.......... 0.050

Year-End	Required Contribution	Cumulative Contributions	Total Accumulation
1	$1,806	$1,806	$1,806
2	1,896	3,701	3,810
3	1,991	5,692	6,029
4	2,090	7,782	8,481
5	2,195	9,977	11,185
6	2,304	12,281	14,160
7	2,420	14,701	17,429
8	2,541	17,242	21,016
9	2,668	19,909	24,944
10	2,801	22,710	29,242
11	2,941	25,652	33,938
12	3,088	28,740	39,062
13	3,243	31,982	44,648
14	3,405	35,387	50,732
15	3,575	38,962	57,351
16	3,754	42,716	64,545
17	3,941	46,657	72,360
18	4,138	50,795	80,840
19	4,345	55,141	90,035
20	4,563	59,703	100,000

Reprinted with permission from *NumberCruncher*, Leimberg & LeClair, Inc.

Question – If I want to withdraw an increasing amount from my retirement fund to keep up with inflation, how will this affect the required capital?

Answer – Increasing the amount of your withdrawals from a fund on a regular basis will add to the amount of necessary capital, or shorten the time that the fund will provide income. For example, a fund of $529,701 will allow you to make withdrawals of $50,000 each year for twenty years assuming an after-tax interest rate of 7%. If you wanted to be able to increase the amount of the withdrawals by 5% each year, ($52,500 in year two, $55,125 in year three, etc.) then you would need to have $785,844 as a beginning capital balance (see Figure 15.2).

Question – How can I increase my savings and investment?

Answer – In the short run, one can increase savings and investment only by reducing spending on discretionary items. And the shorter is one's horizon, the fewer are the discretionary items one can reduce or eliminate. However, in the longer run, almost all spending categories are discretionary. If necessary, for example, over a year or two, a family can sell a home and move to less expensive housing, they can move to a new state or region with better employment opportunities, they can go back to school to upgrade their marketable skills in their current occupation or to change careers to a more highly-compensated occupation.

Probably the most important step families can take to increase their savings and investment levels is to change their attitude and perspective. Many people save and invest what they have left after paying all their "obligations" such as mortgages,

Figure 15.2

LUMP SUM NEEDED TO PROVIDE INCREASING ANNUAL PAYMENTS	
Amount of Initial Annual Payment Desired	$50,000
Desired % Increase in Annual Payments	0.050
Number of Years Payments Should Last	20
After-Tax Return (%) on Invested Capital	0.070
Principal Needed to Fund Annuity	$785,844

Reprinted with permission from *NumberCruncher*, Leimberg & LeClair, Inc.

car payments, taxes, and the like, as well as those "necessary discretionaries" such as cable TV bills, club dues, and the like.

The change they need to make is to put themselves at the front of the payment list, rather than at the end – they have to adopt a "pay yourself first" mentality. This is easiest to achieve if one takes a "split-the-pot" approach to increases in wages or salaries over time and to any bonuses or windfalls. For example, each year, most people get a pay increase based upon inflation and a real increase in pay for merit and experience. Say, for instance, a person gets a 5% raise when inflation is 3%, totaling $6,000 for the year. Most people are reluctant to actually cut their standard of living to increase their saving, so they would want to spend at least 3% or $3,600 of their raise. However, the key now is to pay themselves first, by immediately allocating at least half of their real $2,400 increase to meet their savings and investment objective right off the top. This means they would take $200 right off the top of their monthly pay and save or invest it. This would still leave them with a real $1,200 increase for new discretionary spending.

Although this is not exactly a huge increase in saving, if this approach is followed each year, the numbers really start to add up. For example, assume that the person's salary continues to increase by 5% per year, inflation remains at 3%, and the person continues to "split-the-pot" by increasing real discretionary spending by 1% of the 5% increase and by increasing the saving/investment element by 1% of the 5% increase each year. In 5 years, both the person's real discretionary spending and savings/investment will increase up to $6,631 per year. If this approach continues for 10 years, the amount this person saves each year will increase to almost $15,100.

Assuming this person earns 8% on the savings/investment balances, the balance will grow to about $23,100 after 5 years, but to over $105,000 after 10 years! If this person can continue with this program for another 5 years (15 years total), the savings/investment balance will reach almost $300,000 and this person will still have increased real annual discretionary spending by almost $26,000 per year as well!

It is even easier to apply this system when a person gets a promotion that greatly increases annual income, say by 20%. In this case, if the family has the discipline to only increase their standard of living by 5%, they can immediately increase their savings/investment by 15% of salary. For most people, a real increase in their standard of living of 5% is quite a step up. They just have to take a "pay themselves first" attitude towards their savings/investment goal.

Similarly, suppose a person receives a Christmas bonus of $2,000. The "pay-yourself-first" approach would suggest that the person should simply save the entire amount, since the entire amount is a windfall. However, even saving just half under the split-the-pot approach would increase the family's saving/investment immediately by $1,000. Putting the majority of any bonuses, inheritances, or other windfalls into savings/investments is a "no-cost" savings option, since one is giving up nothing in discretionary spending compared to what one would have had anyway.

Part of the way to make this program work, is to make the savings/investment payments automatic, or nearly so. In other words, make them essentially nondiscretionary. For instance, if your employer offers a savings program, commit your designated percentage of salary and have it automatically taken out of your pay, just like your income tax withholding. Alternatively, banks, money market funds, and mutual funds permit account-holders to have designated amounts automatically deposited to savings or investment accounts from the account-holders' checking account each month. Once you have decided how you are going to "split-the-pot" of any salary increases for a year, set up an automatic deposit program to make the savings/investment payments automatic and, thus, effectively, nondiscretionary.

Taking a "pay-yourself-first" attitude and a "split-the-pot" approach to savings and investment may seem to be just baby steps at first. But as was described above, applied consistently over 10 to 15 years, the cumulative results can be enormous.

Figure 15.3 — Sample family budget

INCOME AND EXPENSES REPORT

Annual Income and Expenses For 2007

Annual Income	Amount	% of Total Income
Salary/Bonus 1:	$125,000	74.4%
Salary/Bonus 2:	$30,000	17.9%
Self-Employment (Business):	0	0.0%
Dividends — Close Corporation Stock:	0	0.0%
Dividends — Investments:	$3,000	1.8%
Interest on Savings Accounts:	$2,000	1.2%
Interest on Bonds, Taxable:	$5,000	3.0%
Interest on Bonds, Exempt:	$3,000	1.8%
Trust Income:	0	0.0%
Rental Income:	0	0.0%
Other Sources:	0	0.0%
Total Annual Income:	$168,000	100.0%
Annual Expenditures - Fixed		
Housing (Mortgage/Rent):	$15,500	9.2%
Utilities & Telephone:	$7,000	4.2%
Food, Groceries, Etc.:	$10,500	6.3%
Clothing and Cleaning:	$7,000	4.2%
Income Taxes:	$28,000	16.7%
Social Security:	$7,700	4.6%
Real Estate Taxes:	$5,000	3.0%
Transportation:	$8,000	4.8%
Medical/Dental Expenses:	$8,000	4.8%
Debt Repayment:	$5,000	3.0%
Housing Supplies/Maint.:	$6,000	3.6%
Life Insurance:	$8,000	4.8%
Prop. & Liability Ins.:	$5,000	3.0%
Current School Exp.:	$4,500	2.7%
Total Fixed Expenses:	$125,200	74.4%
Variable Expenses		
Vacations, Travel, Etc.:	$4,000	2.4%
Recreation/Entertainment:	$5,000	3.0%
Contributions, Gifts:	$7,500	4.5%
Household Furnishings:	$5,000	3.0%
Education Fund:	$5,000	3.0%
Savings:	$3,000	1.8%
Investments:	$2,500	1.5%
Other Expenses:	$5,000	3.0%
Total Variable Expenses:	$37,000	22.0%
Total Expenses:	$162,200	96.5%
Net Saving:	**$5,800**	**3.5%**

Reprinted with permission from *NumberCruncher*, Leimberg & LeClair, Inc.

Figure 15.4 — Alternate Sample family budget

INCOME AND EXPENSES REPORT

Annual Income and Expenses For 2007

Annual Income

	Amount	% of Total Income
Salary/Bonus 1:	$110,000	71.9%
Salary/Bonus 2:	$30,000	19.6%
Self-Employment (Business):	$0	0.0%
Dividends — Close Corporation Stock:	$0	0.0%
Dividends — Investments:	$3,000	2.0%
Interest on Savings Accounts:	$2,000	1.3%
Interest on Bonds, Taxable:	$5,000	3.3%
Interest on Bonds, Exempt:	$3,000	2.0%
Trust Income:	$0	0.0%
Rental Income:	$0	0.0%
Other Sources:	$0	0.0%
Total Annual Income:	$153,000	100.0%

Annual Expenditures - Fixed

Housing (Mortgage/Rent):	$15,500	10.1%
Utilities & Telephone:	$7,000	4.6%
Food, Groceries, Etc.:	$10,500	6.9%
Clothing and Cleaning:	$7,000	4.6%
Income Taxes:	$23,500	15.4%
Social Security:	$7,500	4.9%
Real Estate Taxes:	$5,000	3.3%
Transportation:	$8,000	5.2%
Medical/Dental Expenses:	$8,000	5.2%
Debt Repayment:	$5,000	3.3%
Housing Supplies/Maint.:	$6,000	3.9%
Life Insurance:	$8,000	5.2%
Prop. & Liability Ins.:	$5,000	3.3%
Current School Exp.:	$4,500	2.9%
Total Fixed Expenses:	$120,500	78.8%

Variable Expenses

Vacations, Travel, Etc.:	$4,000	2.6%
Recreation/Entertainment:	$5,000	3.3%
Contributions, Gifts:	$7,500	4.9%
Household Furnishings:	$5,000	3.3%
Education Fund:	$5,000	3.3%
Savings:	$3,000	2.0%
Investments:	$2,500	1.6%
Other Expenses:	$5,000	3.3%
Total Variable Expenses:	$37,000	24.2%
Total Expenses:	$157,500	102.9%
Net Saving:	**$-4,500**	**-2.9%**

Reprinted with permission from *NumberCruncher*, Leimberg & LeClair, Inc.

Figure 15.5 — Blank budget form

Budget — Annual Income and Expenses for:		2007
Annual Income	**Amount**	**(%)**
Salary/Bonus 1	0	0.0
Salary/Bonus 2	0	0.0
Self-Employment (Business)	0	0.0
Rental Income	0	0.0
Dividends — Close Corporation Stock	0	0.0
Dividends — Investments	0	0.0
Interest — Savings Accounts	0	0.0
Interest — Bonds, Taxable	0	0.0
Interest — Bonds, Exempt	0	0.0
Trust Income	0	0.0
Rental Income	0	0.0
Other Sources	0	0.0
Total Annual Income	$0	0.0
Annual Expenditures		
Fixed Expenses		
Housing (Mortgage/Rent)	0	0.0
Utilities & Telephone	0	0.0
Food, Groceries, Etc.	0	0.0
Clothing and Cleaning	0	0.0
Income Taxes	0	0.0
Social Security	0	0.0
Real Estate Taxes	0	0.0
Transportation	0	0.0
Medical/Dental Expenses	0	0.0
Debt Repayment	0	0.0
Housing Supplies/Maint.	0	0.0
Life Insurance	0	0.0
Prop. & Liability Ins.	0	0.0
Current School Expense	0	0.0
Total Fixed Expenses	$0	0.0
Variable Expenses		
Vacations, Travel, Etc.	0	0.0
Recreation/Entertainment	0	0.0
Contributions, Gifts	0	0.0
Household Furnishings	0	0.0
Education Fund	0	0.0
Savings	0	0.0
Investments	0	0.0
Other Expenses	0	0.0
Total Variable Expenses	$0	0.0
Total Income	$0	0.0
Total Expenses	$0	0.0
Net Saving (Borrowing)	$0	0.0

Reprinted with permission from *NumberCruncher*, Leimberg & LeClair, Inc.

Chapter 16

PERSONAL FINANCIAL STATEMENTS

WHAT IS IT?

Personal financial statements provide a summary of an individual's financial position. The financial statements most commonly thought of in a business context are the "Balance Sheet" and the "Income Statement." In personal financial planning, the financial statements that are most commonly used are the "Balance Sheet" – the American Institute of Certified Public Accountants (AICPA) refers to this as a "Statement of Financial Condition" – and the "Cash Flow Statement."

As with business financial statements, a personal "balance sheet" reflects a person's assets, liabilities, and net worth as of a given date. A personal "cash flow statement" shows an individual's cash receipts (e.g., income) and cash disbursements (e.g., expenses) for a given period of time. The cash flow statement is often presented in conjunction with a statement of an individual's taxable income.

HOW DOES IT WORK?

The preparation of personal financial statements requires the compilation of the individual's "personal financial data" into the formal statements used in the financial planning process. Some individuals have developed the habit of maintaining financial statements on a regular basis. Other clients will not begin the financial statement process until a specific need arises, and often will need professional help. These statements are essential before a financial planner can effectively begin the planning process.

Figure 16.1 is an example of a personal balance sheet, using the format illustrated in the AICPA's Personal Financial Statements Guide. Such statements of financial condition are generally accompanied by notes, which are an integral part of these statements. Note 1 is a general statement that the assets are stated at their estimated current values, and the liabilities at their estimated current amounts. The other notes are referenced at the end of the description of the specific assets and liabilities to which they apply. They generally describe the methods used to determine the estimated current values of assets and the estimated current amounts of liabilities and any other information warranting disclosure to the users of the statements.

Contingent liabilities are listed on the balance sheet without specific amounts reflected. This is because it is not possible to determine whether or how much the individual may be required to pay. An example of a contingent liability is a personal guaranty of a debt of a closely held corporation controlled by the individual. Such contingent liabilities generally receive substantial explanation in the notes to the financial statements.

Figure 16.2 is an example of a combined personal statement of cash flow and taxable income that can be extremely useful in the financial planning process. (A blank form for this statement suitable for photocopying appears in Figure 16.3 at the end of this chapter.)

WHEN IS THE USE OF THIS TECHNIQUE INDICATED?

1. It is the essential starting point in the determination of personal financial goals. The financial statements are critical in order to determine (a) "what you have" and (b) "what you need to get where you want to be."

2. When an individual would like to borrow money for an investment and must prove to the lender an ability to make debt service payments and assure the creditor that there is adequate security for the loan.

3. When a "tax shelter" or other investment is contemplated and the investor must prove to the promoters that all the financial criteria established in the prospectus can be met. These criteria typically include

   a) a minimum income and marginal tax bracket

   b) a minimum net worth of the prospective investor

Figure 16.1

ROBERT AND REBECCA STONE
STATEMENTS OF FINANCIAL CONDITION
DECEMBER 31, 2007 AND 2006

	December 31, 2007	December 31, 2006
ASSETS		
Cash	$ 7,400	$ 31,200
Bonus Receivable	40,000	20,000
Investments		
Marketable Securities (Note 2)	321,000	281,400
Stock Options (Note 3)	56,000	48,000
RobReb Limited Partnership (Note 4)	96,000	84,000
Stone & Stone, Inc. (Note 5)	1,100,000	950,000
Vested Interest in deferred profit sharing plan	222,800	197,800
Remainder interest in testamentary trust (Note 6)	343,800	257,600
Cash value of life insurance ($87,200 and $85,800), less loans payable to insurance companies ($76,200 and $75,400) (Note 7)	11,000	10,400
Residences (Note 8)	380,000	360,000
Personal effects (excluding art and jewelry) (Note 9)	110,000	100,000
Art and Jewelry (Note 9)	80,000	73,000
	$2,768,000	$2,413,400

	December 31, 2007	December 31, 2006
LIABILITIES		
Income taxes - current year balance	$ 17,600	$ 800
Demand 6.0% note payable to bank	50,000	52,000
Mortgage payable (Note 10)	196,400	198,000
Contingent liabilities (Note 11)	264,000	250,800
Estimated income taxes on the differences between the estimated current values of assets and the estimated current amounts of liabilities and their tax bases (Note 12)	478,000	320,000
Net worth	2,026,000	1,842,600
	$2,768,000	$2,413,400

(The net worth required will vary significantly, depending on such factors as the risk involved in the investment and the amount of future funding the investor may be called upon to provide.)

4. As the starting point for the budgeting process.

5. As the starting point for the income or cash flow projection process. For example, "Do I have enough to retire?"

6. When a "capital needs analysis" is required to determine life or disability income insurance shortfalls.

ADVANTAGES

1. Provides a means for summarizing an individual's financial position in a format commonly used in financial analysis.

Figure 16.2

ROBERT AND REBECCA STONE
STATEMENT OF CASH FLOW AND TAXABLE INCOME
CALENDAR YEAR 2007

	CASH FLOW	TAXABLE INCOME
CASH RECEIPTS & INCOME:		
Salary – Husband	$70,000	$70,000
Wife	90,000	90,000
Bonus – Husband	25,000	25,000
Wife	5,000	5,000
Interest	3,500	3,500
Maturity [Cash-in] of Notes Receivable, etc.		
Dividend	2,500	2,500
Cash Distributed/Taxable Income from Business:		
Assets Sales:		
Sales Proceeds	25,000	$25,000
Less: Basis		(5,000)
Equals: Gain (Loss)		20,000
Rental Property:		
Rental Income	14,000	14,000
Less: Depreciation		(3,000)
Less: Debt Service	(6,500)	(6,500)
Add Back:		
Principal Payments		1,200
Equals: Interest Expense		(5,300)
Less: Other Expenses	(4,500)	(4,500)
Partnership Cash Distributed/Taxable Income (Loss)	3,000	(1,500)
Cash Distributed/Taxable Income (Loss) from Other Investments		
Other Cash Receipts/Taxable Income [Trusts, Gifts, Loans, etc.]	5,000	5,000
Total Cash Receipts & Income	$232,000	$220,700
CASH DISBURSEMENTS & EXPENSES:		
Employee Business Expenses	$2,500	$2,500
IRA-Keogh Contributions*,	8,000	8,000
Alimony Paid,		
Medical Expenses	2,500	2,500
Less: Nondeductible Amount		(2,500)
State & Local Taxes –		
Income	6,000	6,000
Real Estate	2,500	2,500
Personal Property	1,200	1,200
Federal Income Taxes Paid or W/H	50,000	
Other Deductible Taxes		
Nondeductible Taxes (e.g., FICA)	11,950	
Debt Service Payments –		
Mortgage – Interest	9,500	9,500
– Principal	1,200	

Figure 16.2 (cont'd)

	CASH FLOW	TAXABLE INCOME
Debt Service Payments –		
Other – Interest	4,500	
– Principal	8,000	
Charitable Contributions	15,000	15,000
Political Contributions		
Casualty Losses (Net of Insurance Proceeds)		
Other Deductible Amounts	3,000	3,000
Nondeductible Personal Expenses (Food, Clothing, Vacations, Education, Furnishings, Gifts, etc.)	62,000	
Investments	30,000	
Standard Deduction		
Personal and Dependency Exemptions‡		13,600
Total Cash Disbursements & Expenses	$217,850	$ 61,300
Net Cash Inflow (Outflow) & Taxable Income	$ 14,150	$159,400

*Neither spouse participated in an employer-sponsored retirement plan.
‡The couple has two dependent children and the exemption amount for 2007 was $3,400.

2. Provides an individual with an orderly reference point to evaluate his current financial position relative to financial goals.

3. May force an individual to focus realistically on what needs to be done to achieve projected goals and provide motivation for the appropriate action.

DISADVANTAGES

1. May be difficult and time consuming to compile, especially if financial statements are not maintained on a regular basis.

2. A "fair market value" balance sheet may require expensive appraisals and asset valuations. (Balance sheets prepared under "generally accepted accounting principles" are usually based on the original or depreciated cost of assets, rather than their current fair market value. Such statements tend to understate net worth.)

HOW IS IT IMPLEMENTED?

The financial records of most individuals are both informal and incomplete. In many cases, a client will have organized and recorded only a small portion of his assets and liabilities. This means that the financial planner must be prepared to assist the client in gathering the necessary information from numerous sources, such as:

1. income tax returns

2. real estate and personal property tax returns

3. the client's accountant

4. bank records, including checking and savings account statements, loan balance statements, etc.

5. the client's attorney

6. stock brokers' statements

7. property and life insurance records

8. a listing of safe deposit box contents

9. the client

The following basic guidelines (suggested by the Personal Financial Statements Guide of the AICPA) should be considered in creating personal financial statements:

1. Reflect assets and liabilities on an accrual rather than cash basis. For example, if Lara Leimberg, the famous author, had earned $30,000 of royalties which she had not yet received, that amount should be shown as an account receivable on her personal balance sheet. This would be the case even if she reported income for tax purposes on a cash basis.

2. Assets and liabilities should be presented by order of liquidity and maturity. The most liquid assets, such as cash, should be at the top. This helps to highlight the ability to meet immediate cash needs, the amount of liquid assets available for immediate consumption, or to take advantage of investment opportunities. From an estate planning perspective, listing assets in order of liquidity also emphasizes the importance of adequate cash (or equivalents) to meet estate settlement needs.

3. Statements should include only the proportionate interest of a joint or community property owner. The extent of that interest and its value must be determined under the property laws of the appropriate state. An attorney's advice might be necessary to ascertain whether an interest should be included and, if so, to what extent.

4. If a business interest comprises a significant portion of a client's total assets, it should be segregated and shown separately from other investments.

5. If real estate or a business interest is encumbered with a large debt, that debt should be presented separately from the asset. This is particularly true if the liability may be satisfied from sources unrelated to the investment. For example, if Charlee Leimberg, the real estate investor, purchased a $600,000 building and obtained a $400,000 mortgage on which she was personally liable, the real estate and the related mortgage should be presented separately.

6. Assets should be presented at estimated current values. Likewise, liabilities should be shown at their estimated current amounts. The current value of an asset is the amount at which an exchange would occur between a hypothetical "informed and willing" buyer and seller, neither of whom is under compulsion to consummate the transaction.

   Any material transaction costs (such as commissions) should be considered when estimating current values. Taxes on unrecognized gain that would be incurred upon the conversion of the asset to cash are often shown separately as a liability. For instance, assume an investor purchased land for $300,000 which is now worth $700,000. Obviously, upon the sale of the land the investor would recognize a $400,000 gain. The estimated tax liability should be shown in order to realistically reflect the true net worth of the asset. Similarly, if an individual has a vested pension worth $500,000, the tax to be paid when the money is taken should be included on the balance sheet as a liability.

   Value can generally be determined through

   a) recent sales of similar assets

   b) capitalization of past or prospective earnings

   c) liquidation values

   d) adjustment of historical cost based on changes in a specific price index

   e) the use of appraisals (specialists may have to be consulted in estimating the value of works of art, jewelry, real estate, restricted securities, and closely held businesses)

   f) the use of the discounted amounts of projected cash receipts and disbursements

7. Receivables should be discounted using appropriate interest rates as of the date the financial statement is compiled.

8. Marketable securities (which include both debt and equity investments) should be shown at their quoted market prices. If the security is traded on an exchange, the determinative value will be the closing price of the security nearest to the date of the financial statements. If the security is traded over the counter, the mean of the bid prices or of the bid and asked prices will generally provide a fair estimation of current value. These quotations are available from a number of financial reporting services.

9. Adjustments should be made to recognize the importance of a majority, minority, or large block interest in equity securities. A controlling interest may have proportionately more value than a recently sold minority interest, but a large block of stock might not sell at as high a per share price as a small number of shares recently sold.

10. Restrictions on the transfer of a security may indicate the desirability of an adjustment to recent market price.

11. In the absence of a published price for an option, the value of an option should be determined by reference to the value of the assets subject to the option. The planner should also consider both the exercise price and the length of the option period.

12. Life insurance should be valued at its "interpolated terminal reserve" value plus any unearned premium as of the balance sheet date. The amount of any loans against the policy can be netted against the policy value.

WHERE CAN I FIND OUT MORE ABOUT IT?

1. *Personal Financial Statements* (New York, NY: American Institute of CPAs, 1992).

2. Robert J. Garner, ed., *Ernst & Young's Personal Financial Planning Guide* (New York, NY: John Wiley, 2002).

3. Elizabeth Lewin, *Your Personal Financial Fitness Program* New York, NY: (Facts on File Publications, 1987).

4. *NumberCruncher* (Bryn Mawr, PA: Leimberg & LeClair, Inc.).

QUESTIONS AND ANSWERS

Question – How do you estimate the value of a business or other asset through "capitalization of income"?

Answer – The projected flow of income from a business or other asset can be converted into an estimate of its present value. This is called "capitalizing the income." Capitalization of income is a simple, reasonably accurate and commonly accepted means to estimate fair market value.

If a business generates $100,000 of annual earnings, its value would approximate $500,000 if the "capitalization rate" assumed is 20% ($100,000 annual earnings divided by 20% equals the capitalized value of $500,000).

Another way of computing the value of a business or other asset using capitalized earnings is to multiply the annual income amount ($100,000) by the number of years earnings are reasonably estimated to continue (5 years). Thus, an earnings multiplier of "5 times earnings" produces the same value as applying a capitalization rate of 20%.

Two questions must be answered before the financial planner can use a value arrived at through this method: (1) What adjustments must be made to earnings to realistically reflect the "true" earnings of the business or other asset? *and* (2) What capitalization rate is appropriate?

The earnings of a business must be adjusted to take into consideration (1) excessive (or unrealistically low) salaries and other forms of compensation paid to shareholder-employees, (2) excessive (or unrealistically low) rents paid to shareholders, (3) nonrecurring or unusual income or expense items, such as fire losses or insurance recoveries, (4) excessive depreciation, (5) major changes in accounting procedures, (6) widely fluctuating or cyclical profits, (7) strong upward or downward earnings trends, and (8) other factors that may distort the reflection of normal earnings.

In determining the appropriate capitalization rate (earnings multiplier) to be applied to a particular valuation, consider the following:

1. A higher capitalization rate results in a lower value. For instance, a business producing after-tax income of $50,000, capitalized at 6%, would be valued at $833,333. The same income, capitalized at 15%, would result in a valuation of $333,333. (A 6% capitalization rate is the same as using an earnings multiplier of approximately 16.67. A 15% capitalization rate is the same as multiplying the earnings by about 6.67.)

2. A lower capitalization rate (and therefore a higher valuation) is appropriate when you are dealing with a stable business, one with a large capital asset base, and one with established goodwill.

3. A higher capitalization rate (and therefore a lower valuation) is appropriate when you are dealing with a small business, one with little capital, a relatively short financial history, or shallow management resources. A business involved in a speculative venture or one which depends on the presence of only one or two key people will generally warrant a higher capitalization rate.

There are situations where the capitalization of earnings approach is inappropriate or will lead to an unrealistic valuation. For example, raw land, producing no current income, but expected to result in substantial appreciation for the investor, cannot be valued using this method.

Question – When should book value be used in determining the value of a closely held business?

Answer – Book value (book value of assets minus book value of liabilities) is an appropriate method of valuation when the business is

1. an investment company with essentially no intrinsic value other than the underlying value of its assets
2. a real estate development business and land and/or buildings are the major profit making factor
3. dependent on one or two key individuals for its success (Such businesses are typically worth only "liquidation value" upon the death, disability, or termination of employment of such key people.)
4. in the process of liquidation (The financial planner should consider the impact of a sacrifice sale as well as the resulting tax liability in determining the net realizable value to the owner.)
5. highly competitive but only marginally profitable (In such cases profits of the past are an unreliable tool to measure potential future earnings.)
6. relatively new
7. experiencing large deficits

Book value should not be used when invested capital is a minor element in the generation of profits or the client does not have enough voting power to force the liquidation of the business.

Book value should rarely be used as the sole determinant of valuation; it should be used in conjunction with or as a means of testing the relevancy of the capitalization of earnings and other methods.

Question – What adjustments must be made to book value in order for it to result in a realistic valuation?

Answer – Most financial planners begin with an accountant's balance sheet, prepared in accordance with generally accepted accounting principles. Such balance sheets are generally based upon historic data and do not reflect the current market value of the underlying assets.

Consider making adjustments under the following circumstances:

1. when assets are valued at original cost, thus not reflecting any subsequent appreciation or depreciation
2. when assets have been depreciated more rapidly than their economic value has actually declined
3. when one or more assets with significant economic value have been "written off"
4. when the business possesses material "off balance sheet assets," such as a long-term lease at an unusually favorable rent
5. when the business carries franchises, goodwill, results of successful research and development, or other intangible assets on its books at nominal (if any) cost
6. when the business has poor experience in the collection of accounts receivables
7. when the firm possesses inventory that is either obsolete or for some other reason is not readily marketable
8. when the firm's working capital or liquidity position is unfavorable
9. when the assets of the business are encumbered with significant long term debt
10. where the retained earnings are high only because they have been accumulated over a long period of time (Such a business may have poor current earnings and its potential for future profits may be minimal.)

Question – What are "goodwill" and "going concern value"?

Answer – In the broadest sense, goodwill is synonymous with the entire intangible value inherent in the operation of a business. But, in the narrower and more technically accurate sense, the intangible value attributable to identifiable intangible assets, such as franchises, patents, secret formulas, trademarks, exclusive licenses, favorable leases, and customer lists, should be separately identified.

What is left, therefore, is a much more restrictive definition of goodwill; goodwill is the expectation of repeat sales due to such factors as (a) advantageous location, (b) superior management expertise, and (c) relationships built between customers and employees.

Goodwill, in its most restrictive sense, is therefore the ability of location, management expertise, and customer relationships to generate earnings that are in excess of the fair market value and that can reasonably be anticipated on the net tangible and identifiable intangible assets of the business.

Going concern value is that element of value possessed by a firm which is an existing establishment, doing business, with earnings sufficient to realize a fair rate of return on the net tangible assets required for continued business operations.

A planner should examine the following factors to determine if an enterprise has a going concern value: (1) experienced management, (2) trained and functioning sales and production personnel, (3) in-place operating facilities, (4) established sources of supply, (5) an established and operative system for distributing the products and services offered by the business, (6) consumer demand for the firm's products, and (7) the ability to continue – uninterrupted – the business and production functions described above in the event of a change of ownership for any reason. The absence of any of these factors may substantially impair the going concern value of the enterprise.

Figure 16.3

STATEMENT OF CASH FLOW AND TAXABLE INCOME CALENDAR YEAR	CASH FLOW	TAXABLE INCOME
CASH RECEIPTS & INCOME:		
Salary – Husband		
Wife		
Bonus – Husband		
Wife		
Interest		
Maturity [Cash-in] of Notes Receivable, etc.		
Dividend		
Cash Distributed/Taxable Income from Business:		
Assets Sales:		
Sales Proceeds		
Less: Basis		________
Equals: Gain (Loss)		
Rental Property:		
Rental Income		
Less: Depreciation		
Less: Debt Service		
Add Back:		
Principal Payments		________
Equals: Interest Expense		
Less: Other Expenses		

Figure 16.3 (cont'd)

	CASH FLOW	TAXABLE INCOME
Partnership Cash Distributed/Taxable Income (Loss)		
Cash Distributed/Taxable Income (Loss) from Other Investments		
Other Cash Receipts/Taxable Income [Trusts, Gifts, Loans, etc.]		
Total Cash Receipts & Income		
CASH DISBURSEMENTS & EXPENSES:		
Employee Business Expenses		
IRA-Keogh Contributions		
Alimony Paid		
Medical Expenses		
Less: Nondeductible Amount		
State & Local Taxes –		
Income		
Real Estate		
Personal Property		
Federal Income Taxes Paid or W/H		
Other Deductible Taxes		
Nondeductible Taxes (e.g., FICA)		
Debt Service Payments –		
Mortgage – Interest		
– Principal		
Other – Interest		
– Principal		
Charitable Contributions		
Political Contributions		
Casualty Losses (Net of Insurance Proceeds)		
Other Deductible Amounts		
Nondeductible Personal Expenses (Food, Clothing, Vacations, Education, Furnishings, Gifts, etc.)		
Investments		
Standard Deduction		
Personal and Dependency Exemptions		
Total Cash Disbursements & Expenses		
Net Cash Inflow (Outflow) & Taxable Income		

Chapter 17

CREDIT AND DEBT MANAGEMENT

INTRODUCTION

Advisers and their clients are faced with a host of consumer finance and personal financial-planning issues all the time, especially with respect to credit arrangements such as credit cards, home financing or refinancing, home-equity lines of credit, or automobile financing and leasing.

Before someone can get credit, they must be creditworthy. Knowing how to read and understand credit reports and knowing how creditworthiness is scored is critical to maintaining the ability to borrow.

This chapter discusses what characteristics creditors look for when granting credit, debt ratios and their use as guidelines to reasonable and manageable debt limits, how to deal with debt problems and over-borrowing, credit reports, the FICO credit score, how to improve one's credit, how to deal with identity theft, and the major consumer protection laws.

WHAT IS IT?

People get credit by promising to pay in the future for something they receive in the present. Credit is a convenience. It lets people charge a meal on their credit card, pay for an appliance on the installment plan, take out a loan to buy a house, or pay for schooling or vacations. With credit, people can enjoy their purchases while they are still paying for them – or they can make a purchase when they are lacking ready cash.

However there are strings attached to credit too. It usually costs something. And of course what people borrow, they are obligated to pay back. Failure to do so can lead to serious financial consequences ranging from impaired creditworthiness to losses of assets, including even cars and homes, and may cause a significant reduction in one's standard of living. Consequently, people should manage their use of debt judiciously, diligently safeguard their creditworthiness, and strive to keep their debt balances and debt payments at reasonable and manageable levels.

What Creditors Look For

In determining what level of debt balances and debt payments is reasonable and manageable, the best guide is the standards creditors use when granting loans to borrowers. They are the experts with vast experience as to what constitutes a good and bad credit risk.

The Three C's

Creditors look for an ability to repay debt and a willingness to do so – and sometimes for a little extra security to protect their loans. They speak of the three C's of credit:

1. *Capacity* – Can the borrower repay the debt? Creditors ask for employment information: occupation, how long a person has worked, and how much the person earns. They also want to know the borrowers expenses: how many dependents they have, whether they pay alimony or child support, and the amount of their other obligations.

2. *Character* – Will a borrower repay the debt? Creditors will look at borrowers' credit history: how much they owe, how often they borrow, whether they pay bills on time, and whether they live within their means. They also look for signs of stability: how long borrowers have lived at their present address, whether they own or rent their homes, and the length of their present employment.

3. *Collateral* – Is the creditor fully protected if the borrower fails to repay? Creditors want to know what borrowers may have that could be used to back up or secure their loans, and what sources they have for repaying debt other than income, such as savings, investments, or property.

Creditors use different combinations of these factors in reaching their decisions. Some set unusually high standards and other simply do not make certain kinds of loans. Creditors also use different kinds of rating systems. Some rely strictly on their own instinct and experience. Others use a "credit-scoring" such as the FICO score or a statistical system to predict whether borrowers are a good credit risk. They assign a certain number of points to each of the various characteristics that have proved to be reliable signs that borrowers will repay. Then, they rate them on this scale.

And so, different creditors may reach different conclusions based on the same set of facts. One may find a person an acceptable risk, while another may deny that same person a loan.

Debt Ratios

People's debt-to-income ratios (DTI) are a key indicator of their true financial picture. It is definitely the lending industry's leading measure of fiscal health. The debt to income ratio is calculated by dividing monthly minimum debt payments (generally excluding mortgage or rent, utilities, food, entertainment) by monthly gross income. For example, someone with a gross monthly income of $2,000 who is making minimum payments of $400 on debt (loans and credit cards) has a debt to income ratio of 20% ($400 / $2000 = 0.20).

This formula will vary slightly from lender to lender but only slightly. Some lenders include the mortgage but raise the acceptable ratios and others do not. While variations will result in different percentage outcomes, the overall concept is the same: a debt-to-income ratio compares debt load to income.

Most authorities seem to agree that a debt ratio (without a mortgage, utilities, etc.) of 10% or less is great. Debt ratios at 20% or higher are yellow lights since just one financial emergency could put the borrower into a serious financial squeeze.

Front-End Ratio

Mortgage lenders tend to look at two debt ratios when determining whether to grant a home mortgage or home equity line of credit. One is the ratio of the monthly housing expense to the borrower's gross (pre-tax) monthly income. This is called the front-end ratio.

The monthly housing expense is made up of principal, interest, property taxes, and insurance – otherwise know as the PITI. Homeowner's association dues and a mortgage insurance premium are added to the PITI in qualifying borrowers, if applicable.

Let us assume a borrower's gross annual income is $60,000, which gives him a gross monthly income of $5,000 ($60,000 divided by 12 months). If the lender says that the front-end ratio cannot exceed 32%, this means that his PITI divided by his gross monthly income must equal 32% or less.

To calculate the front-end ratio amount, one multiplies the gross monthly income ($5,000 in this example) by 0.32. The result, $1600, will have to cover the monthly housing expense.

Back-End Ratio

The other ratio is called the back-end ratio. This is the ratio between the borrower's total debt (PITI plus other monthly debt payments) to the gross monthly income. If the lender says that the back-end ratio cannot exceed 38%, this means that the total monthly debt, including the PITI, must be no more than 38% of the gross monthly income.

If one multiplies the gross monthly income of $5,000 by 38%, the result ($1900) is the back-end ratio amount. This means that a borrower can have up to $300 in monthly debt in addition to the PITI and the lender will still qualify that person for a loan with a PITI of $1,600 ($1,900 minus $1,600 = $300).

If one's monthly debts (for car payments, student loans, credit card balances that will not be paid off in a few months) exceed $300, the back-end ratio will exceed the 38% lender guideline. In this case, the lender will probably still give the borrower a loan, but a smaller loan than if borrower had less other debt.

If a lender says the ratios are 33/39, this means that the front-end ratio is 33% and the back-end ratio is 39%. While most lenders take both ratios into consideration, some lenders make exceptions. FHA qualifies borrowers based on the back-end ratio alone.

Collateral and Secured Loans

Loans where borrowers have pledged specific resources to repay the loans in the event of default are called collateralized or secured loans. Since mortgages and home equity lines of credit or car loans give lenders recourse to the borrower's home or car in the event of default, these loans are secured loans.

Borrowers with high debt-to-income ratios may be able to get what would generally be a non-secured loan approved if they pledge assets as collateral, or if they open an account with the lender from which monthly mortgage payments can be automatically deducted. Typically such borrowers will pledge investment assets, such as stocks and bonds, business assets, such as equipment, or valuable personal property, such as artwork or jewelry to collateralize these loans.

In the case of investment assets, the amounts of these loans are limited by the Federal Reserve's margin requirements for each particular investment asset class. With regard to the other types of security, the lending limit depends on the lender's assessment as to the quality of the assets. In some cases, the lenders will insist that the borrower provide a professional appraisal of the fair market value of the property being offered as collateral.

However, the credit lending industry, and especially the credit card industry, has become extremely liberal in their lending policies. According to Motley Fool in the article "Our Credit Crunch":

> "...far be it for the credit card industry to poo-poo your request for a line of credit. Even if your debt-to-income ratio is 50% or more, you'll probably have little trouble qualifying for a credit card. Never mind that mortgage lenders preach that your debt level – including mortgage and all revolving unsecured debts – should not exceed 36% of your gross monthly income. In their eyes, that leaves just 8% of your income for non-mortgage debts."

Dealing with Debt Problems

Many people face financial crises at some time in their lives. They may have trouble paying their bills, or may be getting dunning notices from creditors, or having their accounts being turned over to debt collectors. If things get bad, they often worry about losing their homes or cars. Whether the crisis is caused by personal or family illness, the loss of a job, or simple overspending, it can seem overwhelming. However, with proper planning and action, the fact of the matter is that their financial situation does not have to go from bad to worse.

People with debt problems should consider these options: realistic budgeting, credit counseling from a reputable organization, debt consolidation, or bankruptcy. Which will work best depends on their level of debt, their level of discipline, and their prospects for the future.

Developing a Budget

The first step toward taking control of one's financial situation is to do a realistic assessment of how much money comes in and how much money one spends. Start by listing income from all sources. Then, list "fixed" expenses – those that are the same each month – such as mortgage payments or rent, car payments, or insurance premiums. Next, list the expenses that vary, such as entertainment, recreation, or clothing. Writing down all these expenses – even those that seem insignificant – is a helpful way to track spending patterns, to identify the expenses that are necessary, and to prioritize the rest. The goal is to make sure one can make ends meet on the basics: housing, food, health care, insurance, and education. Chapter 15 discusses budgeting and money management techniques.

Contacting Your Creditors

People having trouble making ends meet should contact their creditors. They should tell their creditors why they are having difficulty making payments and try to work out a modified payment plan that reduces their payments to a more manageable level. They should not wait until their accounts have been turned over to a debt collector. At that point, the creditors have given up on them.

Dealing with Debt Collectors

The Fair Debt Collection Practices Act is the federal law that dictates how and when a debt collector may contact you. A debt collector may not call you before 8 a.m., after 9 p.m., or at work if the collector knows that your employer doesn't approve of the calls. Collectors may not harass you, make false statements, or use unfair practices when they try to collect a debt. Debt collectors must honor a written request from you to stop further contact.

Credit Counseling

When people are not disciplined enough to create a workable budget and to stick to it, cannot work out a repayment plan with their creditors, or cannot keep track of mounting bills, they should consider contacting a credit counseling service. Their creditors may be willing to accept reduced payments if the borrowers enter into a debt repayment plan with a reputable organization. In these plans, the borrowers deposit money each month with the credit counseling service. Their deposits are used to pay their creditors according to a payment schedule developed by the counselor. As part of the repayment plan, the borrowers may have to agree not to apply for or use any additional credit while they are participating in the program.

A successful repayment plan requires borrowers to make regular, timely payments, and could take 48 months or longer to complete. Borrowers should ask the credit counseling service for an estimate of the time it will take to complete the plan. Some credit counseling services charge little or nothing for managing the plan; others charge a monthly fee that could add up to a significant charge over time. Some credit counseling services are funded, in part, by contributions from creditors.

While a debt repayment plan can eliminate much of the stress that comes from dealing with creditors and overdue bills, it does not mean borrowers can forget about their debts. They still are responsible for paying any creditors whose debts are not included in the plan. They are responsible for reviewing monthly statements from their creditors to make sure their payments have been received. If the repayment plan depends on their creditors agreeing to lower or eliminate interest and finance charges, or waive late fees, the borrowers are responsible for making sure these concessions are reflected on their statements.

A debt repayment plan does not erase negative credit history. Accurate information about accounts can stay on the credit report for up to seven years. In addition, creditors will continue to report information about accounts that are handled through a debt repayment plan. For example, creditors may report that an account is in financial counseling, that payments have been late or missed altogether, or that there are write-offs or other concessions. A demonstrated pattern of timely payments, however, will help borrowers who go through this process to get credit in the future.

Auto and Home Loans

Debt repayment plans usually cover unsecured debt. Auto and home loans, which are considered secured debt, may not be included. Borrowers must continue to make payments to these creditors directly.

Most automobile financing agreements allow a creditor to repossess a car any time the borrower is in default. No notice is required. If a car is repossessed, the borrower may have to pay the full balance due on the loan, as well as towing and storage costs, to get it back. If someone cannot do this, the creditor may sell the car. If default is approaching or inevitable, borrowers may be better off selling the car themselves and paying off their debt: In this way they would avoid the added costs of repossession and a negative entry on their credit report.

When people fall behind on their mortgages, they should contact their lender immediately to avoid foreclosure. Most lenders are willing to work with borrowers if they believe they are acting in good faith and the situation is temporary. Some lenders may reduce or suspend payments for a short time. When the borrowers resume regular payments, though, they may have to pay an additional amount toward the past due total. Other lenders may agree to change the terms of the mortgage by extending the repayment period to reduce the monthly debt. Borrowers should ask whether additional fees would be assessed for these changes, and calculate how much they total in the long run.

If borrowers and their lenders cannot work out a plan, the borrowers should contact a housing counseling agency. Some agencies limit their counseling service to homeowners with FHA mortgages, but many offer free help to any homeowner who is having trouble making mortgage payments. Borrowers may call the local office of the Department of Housing and Urban Development (HUD) or the housing authority in their state, city, or county for help in finding a housing counseling agency nearby.

Debt Consolidation

Borrowers may be able to lower their cost of credit by consolidating their debt through a second mortgage or a home equity line of credit. Think carefully before taking this on. These loans require that their homes serve as collateral for the debt consolidation loan. If they cannot make the payments – or if the payments are late – they could lose their homes.

The costs of these consolidation loans can add up. In addition to interest on the loan, borrowers pay "points." Typically, one point is equal to 1% of the amount they borrow. Still, these loans may provide certain tax advantages that are not available with other kinds of credit. The interest paid on up to $100,000 of the balance of these loans is tax deductible, whereas the interest paid on other consumer loans or personal debt is generally not deductible. Consequently, not only will the rate of interest paid on a consolidation loan typically be lower than the average rate paid on the debts being consolidated, but the effective rate will be even lower to the extent the interest is deductible.

Bankruptcy

Personal bankruptcy generally is considered the debt management tool of last resort because the results are long-lasting and far-reaching. A bankruptcy stays on a credit report for 10 years, making it difficult to acquire credit, buy a home, get life insurance, or sometimes get a job. However, it is a legal procedure that offers a fresh start for people who cannot satisfy their debts. Individuals who follow the bankruptcy rules receive a discharge – a court order that says they do not have to repay certain debts.

There are two primary types of personal bankruptcy: Chapter 13 and Chapter 7. Each must be filed in federal bankruptcy court. The basic fees for filing for bankruptcy relief are about $300 but miscellaneous fees (for photocopies, amendments, etc.) may increase that amount somewhat. Attorney fees are additional and can vary widely, frequently ranging from $1,000 to $2,000 or more. The consequences of bankruptcy are significant and require careful consideration.

Chapter 13 allows the filers, if they have a regular income and limited debt, to keep property, such as a mortgaged house or car that they otherwise might lose. In Chapter 13, the court approves a repayment plan that allows the filer to pay off a default during a period of three to five years, rather than surrender any property.

Chapter 7, known as straight bankruptcy, involves liquidating all assets that are not exempt. Exempt property may include cars, work-related tools and basic household furnishings. A court-appointed official – a trustee – may sell some property or turn it directly over to creditors. A person can receive a discharge of debts under Chapter 7 only once every eight years.

Both types of bankruptcy may get rid of unsecured debts and stop foreclosures, repossessions, garnishments, utility shut-offs, and debt collection activities. Both also provide exemptions that allow filers to keep certain assets, although exemption amounts vary. Personal bankruptcy usually does not erase child support, alimony, fines, taxes, and some student loan obligations. Also, unless filers have an acceptable plan to catch up on their debt under Chapter 13, bankruptcy usually does not allow the filer to keep property when their creditor has an unpaid mortgage or lien on it.

The Bankruptcy Abuse and Creditor Protection Act of 2005 (BACPA 2005) tightened the rules for electing Chapter 7 bankruptcy. In order to file under Chapter 7, the debtor must satisfy a two-stage bankruptcy means test. The first stage checks to see if the debtor's monthly average of the last 6 months gross income is below the median income for the debtor's state of residence, Debtors' whose incomes fall below their state's median incomes may file under Chapter 7. If debtors' incomes are slightly higher than their state's median incomes, they can enter stage two where they file a form performing a calculation showing they have certain allowable expenses that still makes them eligible to file under Chapter 7. In any event, BACPA 2005 requires debtors who qualify to jump through two additional hurdles. First, they must take an approved credit counseling course within 6 months before filing. Second, they must complete an approved financial management course before they can be discharged.

CREDIT SCORING

Introduction

Since access to consumer credit depends upon creditworthiness, knowing how to read and understand credit reports and knowing how creditworthiness is scored is critical to maintaining the ability to borrow. These scores affect an overwhelming number of today's lending decisions. The Fair Credit Reporting Act (FCRA) was enacted to promote accuracy and ensure the privacy of information used in consumer reports. Recent amendments to the Act expand consumer rights and place additional requirements on credit reporting agencies (CRAs). Businesses that supply information about borrowers to CRAs and those that use consumer reports also have new responsibilities under the law.

How to Read and Understand a Credit Report[1]

Often, lenders will suggest that people applying for credit get a copy of their credit reports as part of the pre-qualifying process for a loan. The purpose is so that the applicants can see how their credit looks and to clear up any errors that might be in the report. The credit-reporting agency (CRA) must tell consumers everything in their reports, including medical information, and in most cases, the sources of the information. The CRA also must give consumers a list of everyone who has requested their report within the past year-two years for employment related requests.

Principal National Credit Agencies and Costs of Reports

The Fair Credit Reporting Act requires each of the nationwide consumer reporting companies – Equifax, Experian, and TransUnion – to provide consumers with free copies of their credit reports, at their request, once every 12 months. The three companies have set up one central website, one toll-free telephone number, and one mailing address through which consumers can order their free credit reports. The Federal Trade Commission (FTC), the nation's consumer protection agency, wants everybody to know that, if they want to order a free annual credit report online, the *ONLY* authorized website is annualcreditreport.com.[2]

When companies deny people credit, insurance, or a job because of something in their credit report, the companies have to tell them which credit bureau provided the information. These people are entitled to a free credit report from that bureau within 60 days of being turned down, even if they have already received their free report for the year. They may request a free credit report by phone or mail, if they were denied credit, insurance, or a job. The credit bureau will check to see if it indeed provided information to the creditor, insurance company, or employer that turned them down. Because bureaus are not notified when people are denied credit, the CRAs have to take the requestors' word for it.

Anybody who is on welfare, unemployed, and looking for a job, or whose credit report is inaccurate due to fraud (because somebody stole their financial identity) is are entitled to a free credit report.

People who do not qualify for a free report for any of the reasons described above may purchase a copy of their credit reports from any or all of the credit asgencies. Prices vary by state but generally range from $1.00 to $8.50. The actual cost may depends on why consumers are asking for their credit report, where they live, and whether they order by phone, on-line, or mail.[3]

Generally, potential borrowers should order reports from all three agencies since everything is not always the same on all of them. The reports will have different information because it is a voluntary system, and creditors subscribe to whichever agency they want – if any at all.

Ordering a report directly from a credit bureau instead of asking a friend who works at a bank to pull one up for you is generally the best course. The ones the bank receives are written for people who work in the credit industry. The one potential borrowers get from the credit bureau is designed for consumers. The information is almost the same, but the consumer version is easier to read. The report sent to a lender will list the credit bureau member numbers of creditors and it will not have the complete list of every company that has pulled a potential borrower's credit information for promotional purposes, like pre-approved credit card offers.

Credit reports include a lot of numbers, abbreviations and terms that many people have never seen before such as "trade lines," "charge-offs," and "account review inquiries." So, how does one read these reports?

What a Credit Report Contains

A credit report is basically divided into four sections:

1. *Identifying information* – One should review it closely to make sure it is accurate. It is not unusual for there to be two or three different spellings of the consumer's name or more than one Social Security number. That typically arises because some previous lender reported the information that way. The variations will typically stay on the credit report. Other information might include the consumer's current and previous addresses, date of birth, telephone numbers, driver's license numbers, current and previous employers, and the spouse's name.

2. *Credit history*–Sometimes, the individual accounts are called trade lines. Each account will include the name of the creditor and the account number, which may be scrambled for security purposes. Consumers may have more than one account from a creditor. Many creditors have more than one kind of account, or if one moves, they may transfer an account to a new location and assign a new number. The entry will also include:

   - when account was opened
   - the kind of credit (installment, such as a mortgage or car loan, or revolving, such as a department store credit card)
   - whether the account is in borrower's name alone or with another person
   - the total amount of the loan, or the high credit limit or highest balance on a line of credit or credit card

- how much is still owed
- the fixed monthly payments or minimum monthly payment amount
- the status of the account (open, inactive, closed, paid, etc.)
- how well the borrower has paid the account

On Experian's report, payment history is written in plain English, for instance, "never pays late," "typically pays 30 days late," etc. Other comments might include "internal collection and charged off" or "default." Charged off means the creditor has made efforts to collect, given up, and written it off.

Other reports use payment codes ranging from 1 to 9; an R1 or I1 on a report is an indication of a good payment history on a revolving or installment account.

3. *Public records* – This is the part of the report borrowers want to be absolutely blank. Generally, when borrowers have a report or comment in their public record section, they have had a significant problem. This section does not list arrests and criminal activities; just financial-related data, such as bankruptcies, judgments, and tax liens. Those types of records will typically trash one's creditworthiness faster than anything else.

4. *Inquiries section* – This section lists everyone who has asked to see the credit report. Inquiries are divided into two sections. "Hard" inquiries are ones the borrower initiates by filling out a credit application. "Soft" inquiries are from companies that want to send out promotional information to a pre-qualified group or from current creditors who are monitoring the borrower's account.

The FICO Credit Score

A credit score number is often called a FICO score, for Fair, Isaac and Co., the California-based company that developed the system upon which it is based. The score is supposed to distill all the information in a credit report, plus other factors such as one's age and income, whether the borrower owns or rents a house, how long the borrower has lived in a home, and how long the borrower has been in the current job.

The FICO score is designed to give lenders a fast, accurate prediction of the risk involved in giving the potential borrower a loan. Lenders have attested to the score's value in streamlining the underwriting process and creating more opportunities for consumers to get mortgages. Scores range from the 300s to about 900, with the vast majority of people falling in the 600s and 700s (the higher the score, the better).

When determining how high a score will be, five characteristics separate the cream of the crop from everyone else. In order of score significance:

1. *Past delinquency* – People who have failed to make payments in the past tend to do the same in the future.

2. *The way credit has been used* – Someone who is maxed out or close to the limit on a credit card is considered a greater risk than someone who does not look at the high credit line as a license to print money.

3. *The age of the credit file* – Fair, Isaac's model assumes people who have had credit for a long time are less risky.

4. *The number of times a person asks for credit* – The system frowns upon those who have initiated several requests for credit cards, loans, or other debt instruments over a short period of time.

5. *A customer's mix of credit* – Someone with only a secured credit card is generally considered riskier than someone who has a combination of installment and revolving loans. (On installment loans, a person borrows money once and makes fixed payments until the balance is gone, while revolving borrowers make regular payments, each of which frees up more money for future access, such as a store credit account.)

How is credit worthiness gauged using the credit score? It depends on the type of loan a borrower is seeking. For example, a mortgage broker will give more weight to different credit factors than a credit card issuer.

Mortgages

By Freddie Mac standards, borrowers with FICO scores above 660 are likely to have an "acceptable" credit reputation and their loan files need only a basic review. The credit risk is "uncertain" for those with scores between 620 and 660, with a thorough review of the borrower's entire credit history. A score below 620 indicates "high risk" with an unacceptable credit reputation that could make traditional financing difficult to obtain.

Most very good FICO scores come in the mid-700s. One can expect to see standard pricing or interest rates, assuming a FICO score above 680. For a score above 720, the pricing gets better. If potential borrowers score above 750 – with some lenders in some cases – they will see yet another improvement in the points or interest. On the average $200,000 (home purchase), it can mean up to $1,000 to a borrower.

Credit Cards

Credit card lenders place additional weight on credit card-related information, such as how many times a person missed revolving credit payments. And the systems evaluate a college student targeted for a starter card differently than a platinum-toting stockbroker with a summer home in the Hamptons.

Auto Lenders

Auto scores, on the other hand, focus on "deal characteristics" in much the same way the mortgage scores do. They take into account things such as the amount a borrower puts down, as well as a borrower's debt-to-income ratio, length of time at one job, and the like. As with credit card lending, information about past performance on similar types of loans is weighted, so a missed Nissan payment in one's credit history might be more important than an overdue Visa bill when applying for a new car loan.

Improving One's Credit Report

Under the law, both the CRA and the organization that provided the information to the CRA, such as a bank or credit card company, have responsibilities for correcting inaccurate or incomplete information in a report. Long-time lenders say it is common for reports to have errors. Some estimate that as many as 80% of all credit reports have some kind of misinformation. Therefore, to protect all their rights under the law, consumers should contact both the CRA and the information provider if they have a dispute.

First, consumers should tell the CRA in writing what information they believe is inaccurate. Include copies (not originals) of documents that support the position. In addition to providing their complete name and address, their letter should clearly identify each item in the report they dispute, state the facts and explain why they dispute the information, and request deletion or correction. They may want to enclose a copy of the report with the items in question circled. A letter may look something like the one below. Consumers should send their letter by certified mail, return receipt requested, so they can document what the CRA received. They should always keep copies of their dispute letter and enclosures.

CRAs must reinvestigate any items in question – usually within 30 days – unless they consider the dispute frivolous. They also must forward all relevant data the consumer provides about the dispute to the information provider. After the information provider receives notice of a dispute from the CRA, it must investigate, review all relevant information provided by the CRA, and report the results to the CRA. If the information provider finds the disputed information to be inaccurate, it must notify all nationwide CRAs so that they can correct this information in the file.

Disputed information that cannot be verified must be deleted from the file. If the report contains inaccurate information, the CRA must correct it. If an item is incomplete, the CRA must complete it. For example, if the file showed that a consumer was late making payments, but failed to show that the payments were no longer delinquent, the CRA must show that the payments are now current.

If a file shows an account that belongs only to another person, the CRA must delete it. When reinvestigations are completed, the CRA must give consumers the written results and a free copy of their report if the dispute results in a change. If an item is changed or removed, the CRA cannot put the disputed information back in the file unless the information provider verifies its accuracy and completeness and the CRA gives the consumer a written notice of its intent to reinsert the items that includes the name, address, and phone number of the provider.

If requested, the CRA must send notices of any corrections to anyone who received a report in the past six months. Consumers can have a corrected copy of their corrected report sent to anyone who received a copy during the past two years for employment purposes.

If a reinvestigation does not resolve a dispute, consumers should ask the CRA to include their statement of the dispute in the file and in all future reports.

Figure 17.1

Date
Your Name
Your Address
Your City, State, Zip Code

Complaint Department
Name of Credit Reporting Agency
Address
City, State, Zip Code

Dear Sir or Madam:

I am writing to dispute the following information in my file. The items I dispute also are encircled on the attached copy of the report I received.

This item (identify item(s) disputed by name of source, such as creditors or tax court, and identify type of item, such as credit account, judgment, etc.) is (inaccurate or incomplete) because (describe what is inaccurate or incomplete and why). I am requesting that the item be deleted (or request another specific change) to correct the information.

Enclosed are copies of (use this sentence if applicable and describe any enclosed documentation, such as payment records, court documents) supporting my position. Please reinvestigate this (these) matter(s) and (delete or correct) the disputed item(s) as soon as possible.

Sincerely,
Your name

Enclosures: (List what you are enclosing)

In addition to writing to the CRA, consumers should tell the creditor or other information provider in writing that they dispute an item. They should be sure to include copies (not originals) of documents that support their position. Many providers specify an address for disputes. If the provider continues to report the disputed item to any CRA after receiving a consumer's dispute notice, it must include a notice that the consumer disputed the item. When consumers are correct about a disputed item – that is, if the information is not accurate – the information provider may not report it again.

When negative information in a report is accurate, only the passage of time can assure its removal. Accurate negative information generally can stay on the report for seven years. There are certain exceptions:

- Bankruptcy information may be reported for 10 years.
- Credit information reported in response to an application for a job with a salary of more than $75,000 has no time limit.
- Information about criminal convictions has no time limit.
- Credit information reported because of an application for more than $150,000 worth of credit or life insurance has no time limit.
- Default information concerning U.S. Government insured or guaranteed student loans can be reported for seven years after certain guarantor actions.
- Information about a lawsuit or an unpaid judgment against the consumer can be reported for seven years or until the statute of limitations runs out, whichever is longer.

Finally, a credit file may not reflect all one's credit accounts. Although CRAs will include most national department store and all-purpose bank credit card accounts the file, not all creditors supply information to CRAs. Some travel, entertainment, gasoline card companies, local retailers, and credit unions are among those creditors that often do not supply information to CRAs.

When consumers have been denied credit because of an "insufficient credit file" or "no credit file" and they have accounts with creditors that do not appear in their credit file, they may ask the CRA to add this information to future reports. Although CRAs are not required to do so, many CRAs will add verifiable accounts for a fee. However, understand that if these creditors do not report to the CRA on a regular basis, the added items will not be updated in the credit file.

IDENTITY THEFT

What Is It?[4]

Identity theft occurs when an imposter obtains key pieces of information such as Social Security and driver's license numbers to obtain credit, merchandise, and services in the name of the victim. The victim is left with a ruined credit history and the time-consuming and complicated task of regaining financial health.

Identity theft is the fastest-growing crime on the Federal Trade Commission's list of consumer fraud complaints for the third consecutive year. The Identity Theft Resource Center estimates that up to $10 million consumers become the targets of identity theft and a growing number become victims each year.

The 2006 Federal Trade Commission (FTC) *Identity Fraud Consumer Report* provides a more detailed look into identity theft and how it occurs. The report states in the last year, approximately 9 million Americans, 4% of the population, were victims of identity fraud. The average fraud amount per victim increased 21.6% in 2006 to $6,383 per victim. Fortunately, this generally was not the final out-of-pocket expense. Each victim spent approximately 40 hours working with various sources to resolve the damage, a 21.2% increase from 2003. Unlike the TJX breach, 63% of all identity theft cases in 2006 were controllable by the victim.[5] Finally, identity theft and related crimes cost people $57 billion in aggregate.[6] A dollar figure, however, fails to capture the actual personal and financial strain that ultimately afflicts victims of identity theft.

How is Personal Information Stolen and How to Prevent it?

There are a number of ways in which identity thieves obtain valuable personal information. Many of these methods can be safeguarded against by utilizing common sense or a fairly inexpensive paper shredder. Despite what many people think, as well as what many people see on the news, the high-tech ways of stealing personal information still lag far behind as some of the more traditional methods. Many may be surprised by what a thief can acquire from simply eavesdropping on an innocent conversation, a decidedly low-tech method of spying.

Below are the descriptions of some of the most popular traditional methods as well as the newer high-tech methods that are being used increasingly every year to gather sensitive information. In parentheses beside each is the percentage that method represents of the total amount of identity theft cases as reported in the 2006 Identity Fraud Consumer Report.

Traditional Methods

- Lost or stolen information (30%)

The majority of complaints are caused by information in lost or stolen wallets, purses, luggage or vehicles. Many people carry an excess of personal information on them at all times. Experts suggest that a social security card, birth certificate, or passport be carried only when completely necessary. In addition, it is suggested that a person not carry all of his credit cards.[7] This will allow someone to still have a useable credit card in case his wallet is stolen and temporary holds need to be placed on the stolen cards. Finally, quick action in reporting lost or stolen personal identification is the best method to save the victim both time and money.

- Stolen by friends, relatives, or acquaintances (15%)

People often do not recognize friends or relatives as a source for fraud, and, as a result, they often place too much trust in them. The best way to protect against this type of fraud is to ensure that all personal information is kept in a safe location within the home. That way, visitors cannot simply acquire the data while it is in plain sight within the home. Even though friends, relatives, and acquaintances are the source for only 15% of all cases, it represents the highest percentage of total amount of lost or stolen funds, 23%.[8] This occurs because, unlike a stolen purse or wallet, the victim may not be aware of this type of fraud for a much longer time.

- Stolen mail, fraudulent change of address forms, and dumpster diving (9%)

Unattended mail is one of the easiest ways for a thief to get hold of personal information. There are plenty of households with non-locking mailboxes that may hold blank checks, utility bills, paychecks, and credit applications that have all of the necessary data for fraud. In addition, a thief may also be able to acquire a change of address form from the mail which will enable him to receive all future mailings. A lockable mailbox may serve as a deterrent in such situations.

The mail is not safe once it is inside the house either. Many thieves will resort to dumpster diving, which is the practice of searching through trash for discarded personal information. The best defense against this practice it to watch what gets thrown out, and use a high-quality shredder for any personal information.[9]

High-Tech Methods

- Computer viruses, spy ware, and hackers (5%)

Technology and personal computers have revolutionized the identity theft world. A computer user must be proactive in protecting himself from malicious software and viruses. It is difficult to quantify the number of computers in use without adequate virus protection or up-to-date operating system patches. Experts say the best way to safeguard information on your computer is to set your operating system to automatically check for and install security updates, purchase and update anti-virus and anti-spy software, exercise prudence when opening email attachments, work behind a firewall, encrypt wireless signals, and regularly change passwords.[10] These basic steps, coupled with good computing common sense, all but guarantee computer safety.

- Phishing and Pharming (3%)

Phishing is the process by which a thief will attempt to "bait" the victim into providing fraudulent information by pretending to represent a trustworthy entity.[11] These criminals are becoming increasingly creative in their attempts to lure private information, including account numbers, passwords, and banking information. The phishing attempts will often take the form of an email, often appearing to come from a bank or other trusted institution, which will prompt the victim for some type of private information. The thief will often use various fonts and logos to make the email seem official.

Thieves tend to target victims while posing as some of the most popular and trusted online sources. Phishtank, an online phishing tracker, identified PayPal, eBay, and Barclays Bank, as the top three brands fraudulently represented in phishing emails in October 2006. The best defense against phishing attempts is to never reply to suspicious emails, especially since most trusted organizations will never proactively seek the information they should already have. In a slight variation, phishing can take the form of a phone call, when a thief identifies himself as a representative of a trusted organization.

Pharming, on the other hand, occurs when an internet user is directed to a malicious site that looks, through font and graphics, to be legitimate. Pharming is often the result of typographical errors when typing a web address. Proper care should be taken by any internet user to ensure that they are on a trusted, legitimate site.[12]

Apparently the true potential that the internet holds for identity thieves has not completely been realized. The real test is the ability of computer users and security companies to recognize and contain new risks. The rise in popularity of public wireless fidelity, or "Wi-Fi," hotspots exposes another potential weakness in personal computer security. When connected to free Wi-Fi networks, often located in parks or coffee houses, the person next to you, using a simple piece of software readily available to all internet users can track your movement online in a process called "sniffing." Unfortunately, when average users connects to this network, they usually expect the same security they have while at home or work.

Effects of Identity Theft

The consequences of identity theft are many, and frequently even experts have difficult predicting just how severe the consequences will be or how long they will last. The ultimate damage depends upon many factors, including the type of theft, whether the thief sold the information to other thieves, if the thief is caught, and how long it took the victim to detect that his identity was stolen.

An identity thief may use the victim's personal information to commit a number of different crimes. They may successfully enter into long-term financial commitments, such as mortgages or car loans. They may also accumulate a substantial debt, and then file for bankruptcy, ruining the victim's credit history and reputation Some thieves, however, do not steal identities for just for financial gain. For example, the hijackers in the September 11 attacks used fake IDs to board the airplanes and commit grave acts of terrorism. In this case, fraudulent identity was a threat to national security. Thieves have also used a victim's identity to pile up parking tickets or commit felonies. According to The Federal Trade Commission's FTC "Identity Theft Survey Report," the most common identity violations in 2006 were credit-card fraud (25%), phone or utilities fraud (16%), bank fraud (16%), employment-related fraud (14%), government documents/benefits fraud (10%), loan fraud (5%), other identity theft (24%), and attempted identity theft (6%).[13]

The FTC report states that victims incurred an average out of pocket expense of $422. When the thief succeeded in opening a new credit card or bank account in the victim's name, the estimated out of pocket expense escalated to $1,800. Furthermore, it took a victim approximately 40 hours to resolve his incident, while a victim of "new accounts and other frauds" spent approximately 60 hours on resolution. Not surprisingly, there is a distinct correlation between the type of identity theft that occurs and the amount of money that the victim must pay.

Another factor directly related to the amount of money that a victim has to pay out of pocket is the length of time that elapsed before the theft was discovered. Victims who quickly discovered that their personal information was misused were less likely to incur out of pocket expenses. No expenses were incurred by 67% of victims who discovered the theft in less than six months. On the contrary, only 40% of victims who took six months or longer to discover the misuse were able to avoid incurring expenses.

There is some encouraging news in the fight against identity theft. Fortunately, the number of identity theft victims in the United States has recently been declining. However, the fraud amount per victim has been increasing. Figure 17.2 captures data from 2003-2006 regarding the total number of victims and the financial hardship endured.

What to do About it?

If a person suspects he is a victim of identity theft or if he knows he is, what should he do?

1. *Contact one of the three credit-reporting agencies –*

   That agency will notify the others. A "fraud alert" will be automatically placed on each of the victim's credit reports within 24 hours. This alerts creditors to call the victim for permission before any new accounts are opened in his name. Not all creditors pay attention to "fraud alerts." Those who have been subject to identity theft still need to stay vigilant for any new accounts that may be opened.

Figure 17.2

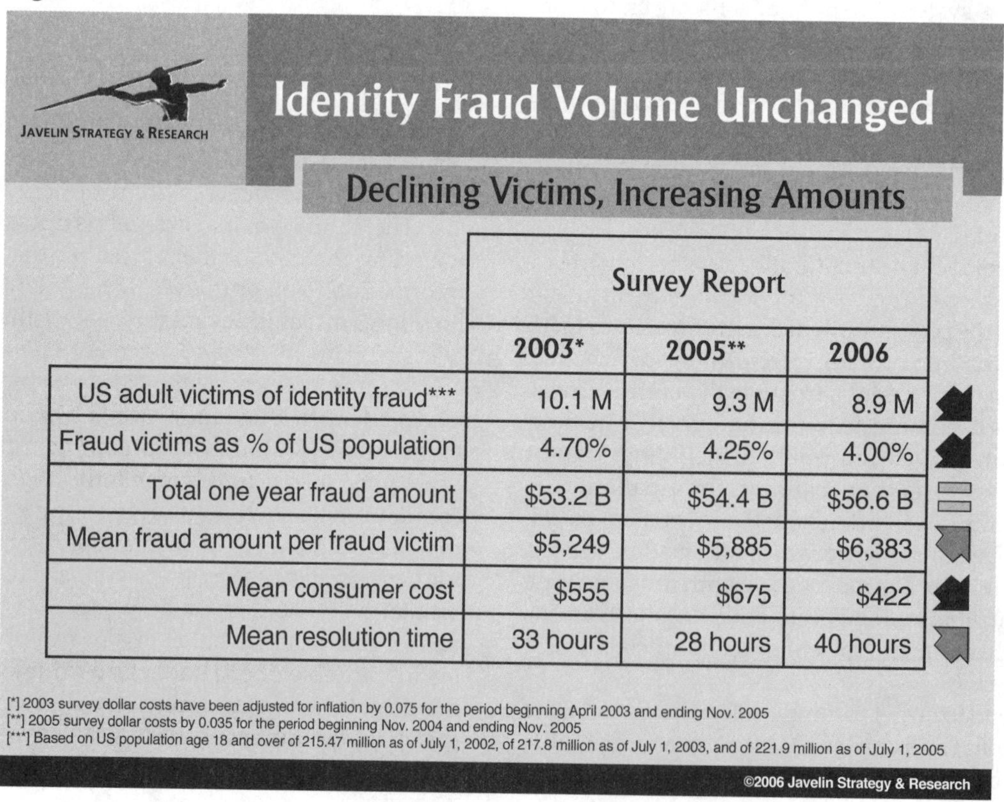

	Survey Report		
	2003*	2005**	2006
US adult victims of identity fraud***	10.1 M	9.3 M	8.9 M
Fraud victims as % of US population	4.70%	4.25%	4.00%
Total one year fraud amount	$53.2 B	$54.4 B	$56.6 B
Mean fraud amount per fraud victim	$5,249	$5,885	$6,383
Mean consumer cost	$555	$675	$422
Mean resolution time	33 hours	28 hours	40 hours

[*] 2003 survey dollar costs have been adjusted for inflation by 0.075 for the period beginning April 2003 and ending Nov. 2005
[**] 2005 survey dollar costs by 0.035 for the period beginning Nov. 2004 and ending Nov. 2005
[***] Based on US population age 18 and over of 215.47 million as of July 1, 2002, of 217.8 million as of July 1, 2003, and of 221.9 million as of July 1, 2005

2. *View credit reports –*

   Once the credit-reporting agencies are notified, the victim automatically receives a free credit report from each of the three agencies, and the victim will be opted out of preapproved credit card and insurance offers. After the victim receives the reports, he should make note of the unique number assigned to his account. This will be valuable in all later communications with the agencies.

3. *Write a victim statement –*

   Write a victim statement explaining the circumstances of the theft, including the credit cards or other credit lines improperly used, the items purchased, the retailer, and other information explaining what happened. Then ask for the victim statement to be added to the credit file at each credit agency.

4. *Contact creditors of tampered accounts –*

   Contact creditors for any accounts that have been tampered with or opened without your knowledge. Put all complaints/explanations in writing.

5. *Contact law enforcement agency –*

   Alert the police in your city. You may also need to report the crime to the police departments where the crime occurred. Make sure the police report lists all fraud accounts. Give as much documented information as possible. Ask each creditor to provide both you and your investigating law enforcement agency with copies of the documents showing fraudulent transactions. Sometimes you may have to fight to get this documentation, but do not give up. You and the law enforcement agency may need these to help track down the perpetrator.

   Get a copy of the report and send it to the creditors and the credit-reporting agencies as proof of the report of the crime. Keep the phone number of your police investigator handy.

6. *Contact the FTC –*

   Contact the FTC at (877) 438-4338. While federal investigators only tend to pursue larger, more sophisticated fraud cases, they monitor identity theft crimes of all levels in the hopes of discovering patterns and breaking up larger rings. More importantly, fill out the ID Theft Affidavit at the FTC's Web site. Then make copies and send them to creditors. The agency also has an on-line complaint form.

7. *Change all you account passwords or PINs –*

   If an account does not have a password, add one. Avoid using your mother's maiden name or the last four digits of your Social Security number as a personal identification number.

8. *Notify the Office of the Inspector General if your Social Security number has been fraudulently used –*

   Also, ask for a copy of your Personal Earnings and Benefits Statement and check for accuracy.

9. *Change your driver's license number –*

   You may need to change your driver's license number if someone is using yours as an ID. Go to the Department of Motor Vehicles to get a new number.

10. *Contact your telephone and utility companies –*

    Contact your telephone and utility companies to prevent a con artist from using a utility bill as proof of residence when applying for new cards.

AVOIDING CREDIT SCAMS

Turning to a business that offers help in solving debt problems may seem like a reasonable solution when bills become unmanageable. Be cautious. Before doing business with any company, check it out with the local consumer protection agency or the Better Business Bureau in the company's location.

Ads Promising Debt Relief May Be Offering Bankruptcy

Consumer debt is at an all-time high. What is more, a record number of consumers – nearly 1.5 million in 2001 – are filing for bankruptcy. Whether the debt dilemma is the result of an illness, unemployment, or overspending, it can seem overwhelming. In the effort to get solvent, be on the alert for advertisements that offer seemingly quick fixes. While the ads pitch the promise of debt relief, they rarely say relief may be spelled b-a-n-k-r-u-p-t-c-y. And although bankruptcy is one option to deal with financial problems, it is generally considered the option of last resort. The reason: it has a long-term negative impact on one's creditworthiness. A bankruptcy stays on one's credit report for 10 years, and can hinder a person's ability to get credit, a job, insurance, or even a place to live.

Advance-Fee Loan Scams

These scams often target consumers with credit problems or consumers who have difficulty getting credit. In exchange for an up-front fee, these companies guarantee that applicants will get the credit they want – usually a credit card or a personal loan.

The up-front fee may range from $100 to several hundred dollars. Resist the temptation to follow up on advance-fee loan guarantees. They may be illegal. Many legitimate creditors offer extensions of credit, such as credit cards, loans, and mortgages, through telemarketing and require an application fee or appraisal fee in advance. But legitimate creditors never guarantee in advance that a person will get the loan. Under the federal Telemarketing Sales Rule, a seller or telemarketer who guarantees or represents a high likelihood of a person getting a loan or some other extension of credit may not ask for or receive payment until the person has received the loan.

Recognizing an Advance-Fee Loan Scam

There are many fraudulent loan brokers and other individuals misrepresenting the availability of credit and credit terms. Ads for advance-fee loans often appear in the classified ad section of local and national newspapers and magazines. They also may appear in mailings, radio spots, and on local cable stations. Often, these ads feature "900" numbers that result in charges on the caller's phone bill. In addition, these companies often use delivery systems other than the U.S. Postal Service, such as overnight or courier services, to avoid detection and prosecution by postal authorities.

Do not confuse a legitimate credit offer with an advance-fee loan scam. An offer for credit from a bank, savings and loan, or mortgage broker generally requires a verbal or written acceptance of the loan or credit offer. The offer usually is subject to a check of one's credit report after a person applies to make sure the person meets their credit standards. Borrowers are usually not required to pay a fee in order to get the credit.

Be suspicious of anyone who calls on the phone and says they can guarantee you will get a loan if you pay in advance. Hang up. It's against the law.

Credit Repair Scams

Every day, companies nationwide appeal to consumers with poor credit histories. They promise, for a fee, to clean up a person's credit report so the person can get a car loan, a home mortgage, insurance, or even a job. The truth is they cannot deliver. After the unfortunate dupes pay them hundreds or thousands of dollars in up-front fees, these companies do nothing to improve credit reports; many simply vanish with the money.

The Credit Repair Organizations Act

By law, credit repair organizations must give clients a copy of the "Consumer Credit File Rights under State and Federal Law" before they sign a contract. They also must give clients a written contract that spells out the clients' rights and obligations. People using these services should read these documents carefully before signing the contract. The law contains specific consumer protections. For example, a credit repair company cannot

- make false claims about their services
- charge clients until they have completed the promised services
- perform any services until they have their clients' signatures on a written contract and have completed a three-day waiting period, during which time clients can cancel the contract without paying any fees

Also, the contract must specify

- the payment for services, including their total cost
- a detailed description of the services to be performed
- how long it will take to achieve the results
- any guarantees they offer
- the company's name and business address

If You Are A Victim – Where to Complain

When people have a problem with any of the scams described here, they should contact their local consumer protection agency, state Attorney General (AG), or Better Business Bureau. Many AGs have toll-free consumer hotlines.

FINANCIAL PRIVACY

Protecting the privacy of consumer information held by "financial institutions" is at the heart of the financial privacy provisions of the Gramm-Leach-Bliley Financial Modernization Act (GLB). The GLB Act requires companies to give consumers privacy notices that explain the institutions' information-sharing practices. In turn, consumers have the right to limit some – but not all – sharing of their information.

The following sections briefly summarize the basic financial privacy requirements of the law.

Financial Institutions

The GLB Act applies to "financial institutions" – companies that offer financial products or services to individuals, like loans, financial or investment advice, or insurance. The Federal Trade Commission has authority to enforce the law with respect to "financial institutions" that are not covered by the federal banking agencies, the Securities and Exchange Commission, the Commodity Futures Trading Commission, and state insurance authorities. Among the institutions that fall under FTC jurisdiction for purposes of the GLB Act are non-bank mortgage lenders, loan brokers, some financial or investment advisers, tax preparers, providers of real estate settlement services, and debt collectors. At the same time, the FTC's regulation applies only to companies that are "significantly engaged" in such financial activities.

The law requires that financial institutions protect information collected about individuals; it does not apply to information collected in business or commercial activities.

Consumers and Customers

A company's obligations under the GLB Act depend on whether the company has consumers or customers who obtain its services. A consumer is an individual who obtains or has obtained a financial product or service from a financial institution for personal, family, or household reasons. A customer is a consumer with a continuing relationship with a financial institution. Generally, if the relationship between the financial institution and the individual is significant and/or long-term, the individual is a customer of the institution. For example, a person who gets a mortgage from a lender or hires a broker to get a personal loan is considered a customer of the lender or the broker, while a person who uses a check-cashing service is a consumer of that service.

Why is the difference between consumers and customers so important? Because only customers are entitled to receive a financial institution's privacy notice automatically. Consumers are entitled to receive a privacy notice from a financial institution only if the company shares the consumers' information with companies not affiliated with it, with some exceptions. Customers must receive a notice every year for as long as the customer relationship lasts.

The privacy notice must be given to individual customers or consumers by mail or in-person delivery; it may not, for example, be posted on a wall. Reasonable ways to deliver a notice may depend on the type of business the institution is in: for example, an online lender may post its notice on its website and require online consumers to acknowledge receipt as a necessary part of a loan application.

The Privacy Notice

The privacy notice must be a clear, conspicuous, and accurate statement of the company's privacy practices; it should include what information the company collects about its consumers and customers, with whom it shares the information, and how it protects or safeguards the information. The notice applies to the "nonpublic personal information" the company gathers and discloses about its consumers and customers; in practice, that may be most – or all – of the information a company has about them. For example, nonpublic personal information could be information that a consumer or customer puts on an application; information about the individual from another source, such as a credit bureau; or information about transactions between the individual and the company, such as an account balance. Indeed, even the fact that an individual is a consumer or customer of a particular financial institution is nonpublic person information. But information that the company has reason to believe is lawfully public – such as mortgage loan information in a jurisdiction where that information is publicly recorded – is not restricted by the GLB Act.

Opt-Out Rights

Consumers and customers have the right to opt out of –or say no to–having their information shared with certain third parties. The privacy notice must explain how – and offer a reasonable way – they can do that. For example, providing a toll-free telephone number or a detachable form with a pre-printed address is a reasonable way for consumers or customers to opt out; requiring someone to write a letter as the only way to opt out is not.

The privacy notice also must explain that consumers have a right to say no to the sharing of certain information – credit report or application information – with the financial institution's affiliates. An affiliate is an entity that controls another company, is controlled by the company, or is under common control with the company. Consumers have this right under a different law, the Fair Credit Reporting Act. The GLB Act does not give consumers the right to opt out when the financial institution shares other information with its affiliates.

The GLB Act provides no opt-out right in several other situations: For example, an individual cannot opt out if

- a financial institution shares information with outside companies that provide essential services like data processing or servicing accounts,
- the disclosure is legally required, or
- a financial institution shares customer data with outside service providers that market the financial company's products or services.

Receiving Nonpublic Personal Information

The GLB Act puts some limits on how anyone that receives nonpublic personal information from a financial institution can use or re-disclose the information. Take the case of a lender that discloses customer information to a service provider responsible for mailing account statements, where the consumer has no right to opt out: The service provider may use the information for limited purposes – that is, for mailing account statements. It may not sell the information to other organizations or use it for marketing.

However, it is a different scenario when a company receives nonpublic personal information from a financial institution that provided an opt-out notice – and the consumer didn't opt out. In this case, the recipient steps into the shoes of the disclosing financial institution, and may use the information for its own purposes or re-disclose it to a third party, consistent with the financial institution's privacy notice. That is, if the privacy notice of the financial institution allows for disclosure to other unaffiliated financial institutions – like insurance providers – the recipient may re-disclose the information to an unaffiliated insurance provider.

Other Provisions

Other important provisions of the GLB Act also impact how a company conducts business. For example, financial institutions are prohibited from disclosing their customers' account numbers to non-affiliated companies when it comes to telemarketing, direct mail marketing or other marketing through e-mail, even if the individuals have not opted out of sharing the information for marketing purposes.

Another provision prohibits "pretexting" – the practice of obtaining customer information from financial institutions under false pretenses. The FTC has brought several cases against information brokers who engage in pretexting.

OTHER CONSUMER PROTECTION LAWS[14]

The *Consumer Credit Protection Act of 1968* – which launched *Truth in Lending* – requires creditors to state the cost of borrowing in a common language so that the customer can figure out exactly what the charges will be, compare costs, and shop around for the best credit deal.

Since 1968, credit protections have multiplied rapidly. The concepts of "fair" and "equal" credit have been written into laws that outlaw unfair discrimination in credit transactions, require that consumers be told the reason when credit is denied, let borrowers find out about their credit records, and set up a way to settle billing disputes.

The *Truth in Lending Law* requires creditors to give consumers certain basic information about the cost of buying on credit or taking out a loan. The required disclosures vary slightly for closed-end credit (e.g., a fixed-term loan) and open-end credit (e.g., a revolving credit card account), but generally include the Annual Percentage Rate (APR) and other key terms of a credit offer.

Consumer Leasing disclosures can help consumers compare the cost and terms of a lease with another lease and with the cost and terms of buying for cash or on credit.

Credit costs vary. By remembering two terms, consumers can compare credit prices from different sources. Under Truth in Lending, the creditor must tell consumers – in writing and before they sign any agreement – the finance charge and the annual percentage rate.

The finance charge is the total dollar amount consumers pay to use credit. It includes interest costs, and other costs, such as service charges and some credit-related insurance premiums.

The APR is the percentage cost (or relative cost) of credit on a yearly basis. It provides a convenient yardstick to compare costs, regardless of the amount of credit or how long one has to repay it.

All creditors – banks, stores, car dealers, credit card companies, finance companies – must state the cost of their credit in terms of the finance charge and the APR. Federal law does not set interest rates or other credit charges. But it does require their disclosure so that consumers can compare credit costs. The law says these two pieces of information must be shown to consumers before they sign a credit contract or before they use a credit card.

The *Real Estate Settlement Procedures Act*, like *Truth in Lending*, is a disclosure law. The Act, administered by the Department of Housing and Urban Development, requires the lender to give borrowers, in advance, certain information about the costs they will pay when they close the loan.

The *Equal Credit Opportunity Act* requires that all credit applicants be considered on the basis of their actual qualifications for credit and not be turned away because of certain personal characteristics. Potential borrowers must still pass the creditor's tests of creditworthiness. but the creditor must apply these tests fairly, impartially, and without discrimination on the basis of age, sex, marital status, race, color, religion, national origin, because they receive public income such as veterans benefits, welfare, or Social Security, or because they exercise their rights under Federal credit laws such as filing a billing error notice with a creditor.

The *Fair Credit Billing Act* sets up procedures requiring creditors to promptly correct billing mistakes; allowing consumers to withhold payments on defective goods; and requiring creditors to promptly credit borrowers' payments. It also spells out how credit-reporting agencies must report disputes in their credit files and the procedures for consumers to report such disputes.

Consumer Pamphlets Available

- Consumer Handbook to Credit Protection Laws
- Consumer Handbook of Adjustable Rate Mortgages
- A Consumer's Guide to Mortgage Closing Costs
- A Consumer's Guide to Mortgage Lock-Ins
- A Consumer's Guide to Mortgage Refinancings
- A Guide to Business Credit for Women, Minorities, and Small Businesses
- Home Mortgages: Understanding the Process and Your Right to Fair Lending
- A Guide to Federal Reserve Regulations
- How To File a Consumer Credit Complaint
- Making Deposits: When Will Your Money Be Available?
- When Your Home is on the Line: What You Should Know About Home Equity Lines of Credit

Copies of these other consumer pamphlets are available upon request from Publications Services, Division of Support Services, Board of Governors of the Federal Reserve System, Washington, D.C. 20551.

CHAPTER ENDNOTES

1. The following sections are adapted from a special report posted at www.Bankrate.com, written by Pat Curry, a freelance writer based in Georgia, and "Facts for Consumers: Building a Better Credit Record," Federal Trade Commission at http://www.ftc.gov/bcp/conline/pubs/credit/bbcr.htm.
2. The FTC also warns consumers to be wary. Many other websites claim to offer "free credit reports," "free credit scores," or "free credit monitoring." But, be careful. These sites are not part of the official annual free credit report program. And in some cases, the "free" product comes with strings attached. For example, some sites sign users up for a supposedly "free" service that converts to one they have to pay for after a trial period ends. If they do not cancel during the trial period, they may be agreeing to let the company start charging monthly fees to their credit card.

   These sites often look like the official site at annualcreditreport.com. Some use terms like "free report" in their names; others have website names that purposely misspell annualcreditreport.com in the hope that users will mistype the name of the official site. Some of these "imposter" sites direct users to other sites that try to sell users something or collect personal information.

Anyone who wants to order a free annual credit report online should carefully type in the name: annualcreditreport.com, or go to the FTC's website which has a link to it. Once users have filled out certain information at annualcreditreport.com, they will be directed to individual websites operated by the three nationwide consumer reporting companies. Users may get offers to buy additional products or services while on the companies' websites, such as credit scores or credit monitoring products, but they are not required to make a purchase to receive their free annual credit reports.

Anyone who gets an email or sees a pop-up ad claiming it is from annualcreditreport.com or any of the three nationwide consumer reporting companies should not reply or click on any link in the message – it is probably a scam. The annualcreditreport.com site will NEVER send users an email solicitation for their free annual credit report, use pop-up ads, or call users to ask for personal information. Forward any email that claims to be from annualcreditreport.com or any of three consumer reporting companies to the FTC's database of deceptive spam at spam@uce.gov.

3. The phone, address, and web site information for the three major credit agencies can be found in Figure 17.3.
4. Much of the material in this section is adapted, with many thanks for a job very well done, from a paper prepared by Daniel Riley and Jacqueline Tyszka, "Identity Theft and Personal Financial Planning," for a class in *Personal Financial Planning* in the Haub Graduate School of Business, St. Joseph's University, Spring 2007.
5. Johannes, Rubina. "2006 Identity Fraud Survey Report." Javelin Strategy and Research Unknown Update. Retrieved 10 April 2007. http://www.javelinstrategy.com/products/99DEBA/27/delivery.pdf.
6. Newman, Graeme R. "Identity Theft." United States Department of Justice. Unknown Update. Retrieved 11 April 2007. http://www.cops.usdoj.gov/mime/open.pdf? Item=1271.
7. "Prevention Tips You Should Know." Pennsylvania Commission on Crime and Delinquency, Identity Theft Action Plan. Unknown Update. Retrieved 8 April 2007. http://www.identitytheftactionplan.com/preventH.html.
8. Johannes, Rubina. "2006 Identity Fraud Survey Report." Javelin Strategy and Research Unknown Update. Retrieved 10 April 2007. http://www.javelinstrategy.com/products/99DEBA/27/delivery.pdf.
9. Koerner, Brian. "Stolen Mail and Your Identity – A Favorite Tactic of an Identity Thief." About: Identity Theft. Unknown Update. Retrieved 11 April 2007: http://idtheft.about.com/od/methodsofthefl/p/StolenMail.htm.
10. "ID Theft." Federal Trade Commission. Unknown Update. Retrieved 10 April 2007. http://www.consumer.gov/idtheft/con_minimize.htm#computer.
11. Watson, David. "Know Your Enemy: Phishing. Behind the Scenes of Phishing Attacks." The Honeynet Project and Research Alliance. 16 May 2005. Retrieved 11 April 2007. http://www.honeynet.org/papers/phishing/.
12. "Phishing and Identity Theft." Privacymatters.com. Unknown Update. Retrieved 11 April 2007. http://identity.privacymatters.com/identity-articles/phishing.aspx.
13. http://www.ftc.gov/bcp/edu/microsites/idtheft/.
14. Source: *Consumer Handbook to Credit Protection Laws*, The Federal Reserve Board, at http://www.federalreserve.gov/pubs/consumerhdbk/cost.htm.

Figure 17.3

Credit Bureau	**Equifax**	**Experian**	**Trans Union**
Phone	(800) 685-1111	(800) 397-3742	(877) 322-8228
Address	Equifax Credit Information Services P.O. Box 740241 Atlanta, GA 30374	Turned down for credit, insurance, or employment: P.O. Box 9600 Allen, TX 75013 On welfare, unemployed, or credit fraud: P.O. Box 9532 Allen, TX 75013	Trans Union Consumer Solutions P.O. Box 2000 Chester, PA 19022-2000
On the Internet	http://www.equifax.com/	http://www.experian.com/	http://www.transunion.com/

Chapter 18

FINANCING ASSET ACQUISITIONS

INTRODUCTION

People finance their investments to enhance their returns through the use of positive financial leverage, to increase the scale of their investments, or to purchase assets, such as real estate and business assets, that they would not be able to afford without borrowing or other financing.

This chapter discusses the following topics:

1. financial leverage
2. margin trading
3. secured vs. unsecured debt
4. long-term vs. short-term debt
5. mortgage loan programs
6. other mortgage financing alternatives
7. refinance loans
8. mortgage (loan) math
9. mortgage and loan financial planning applications
10. fixed-rate versus adjustable-rate loans
11. determining how much home one can afford
12. leasing

FINANCIAL LEVERAGE

Leveraging is the use of techniques that permit investors to control or benefit from an investment with a given dollar value while using less than that given dollar value of the investor's own money. Essentially, as the name implies, it is similar to the action of a lever that permits a person to move a boulder larger than he could move with his hands alone. Leveraging permits investors to control more or larger investment assets than they could control with their own equity alone.

Financial leverage is the use of borrowed funds to supplement the investor's own dollar investment (equity) to increase the scale of investment. For example, an investor can purchase stocks, bonds, and other marketable securities, real estate, business assets, and the like using some combination of investor and borrowed funds. If the investment return on the asset exceeds the interest rate paid on the loan, the investor's return on his equity will rise above the return on the underlying asset (positive leverage). Conversely, if the return on the asset is less than the interest rate paid on the loan, the investor's return will fall below the return on the underlying asset (reverse or negative leverage). Investors may be able to deduct the interest expense against investment income on their tax returns, subject to limitations.

For example, if a person in a 33⅓% combined federal and state tax bracket invests $1,000 for one year at a fully taxable 10% rate of return, she will have $1,066.70 after tax at the end of the year. The after-tax rate of return is 6.67%.

Now suppose the investor can borrow $1,000 at 5% interest and add it to her $1,000 investment. This $2,000 total investment will earn $200 before tax. The investor must pay $1,000 plus $50 interest back to the lender, so the investor is left with $1,150 before tax (assuming the interest is tax deductible) or $1,100 after tax. The investor has increased the after-tax return on her equity from 6.67% to 10% through the use of financial leverage.

Certain types of investments, marketable securities, are subject to government-mandated borrowing limitations, called margin requirements. Margin requirements or borrowing limitations for real estate, business assets, private placements, non-publicly-traded limited partnership interests, and other non-exchange-traded investments are generally not subject to regulation. The equity requirements are generally determined by mutual agreement among the parties to the transaction and the lenders.

MARGIN TRADING

Securities traded on organized exchanges or in the over-the-counter market are subject to minimum investor equity requirements, called margin requirements, as set by the Federal Reserve Board's Regulation T. These rules apply to the amount of equity investors must have and maintain in both securities purchased with financial leverage (e.g., stocks) and those that are inherently leveraged (e.g., futures contracts). These limitations apply regardless of the source of borrowing – brokerage firm, bank, or even family members. The National Association of Securities Dealers (NASD), the New York Stock Exchange (NYSE), and other exchanges have their own rules that generally match the Reg. T requirements, but which may be more restrictive.

If investors borrow money to leverage their investments from their brokerage firm, or trade in securities with inherent leverage, they must set up a margin account. The minimum portion of the purchase price that the customer must deposit is called the initial margin and is the customer's initial equity in the account. Subsequently, investors must maintain a specified minimum level of equity relative to the market value of the investment called the maintenance margin. The maintenance margin requirement is generally lower than the initial margin requirement. If an investor's margin falls below the required maintenance level, the brokerage firm will issue a margin call requiring the investor to deposit additional funds within a specified period of time. If the investor fails to do so, the brokerage firm will sell the assets and close out the investor's position. Brokerage firms may have their own margin requirements that are more restrictive than those spelled out in Reg. T or the NYSE or NASD guidelines.

How do margin requirements vary among different securities?

Margin requirements tend to vary somewhat depending upon each brokerage firms own "house" rules, but competition tends to keep them quite close to Reg. T requirements and the NASD guidelines.

SECURED VS. UNSECURED DEBT

Debts of an individual or business can be either secured or unsecured.

Unsecured debt is debt that does not have any collateral to satisfy the debt in case the debtor is no longer able to pay. Examples of unsecured debt are credit cards, utility bills, medical bills, and other contracts where no collateral is pledged to the creditor. If an unsecured creditor wishes to collect a debt that has not been paid, the only recourse is a lawsuit against the debtor. If the debtor enters bankruptcy, unsecured debt can be discharged by the bankruptcy proceeding.

Secured debt is debt that is backed by some type of collateral. Mortgage debt is an example of secured debt. Also, most car loans are forms of secured debt. A secured creditor is generally in a better position than an unsecured creditor because if the debtor does not pay back the loan, the creditor can take back the property either through repossession or a foreclosure action. After the property is taken back by the creditor, the creditor may be able to collect any additional deficiency if the repossessed property is worth less than the debtor owes. This deficiency would then become unsecured debt. Secured debt is not discharged in a bankruptcy proceeding.

LONG-TERM VS. SHORT-TERM DEBT

Short-term debt can be used by a business to get through the slow times that it may experience, such as a retail store or a restaurant with seasonal business cycle. Short-term loans can last anywhere from 90 days to up to three years, depending on the purpose of the loan. These types of loans might be used to cover accounts payable, pay salaries in the short-term, or provide the business with cash until accounts receivable are paid. Most short-term loans are unsecured loans, although some loans to acquire inventory might be secured by the inventory itself. For accounting purposes, most short-term debt is considered to be a current liability.

Long-term debt is generally classified as debt that is paid off over a period of time that exceeds the one to three years (some commentators and organizations define "short-term" debt as up to one year, others as up to three years). The idea behind long-term debt is to us it to purchase an asset that has a long-term use, such as a home or business equipment that is expected to be used over a long period of time.

MORTGAGE LOAN PROGRAMS

Fixed Rate Mortgages

With fixed rate mortgage (FRM) loans, the interest rate and monthly mortgage payments remain fixed for the term of the loan. Fixed-rate mortgages are available for 10, 15, 20, 25, 30, or even longer in some circumstances. Generally, the shorter the term of a loan, the lower the interest rate the lender will charge on the loan.

The most popular mortgage terms are 15 and 30 years. With the traditional 30-year fixed rate mortgage, monthly payments are lower than they would be on a shorter-term loan. But if a person can afford higher monthly payments, a 15-year fixed rate mortgage allows the borrower to repay the loan twice as fast and save more than half the total interest costs of a 30-year loan.

The payments on fixed rate fully amortizing loans are calculated so that at the end of the term the mortgage loan is paid in full. During the early amortization period, a large percentage of the monthly payment is used for paying the interest. As the loan is paid down, more of the monthly payment is applied to principal. The mathematics of loans are discussed further later in this chapter.

The principal advantages of fixed rate loans are their relative simplicity and the fixed and certain periodic payments. Other types of loans are generally more complicated, but they may offer features and flexibilities that better serve investors' particular needs.

Adjustable Rate Mortgages

An Adjustable Rate Mortgage (ARM) loan is any mortgage loan program that allows the lender to periodically reset or adjust the loan's interest rate, according to agreed measurements and at pre-set periods. The mortgage lender does not have free reign with the adjustments. Today's ARM loan borrowers actually have several protections built into the residential ARM loan program.

Advantages of ARM Loans

The residential ARM loan was first introduced into the national market as the Variable Rate loan. This term still remains in use with credit cards and installment loans, but it has been replaced in the mortgage industry with the more specific and catchy "ARM" description.

Many homebuyers are wary of ARM loans. Older homeowners, who remember the 19% interest rate of the 1970s, are especially leery of the inherent risks of ARM programs. However, ARM loans do have their advantages, which make them ideal for people who can see the home or property purchase as a financial investment. In fact, ARM loans are the programs of choice for experienced real estate investors.

When homebuyers are planning on keeping the home for three years or less, they will save money virtually all the time by selecting an ARM loan, instead of a fixed-rate loan. After the third year, depending on how the market reacts, the fixed-rate or balloon loans are generally better. Even if they decide to stay past the third year, many ARMs have a conversion option and some lenders provide no-lender-cost refinances.

With the development of 3/1, 5/1 and 7/1 ARMs, which will be discussed in more detail below, ARM programs now offer an even greater opportunity for homebuyers planning on up to a seven-year ownership period with any one property.

The reason for the ARM loan's advantage is that even with any wild increases in the market's current interest rates, the rate increase caps – or limits – means that monthly payments normally remain lower with the ARM loan for at least two years to three years.

Second, ARM loans are attractive during periods of high interest rates. History has shown that interest rate fluctuations are normal and tend to be cyclical. During times of comparatively higher rates, borrowers can elect to go with an ARM loan that has a much lower interest rate than the regular 30-year fixed-rate. When the market finally improves to lower rates, the borrower can refinance his or her loan.

Even if homeowners plan to keep their newly found property forever, if they are searching for a mortgage loan during a period of relatively higher interest rates, they should consider going with the lower "teaser rate" of the ARM loan. Then, once interest rates have decreased, they may just refinance the mortgage loan to a lower rate – preferably a fixed-rate program. Sometimes, their current lender will give them a free refinance, just so they can keep them as a borrower.

ARM Loan Details

An adjustable-rate mortgage (ARM) allows the lender to change the interest rate – at periodic intervals – without altering other conditions of the loan agreement. When the lender adjusts the interest rate, they also adjust the monthly principal and interest (P&I)

payment. By so doing, the ARM loan allows the borrower to share more of the loan's risk. This lowers the lender's relative risk exposure, so the interest rate on ARMs is usually much lower than those on comparable fixed-rate loans. Several distinct features of the ARM loan are

1. *ARM periods* – The period is the span of time that a lender must wait before it can readjust the interest rate of the ARM loan. The lender may only change the interest rate on a loan once each period, normally on the anniversary date of each period. The exceptions are ARM loans based on the prime rate, which normally have no set period. This is the case with many credit cards, business loans, and commercial loans. Many home equity lines of credit also use the prime rate and are subject to interest rate changes with only one month's notice. Banks adjust the prime rate according to overall market conditions. The prime rate may not change for two years in a row; then it may increase five times in one month.

   Readjustment periods can range from one month to several years, with one-year ARM periods being the most common. Generally speaking, ARMs with shorter periods usually provide lower interest rates, since shorter periods give the lender more opportunities to adjust the interest rate – and thus further lower the lender's overall risk exposure. (Do not confuse the loan term or amortization with the period. A 30-year amortization is the norm for all ARM loans, although shorter amortization settings and terms are also available.) As the table below shows, the ARM period does not affect the term and amortization. The ARM period merely indicates how often the loan's interest rates – and consequently, its monthly payments – are adjusted.

	Rates adjust every	Term	Amortization
3-month ARM	3 months	30 years	30 years
6-month ARM	6 months	30 years	30 years
1-year ARM	1 year	30 years	30 years
3-year ARM	3 years	30 years	30 years

   In addition to the above standard ARM programs, *balloon* or *two-step ARM* programs have also become more popular. The most common are 3/1, 5/1, 7/1, and 10/1 ARMs.

	Rates adjust every	Term	Initial Amortization
3/1 ARM	1 year; after the 3rd year	30 years	30 years
5/1 ARM	1 year; after the 5th year	30 years	30 years
7/1 ARM	1 year; after the 7th year	30 years	30 years
10/1 ARM	1 year; after the 10th year	30 years	30 years
2-year/6-month	6-month; after the 2nd year	30 years	30 years

   These ARM loans are one-year ARM loans, however the interest rate is fixed for the first three, five, seven or ten years, depending on the program. For example, a 3/1 ARM is basically a one-year ARM loan with one-year periods. However, for the first three years, the ARM loan's rate is fixed (will NOT adjust). After the third year, the ARM loan's rate will begin adjusting as normal. The 2-year/6-month ARM is primarily used by non-conforming[1] loan programs. The interest rate is fixed for the first two years; after that fixed period, the loan's interest rates begin adjusting every six months.

2. *Index and margin* – When lenders adjust an ARM loan's interest rate, they must do so according to the agreement set forth in the original promissory note signed at the closing. The standard method for adjusting ARM interest rate is to add the defined "margin" to the current "index" rate. With straight ARM loans, the interest rates and monthly payments are adjusted on the anniversary date of the loan.

   The margin is a constant amount – usually 2.750 to 3.250 for most conforming[2] ARM loans – which is added to the index to determine the new interest rate. The margin is set when the borrower signs the loan note at the closing and it stays the same throughout the life of the loan.

   Although the margin remains constant, the index may change and is the basis of the ARM loan's adjustments. The interest rate on ARM loans is tied to the rates of securities, financial papers, or a basket of indicators that adequately reflect market conditions. This indicator rate is normally called the index rate. The most popular and commonly known indexes are

   a) *U.S. Treasury Bills* – The T-Bill index rate is based on the yield prices established by the daily sale and trade of the U.S. Treasury Bills on the financial markets. There are actually several T-Bills (2-year, 6-month,

3-year, etc.), but the one-year T-Bill is the most commonly used index.

b) *Prime rate* – The prime rate is the rate that banks charge to their best customers, usually commercial. The prime rate is actually higher than other indices because it factors in the bank's profit margin. Although, each bank sets its own prime rate, they tend to be uniform as they are all based on the same market data.

c) *Cost-of-Funds index (COFI)* – The COFI index is calculated by each of the Federal Reserves' regional districts, the most popular of which is the 11th District. The Cost-of-Funds index is a monthly survey of the cost to the banks of the money they have at their disposal. Thus, the COFI index takes into account current CD rates, savings account rates and other costs that banks must pay for funds.

d) *London InterBank Offered Rate (LIBOR)* – The LIBOR index has become the index of choice for non-conforming lenders, especially with sub-prime (B/C/D/E) credit loans. The LIBOR rate tends to remain close to – though slightly higher – than the T-Bill rate.

The index is a publicly available and trusted mechanism that measures changes in the economy (generally) and the mortgage industry and real estate market (specifically). The index measures fluctuations in the financial markets on a continuous basis. The loan's promissory note will indicate the specific index the lender will use to adjust interest rates.

3. *Caps* – At the anniversary (one-year, six-month, etc., depending on period) of the ARM loan, the lender adjusts the interest rates and payments by adding the constant loan margin to the index rate. However, this raw index-plus-margin number is not necessarily the borrower's new interest rate. This preliminary rate must be within the restrictions established by the specific loan program's caps. The new interest rate and monthly payment is the index plus margin, less whatever restrictions are required by the program's caps. Caps protect the borrower by limiting the movement of the interest rate, payments and principal balances, normally associated with ARM loans. There are four types of caps that can be involved with each ARM loan: periodic, lifetime, payment, and principal.

a) The *periodic cap* limits how much the loan's interest rate may change from one period to the next. The norm for most conforming lenders is a periodic cap of one or two percentage points. For example, if the loan program specifies a periodic cap of 2.00 percentage points, then the borrower's loan rate cannot increase (or decrease) by more than two percentage points from one period to the next. Thus, if the borrower had an interest rate of 5.5%, even if the index shot up to 8%, the most that the borrower's new rate can be is 7.5%. If, in the next period, the index jumps again, say, to 11%, the most the lender can increase the rate is again 2% over the previous rate of 7.5%, or to 9.5%. Now, if the index stays at 11%, in the next period the lender could increase the rate by 1.5% to 11%.

b) The *lifetime cap* establishes a maximum – and sometimes minimum – level that the interest rate may never surpass during the entire life of the loan. Most conforming loan programs set a lifetime cap of five or six percentage points, applied to the start rate. For example, an ARM loan with a 6% life cap and a starting rate of 5.50 would have a maximum limit of 11.50%. This means that even if the index would increase to 17.50% (which happened in the late 1970s), this ARM loan's interest rate would never exceed 11.50%. For many ARM loans, the start rate is the lifetime "floor" cap. The loan's interest rate will never go below that start rate. Obviously, this is a great benefit for lenders when rates really drop.

c) The *payment cap* limits how much the loan's monthly payment (not rate) may change from one period to the next. The typical payment cap, if any, would be 7% to 12% of the current payment. For example, if an ARM loan had a payment cap of 7% and a current mortgage payment of $1,000, the new payment would be a maximum of $1,070 per month ($1000 x 1.07). However, payment caps do not limit the increases of interest rates. Consequently, payment caps may induce negative amortization, which means that the principal balance increases instead of decreases.

d) The *principal cap* often accompanies loans with payment caps, by placing a ceiling on negative amortization. The principal cap limits the principal from increasing more than some specified percentage of the original loan balance. For example, on a 100,000 mortgage, if the principal cap percentage is 125%, the principal amount increase will never exceed 25% of the original loan balance, or $125,000.

4. *Negative amortization* – Negative amortization occurs in some ARM loans with payment caps whenever the monthly payments are not enough to cover the interest due on the debt. Unless the loan explicitly waives this unpaid interest, that deficit amount is added to the principal balance. Worse yet, as unpaid interest is added to the principal balance, the borrower will be charged interest on the unpaid interest. Because this situation could lead to endlessly increasing principal balances, ARM loans with payment caps usually also contain principal caps, as a protection against negative amortization. Principal caps still allow negative amortization to increase the principal balance, but sets limits on how high the principal may increase. The lender usually waives any unpaid interest that arises after the loan reaches the principal limit.

Most borrowers perceive negative amortization as very undesirable. However, ARM loans with payment caps and potential negative amortization are still prevalent, because they usually offer very low start rates. For borrowers who intend to keep a loan for only a year or so – even though the loan is amortized for 30 years – these loans could be wise investments.

5. *Conversion option* – The conversion option is an additional protection for most ARM and balloon loan borrowers that permits them to convert the ARM into a long-term fixed-rate loan. The conversion option is not a refinance, although it looks and acts like one. Rather, the conversion option amends the original mortgage loan note, without substantially changing the mortgage and title record. For example, an ARM loan borrower who is in the third year of her loan can convert it into a 27-year fixed-rate loan. The interest rate of the new fixed-rate loan will be based on the market rates at the time the loan is converted, as predefined in the conversion option clause. Most lenders charge a fee of $200 to $500 to prepare, execute and record the conversion documents. Borrowers must also meet certain requirements to exercise the conversion option. They cannot be delinquent on the account or have an unacceptable payment history. In addition, the option to convert typically has a time limit. In most cases, borrowers must exercise the conversion option sometime after the first full year and before the end of the fifth year of the loan.

6. *Adjustment Process* – As the rate is adjusted at the beginning of each period, the new payment is not calculated on the same 30-year amortization as the beginning payments. The amortization for the new payment calculation is usually only for the remaining term. The lender, as does the borrower, normally wants the loan to be completely repaid within the standard 30-year period. Consider the following graph of how payments are adjusted at the beginning of each year of a one-year ARM:

ARM Period	Interest Rate	Loan Amount	Amortization Period
Year 1	Start Rate	Original Loan	360 (30 years)
Year 2	Margin + Current Index	Current Balance	348 (29 years)
Year 3	Margin + Current Index	Current Balance	336 (28 years)
Year 4	Margin + Current Index	Current Balance	324 (27 years)

Because the amortization period is constantly decreasing, the monthly payment will remain the same or increase – even as the loan balance decreases or if the interest rate remains the same. In cases of negative amortization, the loan promissory note will make arrangements for paying the additional balance during the latter years of the loan or as a balloon amount at the conclusion of the term.

Disadvantages of ARMs

The primary disadvantage of the ARM loan is the adjusting interest rate. The caps provide some degree of protection; however, any rate and payment adjustment could hurt. Also, if the ARM starts with a teaser rate, a lower-than-market introductory rate, then the new adjusted rate is bound to be higher – even if the market rate does not increase.

A second minor disadvantage of the ARM loan is that the mortgage insurance, if any, will be slightly higher than the with a fixed-rate loan. The mortgage insurance premiums for ARM loans will normally be 10% to 20% higher than the mortgage insurance for comparable fixed-rate programs. This is because ARM loans do tend to carry more risk for the borrower. Remember that ARM loans allow the borrower to share more of the loan's risk with the lender. The mortgage insurance is merely a reflection of that increased borrower risk, which is borne out by higher default levels of ARM loans.

Home Equity Line of Credit

The Home Equity Line of Credit, sometimes referred to by its acronym HELOC, is a variation of the home equity loan. In most cases, both the HELOC and home equity loan are typically second mortgages. The line of credit is a cross between a mortgage loan and a credit card. Instead of providing the borrower with a check for the loan sum, the line of credit provides the borrower with a check book, which taps into a mortgage loan. This article explores the two opportunities that HELOCs offer to homeowners:

- financial planning tool
- investment tool

After the closing, the homeowner with a line of credit can write checks against the credit line established by this type of financing. There is usually no restrictions on the usage of the funds. As long as the borrower is not in default with his or her HELOC, the borrower will not have to obtain any lender approval before writing a check.

This credit line is still a legally recorded mortgage lien. However, the actual principal balance will increase or decrease according to how much the homeowner takes out or pays back.

Financial Planning Tool

The line of credit is an excellent safety net for the homeowner, as well as an unparalleled financing tool for investors. If the homeowner is faced with an emergency and needs funds, the line of credit can provide the needed money. If the investor or entrepreneur discovers an investment opportunity, the line of credit can provide quick capitalization.

By contrast, the unprepared homeowner would have to apply for a second mortgage, which could take 4-6 weeks to close. If the homeowner is already in an emergency situation, because of a job lay-off or sudden medical crisis, the lender may reject or severely restrict that borrower's application.

Unlike home equity loans, the credit line borrower only pays interest on the current principal balance used. If the borrower maintains zero balance on the credit line, no interest payments are due. Homeowners who wish to have this home equity safety net can simply put aside their HELOC checkbook in a safety deposit box. If the homeowners never use it, they are never charged any interest. But if an emergency ever arises, they will be able to feel more secure.

As with home equity loans, the home equity credit line interest rates are lower than credit cards and are often tax-deductible.

Homeowners who wish to consider the HELOC should understand three important elements of the typical line of credit:

1. *Cost* – As mentioned above, the borrower only pays interest on the balance that the borrower maintains on their home equity credit line account. That interest is usually tax-deductible for most homeowners. The cost to obtain a home equity line of credit will be the same as the closing costs required to obtain a standard home equity loan. Most homeowners can expect a flat fee of $500-$800 dollars, some of which may be tax-deductible. Most lenders will charge an annual fee of $25-$50, especially if the borrower does not use the credit line. Some banks are willing to waive this fee for its favored borrowers. Also, this fee may be tax-deductible: please consult your tax preparer or accountant.

2. *Mechanics* – The home equity line of credit is similar to the home equity loan. The primary difference is that the line of credit provides the borrower with a checkbook, instead of one lump-sum check. The borrower can use the home equity credit line checkbook to withdraw

funds for any purpose. Most home equity line of credit will divide the credit line's term into two phases:

- *Revolving* – During the revolving phase, the borrower can withdraw funds from the credit line, until the credit limit is reached. Some lenders may extend this credit limit, especially as the property appreciates. This revolving stage usually lasts five to ten years, with seven years being the most common term. The minimum payment due each month is usually the interest due for that particular month. As such, the HELOC is essentially an interest-only balloon loan during the revolving state. If the borrower wishes to reduce the principal balance during this interest-only phase, the borrower simply increases the payments above the minimum.

- *Amortized* – When the revolving period is complete, the lender provides the borrower with an option to convert the current balance into a standard fully amortizing loan. During the amortized period, the home equity credit line is essentially converted into a home equity loan. Most of these loans are usually for 15-year terms, with the monthly payments paying down the principal balance, as well as paying the interest due. However, some lenders will allow positive borrowers to renew their home equity line of credit by simply refinancing it with a new credit line.

3. *Interest rate* – Although some credit lines are fixed-rate, most are adjustable-rate mortgage (ARM) financing. These ARM programs also tend to be tied to the Prime Rate (although see the discussion of ARM mortgages above for other indexes), which is the rate charged by commercial banks to their best customer. Note, however, that the borrower's actual interest rate is normally higher than the prime rate, depending on the borrower's available equity and credit grade.

For example, Charlie has good credit and plenty of equity. If his home equity credit line and his first mortgage account for only 80% of the property's value (80% LTV), then his interest rate will probably be set at the prime rate. On the other hand, if Charlie's home equity line of credit takes up all of the property's available equity, his interest rate will probably be two to three percentage points over the prime rate. If Charlie's particular credit line stipulates an interest rate two percentage points over the prime rate index and if the prime rate is currently at 6.50%, his interest rate would be 8.5% (index 6.5% + constant 2%).

Investment Tool

For entrepreneurs and fledgling real estate investors, the home equity line of credit can be one of their best financing weapons. It provides them with liquidity, through a low-cost source of funds.

For example, Kathy is starting a Curves franchise – a workout center for women. She has found the perfect place to put her strong business plan and experience to good use. Kathy has already saved just about enough money to get this business started; but she is worried about how tight her finances will be and weathering any possible adverse economic circumstances.

Kathy obtains a home equity line of credit of $100,000 against her home. She can use these funds for the actual capitalization or simply as a safety net to help her through the initially dry months she anticipates. She knows that this business venture will be a success, but she does not want to endanger her credit rating, home mortgage payments, and overall financial situation. This line of credit will provide Kathy with a sense of security that she can withstand a strenuous six-month to one-year starting period, if necessary.

Balloon Loans

The balloon mortgage loan is an installment note whose amortization is longer than its term. Simply, the payments are calculated for a long-term period, but the loan's actual life is relatively short-term – with the "balloon" mortgage balance due at the end of that short term. The balloon loan used to be one of the chief alternatives to the fixed-rate program, because it offered lower rates without the increased risk of the ARM loan. With the evolution of the 3/1, 5/1, and other Two-Step ARM programs, the balloon program is not popular with homebuyers and homeowners. However, it is still widely used for commercial and non-conforming loans. The most common types of residential balloon mortgage loans are the five-year and seven-year balloons for conforming loan programs. However, 10-year and 15-year balloons are also prevalent among non-conforming programs. The majority of commercial and apartment building loans today are balloon loans.

Advantages and Disadvantages of Balloons

Balloon mortgage loans have two important elements that provide a considerable advantage to the borrower: a shorter term and a longer amortization. The shorter term (as compared to a standard 30-year loan) means a relatively lower risk exposure for the lender and so a lower interest rate. The interest rate for a conforming five-year balloon, for example, is typically 0.500 to 1.000 percentage points less than conforming 30-year fixed-rate loans. At the same time, the balloon loan's longer amortization (usually 30 years) provides the borrower with lower monthly payments than short-term loans, such as a 15-year mortgage. Except for the short-term, the conforming (Fannie Mae or Freddie Mac) balloon loans are very similar to the 30-year fixed-rate program.

In many respects, a balloon mortgage loan is a compromise between the fixed-rate and the adjustable-rate mortgage (ARM) loans. The balloon loan's interest rate, for starters, is usually lower than comparable fixed-rate loans, though higher than comparable ARM programs. The balloon program also provides a middle ground between risk and stability. Whereas the ARM loan's fluctuation in interest rate and payments means more instability for the borrower, the conforming balloon loan is fixed rate. Therefore, the balloon loan can offer a bit of the best of both worlds: a lower rate than fixed-rate programs, but more stability than ARM loans. Homebuyers that anticipate staying in their home for no more than five to seven years may find the balloon loan an attractive alternative. It has all the stability of a 30-year fixed-rate loan (during that period) but at a lower interest rate and a correspondingly lower payment.

Even homebuyers who plan to stay longer than five to seven years in the property may still find a balloon mortgage loan a wise choice. The buyer can always refinance to a standard fixed-rate loan at the end of the balloon term and, in some cases, exercise a conversion option.

The main disadvantage of the balloon loan, as compared to the 30-year fixed-rate loan, is that conforming balloon loans typically require at least 10% down payment.

Balloon Mechanics

Although the monthly payments of a balloon loan are calculated with a long-term amortization of (usually) 30 years, the balloon has a relatively short life. At the end of the balloon's term the loan will have a large loan principal balance still remaining. The borrower must either pay off the loan in full or refinance the remaining balance. This final, very large "balloon" payment is the origin of this program's name.

1. *Amortization* – The most important aspect of the balloon program is how its amortization differs from its term. For example, the conforming five-year balloon has an amortization of 30 years and a term of five years. The monthly payments are calculated with a 30-year amortization; however, at the conclusion of the five-year term, the remaining loan balance must be paid off, converted or refinanced. For example, a five-year balloon loan with a loan amount of $100,000, an interest rate of 7.5%, and an amortization period of 30 years has monthly payments of $699.21 – exactly the same as a 30-year fixed-rate mortgage. However, at the conclusion of the five-year term, the remaining loan balance will be $94,617. (The loan balance does not decrease very quickly during the first years of a 30-year amortization.) This balance must be paid off, refinanced or, if applicable, converted at the end of the five-year term. The most common types of balloon mortgage loan programs are five-year and seven-year balloons, but lenders also offer three-year and ten-year programs. The three most common balloon loan variations include

   a) *Two-step balloons* – The most typical conforming variations of balloon programs are the 5/25 and 7/23 two-step balloons. At the end of the balloon term, if the borrower meets certain conditions he may automatically convert the loan into a long-term loan. For example, the 5/25 balloon is initially a five-year loan. At the end of the fifth year, the borrower would have the option of converting the balance into a 25-year fixed-rate loan. To exercise this option, the borrower's account must not be delinquent and the borrower's payment history must be good. The interest rate of the 25-year loan would be based on the current rates at the end of the fifth year.

b) *Balloon ARMs* – Recently, the most popular variation of the balloon programs have been the 3/1, 5/1, and 7/1 balloon ARMs. These programs start with a fixed-rate balloon, but automatically convert to a long-term ARM loan. For example, the 7/1 ARM has a fixed interest rate during the first seven years of the loan. At the end of the seventh year, this loan converts into a one-year ARM loan with a 23-year initial amortization. This conforming program would have the adjustment caps of comparable ARM programs, except for the initial adjustment at the end of the seventh year. The first adjustment normally has either no cap or an extra-high cap.

c) *Interest-only balloons* – Some home equity credit lines and other balloon loans are designed as interest-only balloon loans. During the balloon's term, the monthly payments are only for the interest due on the loan. Thus, the monthly payments are lower than standard balloons. At the balloon's maturity date, the borrower must repay or refinance the entire original loan balance. The interest-only balloon is also known as a "term loan" or as a "straight mortgage note." The payments are lower than standard balloon loans; however, the principal never goes down.

2. *Conversion option* – Most conforming and some non-conforming balloon programs offer the borrower a conversion option. This option allows the borrower to convert the balloon mortgage loan into a standard long-term loan, either fixed-rate or ARM, at the current rates at the time of conversion. Generally, the borrower may exercise the conversion option only after the one-year anniversary of the loan and before the end of the balloon term. Many lenders require that the borrower demonstrate a timely payment history with the balloon mortgage loan. The conversion loan will usually charge a small administrative fee, as well as any pertinent legal recording fees. The new term and amortization period of the loan is usually 30 years, less the age of the balloon loan. For example, if the balloon loan is converted after two years into a fixed-rate loan, the new loan will usually have a 28-year term with the interest rate fixed at the prevailing market rate at the time of conversion.

Buy-Down Programs

Buy-down programs involve a reduction of the interest rate through prepayment of the loan's interest. At the closing, the buyer, lender, seller or other related parties pay points in order to provide the borrower with a lower interest rate. There are two basic types of buy-down programs – permanent and temporary. With the permanent buy-down loan, the borrower usually pays the points to reduce the monthly payments on the loan. In the case of temporary buy-down loans, frequently the property seller or the lender will pay the prepaid interest points as an incentive to buyer/borrowers.

Permanent Buy-Downs

A permanent buy-down lowers the interest rate for the entire term of the loan. At the initiation of the loan, the borrower (or sometimes the seller or lender) pays discount points, which are interest charges paid in advance. This tactic can be advantageous for those borrowers who can afford it because of the long-term benefits, which include (1) reduced interest payments long-term, (2) tax-deductible points, (3) lower monthly payments, and (4) qualification for a higher loan amount.

For example, consider a 30-year fixed-rate $100,000 loan with a current market interest rate of 8%. The monthly principal and interest (P & I) payment for this loan is about $733. However, suppose that by paying one discount point of prepaid interest (in this case, $1,000), the borrower can lower the interest rate to 7.75%. The monthly mortgage payment drops to about $716, or by $17 a month. The savings are $204 per year, or $6,120 throughout the entire 30-year term of the loan. Plus, the discount point/fee is normally tax-deductible.

The permanent buy-down program is usually not recommended for homebuyers who plan to stay in the new property for less than five years. Also, borrowers who think they may refinance their loan within the next three to five years generally should avoid paying any discount points. Of course, the "break even" period until the borrower will recoup the prepaid interest points depends of the interest rate differential and may be shorter or longer than three to five years.

Temporary Buy-Downs

The temporary buy-down programs (often called "teaser" programs) reduces the interest rate for only a short period of time, usually two years. The most common temporary buy-downs are the 2-1 and 1-1 temporary buy-down programs. The 2-1 buy-down reduces the interest rate by two percentage points during the first year of the loan and by one percentage point during the second year of the loan. The loan returns to the note rate in the third and subsequent years. By comparison, the 1-1 buy-down program reduces the interest rate by one percentage point during the first two years of the loan and returns to the note rate in the third year.

The temporary buy-down program is advantageous for borrowers who wish to qualify for a larger loan amount than the amount for which their income would normally qualify them. By lowering the interest rate and, as a result, the monthly payments during the first years of the loan, the prospective borrower may qualify for a higher loan amount. Often, developers offer to subsidize such buy-downs to more quickly market their newly built homes. The temporary buy-down is normally applied only to conforming fixed-rate loans. However, some lenders allow this option on certain balloon and ARM programs as well.

The main disadvantage of the temporary buy-down program is that its note rate is generally higher than on a conventional loan. This high note rate is offset by the low start rate. However, once the buy-down period is complete, the loan's interest rate will be relatively higher (than standard loan programs) for the rest of its term. For example, if the current market rate for a 30-year fixed-rate loan is 7%, the note rate of the same program with a 2-1 buy-down would probably be about 8%. During the first year, the start rate will be 6% (8% note rate less 2-point first-year reduction). In the second year, the interest rate will increase to 7% (8% note rate less 1-point second-year reduction). In the third and subsequent years of the loan, the interest rate will return to the note rate of 8%. Fortunately, most buy-down programs do not have prepayment penalties; so the borrower can refinance to lower rate, if currently available.

The temporary buy-down programs are options that the lender may offer on select programs. The restrictions of those specific programs guide the requirements imposed upon the borrower. However, many 2-1 temporary buy-down programs will require that the prospective borrower demonstrate potential for increased income. This is usually accomplished with a standard verification form completed by the employer or documentation of steadily increasing income.

Most temporary buy-downs establish an interest-subsidy escrow account for the period of the temporary buy-down. The funds in this escrow account are essentially prepayment of the interest during the first years of the loan. Either the lender or the seller/developer normally provide the funds for this interest-subsidy escrow account. A seller or developer may provide such buy-down funds as an incentive or assistance for buyers.

Construction Loans

For some homebuyers, the dream home is a truly custom-made, newly constructed home. For these construction purposes, a simple mortgage loan will not and cannot suffice – a construction loan is required. The typical construction loan will contain elements with different characteristics than found in a standard purchase or refinance loan. Four items are of particular importance: loan commitment, rate lock, method of disbursement, and lower LTV ratio limits.

Upon approval of the construction loan application, the borrower will receive a *loan commitment* from the lender. Most lenders do levy a loan commitment fee for construction loans. This loan commitment normally lasts for nine months, though longer or shorter commitments are also used. The lender locks-in the interest rate for the entire term of the construction loan. The primary purpose of the *rate lock* is not related to the construction loan, per se, but rather to fix the rate for the permanent refinancing mortgage loan at the conclusion of the construction.

Keep in mind, when constructing a custom property, the borrower needs two distinct loans – a short-term construction loan during the actual construction period and a long-term permanent mortgage loan after the property is built. Large-scale tract developers usually do NOT require buyers to obtain construction financing. Instead, most developers will require that the borrowers be approved for "purchase" mortgage loans. The actual construction of the property is funded with the developer's own cash, assets, or loans. The buyer's mortgage loan commitment is simply a guarantee to the developer that the buyer is qualified and will be able to purchase the newly constructed property immediately after construction is completed. People who are building custom homes, however, need to secure a construction loan to pay the builder/general contractor.

Jumbo Loans

A jumbo loan is any loan whose amount exceeds conforming guidelines. Conforming loans, which typically have the best interest rates and loan terms in the market, are loans sold to federally chartered agencies such as Fannie Mae and Freddie Mac. Such loans must satisfy or "conform" to these agencies' guidelines in order to be purchased.

Conforming Loan Limits

The definition of jumbo loans depends on the current conforming loan limits. Loan limits are adjusted by Fannie Mae and Freddie Mac - usually in cooperation with each other – to reflect increases in average home prices and mortgage loan amounts. In addition, they vary according to the number of units in the subject property. Each unit refers to one legal apartment. As of January 2007, the Fannie Mae maximum loan amount limits for conforming loan programs are as follows for first mortgages: single-unit or condominium loans: $417,000; two-unit residential loans: $533,850; three-unit residential loans: $645,300; four-unit residential loans: $801,450. (Note: One- to four- family mortgages in Alaska, Hawaii, Guam, and the U.S. Virgin Islands are 50% higher than the limits for the rest of the country.) For second mortgages, the loan limit is $208,500 (In Alaska, Hawaii, Guam, and the U.S. Virgin Islands the limit is $312,750.) The FHA sets lower loan amount limits than do Fannie Mae and Freddie Mac.

Because jumbo loans are non-conforming, they charge relatively higher interest rates than similar conforming programs.

Alternative Option: Jumbo Loans without Jumbo Pricing

There are ways to minimize the higher interest rates of jumbo loans. Obviously, the buyer can always make a larger down payment so that the loan amount finally required fits within the conforming limit. Depending on the sales price of the home, however, this can prove to be a very expensive approach.

A more advantageous approach is to purchase the property with two mortgages: a standard conforming first mortgage and a second mortgage loan. In this scenario, the first mortgage is a standard conforming program with a loan amount at the maximum limit. The second mortgage is for whatever amount the buyer needs to cover the difference required for financing.

Example. Chaka wants to buy a $700,000 property, and she only wants to make a down payment of 20%, or $140,000. She could obtain a jumbo loan for $560,000, but their interest rates are typically 0.25 to 1.00 percentage points higher than conforming loan programs. If the jumbo rate on that $560,000 loan were 7%, her monthly payment would be $3,725.69.

Instead, Chaka obtains a conforming 30-year first mortgage of $417,000. She then obtains a 30-year purchase second mortgage of $143,000; the two mortgages combine for the necessary $560,000 in mortgage financing. If the conforming rate were only 6.25%, the monthly payment would be $2,567.54. Even if the second mortgage's rate were at 7% (the rate for the jumbo mortgage), that monthly payment would be $951.38. Thus, her total combined mortgage payment would be $3,518.92, or $206.77 less per month than with the jumbo mortgage. That savings is about a 5.65% of the jumbo's monthly payment – enough to pay for most people's monthly cable TV and internet service!

No Income Verification (NIV) Loans

One of the most common non-conforming loan programs is the no income verification (NIV) loan. The NIV program allows the borrower to qualify for mortgage financing, regardless of the borrower's income. A review of the different types of NIV programs, as well as a discussion of costs and practical applications, follows.

Various lenders have different interpretations and application of the NIV option. The basic element is that the borrower's income, as reflected on the application, does not require verification. The NIV loan merely accepts the applicant's stated claim about his or her income – within reason. Although the NIV program will not verify the applicant's income, it will require that the stated income makes sense: it is acceptable for a doctor, lawyer, or other professional to state that he or she makes $100,000 a year; however, it is not acceptable for a janitor or clerical employee to state the same thing.

Most NIV loans will still insist on verifying employment, especially if the borrower is not self-employed. If the borrower is self-employed, the self-employment must be documented with a business license, past receipts and/or advertisements. Some lenders only offer NIV loans to self-employed borrowers. In fact, the NIV loan was initially developed primarily for self-employed borrowers, who had a difficult time documenting their income.

Until recently, practically all NIV programs were non-conforming loans. In recent years, however, some conforming programs have started to offer a limited NIV option for borrowers with very good credit. The interest rates on such conforming NIV programs are much better than standard non-conforming NIV

Applicable Situations

The no income verification loan is ideal for self-employed applicants and for borrowers who have unstable income, such as commissioned employees, recently employed borrowers and applicants who receive a large amount of cash (undocumented) income. However, salaried borrowers who cannot otherwise qualify for a loan based on their documented income use the NIV program.

The NIV option is available – at a cost (see below) – to borrowers with a wide range of credit and employment situations. Thus, applicants with D-credit in the middle of a bankruptcy or foreclosure can still qualify for a NIV loan.

Cost of NIV Programs

The NIV loan is more risky for the lender than standard "full documentation" loans, because the income calculation provides the lender with a statistical analysis of the borrower's ability to repay the loan. Without the income qualification of full documentation loans, lenders are assuming a higher level of risk. To offset these risks, NIV loans charge higher prices and require larger down payments than comparable full documentation programs.

Most NIV programs charge interest rates that are 1.50 to 4.00 percentage points higher than comparable full documentation loans. For example, if a conforming ARM loan is currently at 6%, an A-credit NIV ARM loan would probably be around 7.5% to 10%.

The most serious cost of the NIV option, however, is the down payment requirement. Most NIV programs require at least 20%-25% down payment for A-credit borrowers; C-credit and D-credit borrowers should expect to make at least 30%-40% down payments.

OTHER MORTGAGE FINANCING ALTERNATIVES

The following table briefly summarizes other mortgage financing options.

REFINANCE LOANS

Mortgage refinancing occurs when an old loan is paid and closed with the proceeds of the new loan. Most borrowers refinance loans for at least one of the following four reasons:

1. *Better interest rates* – When current interest rates are much lower than the rate on the borrower's original mortgage loan, a refinance would be a wise financial investment for the borrower.

2. *Change of term* – The term is the life of the loan and relates to the amortization of the loan. The longer the term and amortization, the smaller the monthly payments. However, shorter terms and amortization save money in the long run and build equity faster.

3. *Consolidation of debt* – Refinance loans are often used to consolidate several long-term liabilities. Credit cards charge exorbitant rates, and many installment loans are not much better. A consolidation refinance loan rolls these debts into one mortgage loan with lower and tax-deductible interest rates.

Figure 18.1

MORTGAGE FINANCING ALTERNATIVES
Renegotiable Rate Mortgage (Rollover). Interest rate and monthly payments are constant for several years; changes possible thereafter. Suitable for buyers with rising incomes.
Seller Take-back. Seller provides all or part of financing with a first or second mortgage. May offer a below market interest rate; may have a balloon payment requiring full payment in a few years or refinancing at market rates, which could sharply increase debt payments.
Growing Equity Mortgage. Fixed interest rate but monthly payments may vary according to agreed-upon schedule.
Contract Sale. Seller retains original mortgage. No transfer of title until loan is fully paid. Low down payment. Equal monthly payments with unpaid principal due at loan end. Contracts often made for 2 or 3 years, with "balloon payment" (balance due) at end. Buyer must refinance. Buyer has less protection than with mortgage financing. Legal advice strongly recommended. If buyer can't refinance, may have to sell property to pay off contract.
Rent with Option. Renter pays "option fee" for right to purchase property at specified time and agreed upon price. Rent may or may not be applied to sales price. Enables renter to buy time to obtain down payment and decide whether to purchase. Locks in price during inflationary times. Failure to take option means loss of option fee and rental payments.
Federal Housing Administration (FHA). Insured by FHA, local lending institution provides money. Below-market interest rates. Loan limits and down-payment requirements. Borrower pays for FHA mortgage insurance. Extra time needed for paper work.
Veterans Administration (VA) Loan. Guarantees payment to qualified veterans and surviving spouses. Below-market interest rates and down-payment requirements. Loan amount limited to repayment ability. Several mortgages available. Extra time needed for paper work.
USDA Rural Housing Service Loan. People in rural areas are eligible. Home must be of modest cost and design. Below market interest rates and down payment vary according to family income. Income and loan amount caps for this program. Contact local USDA Rural Development Office for information.
Community Reinvestment Loan Programs. Participating banks and savings and loans offer loans to low- and moderate-income consumers for purchase and remodeling. Lending requirements may be less restrictive.
Federal Home Loan Bank Board. Participating banks provide up to $8,000 to first-time home buyers whose incomes are below 80 percent of median county income. Money can be used to meet down payment requirement or to help pay closing costs.
Fannie Mae. Several programs created by Fannie Mae are offered by participating lenders. Low down payments are typical. Some have no income limitations.

4. *Extra cash* – The mortgage refinance is also a good way to raise extra cash for special purposes, such as sending a child to college, financing a special vacation or investing in a new business.

Cash-Out Refinance

Cash-out refinancings provide the borrower with additional cash from an increased loan amount. This privilege comes at a price. Conforming lenders set lower limits on cash-out loans, as compared to non-cash-out refinances. For conforming programs, the maximum total loan-to-value (LTV) ratio for cash-out refinances are usually as follows:

- single-family, owner-occupied residential property: 80%
- two-unit to four-unit, owner-occupied residential property: 75%
- all non-owner-occupied residential properties: 65%

Rate and term (no cash out) refinances, by comparison, regularly allow up to 90% of the property's value. Some programs actually allow LTVs of 100% and 125%.

Strictly speaking, the cash-out refinance – and its lower loan limits – applies to the following three situations:

1. *Cash back to the borrowers* – The borrower can receive surplus cash from applicable equity in the property. However, most conforming lenders limit the cash-out amount (after all other costs and pay-offs) to only $50,000. Non-conforming lenders also often set cash-out limits; but these limits are usually higher than those for conforming.
2. *Debt consolidation* – Conforming lenders classify any refinance that consolidates non-mortgage debts, such as credit cards and other personal loans, as cash-out refinances. Those consolidation funds are essentially cash-out of the property's established equity.
3. *Replace a first or second mortgage that is less than one year old* – If a borrower is refinancing a first or second mortgage loan that is less than one year old – regardless of whether the borrower is receiving cash back – conforming lenders classify the refinance as a cash-out.

Rate and Term (No Cash-Out) Refinance

The rate and term refinance, or no cash-out mortgage, deals with a straightforward refinance of an existing loan. The loan-to-value (LTV) ratios for non-cash-out refinances are higher than for cash-out, because cash-outs increase the lender's risk exposure. Strictly speaking, conforming rate and term (non-cash-out) refinances – and their higher loan-to-value (LTV) ratios – are applied to the following situations:

1. *Refinance of a first mortgage that is at least one year old* – Rate and term (non-cash-out) refinance may cover any loan that is paying off any first mortgage loan that is at least one year old. If the existing loan is less than one year old, many lenders consider this refinances a cash-out and apply a lower LTV ratio.
2. *Consolidation of multiple mortgages* – Rate and term refinance may cover a consolidation of mortgage loans. However, the junior liens (second and third mortgages) must be at least one year old.
3. *Refinance that also pays closing costs and prepaid expenses* – The loan amount of a rate and term (non-cash-out) refinance mortgages may be increased to cover the closing costs, discount points and pre-paid expenses of the refinance transaction.
4. *Limited cash back* – The borrower may receive a cash surplus with the rate-and-term refinance, but the cash-out may not exceed 1% of the mortgage amount. Because it is considered a rate and term refinance, the borrower can actually qualify for a higher loan amount.

Refinance Requirements

Mortgage refinances tend to be simpler than purchase loans. It has now become common practice among homebuyers to take future refinances into consideration when buying a home. During periods of relatively higher interest rates, homebuyers now often select ARM loans. ARMs have lower initial rates; and most homebuyers figure wisely that they can always refinance to a long-term fixed-rate loan when interest rates have cycled back down to more attractive levels.

As many homeowners have found, refinances have slightly differing requirements than do purchases for a few items.

1. *Investment consideration* – Although a refinance can lower your monthly payments, it may not always be a good idea. A homeowner who has already paid off ten (10) years of a 30-year loan would be unwise to refinance to another 30-year loan – even if the rate were lowered. It may even be unwise to refinance to a 20-year or 15-year loan.
2. *Appraisal value* – Most residential lenders require appraisal reports to be no more than three

months old at the time of closing. Many will accept appraisals that are up to one year old; however, the appraiser will have to issue a re-certification letter that confirms the applicability of the report's value estimate. Often, however, it is in the borrower's best interest to obtain a new appraisal. The new appraisal could include value appreciation to provide a higher appraisal value. A higher value could lower the LTV ratio, which can affect the mortgage insurance and available equity.

Example. Bill and Hillary bought a house for $300,000 three years ago with an $270,000 (90% LTV) loan. They have the property reappraised and the appraiser estimates their current value at $340,000. By this time, their loan balance is now $267,000. With this new appraisal, they can refinance their current loan at an LTV of 78.5%. This could eliminate their $107/month mortgage insurance payments. They could also opt to take out a home equity loan against their increased equity to consolidate debt or make improvements.

The loan underwriters automatically review all appraisals and, if there is a significant appreciation in value, the underwriters will have a third party review the new appraisal report. The appraisal review can reject or accept the appraisal, or require additional information or comparables (recent sale prices for comparable homes in the area) to support the valuation.

3. *Payoff statement* – Refinances further require that the loan officer or processor acquire a payoff statement from all institutions and lenders who will be paid by the proceeds of the refinance loan. The payoff statement will indicate how much the borrower owes the creditor. In most situations, the most important payoff statement required will be from the current mortgage lender. If the new loan is a first mortgage, that new first mortgage lender wants to ensure that all current mortgages on the property are all paid off and removed.

Refinancing When There Are Two (or More) Current Mortgages

If the borrower in a refinance has at least two mortgages – both a first mortgage and a second mortgage – on the subject property, that borrower will have three refinancing options, each of which have different challenges.

1. *Consolidation* – The borrower may choose to pay off both loans with a new refinance loan. This refinance loan in effect consolidates the primary and junior mortgage loans. If the second mortgage is at least one year old, then this would be considered a rate and term (non-cash-out) refinance and have higher loan-to-value (LTV) ratios.

2. *Refinance the second mortgage only* – The borrower may choose to refinance only the junior mortgage and leave the primary mortgage as it is. The new loan will have to be a second mortgage loan.

3. *Refinance the first mortgage only* – The borrower may elect to refinance only the primary mortgage and leave the junior mortgage as it is. However, this requires subordination of the existing second mortgage. (Liens are recorded chronologically. The new first mortgage loan wants to have first lien. The lender on the second mortgage loan must agree in writing that the new first mortgage will assume priority lien over that existing second mortgage. The existing second mortgage "subordinates" itself to the new first mortgage.)

MORTGAGE (LOAN) MATH

Amortization

Amortization is the process of apportioning interest and principal for each payment over the term of the loan. The interest portion of each payment is equal to the loan balance at the beginning of the period times the interest rate applicable for the period. The principal amount of each payment is then simply the payment amount less the interest paid.

For example, Figure 18.2 shows the first year amortization schedule for a $200,000 10-year mortgage with a stated interest rate of 7% and monthly payments of $2,322.17.

The interest due in the first month is computed by multiplying the beginning-of-period (BOP) balance in of $200,000 in column 2 by 7% to derive $1,166.67 in column 4. The principal due of $1,155.50 in the first month is equal to the payment amount of $2,322.17 in column

Figure 18.2

AMORTIZATION SCHEDULE					
Month (1)	BOP Balance (2)	Payment (3)	Interest Due (4)	Principal Due (5)	EOP Balance (6)
1	200,000.00	2,322.17	1,166.67	1,155.50	198,844.50
2	198,844.50	2,322.17	1,159.93	1,162.24	197,682.25
3	197,682.25	2,322.17	1,153.15	1,169.02	196,513.23
4	196,513.23	2,322.17	1,146.33	1,175.84	195,337.39
5	195,337.39	2,322.17	1,139.47	1,182.70	194,154.69
6	194,154.69	2,322.17	1,132.57	1,189.60	192,965.09
7	192,965.09	2,322.17	1,125.63	1,196.54	191,768.55
8	191,768.55	2,322.17	1,118.65	1,203.52	190,565.03
9	190,565.03	2,322.17	1,111.63	1,210.54	189,354.49
10	189,354.49	2,322.17	1,104.57	1,217.60	188,136.88
11	188,136.88	2,322.17	1,097.47	1,224.70	186,912.18
12	186,912.18	2,322.17	1,090.32	1,231.85	185,680.33

3 minus the interest due of $1,166.67 in column 4. The end-of-period (EOP) balance of $198,844.50 in column 6 at the end of the first year is equal to the beginning balance of $200,000 in column 1 minus the principal due of $1,155.50 in column 5. The ending balance in column 6 then becomes the beginning of period balance in column 2 in the following month and this process continues until the end of the term of the loan.

Figure 18.3 shows how the portion of each payment attributable to interest and principal changes over the term of the loan. The original loan amount in Figure 18.3 is equal to $200,000 with a stated annual interest rate of 9% and monthly payments of $1,609.25 for 360 months (30 years). The figure also shows the declining balance of the loan over the 30-year term relative to the right-hand axis of the graph. As the figure shows, the largest portion of the early payments is allocated to interest and so the principal balance declines only slowly. Over time, however, the portion of each payment allocated to principal increases and the portion allocated to interest decreases at accelerating rates. Consequently, the principal balance of the loan declines at an accelerating rate as one moves further towards the end of the term of the loan.

Figure 18.3

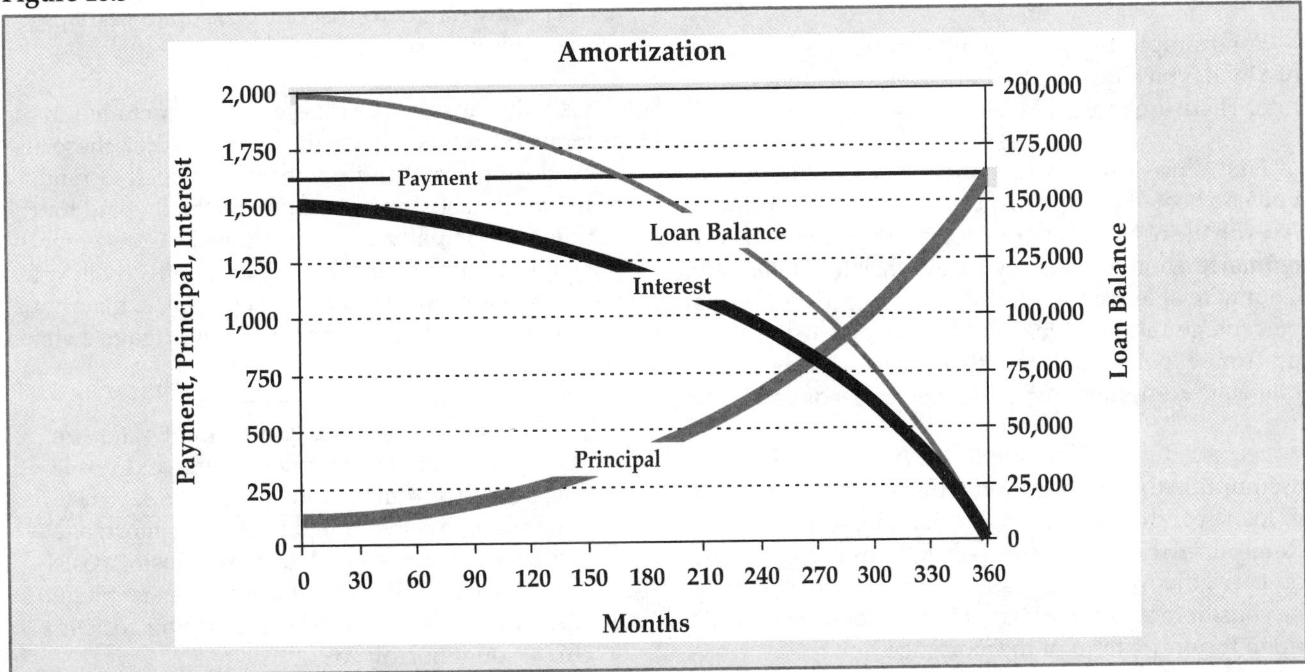

Computing the Payment Amount

If one knows the mortgage balance, Bal_0, and the interest rate, r, and the term, n, one can determine the required payment with the following formula:

$$Pmt = Bal_0 \times \left[\frac{r}{1 - (1+r)^{-n}} \right]$$

Example. Assume borrower wants to determine the monthly payment on an auto loan of $25,000 at 6% (annual) for a period of 36 months. The monthly interest is 0.5% (6% / 12), so the payment is, $760.55, determined as follows:

$$Pmt = 25{,}000 \times \frac{0.005}{[1 - (1 + 0.005)^{-36}]}$$

$$= 25{,}000 \times \frac{0.005}{0.164355} = 25{,}000 \times 0.030422 = \underline{\underline{760.55}}$$

MORTGAGE AND LOAN FINANCIAL PLANNING APPLICATIONS

Basics of Loan Rates

The mathematics of loan finance are basically pure-vanilla time-value computations, but certain concepts may not be well understood or may be misunderstood.

For example, the stated annual rate (or contract rate) of a loan typically is not the borrower's effective annual rate. There are three reasons for this.

First, since acquiring a mortgage or loan usually involves a host of up-front expenses and fees, the rate one pays on the net proceeds one actually borrows to buy or refinance a home is actually greater than the stated rate. Commercial lenders typically provide an APR (annual percentage rate) that takes into account most of these up-front expenses and reports the rate as if the stated rate were computed just on the net proceeds received.

Second, the lenders compute the APR based upon the assumption that the borrower will pay off the mortgage or loan over the stated term, say, 5, 10, 15, 20, or 30 years. Rarely does this actually happen. If the mortgage is paid off early, the APR for that shorter period will generally be considerably higher than the APR computed based upon the entire term of the mortgage.

Third, neither the stated rate nor the APR account for the compounding of interest over the year. For example, lenders typically determine the monthly interest by dividing the stated annual rate by 12. If the stated interest is 7%, then they would use a rate of 0.07/12, or 0.00583 for the monthly rate in computing the monthly payments on the mortgage. However, when the monthly payments are computed this way, the effective annual rate is actually 7.229%.[3]

Effect of Points and Closing Costs on the APR

When borrowers are considering alternative mortgages or loans, they may typically select from an array of mortgages or loans with different combinations of interest rates and points.

Points are prepaid interest, typically quoted as some percentage of the loan amount. For instance, a lender may offer mortgages at 7.5% with no points, 7.25% with one point, 7% with two points, and 6.75% with three points.

In addition, securing a mortgage or loan typically involves various fees and other up-front closing costs. These closing costs include such things as application fees, broker's fees or commissions, title insurance, appraisal fees, advance payments of real estate taxes and mortgage insurance, copying, filing, recording, and notarization fees, escrow fees, other miscellaneous fees, and sometimes, legal and/or accounting fees. These fees can typically range from about 1.5% up to perhaps 4% of the amount borrowed.

Usually, most or all of these fees are included in the amount borrowed. Regardless of whether these up-front closing costs[4] and points are financed or paid all or in part in cash, they affect the rate being paid for the net amount actually being borrowed.[5] Consequently, the rate of interest the borrower is effectively paying over the term of the mortgage, called the annual percentage rate, is higher than the mortgage's stated annual rate.

Example 1. Assume your client, Hausen Hunter, is purchasing a new home and needs net proceeds from the mortgage to be $200,000. The stated interest rate on a 30-year mortgage with two points is 7%. Additional closing costs total $3,637.83. What is the annual percentage rate if your client includes the closing costs in his amount borrowed?

If the net proceeds need to be $200,000, the total amount borrowed has to be grossed up for the closing costs of $3,637.83 plus the 2% points on the amount borrowed. But the 2% points increase the amount borrowed, so it is a circular calculation. You can determine the gross-up amount with the following formula:

$$\text{Amount Financed} = \frac{(\text{Net Proceeds} + \text{Other Fees \& Charges (excluding points)}}{(1 - \text{points\%})}$$

In this case, the amount financed would need to be:

$$\text{Amount Financed} = \frac{(\$200{,}000 + \$3{,}637.83)}{(1 - 0.02)}$$

$$\text{Amount Financed} = \frac{\$203{,}637.83}{0.98} = \mathbf{\$207{,}793}$$

The real effective annual rate is computed by first determining the monthly payment for the amount financed for the given term at the stated rate of interest using the standard time value formula for computing the level periodic payments of an annuity given the present value (the amount financed). Next, the closing costs are subtracted from the amount financed to determine the real net proceeds. Then, solve for the interest rate that would have to apply for the given level periodic payments to be consistent with the reduced net proceeds as the present value, rather than the actual amount financed.[6]

Effectively, Hausen is paying almost 7.4%, rather than 7%, assuming he holds the mortgage to maturity because of the effects of points and other closing costs. Note that Hausen will reduce his monthly payments from $1,382.46 to $1,330.60, a decrease of $51.86 a month, if he pays the closing costs in cash rather than financing them. However, his effective annual rate actually increases, rather than decreases, because the no-point closing costs remain the same, regardless of whether or not he finances those costs. Since the total amount being financed is less, the total closing costs represent a greater percentage of the amount being financed, thus increasing the effective rate he actually pays.

Finally, the effective APR takes account of the fact that interest is charged monthly. The interest rate charged each month by the lender is determined by taking the annual rate and dividing by 12. If this monthly rate is compounded over the twelve months, it gives one the effective annual rate. The effective annual APR is slightly greater than the nominal APR due to monthly compounding.

Effect of Early Payoff on the APR

It is the rare person indeed who buys a first home, acquires a mortgage, and then never moves from that home, who never considers refinancing in periods of lower interest rates, or who never considers refinancing to consolidate debts or to tap the equity in the home for business or personal purposes.

Our society is becoming more mobile all the time. Fifteen years ago, the average homeowner lived in their home for an average of seven years. Today that average has fallen to under five years. So if your clients are about average, you can expect that about one in every five each year will be moving, selling their homes, buying new homes, and facing decisions regarding their new mortgage. Furthermore, with the advent of ever more creative and complex financing arrangements, the greater fluctuation of interest rates than in prior decades, the deductibility of mortgage interest (as compared to the nondeductibility of other personal interest), and the increasing use of home equity to finance the baby boomer's lifestyle and expenses, such as their children's college educations, it is no surprise that the time until the average homeowner now sells his home or refinances is under four years.

Obviously, the pace accelerates in periods of lower interest rates, such as we have generally experienced in recent years. How long have you had your current mortgage? Are interest rates favorable enough to consider refinancing? How many of your clients have mortgages that are eight, 10, 15 years old or older with interest rates that are comparably high by today's standards?

Keep in mind that the time a person realistically expects to keep a mortgage has a huge impact not only on the cost of any given mortgage, but also on the type of mortgage that is most suitable for his or her planning horizon.

As was discussed in the previous section, the true cost of a mortgage is reflected in the APR, or the effective, rather than the stated, annual rate. APRs are standard fare for virtually all commercial mortgages. However, those APRs are based upon the assumption that the borrower will pay off the mortgage over its stated term, typically 15, 20, 30, or even 40 years, in some cases. But the average homeowner either sells and buys a new home or refinances, for any number of reasons, at the rate of once every four years or so. How does the actual cost of borrowing change when more realistic assumptions are used concerning when the homeowner is most likely to pay off the mortgage, either because he will sell his house and move or refinance the mortgage?

Assume a $200,000, 6.5% mortgage for 30 years has an APR of 7.075%. If the mortgage is paid off in five years and the closing costs are financed, the APR rises to 7.928%.

The effective rate is computed essentially in the same way as for the full term. First calculate the required monthly payment for the 30-year period based upon the stated rate and the amount financed. That monthly payment amount is used in the analysis once again, only now for just a five-year (60-month) period. Since the period covers just five years, you must include the payment of the remaining balance of the loan at the end of the five-year period. The remaining balance is calculated simply by finding the present value of the remaining 300 monthly payments at the stated interest rate. This is computed just as if you were finding the original loan amount for a mortgage with the same annual payments as the existing loan and at the same interest rate, but for a period of 300 months, rather than 360 months.

The effective annual interest rate is determined by finding the interest rate that will equate the present value of this 60-month payment stream plus the present value of the principle balance at the end of the 60-month period with the net proceeds. Excel's RATE function can be used to find the interest rate that equates the present value of this 60-month payment stream and the final remaining balance balloon payment to the net proceeds.

By projecting that the payoff will occur in five years rather than 30 years, the APR rises from just under 7.1% to over 7.9%. This is over a 12% increase in the effective rate of interest one would pay, if the mortgage were paid off in five years rather than 30 years.

Refinancing

New Loan

The original loan has a remaining term of 300 months, a stated annual rate of 8.5%, and payments of $1,576.27 per month. The prospective loan has a stated annual rate of 7.25%, assumed total refinancing fees of $6,750, a term of 360 months, and monthly payments of $1,381.44. Therefore, the new loan will reduce monthly payments by $194.83 per month. Of the total refinancing fees, $2,025.05 is assumed to be amortizable prepaid interest points. The borrower is assumed to be in a 30% combined state and federal marginal income-tax bracket.

An analysis might assess the feasibility of the new loan in the event the borrower refinances again, cashes out, or sells his home in 60 months (five years). To determine whether the refinancing option is advantageous, the analysis computes all the cash flows for each mortgage over the 60-month period. This includes the remaining balances at the end of the 60-month period as well as the different monthly payment streams in the intervening period.

Simply summing the differences in the total payments, the borrower can expect to pay $2,203.31 less over the 60-month period if he refinances than if he stays with his existing mortgage. Although this simple summing procedure is commonly used and certainly suggests that the borrower should refinance in this case, it is not always a reliable method.

Simply summing the differences in the cash flow streams of the mortgages over the 60-month period does not properly account for potential differences in the timing of the payments. A dollar today is always worth more than a dollar tomorrow, so if one mortgage requires a lot more payments in the early years than the other one, it may not be the better alternative, even if the total payments are less.

In this particular case, the simple summing method actually understates the benefit of the refinancing alternative. To adjust for the differences in the timing of payments with the two loans, the payments must be discounted to a present value.

There are different schools of thought on the matter of how to properly discount the cash flows, but the author feels strongly that one approach is superior to the others when comparing refinancing alternatives.

The analysis here discounts the payments in the following manner. All payments that would be made on the new loan are discounted at the original mortgage's interest rate. The rationale for this approach is straight forward. The borrower is either going to keep his existing mortgage, or he is going to refinance it with another mortgage. In either case, he is still going to owe a certain amount of money. He does not have the option of investing this money elsewhere, so what rate of return he could earn on investments elsewhere is immaterial. However, by discounting the cash flows of the prospective mortgage at the original mortgage's interest rate, the prospective mortgage's payments are evaluated as if they were a restructuring of the original mortgage at the original mortgage's interest rate. If the present value of the payments on the prospective mortgage is less than the balance currently remaining on the original mortgage, refinancing is essentially equivalent to having the original lender agree to reduce the current balance of the original loan. If the present value of these payments on the new mortgage is greater than the current balance on the original mortgage, then refinancing is essentially equivalent to a restructuring where the mortgage lender increases the current balance of the original mortgage.

Obviously, if the present value of the difference in payment streams is negative, the new loan is clearly superior to the old mortgage. It is essentially the same as having the original mortgage lender forgive a part of the current debt.

In this case, the difference in the present values of the two mortgages' cash flows is -$3,284.98, so the new loan is the better deal. The new loan is financially equivalent to the original mortgage lender immediately writing down the current balance of the loan by $3,284.98. In fact, when properly accounting for the differences in the timing of cash flows, refinancing appears to be even a better deal than was suggested when using the simple summing method.

The advantage of the new loan can also be expressed in terms of the monthly payment on the original mortgage. If $3,284.98 of the original mortgage's current balance were immediately forgiven by the lender, the borrower's monthly payments would fall by $26.45 per month, or $317.40 per year, over the remaining full term of the original mortgage.

Many refinancing analyses stop here, but tax effects are also important. Taxpayers are permitted to deduct the interest payments on home mortgages and home equity loans up to their qualified loan limit. The interest payments on original acquisition debt (up to $1 million) and up to an additional $100,000 of home equity debt are generally tax deductible.[7] For most taxpayers a significant portion, if not all, of their home mortgage interest payments are tax deductible.

Since refinancing can involve significantly different terms, interest rates, and allocations of points, the amounts and timing of deductible interest expense can vary greatly between a prospective refinancing loan and the original loan, and between refinancing alternatives. For instance, if a taxpayer refinances a loan with five years remaining until it is paid off with a new 30-year mortgage, interest expense will constitute a significantly larger portion of each payment on the new loan than on the old loan. But also, almost certainly, the payments on the new loan will be smaller than on the old loan. So the deductible interest expense may be greater than, close to equal to, or less than what is being deducted now on the old loan. These differences in the timing and amounts of tax savings are just as important as differences in the payment cash flows.

Here, the taxpayer's qualified loan limit is set high enough so that all interest payments are fully tax deductible. It is also assumed that there are no amortizable points on the original mortgage, but that the new mortgage has prepaid interest points equal to about 2% of the loan amount. Since this is a refinancing, the deduction of the points generally must be allocated to the entire term of the loan, rather than written off immediately in the year the loan is acquired.[8]

It is assumed that the taxpayer is in a 30% marginal combined state, local, and federal income-tax bracket and itemizes his deductions. Therefore, each dollar of deductible interest expense represents a $.30 income-tax savings.

In this case, the borrower will pay $6,928.26 less in interest on the new mortgage than he would have on the original mortgage over the 60-month period until it is assumed either loan will be paid off. In addition, $1,715.12 of his amortizable points will not be deductible until the loan is paid off in 60 months. Consequently, if he refinances, he not only has less deductible interest and, therefore, less tax savings, over the 60-month period, but the interest he does get to deduct is somewhat more "back-ended." Therefore, over the 60-month period he can expect to have $2,078.48 more tax savings with the original mortgage than with the new mortgage. When discounted using the interest rate of the original mortgage, the present value of the tax savings favors the original loan by $1,532.55.

Therefore, when the analysis incorporates the tax effects of interest deductibility, the advantage still goes to the refinance loan, but not by as much as was originally thought when this tax factor was ignored. The net benefit in present value terms after tax is just $1,752.43, not $3,284.98.

However, assuming that the borrower does not expect to sell his home, or pay off or refinance his home within five years, the new loan is the better deal, to the tune of $1,752.43.

Effect of Biweekly Payments

By paying half the regular monthly payment on a mortgage biweekly, the remaining term of a mortgage can be significantly reduced. For most borrowers, splitting the monthly payment in half and paying it once every two weeks (26 payments a year), rather than the full amount monthly (12 payments a year), is not an undue hardship. In fact, for most borrowers, the difference is hardly noticeable, but the benefits are sizeable.

In this case, assume that the current balance on the mortgage is $150,000 and that the remaining term is 240 months. For this mortgage, the monthly payment would be $1,185.56. If the borrower pays half this amount, $592.78, every two weeks instead of the monthly payment, the mortgage will be paid off 37.5 months sooner and the borrower will save $24,624.07 in interest payments over the term until the mortgage is entirely paid off.

DETERMINING HOW MUCH HOME ONE CAN AFFORD

People's debt-to-income ratios (DTI) are the principal indicators of their true fiscal health. It is definitely the lending industry's leading measure of borrowing capacity.

Front-End Ratio

Mortgage lenders tend to look at two debt ratios when determining whether to grant a home mortgage or home equity line of credit. One is the ratio of the monthly housing expense to the borrower's gross (pre-tax) monthly income. This is called the front-end ratio.

The monthly housing expense is made up of principal, interest, property taxes and insurance – otherwise known as the PITI. Homeowner's association dues and a mortgage insurance premium are added to the PITI in qualifying borrowers, if applicable. Let us assume a couple's gross annual income is $96,000, which gives them a gross monthly income of $8,000 ($96,000 divided by 12 months). If the lender says that the front-end ratio cannot exceed 32%, this means that the couple's PITI divided by their gross monthly income must equal 32% or less.

To calculate the front-end ratio amount, one multiplies the gross monthly income by 0.32. The result, $2,560 ($8,000 x 0.32, in this example), is the maximum monthly housing PITI payment the family's income can reasonably support according to the lender's criteria.

Determining the Maximum Mortgage Amount

How much "house" the family can afford now depends on how much the family can put down on the home as well as on the terms of the mortgage financing. The total amount the family can afford to pay for a home is equal to the amount they can afford to put down plus their maximum qualifying mortgage amount less mortgage closing costs and points on financing.

For example, assume the family is interested in a home that they think someone could buy for $325,000. Can they afford that much house?

The property taxes and insurance for the home are estimated to be $6,000 and $1,800 per year, respectively, or about $650 per month together. Based upon the lender's criteria, the family can afford to pay about $1,910 ($2,560 - $650) in monthly mortgage payments (principal and interest). To determine the qualifying mortgage amount, one has to calculate what mortgage amount generates monthly payments of $1,910 per month. The factors in this calculation are the monthly payment ($1,910 in this case), the term of the loan in months, the stated annual interest rate (then converted to the monthly rate), the estimated closing costs, and the prepaid interest points, if any.

Assume the annual interest rate is six percent (monthly rate (r) = 6%/12 = 0.5%), the term (n) is 360 months (30 years), estimated closing costs (cc) are $3,200, and the lender is charging one interest point (p). The maximum monthly payment for principal and interest (pmt) is $1,910. The formula for computing the maximum qualifying mortgage amount (MQMA) is simply the present value of an immediate annuity formula:

$$MQMA = pmt \times \frac{[1 - (1+r)^{-n}]}{r}$$

Substituting the appropriate values into the formula, the result is:

$$MQMA = \$1{,}910 \times \frac{[1 - (1 + 0.005)^{-360}]}{0.005}$$

$$= \$1{,}910 \times \frac{(1 - 0.166042)}{0.005}$$

$$= \$1{,}910 \times \frac{0.833958}{0.005}$$

$$= \$1{,}910 \times 166.7916 = \underline{\underline{\$318{,}572}}$$

Therefore, the maximum qualifying mortgage amount is about $318,600. To compute the portion of that amount that is available for the purchase price of the house, subtract out the closing costs and prepaid interest or points. Out of the total $318,200, $3,200 is going to pay closing costs and 1% of the total, or about $3,186, is going to cover the one point prepaid interest, for a total of about $6,400. Therefore, the portion of the total qualifying amount actually available to pay for the price of the home is about $312,200.

Assuming the family has, say, $35,000 to put down on the home, they could afford a home with a price tag as high as about $350,000 ($312,200 + $35,000 = $347,200 ≈ $350,000). At least according to the lender's criteria, the family can afford to buy their dream home for $325,000 with almost $25,000 of borrowing capacity to spare.

Back-End Ratio

A second ratio used by mortgage lenders is called the back-end ratio. This ratio helps lenders determine the mortgage payment people can afford given both their level of income and their other minimum required monthly debt payments. The back-end ratio is the ratio of the borrower's total debt (PITI plus other minimum monthly debt payments) to the gross monthly income. If the lender says that the back-end ratio cannot exceed 385, this means that the total monthly debt, including the PITI, must be no more than 38% of the gross monthly income. The acceptable ratio varies by lenders and circumstances, but typically ranges from about 36% to 42%.

For instance, multiplying a person's gross monthly income of $8,000 by 38% results in a back-end ratio amount of $3,040. Assume a person with an $8,000 monthly income has $1,000 of total required monthly minimum car, student loan, credit card and other consumer or installment debt payments that will not be paid off within the next few months. These payments represent 12.5% of monthly income. This means that this person can qualify for a mortgage with monthly payments (PITI) totaling no more than 25.5% of monthly income, or $2,040.

If a lender says the ratios are 33/39, this means that the front-end ratio is 33% and the back-end ratio is 39%. Basically, most mortgage lenders use the front-end ratio to determine the absolute maximum they would be willing to lend to a given borrower. They use the back-end ratio to adjust their maximum lending limit downward in light of the borrower's other required debt payments. While most lenders take both ratios into consideration, some lenders make exceptions. The Federal Housing Administration (FHA) qualifies borrowers based on their back-end ratio alone for FHA loans (currently using a maximum ratio of 41%). This means that home mortgage borrowers with relatively little other debt may qualify for larger FHA-sponsored mortgages than for other commercial mortgages.

REVERSE MORTGAGES

The previous analyses have discussed how to finance the purchase of a home. However, as people who purchased homes years ago approach retirement, in many cases their problem is not the financing of home purchases, but rather, how they can effectively tap into the equity they have built up over the years without jeopardizing the security of the "roof over their heads." In some cases, what are called "reverse mortgages" may provide the answer.

What is a reverse mortgage? It is a loan against the borrower's home that requires no repayment for as long as the borrower lives there.

How is it different than a traditional mortgage? To qualify for most loans, the lender checks the applicant's income to see how much the applicant can afford to pay back each month. But with a reverse mortgage, the borrower does not have to make monthly repayments. So income generally has nothing to do with getting the loan or the amount of the loan.

With most home loans, if the borrower fails to make monthly repayments, the borrower could lose the home. But with a reverse mortgage, the borrower does not have any monthly repayments to make. So the borrower cannot lose the home by failing to make the payments.

Who qualifies for reverse mortgages? Qualifying persons include those persons who own their homes and, generally, owners must be at least 62 years old. The home generally must be the owners' "principal residence," which means the owners must live in it more than half the year.

For the federally insured "Home-Equity Conversion Mortgage" (HECM), the home must be a single-family property, a 2-4 unit building, or a federally approved condominium or planned unit development (PUD). For Fannie Mae's "HomeKeeper" mortgage, the dwelling must be a single family home or condominium.

Reverse mortgage programs generally do not lend on cooperative apartments or mobile homes, although some "manufactured" homes may qualify if they are built on a permanent foundation, classed and taxed as real estate, and meet other requirements.

If the owner has any debt against the home, the owner generally must either pay it off before getting a reverse mortgage or -- as most borrowers do -- use an immediate cash advance from the reverse mortgage to pay off the existing mortgage. If the owner does not pay off the debt or does not qualify for a large enough immediate cash advance to do so, the owner generally cannot get a reverse mortgage.

How much cash can an owner get from a reverse mortgage? The amount of cash owners can get from a reverse mortgage depends on the program selected and, within each program, the owner's age, home value, and interest rates. It can vary by a large amount from one program to another. A typical consumer might get $30,000 more from one program than from another. But no single program works best for everyone. For all but the most expensive homes, the federally insured "Home-Equity Conversion Mortgage" (HECM) or Fannie Mae's "HomeKeeper" mortgage generally provides the most cash. They are also the most widely available reverse mortgage programs. In general, the most cash goes to the oldest borrowers living in the homes of greatest value at a time when interest rates are low. On the other hand, the least cash generally goes to the youngest borrowers living in the homes of lowest value at a time when interest rates are high.

But remember, the total amount of cash an owner will actually end up getting from a reverse mortgage will depend on how it is paid to the owner, in addition to other factors.

How is the money paid? That is up to the borrower. The borrower could take it:

- As an immediate cash advance at closing, that is, a lump sum of cash paid to the owner on the first day of the loan;
- As a credit line account that lets owners take cash advances whenever they choose during the life of the loan -- until it is all used up; or
- In some form of a monthly cash advance, that is, as an annuity.

If the owner takes the annuity option, the payments can be arranged:

- For a specific number of years;
- For as long as the owner lives in the home; or
- For the rest of the owner's life or for the rest of owner's life and the spouse's life until the second death, no matter where the couple lives.

Finally, the borrower can usually arrange to take payments as any combination of immediate cash advance, credit line account, and monthly cash advances.

If owners take a credit line account, the total amount of cash they actually get will depend on two things: how much of their credit line they use, and whether the credit line is "flat" or "growing."

With a flat credit line, the amount of remaining available credit at any time only changes if they take a cash advance, at which point it decreases by the amount of the advance. For example, if a borrower has a flat $50,000 credit line and takes out $10,000, there will be $40,000 left whenever the borrower decides to take more.

With a growing credit line, the remaining available credit grows larger by a given rate. For example, if a borrower takes $10,000 from a $50,000 credit line that grows by eight percent each year, and then comes back for more three years later, there will be over $50,000 left to use because the remaining $40,000 growing at eight percent per year will become $50,388 after three years.

Therefore, a growing credit line can give the borrower more cash over time than a flat one. That is why borrowers need to look at more than the size of a credit line when a reverse mortgage starts. They also should consider how much available credit will be left in the future. The amount remaining in future years will also depend, of course, on how much money they take out over time and when they take it.

The credit line in the Home-Equity Conversion Mortgage (HECM) program grows larger each month by the same rate as the rate charged on the loan balance. It keeps growing for as long as there is any credit left, that is, until all of the remaining credit is withdrawn.

Fannie Mae's HomeKeeper credit line is flat. The remaining available credit does not increase.

One might wonder why anyone would opt for the "flat" plan when they could get a "growing" plan. The plans with "growing" credit lines inevitably start with a lower initial balance than "flat" plans. If borrowers need or want to use the money right away for some large expenditure, the "flat" plan will give them a much larger initial balance to draw upon. If they plan to withdraw the cash in relatively small amounts over time, the "growing" plan will start with a smaller balance than the "flat" plan but still permit greater total withdrawals over the years.

If borrowers elect to take monthly loan advances, the total amount of cash they actually get will depend on whether they select a plan that sends the payments to them for a specific number of years, or for as long as they live in their homes. It will also depend how long they actually live in their homes.

If borrowers elect to use a reverse mortgage to buy an annuity, the total amount of cash they actually get will depend on how long they live, no matter where they live. The net value of the cash they will receive over time, however, may depend on other factors.

What happens to the debt? The debt grows larger and larger as the borrower keeps getting cash advances, makes no repayments, and interest is added to the amount owed (the "loan balance"). That is why reverse mortgages are called "rising debt, falling equity" loans. As the amount owed grows larger, the owner's equity in the home declines.

Why it is called "reverse?" In a "forward" mortgage (the kind normally used to buy a home), the borrower's regular monthly repayments make the debt go down over time until it is entirely paid off. Meanwhile, the borrower's equity in the home is rising as the debt declines, and as the property value grows (appreciates). Therefore, forward mortgages are "falling debt, rising equity" loans, just the opposite of reverse mortgages.

In other words, in a forward mortgage, you use debt to turn income into equity. In a reverse mortgage, you use debt to turn equity into income. With a reverse mortgage, the borrowers are reversing the deal they used to buy their homes. When the home was initially purchased, the purchaser had income and wanted equity. Now, the owner has equity and wants income. In both cases debt is used to turn what the person has into what he wants.

When is the debt repaid? The reverse mortgage debt is repaid when the last surviving borrower dies, sells the home, or permanently moves away. "Permanently" generally means the borrower has lived in a new (different) home for at least 12 months in a row. Borrowers might also be required to pay back the loan if they fail to pay property taxes, fail to keep up their homeowner's insurance, or fail to maintain the home. But if borrowers fail to do any of these things, the lender may be able to make extra cash advances to cover these expenses. Just remember, reverse mortgage borrowers are still homeowners and therefore are still responsible for taxes, insurance, and upkeep.

How much will the borrower owe? The total amount borrowers will owe at the end of the loan (the "loan balance") equals all the cash advances they have received (including any that were used to pay loan fees or costs) plus all the interest on the loan up to the loan's "nonrecourse" limit (described below).

Interest rates can change based on changes in published indexes similar to regular adjustable rate mortgages. But the more adjustable the rates are, the lower they are to start with. Therefore, if the rates are more adjustable, initially borrowers can receive larger cash advances. More adjustable rates will always continue to be lower than less adjustable rates until such time as index rate changes push the rates up to and over the caps on the less adjustable rates. For example, a borrower might be able to choose between an initial adjustable rate of six percent, with a cap of 10 percent or an initial adjustable rate of seven percent with a cap of nine percent. As long as the underlying index used to compute the adjustable rates remains under nine percent, the rate the borrower will pay on the six-percent/10-percent reverse mortgage will always be less than the rate he would pay on the seven-percent/nine-percent reverse mortgage.

What is the most a borrower can owe? Borrowers can never owe more than the value of their homes at the time the loan is repaid. Reverse mortgages are "nonrecourse" loans, which means that in seeking repayment the lender does not have recourse to anything other than the value of the home. If the value of the home is insufficient to repay the loan entirely, the lender may not go after the borrower's income or other assets, or the borrower's heirs' income or assets.

So even if a borrower receives monthly loan advances until age 115, and/or the home declines in value between closing and the time the loan comes due, and the total of monthly advances becomes greater than the home's value, the borrower can still never owe more than the value of the home. If the home is sold in order to pay off the loan, the debt is generally limited by the net proceeds from the sale of the home.

How is the loan repaid? If a borrower sells the home and moves, the borrower would most likely pay back the loan from the money he gets from selling the home. But borrowers may repay the loan from other funds, if they have them.

If the loan ends due to the death of the last surviving borrower, the loan must be repaid before the home's title can be transferred to the borrower's heirs. The heirs could repay the loan by selling the home, using other funds from the borrower's estate or their own funds, or by taking out a new forward mortgage against the home.

Not all reverse mortgage borrowers end up living in their homes for the rest of their lives. Some who expect to remain living there change their minds. Others sometimes face later health problems that require a move. It therefore makes sense to plan for borrowers to consider the possibility that they may sell and move some day. If, at the end of the loan, the loan balance is less than the value of the home (or the net sale proceeds if the house is sold), then the borrower or the heirs keep the difference. The lender does not "get" the house. The lender gets paid the amount owed and the borrower or the heirs keep the rest.

Note: If a borrower takes the loan as a credit-line account, the borrower should be sure to withdraw all remaining available credit before the loan ends. The borrower will have the money sooner that way, and it could be more than otherwise might be left. For example, a growing credit line could become greater than the leftover equity in some cases.

If a borrower has purchased an annuity and then sold the home, the borrower could continue receiving monthly annuity advances for the rest of the borrower's life. If the loan ends due to the death of the last surviving borrower and if the annuity purchased by the borrower includes a death benefit or "period certain" payments, then the annuity's beneficiaries would receive additional cash.

What is the out-of-pocket cost? The out-of-pocket cash cost is most often limited to an application fee that covers a property appraisal (to see how much the home is worth) and a minimal credit check (to see if the borrower is delinquent on any federally-insured loans). Most of the other costs can be "financed" with the loan. This means that borrowers can use reverse mortgage funds advanced to them at closing to pay the costs due at that time, and later advances to pay any ongoing costs. The advances are added to the loan balance, and become part of what they owe and pay interest on. If a lender charges an origination fee that is greater than the amount that can be financed with the loan, borrowers have to pay the difference in cash at closing.

What are the other costs? The specific cost items vary from one program to another. Many of them are of the same type found on "forward" mortgages: interest charges, origination fees, and whatever third-party closing costs (title search and insurance, surveys, inspections, recording fees, mortgage taxes) are required in the borrower's area. Other types of costs can be more exotic, and unique to reverse mortgages: monthly servicing fees, "equity-sharing" fees, "shared appreciation" fees, "maturity" fees.

Although total loan costs between the HECM and HomeKeeper programs can vary enormously, many of the individual cost items within each program do not vary from one lender to another. Within each program, the costs that may be different from one lender to another are generally the origination fee and the servicing fee.

The largest total cost differences one will find are those between different programs, for example, between the HECM and HomeKeeper programs. But it is virtually impossible to evaluate or compare the true, total cost of reverse mortgages unless the borrower considers his Total Annual Loan Cost (TALC) rates.

What is the total annual loan cost? Federal Truth-in-Lending law requires reverse mortgage lenders to disclose the projected annual average cost of these loans in a way that includes ALL of the costs and benefits, and also takes into account the nonrecourse limits. This Total Annual Loan Cost (TALC) disclosure shows borrowers what the single all-inclusive interest rate would be if the lender could only charge interest and not charge any other fees. Specifically, it tells borrowers the annual average rate that would produce the total amount owed at various future points if only that rate were charged on all the cash advances they get that are not used to pay loan costs. In other words, it shows them what they are paying in total for the money they get to spend.

How does the total annual loan cost (TALC) vary? On any given loan, TALC rates depend on two major factors: time and appreciation. TALC rates are generally greatest in the early years of the loan and decrease over time, for two reasons. First, the initial fees and costs become a smaller part of the total amount owed. Second, over time it becomes increasingly likely that the rising loan balance will catch up to, and then be limited by, the nonrecourse limit.

A major exception to this general rule is the "cost bubble" created by Fannie Mae's "equity-sharing" fee on HomeKeeper loans. In this arrangement, the equity-sharing provision "kicks in" two years after the loan is in place with the effect that the TALC jumps drastically at that time.

The less the home appreciates, the greater is the possibility that a rising loan balance will equal or exceed the home's value. On the other hand, when a home appreciates at a robust rate, the loan balance may never catch up to (and be limited by) the home's value. Consequently, if a borrower ends up living in the home well past life expectancy or the home appreciates at a low rate, the borrower might get a true bargain. But if the borrower dies, sells, or moves within just a few years or the home appreciates a lot, the true cost could be very high.

There is no way of avoiding this fundamental risk. Borrowers just need to understand it in general, assess the potential range of TALC rates on a specific loan, and decide if it is worth the benefits they expect they will get from the loan.

Just remember, TALC rates are not really comparable to the Annual Percentage Rates (APRs) quoted on "forward" mortgages. Unlike APRs, TALC rates include all the costs. Also, unlike APRs, TALC rates do not assume the borrower will take the entire loan on the first day (if they did, TALC rates would be much closer to APRs).

Also, remember that borrowers get benefits from reverse mortgages that they do not get from "forward" mortgages. Borrowers make no monthly repayments, and no repayments of any kind for as long as they live in their home. They get an open-ended monthly income guarantee, or a guaranteed credit line (which may grow larger until they use it all). The total debt limit cannot exceed the net value of the home, the "nonrecourse" limit. This limit applies even if it is less than what the loan balance would otherwise have been based on the amounts the borrower has received, no matter how long the borrower lives, and no matter what happens to the value of the home.

So borrowers may pay more for a reverse mortgage than they would with a traditional mortgage. But the benefits are not available on any other type of debt. And if the borrowers live long, or if the property value does not grow much, they can end up with a lower than expected cost.

If borrowers are considering a credit line, however, the official TALC disclosures do not account for the added value of growing credit lines. Also, the official TALC disclosures are all based on the life expectancy of single owners. Therefore, if the reverse mortgage is based upon the joint lives of a husband and wife, for instance, the TALC figures will not entirely reflect the costs over the joint life expectancy.

What is it worth? Only borrowers can decide what a reverse mortgage is worth to them. It probably depends most on what they plan to use the proceeds for. Reverse mortgages are typically used to:

- Increase monthly income;
- Create a cash reserve (credit line account) for irregular or unexpected expenses;
- Pay off debt that currently requires monthly repayments;
- Repair or improve a home;
- Pay for personal services needed to remain independent; or
- Generally improve the quality of one's life.

It may be helpful in evaluating the worth of a reverse mortgage to consider the principal alternative -- selling the home and moving. Does the borrower have any idea how much money could be made by selling the home or what it would cost to buy and maintain or rent a new one?

If borrowers look into purchasing new homes, they may find a different home, neighborhood, or community with an array of services or amenities that is much more attractive than they had expected to find. Otherwise, they may simply confirm that where they live now is the best place for them to be. Either way, looking carefully at the possibility of selling and moving will give borrowers a much better idea of the overall costs and benefits of staying versus moving.

Also potential borrowers should take a look at other financial and services options that they may prefer to or wish to combine with a reverse mortgage.

How do reverse mortgages affect public benefits? Social Security and Medicare benefits are not affected by reverse mortgages. But Supplemental Security Income (SSI) and Medicaid are different. In general, these programs count loan advances differently than annuity advances.

Loan advances generally do not affect benefits if they are spent during the calendar month in which they are received. But if a borrower keeps an advance past the end of the calendar month (in a checking or savings account, for example), then it will count as a "liquid asset." If total liquid assets at the end of any month are greater than $2,000 for a single person or $3,000 for a couple, borrowers could lose their eligibility.

Annuity advances reduce SSI benefits dollar-for-dollar, and can make a borrower ineligible for Medicaid. Therefore, if borrowers are considering an annuity, and if they are now receiving, or expect someday they may qualify for, SSI or Medicaid, check with the SSI, Medicaid, and other program offices in the community. Get specific details on how annuity income would affect these benefits.

What are the tax consequences of a reverse annuity? An American Bar Association guide to reverse mortgages advises that generally the IRS does not consider loan advances to be income. Annuity advances will generally be partially taxable, just as any commercial annuity is taxed under the rules of Internal Revenue Code Section 72. Interest charged on the loan is not generally deductible until it is actually paid, that is, at the end of the loan.

What about "borrowing?" Many people have been well served by these borrowing cautions:

- Do not borrow in general; and

- Do not borrow against your home in particular.

Borrowing usually means using money one has not earned yet. One borrows today in the hope of earning enough in the future to repay it. Therefore, people are typically borrowing against their uncertain future earnings. This sounds much like "counting your chickens before they hatch." That is generally not a good idea without a steady job and good earning prospects.

But this caution does not really apply to reverse mortgages because borrowers are not really borrowing against future income. In fact, they are borrowing against home equity that they have already earned. So they are not counting their chickens before they hatch. They are hatching the nest egg they have already earned.

Traditional borrowing against home usually means paying back a loan every month. But if borrowers lose their jobs or their income drops, they could miss some payments and lose their home to foreclosure. That is why it is generally not a good idea to borrow against one's home unless it is for a very basic purpose.

But this caution does not apply to reverse mortgages. No monthly repayment is required. Borrowers cannot lose their homes by missing a payment on a reverse mortgage because there are no payments to make.

What about "spending?" Many people have also been well served by these spending cautions: "You do not know how much you will need and how long you will live. So do not spend your savings. Wait until you really need them."

This makes a lot of sense. But, if everyone literally followed these cautions forever, they would never use any of the money they spent a lifetime building up. That does not make much sense. Why go to the trouble of earning the money and saving it if they are never going to use any of it? Therefore, in retirement, this spending caution should be revised to a related question: when should people consider using their savings and how much of their savings should they use? The follow-up question is: which savings (for example, home equity) should one use first?

As amended, this caution clearly does apply to reverse mortgages. Because the more home equity "savings" people use now, the less they will have later. So the question now becomes: if people ever do take a reverse mortgage, should they do it now or wait until later to decide? In the future, they may be eligible for more cash because they will be older and their home may be worth more. On the other hand, interest rates may be higher, and that would decrease the amount otherwise available. Furthermore, if they take a reverse annuity now, how should they take it: credit line, monthly, or a combination? If they take a credit line, how much of it should they use now versus later? If they take a monthly advance, should they select a specific number of years, for as long as they live in their home, or should they buy an annuity providing lifetime advances no matter where they live?

What about "investing"? Should borrowers consider taking a lump sum of cash from a reverse mortgage and investing it someplace? Except for purchasing a sound annuity, that is generally a risky idea, unless, of course, they can afford to lose money. Remember, to come out ahead on any investment, a person must earn a greater rate of return on the investment than the TALC rate they are paying on the reverse mortgage. And the odds against doing that safely are very long. A much better alternative is to take a HECM credit line. Interest is only charged on the cash advances actually taken, and the remaining available credit grows larger every month. Furthermore, this growth is not an "interest" earning, so borrowers are not taxed on it.

LEASING

Types of Leases

Basically, a lease is a contractual agreement between a lessee and lessor. The lessor owns the asset and for a fee allows the lessee to use the asset. From an economic standpoint, there are two basic types of leases: operating leases and financial leases.

1. *Operating leases* – Operating leases usually are not fully amortized. That is, the lessee does not "pay" for the asset in its entirety over the term of the lease. The lease usually requires the lessor to maintain and insure the asset and the lessee typically enjoys an option to cancel the lease before the end of the term of the lease, perhaps with prepayment penalties. As the name implies, the lessor is the economic owner and the lessee rents the asset from the lessor.

2. *Financial Leases* – Financial leases are exactly the opposite of an operating lease. Generally, the lessor does not provide for maintenance or service of the asset. The financial leases are fully amortized. The lessee usually has a right to renew the lease at expiry. Finally, generally, the lessee cannot cancel a financial lease. Although termed "leases," from an economic standpoint the lessee is essentially buying the asset and the lease is effectively a form of owner/seller financing – hence the term financial lease. There are common variations on the financing lease model, including sale and lease-backs and leverage leases.

   a) *Sale and lease-back* – The sale and lease-back is a particular type of financial lease. It occurs when a company sells an asset it already owns to another firm and immediately leases it from them. Two sets of cash flows occur: the lessee receives cash today from the sale and the lessee agrees to make periodic lease payments, thereby retaining the use of the asset.

   b) *Leveraged lease* – A leveraged lease is another type of financial lease. It is a three-sided arrangement between the lessee, the lessor and a third-party lender. The lessor owns the asset and for a fee allows the lessee to use the asset. The lessor borrows to partially finance the asset, typically using a nonrecourse loan. This means that the lessor is not obligated to the lender in case of a default by the lessee.

Lease Accounting

In the past, leases led to off-balance-sheet financing. Today that is not necessarily the case. It depends on how the lease is classified. If a lease is classified as an operating lease, the lease does not appear on the balance sheet. If is classified as a capital lease, it does appear on the balance sheet – the present value of the lease payments appears on both sides.

For example, assume a company has land worth $100,000 and wants to acquire equipment worth $100,000. The tables below show how the balance sheet would appear if the company buys the equipment with 100% loan financing, acquires the use of the equipment through an operating lease, or acquires the use of the equipment with a capital lease.

Balance Sheet

Equipment is purchased with debt

Equipment	$100,000	Debt	$100,000
Land	$100,000	Equity	$100,000
Total Assets	$200,000	Total Debt & Equity	$200,000

Operating Lease

Equipment	$0	Debt	$0
Land	$100,000	Equity	$100,000
Total Assets	$100,000	Total Debt & Equity	$100,000

Capital Lease

Leased Assets	$100,000	Obligations Under Capital Lease	$100,000
Land	$100,000	Equity	$100,000
Total Assets	$200,000	Total Debt & Equity	$200,000

When Is a Lease a Capital Lease?

The lessee must capitalize a lease if any one of the following criteria is met:

- The present value of the lease payments is at least 90% of the fair market value of the asset at the start of the lease.
- The lease transfers ownership of the property to the lessee by the end of the term of the lease.
- The lease term is 75% or more of the estimated economic life of the asset.
- The lessee can buy the asset at a bargain price at the expiration of the term of the lease.

Taxes

The principal benefit of long-term leasing is tax reduction. Leasing allows the transfer of tax benefits from those who need equipment but cannot take full advantage of the tax benefits of ownership to a party who can. Not surprisingly, the IRS seeks to limit this type of tax transfer, especially if the lease appears to be set up solely to avoid taxes without any real economic transfer of risk.

The lessee can deduct lease payments if the lease is *qualified* by the IRS. To be qualified

- The term must be less than 30 years.
- There can be no bargain purchase option.
- The lease should not have a schedule of payments that is very high at the start of the lease and low thereafter.
- The lease payments must provide the lessor with a fair market rate of return.
- The lease should not limit the lessee's right to issue debt or pay dividends.
- Renewal options must be reasonable and reflect fair market value of the asset.

Reasons for Leasing

Leasing may often be more costly than purchasing. However, even in such circumstances leasing may still be preferred, for several reasons:

- Taxes may be reduced by leasing.
- The lease contract may reduce certain types of uncertainty. For instance, with most operational leases, the lessee may cancel the lease if the asset is no longer needed or becomes technologically obsolete.
- Transactions costs can be higher for buying an asset and financing it with debt or equity than for leasing the asset.

CHAPTER ENDNOTES

1. Conventional mortgages that are not eligible for sale to either the FNMA, GNMA, or FHLMC. Nonconforming loans (which are generally more expensive) are an alternative to the highly selective and restrictive conforming loans acceptable to Freddie Mac and Fannie Mae. Nonconforming loans are still sold on the secondary market – just not to Fannie Mae and Freddie Mac.
2. Conforming programs can be fixed-rate, ARMs, balloons, or temporary buy-downs. The term conforming essentially apply to those conventional mortgage loans that "conform" to the guidelines established by Fannie Mae (FNMA, or the Federal National Mortgage Corporation), Freddie Mac (FHLMC, the Federal Home Loan Mortgage Corporation) and Ginnie Mae (GNMA, the Government National Mortgage Association).

   Conforming programs carry lower risk for the lender and investors. Consequently, conforming programs have lower interest rates than comparable loan programs. These lower risk levels and interest rates are due to explicit or implied government backing of the mortgage-backed securities formed by conforming loan programs.

3. This amount is computed by taking one plus the monthly rate and compounding it for 12 months, then subtracting one. Specifically, $(1.00583)^{12} - 1 = 7.229\%$.

4. Generally, points are deductible in the year paid when they are incurred to secure financing for the purchase or improvement of a principal residence. Points paid on home mortgage refinancings, typically must be amortized over the life of the loan. IRC Sec. 461.

5. If these costs are financed by increasing the loan amount, they will be directly reflected in the loan repayment amount. If they are paid in cash, the loan repayment amount will be lower, but these up-front cash payments should still be treated as a cost or payout of borrowing and included in the calculation of the APR, as will be shown below.

6. This is, in effect, a type of internal rate of return calculation. The analysis here uses Excel's RATE function to compute the interest rate value.

7. Also, home mortgage debt acquired before 1987 is grandfathered and may increase a taxpayer's qualified loan limit. See IRS Publication 936, *Home Mortgage Interest Deduction*, and Publication 535, *Business Expenses*, Part 5, "Interest," for a discussion of the qualified loan limit, allocation rules, points, and computational rules.

8. In certain circumstances, points paid on a mortgage acquired to buy or improve a primary residence or one second home may be deductible in the year the points are paid. In most refinancing cases or in the case of a home equity loan or a home equity line of credit, the points must be allocated to the entire term of the loan. Once again, see IRS Publications 936 and 535 for more information.

Chapter 19

ECONOMIC CONCEPTS

INTRODUCTION

This chapter explores the key concepts of economics. A complete and in-depth discussion of all aspects of economic theory is far beyond the reach of this chapter. However, this chapter does discuss certain basic and universal concepts, the components of the microeconomic theory (such as consumer behavior and price elasticity based on demand) and macroeconomic theory (such as Keynesianism, Monetarism, rational expectations, supply-side economics, government fiscal and monetary policies, inflation, and interest rates). Given the importance of business cycles to both investors and businesses, the chapter looks at the features of business cycles and the composite economic indicators economists use to predict turns in the growth in the economy. In the final sections, the chapter discusses inflation, deflation, and disinflation; and explores yield curves and what they may reveal regarding future economic activity.

BASIC CONCEPTS

Despite the fact that the economies of the United States and most of the western world are based, more rather than less, on capitalist principles, average citizens and even many businesspersons are woefully ignorant of the tenants of capitalism and general economic concepts. Although capitalism is not the only organizing basis for economic systems, it has generally proven to be the most efficient or effective at allocating and using scarce resources to enhance economic prosperity when combined with political systems that maintain the rule of law, the rights to contract, the courts and tort system, and competitive market structures.

Scarcity

A key concept of economics is scarce resources. Regardless of which economic system one is talking about, they all deal with the issue of the allocation of scarce resources. Resources are the inputs to any economy – the land, labor, minerals, knowledge, technology, time, etc. – necessary to produce outputs or goods (homes, cars, food, entertainment, medical care, services, and all the other gizmos we use and consume). All resources are scarce. Therefore, the objective of the economic system and business is to use these scarce resources in the most effective and efficient way possible so as to produce the greatest possible amount of goods with the given inputs, while minimizing waste.

The practical implication of this concept of scarce resources is captured perfectly by Nobel Prize-winning economist Milton Friedman's universal and timeless maxim: "There is no free lunch."

Opportunity Cost

Every output – each "lunch" – uses up inputs, whether one personally pays for them or not. The cost for this lunch is equal to whatever else could have been produced with those inputs used in their most effective and efficient manner. In other words, there is always a trade-off and the cost is the opportunities foregone as a result of using the inputs for one purpose, rather than some other purpose; hence, the term "opportunity cost."

Time Value

Another universal economic concept is a corollary of the concepts of scarcity and that is "time is money." A dollar today is always worth more than a dollar tomorrow. Money is simply a convenient medium of exchange that represents claims on the economy's resources. A dollar today can be consumed (used to purchase goods) or invested (used to purchase inputs). In either case, it is worth more than a dollar tomorrow, or next year, or 10 years from now, since it could be used to purchase inputs that could be employed to produce more than one dollar's worth of outputs or goods in the future.

Supply, Demand, Marginal Pricing, and Equilibrium

All economics is about supply and demand. The basic premise is simple and obvious. All goods are scarce in the sense that if the good were free, people would want to consume more of it than is available. Faced with a shortage at a given price of some good that some consumers desire more than other goods they can acquire for the same expenditure, these consumers will offer to pay more for that good. They will bid the price of that good up to the level where the value of what they feel they are getting from this good (called their marginal utility) exactly matches the value of what they are giving up in terms of other goods they could otherwise purchase with the money spent on this good (the opportunity cost).

Of course, for a given supply of this good, these consumers will be able to acquire the good only if some other consumers drop out of the bidding. So the price that clears the market and matches supply and demand will be the price where the value to the ultimate winners in the bidding for this good (the marginal utility) exactly matches the value (the marginal utility) to those buyers of the other goods they have to give up to purchase this good. All the potential buyers who perceive the value to them to be less than what they could otherwise buy at that price drop out of the bidding. So the price for the good is set at the margin – at the price where the perceived value or marginal utility of all but the "winning" bidders is less than the price. If one more consumer now enters the market and perceives the value or marginal utility of the good to be greater than the price, he would bid up the price until one of the other consumers dropped out of the bidding. So the market price is set at the margin and reflects the marginal value placed on that good by the last buyer.

But, as was explained above, nothing is free. Producing one sort of good always comes at the cost of foregoing the production of some other sort of good. So producers will continue to produce a good only as long as it is more profitable than producing something else. As long as they can continue to produce the good and sell it for a profit, they will increase their production until they break even relative to what they could earn by producing something else. In other words, they will increase production until the marginal cost of producing one additional unit of the product exactly matches the marginal revenue.

There will always be some point where marginal costs equal marginal revenues, for two reasons. The first is the principle of scarcity discussed above. A producer's inputs, just like all other goods, are scarce resources. Producers can only make more goods by employing more inputs. However, since the inputs are limited, they ultimately can acquire more inputs only by paying higher prices, so the cost of producing more units must ultimately rise and cut into their profit. Second, as they produce more units of their good, the price at which they can sell those additional units will ultimately have to fall in order to induce more consumers to buy the product.

In summary:

- The basic law of economics is this: supply equals demand for a price.
- Equilibrium is the point where market price matches the demand with the supply.
- In general, demand increases with a relative fall in price while supply falls; demand falls with a relative increase in price while supply increases.

Figure 19.1

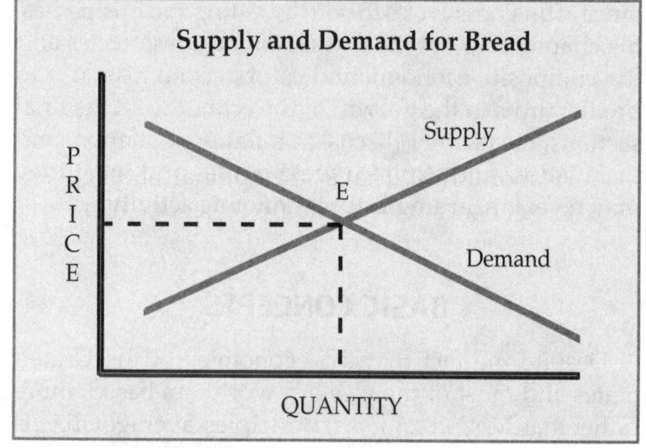

MICROECONOMICS

Microeconomics (also called price theory) is the study of individual economic decisions and their aggregate consequences. This approach to economic theory builds concepts from the perspective of the small (individuals' and firms' actions) and moves up toward the large (government policies, international trade). Components of microeconomic theory include:

- the theory of the firm
- consumer behavior and utility
- opportunity costs
- marginal utility
- elasticity

- competitive market structures
- asset pricing (discussed in Chapter 28, "Investment Planning")

Theory of the Firm

The theory of the firm is about the economics of business operations and profit maximization. Generally postulating a multiplicative model of two basic inputs, capital and labor, it seeks to find the theoretical capital and labor mix that maximizes firm value. Among the common-sense conclusions derived are that in competitive markets

1. Firms should expand production until the marginal cost (MC) of producing another unit of output equals the marginal revenue (MR) received when selling that unit, i.e., MC = MR.

2. Firms should select their optimum mix of labor and capital by balancing the marginal product of capital (MPC) with the marginal product of labor (MPL). That is, the optimal labor/capital mix occurs where adding either one more unit of labor or one more unit of capital will produce the same increase in output, i.e., MPC = MPL.

In addition, the theory of the firm looks at the question of the optimal capital structure between debt and equity to maximize firm value. Franco Modigliani and Merton Miller showed (their "irrelevance proposition") that in an economist's ideal world of complete and perfect capital markets (without differential taxation) and with full and symmetric information among all market participants, the total market value of all the securities issued by a firm is governed by the earning power and risk of its underlying real assets and is independent of how the mix of securities issued to finance it is divided between debt instruments and equity capital. Basically, this proposition says that the value of a firm, like the size of a pizza, remains the same, regardless of how one slices it up (between debt and equity).

However, in the real world, where debt securities are taxed differently than equities, the mix between debt and equity can affect the overall value of both the debt and equity. In this environment, the objective of management is to choose the mix between debt and equity so as to maximize the value of the (owners') equity in relation to its risk.

Marginal Revenue (MR) and Marginal Cost (MC)

This refers to the incremental cost or revenue associated with the next unit of production and sales.

In competitive markets, the optimal level of production and sales is the level where, for the last unit, marginal revenue equals marginal cost (MR = MC).

For a small producer in a competitive market, MR equals price, a constant essentially given to the producer by the market (he is too small to influence the price). For large producers in protected or otherwise not completely competitive markets, MR tends to decline with the level of production and sales. In other words, additional buyers, beyond those who have purchased at the current price, can be enticed to buy only if they can buy at a lower price.

For most producers, MC may fall as economies of scale (efficiencies of size) reduce costs, but, ultimately, will rise as the scale of production rises.

Figure 19.2

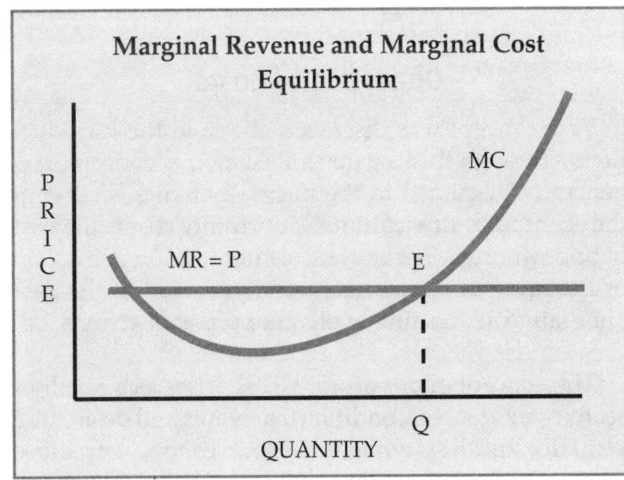

Consumer Behavior and Marginal Utility

The basic concept here is that consumers seek to maximize the utility of their consumption, subject to the constraints of their income and wealth. Marginal utility (MU) is the added value, usefulness, or benefit of the next unit of a product consumed by the consumer.

In general, the "law of diminishing marginal utility" holds that the added utility of one additional unit of a good is less than that added by the previously consumed unit. In other words, marginal utility declines as the number of units consumed increases. For instance, the first minute in a shower after a tough tennis match is sheer bliss, but after 20 minutes, the value of one additional minute in the shower becomes negligible, maybe even a disutility. Consumers maximize utility by purchasing just so many units of each desired good that the marginal utility of each good per dollar spent is equal. This will occur where the consumer's marginal utility equals the cost (C) of one additional unit, i.e., MU = C.

The theory of consumer behavior also addresses such questions as: hours of labor supplied versus leisure hours consumed, and consumption today versus saving and consumption tomorrow. Essentially, the same principles apply in these cases whereby consumers will offer more labor until the value (marginal utility) of what they are paid per hour is equal to the value (marginal utility) of an additional hour of leisure. Similarly, people will save and invest, rather than spend, current income up to the point where the marginal utility of an additional unit of future consumption equals the value of current consumption. It is generally assumed that people act to maximize the utility of their lifetime consumption, where, among other things, desired bequests or legacies are weighed and valued just like any other good.

Opportunity Costs

This concept was discussed above in the introduction. Although this is a general economic concept, it is generally discussed in the microeconomics section of the economics curriculum. Opportunity cost is the cost of opportunities forgone as a result of taking one action or pursuing one economic activity instead of the best alternative action among all other possible actions.

The concept of opportunity cost arises as a result of scarcity, the general condition that wants and desires are virtually limitless, while the resources to satisfy those wants and desires are limited.

Price Elasticity of Demand

Price elasticity of demand is a measure of the buyer's responsiveness or sensitivity to changes in price. In some circumstances, such as would certainly be the case with respect to the charge for the antidote to a potentially fatal snake bite, people will be quite insensitive to changes in prices. In other circumstances, such as when buying common 3-inch steel nails or other commodity-like products for which there are many competitors, consumers will shift from one competitor to another at the slightest difference in price.

<u>Formula for the elasticity of quantity demanded.</u>

$$\text{Elasticity of Quantity Demanded} = \frac{\text{\% Change in Quantity Demanded}}{\text{\% Change in Price}}$$

1. If the elasticity coefficient is greater than 1, the product is price elastic.

2. If the elasticity coefficient is less than 1, the product is price inelastic.

3. Elasticity tends to vary at different price levels and quantities, typically being less elastic at low quantities and high prices (buyers who want it, need it, so they are less sensitive to price) and more elastic at high quantities and lower prices (buyers want it, but they do not need it, so they are more sensitive to price).

Figure 19.3

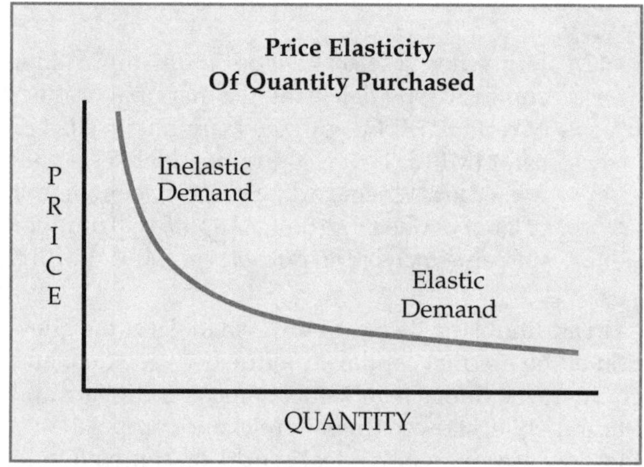

<u>Formula for the elasticity of total revenue.</u>

$$\text{Elasticity of Total Revenue} = \frac{\text{\% Change in Total Revenue}}{\text{\% Change in Price}}$$

The following table illustrates elasticity of demand.

Elasticity of Demand for Hamburger							
Price Per Lb.		**Total Lbs. Demanded**		**Total Revenue**		**Elasticity Quantity**	**Elasticity Revenue**
$5.00		1,000		$ 5,000			
	+25%		-50%		-38%	2.00 **E**	1.50 **E**
4.00		2,000		8,000			
	+33%		-50%		-33%	1.50 **E**	1.00 **E**
3.00		4,000		12,000			
	+50%		-56%		-33%	1.10 **E**	0.67 **I**
2.00		9,000		18,000			
	+100%		-44%		+13%	0.43 **I**	0.13 **I**
1.00		16,000		16,000			
E = *Elastic*		**I** = *Inelastic*					

Competitive Market Structures

The type of market structure influences firm behavior, strategies, and tactics. The key determinants of market structure are product pricing, supply, barriers to entry, efficiency, and competition. When there is a high degree of competition and few barriers to entry in industry, the market is characterized by pure (or close to perfect) competition. Where there is only one firm and/or very high barriers to entry in an industry, the market is characterized by pure monopoly. Of course, these extremes are actually quite rare, so most markets are characterized by some degree of competition in between pure competition and pure monopoly.

Essentially, market structure depends on (1) how free firms are to enter or exit a market and whether there are any natural, legal, or governmental barriers to entry; (2) whether the product is homogeneous (fungible, e.g., nails) or to what degree each firm can differentiate its product within the market (e.g., perfumes); (3) how much control each firm has over the supply or output of the industry; and (4) how much control the firms have over the price they can charge for the product. Obviously, to some extent, all of these factors are interrelated.

Pure Competition

A purely competitive market is characterized by (1) entirely free entry and exit to the industry; (2) a homogeneous and undifferentiated product (e.g., commodities such as corn, iron ore, etc., where no consumer has any grounds for preferring one company's product over that of another); (3) large number of buyers and sellers so that no individual seller can influence price; (4) sellers are price takers (they have to accept the market price); and (5) perfect or close to perfect information is available to buyers and sellers so that no buyer or seller can exploit the ignorance of others.

Examples of pure (or close to perfect) competition markets are U.S. financial markets, such as the stock exchanges, currency markets, bond markets, and the agricultural and commodities markets. The advantages of perfect competition include that a high degree of competition helps allocate resources to most efficient use, prices are set equal to marginal costs, firms make a "normal" profit in the long run, firms tend to operate at maximum efficiency, and consumers benefit from these efficiencies.

When a firm has a new idea in a competitive market, the firm generally makes short-term abnormal profits. However, other firms quickly emulate or replicate the idea and enter the market to take advantage of abnormal profits. These new firms increase supply and prices fall in the long run to the price at which firms make "normal" profits for the risks undertaken in this market.

Pure Monopoly

In the case of pure monopoly, the industry is the firm! In actuality, there have been very few examples of pure monopoly. Even in cases where one firm basically controls all or virtually all of the market, such as was the case of DeBeers for years in the wholesale diamond market, there are always imperfect substitutes. If the price of diamonds becomes too high, consumers can substitute emeralds or opals, or other, perhaps less pricey, baubles. Basically, close substitutes virtually always erode monopoly power. For example, if prices for professional basketball tickets are set too high, consumers can substitute college basketball, or professional hockey, or even more time spent at the movies (pro basketball is really just entertainment, is it not?).

From a practical standpoint, a firm may have close to monopoly control of the market when the firm controls 25% or more of the market for the product. Also, some industries tend towards what is called *natural monopoly* because of high barriers and/or costs to entry and/or physical limitations or natural advantages to larger scales of operation. For example, the gas, electric, water, telecommunications, and rail industries all have these basic characteristics.

Monopolistic firms, unless regulated (as is typically the case with natural monopolies), may control price or output/supply, earn abnormally high profits in the long run (set prices above their marginal cost of production), and charge different prices to different consumers based upon each consumer's perceived need and ability to pay.

Although monopolistic markets "exploit" consumers by both limiting their choices and extracting more in price than the firm's marginal cost (called extracting monopoly rents), monopolistic markets sometimes provide certain advantages. The monopolistic rents earned by the firm may permit the firm to undertake greater research and development and accelerate innovation, at least to the extent that some products might not be developed because of great costs and risks unless producers had some guarantee of monopoly in production. Actually, every time a firm, such as a drug company, receives a patent on a new product, such as a new wonder drug, the government is granting the firm a "monopoly" for that product for a certain number of years. This rewards companies with monopoly marketing rights for the tremendous expense and risk associated with spending hundreds of millions of dollars in research and development on the gamble they will ultimately achieve the desired technological breakthrough. Through this temporary monopoly mechanism, consumers enjoy many goods and services that might otherwise never have been developed.

The disadvantages associated with monopolies are several. In general, consumers pay higher prices than they would in the presence of pure competitive markets. Often, supply is intentionally limited to increase prices, thus limiting or pricing certain consumer choices out of the range of the budgets of many potential consumers. In addition, monopoly market power may breed complacency and lead to inefficient production and control over costs, which is a dead-weight loss in economic efficiency shared in part by all consumers.

Monopsony

Monopsony is a state in which demand comes from one source. If there is only one customer for a certain good, that customer has a monopsony in the market for that good. The concept is analogous to monopoly, but as applied on the demand side of the market, not the supply side. For example, for some workers in an isolated company town that was created by and is dominated by one employer, that employer is a monopsonist for some kinds of employment. For some kinds of U.S. medical care, such as in the case of the government program Medicare, the federal government is a monopsonist.

A common theoretical implication is that the price of the good is pushed down near the cost of production. The price is not predicted to go to zero, because if it went below where the suppliers are willing to produce they would not produce at all.

The term "market power" is often used to describe the continuum from perfectly competitive markets with many buyers to a monopsony market with only one buyer and there is an extensive practice/industry/science of measuring the degree of market power, or control over price.

Oligopoly

An oligopoly market structure is an industry dominated by a small number of large sellers, although the industry may have a large number of smaller firms. Typically, there are high barriers to entry in the market (e.g., initial scale of investment required, specialized know-how, physical barriers), at least with respect to reaching a dominant status. It follows that these sellers are also dominant buyers in the industry – this is termed "oligopsony."

Examples of oligopolistic market structures are supermarkets, the banking industry (e.g., Citibank, Bank of America, Chase Manhattan), brewers (e.g., Anheuser-Busch, Miller), fast-food outlets (e.g., McDonald's, Burger King, KFC, Starbucks), soda pop (e.g., Coca-Cola, Pepsi), bookstores (e.g., Borders, Barnes & Noble), detergents (e.g., Unilever, Proctor & Gamble), entertainment (e.g., Time-Warner, Disney), chemicals and medicinal drugs (e.g., Glaxo Smith Kline, Dupont), oil (e.g., AMOCO, Mobil), electrical goods (e.g., Sony, GE), and broadcasting (e.g., ABC, NBC, CBS, TBS). Products in these markets are sometimes highly differentiated (medicinal drugs) or close to homogenous (oil and gasoline). The major firms tend to rely on non-price competition (e.g., better service, easier access, brand name recognition, etc.). Smaller firms within these industries tend to differentiate their product, or sell in niches, but tend to be price-takers.

Oligopolies are characterized by periods of fierce competition interspersed within generally longer periods of "cooperative" pricing or outright collusion. For example, occasionally consumers will see gasoline "price wars" between competing oil companies, at least in local markets. But generally, the price for a gallon of gasoline for any major company tends to remain within pennies of the other major companies' prices.

Signaling. Oligopolies have the potential for collusion among the major players in setting prices and controlling output. Although active collusion is generally illegal under anti-trust laws, it can be achieved in indirect ways through "signaling." Signaling is the tactic of legally informing competitors what actions they are planning to initiate or will take in response to another competitor's actions. Since direct contact or collusion is usually illegal under the antitrust laws, companies use signals to communicate with competitors.

The objectives of signaling are, principally, to avoid potentially costly price wars and to bluff competitors into responses to which a company can capitalize. Companies send signals in essentially 6 ways:

1. *Price movements* – These are used to signal intentions and penalize unacceptable behav-

ior. For example, one gasoline company, say ARCO, lowers its wholesale price per gallon in a given region a cent or two hoping to attract customers from its competitors. A competitor, say AMOCO, quickly drops its price by five or more additional cents below ARCO's new price. Basically, AMOCO is saying to ARCO, if you want to play this game it could get nasty. If ARCO immediately raises its prices they are signaling, in effect, that they will call a truce. If they do not raise their price, they are signaling that they intend to do battle.

2. *Prior announcements* – These are used to threaten, to test competitor's resolve, and to avoid surprises. For example, Coor's Beer in the early '80s announced that it was exploring the possibility of expanding its market from just the west-central United States to the entire U.S. market. They were hoping to test the response of the other national brewers to their announcement to see what counter-measures, if any, they could expect from these competitors.

3. *Media discussions* – These are used to communicate a company's rationale for actions and to convey the company's thoughts to the competition. This is a very typical signaling device, especially in the banking industry. When, say, CitiBank, decides that it thinks the prime rate it charges its best and most financially sound customers should be raised by half a percent, CitiBank's chief economist will almost certainly be seen on one of the Sunday morning national news talk shows discussing the economy and why Citibank thinks the prime rate will have to rise a half a percent. Inevitably, the chief economists for BankAmerica, Chase Manhattan, and other large banks will be seen soon thereafter on similar shows voicing their opinions on the matter. If they agree, each bank feels safe to raise their prime rate without risking that they will lose customers to their competitors. However, if one or more of the economists do not follow the "party line," they are indicating that their bank is not willing to play along. In this case, CitiBank has determined what the competition plans to do without illegally colluding to set the price of money (the prime rate).

4. *Counterattack* – This is used to attack a competitor's principal market with a price cut or promotion in retaliation for its entry or encroachment in your principal markets. Say U.S. Airways starts a low cost-promotion on flights from Detroit to San Francisco, one of Northwest's principal routes. Northwest might retaliate by offering low-cost flights from Philadelphia to Orlando, one of U.S. Airways principal routes.

5. *Announce results* – This is used to communicate clearly to the competition the results of an action to avoid costly misunderstanding. For example, a competitor could announce that a price cut is for a limited time in order to avoid signaling a long-term intention to keep prices low.

6. *Litigation* – This is used to tie up a competitor in court. There are innumerable examples of when this tactic has been used both for more legitimate and less legitimate purposes. When Kodak entered the instant photography business, Polaroid sued Kodak for patent infringement. Kodak said that it would fight with all the resources at its disposal, hoping, presumably, that Polaroid might find it better to compromise than fight. However, fight Polaroid did, and prevailed, with Kodak ultimately abandoning the instant photography business and paying Polaroid a $1 billion settlement. In this case, Kodak was hoping its larger size, resources, and the cost of potential litigation would intimidate Polaroid into settling and permitting Kodak to remain in the business. However, Polaroid called Kodak's bluff and won. In many other cases, companies are intimidated into capitulation or compromise.

Concentration – The more an industry is dominated by just a few firms within the industry, the more control and sway the major firms have on the price and quantity of output. The degree of oligopoly is measured by what is called the "concentration ratio," the proportion of market share accounted for by the top X number of firms within the industry. For example, a five firm concentration ratio of 80% means that the top five firms account for 80% of the market.

Monopolistic Competition

Monopolistic competition is a market structure with many buyers and sellers and where entry and exit is relatively free, but where products are highly differentiated. Each firm may have a tiny "monopoly" because of the differentiation of their product and therefore has some control over price and output for its particular version of the "product." Examples include restaurants, fast-food outlets, professions, copy stores, perfumes, sneakers, clothing stores or lines, and cereals. Price-fixing flexibility is limited by imperfect substitutes. For example, if the price of Chanel No. 5 is too high, customers may switch to Canoe or Beautiful; if McDonald's Big Mac is too expensive, customers may switch to Burger King's Whoppers or to KFC's fried chicken instead.

Monopolistic competition is perhaps the most prevalent market structure in the U.S. In fact, much of the curriculum, especially the marketing curriculum, in the MBA programs throughout the country is focused on how to make products more "high involvement" by differentiating a firm's products from the competition to enhance the firm's control of price and output and, thus, potential profits. For example, 40 years ago, jeans were perceived exclusively as work clothes, so they were priced essentially as a commodity item. Although Lee and Levi jeans had slight differences, they were priced nearly identically and cost substantially less than dress slacks. However, once Jordache entered the market with its distinctive pocket stitching and with the pitch that jeans were not just for work anymore (i.e., had become an item of fashion apparel), the market for jeans with all sorts of distinctive fashion uses grew exponentially. Today, one is likely to pay as much or more for a pair of jeans as one pays for a pair of dress slacks.

MACROECONOMICS

Components of macroeconomic theory include

- fiscal versus monetary policy
- Keynesian theory
- monetary theory
- rational expectations
- supply-side economics
- business cycles
- inflation, deflation, and disinflation
- interest rates and the yield curve

Macroeconomics is the study of the entire economy in terms of the total amount of goods and services produced, total income earned, the level of employment of productive resources, and the general behavior of prices. Macroeconomics is economic theory from the perspective of the large (government policies, money supply, international trade, taxation, econometric modeling) and moving down to the effects on the small (individuals, firms). Macroeconomics is used to analyze how best to influence policy goals such as economic growth, price stability, full employment, and the attainment of a sustainable balance of payments.

Until the Great Depression of the 1930s, most economic analysis concentrated on individual firms and industries. However, after the Great Depression, together with the development of the concept of national income and product statistics, the field of macroeconomics began to expand. Particularly influential were the ideas of John Maynard Keynes, who used the concept of aggregate demand to explain fluctuations in output and unemployment. Keynesian economics is based on his ideas.

One of the challenges of economics has been a struggle to reconcile macroeconomic and microeconomic models. Starting in the 1950s, macroeconomists developed micro-based models of macroeconomic behavior (such as the consumption function). The first global macroeconomic model, Wharton Econometric Forecasting Associates LINK project, was initiated by Lawrence Klein and was mentioned in his citation for the Bank of Sweden Prize in Economic Sciences in Memory of Alfred Nobel in 1980.

Theorists such as Robert Lucas Jr suggested (in the 1970s) that at least some traditional Keynesian macroeconomic models were questionable, as they were not derived from assumptions about individual behavior. However, New Keynesian macroeconomics has generally presented microeconomic models to shore up their macroeconomic theorizing, while the Lucas critique has fallen from favor.

Today the main schools of macroeconomic thought are as discussed in the following paragraphs.

Keynesian economics focuses on aggregate demand to explain levels of unemployment and the business cycle. That is, business cycle fluctuations should be reduced through fiscal policy (the government spends more or less depending on the situation) and monetary policy. Early Keynesian macroeconomics was "activist," calling for regular use of policy to stabilize the capitalist economy, while some Keynesians called for the use of incomes policies.

Monetarism, led by Milton Friedman and the Chicago School, holds that inflation is always and everywhere a monetary phenomenon. It rejects fiscal policy because it leads to "crowding out" of the private sector consumption and investment. Further, it does not wish to combat inflation or deflation by means of active demand management as in Keynesian economics, but by means of monetary policy rules, such as keeping the rate of growth of the money supply constant over time and maintaining the level of interest rates.

New classical economics emphasizes the idea of rational expectations. The original theoretical impetus for this "resurgence" of classical economics was the charge that Keynesian economics lacked microeconomic foundations (i.e., its assertions were not founded in basic economic theory). This school emerged during the 1970s lead by Robert Barrow and others. This school assumes that at any one time, there is only one "market clearing" equilibrium and that the economy automatically gravitates to that equilibrium. Fluctuations occurred due to changes in potential output (i.e., changes in aggregate supply). It is the position of the new classicists that the efforts of the government to "manage" the economy through activist policies are one of the principle destabilizing factors in the economy.

New Keynesian economics arose partly in response to new classical economics. It strives to provide microeconomic foundations to Keynesian economics by showing how imperfect markets can justify demand management.

Supply-side economics emphasizes incentives to production and supply. The focus for monetary policy should be purely on the price of money as determined by the supply of money and the demand for money. It advocates a monetary policy that directly targets the value of money. Typically the value of money is measured by reference to gold or some other reference. The focus of fiscal policy is to raise revenue for worthy government investments, with a clear recognition of the impact that taxation has on domestic trade.

Fiscal Versus Monetary Policy

Fiscal policy deals with government tax and spending as it affects the economy. The basic philosophy is that government intervention can improve the performance of the economy. By spending more and taxing less when the economy is down or in recession, the government can spur economic activity, raising incomes and production, and reducing unemployment. Conversely, by spending less and taxing more when the economy is overheating, government action can dampen inflationary pressures. This school of thought, called the Keynesian school, was fathered by John Maynard Keynes, the author of *The General Theory of Employment, Interest, and Money* (1936) and has been the predominant economic theory applied by Democratic administrations since Franklin Roosevelt, although Republican administrations have practiced these policies as well.

Monetary policy deals with the effect of the money supply on economic activity. The philosophy of this school of thought is that the economy is more responsive to changes in the money supply and interest rates through the independent actions of businesses and individuals, than to government tax-and-spend policies. The concept is that increases in the money supply through the actions of the Federal Reserve can lower interest rates and increase liquidity in economic downturns, thus spurring businesses to make additional investments and spurring consumers to increase consumption spending to drive economic activity back up to a desired growth rate. Conversely, reductions in the money supply can raise interest rates and reduce liquidity, which raises the cost of investment and consumption to help quell an overheating economy. Nobel Prize-winning economist Milton Friedman was and is the leading proponent of this theory, notably identified with the Chicago School of Business and Economics.

The Changing Debate

The clear failings of the application of either theory to successfully "manage" the economy, with the period of "stagflation" (high inflation and recession) in the 1970s being just one the most obvious examples, has changed the debate from which theory is the best tool to manage the economy to whether or not the government can effectively manage the economy at all. Many of the economists associated with the Keynesian school of thought have tended to continue to support an "activist" government role, while those of the Monetarist-Chicago school have seen government intervention as more a source of instability and economic inefficiency than the contrary. The Keynesians are for "micro management" by the government for both political and social ends. The Monetarist-Chicago school believes that the government's role is limited to ensuring stability and eliminating the barriers to free and unfettered enterprise.

The debate is not simply about which theories when applied are the most effective, but about the role of government itself, in other words, about social policy. The discipline now called economics has been called, and still is called, the study of political economy.

Rational Expectations Theory

In the 1970s and 1980s a new "rational expectations" or "anticipations" theory was proposed, and supported by empirical evidence, that has questioned the efficacy of any government attempts to manage economic affairs. It is based on the simple notion that in order for most government fiscal or monetary policies to work, people must either be ignorant of the policies or not understand the implications of the policies on economic activity. For instance, in order for an increase in the money supply to increase economic activity, it must be presumed that people behave as though this will not increase prices, or that they will adjust their anticipations only slowly. Of course, once people come to realize that increases in the money supply, all else being equal, will result in higher prices, they will rationally anticipate the increases and adjust their behavior immediately. This will mute the effect of the policy. Similar arguments can be made for fiscal policies. The only lasting effect is the inefficiencies associated with people's attempts to outmaneuver the government policies.

A further conclusion of the rational expectations theory is that government policies themselves, if not entirely anticipated, in fact create shocks to the economy that create or exacerbate the instability the government is trying to eliminate. In other words, government activism tends to be the problem, not the solution.

Gross National Product, Inflation, and the Keynesian View

Terms

- *Gross national product* (GNP) is the total market value of all final goods and services produced by the economy in a year. The values of intermediate goods are not counted directly, but rather, to avoid double counting, are only counted in the value of the final product in which they are a part.

- *Gross domestic product* (GDP) is only that part of GNP that is produced within the country's borders. The adjustment is relatively small and so GDP is almost the same as GNP.

- *Nominal* GNP or GDP is the GNP or GDP expressed in current dollars.

- *Real* GNP or GDP is the GNP or GDP adjusted for inflation or expressed in constant-value dollars.

- The GNP or GDP *deflator* is the factor adjusting nominal GNP or GDP to real (inflation-adjusted) GNP or GDP in terms of some base year.

- The *consumer price index* (CPI) measures the price changes of a specifically designed, "representative" basket of consumer goods and services that most people buy. There are actually several variations of this index for large urban areas, small urban areas, rural areas, and even geographical regions of the country.

- The *producer price index* (PPI) measures price changes of a collection of raw materials used most often by producers.

- *Net national product* (NNP) is the GNP adjusted for economic depreciation (i.e., adjusted for the amount of capital, such as machinery, factories, buildings, and equipment, that is used up in the process of production each year).

<u>Keynesian formula for GNP.</u>

$$GNP = C + I + G + X$$

where C is personal consumption
I is private investment
G is government purchases
X is net exports over imports

According to this equation, GNP can be increased by increasing any of the four components of GNP.

Fiscal Multiplier

Any increase in government spending has a multiplier effect on GNP. The marginal propensity to consume (MPC) is the ratio of the amount an average person will spend to the total amount received when receiving additional income. The greater is the MPC, the greater is the potential effect of an increase in income on the GNP. The formula is usually stated as follows:

$$\text{Government spending multiplier} = 1 \div (1 - \text{MPC}).$$

Example. If, in the economy as a whole, people tend to spend 90% of any additional income they receive and save only 10%, the MPC is 90%. Therefore, if the government spends an additional $100 million on a public-works project, the result would be another $1 billion in the economy: $100 million x (1 ÷ 0.10) = $100 million x 10 = $1 billion.

One of the fallacies of this notion is that it ignores the fact that in order to spend $100 million, the government has to get the money from some place. They have basically three choices: raise taxes, borrow, or print money.

1. *Raise taxes* – If the government raises taxes by $100 million, they will be taking $100 million out of the economy at the same time as they are putting $100 million into the economy. Sounds like it is a wash, right? No, not according to the Keynesian theory. If the government puts $100 million in, total spending increases through the multiplier by $1 billion. Therefore, the net effect is an increase in total spending of $900 million, theoretically.

   However, taking $100 million out of the economy in taxes also has a negative spending multiplier effect, does it not? So it really is a wash, right?

   No, once again. According to Keynesian theory, the net effect leaves us with a net increase in spending of the original $100 million spent by the government. The argument is that of the $100 million taxed from individuals, only $90 million would actually have been spent, the rest would have been saved. Therefore, taxing $100 million really only takes $90 million of spending out of the economy. Therefore, when government both taxes and spends $100 million, the theory asserts, there is a net first-round spending increase of $10 million. When the multiplier is applied to this net $10 million increase in spending, total spending increases by $100 million, the same as the initial amount of government spending.

   This is called the *balanced budget multiplier*, but it does not wash. What happens to the amount that would otherwise have been saved? When money is saved by individuals, it is not "taken out" of the economy. It ends up in some bank where it is loaned so someone else can spend it on consumer or investment goods. Therefore, it re-enters the economy as additional spending. So, there is actually no additional spending.

   How can $100 million spent by the government have a greater effect than $100 million spent by the people themselves? The only way that money spent by the government can have a greater economic effect than the same amount spent by the people themselves is if it is spent or invested by the government more effectively and efficiently than it would be by the people.

2. *Borrow* – If the government borrows the money, they are also, once again, taking purchasing power out of the economy. There has been considerable debate and research into the question of "crowding out," the question of whether government borrowing reduces or otherwise crowds out borrowing and investment that would otherwise have been made by the private sector. The arguments that it does not are weak.

   Money is fungible. What makes borrowing by the government any different than borrowing by anyone else? If government borrowing increases the demand for loan funds above what it would be without the government borrowing, interest rates, the price of debt, will rise, choking off private borrowing and investment by those who would have found it attractive at lower rates but not at the higher rates.

3. *Print money* – If the government does not want to tax people and cannot or will not borrow the money, it can simply print it! It does not actually print money, not usually, that is. Rather, it borrows the money through the Federal Reserve, which simply creates bookkeeping entries and increases the banking reserves. This is called *monetizing the debt.* It is just such monetization that created the double-digit inflation of the 1970s. If the money supply increases faster than the growth in the economy, inflation is inevitable. More dollars chase fewer goods.

IS/LM Curve of the Investment/Spending and Money Markets

The IS/LM curve (Investment-Saving/Liquidity-Money curve) shows the relationship or tradeoff between investment and saving versus liquidity. High interest rates choke off both investment and consumer spending, especially of consumer durables, which are frequently financed. The downward sloping curve describing this relationship is called the investment and spending curve (IS).

In Keynesian theory, higher interest rates increase the preference for money (short-term liquid money-market instruments) or increase liquidity preference. In contrast, when interest rates are low, people shift to stocks or long-term, less-liquid bonds with higher yields. This relationship is described by an upward-sloping liquidity and money curve (LM).

At the point where the IS and LM curves cross is the equilibrium interest rate and GNP.

Figure 19.4

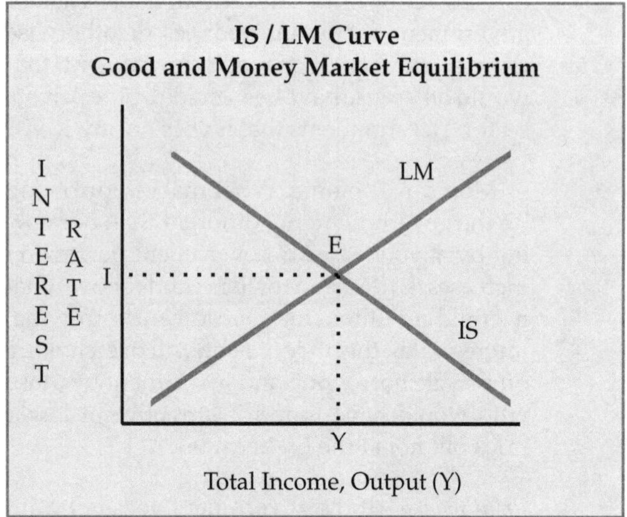

The IS/LM curves will shift with changes in fiscal and monetary policy. For example, if government spending increases, total spending will rise (according to the free-lunch notions of Keynesianism) and the entire IS curve will shift upward, resulting in higher equilibrium interest rates and higher GNP. If the money supply is also increased in the right amount corresponding to the increase in spending, the LM will shift outward. The net result could be an increase in GNP while interest rates remain level.

Figure 19.5

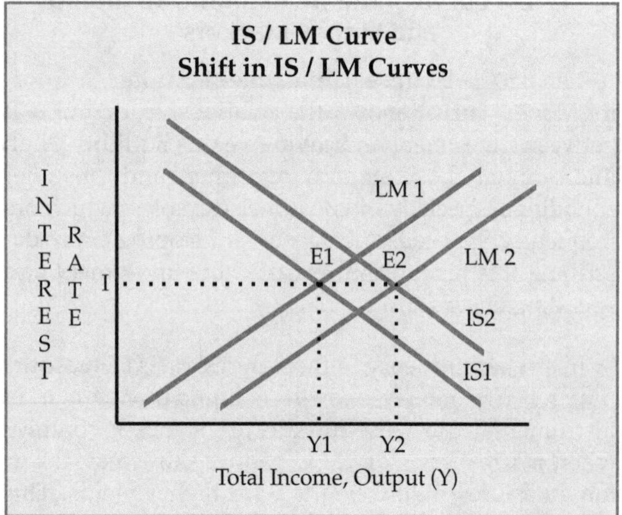

Economic Growth and the Monetarist View

Money includes currency and "money equivalents," such as checking accounts and money-market funds. M1 is defined as cash, checking account balances, and nonbank traveler's checks. M2 is defined as M1 plus savings accounts and money-market accounts.

Quantity-theory-of-money formula.

Money (M) x Velocity (V) = Nominal GNP
Money (M) x Velocity (V) = Price Level (P) x Real GNP (Q)
$M \times V = P \times Q$

where Velocity is defined as the rate at which money turns over in the economy.

The quantity theory asserts that the velocity is relatively constant, therefore, increases in the supply of money will increase nominal, but not necessarily real, GNP.

Monetary Policy Tools: The Federal Reserve

1. *Change the discount rate* – This is the rate at which banks can borrow from the Federal Reserve to increase their lending to customers. By increasing the discount rate, the Federal Reserve, or the Fed, as it is called, discourages bank borrowing and, hence, reduces overall demand in the economy.

2. *Buy or sell government securities* – Through what are called open-market transactions, the Fed buys or sells Treasury bonds to the public. Selling the bonds to the public takes money out of the economy; buying them puts money into the economy.

3. *Change the reserve requirements of financial institutions* – By changing the reserve requirements, the Fed either puts more liquidity into or takes more liquidity out of the banking system. Banks must keep a certain proportion of their deposits secured by reserves. By adding to or taking away from these reserves, the Fed either expands or contracts the available funds for loans and money supply.

Supply-Side Economics

During the recent debate in our nation's capital over how best to get the U.S. economy moving, two opposing camps coalesced. The first, and larger, camp emphasized more government spending, accompanied by tax rebates and temporary tax cuts geared primarily at low-income earners. These were the Keynesians, and their emphasis was on consumption. The second camp emphasized the need for permanent tax relief that boosts incentives for working, investing, and risk taking, and helps the economy in both the short run and over the long haul. These were the supply-siders, and their emphasis was on production, subject to the free market.

What has recently been called supply-side economics is really a re-emergence of classical economic theory in response to the failures of both the Keynesian and Monetarist policies in the decade of the 1970s. Its basic premise is that the most effective and efficient form of government action is to provide incentives to market participants and let the competitive market work without too much interruption and interference from government. The fundamental principle involved is that the actions of millions of market participants, where all individuals are pursuing their own enlightened self interest, allocates resources more efficiently than government-mandated spending policies.

In summary, supply-side economics is built on the following tenets:

- *Incentives matter* – Individuals naturally respond to incentives. For example, the relative prices, or costs, of consumption versus investment, or risk avoidance versus risk taking, influence the behavior of individuals, families, and businesses.

- *Markets work* – The free, unfettered market provides clear incentives (through price and profit signals) that assure that resources are allocated to their most efficient and beneficial uses. So while supply-side economics emphasizes production (see next point), it is production within the context of the free market. In order to be of value, production must meet or create a demand. After all, the end point of the entire economic process is consumption.

- *Supply comes before demand in the economic process* – There are two aspects to the idea that supply takes precedence over demand in the economic hierarchy. First, in the marketplace, one must supply a marketable good or service before one can legitimately demand or consume. That is, one must supply something in order to be able to exchange it to meet one's own needs and desires. Or more plainly, you can't get something for nothing.

- *Supply creates demand* – Indeed, no general demand existed for televisions, home computers, or most other products or services, until someone invented and improved upon such products and services.

- *The engines of economic growth (working, saving, investing, risk taking, innovating, inventing, and creating) are all supply-side endeavors* – Economic growth can only occur through a boost in resources used for production purposes and/or greater efficiencies, innovations, and inventions.

- *The entrepreneur, not the government, drives the economy* – Supply-side economics recognizes the critical economic role played by the entrepreneur. As the source of new products, services, inventions, and innovations, the entrepreneur serves as the ultimate source of economic growth.

- *A healthy economy depends upon sound money* – Price instability and inflation are monetary phenomena that increase the risks and costs of saving, investing, and risk taking. Sound money (knowing that a unit of currency will maintain its value months, years, and decades from now) is the necessary foundation upon which an economy can prosper.

Supply-Side Policies

Supply-side policy is driven by two "policy levers." The first is the fiscal lever – tax, regulatory, and spending policies geared toward establishing a pro-growth economic environment. The second is the monetary lever – monetary policy geared to establish price stability upon which an economy can function and flourish. Under the supply-side economics model, and in contrast with Keynesian notions and the Phillips curve theory, economic growth and price stability are not at odds with one another, but are actually complimentary. The most accurate definition of inflation remains "too much money chasing too few goods." Therefore, economic growth, or the production of more goods and services, is anti-inflationary.

As for the fiscal policy lever, the following policy prescriptions are deeply rooted in supply-side economic thinking:

- *Low marginal tax rates* – Marginal tax rates (i.e., the tax rate on the next dollar of income earned) influence economic decisions. For example, the marginal tax rate helps determine the relative price of work vs. leisure, investment vs. consumption, risk taking vs. risk avoidance, and so on. Therefore, supply-side economics places significant importance on reducing marginal income tax rates in order to boost incentives for working, investing, and risk taking. In addition, the supply-side belief that supply comes before demand in the economic order leads to a preference for taxing consumption rather than production. After all, consumption is the eventual end point of all economic activity and seems the most logical point in the economic process to reflect the total cost of government. Of course, as is the case with all taxes, taxing consumption too heavily would cripple an economy.

- *A light regulatory burden* – Under supply-side economics, regulation is simply another form of taxation. Regulations raise the costs of investment and entrepreneurship, and thereby restrain economic growth and job creation.

- *Small, limited government* – Under supply-side economics, the primary emphasis is on the total size of government. That is, what are the total resources being diverted from more productive private-sector ventures to less productive government endeavors, whether through borrowing or taxing. Basically, government operates without normal economic incentives. Without the disciplines of prices, profits, losses, and private ownership, government is inherently wasteful, and, therefore, should be quite limited in its duties. On the secondary level, the relative mix of how government is then financed gains supply-side attention. For example, the relative economic costs of borrowing versus taxing must be considered. Of course, in the long run, most government expenditures are eventually paid for with taxes and fees (or through inflation). However, the mix, timing, levels, and types of taxation help determine the size and growth of the economy.

- *Free trade* – From a supply-side point of view, eliminating international barriers to trade lowers costs, expands and opens markets and opportunities, enhances incentives for production, boosts competition, improves quality, reduces consumer costs, and expands consumer choices.

As for the monetary policy lever, the only objective of monetary policy should be price stability. A sound currency and stable prices create an environment where investment and the economy can flourish. Anchoring the dollar to gold – as was the case, to varying degrees, from the end of the 1870s to the late 1960s – still serves as the surest path to price stability.

THE BUSINESS CYCLE

Business activity always expands and then contracts. Periods of surging production, employment, and profits are followed by periods of shrinking outputs and profits and increases in unemployment. Then the entire cycle repeats itself again.

The cycle is certain and inevitable. What is uncertain is exactly why business and economic activity fluctuates as it does. The more important question from a practical perspective is how to determine when current trends in business and economic activity will change.

No one yet has been able to accurately predict the length and course of each cycle. This is, in part, because the economy is not like a scientific experiment where conditions can be controlled to isolate the underlying "laws" that govern the movements in the economy like the balls on a pool table. The basic economic conditions for each historical "experiment" or observation of changes in the economy are always somewhat different from the previous cycle.

This does not mean that certain "laws" or principles do not influence the business cycle, but rather that our observations of these laws are "fuzzy." We cannot be sure that we have properly accounted for all the factors and circumstances that conditioned the subsequent events. Therefore, we can only glean general tendencies of what economic or business conditions might or generally should follow another set of economic or business conditions.

Yet, several things are certain: the business cycle is generated by forces within the economic (and political) system, not by any preternatural outside forces. Forces and conditions within the economic system drive the alternating periods of expansion and contraction. Consequently, certain critical features of the cycle endure.

1. *The forces of supply and demand condition every business cycle* – To increase income, one must produce more. But the level of demand must justify this output. With sufficient demand, the level of production will be sustained and will grow, and income will increase. If demand is

insufficient, the reverse will occur. During the expansion phase of the cycle, demand outpaces supply, which permits the growth of production and income; during the contraction phase, supply outpaces demand and the growth of production and income slows or falls.

Exactly why these disparities in the forces of supply and demand exist and why they change is uncertain. However, certain economic statistics and indicators tend to reflect the effects of changes in these forces even before or just as these forces begin to affect the economy as a whole.

2. *Credit drives consumption and business investment* – Consumers may increase consumption and businesses may increase investment in productive capacity by borrowing money if their current income is insufficient to sustain their desired expenditures. Spending borrowed funds permits demand to take on a life of its own and bid up a constantly and rapidly growing level of production. This supports the expansionary phase of the business cycle.

   This expansion of credit and production is only sustainable as long as the borrowers and the lenders continue to have confidence in the trend of the expansion. But as the expansion continues, the availability of credit tightens, interest rates increase, and the cost of borrowing to finance either consumption or investment increases. Simultaneously, to continue the expansion, producers must expand their production in less and less lucrative investment opportunities as the most lucrative investment (production) opportunities become fully exploited. Inevitably, the potential returns just do not seem to warrant the increased cost, demand falls, and with it, the level of production and income. The contraction has begun.

   Once again, it is difficult to determine just when the turnaround will occur, but various credit-market and interest-rate statistics and indices can send out "warning" signals that the inevitable downturn cannot be far behind.

3. *Every expansion inevitably leads to contraction* – As described above, sooner or later businesses realize that the expected level of sales will not support additional plant and equipment, and inventories begin to grow above desired levels. Consumers realize that they will have difficulty paying for that new home or car. Businesses and consumers begin to curtail their borrowing and expenditures. Since production and income have spurted ahead to meet the growth in demand, they fall when the inevitable contraction in demand takes place.

   Various business and consumer statistics provide evidence of reduced demand and excess supply.

4. *During contractions, production and income recede to a level that does not rely on a continuous growth in credit* – Predicting the end of a contraction is as difficult, if not more so, than predicting the downturn of an expansion.

5. *Every contraction sows the seeds of the subsequent recovery* – Eventually, as consumers and businesses repay their debts, the lower debt burdens and reduced interest rates encourage consumer and business borrowing and demand once again. The economy begins to expand once more.

   Despite downturns, some of the gains of the prior expansions have historically survived. To some extent, contractions can be attributed to the continued, and even expanded, investment in productive capacity in markets and technologies that are being replaced by new markets and technologies. Like the cycle of life itself, the old gives way to the new. The businesses that, through design or simply through the good fortune of being in the right place at the right time, invest in the emerging markets and employ efficient technologies survive and prosper. Contractions continue until the "misspent" investment of the prior expansion is absorbed and reallocated to the industries and markets where it can be more productively used. As investment and human (labor) capital is more efficiently allocated, productivity increases, spurring a recovery and expansion.

Composite Economic Indicators

1. *Where do they come from?* In December 1995, the Conference Board became the official source for the widely publicized composite indexes of leading, lagging, and coincident indicators. For almost 30 years, these economic data series, often referred to as "the leading index" or "the leading indicators,"

were compiled and published by the U.S. Department of Commerce. The Conference Board has also assumed responsibility for compiling a larger set of economic indicators that was also previously provided by the federal government in both a conventional publication, the *Survey of Current Business*, and in electronic format (both diskettes and on the Internet). The Board publishes this under the title *Business Cycle Indicators*.

2. *General overview* – The composite leading, coincident, and lagging indexes are the key elements in an analytic system designed to signal peaks and troughs in the business cycle. Because they are averages, they tend to smooth out a good part of the volatility of the individual series and thereby serve as handy summary measures of the business cycle. Historically, the cyclical turning points in the leading index have occurred before those in aggregate economic activity, while the cyclical turning points in the coincident index have occurred at about the same time as those in aggregate economic activity. The cyclical turning points in the lagging index generally have occurred after those in aggregate economic activity. A change in direction in a composite index does not signal a cyclical turning point unless the movement is of significant size, duration, and scope. It is important to recognize that the timing of the leading index has been irregular and "false signals" are inevitable. The main value of the leading index is in signaling that either the risk of a recession has increased or that a recession may be coming to an end.

   Although it is often stated in the press that three consecutive downward movements in the leading index signal a recession, the Conference Board does not endorse the use of such a simple, inflexible rule. For example, the January 1997 issue of *Business Cycle Indicators* discusses how a 1% decline (2% when annualized) in the leading index, coupled with declines in a majority of the 10 components, provides a reliable, but not perfect, recession signal.

3. *Predictive accuracy* – Unfortunately, economists have never agreed on a single economic indicator to predict the future of the business cycle. Some indicators are better than others, but none is consistently accurate; all give false signals on occasion. The index of leading economic indicators was devised to combine a number of statistical series drawn from a broad spectrum of economic activity, each of which tends to move up or down ahead of the general trend of the business cycle.

   a) *Predictive accuracy of the index* – The index has accurately forecast eight of the ten recessions since 1950, by an average of five months in each of the eight accurate cases. In 1981-82, the index sent mixed signals because it actually turned down about a half year before the recession, only to turn up again about four months before the recession and then down again about two months before the recession. For 1990-91, there was no advance warning, although some experts observed that there would have been no recession in 1990-91 had it not been for the Persian Gulf crisis. This observation simply illustrates that the index is only a general barometer composed of a limited, albeit broad, array of ongoing economic indicators. Many other exceptional factors or irregular circumstances may affect economic activity. One should always be on the lookout for such exceptional factors or irregular circumstances when attempting to forecast business and economic activity.

   b) *False alarms* – Since 1950, the index has also predicted four recessions that never arrived. In 1962, 1966, 1984, and 1987, the index fell for at least three consecutive months although no recession followed. The clear conclusion once again is that the index is a good general barometer of the business cycle, but it is neither flawless nor complete. One should always assess the individual components of the index, as well as the general economic and political environment and other domestic and world economic conditions and circumstances, when attempting to forecast future economic activity.

4. *Criteria for inclusion in index* – Ten statistical series comprise the index. There are four general criteria for inclusion in the index:

   - Each series must accurately lead, be coincident with, or lag the business cycle, depending on the economic index.
   - The various series should provide comprehensive coverage of the economy by representing a wide and diverse range of economic activity.
   - Each series must be available monthly, with only a brief lag until publication.
   - Each series must be free from large subsequent revisions.

The composite economic indicators meet these criteria, and weaving these series into a comprehensive composite provides a statistic that is more reliable and less erratic than any individual component by itself.

Some of the indicators measure activity in physical units, others in current dollars, still others in constant dollars, and some with an index form. This variety of measurements is reduced to an index with 1996 assigned a base value of 100. All other months and years are expressed as a percentage of the base year.

5. *Components* –

a) *Unemployment claims* – The average weekly initial claims for unemployment insurance (state programs) gives a sense of the number of people losing their jobs. A falling number is a sign that the economy is growing.

b) *Orders for consumer goods* – Manufacturers' new orders, consumer goods, and materials industries, if rising, are a signal consumers are spending more freely. Reduced reported orders suggest greater consumer uncertainty and decreasing overall demand.

c) *Building permits* – The number of new private housing units authorized by local building permits is one of the most widely watched measures of economic health. The housing market is extremely sensitive to the business cycle and consumer sentiment. If consumers are becoming more pessimistic about economic prospects, it is quickly reflected by a drop in new housing demand. Conversely, if consumer sentiment turns optimistic, housing demand typically rebounds quickly.

d) *Interest-rate spread* (10-year Treasury bonds less federal funds) – As demands for loan funds goes up (a bullish sign), bank reserves get tighter and the price (interest rate) that banks must pay to acquire overnight funds to meet reserve requirements goes up. As a result, the spread between the 10-year Treasury bond rate and the federal funds rate declines. In contrast, when demand for loan funds falls, the spread increases, which suggests that the market may be heading toward a downturn.

e) *Workweek* – The average weekly hours of production for nonsupervisory workers in manufacturing is a complement to the factory-orders indicator. If both components are up, it is a bullish indicator. If orders are up, but the average weekly hours of production has not also increased, it may indicate that manufacturers are not overly optimistic that the level of demand will be sustained. In contrast, if orders have not increased, but weekly hours are up, it suggests that manufacturers anticipate higher demand, a bullish indicator. Clearly, if both indicators are down, it is a very bearish indicator of future economic activity.

f) *Slower deliveries* – Vendor performance (slower deliveries diffusion index) is a complement to the order-backlog indicator. As demand increases, deliveries tend to get slower as vendors try to fill orders. In contrast, as demand subsides, vendors are able to fill orders more quickly.

g) *Plant and equipment orders* (manufacturers' new orders for nondefense capital goods) – Contracts and orders for plant and equipment (and machine tools) increase when producers plan to expand their productive capacity; a clearly bullish indicator, since it is both a sign of increasing demand (by producers) and a sign of optimism on the part of producers that future demand for their products will be sufficient to justify the additional investment in plant and equipment.

h) *Stock prices* – The S&P 500 Index of common stocks has typically led economic recoveries and recessions by about nine months. Since the S&P 500 Index is a measure of the overall value of the industrial capacity of the economy and the value of the stock market reflects the beliefs and sentiments of essentially the entire universe of economic participants, it is not surprising this indicator tends to lead the business cycle. The problem with this indicator alone is similar to that of the leading economic indicators taken together, only worse. As one economist summed it up, "the S&P 500 Index has predicted 15 of the last nine recessions." Consumer sentiment clearly has an impact on economic activity, but like a large ocean-going vessel, it takes considerable and sustained waves and current (negative or pessimistic expectations) to drive the vessel (or economic activity) off course. In contrast, the stock market can respond quickly, even to ephemeral changes in investor sentiment. Consequently, stock prices are much more volatile than the business cycle itself and, alone, cannot be reliably used to forecast economic activity.

i) *Money supply (M2)* – When the Federal Reserve ceases to pump enough money into the economy, short-term interest rates rise as borrowers compete for fewer available dollars. As interest rates rise, the cost of credit purchases, as well as the carrying costs for inventory, also increase, inevitably reducing consumer demand while raising producer's costs. The net effect is bearish. In contrast, an increase in the money supply can reduce short-term rates (at least in the short run) with a stimulative effect on the economy. The problem with increases in the money supply is that if the increases become excessive, inflation will rise, as will interest rates, once again with a negative impact on overall demand.

j) *Index of consumer expectations* – If consumers feel good about their current situation and about the future, they tend to spend more freely, which boosts economic growth. If they are worried about things like job security, they tend to save more and spend less, slowing economic growth and the economy.

Consumer sentiment is measured in several different ways. Three of the principal guides that economists use are:

(i) *The index of consumer expectations* – The University of Michigan Institute for Social Research, which compiles the index of consumer expectations, asks a number of questions, including whether consumers are confident enough to take on debt for such big-ticket items as cars and appliances. Responses are tabulated according to whether conditions are perceived as better than or worse than a year earlier. An index is constructed comparing the outcome to that for a base year.

(ii) *The index of consumer confidence* – The Conference Board index focuses on consumer worries about job security. This index is closely correlated with the index of consumer expectations, but tends to be more volatile.

(iii) *The Sindlinger report* – The Sindlinger report focuses on consumer's willingness to spend money on short-term purchases. It also compares the confidence levels of investors and noninvestors, which can be influenced by the performance of the financial markets.

6. *Coincident and lagging economic indicators* – The *Wall Street Journal* and other business/finance publications typically report the indexes of coincident and lagging economic indicators when it reports the index of leading economic indicators. These indexes, like the leading index, are composite indexes of several economic series that tend to move concurrently with and after changes in the general level of economic activity, respectively.

The coincident index is composed of four indicators that tend to move in concert with the business cycle:

- employees on nonagricultural payrolls
- personal income less transfer payments
- industrial production
- manufacturing and trade sales

The lagging index is composed of seven indicators that tend to lag the business cycle:

- average duration of unemployment
- inventory-to-sales ratio, manufacturing and trade
- labor cost per unit of output, manufacturing
- average prime rate
- commercial and industrial loans
- consumer installment credit to personal income ratio
- consumer price index for services

So, what value would such indexes have for forecasting economic activity? Economists have discovered that the ratio of the indexes of coincident indicators to lagging indicators provides, in general, an even greater lead time in predicting changes in economic activity than the leading index. This ratio has given a warning of a recession about four months earlier than the leading index, on average.

Thus, when both the leading index and the ratio of the indexes of the coincident and lagging indicators are up, it is a very strong bullish signal. However, when the leading index is up or level, but the ratio of coincident to lagging indexes is down, one should keep an especially wary eye on the leading economic indicators and other indicia of economic activity. A slowdown in the economy may be just around the corner.

Other Economic Indicators

Consumer Demand and the Business Cycle

If consumer demand would grow at a relatively constant sustainable rate, there would be far fewer fluctuations in economic activity and little or no business cycle. So why does consumer demand fluctuate?

As noted above, each expansion sows the seeds of the following recession because every expansion is fueled by credit. Consumers and businesses borrow to buy new homes, cars, factories, and machinery. The more they borrow and spend, the faster demand grows, pushing production into higher gear in order to keep pace with demand. But sooner or later, the upward spiral of borrowing and spending comes to an end. The strain on productive capacity forces costs higher, pushing up prices. Inflation depresses consumer sentiment and consumers respond by curtailing their expenditures. Consumers also find that their incomes cannot support the burden of additional debt repayment. Businesses, having accomplished their targeted growth in plant and equipment, cut back or cease their expenditures in this area. Once business and consumer borrowing and spending start to decline, the slump begins and production and income falls. Subsequently, inflation subsides with the drop in demand. Debt is repaid. As the demand for borrowing declines, the cost of borrowing (interest rates) also declines. Businesses that have cut back on production eventually begin to deplete their inventories. With lower borrowing costs and generally lower relative materials prices and wages, producers ultimately must increase production to meet demand. Jobs increase, layoffs are called back to work, consumer sentiment rises, and with it, consumer spending. The cycle is ready to repeat itself.

Several statistical series are especially indicative of consumer demand, including the CPI, auto sales, consumer credit, and housing starts.

1. *Consumer price index (CPI)* – The fluctuations in the CPI chart the course of inflation. Lower inflation leads to improved consumer sentiment and demand, which drives economic expansion forward.

   The CPI measures relative price changes over time. The CPI is calculated by compiling a list of goods and services purchased by the typical consumer, including such items as food, clothing, shelter, public utilities, and medical care, which make up a "market basket." The price of each item is recorded and assigned a weight according to its relative importance in the basket. Changes in the prices of each item are noted and the percentage change in the total price is reflected in the change of the index number.

   The basket of goods and services included in the index is changed periodically to reflect changes in tastes and the introduction of new goods and services or improvements in old goods and services. Although it is designed to measure overall changes in prices, it is not really a cost-of-living index. The market basket is relatively fixed. However, consumers typically substitute one good or service for another as relative prices change or with changes in income. Consequently, it is not necessarily a good measure of changes in the cost of living for any particular individual. However, it is a relatively good measure of the overall economy-wide cost of living. In addition, the CPI is the basis for adjusting Social Security payments and determining cost-of-living increases in pensions and wages, as well as for indexing of tax-rate tables and many other tax-related variables and limitations.

2. *Auto sales* – This is a critical statistic because domestic auto sales historically have led the cycle into both expansion and contraction. The auto industry, along with the cluster of industries that depends upon it (e.g., rubber tire, steel, glass, upholstery, gasoline) represents a significant share of the total economic activity. In addition, although what may be good for GM may not necessarily be good for America, GM's sales (and those of the other domestically produced autos, including foreign cars domestically made, such as Mitsubishi, Honda, and Toyota, as well as others) are a reliable indicator of overall economic activity.

3. *Consumer credit* – The *Wall Street Journal* publishes the Commerce Department's release on

consumer installment debt in the second week of the month. Changes in consumer credit have been an important barometer of consumer activity because consumers have typically borrowed heavily to finance purchases of autos and other expensive and postponable items such as appliances, furniture, home improvements, and vacations.

Both consumer sentiment and consumer credit fell steeply in the 1990-91 recession. Historically, increases in consumer credit trailed off with surges in inflation and drops in consumer sentiment. Then with each recession and the ultimate return of consumer confidence, consumer credit rebounded.

4. *Housing starts* – The Commerce Department's monthly release on housing starts is usually published in *The Wall Street Journal* between the seventeenth and twentieth of the month.

   The cyclical sensitivity of housing starts to consumer sentiment and the availability of mortgage credit is striking. Housing starts turn down well before the onset of recession, as soon as rising inflation reduces consumer confidence. The Federal Reserve's actions to reduce money supply to curtail inflation are quickly reflected in mortgage rates, which have a dramatic impact on housing demand. Typically, however, housing starts increase even before a recession has ended as consumer confidence increases and the Fed switches to an easier money policy.

   Similar to the auto industry, the housing construction industry has a significant impact on a number of supporting industries, including lumber, cement, glass, roofing, materials, heating, plumbing and electrical supplies, kitchen and laundry appliances, and furniture and furnishings.

Consumer debt and consumer demand have been the leading edge of the post-World-War-II business cycle. Ironically, their strong growth has led to cyclical problems with inflation, which periodically tended to choke off credit, demand, and economic expansion, generating recession.

As the cycle has moved from peak to contraction, rapidly rising inflation depressed consumer real income and consumer sentiment, bringing on collapse in consumer demand and inevitable recession.

CPI ↑ ➔ Consumer Sentiment ↓ ➔ Consumer Demand ↓

As the cycle has moved from contraction to recovery, reduced inflation spurred consumer sentiment and consumer demand, inevitably leading to another round of excess credit demand and inflation.

CPI ↓ ➔ Consumer Sentiment ↑ ➔ Consumer Demand ↑

Output and Efficiency

Gross national product (GNP), industrial production, and capacity utilization measure the economy's output; productivity measures its efficiency. As output increases, efficiency decreases, and inflation (as reported by the producer price index) inevitably increases.

At the peak of the cycle, when output is at its maximum, production facilities are strained to the point where production costs rise sharply. Overburdened equipment fails, accelerating the expense of maintenance and repair. The quantities of labor added to the production process are relatively greater than the increase in output. Inevitable inefficiencies force up costs, and consequently prices, even though the product itself has not changed. As the obvious result, inflation increases rapidly. With a recession's drop in production, the strain on facilities and labor eases. Costs fall, inflation declines, and the stage is set for a new round of expansion and growth.

- *Gross domestic product (GDP)* – GDP measures the total value of all the goods and services produced in the United States and is the official scale with which fluctuations in the economy are measured. The *Wall Street Journal* reports GDP about three weeks after the close of each quarter.

- *Constant-dollar (real) GDP* – Measures the final output of goods and services produced in the U.S. in one year, without including the impact of changed prices on the value of those goods. The base year is 1987. An annual change of three percent is considered good and sustainable. Growth of more than five percent is unusual and unsustainable for any lengthy period of time. The economy simply cannot produce more than that without an increase in prices because of the limits on our productive capacity at any given moment. Real GDP should increase with increases in population and technological advances. If the work force grows at a higher rate, then real GDP should grow at a higher rate, but there are limits on the rate of technological improvements and the investment capital to implement those improvements, which limit overall sustainable growth above certain limits.

- *Current-dollar (nominal) GDP* – The CPI is not the only, or even the best, measure of inflation. The *fixed-weight price index for gross domestic purchases*, which includes everything bought in the U.S., including imports, is the broadest measure of price increases. The *producer price index*, which covers wholesale prices of goods, but not services, shows the changes in prices charged by producers of finished goods.

- *Industrial production* – The index of industrial production measures changes in the output of the mining, manufacturing, and gas and electric utility sectors of the economy. It is a narrower concept than GDP because it excludes agriculture, construction, wholesale and retail trade, transportation, communications, services, finance, and government. It is more volatile than GDP, because GDP includes services, finance, and government, which are less sensitive to cyclical fluctuations.

- *Capacity utilization (factory operating rate)* – Capacity utilization is the rate at which mining, manufacturing, and public utilities industries operate, expressed as a percentage of the maximum rate at which they could operate under existing conditions. Essentially, it is a measure of what these industries are currently producing compared to the most they could produce using all their present resources.

  Capacity utilization is a short-run concept determined by a company's current physical limits; at any moment in which capacity utilization is reported, it is assumed that the company's plant and equipment cannot be increased, although labor and other inputs can.

  What bearing does capacity utilization have on the efficiency or productivity of industry? Similar to a car and its speed, industrial plant and equipment operate at greater efficiency at lower levels of utilization. As capacity utilization increases, returns diminish, just like the fuel economy of a car at higher speeds. At a certain level of utilization, the industry passes the point of diminishing returns. The point will ultimately be reached where the percentage increases in output will become smaller than the percentage increases in inputs.

  The reasons for this are numerous and reasonable. At low levels of utilization there is ample time to inspect, maintain, and repair equipment; accidental damage can be held to a minimum; and production increases can be achieved easily in a smoothly efficient plant. However, as the operating level increases, it becomes more difficult to inspect, maintain, and repair equipment.

  Furthermore, as production increases, more labor is hired, and these workers are generally less experienced and usually less efficient than the older workers. If more hours are scheduled, errors caused by fatigue and accidents will increase.

- *Labor productivity and unit labor costs* – Labor productivity measures output or production per unit of labor input (e.g., output per hour) and is the most important gauge of our nation's efficiency. Its significance cannot be overemphasized since per capita real income cannot improve, and therefore the nation's standard of living cannot rise, without an increase in per capita production.

  Unit labor cost measures the cost of labor per unit of output. It is the inverse of labor productivity. It tells one how much added labor is required to produce an additional unit of output.

Inventories

Inventories are stocks of goods on hand: raw materials, goods in process, or finished products. Individual businesses use them to bring stability to their operations, but they actually have a destabilizing effect on the business cycle overall.

Inventories are expensive. Money tied up in inventories could be invested, so the opportunity cost of inventories is the amount that could be earned by investing the money. Businesses generally want to maintain minimum inventories, but they need inventories to meet fluctuations in demand for their products, variations in the production schedules, etc. in order to maintain smooth operations and to keep customers satisfied.

How do inventories, which are so necessary to the smooth functioning of an individual business, exacerbate the business cycle?

During an expansion, as demand grows, companies will increase inventories faster than the demand to avoid shortages and possible loss of customers. As a result, industrial production increases more vigorously than it otherwise would, accentuating the cyclical expansion and the swift rise in capacity utilization. For the economy as a whole, production grows more rapidly than sales, which hastens the inevitable decrease in labor productivity and increase in unit labor costs. Thus, inventory accumulation adds to inflationary pressures.

When the economy turns down, businesses curtail production in order to prevent involuntary inventory accumulation. In fact, in anticipation of declining demand, companies rush to reduce output and to begin to liquidate inventory. But as goods are sold from inventory, output and employment are reduced more than sales. This aggravates the cycle's downturn.

Therefore, inventories are destabilizing since inventory accumulation boosts output above sales during the expansion phase of the cycle and inventory liquidation depresses output during the contraction phase.

The *inventory-sales ratio,* which is typically reported along with other business inventory statistics, is a critical statistic. It measures the number of months it would take businesses to run through stockpiles at the current sales rate. In the past, an inventory-sales ratio exceeding 1.6 was taken as a sign that inventories had become bloated and that either demand was waning or that businesses would soon begin to cut production to bring inventories more in line with sales. In either case, it was an indication that industrial production was more likely than not to fall and that a recession was looming on the horizon.

INFLATION, DEFLATION, AND DISINFLATION

Inflation is a sustained increase in price levels. Deflation is the opposite of inflation; deflation is a sustained decrease in price levels. Disinflation is a level of inflation that is declining.

Through most periods of modern history, there has been some level of inflation. At times, the rate of inflation has declined so that there was disinflation. Long periods of deflation have generally been associated with economic depressions. However, there have also been periods of stagflation where inflation has been high during periods of recession.

As described above, the consumer price index (CPI) measures relative price changes of a basket of goods over time. The CPI is often used as an overall measure of inflation.

As discussed above, inflation is often used as one of many economic indicators.

YIELD CURVES

At any point in time, a yield curve shows the relation of current interest rates to different time horizons. For example, the interest rate for an investment that matures in one year might be 2%, for 5 years 5%, and for 10 years 8%.

All other things being equal, an investment for a longer period of time is generally regarded as riskier and is rewarded with a higher interest rate than an investment for a shorter period of time. Thus, the yield curve generally reflects higher interest rates for longer investment horizons and is upward sloping.

However, there have been times when the yield curve has been downward sloping. At such times, the yield curve has reflected higher interest rates for shorter investment horizons than for longer investment horizons. During such times, the expectation is usually that interest rates in the future will be lower.

As discussed above, interest rates are often used as one of many economic indicators.

Chapter 20

TIME VALUE OF MONEY AND QUANTITATIVE ANALYSIS

WHAT IS IT?

The time value of money is an important concept for sound financial decisions. Present and future value computations provide quantitative techniques for determining the value of time in tax and financial decision-making and are essential in understanding:

1. the effect of time on the profitability of an investment

2. how the projected value of an investment's future economic returns affects the price that should be paid for it

3. how to compute the value of an investment's future economic return

Sound financial decisions depend on an understanding of the basic mathematics of compound interest. This concept is essential in analyzing the financial consequences of almost any investment.

The concept of investment, by definition, implies a delay in consumption or enjoyment. For an individual to forego current consumption or enjoyment in favor of future consumption, there must be some reward. That reward is called "profit," which must be large enough to justify (at least in the mind of the investor) the expected delay. The measure of the profit is typically called the "rate of return," or the "rate of interest."

The concept of time value of money is also crucial to the larger picture of any cash flow or goal based financial planning. Planning for the future often involves projecting current and future cash flows and needs, such as for education funding, retirement planning, and estate planning. Effective planning for the future generally involves some estimation of present or future values, so as to put such outflows and inflows on a common footing that can be evaluated. In addition to rates of returns, rates of inflation, growth, tax, and probabilities may be modeled into such planning.

For more information on the technical aspects of the time value of money and of measuring investment returns, please consult our sister-publication the *Tools & Techniques of Investment Planning*.

HOW DOES IT WORK?

The particular type of investment that a given individual will make depends both on his financial resources and risk preferences. But regardless of preferences, there are three basic underlying rate of return principles that should govern every investment: (1) "timing," (2) "quality," and (3) "quantity."

1. *Timing* – An early return of principal and income is preferable to a later return. For example, given two potential investments, one providing $1,000 now and the other providing $1,000 a year from now, the former investment should be the one selected.

   This "sooner is better than later" concept will be referred to as "timing." Tax law provides a good example of the advantages of timing. An important technique in income tax planning, and an integral part of a tax shelter investment, is the use of accelerated depreciation to recover the investor's capital more quickly. The timing benefit of accelerated depreciation as compared to straight-line depreciation is the result of keeping tax dollars in the hands of the taxpayer for a longer period of time. This provides a quicker recovery of cost than would be possible through a slower form of depreciation.

2. *Quality* – An investment with less risk is preferable to one with greater risk. Therefore, if two alternative investments offer the same rate of return, but it is more likely that the principal of the second investment could be lost, the former investment should be the one selected. This "likelihood of pay back" concept is referred to as "quality."

3. *Quantity* – Assuming investment risks are equal and the timing of the return is identical, the investment with the highest rate of return is

preferable. Therefore, if two investments have equal timing and are equally risky, but one has a higher rate of return, it should be the one selected. This "more is better than less" concept will be referred to as "quantity."

This chapter focuses on the principles inherent in the first and third of these three concepts (timing and quantity) and their interrelationship. It is only through a "time adjusted analysis" that an investment with a higher yield but a longer investment life can be effectively compared with an investment with a lower yield but a shorter life span.

In summary, the proper measure of the financial consequences of investment alternatives will focus not only on risk and the sum of the cash flows, but also reflect the differences in the expected timing of their receipt.

WHEN IS THE USE OF THIS TECHNIQUE INDICATED?

1. When an investor wishes to analyze an investment or compare alternative investments where any of the following factors is involved:

   a) "timing" (When and/or how often must cash be put in and/or taken out of the investment?)

   b) "quantity" (At what interest rate is the investment earning or growing?)

2. When planning for future financial needs (e.g., education, retirement, estate planning) while taking into consideration future income sources (e.g., investments, insurance, social security, retirement benefits).

ADVANTAGES

1. Makes it possible to determine whether an investor can afford to commit funds to a particular investment for the length of time required.

2. Permits a quantitative comparison of alternative investments with different rates of return and different investment life spans.

3. Allows future funding shortfalls to be identified and steps taken to address such needs as soon as possible.

DISADVANTAGES

1. Heavy reliance on quantitative techniques for evaluating alternatives may overshadow the need to review subjectively the appropriateness of an investment. There are times when an investor should rely on his "gut feelings" and "play a hunch."

2. There are such a large number of measurement devices that the choice of the wrong one in a given situation may easily occur. For example, what would be the appropriate measuring tool to use in estimating the value of an investment 10 years from now? It would not be helpful to measure the future value of a *series* of payments during that period. It would, however, be appropriate to compute the future value (in 10 years) of a single, lump sum invested today.

3. The results of any quantitative analysis are only as good as the initial information provided. Financial analysis is subject to the same danger often raised by computer users: "Garbage in, garbage out." For example, in evaluating the present value of a retirement fund needed 10 years from now, it would be a mistake to use an interest rate of 14% if it is known that an investment can never earn at a rate greater than 10% per year. The use of a 14% interest assumption would provide an overly optimistic and misleading answer. In turn, this would lead to the possible underfunding of retirement needs.

PRESENT VALUE AND FUTURE VALUE

The right measurement device in a particular situation depends upon the nature of the problem to be solved. In this section, each of the basic time value of money concepts used in financial planning will be reviewed. These present value and future value concepts can also be used as the building blocks for other time value of money calculations.

I. Computing the Future Value of a Lump Sum

PROBLEM: If I have a lump sum of $______ today, how do I calculate the value of that lump sum ______ years in the future assuming I earn ____% on my investment?

SOLUTION: Go to Appendix D, Compound Interest Table (future value of a lump sum). This table reflects the amount $1 will be worth in a given number of years at various interest rates. For example, to find how much \$10,000 invested today will be worth in 5 years, if it grows at the rate of 10% per year, you would multiply \$10,000 by the factor found in the "5-year" row under the 10% column. That factor is 1.6105. Therefore, \$10,000 invested today will be worth \$16,105 in 5 years.

This compound interest table provides a quick way to determine the future value of an investment or other asset such as a family home. However, this table contains only a limited number of years and interest rate assumptions. To compute the future value of an asset where the number of years or interest rate is not covered by the table, it may be necessary to utilize the following formula:

Equation FVLS

$$FV = PV \times (1 + i)^n$$

In this formula,

n = The Number of Years (Periods) in the Future

FV = Future Value Amount

PV = Present Value Amount

i = Interest Rate for Each Year (Period)

Applying the formula to our example,

$$FV = PV \times (1 + i)^n$$

$$FV = \$10{,}000 \times (1 + 0.10)^5$$

$$FV = \$16{,}105$$

The formula is a shortcut way of expressing the annual 10% compounding, in our example, of the initial \$10,000 investment for the 5-year investment period. The actual, manual computation for the entire investment period can be charted as follows:

	Beginning Balance		Interest @ 10%		Ending Balance
Year 1	\$10,000	+	\$1,000	=	\$11,000
Year 2	\$11,000	+	\$1,100	=	\$12,100
Year 3	\$12,100	+	\$1,210	=	\$13,310
Year 4	\$13,310	+	\$1,331	=	\$14,641
Year 5	\$14,641	+	\$1,464	=	\$16,105

The Compound Interest Table in Appendix A carries compounding factors to four decimal places; other compound interest tables may show more or fewer decimal places and therefore cause the final result to be different. A further shortcoming of tables is evident when, for example, the interest rate or the compounding period is more complex (such as an interest rate of 10.375%, or a compounding period of 20 years, 7 months). In such cases, interpolation between numbers in the tables could be used.

A pocket calculator can handle the multiple computations necessary. Many financial calculators are sophisticated enough to perform the calculation by merely entering the **P** (principal), **n** (number of periods), and **i** (interest rate) numbers. In addition, personal computers easily can be programmed to perform the formula computations, as well as provide a printout of the future value at any interim period.

II. Computing the Present Value of a Future Lump Sum

PROBLEM: If I will have a lump sum of \$______ in ___ years, how do I calculate the present value of my investment, assuming it will earn interest at the rate of ___? In other words, what is the equivalent today of \$______ payable as a lump sum ___ years in the future?

SOLUTION: Go to Appendix A, Present Value Table (present value of a future lump sum). This table reflects the present value of \$1 received at the end of a given number of years in the future at various interest rates. For example, to find out the present value of \$100,000 to be received in 20 years, assuming a growth rate of 10% per year, you would multiply \$100,000 by the factor found in the "20-year" row under the 10% column. That factor is 0.1486. Therefore the \$100,000 to be received in 20 years has a present value of \$14,860.

This present value table was compiled using the following mathematical formula that can be used in cases that are not included in the table:

Equation PVLS

$$PV = \frac{FV}{(1+i)^n}$$

Again, in this formula,

PV = Present Value Amount

FV = Future Value Amount

n = The Number of Years (Periods) Until the Future Payment

i = Interest Rate for Each Year (Period)

Applying the formula to our example,

$$PV = \frac{FV}{(1 + i)^n}$$

$$PV = \frac{\$100{,}000}{(1 + 0.1)^{20}}$$

$$PV = \$14{,}860$$

A careful look at these first two formulas will reveal that they are really the same formula, but used to solve for different unknown elements. The first formula is used to determine the future value of a lump sum when the present value, number of years, and interest rate are known. The second formula is used to determine the present value when the future value, number of years, and interest rate are known. Either formula can be used to compute any one of the four factors in the equation, so long as the other three are known.

For example, either formula could be used if you wanted to know how many years it would take for a present value of $14,860 to grow to $100,000, if the annual interest rate earned on the amount was 10%. You could also use either the table in Appendix A or Appendix D, provided the three known elements can be located in the table. For example, using the table in Appendix A, the Present Value Table, looking under the 10% column we can see that it will take 20 years for a present value of 0.1486 to grow to $1. Multiplying these amounts by 100,000, we see that it will take 20 years for a present value of $14,860 to grow to $100,000.

If the present value in the above example were $15,000, rather than $14,860, the present value table could be used only to estimate the actual period needed to compound the $15,000 to $100,000 at a 10% interest rate. In this case the formula would be needed to arrive at the actual compounding period required. It would then make sense to use a financial calculator or a computer to solve the problem.

Plugging this information into the second formula, the solution would look like this:

$$PV = \frac{FV}{(1 + i)^n}$$

$$\$14{,}860 = \frac{\$100{,}000}{(1 + 0.10)^n}$$

$$n = 20 \text{ years}$$

As a further example, let's calculate the interest rate at which $14,860 would have to grow in order to compound to $100,000 in 20 years. Using the second formula:

$$PV = \frac{FV}{(1 + i)^n}$$

$$\$14{,}860 = \frac{\$100{,}000}{(1 + i)^{20}}$$

$$i = 0.10 \text{ or } 10\%$$

III. Calculating the Future Value of a Regular Series of Payments

PROBLEMS:

A. If, beginning today, I invest $______ a year for ___ years, how do I calculate what the value of that series of investments would be ___ years from now assuming I earn a compounded interest rate of ___% on my investments?

This type of problem requires the calculation of the future value of a regular series of payments. Where each payment is made at the beginning of a compounding period (for example, at the beginning of each year), the process is known as an "annuity due" or an "annuity in advance."

B. What if the first payment in my series of investments is not made until one year from now? In this case the process is known as an "ordinary annuity" or an "annuity in arrears."

SOLUTIONS:

A. Go to Appendix E, Compounded Annual Annuity (In Advance) Table (future value of an annuity due). This table reflects the amount to which $1 deposited at the beginning of each year will accumulate at compound interest for a given number of years at various interest rates. For example, to find out how much $1,000 a year, invested at the *beginning* of each year, will be worth at the end of 20 years, if the invested annual payments grow at the rate of 10% per year, multiply $1,000 by the factor found in the "20-year" row under the 10% column. That factor is 63.0025. Therefore, the investments of $1,000 per year, as of the beginning of each year, would be worth $63,002.50 at the end of 20 years.

This annuity table was compiled using the following formula that can be used in cases not included in the table:

Equation FVAD

$$FV = A \times (1 + i) \times \left[\frac{(1 + i)^n - 1}{i} \right]$$

In this formula,

FV = Future Value Amount

A = The Amount of the Annual (Annuity) Investment (Payment)

n = The Number of Years (Periods) of Annual Investments (Payments)

i = Interest Rate for each Year (Period)

Applying the formula to our example,

$$FV = A \times (1 + i) \times \left[\frac{(1 + i)^n - 1}{i} \right]$$

$$FV = \$1{,}000 \times (1 + 0.10) \times \left[\frac{(1 + 0.10)^{20} - 1}{0.10} \right]$$

$$FV = \$63{,}002$$

In an investment context, a common example of an "annuity due" is the amount an investor would deposit at the beginning of each year in order to provide funds for retirement at a specified retirement age.

B. Go to Appendix F, Compounded Annual Annuity (In Arrears) Table (future value of an ordinary annuity). This table reflects the amount to which $1 deposited at the end of each year will accumulate at compound interest for a given number of years at various interest rates. For example, to find out how much $1,000 a year, invested at the end of each year, will be worth at the end of 20 years, if the invested annual payments grow at the rate of 10% per year, multiply $1,000 by the factor found in the "20-year" row under the 10% column. That factor is 57.2750. Therefore, the investments of $1,000 per year, as of the end of each year, would be worth $57,275 at the end of 20 years.

This annuity table was compiled using the following mathematical formula that can be used in cases not included in the table:

Equation FVOA

$$FV = A \times \left[\frac{(1 + i)^n - 1}{i} \right]$$

In this formula,

FV = Future Value Amount

n = The Number of Years (Periods) of Annual Investments (Payments)

A = The Amount of the Annual (Annuity) Investment (Payment)

i = Interest Rate for each Year (Period)

Applying the formula to our example,

$$FV = A \times \left[\frac{(1 + i)^n - 1}{i} \right]$$

$$FV = \$1{,}000 \times \left[\frac{(1 + 0.10)^{20} - 1}{0.10} \right]$$

$$FV = \$57{,}275$$

In an investment context, an example of an "ordinary annuity" is the deposits an investor would make at the end of each year in order to provide funds for retirement at a specified retirement age.

It is important to compare the future value of the series of payments made at the beginning of each year ($63,002) with the future value of the series of payments made at the end of each year ($57,275). This $5,727 difference results from the additional compounding on all of the payments.

If interest is equal to 0%, then the future value of an annuity (ordinary or due) equals the sum of all payments, or A x n.

IV. Computing the Present Value of a Regular Series of Receipts

PROBLEM: If, beginning one year from today, I receive $______ a year for ___ years, how do I calculate the present value of that series of payments, assuming a ___% discount rate?

SOLUTION: Go to Appendix C, Compound Discount Table (present value of an ordinary annuity). This table reflects the present value of $1 received annually at the end of each year for a given number of years at various discount rates.

For example, to compute the present value of $1,000 received at the end of each year for a 20-year period, discounted at the rate of 10% per year, multiply $1,000 by the factor found in the "20-year" row under the 10% column. That factor is 8.5136. Therefore, the receipt of $1,000 at the end of each year for the next 20 years has a present value of $8,513.60.

This annuity table was compiled using the following formula that can be used in cases not included in the table:

Equation PVOA

$$PV = A \times (1 \div i) \times \left[1 - \frac{1}{(1+i)^n} \right]$$

In this formula,

P = Present Value Amount

A = The Amount of the Annual (Annuity) Receipts

i = Interest Rate for each Year (Period)

n = The Number of Years (Periods) of Annual Receipts

Applying the formula to our example,

$$PV = A \times (1 \div i) \times \left[1 - \frac{1}{(1+i)^n} \right]$$

$$PV = \$1{,}000 \times (1 \div 0.10) \times \left[1 - \frac{1}{(1+0.10)^{20}} \right]$$

$$PV = \$8{,}513$$

The corresponding factor for the present value of an annuity with payments at the beginning of each year can be found in Appendix B, Compound Discount Table (present value of an annuity due). The corresponding formula is:

Equation PVAD

$$PV = A \times (1 \div i) \times \left[1 - \frac{1}{(1+i)^n} \right] \times (1+i)$$

If interest is equal to 0%, then the present value of an annuity (ordinary or due) equals the sum of all payments, or A x n.

V. Practical Examples

1. PROBLEM: Rich Stevens, age 53, has just inherited $100,000 which he would like to use as part of his retirement nest egg. Rich would like to know just how much the $100,000 will be worth in 12 years, when he will reach age 65, assuming the funds can be invested for the entire period at a 12% annual rate. He would also like to know what the future value of the $100,000 would be in only 7 years, when he reaches age 60, in case he decides to retire early.

SOLUTION: Using the table in Appendix D, the future value of the $100,000 at the end of 12 years and 7 years can be computed as follows:

	Present Value		12% Interest Factor		Future Value
12 Years	$100,000	x	3.8960	=	$389,600
7 Years	$100,000	x	2.2107	=	$221,170

2. PROBLEM: Now that Rich knows how much the $100,000 inheritance will be worth in both cases, he would like to know how much he could withdraw from the fund in equal installments at the end of each year from the year he reaches age 65 until he reaches age 70½, the year he must start withdrawing funds from his individual retirement account (IRA). Rich assumes the funds will continue to earn at a 12% annual rate. In other words, Rich would like to know the annual year-end payment from (1) a 6-year annuity (from age 65 to the year he will be 70½), earning 12% annually on a principal sum of $389,600, and (2) an 11-year annuity (from age 60 to the year he will be 70½), earning 12% annually on a principal sum of $221,070.

SOLUTION: Using the table in Appendix C, the year-end annual annuity payment amounts can be computed as follows:

	Principal Sum		12% Annuity Factor		Annual Annuity Amount
6-Year Annuity	$389,600	÷	4.1114	=	$94,761
11-Year Annuity	$221,070	÷	5.9377	=	$37,232

3. PROBLEM: Rich has determined that he will need $60,000 per year from the inheritance fund to handle his living needs until he reaches age 70½. Assuming the fund will continue to earn 12% annually, at what age can Rich afford to retire? (Rich has already decided not to touch his IRA funds until the latest possible date, believing he can cover his living costs with the inheritance until that time. He is even willing to adjust his retirement date by a year or so if need be.)

SOLUTION: This problem is more difficult, but a reasonably accurate answer can be computed using "trial and error" and the tables in Appendix C and Appendix D.

We have already determined that if Rich waits until age 65 to retire, the inheritance will grow, at a 12% annual interest rate, to $389,600 when he retires. The $389,600 will provide him with a 6-year annual annuity of $94,761, until he reaches age 70½. This annual annuity is $34,761 per year more than the $60,000 Rich believes he needs. Therefore, Rich should be able to retire before reaching age 65.

On the other hand, we have also computed that Rich's inheritance will grow, at a 12% rate, to only $221,070 by the time he reaches age 60. In this case the resulting annual annuity would be only $37,232 until he reaches age 70½, 11 years after retiring. This annual annuity is $22,768 ($60,000 – $37,232) per year short of Rich's $60,000 estimated annual need until reaching age 70½. Consequently, it does not appear that Rich can retire as early as age 60.

On a trial and error basis, let's compute what would happen if Rich retires at age 62. The $100,000 would grow for 9 years at 12% to $277,310, computed as follows, using the table in Appendix D:

	Present Value		12% Interest Factor		Future Value
9 Years	$100,000	x	2.7731	=	$277,310

The $277,310 would provide Rich an annuity for 9 years at 12%, until he reaches age 70½, of $52,046, computed as follows, using the table in Appendix C:

	Principal Sum		12% Annuity Factor		Annual Annuity Amount
9-Year Annuity	$277,310	÷	5.3282	=	$52,046

On this basis, Rich falls $7,954 short of reaching his goal of a $60,000 annual annuity if he retires at age 62. Let's see what happens if he retires at age 63. The $100,000 would grow for 10 years at 12% to $310,580, computed as follows, using the table in Appendix D:

	Present Value		12% Interest Factor		Future Value
10 Years	$100,000	x	3.1058	=	$310,580

The $310,580 would provide Rich an annuity for 8 years at 12%, until he reaches age 70½, of $62,521, computed as follows, using the table in Appendix C:

	Principal Sum		12% Annuity Factor		Annual Annuity Amount
8-Year Annuity	$310,580	÷	4.9676	=	$62,521

On this basis, Rich will exceed his goal of a $60,000 annual annuity by $2,521, if he retires at age 63. Therefore, although the tables in Appendix C and Appendix D cannot provide an exact retirement date, they can be used to provide a reasonable approximation. In this case,

Rich Stevens can attain his retirement goal of a $60,000 annual annuity, to last until he reaches age 70½, using his $100,000 inheritance, if he retires sometime just before attaining age 63.

4. PROBLEM: Rich has decided that he wants to retire at age 60. He would like to know how much of his other funds need be set aside with his $100,000 inheritance in order to reach his goal of a $60,000 annuity from age 60 until the year he reaches age 70½. Rich assumes the funds can continue to earn at a 12% annual rate.

SOLUTION: The first step in determining the amount that must be added to the $100,000 inheritance is to determine the lump sum needed as of the anticipated retirement date in 7 years (age 60). At age 60, Rich will need $356,262 in order to provide an annual annuity of $60,000 for the 11 years from age 60 until the year he reaches age 70½. This lump sum can be computed as follows, using the table in Appendix C (present value of an annuity):

	Annual Annuity Amount		12% Annuity Factor		Principal Sum
11-Year Annuity	$60,000	x	5.9377	=	$356,262

In order for Rich to accumulate $356,262 by the time he retires at age 60, he must currently invest, at a 12% annual rate, a lump sum amount of $161,137, which can be computed in the following manner, using the table in Appendix A:

	Future Value		12% Interest Factor		Present Value
7 Years	$356,262	x	0.4523	=	$161,137

Since Rich has $100,000 from his inheritance, he must add $61,137 in order to accumulate the $356,262 needed to fund an 11-year, $60,000 annuity, to begin in 7 years, when Rich reaches age 60.

5. PROBLEM: Suppose Rich Stevens does not have $61,137 of other funds? How much must he set aside at the beginning of each year over the next seven years, together with the $100,000 lump sum from his inheritance, to reach his $356,262 objective at age 60?

SOLUTION: The $100,000 will grow to $221,070 in the 7 years until Rich reaches age 60, assuming a 12% annual interest rate (see the solution to Problem 1 for this computation). The shortfall at age 60 would be $135,192, the difference between the $356,262 needed and the $221,070 compounded from the original $100,000 inheritance. The $135,192 shortfall can be funded with annual investments of $11,964 computed as follows, using the table in Appendix E:

	Future Value		12% Interest Factor		Annual Investment
7 Years	$135,192	÷	11.2997	=	$11,964

TAXES, INFLATION, AND GROWTH

At times it will be necessary to factor taxes, inflation, and growth into the time value of money concepts of present and future values. Taxes and inflation may reduce the time value of an investment. Sometimes, annuity payments may be determined in a way that takes into account growth in payments, perhaps to reflect inflation.

I. Taxes

Taxes reduce the effective rate of return on investments. However, different investments may be subject to tax at different times. Also, different taxpayers and different investments may be subject to different rates of tax. Furthermore, tax rates may be different in different years. All other things being equal, a higher tax rate reduces the rate of return more than a lower tax rate.

If an investor is taxed annually on investment income, the rate of return can be adjusted to an after-tax rate of return by multiplying the rate of return by one minus the investor's tax rate. For example, an investor earns 8% before tax and is subject to a 25% tax on such earnings. The investor has an after-tax rate of return of 6% [8% x (1 – 25%)]. This after-tax rate of return could be used as the rate of return in any of the present and future value formulas above.

If the investor is taxed only at some later time (i.e., tax is deferred), perhaps on distribution or disposition, the investment could be valued using a before-tax rate of return with tax subtracted at the later time. For example, an investor makes a deductible (before-tax) contribution of $2,000 to a traditional IRA. The IRA contribution grows at an 8% before-tax rate of return to $10,000, when it is distributed. If the distribution is subject to a 25% tax, the investor is left with $7,500 [$10,000 x (1 – 25%)]. [The investor would also have received a tax deduction at the time of contribution worth $400 ($2,000 x 25%) which could also be invested.]

Assume instead that the investor makes a nondeductible (after-tax) contribution of \$2,000 to a traditional IRA. The IRA contribution grows at an 8% after-tax rate of return to \$10,000, when it is distributed. If the distribution is subject to a 25% tax, the investor is left with \$8,000 [\$2,000 + (\$10,000 - \$2,000) x (1 – 25%)].

When capital gains are factored in and taxed periodically, while dividends are received and taxed annually, the calculation of present and future values can become quite complex. Generally, the way to make such complex calculations is to break the valuation down into its separate parts. A spreadsheet is often useful.

II. Inflation/Growth

Often investment analyses and other financial planning problems involve adjustments for inflation or for expected systematic increments or decrements of payments or cash flows over time. For example, when planning for how much one must accumulate for retirement, it is common to assume that the amount needed each year in retirement will increase as a result of inflation. The annuity formulas presented earlier will compute the present value of a series of level payments for a specified number of years, but how does one compute the present value if the payments are assumed to be increasing at some constant rate rather than remaining level?

Actually, the formulas given above are generally still perfectly applicable, with some slight modification, if one substitutes inflation-adjusted or growth-adjusted rates for nominal rates.

The inflation- or growth-adjusted rate of return, ρ, is defined as follows, where r is the nominal rate of return and g is the inflation or growth factor:

Equation RIA

$$\rho = (r - g) \div (1 + g)$$

For example, an investor earns 12% on her investment for the year. However, inflation for the year is 4%. Her real inflation-adjusted rate of return is calculated as follows.

$$\rho = (12\% - 4\%) \div (1 + 4\%) = 7.69\%.$$

Example. A client's child will be attending college in 5 years. The client wants to know how much she will need to set aside today to pay the first year's tuition and fees. Assume current tuition and fees are \$36,000, and inflation for college costs averages 6%, and she can earn 5% on the money she invests for this purpose. The amount needed can be computed directly using just the present value equation PVLS above with the inflation-adjusted rate of return of –0.9434% [(5% - 6%) ÷ (1 + 6%)] (ρ), 5 years (n), and the \$36,000 goal (FV). She will need to invest \$37,747 today.

$$PV = \frac{FV}{(1 + \rho)^n}$$

$$PV = \frac{\$36{,}000}{(1 - 0.9434\%)^5}$$

$$PV = \$37{,}747$$

Inflation/Growth Adjusted ROR and Annuities

The inflation/growth-adjusted rate becomes much more useful when dealing with calculations involving annuities. For inflation-adjusted ordinary annuities where the payment is assumed to grow at g% per period, the present and future values can be computed by adjusting the annuity formulas for the growth of payments. Annuities with such fixed adjustments for inflation are sometimes referred to as serial payments. The inflation/growth adjusted formulas for such annuity payments follows.

Equation PVOAg

$$PV = Pmt \times \left[\frac{1 - (1 + \rho)^{-n}}{\rho}\right] \times (1 + g)^{-1}, \text{ if } \rho \neq 0$$

$$PV = Pmt \times n \times (1 + g)^{-1}, \text{ if } \rho = 0$$

Equation PVADg

$$PV = Pmt \times \left[\frac{1 - (1 + \rho)^{-n}}{\rho}\right] \times (1 + \rho), \text{ if } \rho \neq 0$$

$$PV = Pmt \times n, \text{ if } \rho = 0$$

Equation FVOAg

$$FV = Pmt \times (1 + g)^{n-1} \times \left[\frac{(1 + \rho)^n - 1}{\rho} \right], \text{ if } \rho \neq 0$$

$$FV = Pmt \times n \times (1 + g)^{n-1}, \text{ if } \rho = 0$$

Equation FVADg

$$FV = Pmt \times (1 + g)^{n-1} \times \left[\frac{(1 + \rho)^n - 1}{\rho} \right] \times (1 + r), \text{ if } \rho \neq 0$$

$$FV = Pmt \times n \times (1 + g)^{n-1} \times (1 + r), \text{ if } \rho = 0$$

Example. A client's child will be attending college in 5 years. The client wants to know how much she will need to set aside today to pay four years of tuition and fees. Assume current tuition and fees are $36,000, and inflation for college costs averages 6%, and she can earn 5% on the money she invests for this purpose. She will need to invest $153,160 today.

One way to calculate the amount required derives from realizing that the present value of a 4-year annuity due commencing at the end of 5 years is equal to the value of a 9-year annuity due commencing today less the value of a 5-year annuity due commencing today.

Using equation PVADg with n = 9, ρ = –0.9434%, and Pmt = $36,000 (use the current college cost value since the analysis starts from today), the present value of a 9-year inflation-adjusted annuity is $336,621. Similarly, using equation PVADg with n = 5, ρ = –0.9434%, and Pmt = $36,000, the present value of a 5-year inflation-adjusted annuity is $183,461. The difference is $153,160 ($336,621 - $183,461).

NET PRESENT VALUE AND INTERNAL RATE OF RETURN

Often, an investment will consist of one of more amounts paid by the investor (negative cash flow) and one or more amounts received by the investor (positive cash flow). Furthermore, the cash flows may be irregular, with different amounts paid or received in different years. Net present value calculations apply the present value building blocks above to calculate a net present value for such negative and positive cash flows. Alternatively, internal rate of return calculations can be used to estimate what an investment with negative and positive cash flows would earn, building on the same present and future value building blocks. A couple of other simple methods for evaluating investments are also discussed here.

Alternative investments can be compared using the following methods.

1. *Net present value* is the difference between the present value of all future benefits of an investment and the present value of all capital contributions. This method measures the tradeoff between the cash invested and the benefits projected.

2. *Internal rate of Return* is that rate at which the present value of all the future benefits an investor will receive from an investment exactly equals the present value of all the capital contributions the investor will be required to make. IRR is generally used to compare the *effective* interest rates of two or more investments.

3. *Adjusted rate of return,* often called "effective rate of return," is calculated by assuming that all of the investment's benefits (not only cash inflows but also tax savings) are invested at the "alternative reinvestment rate." The alternative reinvestment rate is the after-tax rate at which money can be safely invested.

4. *Pay back period* measures the relative periods of time needed to recover the investor's capital (income received after the pay back period will be considered gain).

5. *Cash on cash,* as its name implies, analyzes an investment by dividing the annual cash flow by the amount of the cash investment in order to determine the cash return on the cash invested.

I. Net Present Value

Net present value is an extension of the present value concepts discussed above. Present value is the amount that must be invested now to produce a given future value. For instance, if I assume I can invest money at 10%, I must have $1,000 now in order to have it grow to $1,100 one year from now. $1,000 is the present value of $1,100 to be received in one year. Obviously, the present value is affected by (1) the interest (investment analysts call this the "discount") rate, as well as (2) the length of the investment period.

Present value is a simple means of comparing two investments. For example, I am considering an investment of $1,000 that will pay me $1,200 three years from now. I can also invest the $1,000 in an alternative investment of equal risk and earn 10% on my money. Which investment should I make?

An easy way to compare the investments is to compute the present value of the $1,200 payable three years from now at a 10% discount rate. The present value of the first investment is only $902, while obviously the present value of $1,000 in hand today is $1,000. Therefore, from a pure present value standpoint, the proposed investment is inferior to the alternative of simply investing the $1,000 at 10%.

"Net" present value is the difference between (1) the present value of all future benefits to be realized from an investment and (2) the present value of all capital contributions into the investment. A negative net present value should result in an almost automatic rejection of the investment. A positive net present value indicates that the investment is worth further consideration since the present value of the stream of dollars the investor will recover exceeds the present value of the stream of dollars the investor will have to pay out.

The problem is what discount rate should be used in computing the present values of the cash inflows and cash outflows? Usually this discount rate will be the minimal acceptable rate of return. This is usually found by determining the cost of capital or, as in the example above, determining the rate an alternative investment of similar quality can earn. In the example above, the rate was 10%. Once this so-called "reinvestment rate" is determined, it can be used as the discount factor to compute the present value of the money invested and the present value of the expected return.

These present value amounts are then netted against each other. If the result is positive, the investment will exceed the reinvestment rate and should be considered. If the net present value is a negative number and falls short of the reinvestment rate, the investment under consideration should be rejected.

To the extent that a proposed investment yields a positive net present value, the investment provides a potential "cushion" for safety. It may also allow the investor to incur certain additional costs (such as attorney's, accountant's, or financial planner's fees in connection with the analysis of the investment) and still achieve the desired reinvestment rate.

An example of the use of net present value analysis may be helpful.

Assume that at the beginning of the year an individual has been shown an investment opportunity requiring a lump sum outlay of $10,000. Currently the funds he would use for this investment are in a money market fund earning 6% annually, net after taxes. The investment proposal projects the following after-tax cash flows at the end of each year.

Year	Amount Received
1	$ 2,000
2	1,500
3	750
4	500
5	10,000
Total Receipts	$14,750

Based solely on net present value analysis, should he make the investment?

The first step in the analysis would be to determine the appropriate reinvestment rate. In this example, the investor currently is earning a net after tax return of 6% in what he believes is a "safe" investment. To warrant any further consideration, this proposed investment must have a net present value of at least the benchmark reinvestment rate of 6%.

Does the proposed investment meet that benchmark? The stream of dollars projected to be received from the proposed investment has a present value of $11,720 assuming a 6% discount rate. The net present value is a positive $1,720 (the difference between the present value of the future stream of cash inflows, $11,720, and the $10,000 present value of the lump sum outflow of $10,000). Therefore, the proposal does deserve further consideration.

But what if the investor demands a rate of return from the proposed investment higher than his benchmark rate of 6% in order to compensate for the additional risk? If he sets a 15% rate as his minimum, the present value of the stream of dollars from the proposed investment is only $8,624. The net present value is a negative $1,376 (the difference between the present value of the future stream of cash inflows, $8,624, and the $10,000 present value of the lump sum outflow of $10,000). Therefore, the proposal does not deserve further consideration.

What discount rate when applied to the expected stream of cash inflows from the proposed investment has a present value exactly equal to the $10,000 lump sum investment? That discount rate is 10.5%. This computation illustrates the concept of Internal Rate of Return, discussed more fully below.

How to Compute Net Present Value

A. Lump Sum Investment, Single Future Receipt

Assume an individual makes a lump sum investment at the beginning of year one of $10,000. The expected return on this investment is $15,000 (after tax) to be received as a single amount at the end of year five. The investor's discount rate (for an alternative "safe" investment) is 6% after tax. What is the net present value of the investment under consideration?

To compute the net present value of the investment, the following basic steps are necessary.

1. Compute the present value of the $10,000 investment. Since only one payment is required (immediately at the beginning of the cash flow period), the present value of that payment would be $10,000.

2. Compute the present value of the $15,000 future amount to be received (at the end of year five) using the 6% discount rate. Refer to the Present Value Table in Appendix A. The applicable factor for the present value of $1 at the end of 5 years, using a 6% discount rate, is 0.7473. This factor is multiplied by the $15,000 amount to be received in the future. The present value is therefore $11,210 ($15,000 x 0.7473).

3. Subtract the present value of the $10,000 lump sum investment ($10,000) from the present value of the $15,000 single payment to be received ($11,210). The net amount is +$1,210; a "positive" net present value. [Note that if the $15,000 were not received until the end of seven years, the present value of the receipt would be only $9,977 ($15,000 x 0.6651 discount factor), resulting in a "negative" net present value of $23.]

B. Lump Sum Investment, Multiple Future Receipts

Assume an individual makes a lump sum investment at the beginning of year one of $10,000, the present value of which is $10,000 [Step (1)].

The expected return on this investment (received at each year end) and the present value of each receipt, discounted at 6% are as follows [Step 2].

Year	Amount Received	PV @ 6%
1	$ 2,000	$ 1,887
2	1,500	1,335
3	750	630
4	500	396
5	$10,000	$7,473
Total Receipts	$14,750	$11,721

[The present value amounts in this table were computed using the Present Value Table in Appendix A. Computations made using different tables or software may vary slightly due to rounding differences, including the number of decimal places that factors are rounded.]

The net present value is therefore $1,721 ($11,721 present value of the future flow of receipts, less $10,000 present value of the lump sum investment) [Step 3].

C. Multiple Investments, Multiple Future Receipts

Continuing the above example, assume that instead of one $10,000 investment at the beginning of year one, there will be two $5,000 payments, one at the beginning of year one, and the other at the beginning of year two. The present value of the investment, using the same 6% discount rate would be computed as follows [Step 1].

	Year	Payment	PV @ 6%
[Beginning]	1	$ 5,000	$ 5,000
[Beginning]	2	5,000	4,717
Total Payments		$10,000	$ 9,717

When multiple investment payments are required over a period of time, the present value of these payments must be determined. In this example, the present value of the first $5,000 investment is $5,000. The present value of the second $5,000 is $4,717, $5,000 multiplied by the present value factor of 0.9434 (since the payment is made at the beginning of the second year, the present value factor for the end of the first year is appropriate). If it is assumed that the present value of the receipts are the same as above, $11,721 [Step 2], then the net present value of this investment is $2,004 ($11,721 - $9,717) [Step 3].

II. Internal Rate of Return

When the concept of net present value (NPV) was introduced above, it was defined as the difference between the present value of all future benefits to be realized from an investment and the present value of all capital contributions into the investment. The discount (interest) rate at which these two present values will be equal is the internal rate of return (IRR) of the investment.

Stated in other terms, in computing IRR the interest rate sought is that rate at which inflows and outflows of cash, discounted to present value, will equal the original principal. It is a method of determining what percentage rate of return cash inflows will provide based on a known investment (cash outflow) and estimated cash inflows.

Internal rate of return is really the same as a present value computation except that the discount rate is either not known or not given. The financial advisor is therefore attempting to find that rate which will discount the future cash inflows so that they will precisely equal the investor's initial investment.

Confused? Let's try an example.

Assume your client is considering the purchase of a $100,000 unit of a limited partnership. The full $100,000 is due at the beginning of the year. You have estimated that, after taxes, she should be receiving the following cash inflows at the end of each year.

End of Year	In-Flow
1	$ 10,000
2	10,000
3	120,000

If we were to do a NPV analysis of this investment, looking at several alternative rates of return, it would look as presented in Figure 20.1.

At an 8% rate, this investment has a positive net present value of $13,092. That is, if you had invested $100,000 at 8% (for example, in a certificate of deposit) the present value of the future cash inflow should be $100,000. But, in the investment above, the present value of the expected cash inflows is actually $113,092, $13,092 higher than it should be at 8%. Therefore, it is obvious that the investment is generating a significantly higher rate of return than 8%.

At a 10% rate, this investment has a positive net present value of $7,513. That is, if you had invested $100,000 at 10% the present value of the future cash inflow should be $100,000. But, in the investment above, the present value of the expected cash inflows is actually $107,513, $7,513 higher than it should be at 10%. Therefore, it appears that the investment is generating a higher rate of return than 10%.

At a 20% rate, this investment has a negative net present value of $15,279. That is, if you had invested $100,000 at 20% the present value of the future cash inflow should be $100,000. But, in the investment above, the present value of the expected cash inflows is actually $84,721, $15,279 lower than it should be at 20%. Therefore, it is

Figure 20.1

Outflows	Amount Paid	Present Value of Amount Paid @ 8%	10%	12.9%	20%	
Year 1	-$100,000	-$100,000	-$100,000	-$100,000	-$100,000	(Beginning of year)
Inflows	**Amount Received**	**Present Value of Amount Received @ 8%**	**10%**	**12.9%**	**20%**	
Year 1	$ 10,000	$ 9,259	$ 9,091	$ 8,857	$ 8,333	(End of year)
2	10,000	8,573	8,264	7,845	6,944	
3	120,000	95,260	90,158	83,387	69,444	
Total of Present Value of Inflows		$113,092	$107,513	$100,089	$84,721	
Net Present Value (NPV)		$ 13,092	$ 7,513	$ 89	-$15,279	

obvious that the investment is generating a lower rate of return than 20%.

What is the actual rate of return on this investment? Obviously somewhere between 10% and 20%. Internal rate of return is a method of computing that exact rate. The chart in Figure 20.1 illustrates that the internal rate of return of the investment is approximately 12.9%. That is, the present value of the cash outflows ($100,000) is roughly equal to the present value of the cash inflows ($100,089) when discounted at a 12.9% rate.

How to Compute Internal Rate of Return

In manually computing the IRR of this investment the first step is to compute the NPV using a preliminary estimate of the IRR. If the first computation results in a positive NPV, a second calculation, using a higher discount rate, will be necessary. If a negative NPV is computed, the recalculation will require a lower discount rate. The process would have to continue until you arrive at a NPV of $0 (i.e., the rate at which the present value of the cash outflows equals the present value of the cash inflows).

If we use 8% as our initial (test) discount rate, we find a positive net present value, and therefore must try a higher discount rate. On our second attempt, using 10%, we still have a positive NPV. Our third computation, using 20%, yields a negative NPV. Therefore, the IRR must be between 10% and 20%.

After several attempts, we finally try a rate of 12.9% that results in a positive NPV of only $89. We're getting close. For most planning purposes, this would be close enough. To do the job more accurately and efficiently, we could use a business calculator or a computer.

Shortcomings of the IRR Method

What are the shortcomings of the IRR? There are several, but to some extent the shortcomings arise from widespread misconceptions and misunderstandings about the theoretical underpinnings as well as the proper application of the method, even among the most elite and sophisticated investors and investment advisers. Consequently, although IRR is one of the most commonly used tools, it is also the least understood and most misapplied method of evaluating alternative investments.

One of the most common misconceptions, even appearing in many, if not most, of the finance and investment textbooks used by our country's leading business schools, is that the IRR method inherently assumes that the cash flows from an investment being evaluated are implicitly reinvested at the computed internal rate of return of the investment itself. This is decidedly *not* the case, but this generally held misconception is one of the principal reasons the IRR is often misapplied.

The fact is that the IRR assumes that the cash flows are *not* reinvested, at *any* rate. Rather, it assumes cash flows from an investment are consumed when paid and never enter the analysis again. If it were assumed they are reinvested at the IRR, they would not be, or should not be, shown as cash flows.

The reality is that the IRR measures the rate of return on the *unrecovered* investment over time. Cash flows from an investment represent money taken out of the investment. Over time, only the investor's, as yet, unrecovered investment implicitly continues to earn the IRR. The following example shows five alternative investments and demonstrates the point. In each case: only the unrecovered investment earns the IRR; cash flows from the investments do not earn anything.

Project Cash Flows

Year	A	B	C	D	E
0	($1,000)	($1,000)	($1,000)	($1,000)	($1,000)
1	100	50	(200)	200	600
2	100	50	(200)	200	600
3	1,100	1,215	1,793	869	(55)
IRR	10%	10%	10%	10%	10%

Each project has a 10% IRR.

Project A earns 10%, but also pays out $100, or 10% of the initial $1,000 investment, each year. Therefore, the unrecovered investment earning 10% remains at $1,000 each year, which is similar to a 10% coupon bond purchased at par value.

Project B, in contrast, is similar to a bond that has been purchased at a discount. It earns 10% on the initial $1,000 investment, but it only pays out $50 each year. Therefore, Project B's unrecovered investment increases each year.

Year	Unrecovered Investment	Earnings @ 10% IRR	(Payout) Pay in	Increase (Decrease) In Unrecovered Investment
0-1	$1,000	$100.00	$50.00	$50.00
1-2	1,050	105.00	50.00	55.00
2-3	1,105	110.50	1,215.50	(1,105.00)
3	0			

Project B is the same as Project A with all but $50 of the yearly cash flows essentially reinvested in the project at 10%. These implicitly reinvested earnings increase the unrecovered investment and earn the 10% IRR rate.

Project C has an even greater increasing unrecovered investment over time.

Year	Unrecovered Investment	Earnings @ 10% IRR	(Payout) Pay in	Increase (Decrease) In Unrecovered Investment
0-1	$1,000	$100.00	$(200.00)	$300.00
1-2	1,300	130.00	(200.00)	330.00
2-3	1,630	163.00	(1,793.00)	(1,630.00)
3	0			

Since none of the earnings are taken out of Project C until the end, all of the implicit earnings are essentially reinvested in the project at 10%.

Project D has a decreasing unrecovered investment over time.

Year	Unrecovered Investment	Earnings @ 10% IRR	(Payout) Pay in	Increase (Decrease) In Unrecovered Investment
0-1	$1,000	$100.00	$(200.00)	($100.00)
1-2	900	90.00	(200.00)	(110.00)
2-3	790	79.00	(869.00)	(790.00)
3	0			

In this case, the project throws off cash flows that are more than the implicit earnings each year, thereby reducing the unrecovered investment over time and, as a result, the implicit earnings.

Project E has decreasing and, ultimately, negative unrecovered investment over time.

Year	Unrecovered Investment	Earnings @ 10% IRR	(Payout) Pay in	Increase (Decrease) In Unrecovered Investment
0-1	$1,000	$100.00	$(600.00)	($500.00)
1-2	500	50.00	(600.00)	(550.00)
2-3	(50)	(5.00)	55.00	50.00
3	0			

Project E can actually be viewed as a combination of investment and loan since it requires the investor to contribute additional dollars at the end to "pay back" early "withdrawals" in excess of his remaining unrecovered investment. Since there are no explicit payments on the loan, except to pay off the entire amount at the end, the implicit loan does, in fact, "charge" interest at a rate equal to the 10% IRR.

Although it is true that *if* the cash flows were reinvested at the IRR, the computed IRR would not change, this misconception about the IRR and reinvestment of cash inflows leads to errors in the application of the method. In some cases, it does not matter at what rate an investor can reinvest cash flows; in other cases, it makes all the difference in the world.

Specifically, when investors want to know what rate of return they will earn on an investment, their potential reinvestment rate for the cash flows is immaterial, generally. The IRR is the rate of return they will earn on the investment itself.

However, when investors want to use the IRR to compare investments that involve different initial outlays, cash-flow patterns, and/or investment terms, they must *explicitly* account for the differences in cash flows, otherwise *they*, not the IRR method, *are* implicitly assuming cash flows are reinvested at the IRR. When reinvestment at the IRR is not realistic, the IRR method, improperly used, leads to poor choices *among* investments.

For instance, an investor is offered an immediate annuity paying $5,092.61 per year for 20 years for an initial investment of $50,000. He computes the IRR and finds that it is 8%. Whether he spends the cash flows or reinvests them is immaterial; the IRR method does not care. Whatever rate he might earn by reinvesting the cash flows paid to him does not change the return on the investment in the annuity. The annuity is paying 8%, and that is a fact regardless of whether or not and at what rate he reinvests those cash flows.

Now, however, assume he is also offered another annuity that will pay him $6,021.02 per year for 15 years for the same $50,000 initial investment. He computes the IRR for this annuity and finds that it is 8.5%. Is this the better deal? Not necessarily, even though it is, in fact, paying a half a percent more on his investment.

The 8.5%, 15-year annuity might be the better deal if he could reinvest part or all of the $928.41 annual difference in cash flows for the first 15 years so that he could at least match the cash flows he would otherwise receive for the last five years of the 8%, 20-year annuity. But if he cannot, the 8% annuity would be the better deal, even though it really is paying one-half percent less on his money.

Assume the investor feels he could earn 5% by reinvesting the difference in cash flows in an investment with the same level of safety and security as the annuity. The $928.41 annual difference invested each year at 5% would grow to $20,033.81 in 15 years. If this amount continues to earn 5%, he could withdraw $4,627.31 each year for the next 5 years before exhausting the fund. But that is $465.30 per year less than he would receive from the 8%, 20-year annuity. So he would be worse off investing in the 8.5%, 15-year annuity than if he invested in the 8%, 20-year annuity.

Obviously, if his best alternative investment with the same level of safety and security earns only 5%, then both of these annuities are "good" investments for him. The IRR of either one is greater than his opportunity cost rate or hurdle rate of 5%. If he had $100,000 to invest and was limited to a $50,000 investment in each annuity, he should invest in both of them. However, if he *ranked* the annuities based on their IRRs in order to choose between them, he would have made the wrong choice.

In addition to it being often misunderstood and misapplied, the IRR method has other real weaknesses, which can be overcome with proper use of the method. The weaknesses include

- As described above, investors cannot use the unmodified IRR method to compare (directly) mutually exclusive investments (the investment with the highest IRR is not necessarily the "best" investment among a mutually exclusive set).

- The unmodified IRR method does not consider realistic reinvestment rates for positive cash flows or realistic borrowing rates for negative cash flows over the holding period.

- An investment project may have multiple IRRs.

- Solving for the IRR often requires a series of iterative calculations to successively home in on the IRR since, for many types of IRR calculations, there is no single, closed-end formula to compute the IRR. However, financial calculators and computer software programs, such as the ubiquitous spreadsheet programs, have built-in functions that are adequate to solve for the IRR in most cases.

Let us start with the problem of multiple IRRs. The other issues will be discussed in later sections of this chapter.

How can an investment have more than one IRR?

Let us prove it first and then explain why. Figure 20.2 shows an admittedly odd hypothetical investment that has four IRRs. The investment involves an initial outlay of $1,000, a pay-in of $4,700, another outlay of $8,277.50, another pay-in of $6,356.75, and then one last payout of

Figure 20.2

MULTIPLE INTERNAL RATES OF RETURN

	Period 0	Period 1	Period 2	Period 3	Period 4
Cash Flow	(1,000.00)	4,700.00	(8,227.50)	6,356.75	(1,828.78)
Interest -5%	1.00000	1.05263	1.10803	1.16635	1.22774
PV CF	(1,000.00)	4,947.37	(9,116.34)	7,414.22	(2,245.23)
Cum. PV CF	(1,000.00)	3,947.37	(5,168.98)	2,245.23	0.00
Interest 10%	1.00000	0.90909	0.82645	0.75131	0.68301
PV CF	(1,000.00)	4,272.73	(6,799.59)	4,775.92	(1,249.06)
Cum. PV CF	(1,000.00)	3,272.73	(3,526.86)	1,249.06	0.00
Interest 25%	1.00000	0.80000	0.64000	0.51200	0.40960
PV CF	(1,000.00)	3,760.00	(5,265.60)	3,254.66	(749.06)
Cum. PV CF	(1,000.00)	2,760.00	(2,505.60)	749.06	0.00
Interest 40%	1.00000	0.71429	0.51020	0.36443	0.26031
PV CF	(1,000.00)	3,357.14	(4,197.70)	2,316.60	(476.04)
Cum. PV CF	(1,000.00)	2,357.14	(1,840.56)	476.04	0.00

$1,828.78. As the table shows, if this cash flow stream is discounted at -5%, 10%, 25%, and 40%, in each case the net present value is zero. By definition, an IRR is a discount rate that equates the net present value of the cash flows to zero, so these rates are all IRRs.

Potentially, an investment has as many different real IRRs are there are changes in the sign, or direction, of the cash flows over time. In most cases when there is a single initial investment (a payout), or a series of investment payouts, and, subsequently, a series of cash pay-ins, there is only one distinct IRR, since there is only one change in the direction of cash flows. However, if the investment involves a series of payouts mixed over time with a series of pay-ins, then each time the cash flow stream changes from payouts to pay-ins, or vice versa, there could potentially be more IRRs.

One problem with multiple IRRs is that it is not always easy to find them all and most software solutions will find just one, or refuse to solve for any at all if there could be more than one IRR. Regardless of the initial guess or "seed" one picks to start the search for multiple IRRs, the calculator or software program may home in on a particular IRR, even if it happens to be the one furthest away from the initial guess. There is generally no assurance that picking a "seed" closer to one of the IRRs than the others will cause the solution algorithm to find the nearest IRR. Consequently, even if you know that there is more than one IRR, after you find one, changing your guess or seed to find the next IRR will not always be successful. Finding each successive IRR tends to become increasingly difficult.

In addition, just because there could be several distinct real IRRs does *not* mean that there actually *are* several distinct real IRRs. In some cases, some of the IRRs are in the realm of imaginary numbers: those odd numbers that involve the square root of -1. Although such numbers have real-world significance in the arena of physics and electronics, for example, they have no practical significance in the realm of finance and investments.

Even if one finds all the real IRRs, the question remains: which is the "right" one? Mathematically, they are all correct, but which is the correct one financially? Suppose you find that an investment has two IRRs, -10% and +25%. If you invest in the project are you losing 10% or making 25%? Perhaps both? Could you be both making 25% and losing 10%, thereby averaging 7.5%? Hardly!

The only way to solve the dilemma is to use one of the modified IRR methods discussed in the next section. Depending on how you actually will handle the cash flows from the project, you can determine which IRR is in fact closer to the rate you will actually earn on the investment. The added bonus of learning about modified IRR methods is that they are also necessary whenever you want to compare or rank investment alternatives, one against another.

III. Modified Internal Rate of Return Methods

As noted above, at times it may be useful to apply a different rate of return to amounts distributed from an investment. Or a different rate of return might be used where some additional investment is required in later years after the initial investment. The question arises: What interest rate should be used for the amounts while they are held outside the investment being analyzed?

One rate of return that is useful is the safe rate of return. This is the rate of return that could be earned on a risk-free investment such as treasury bills. Another rate of return that could be used is the reinvestment rate that the investor could obtain in other investments. Still another rate of return is the rate at which the investor could borrow the money. Depending on how the cash flows from the project will actually be handled, one can determine which IRR is in fact closer to the rate that will actually be earned on the investment.

IV. Pay Back Period

Pay back period analysis is a "time value of money" concept. This method compares alternative investments by measuring the length of time required to recover the original investment. From this perspective, the investment that returns the original capital in the shortest period of time is the "best" investment.

The major flaw in this analytical technique is obvious: taken to its extreme, an indiscriminate investor would choose a deal requiring a $10,000 investment which paid back $15,000 in one year rather than an alternative which required the same capital outlay but returned $25,000 in two years.

V. Cash on Cash

Cash-on-cash analysis, as its name implies, focuses on the *amount* of cash generated by the investment. It ignores both taxes and the potential gain from any sale.

To compute cash on cash return, divide the annual cash flow by the cash investment. For example, a woman plans to invest $10,000 in the stock of Z-Rocks Corp. Each year she would receive a dividend of $1,000, and expects to receive $15,000 upon the sale of the stock in three years.

She is considering an alternative investment for the $10,000, Eye-B-Em Stock, which yields a cash distribution of only $600 per year, but which she believes will be worth $25,000 at the end of the three-year investment period. Under the cash-on-cash method, her return on the first investment is 10% per year ($1,000 dividend divided by the $10,000 investment), while the return on the alternative is only 6% per year ($600 divided by the $10,000 investment).

Using only the cash-on-cash method to evaluate the investments, she would choose the Z-Rocks stock, because of the higher annual dividend. However, if she had compared the investments by looking at their relative internal rates of return or adjusted rates of return, she would probably have chosen the alternative.

RISK, PROBABILITIES, AND MODELING

Investments are subject to numerous risks. In addition, financial planning involves other risks, such as that a client may die or become disabled. We will look briefly at risk and modeling for the probability of risk here in the context of time value of money. However, an extensive examination is beyond the scope of this book. For an extensive look at risk and the measurement and handling of risk, see the *Tools & Techniques of Investment Planning*.

Without careful planning, the death of a client may leave the client's financial plan incomplete. The client's earnings, or perhaps other sources of income, may stop at death. However, the client may wish to provide for others after his death, including general support for living, or more specialized needs such as for education funding. Life expectancy is often used as a substitute for the probability of death (or how long a person may continue to live) in financial planning. Time value of money calculations often use life expectancy as a period of years. And, of course, life insurance is specifically targeted at such risk.

The disability of a client may also leave the client's financial plan incomplete. The client's earnings, or perhaps other sources of income, may also stop at disability. And, once again, the client may still wish to provide for others despite his disability. However, with a disability, the client continues to have expenses, perhaps even increased, after the disability. Disability is often overlooked in financial planning. However, the probability of disability at a particular age is often significantly greater than the probability of death. Time value of money calculations should probably also take into account the probability of disability. And, of course, disability insurance is specifically targeted at such risk.

Investments are subject to an endless list of risks: market, financial, interest rate, business, industry, country, default, inflation, and so on. The rate of return, or the range of rates of returns, used in time value of money calculations should reflect such risks. The management of investment risks often involves diversification, asset allocation, and professional management.

In making time value of money calculations, a series of calculations might be made using a number of rates of returns to reflect the range of returns that might be expected given all the probabilities that any particular rate of return might be achieved. Probabilities might be assigned based on standard deviations (a measure of how much actual returns deviate from the average return). A Monte-Carlo simulation on a computer might attempt to take all these probabilities into effect.

Monte-Carlo Simulation

Expected returns and standard deviation are not necessarily constant over time. Nor is the return in an individual period predictable. Returns in each asset class are probabilistic. Investors may also make periodic deposits and withdrawals, further increasing the difficulty in predicting long-term returns and risk. If an investor desires a certain level of retirement income, what is the assurance that this level of income is likely to be obtained?

Monte-Carlo simulation is the process of assessing the likelihood of an expected outcome. In a Monte-Carlo simulation, a computer program is used to randomly choose returns from an expected distribution of returns for each period (perhaps, rebalancing the asset allocation as required under the strategy). Each run results in an ending expected portfolio value. The process is run many times (perhaps 1,000), to achieve a distribution of ending values. This process can help assess the probability of achieving a certain value or income in the future (including the possibility that an individual will outlive his retirement assets.)

WHERE CAN I FIND OUT MORE?

1. Leimberg et al, *Tools & Techniques of Investment Planning* (Cincinnati, OH: National Underwriter Company, 2004).

2. Frank Fabozzi, *Fixed Income Mathematics: Analytical and Statistical Techniques* (Chicago, IL: Irwin Professional Publishers, 1996).

3. David Spaulding, *Measuring Investment Performance: Calculating and Evaluating Investment Risk and Return* (New York, NY: McGraw-Hill, 1997).

4. Robert Rachlin, *Return on Investment Manual: Tools and Applications for Managing Financial Results* (Armonk, NY: Sharpe Professional, 1997).

5. Arefaine Yohannes, *The Irwin Guide to Risk and Reward* (Chicago, IL: Irwin Professional Publishers, 1996).

6. Birrer & Carrica, *Present Value Applications for Accountants and Financial Planners* (New York, NY: Quorum Books, 1990).

7. Charles Akerson, *The Internal Rate of Return in Real Estate Investments* (Chicago, IL: American Inst. of Real Estate Appraisers, 1988).

8. David Leahigh, *A Pocket Guide to Finance* (Fort Worth, TX: Dryden Press, 1996).

9. *Calculator Analysis for Business and Finance* (New York, NY: McGraw-Hill).

10. *HP-12C Owner's Handbook and Problem-Solving Guide* (Hewlett-Packard Co.).

QUESTIONS AND ANSWERS

Question – Assume you are offered a 10% rate of return on one investment, compounded annually. You are examining alternative investments but they are all compounded on a semiannual or monthly basis. How can you determine which investment will yield the greatest return?

Answer – The question can be restated by asking, "What is the 'effective' yield on an investment that has a 'stated' or 'nominal' annual interest rate, but compounds more frequently (most commonly semiannually, quarterly, monthly, or daily)?"

Where the number of compounding periods differs from the number of payment periods, to compare alternative investments it is sometimes necessary to convert the stated interest rates to equivalent effective interest rates.

For example, if a $1,000 investment compounds semiannually at an annual stated rate of 10%, the interest earned in the first six months will be added to the original amount of the investment and will thus earn interest for the remainder of the year. Therefore, at the end of 6 months, $50 (10% x $1,000 x ½ year) will be added to the original $1,000 principal. For the balance of the year, $1,050 will be earning interest at the annual rate of 10%. A sum of $52.50 will be earned in the second half of the year (10% x $1,050 x ½ year). The total interest earned for the year on the initial $1,000 is $102.50, resulting in a 10.25% effective rate for the year, compounded on a semiannual basis.

The more frequently an investment is compounded the higher the effective annual interest rate. For example, a monthly compounding of an investment with a 10% stated annual interest rate has an effective annual rate of 10.471%.

Use the following formula to determine the effective annual interest rate where the nominal annual interest rate is compounded more frequently than annually:

$$\text{Effective Rate} = (1 + (i \div n))^{n} - 1$$

In this formula,

n = The Number of Compounding Periods in a Year

i = Nominal Annual Interest Rate

Applying the formula to a nominal annual interest rate of 10% that is compounded quarterly:

$$\text{Effective Rate} = (1 + (i \div n))^{n} - 1$$

$$\text{Effective Rate} = (1 + (0.10 \div 4))^{4-1}$$

$$\text{Effective Rate} = 10.381\%$$

Thus, a quarterly compounding of an investment with a 10% stated annual interest rate has an effective annual rate of 10.381%.

Chapter 21

FINANCIAL INSTITUTIONS

WHAT IS IT?

The primary function of any financial system is to facilitate the allocation and deployment of economic resources both spatially and temporally and in an uncertain environment. In other words, the financial system needs to get people with investable funds together with people who need investable funds in the most efficient manner possible. The basic and essential functions to be performed by any financial system are

- methods for clearing and settling payments
- mechanisms for pooling resources (large-scale indivisible enterprise)
- ways to transfer economic resources through time and across distances
- methods of managing risk and uncertainty
- price information to help coordinate decentralized decision-making
- ways of dealing with incentive problems created when one party to a transaction has information that another party does not or when one party acts as an agent for another (moral hazard, adverse selection)

In a world of perfect information, costless transactions, absence of economies of scale, absence of moral hazard and adverse selection, and no uncertainty – in other words, in a frictionless world – financial intermediaries would be unnecessary. But we do not live in such a world. Consequently, various financial institutions and intermediaries have evolved to overcome these frictions and to improve the allocation of resources and economic efficiency.

Figure 21.1 shows a basic diagram of the financial system for transferring resources from those people/businesses without investment opportunities to those who have them. Broadly speaking, there are two channels from lender/savers to borrower/spenders. The most direct route is through the financial markets – the various stock, bond, commodity, and other exchanges. However, even these exchanges are a sort of intermediary, since they provide a time and place for transactions, set rules and procedures, and monitor compliance. In other words, lender/savers are still not directly transacting with borrower/lenders.

The second route is through various financial intermediaries: commercial banks and other depository institutions, investment banks and brokerage firms, investment companies, mutual funds, and other pooled investment intermediaries, and insurance companies, as well as other financial institutions.

Basically, households save for different reasons than firms invest. Households try to minimize risk and have their savings readily accessible, or liquid. Firms are risk takers and need funds that will be tied up for a long time. By pooling the funds of savers and making loans to individual businesses, financial intermediaries reduce the costs of negotiation and search. They also acquire expertise in both evaluating and monitoring investments. Some financial intermediaries also provide the liquidity households demand. Financial intermediaries reduce risk through diversification. They invest in a large number of projects whose returns, although uncertain, are independent of one another. Every household has a small stake in many projects. Together, financial intermediaries can achieve the average return on investment with greater certainty than any single household can.

This chapter will explain the role of banks and other depository institutions in the economy, the differences among the various depository institutions, the role of bank regulators, including both state and federal regulators, the role of the Federal Reserve System and the workings of the deposit insurance programs, the banking structure in the U.S., and the purpose and characteristics of a number of other financial intermediaries. These other financial institutions include finance companies, investment banks and brokerage firms, investment companies and mutual funds, and a number of other pooled investment financial intermediaries – unit trusts, REITs, mortgage-backed bonds, REMICs, exchange-traded funds, and insurance companies.

Figure 21.1

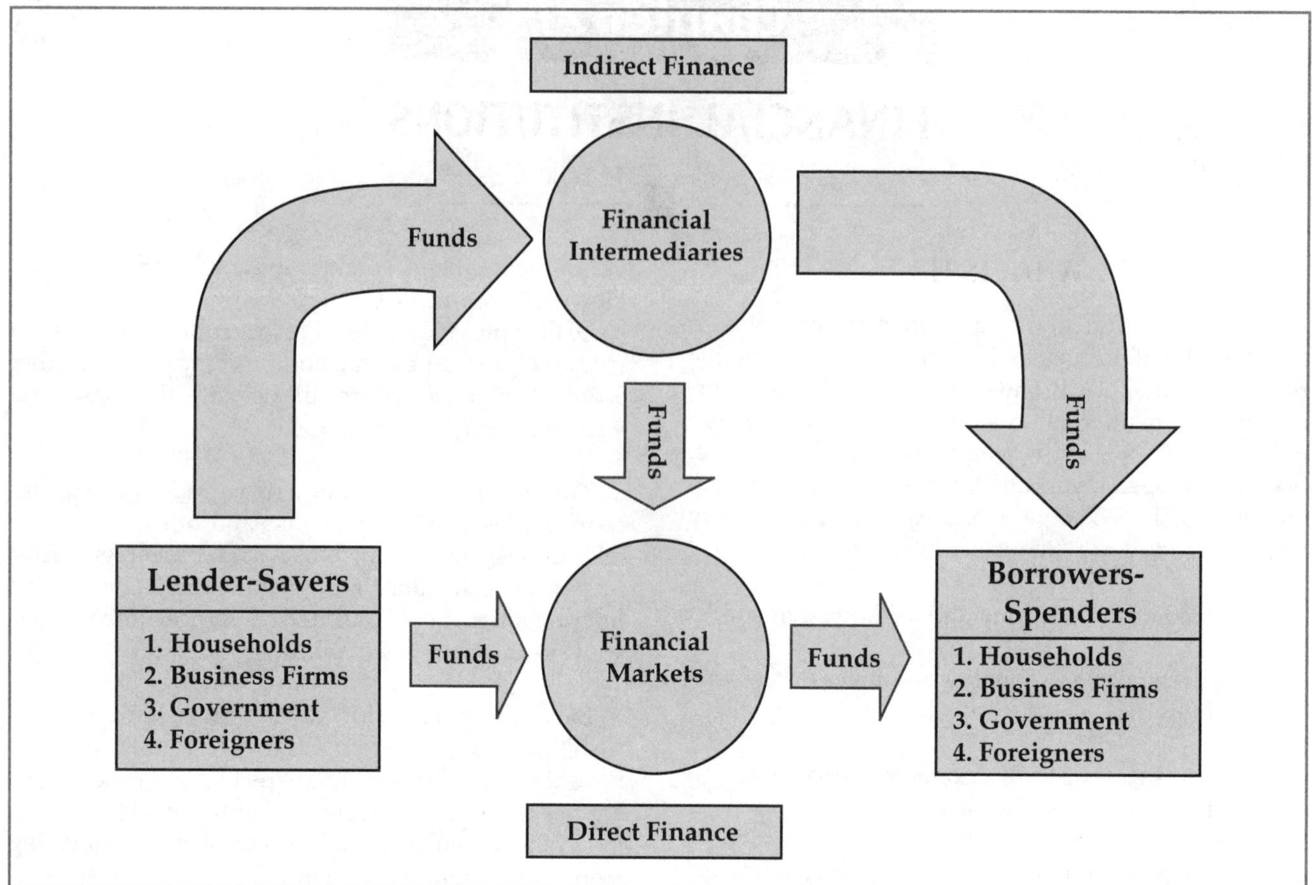

BANKS AND THE ECONOMY

"Bank" is a term people use broadly to refer to many different types of financial institutions. What people call "their bank" may be a bank and trust company, a savings bank, a savings and loan association, or other depository institution.

What Is a Bank?

Banks are privately owned institutions that, generally, accept deposits and make loans. Deposits are money people leave in an institution with the understanding that they can get it back at any time or at an agreed-upon future time. A loan is money lent out to a borrower to be generally paid back with interest. This action of taking deposits and making loans is called financial intermediation. A bank's business, however, does not end there.

Most people and businesses pay their bills with bank checking accounts, placing banks at the center of our payments system. Banks are the major source of consumer loans – loans for cars, houses, and education – as well as main lenders to businesses, especially small businesses.

Banks are often described as our economy's engine, in part because of these functions, but also because of the major role banks play as instruments of the government's monetary policy.

How Banks Create Money

Banks cannot lend out all the deposits they collect, or they would not have funds to pay out to depositors. Therefore, they hold primary and secondary reserves. Primary reserves are cash, deposits due from other banks, and the reserves required by the Federal Reserve System. Secondary reserves are securities banks purchase that may be sold to meet short-term cash needs. These securities are usually government bonds. Federal law sets requirements for the percentage of deposits a bank must keep on reserve, either at the local Federal Reserve Bank or in its own vault. Any money a bank has on hand after it meets its reserve requirement is its excess reserves.

These excess reserves create money. The process works as follows (using a theoretical 20% reserve requirement): Mr. Saver deposits $500 in FirstBank. FirstBank keeps $100 of the deposit to meet its reserve requirement, but lends $400 to Ms. Loan. She uses the money to buy a car. The Motor Car Dealership deposits $400 in its account at SecondBank. SecondBank keeps $80 of the deposit on reserve, but then lends out the other $320 as its own excess reserves. When SecondBank lends that money, it gets deposited in ThirdBank, and the cycle continues. Therefore, in this example, the original deposit of $500 becomes $1,220 on deposit in three different institutions. This phenomenon is called the multiplier effect. The size of the multiplier depends on the amount of money banks must keep on reserve.

The Federal Reserve can contract or expand the money supply by raising or lowering banks' reserve requirements. Banks themselves can contract the money supply by increasing their own reserves to guard against loan losses or to meet sudden cash demands. A sharp increase in bank reserves, for any reason, can create a "credit crunch" by reducing the amount of money banks have available to lend.

How Banks Make Money

While public policymakers have long recognized the importance of banking to economic development, banks are privately owned, for-profit institutions. Banks are generally organized as corporations owned by stockholders. The stockholders' stake in the bank forms most of its equity capital, which is a bank's ultimate buffer against losses. At the end of the year, a bank pays some or all of its profits to its shareholders in the form of dividends. The bank may retain some of its profits to add to its capital. Stockholders may also choose to reinvest their dividends in the bank.

Banks earn money in three ways:

1. They make money from what they call the spread, or the difference between the interest rate they pay for deposits and the interest rate they receive on the loans they make.

2. They earn interest on the securities they hold.

3. They earn fees for customer services, such as checking accounts, financial counseling, loan servicing and the sales of other financial products (e.g., insurance and mutual funds).

Banks earn an average of just over 1% on their assets (loans and securities) every year. This figure is commonly referred to as a bank's "return on assets," or ROA.

A Short History

The first American banks appeared early in the 18th century, to provide currency to colonists who needed a means of exchange. Originally, banks only made loans and issued notes for money deposited. Checking accounts appeared in the mid-19th century, the first of many new bank products and services developed through the state banking system. Today banks offer credit cards, automatic teller machines, individual retirement accounts, home equity loans, and a host of other financial services.

In today's evolving financial services environment, many other financial institutions provide some traditional banking functions. Banks compete with credit unions, financing companies, investment banks, insurance companies and many other financial services providers. While some claim that banks are becoming obsolete, banks still serve vital economic goals. They continue to evolve to meet the changing needs of their customers, as they have for the past two hundred years. If banks did not exist, we would have to invent them.

Banks and Public Policy

Our government's earliest leaders struggled over the shape of our banking system. They knew that banks have considerable financial power. Should this power be concentrated in a few institutions, they asked, or shared by many? Alexander Hamilton argued strongly for one central bank. That idea troubled Thomas Jefferson, who believed that local control was the only way to restrain banks from becoming financially (and, therefore, politically) too powerful.

The U.S. system has tried both ways and found each lacking in some way. The system has evolved so that the current system is a compromise or composite of both approaches. The U.S. financial system allows for a multitude of banks, both large and small. Both the federal and state governments issue bank charters for "public need and convenience," and regulate banks to ensure that they meet those needs. The Federal Reserve controls the money supply at a national level. The nation's individual banks facilitate the flow of money in their respective communities.

Since banks hold government-issued charters and generally belong to the Federal Bank Insurance Fund, state and federal governments have considered banks as instruments of broad financial policy beyond money supply. Governments encourage or require different types of lending. For example, they enforce nondiscrimination policies by requiring equal opportunity lending. They promote economic development by requiring lending or investment in banks' local communities and by deciding where to issue new bank charters. Using banks to accomplish economic policy goals requires a constant balancing of banks' needs against the needs of the community. Banks must be profitable to stay in business, and a failed bank does not meet anyone's needs.

DIFFERENCES AMONG BANKS, THRIFTS, AND CREDIT UNIONS

Three major types of depository institutions exist in the United States: commercial banks, thrift institutions (which include savings and loan associations and savings banks) and credit unions.

These three types of institutions have become more like each other in recent decades, and their unique identities have become less distinct. They still differ, however, in specialization and emphasis, and in their regulatory and supervisory structures.

Commercial banks are the traditional "department stores" of the financial services world. Thrift institutions and credit unions are more like specialty shops that, over time, have expanded their lines of business to better compete for market share. (Many states, in fact, grant thrift institutions the same powers as commercial banks).

Commercial Banks

Commercial banks are generally stock corporations whose principal obligation is to make a profit for their shareholders. Basically, banks receive deposits and hold them in a variety of different accounts, extend credit through loans and other instruments, and facilitate the movement of funds. While commercial banks mostly specialize in short-term business credit, they also make consumer loans and mortgages, and have a broad range of financial powers. Their corporate charters and the powers granted to them under state and federal law spell out the range of their activities.

States and the federal government each issue bank charters. State-chartered banks operate under state supervision and, if they fail, are closed under provisions of state as well as federal law. National banks are chartered and regulated by the Office of the Comptroller of the Currency (OCC), a division of the Treasury Department. Banks can choose between a state and federal charter when starting their business, and can also convert from one charter to another after having been in business. Commercial banks receive deposit insurance from the Federal Deposit Insurance Corporation (FDIC) through the Bank Insurance Fund (BIF). All national banks, and some state-chartered banks, are members of the Federal Reserve System.

Savings and Loan Associations and Savings Banks

Savings and loan associations and savings banks typically specialize in real estate lending, particularly loans for single-family homes and other residential properties. They are organized either as corporations owned by stockholders or as mutual companies owned by their depositors and borrowers. These institutions are referred to as "thrifts," because they originally offered only savings accounts, or time deposits. Over the past two decades, however, they have acquired a wide range of financial powers and now offer checking accounts (demand deposits) and make business and consumer loans as well as mortgage loans. Most of these institutions still invest the bulk of their money in mortgages and real-estate-related loans.

Both savings and loan associations and savings banks may get their charters either from the federal Office of Thrift Supervision (OTS) or from a state government regulator. The Savings Association Insurance Fund (SAIF) insures most savings and loan associations. The Bank Insurance Fund (BIF) insures savings banks.

Generally, savings institutions must hold 65% of their loan portfolio in housing-related assets (loans) or other qualified assets to retain their charter, as well as their membership in the Federal Home Loan Bank System. This is called the "qualified thrift lender" (QTL) test. Recent liberalization of the QTL test has allowed thrifts to use some non-housing assets to meet this requirement.

The number of thrifts declined dramatically in the late 1980s and early 1990's as a consequence of the savings and loan crisis of the 1980s. Many thrifts closed or merged with others under the direction of the Resolution Trust Corporation, at an extraordinary cost to the U.S.

taxpayers. However, the thrift industry has rebounded in recent years. The recapitalization of the thrift fund, a revitalized industry and legislative changes have made the charter – once thought doomed to extinction – an appealing route to financial modernization for some. Due to liberalization of the qualified thrift lender test, many insurance companies and securities firms, as well as commercial firms, are now able to qualify as unitary thrift holding companies and to own depository institutions, bypassing prohibitions in the Glass Steagall Act and the Bank Holding Company Act. Critics of a revitalized thrift charter have said that it has been too advantageous for a certain class of financial institutions, highlighting the need for broader financial modernization through federal legislation.

Credit Unions

Credit unions are cooperative financial institutions, formed by groups of people with a "common bond." These groups of people pool their funds to form the institution's deposit base. The group owns and controls the institution together. Membership in a credit union is restricted to people who share the common bond of the group that created the credit union and is, therefore, not open to the general public. For example, people working for the same employer, belonging to the same church or social group, or living in the same community would share a common bond that might serve as the organizing criteria for the credit union. Credit unions are nonprofit institutions that seek to encourage savings and make excess funds within a community available at low cost to their members.

Credit unions accept deposits in a variety of accounts. All credit unions offer savings accounts, or time deposits. The larger institutions also offer checking and money market accounts. Credit unions' financial powers have expanded to include almost anything a bank or savings association can do, including making home loans, issuing credit cards, and even making some commercial loans. Credit unions are exempt from federal taxation and sometimes receive subsidies, in the form of free space or supplies, from their sponsoring organizations and/or communities.

Credit unions were first chartered in the U.S. in 1909, at the state level. The federal government began to charter credit unions in 1934 under the Farm Credit Association, and created the National Credit Union Administration (NCUA) in 1970. States and the federal government continue to charter credit unions. Almost all credit unions are insured by the National Credit Union Share Insurance Fund (NCUSIF), which is controlled by the NCUA. In many states, state-chartered credit unions are supervised by the state Department of Banking.

BANK REGULATORS

Bank regulation, or supervision, involves four federal agencies and fifty state agencies. At first glance this regulatory scheme seems hopelessly complicated, but it is not that hard to understand once one knows what each agency does.

State and Federal Charters

The system is often described as a "dual banking system." This refers to the fact that both the states and the federal government issued bank charters for the need and convenience of their citizens. The Office of the Comptroller of the Currency (OCC) charters national banks. The state banking departments charter state banks. In addition, the Office of Thrift Supervision (OTS) charters federal savings banks and savings associations. The words "national," "federal" or "state" in an institution's name have nothing to do with where it operates – rather they refer to the type of charter the bank holds.

Chartering agencies ensure that new banks have the necessary capital and management expertise to meet the public's financial and security needs. The chartering agency is an institution's primary regulator, with front-line duty to protect the public from unsafe and unsound banking practices. Chartering agencies conduct on-site examinations to assess banks' condition and monitor compliance with banking laws. They issue regulations, take enforcement actions and close banks if they fail.

The Federal Reserve System (Central Bank)

After the banking panics in 1893 and 1907, commercial banks supported provisions in the 1913 Federal Reserve Act that gave power to Federal Reserve Banks to provide an elastic money supply through their reserve lending to banks, control of the discount rate, and the Fed's ability to supply or curtail credit through its open-market operations buying or selling government bonds. The passage of the Federal Reserve Act in 1913 was meant to correct some of the shortcomings of the national bank system that became apparent during the financial crisis of 1907. The legislative goals were to establish (1) a monetary authority that would expand and contract the money supply in concert with the needs of the economy, (2) a

Figure 21.2

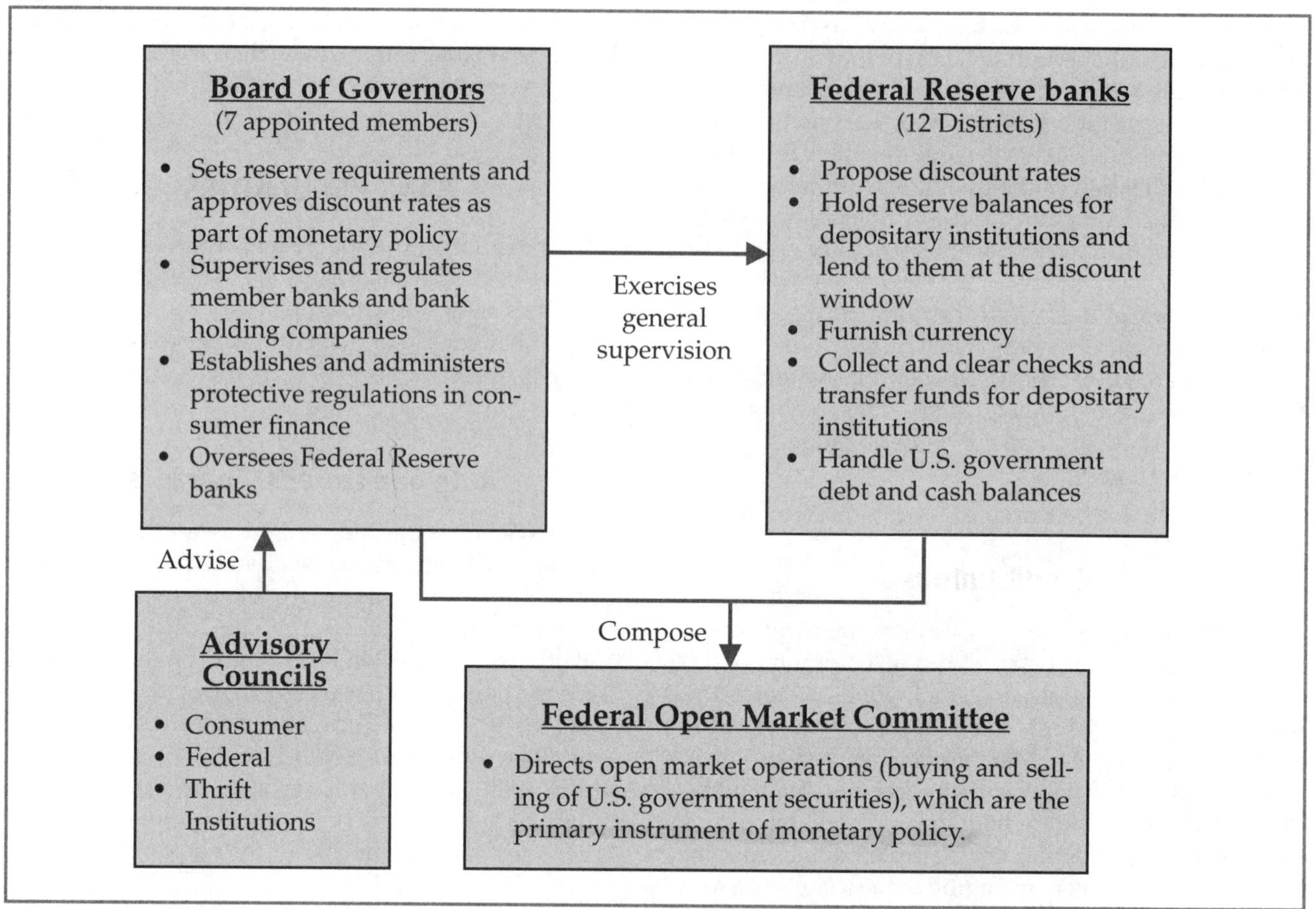

lender of last resort that could supply additional reserves in times of financial contraction, (3) an efficient check clearing and collection system throughout the country, and (4) a more vigilant system of bank oversight and monitoring.

The organizational structure, goals, and role of the Federal Reserve System have evolved over the years with the changing political and economic environment. Today, most of the authority in the system resides in the seven-member Board of Governors and the Chairman of the Federal Reserve rather than in the 12 regional Federal Reserve Banks. The Federal Open Market Committee (FOMC) consists of the seven-member Board of Governors plus five of the presidents of the 12 Federal Reserve banks. (See Figure 21.2 for a diagram of the Federal Reserves Organization and Function.)

The principal functions of the Federal Reserve are economic stabilization through management of the nation's money supply and through its role as "lender of last resort." The FOMC's role in the banking system and the economy as a whole is extremely important since it sets the nation's monetary policy and the level of financial institutions' reserves. Therefore, it is responsible for the amount of money in circulation and for controlling the monetary base and, thus, the overall level of economic activity.

The Federal Reserve also regulates all bank holding companies. Its regulatory focus is not so much on the banks within a holding company as on the umbrella structure of the holding company itself. Holding companies must apply to the Federal Reserve to acquire new subsidiaries or to engage in new activities. The Fed monitors the capital condition and general financial health of holding companies, and may take enforcement actions against them. The Federal Reserve is also responsible for federal oversight of foreign banks operating in the United States.

With banks more able to meet an onslaught of deposit withdrawals through borrowing from the Fed at low interest rates (the discount rate) during periods of financial crisis, it was anticipated that the banking system could avoid future bank panics. Unfortunately, these aspirations were clearly thwarted in the Great Depression of the 1930s. Monetarist Milton Friedman has said the crash occurred because the Fed failed to do its job. It let the money supply contract by one-third, creating an oppressive deflation that caused tremendous hardships for debtors, business firms, and banks. Over half the banks operating in the late 1920s failed during the Great Depression.

In the Fed's defense, at the time, it was only empowered by the Federal Reserve Act to be the lender of last resort to commercial banks that were members of the Federal Reserve System – a minority of all banks. In addition, it could lend only to banks that could present "eligible collateral." However, the Fed did not take aggressive enough action to expand bank credit sufficiently through its open-market operations. With half the banks failing within four years, clearly something more was needed to restore confidence in the banking system. One approach was to provide some form of federally-sponsored deposit insurance.

The Deposit Insurer

The Vandenberg Amendment to the Banking Act of 1933 authorized the creation of a federally-sponsored deposit insurance program. This was formalized with the creation of the Federal Deposit Insurance Corporation (FDIC) on January 1, 1934. Initially, deposit insurance was to cover only $2,500 per deposit. The level of insurance coverage was quickly raised to $5,000 per deposit, where it remained until after World War II. The coverage was raised to $10,000 per account in 1950, to $20,000 in 1969, to $40,000 in 1974, and ultimately to $100,000 in 1980.

The Federal Deposit Insurance Corporation (FDIC) currently insures the deposits of banks up to a maximum of $100,000 per account holder. All states require newly-chartered state banks to join the FDIC before they can accept deposits from the public. Under the 1991 Federal Deposit Insurance Corporation Improvement Act (FDICIA), both state-chartered and national banks must apply to the FDIC for deposit insurance. Previously, national banks had received insurance automatically with their new charters.

The FDIC is the federal regulator of the approximately 5,000 state-chartered banks that do not belong to the Federal Reserve System. It cooperates with state banking departments to supervise and examine these banks, and has considerable authority to intervene to prevent unsafe and unsound banking practices. The FDIC also has backup examination and regulatory authority over national and Fed-member banks.

The FDIC deals with failed institutions by either liquidating them or selling the institutions to redeem insured deposits.

Savings and loan associations originally obtained federal deposit insurance from the Federal Savings and Loan Insurance Corporation (FSLIC), which was established by the National Housing Act of 1934. The FSLIC was allowed to offer insurance on the same terms as the FDIC. The FSLIC, however, incurred too many losses because of savings and loan failures during the savings and loan crisis of the 1980s. To preserve public confidence in deposit insurance, the FSLIC was eliminated in 1989 and replaced with the Savings Association Insurance Fund (SAIF) under the jurisdiction of the FDIC.

Since 1970, National Credit Union Share Insurance Fund (NCUSIF) has insured deposits in credit unions. The terms of the insurance are similar to FDIC insurance. Participating credit union accounts are federally insured up to $100,000. All federally chartered credit unions must be insured by the NCUSIF, and state-chartered credit unions can elect to obtain NCUSIF insurance, provided they comply with NCUSIF requirements.

Federal deposit insurance is not free. Each insured institution can be assessed a fee, expressed as a percentage of deposits, to make sure the insurance funds will have sufficient reserves to cover all their losses. In addition, each insured institution must be federally examined and comply with appropriate federal laws and regulations to ensure that they are not taking excessive risks. Deposit insurance is valuable to the insured institutions, however, because it helps them retain public confidence and usually allows them to pay lower interest rates to depositors than they would have to pay if they were not insured.

Why So Many Different Regulators?

Many people have said that we would never design our current regulatory system as it is if we were starting from scratch. But our current system has evolved with the country, and has changed with the country's needs.

The states were the first to charter banks in the United States. The federal government chartered the First and Second Banks of the United States in the early 19th century. These were the first national banks, and they performed functions similar to today's Federal Reserve System. From 1837, when the Second Bank's charter expired, to 1863, there were no national banks and no federal regulators.

The National Bank Act of 1863 created the Office of the Comptroller of the Currency, and authorized it to charter national banks. The original purpose of both the OCC and national banks was to circulate a universal currency, thus making tax collection easier and helping to finance the Civil War. The dual banking system took shape in the late 19th century, as states reformed their chartering policies and regulatory systems in response to the National Bank Act.

A series of money shortages early in the 20th century made it clear that the country needed some central authority to monitor and control the money supply. The Federal Reserve Act of 1913 established this authority through a network of twelve Federal Reserve Banks, overseen by a Board of Governors. The Federal Reserve System had regulatory authority over all its member banks. This was the first time a federal agency had direct authority over state-chartered banks, although state bank membership in the Federal Reserve was voluntary.

The Banking Act of 1933 created the FDIC, as noted above, in response to the avalanche of bank failures that followed the stock market crash of 1929. The 1933 Banking Act also required all state-chartered banks to join the Federal Reserve within a certain period of time or lose their deposit insurance, but this requirement was eventually repealed. The FDIC established its own standards for state nonmember bank acceptance into the fund.

Bank holding companies were new corporate entities that began appearing in the 1940s. The banks were all regulated, but no one regulated the holding company subsidiaries that were not banks, and no one watched the flow of resources among affiliates within the holding company. The Bank Holding Company Act of 1956 gave the Federal Reserve regulatory responsibility for these companies, while leaving the supervision of banks within holding companies in the hands of their traditional regulators.

In 1989, the Financial Institutions Reform, Recovery, and Enforcement Act (FIRREA) expanded the FDIC's supervisory and enforcement authority, and extended its responsibilities to include the thrift deposit insurance role formerly held by the Federal Savings and Loan Insurance Corporation (FSLIC).

Most recently, 1991's FDICIA also expanded the authority of federal regulators to intervene in troubled institutions. FDICIA also mandated specific enforcement actions for unhealthy institutions – the first time prescribed "early intervention" provisions had been included in federal statutes.

BANK GEOGRAPHIC STRUCTURE

In banking, the term geography refers to the area in which banking activities are allowed to take place, such as interstate banking, and intrastate and interstate branching. While even banking experts often confuse the terms, they have distinctly different meanings.

Intrastate Branching

Intrastate branching refers to branching within a particular state. Permitting banks to open more than one office or branch originated at the state level, and the states have directed the expansion of banks' geographic boundaries. Earlier in this century, few banks had more than one office. Today, most banks can open branches throughout their respective states. A great majority of the 50 states allow statewide branching, and other states allow limited branching. Many banks have expanded their branch network to better meet the needs and convenience of their customers.

The 1927 McFadden Act sought to give national banks competitive equality with state-chartered banks by letting national banks branch to the extent permitted by state law. The McFadden Act specifically prohibited intrastate branching by allowing a national bank to branch only within the city in which it is situated. Although the Riegle-Neal Interstate Banking and Branching Efficiency Act of 1994 repealed this provision of the McFadden Act, it specified that state law would continue to control intrastate branching, or branching within a state's borders, for both state and national banks.

Of note, there are approximately 9,500 savings and loan branches that, because of preemptive authority in the law establishing the thrift charter, are subject to neither intrastate nor interstate branching restrictions. This preemptive authority was intended to foster a national market for home mortgages.

Interstate Banking

Interstate banking refers to the ability of a bank holding company to own and operate banks in more than one state. Under the Douglas Amendment to the Bank Holding Company Act of 1956, states controlled whether, and under what circumstances, out-of-state bank holding companies could own and operate banks within their borders.

The need for the Douglas Amendment grew from the concern that bank holding companies were evading the McFadden Act and state branching laws by acquiring numerous subsidiary banks in various states, and then operating these banks as if they were branches. The development of these interstate bank networks was a significant factor leading to Congress' passage of the Bank Holding Company Act of 1956. Senator Douglas emphasized that a primary purpose of his amendment was "to prevent an undue concentration of banking and financial power, and instead keep the private control of credit diffused as much as possible."

The Riegle-Neal Interstate Banking and Branching Efficiency Act of 1994 repealed the Douglas Amendment. On September 29, 1995, federal law allowed full nationwide banking across the country, regardless of state law. Another provision of the Riegle-Neal Act allows affiliate banks within bank holding companies to effectively act as branches for each other, accepting deposits, collecting payments, and providing other customer services.

Interstate banking has resulted in increased consolidation and concentration in the banking industry. While the United States had 14,399 banks in 1940, the country has fewer than 9,000 banks today. However, while consolidation among banks has certainly been the trend, the number of branches in the U.S. has steadily increased. In other words, consumers have more banking outlets than ever in our country's history.

Interstate Branching

Interstate branching means that a single bank may operate branches in more than one state without requiring separate capital and corporate structures for each state, that is, without the holding company organizational structure. The state of New York approved the first interstate branching statute in 1992. This law set several requirements and conditions on New York branches of out-of-state banks. It also required reciprocity; that New York banks were allowed to branch into the home states of banks that branch into New York. Other states passed similar laws.

The 1994 Riegle-Neal Interstate Banking and Branching Efficiency Act allowed national banks to operate branches across state lines after June 1, 1997. This federal law allows branching through acquisition only, which means that a bank must acquire another bank and merge the two structures in order to operate branches across state lines.

The Riegle-Neal Act allowed states to "opt-out" of interstate branching by passing a law to prohibit it before June 1, 1997. A state that "opted-out" of interstate branching prevented both state and national banks from branching into or out of its borders. Texas and Montana were the only states to "opt-out" of interstate branching.

States also have the power to authorize "de-novo" branching across state lines, which would allow a bank to simply open a new branch in another state instead of having to acquire an entire bank. Several states have decided to allow de-novo branching; however, most of them have done so on a reciprocal basis.

In 1997, the Riegle-Neal Amendments Act was signed into law ratifying an agreement between the states, the FDIC and the Federal Reserve allowing "seamless" supervision for state-chartered banks that branch across state lines.

Foreign Banks

The term "foreign bank" generally refers to any United States operation of a banking organization headquartered outside of the U.S.

The first foreign banks established their presence in the United States in the mid-1800s with New York being the first state to license or regulate these institutions. While state governments took the lead in welcoming foreign banks to the United States, the federal government has also acted to ensure that American markets are open to banks from all nations.

Today foreign banks are a significant presence in the American financial system, providing many important benefits to individuals, businesses, and the general economy. In fact, foreign banks make almost 40% of all loans to American businesses.

Foreign banks most often come to the United States to provide services to American subsidiaries of clients in their home countries or to a specific group of individuals. Once here, however, they provide a wide range of wholesale banking services. They are most active in New York, California, Florida, Illinois and Georgia, but also maintain operations in several other states.

Foreign banking organizations can acquire or establish freestanding banks or bank holding companies in the United States. These banks are regulated and supervised as domestic institutions. Generally, however, it is more cost-effective and productive for foreign banking organizations to operate as another of several available structures: branches, agencies, loan production offices, representative offices, and Edge Act (described below) or agreement corporations. Each of these business structures has a different set of powers and regulatory requirements.

Branches and agencies are the most common structures of foreign banking organizations in the United States. The major difference between these two types of banking offices is that branches may accept deposits, while agencies generally may not. Both structures can make and manage loans, conduct foreign exchange activities and trade in securities and commercial paper. These offices may conduct most of the activities a domestic bank performs. The primary exception is that foreign banks and branches may not accept deposits of less than $100,000 unless they had FDIC insurance prior to December 19, 1991. State governments and the Office of the Comptroller of the Currency separately license and supervise foreign bank branches and agencies. The Federal Reserve serves as the federal regulator of state-licensed foreign bank branches and agencies, in a system similar to that for domestic banks. More than 85% of the foreign bank branches and agencies in the U.S. are state licensed/chartered.

Foreign banks may also establish representative offices in the United States. Representative offices have more limited powers than branches or agencies. Foreign banks often open representative offices as a first step in establishing a presence in America. These offices serve as a liaison between the parent bank and its clients and correspondent banks in the U.S. They may develop relationships with prospective clients, but they cannot conduct any banking transactions themselves. Representative offices must register with the Federal Reserve, and may be licensed by states as well.

Edge Act and agreement corporations are foreign bank offices chartered by the Federal Reserve (Edge Act) or states (representative corporations) to provide financing for international trade. Domestic banking organizations may also establish Edge Act or agreement corporations. These offices have a broader range of powers than other banking organizations, but all of their activities must relate to international trade. Other structures available to foreign banks are commercial lending corporations, licensed by New York State, and export trading companies.

In order to protect American consumers and the overall stability of the U.S. financial system, states and federal banking agencies regulate and supervise foreign banking operations in the United States. The major Federal laws affecting foreign banks in the United States are the International Banking Act (IBA) of 1978 and the Foreign Bank Supervision Enhancement Act (FBSEA) of 1991. The Riegle-Neal Interstate Banking and Branching Efficiency Act of 1994 and the Gramm-Leach-Bliley Financial Modernization Act of 1999 also address foreign bank operations in the U.S.

State and federal bank supervisors recently unveiled a new system for supervising and examining foreign banks in the United States. Under this system, state and federal bank regulators work together to provide a seamless overview of a foreign bank's entire U.S. operation – which may encompass several states. Since foreign bank branches and agencies are arms of their parent banks, their supervisory structure must be slightly different from that used for domestic institutions. Supervisors evaluate an office's risk management, operational controls, compliance with state and federal laws, and asset quality. The Federal Reserve also looks at the overall support U.S. offices receive from their parent banks. Foreign-owned banks that have deposit insurance must comply with all U.S. consumer laws and pay premiums to the FDIC. All lenders must comply with federal fair lending issues.

Foreign banks in the United States are an important source of new capital for American businesses. Since their parents are not as deeply affected by fluctuations in the U.S. economy as their domestic counterparts, U.S. offices of foreign banks can provide credit even during domestic "credit crunches." In short, foreign banks in the United States are valuable corporate citizens and an essential part of the American financial system.

OTHER FINANCIAL INTERMEDIARIES

Trust Companies

A trust company is a corporation authorized to act as a trustee or in other fiduciary capacities. It is somewhat of a historical accident that corporate trustees are regulated as banking institutions, but a trust company does not necessarily need to be a "bank" in the normal sense of the term. Some trust companies act as stand-alone trust companies that do not take deposits or make loans and which may or may not be affiliated with a bank. Many banks, of course, exercise trust powers directly through trust departments. Three alternative forms of trust company charters currently are used:

- State-Chartered Trust Company. The laws of approximately 40 states, including California, allow the establishment of stand-alone trust companies that do not take deposits or make loans and are not affiliated with a bank. The California Department of Financial Institutions ("DFI") licenses trust companies in California.

- National Trust Company. The Office of the Comptroller of the Currency ("OCC"), which charters and regulates national banks, may authorize the creation of a "national trust company," i.e., a bank that limits its activities to the exercise of trust powers.

- Thrift Limited to Trust Powers. The Office of Thrift Supervision ("OTS"), which charters federal savings associations (commonly called "thrifts"), recently has begun to issue charters for federal thrifts limited to trust powers.

While particular regulatory requirements and limitations must be examined on a case-by-case basis, practically anyone can establish, own, and operate a trust company. This includes natural persons, financial services institutions such as broker-dealers, investment advisory firms, insurance companies, and national or state-chartered banks and savings associations (or their holding companies), and non-financial commercial or industrial firms.

The fundamental trust company franchise is the legal authority to engage in the business of holding and managing other people's money for compensation. Technically, this means acting in a fiduciary or representative capacity (e.g., trustee, executor, guardian, conservator, investment adviser or manager, agent, custodian, and similar capacities) and providing services necessary or incidental to carrying out responsibilities imposed by fiduciary laws. The specific nature and scope of trust company business activities are defined by state law. (Federally-chartered trust institutions are authorized to engage generally in activities co-extensive with those permitted by competing state-chartered institutions.)

Statutory and regulatory minimum capitalization requirements for state-chartered institutions vary widely, ranging from as low as $100,000 to as high as $8 million. Applicants for federal charters can expect minimums in the vicinity of $3-5 million. The amount required also will depend on the nature and scope of the trust company's business activities.

Trust companies have two sets of legal and regulatory requirements to contend with:

- Federal and state laws applicable to particular fiduciary relationships govern a trust company's responsibilities as trustee or fiduciary. The Employee Retirement Income Security Act of 1974 (ERISA), for example, imposes standards and responsibilities on trustees and fiduciaries of private employee benefit plans. State laws, such as the Trust Law contained in the California Probate Code, govern fiduciary responsibilities to personal trusts and other non-ERISA trusts.

- A trust company also is subject to intersecting and sometimes inconsistent and overlapping laws governing the activities of the trust company itself as a business entity. As a result, choosing a trust company charter requires careful consideration of the applicable regulatory scheme in light of the organizers' business objectives. A few examples of these regulatory issues are referenced in a chart towards the end of this Client Alert.

Because trust companies are subject to regulation substantially similar to that applicable to banks, they enjoy many of the same exemptions from securities and other laws.

The laws of many states on the geographic limits on trust company operations are based on the notion that trust institutions are authorized to market and provide trust services only to citizens of the state in which the institution is based and chartered. While efforts are being made to ease barriers to interstate operations, these laws pose obstacles at least for state-chartered trust companies. The OCC and the OTS, on the other hand, have issued opinions to the effect that national trust companies and federal thrifts may establish limited purpose trust offices in any state that allows state-chartered banks and trust companies and other institutions the right to act as fiduciaries. Although federally-chartered institutions are subject to certain state requirements (e.g., security deposits with the state treasurer), laws restricting or prohibiting out-of-state institutions from providing or marketing fiduciary services in or to the state are, according to the OCC and OTS, preempted.

In short, federally-chartered trust companies currently have a clear advantage over state-chartered trust companies in terms of interstate operations. Nevertheless, this is an evolving and still somewhat confused area. The

OCC and OTS interpretations have not been tested in court, and several states have been reluctant to concede jurisdiction over out-of-state institutions, whether federal or state chartered. Institutions considering interstate operations thus should monitor current developments on a state-by-state basis. One thing, however, is clear: the modern mobility of customers, increasing competition from national financial services providers, and the communications revolution has made the trust and investment management business a truly national, indeed international, business.

Finance Companies

Finance companies make loans to both consumers and business. Like credit unions, consumer finance companies were established in the early 1900s to provide a source of funds for small borrowers. Because commercial banks did not serve the needs of small consumer borrowers at the beginning of the 20th century, many people borrowed from loan sharks, who charged exorbitant interest rates and frequently used quite abusive collection practices for bad debts. The problem was that small loans were so costly to service that no legal lender could afford to make such loans at the prevailing legal rate ceiling as set by the usury laws of the time in each state. Given this problem, many states enacted laws that (1) would allow specially chartered consumer finance companies to charge relatively high legal loan rates on small loans and (2) severely restricted the type of collection methods that such institutions could use.

Finance companies generally do not have federal insurance (some finance companies have obtained "industrial bank" charters in a few states or have qualified as "non-bank banks" so they can issue FDIC-insured deposits). They also do not have a specific federal regulator. However, they are subject to state regulation and to the Fair Trade and Debt Collection Practices rules of the Federal Trade Commission. In addition, they are potentially subject to antitrust laws. Finally, they are subject to Federal Reserve regulations that regulate credit rate disclosure, prohibit credit discrimination, etc. In general, finance companies tend to hold more capital in reserve relative to their assets than other depository institutions because their deposits are not federally insured.

Investment Banks and Brokerage Firms

Investment banking identifies, structures, and executes diverse and innovative public and private market transactions, helping clients in both developed and emerging markets to achieve their most important strategic and financial objectives. More specifically, an investment bank is an individual or institution that acts as an underwriter or agent for corporations and municipalities issuing securities. Most also maintain broker/dealer operations, maintain markets for previously issued securities, and offer advisory services to investors. Investment banks also have a large role in facilitating mergers and acquisitions, private equity placements, and corporate restructuring. Unlike traditional banks, investment banks do not accept deposits from and provide loans (other than margin loans) to individuals.

An investment bank is a financial institution that generally has two primary focuses: (1) sales and trading of securities and (2) investment banking. The sales and trading side, called the retail or brokerage side, deals with all types of securities and how both individuals and institutions wish to invest their money. The investment banking side primarily deals with corporate finance and all types of transactions pertaining to it.

The brokerage side is the part of the investment banking business with which most small investors are most familiar. Investors wishing to invest in individual securities must set up an account with a brokerage firm to handle the transactions. The types of brokerage accounts include cash accounts, margin accounts (which permit the investors to borrow to buy securities and to sell securities short), and managed accounts (where the brokerage firm is given authority to make transactions on behalf of the investor, rather than just executing the trades indicated by the investor).

Through the brokerage account, investors place their buy and sell orders for stocks, bonds, options, futures, and other securities and the brokerage firm executes the trades for a fee, called the commission, through its representative on the floor of the appropriate exchange or market. Investors can place a number of different types of orders such as market orders (to buy or sell immediately at the current market price), limit orders (which include good-until-canceled orders – keep the order open and buy or sell when the security reaches the specified price or until cancelled, fill-or-kill orders – if the order cannot be executed at the specified price immediately, it is cancelled, and day orders – if the order is not executed by the end of the day, it is cancelled), and stop-loss orders (buy or sell the security if it reaches a specified price).

The brokerage firm keeps track of all trades and issues regular reports, accounts for all cash received on sales and paid for purchases, credits the accounts for all dividends and interest received on securities held in street name[1] as well as debiting the accounts for any interest paid on margin loans, monitors the adequacy of margin and issues margin calls when necessary to meet margin requirements, and monitors all pending or outstanding orders. In addition, firms may provide more or less in the way of investment research, advice, and recommendations. Typically, the commission that investors pay on purchases and sales of securities depends on the level of service. Full service brokers who provide extensive research and advice charge higher commissions. However, most brokerage firms now offer discount, no-frills, brokerage services that provide no specific advice or recommendations and just complete the investor's desired transactions. The commissions are correspondingly lower. In the case of managed accounts, the brokerage firm often does not charge commissions, per se, but rather charges a regular comprehensive fee as a percentage of the value of assets being managed.

The major "players" in the industry, when classified on the basis of size, include Goldman Sachs, Morgan Stanley Dean Witter, Salomon Smith Barney, Bear Sterns, Lehman brothers, Donaldson, Lufkin & Jenrette, and Merrill Lynch. These large firms are known as the "bulge bracket" but a large number of other firms form the sizeable second tier of investment banks. When viewed from the perspective of providing pure investment banking services as compared to a mix of financial services, Goldman Sachs is an example of a bank dealing almost exclusively in investment banking services. JP Morgan Chase and Deutsche Bank, on the other hand, have diversified by providing a combination of investment and commercial banking services. There are also some small, specialized banks, called boutiques, such as Allen & Co. and Lazard Freres, that are oriented towards a specific aspect or niche of investment banking like bond trading, merger and acquisition advisory, or technical analysis.

The revenues from investment banking crossed $200 billion in 2000, amounting to 0.6% of the world's GDP. It is very difficult to gauge the exact size of the industry simply because the industry environment is extremely volatile and a lot of the firms are still private firms. A fair idea about the seriousness of investment banking can be gauged from the fact that global securities underwriting (one of the key investment banking services), despite a slump of 5.1% in 2002, stood at $3.9 trillion. As far as profits go, an investment-bank, through underwriting, typically makes four times the profit that a traditional bank does through issuing an ordinary loan.

The scope of investment banking has widened in the U.S. since 1999 with the repeal of Glass-Steagall Act and the passing of the Gramm-Leach-Bliley Act. This legislation has brought down the barriers between commercial and investment banking. As a result, investment banks are increasingly venturing into the markets and financial services traditionally performed by commercial banks. Under the new legislative environment, a broader and better definition of investment banking is as an industry that either trades directly in capital market products or uses the underlying capital markets to construct different financial products.

In this new emerging and competitive environment, the kinds of services investment banks are offering include

- underwriting initial public equity offerings (IPOs) of traditional and new equity issues and bond issues such as mortgage bonds, Eurobonds, etc.

- sales and trading of fixed income products like government bonds, Eurobonds, money market instruments, asset swaps, corporate bonds, municipal bonds, asset-backed securities, floating-rate notes, mortgage bonds, bond options and more

- sales and trading of stocks listed on stock exchanges or unlisted securities

- sales and trading of the whole range of derivative instruments based on underlying equity, fixed income, foreign exchange, credit, and commodity markets (e.g. sugar, oil, and gold)

- advising, structuring, launching, and financing mergers and acquisitions of companies

- management of funds on behalf of pension funds, life insurance companies, and other institutional portfolios in global capital markets

- helping companies raise funds needed for new projects by determining the amount of funds needed and the means of raising it (through equity, debt, convertibles, preferred, asset-backs or derivative securities)

- conducting research on markets, industry, economic conditions, credit, to give buy or sell recommendations to investors regarding specific stocks or bonds or other securities

- managing investment assets of private wealthy individuals
- providing private banking services for large individual investors

Investment Companies and Mutual Funds

Investment companies allow a large number of relatively small investors to pool their resources and purchase shares in a diversified portfolio. Diversification permits investors to participate in relatively risky investments since only a small percentage of their assets are actually invested in the securities of any one company. To achieve this level of diversification without resorting to mutual fund ownership, an investor would have to have a substantial amount of capital. Purchasing a large number of different securities in less than round lots, that is, in lots of less than 100 shares, is rather expensive. Also, the record keeping involved would be rather burdensome.

Open-End Funds and Closed-End Funds

Investment companies come in essentially two flavors: open-end funds and closed-end funds. Open-end investment companies are usually referred to as mutual funds. Mutual funds are by far the dominant form of investment company. The number of shares outstanding in a mutual fund depends on investor demand. When investors buy shares in the mutual fund, the mutual fund issues new shares. When investors redeem shares, the mutual fund reduces the number of shares it has outstanding. The net asset value (NAV) of a mutual fund is calculated at least once each day. Net asset value is found by taking the total market value of all securities and other assets owned by the fund, subtracting any liabilities, and dividing by the number of shares in the fund. For example, if at the end of the day a mutual fund has a net asset value of $100 million and 2.5 million shares outstanding, the fund has a net asset value of $40 a share.

Closed-end investment companies have a fixed number of shares outstanding. Once they commence operations, they do not normally issue and redeem shares of stock in the fund. Their purpose is to purchase (invest in) other securities. To purchase shares in a closed-end investment company, an investor must buy them in the market from another investor who wants to sell. The investor does not purchase shares from the investment company. At any moment, the value of the shares of a closed-end investment company is determined by the supply and demand for those particular securities. While net asset value is important, there is no guarantee that the fund will be selling at or near its net asset value. Often closed-end investment companies trade at a discount or premium to net asset value. It is possible to find the prices of closed-end investment company stocks selling 15 to 20% greater or less than their net asset value.

Why Investment Companies Arose

Investment companies arose and are considered financial intermediaries because they were able to provide small investors with a number of advantages that they, usually, could not achieve in the securities markets on their own. These advantages included professional management, better investment diversification, a broader range of investment opportunities, convenience, better record-keeping and other investment information, greater liquidity, and protection through regulation.

Professional management – Professional management helps investors because most small investors do not have the time to properly select and manage a portfolio of securities. This often requires research and the analysis of extensive amounts of data. This job often is best turned over to a professional portfolio manager who specializes in investing and managing investments for others. Professional portfolio managers have greater access to the quantitative tools needed to evaluate financial data, to evaluate the quality and ability of a firm's management, and to assess the level of competition in an industry. Thus, they can better make an informed judgment as to the timing of buying and selling individual securities.

Diversification – Purchasing shares of a mutual fund gives the investor immediate diversification. An investor can acquire a portfolio of securities that meet the investor's objectives. For instance, if the investor's objective is aggressive growth, the purchase of a mutual fund with this same stated objective for several thousand dollars could result in a portfolio of 50 or 100 stocks that together meet the investment criteria.

There are many different types of diversification:

- One can diversify among different asset categories, for example, stocks versus bonds versus money market instruments versus real estate.
- One can diversify among different industries, for example, computer versus autos versus entertainment versus retailing.

- One can purchase shares of, and thus diversify, among different companies such as IBM, Wal-Mart, General Motors, and AT&T.

- One can also diversify among different countries by purchasing stocks of companies headquartered in the United States, Germany, Great Britain, and Australia.

Range of investment opportunities – There are thousands of funds from which to choose. Mutual fund companies typically offer investors a family of funds, each having different investment objectives. For example, some of the funds may be growth funds, growth and income funds, or specialty funds that concentrate investments in a specific industry such as health care. Also, within a family of funds, investors are able to move from different types of investments, that is, they can shift money from stock funds to bond funds. Care should be taken however when switching from one fund to another, even within a family. For instance, unless the investment is in a tax-deferred account such as a 401(k) plan or an IRA, every time one fund is sold and another purchased there are income-tax consequences – if there is gain on the shares of the fund sold, taxes are recognized on the gain. Also, attempts at market timing by switching into and out of various mutual funds or between stocks and cash are rarely successful.

Convenience – Mutual funds generally offer automatic reinvestment plans through which dividends and capital gains are reinvested in additional shares of the fund. Also, transfers between funds in the same family can usually be made by telephone or electronic account transfers. This provides investors with additional flexibility if they decide to change their asset allocation.

Record keeping and investor information – Whenever transactions are made, statements are sent to the investor confirming the transactions. They typically show the date and the amount of shares purchased or sold. Also, investors receive periodic statements from mutual fund companies showing the balance in their account and any activity during the statement period. Mutual fund statements also serve as a convenient source of information when preparing income taxes. Some mutual fund companies provide investors with a statement of the average cost of the shares that they have sold. This aids in calculating the gain or loss for tax purposes. Finally, most mutual fund companies provide telephone and even on-line access to account information. The investor can get up-to-date information on the balance of the investor's account, the date of the next dividend, as well as general facts about the fund.

Liquidity – Investors can sell closed-end fund shares whenever the markets are open or redeem mutual fund shares daily at net asset value, giving the investor quick access to the funds.

Regulation – Investment companies are highly regulated, which helps to insure that management treats investors in a legal and ethical manner.

Low cost – Investing in no-load mutual funds is a very low-cost method of acquiring a diversified portfolio.

Money-Market Mutual Funds (MMMFs)

Perhaps the closest substitute for a depository account in a bank is the money-market mutual fund. MMMFs were designed to invest in short-term, highly liquid money-market securities, such as T-bills, CDs, commercial paper, and other notes generally with a term to maturity of less than one year and offer yields that are generally quite favorable compared to interest paid on deposits in bank checking and savings accounts. In addition, most money market mutual funds and some short-term bond funds offer check-writing privileges, so they are essentially direct competitors to bank checking accounts. Generally, the owner can write checks against the balance in the owner's account, usually subject to a minimum, such as $100, $250 or $500 per check.

Other Pooled Investment Intermediaries

A whole host of additional pooled investment opportunities have arisen for investors for the same reasons as those that led to the growth of investment companies, and the number keeps growing. Among these pooled investments are unit trusts, real-estate investment trusts (REITs), mortgage-backed bonds, real-estate mortgage investment conduits (REMICS), and exchange-traded funds (ETFs). A brief description of each of these types of pooled investments follows.

Unit Trusts

A unit investment trust is a pool of unmanaged investments. A trust agreement is drawn up under which the trust holds a portfolio of securities for safekeeping. Once the portfolio is established, it is not actively traded. More often than not, they invest in fixed-income investments such as corporate and/or government bonds or mortgages. As the bonds mature, the proceeds are distributed, rather than reinvested, as would generally be the case with a closed-end investment company. Brokerage houses usually put these trusts together. Units in the trust are then sold to the public, usually at a price of $1,000 a unit. The sponsoring organization handles routine record keeping, collects any coupons or dividends, and distributes the income to the trust holders.

REITs

Real estate investment trusts (REITs) are essentially publicly traded closed-end investment companies that invest in a managed, diversified portfolio of real estate or real estate mortgages and construction loans rather than in financial securities such as stocks and bonds. Although REITs are corporations or trusts, they are not subject to tax at the corporate level if they distribute at least 95% of their net annual earnings to shareholders and meet certain other requirements. Investors must pay the tax on a REIT's earnings as the earnings are distributed. Therefore, REITs allow investors to share, with limited liability, the financial and tax benefits of real estate while avoiding the double taxation inherent in corporate ownership.

Investors have three types of REITs from which to choose: (1) equity REITs, (2) mortgage REITs, and (3) hybrid REITs. Equity REITs acquire ownership interests in commercial, industrial, or residential properties. Income is primarily received from the rentals of these properties. Mortgage REITs invest in real estate indirectly by lending funds for construction and/or permanent mortgages. In some cases, mortgage REITs invest in mortgage-backed securities such as Ginnie Maes or other mortgage-backed obligations. Hybrid REITs combine the features of both equity and mortgage REITs by investing both in real estate and mortgages or loans secured by real estate, similar to a balanced mutual fund investing in stocks and bonds.

Mortgage-Backed Securities

A mortgage-backed bond or security is a debt issue that is backed or secured by a pool of mortgages. For instance, the Government National Mortgage Association (GNMA) assembles home mortgages and issues securities based on the total amount of mortgages in the pool. Such securities are referred to as pass-through securities or participation certificates, and investors can purchase them in denominations of $25,000. The average life of these securities is around eight to 10 years, even though the original maturities may be as long as 30 years. Since the securities are backed by home mortgages, as mortgages are paid off early, the life of the securities is typically less than the original maturity date would indicate.

If interest rates drop, the rate at which these mortgage-backed obligations are paid off usually increases. The problem here is that investors do not lock in a high interest rate for as long a period as they originally hoped. On the other hand, if mortgage interest rates rise, the rate at which these mortgages are paid off should slow down and investors will be stuck holding securities that pay lower than current market interest rates for a longer period of time than they might like. Also, the security holder has to realize that the payments being received are part interest and part principal. Unlike traditional bonds, at maturity there is no lump-sum principal to be received. The investor should be reinvesting principal payments and not treat the interest portion of the distributions as spendable income.

REMICs

Real estate mortgage investment conduits are limited-life, self-liquidating entities that invest exclusively in real estate mortgages or in securities backed by real estate mortgages. They issue two types of securities – regular interests and residual interests. There may be many classes of REMIC regular interests, that is, REMIC bonds, but only one class of residual interest. REMIC bonds are treated for tax purposes as debt securities. The bonds receive a specified cash flow from the underlying pool of mortgages, similar to mortgage-backed bonds such as Ginnie Maes.

Real estate mortgage investment conduits were developed to solve the problem of the prepayment uncertainty that exists with typical mortgage-backed securities. A REMIC divides the payouts on a pool of mortgages into tranches, or segments, based on the investors' preferences for a short-term, intermediate term, or long-term investment. Typically, all investors receive periodic interest payments, but principal payments are another matter. The short-term class receives principal payments first. After those securities are retired, the next or intermediate-term tranche receives principal payments until those securities are retired. Finally, principal payments go to the long-term investors.

REMICs are essentially derivative securities – securities that were created from other securities, in this case from mortgage-backed bonds. The mortgage-backed bonds are placed in a trust and REMIC interests, which are participation certificates in the trust, are sold to the public. Their credit ratings are very high since they are typically made up of mortgage-backed bonds that are backed or guaranteed by the U.S. government.

Regular REMIC interests are not subject so much to default risk as they are to prepayment risk. Some of the short-duration tranches have very little or no prepayment risk. Other longer-term tranches carry a disproportionate share of the prepayment risk and their price movements are very volatile.

Residual interests are treated for tax purposes much like interests in a partnership or trust. They are roughly comparable to an equity interest in the REMIC entity. Whatever income is not paid to the REMIC bondholders goes to the residual interest holders in the REMIC.

REMICs are flow-through entities, similar to mutual funds, and are typically exempt from the federal income tax. A REMIC terminates when all mortgages are repaid.

Exchange-Traded Funds

On the simplest level, as the name implies, an exchange-traded fund (ETF) is a basket of securities, like a mutual fund. However, ETFs are traded, like individual stocks, on an exchange. They are something of a hybrid, combining features of both closed-end and open-end mutual funds, as well as other unique features.

ETFs represent shares of ownership in funds, unit investment trusts, or depository receipts that hold portfolios of common stocks that closely track the performance and dividend yield of specific indexes. They give investors the opportunity to buy or sell an entire portfolio of stocks in a single security as easily as buying or selling a share of stock. They offer a wide range of investment opportunities.

ETFs bear exotic names, such as Qubes, SPDRs, sector SPDRs, MidCap SPDRs, HOLDRs, iShares, VIPERs, and DIAMONDS. All of them are passively managed, tracking a wide variety of sector-specific, country-specific, and broad-market indexes. In addition, new ETFs covering various market sectors, market indexes, or international markets are being created nearly every day.

Broad-based funds track a broad group of stocks from different industries and market sectors. For example, iShares S&P 500 index fund (symbol IVV) is a broad-based ETF that tracks the S&P 500. Sector funds track companies represented in related industries. Another, iShares Dow Jones U.S. Healthcare Sector Index Fund (symbol IYH), is a sector ETF that tracks the Dow Jones Healthcare sector. International funds track a group of stocks from a specific country or a broad index of international stocks such as the MSCI – EAFE index. The iShares MSCI-Australia (symbol EWA) tracks the Morgan Stanley Capital International index for Australian stocks.

While similar to index mutual funds, ETFs differ from mutual funds in significant ways. Unlike index mutual funds, ETFs are priced and can be bought and sold throughout the trading day. Furthermore, ETFs can be sold short and bought on margin. Essentially, anything investors might do with an individual stock, they can do with an ETF.

One of the most important characteristics that make ETFs different from mutual funds or closed-end funds is the redemption feature.

ETFs can be redeemed for the underlying securities. Generally, only large institutional investors or very wealthy investors can avail themselves of this feature, since the minimum in-kind redemption is generally at least 50,000 shares. However, this creates an arbitrage opportunity if prices in the market differ significantly from the net asset value. Consequently, in contrast with closed-end mutual funds, market arbitrage generally keeps ETFs trading close to their net asset values. Although the trading prices for ETFs do not always equal their net asset values, they rarely, if ever, trade at the significant discounts and premiums from net asset value that characterizes market prices for closed-end funds.

Insurance Companies

Life Insurance Companies

Insurance companies are essentially another type of investment pooling intermediary with a twist. The twist is that they also provide a mechanism for risk sharing and risk transfer.

Similar to other investments, the principal economic purpose of life insurance is to accumulate capital. Although most commentators stress that life insurance should not be viewed principally as an investment, the authors of this text disagree. That is what life insurance really is: a superb "investment" vehicle. All conventional investment vehicles serve the same purpose, but the unique feature of life insurance is that it assures a desired accumulation at a specific, but uncertain, time, namely at the time of the insured's death. No other investment makes such a guarantee. It accomplishes this goal by pooling the investments of many investors and, through actuarial calculations, sharing the risk among all investors so that each will receive the desired investment accumulation at their uncertain time of death.

If the time of death were not uncertain, life insurance would be unnecessary. A person could accumulate any desired target amount by investing in a traditional investment vehicle and employing a systematic plan of saving, or what is called a sinking fund. For example, if a person's objective is to accumulate $1,000 in five years and he or she could be assured of surviving that long, this person could simply invest a specific lump-sum amount today in a traditional investment vehicle that with interest would grow to $1,000 in 5 years. For instance, if $620.92 is invested today at 10% interest, the fund will grow to $1,000 in 5 years. Alternatively, if this person does not have $620.92 to invest today, he or she could finance the accumulation over time, for instance, by investing $148.91 at the beginning of each year for the next five years. However, if this person died anytime before the end of the 5-year period, the amount accumulated at the time of death would be less than the desired $1,000. Life insurance is essentially an investment mechanism that assures the desired accumulation by the time of death regardless of when death occurs.

Most discussions of life insurance describe it as a combination of "pure death protection" that decreases and "saving" or "investment" that increases over a person's lifetime. This distinction can be confusing and misleading since life insurance should be viewed in its entirety as a special type of investment or accumulation vehicle that matures at death. However, this bifurcation between "death protection" and "savings" elements can be useful, if it is understood for what it really is. The savings component is the noncontingent part of the overall investment accumulation that is available not just at death, but also during life, similar to any conventional investment or savings instrument.

What is described as the pure death protection component is properly viewed as a contingent investment; that is, the part of the overall investment accumulation that matures or becomes available only at death. The relative size of these two components depends on the life product and how the life insurance is financed. At one extreme is annually renewable term insurance, which is essentially 100% pure death protection and 0% savings. At the other extreme are deferred annuities during the accumulation phase (and other conventional investments) that are essentially 0% pure death protection and 100% savings.[2] The other life insurance products lie somewhere between these extremes.

Making the distinction between the "pure death protection" and "savings" components actually ignores half the spectrum of "life" products. Annuities may be described in a manner analogous to life insurance, as a combination of "pure life protection" and "savings" elements after the annuity starting date. The savings component of annuities is the noncontingent part of the overall investment that is available regardless of whether one lives or dies, similar to any conventional investment or savings instrument.

In other words, the savings component is the guaranteed or refund amount provided by some annuities that is payable even if the annuitant dies. The pure life protection component is a contingent investment that matures or is available only if the annuitant lives. At one end of this spectrum are full-refund or term-certain annuities (or conventional investments) that are essentially 100% savings and 0% pure life protection. At the other end of the spectrum are no-refund life annuities that are 0% savings (theoretically) and 100% pure life protection.[3]

Figure 21.3 shows how various "life" products from term insurance to annuities fall within the pure death/life protection and savings element spectra. But keep in mind that both components comprise the total investment. Any assessment that evaluates the "investment" potential of a life product by looking only at the savings element (the amounts which are available regardless of whether a person lives or dies) ignores the fact that the pure death/life protection component is properly viewed as a type of contingent investment that matures or is available only when the death or life contingency occurs.

A common misconception about life insurance is that the risk of premature death is transferred to the insurance company. Although insurance companies must have a certain amount of surplus or paid-in capital to cover potential excess losses, they price their products to maintain or even increase the surplus and paid-in capital over time. Therefore, risk is shifted to or shared among all insureds in the insurance pool. Those policyowners who live a long time carry the economic burden for those who do not. However, there is less risk sharing with premium-payment plans that generate a greater "savings" component, such as single-premium life insurance, than with those that have a greater "pure death protection"

Figure 21.3

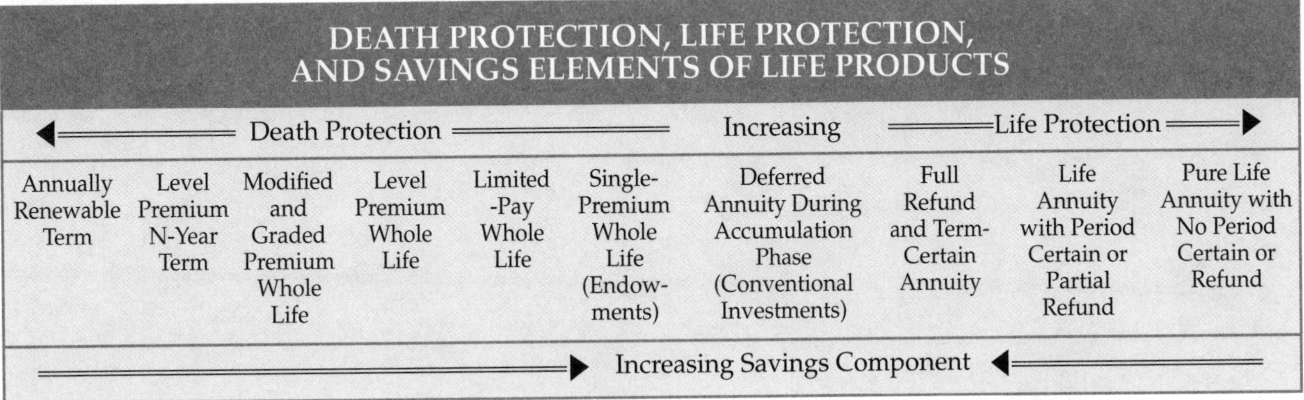

component, such as annually renewable term. The savings component, similar to other investments, can be viewed as a form of self-insurance, since it is available regardless of whether the insured lives or dies. If the self-insurance component is greater, the amount of risk that must be shared among all participants in the pool is obviously less.

Property, Casualty, Liability, Health, Disability and Other Insurance Companies

Similar to life insurance companies, these other insurers are intermediaries that pool the resources of many people to share and transfer the risk of various potential loses. Through payment of actuarially determined premiums, all the policyholders essentially split the cost of any loses for any of the insureds so that no one insured has to bear the burden of a catastrophic loss. Once again, if the timing, incidence, and magnitude of all losses could be accurately predicted for each insured, there would be no market for this insurance. But since nobody knows for sure just who will incur losses, when they will occur, or the magnitude of the losses, people are willing to pool their resources and share the losses for the betterment of everyone.

CHAPTER ENDNOTES

1. Most cash accounts and all margin and managed accounts are in street name, meaning, the securities are actually held in the brokerage firm's name. Entries are placed in the individual investor's accounts indicating their ownership of various securities held by the firm in street name. The investor accounts do not actually have the stock certificates or bonds or other evidences of securities in their accounts.
2. The life insurance product "closest" to a 0% pure death protection and 100% savings combination is a single-premium endowment policy. An endowment policy is essentially a whole life policy that will mature or "endow," that is, pay the face amount of coverage, if the insured is still alive at a specified age, such as age 65. Similar to other life insurance products, it also pays the face amount if the insured dies before the policy endows. By analogy, traditional whole life policies are really endowment policies that endow at age 95 or 100.
3. Even "pure" no-refund life annuities may be considered to have some "savings" component or provide some element of recovery even in the event of death since they may sometimes be exchanged for annuities with refund or guaranteed features, companies may permit the annuitant to "surrender" all or a part of the annuity for its commuted value, or, in very limited circumstances and in limited amounts, the annuitant may be permitted to take loans.

Part 4:

LEGAL

Chapter 22

BUSINESS ENTITIES

WHAT IS IT?

A "business entity" is simply an organization that operates a business in some way. Even an operation run out of one's home on a strictly part-time basis with absolutely no formalities is still operating as a business entity, namely a sole proprietorship.

Business entities run the gamut from the one-person sole proprietorship to corporations with thousands of employees. These different entities have different rules on how they may be formed and governed as well as different tax consequences.

SELECTING THE ENTITY

A person, or group of persons, who are considering entering into a business face a number of choices with regard to the type of entity to use for the potential business. Among the entities that could be chosen are a sole proprietorship (for a single owner), partnership (either general or limited), or a corporation. Importantly, when the owners choose the business form, they are not stuck with that form. The owners can decide to change the form of business if conditions change, although there may be significant costs involved in changing business entities. The form of the business entity is an important decision for a new business because it will affect the costs to start up the business, how the entity will be governed on a day-to-day basis, and perhaps most importantly, what the personal liability of the owners will be.

SOLE PROPRIETORSHIPS

A sole proprietorship is defined as an unincorporated, one-person business, entirely owned and directed by a single person. It is the simplest form of business organization and, as distinguished from a partnership or corporation, a sole proprietorship may be started with a minimum of legal formality. There is seldom need for government approval, with some notable exceptions.

A sole proprietorship does not exist apart from its owner. The sole proprietor and the business are one, and the assets of the business are, at the same time, a part of the proprietor's personal estate. All assets of the business, both tangible and intangible, belong to the sole proprietor. All profits are his or her personal property.

A sole proprietorship may be in order when a prospective business owner wishes to begin operations quickly, with a minimum of paperwork and regulation. For example, to set up a retail store, local regulations may require only a vendor's license and a filing to do business under an assumed name. The new entrepreneur then needs only to find a shop, stock the shelves, and open for business. However, it is true that some sole proprietorships do involve prior government approval. Typically, restaurants, bars, beauty and barber shops, drug stores, and other businesses that may affect public health, safety, or morals must meet additional requirements.

The requirements for operating a business as a sole proprietorship are minimal and generally center on the type of business conducted. However, it should be recognized early in the life cycle of the business that the continued operation of a sole proprietorship is totally dependent upon the ability and personality of one person with continued success and prosperity depending to an enormous extent upon the continuing life and health of the proprietor.

The sole proprietor and his business are taxed as a single unit, and, for federal income tax purposes, he files Form 1040, the individual income tax return along with Schedule C or Schedule C-EZ. All of the proprietor's personal and business income is subject to regular personal tax rates ranging currently from 10% to 35%. There is no separate proprietorship income tax reporting.

PARTNERSHIPS

A partnership is an association of two or more persons to carry on as co-owners of a business for profit. Generally, there are two types of partnerships:

1. *General partnerships* – This is the type in general use. Each partner is a principal, fully active in

the business with a voice in its management; each is an agent of the other with authority to act for the firm within the scope of its business activities; each is fully liable for firm debts; and each shares in the profits.

2. *Limited partnerships* – A limited partnership is defined under some type of state statutory authority such as the Uniform Limited Partnership Act. It is defined as a partnership formed by two or more persons having as members one or more general partners and one or more limited partners. The limited partner's financial liability is limited to his investment in the firm. Note, however, that a limited partnership must have at least one general partner with full liability.

Like a sole proprietorship, a partnership is an unincorporated business entity that is uniquely personal and created by the voluntary acts of the partners, themselves. (Distinguish this from the corporation, which is essentially a creature of the state.) Then, too, a partnership may arise from simply an oral agreement between two or more competent parties to carry on a business for profit. Such an implied partnership is totally dependent upon the close, daily, personal trust and agreement of the parties.

A partnership, itself, is not taxed.[1] However, the partnership must file an informational income tax return with the IRS. The partnership is considered an entity for purposes of determining taxable income and business expenses of the partnership may be deducted. Each partner must report his share of partnership profits, whether or not distributed, on his individual income tax return.[2]

A *family limited partnership* is a limited partnership that exists between members of a family (defined for income tax purposes as including only an individual's spouse, ancestors, lineal descendants, and any trusts established primarily for the benefit of such persons). If a partnership among family members is a genuine partnership, it will be treated tax-wise the same as any other partnership and the same rules will apply. The family limited partnership is a technique frequently used as a means of shifting the income tax burden from parents to children or other family members. However, the benefit of shifting income to children under age 18 has been substantially eliminated. For children under age 18, unearned income in excess of $1,700 (as indexed for 2007) generally will be taxed at the parent's top marginal rate under the "kiddie tax" rules. Starting in 2008, the kiddie tax could affect full-time students up to the age of 24 (see Chapter 27).

A *limited liability partnership* (LLP) is a general partnership that is typically available to only certain professions such as accountants, doctors, and lawyers. Roughly 40 states recognize some form of LLP. The main distinguishing feature of an LLP is that the partners are not liable for the professional malpractice of another partner. Note that no matter the type of business entity someone uses, they cannot insulate themselves from their own professional malpractice.

Partnerships can generally be formed on a tax-free basis. Neither the partnership nor its partners will recognize any gain (or loss) when the partnership receives money or property in exchange for partnership interests.[3]

On the sale of a partnership interest, if the amount a partner realizes exceeds his adjusted basis in his partnership interest, the gain is capital gain *except* that if part of the *amount realized* (whether it is more or less than his basis) is attributable to his share of certain ordinary income property (i.e., partnership assets which, if sold, would result in ordinary gain), part of the amount realized (not just part of the gain) will generally have to be treated as ordinary income.[4]

LIMITED LIABILITY COMPANIES

A limited liability company (LLC) is a hybrid business entity created under state law. It typically combines the limited liability normally associated with a corporation and the pass-through tax treatment accorded to a partnership. All states allow the formation and operation of LLCs but the requirements, operating rules, and tax treatment vary widely among the states. For instance, some states allow single-owner LLCs while other states require two or more owners. Some states impose a state income tax on LLCs while others do not.

An LLC might be appropriate when the owners of the business entity would like the limited liability treatment normally associated with corporations, but also desire flexibility in choosing the tax treatment under federal law. An LLC can choose to be treated, for federal income tax purposes, as either a corporation (a C or S corporation) or a partnership. An LLC may also be appropriate when the owners of a business require flexibility in ownership structure. LLC owners ("members") can be individuals, partnerships, trusts, corporations, or other LLCs, and there is no limitation on the number of members. By contrast, there are significant restrictions on both the type and number of shareholders that can own S Corporation stock.

To form an LLC, articles of organization must typically be filed with a state's office of the secretary of state. The articles of organization contain basic information about the LLC, such as its name, principal place of business, purpose, agent, etc. Some states also require that an operating agreement be filed along with the articles of organization. Even if not required, however, an operating agreement is important to set out the rules for the management of the LLC.

By default, two or more members in an LLC are taxed as if they are partners in a partnership. This means that the income, deductions, capital gains and losses, charitable contributions, stock dividends, and other tax attributes of the business pass through to the members' individual income tax returns. Single-member LLCs are generally taxed as sole proprietorships.[5]

Under the "Check-the-Box" regulations, the members of LLCs may choose the tax treatment afforded to the LLC. LLCs with two or more owners may be treated as a partnership, or the members may file an election to opt for treatment as a corporation. LLCs with a single member may be disregarded as an entity for tax purposes, treating the business as a sole proprietorship, or the member may elect to have the LLC treated as a corporation.[6]

C CORPORATIONS

A corporation is a business entity that limits the liability of its owners. Legally, a corporation is a separate entity from its owners and employees. A corporation can own property in its own name, enter into contracts in its own name, and can sue and be sued in its own name.

A corporation may be indicated when the owners of a business entity want to limit their liability in the business venture. Note, however, that business owners who are also employees of the corporation cannot limit their negligence liability for actions that they themselves commit. Furthermore, an owner of a closely-held or family-owned corporation is often required to personally co-sign, with the corporation, for loans and, thus, may be unable to limit his liability completely.

Almost all states require a corporation to file certain papers with the state. These papers will include at least the corporation's legal name, its purpose, and the name and address of an agent who can be served should the corporation be sued. Some states may also require a corporate charter and corporate bylaws to be filed. Depending on the law of a particular state, a corporation generally must have a shareholder meeting once a year and periodic meetings of the board of directors. There generally must be formal elections of directors and records must be kept of the minutes of shareholder meetings and meetings of the board of directors.

A corporation is a separate taxable entity from its owners and pays federal income tax at its own income tax rates.[7] The taxable income of a corporation is calculated in much the same way as for an individual. Generally, a corporation may take the same deductions as an individual, except those of a personal nature (such as deductions for medical expenses and the personal exemptions). Employee benefits provided for employees are, generally, deductible as ordinary and necessary business expenses, even for those employees who are also owners of the corporation. A corporation is not allowed a standard deduction. When the corporation distributes its profits as dividends to its shareholders, the shareholders are taxed, but the corporation is not allowed a deduction for dividends that are distributed. This is what causes the so-called "double tax" on corporate income. Income is taxed first at the corporate level and then again when profits are distributed to shareholders as dividends.

Corporations can generally be formed on a tax-free basis. The corporation will not recognize any gain (or loss) when it receives money or property in exchange for its own stock, whether the stock is newly issued or treasury stock.[8]

Also, generally, a party who transfers money or property to a corporation will not recognize gain or loss when property is transferred to a corporation in exchange for the corporation's stock. But this ability to transfer even appreciated assets in return for corporate stock tax free applies only if all the parties who contribute property and receive the stock control 80% or more of the stock after the transaction.[9] If the persons who contribute property to the corporation receive additional property or money in the transaction, i.e., "boot," gain will be recognized, but the gain will not exceed the amount of any money received plus the fair market value of the property that is received.[10]

Generally upon the complete liquidation of a corporation, the shareholders will receive money or property from the corporation in exchange for the stock that they own. If they receive more than the basis they have in their stock, they will have a capital gain. If they receive less than the basis in their stock, they will incur a capital loss.

S CORPORATIONS

An "S" corporation is a corporation that has elected to have its income, deductions, capital gains and losses, charitable contributions, and credits passed through to its shareholders.[11] For federal income tax purposes, an S corporation is treated much like a partnership. For almost all other purposes, an S corporation is treated as a "regular," or "C" corporation.

An S corporation may be appropriate when the owners of the business entity would like the limited liability that is available with a corporation, but also desire pass-though treatment for federal (and, in most but not all cases, state) income tax purposes. The pass-through treatment is advantageous both because the income of the corporation will be taxed only once, and because it allows the owners to deduct any losses that the corporation may incur. This is in contrast to the income of a C corporation which is taxed both when it is earned at the corporate level and then when it is paid out to shareholders in the form of dividends. Also, any capital gains earned by a C corporation are generally taxed at the C corporation's regular tax rate. Also, the ability to deduct losses may be especially important in the early years of a corporation. Some corporations are formed as S corporations to take advantage of the owners' ability to deduct losses in the early years, and then when the company becomes profitable, the S election is terminated.

Much like a partnership, an S corporation is generally not subject to tax at the entity (corporate) level.[12] Whether the S corporation's profits are distributed to them or not, S corporation shareholders are taxed on the S corporation's taxable income. Shareholders take into account their shares of income, loss, deductions, and credit on a per-share, per-day basis.[13]

S corporation income that could directly affect the tax liability of the shareholder is passed directly through the corporation to the shareholder. Also, any loss or deduction that the S corporation takes that could directly affect the liability of the shareholder is also passed directly through to the shareholder. An example of this "separately stated" income is the treatment of capital gain income, which is taxed at a different rate than ordinary income. Another example is the treatment of charitable deductions of an S corporation, which are passed directly through to the shareholder.

PROFESSIONAL CORPORATIONS

A professional corporation is simply a C corporation or S corporation in which all the shareholders are members of a profession such as doctors, lawyers, or accountants. A group of professionals might form a corporation so that the owners can take advantage of certain fringe benefits that are available only to employees of C corporations.

ASSOCIATIONS

An association is not really a "business" entity, but is generally a voluntary organization of people under a common name to accomplish some purpose. Associations are generally unincorporated, but they usually will have articles of association or a charter or bylaws for a governing document. Unincorporated clubs, for example, and labor unions would be examples of associations.

TRUSTS

A trust is an entity established either through a will or during an individual's life. In creating a trust, assets are placed in the trust by the grantor (also referred to as the settlor, creator, or trustor). These assets, called the corpus of the trust, are then managed by the trustee (sometimes referred to as the fiduciary) for the beneficiaries. The beneficiaries may receive either the income from the trust or the remainder of the trust, which is the corpus at the time the trust ends, or both. The trustee manages and holds legal title to the property while the beneficiaries hold beneficial title.

Trusts take many forms and are established for different reasons, but they are commonly set up for probate avoidance and tax purposes. For example, a revocable trust avoids probate and can serve as a will substitute by governing the distribution of the grantor's property. Because the grantor has not parted with control of the property, the grantor incurs no gift tax when the trust is set up; the grantor is responsible for the income tax on the income from the trust property; and the trust property is included in the grantor's estate for estate tax purposes when he or she dies.

In contrast, irrevocable trusts are often set up to obtain a trustee's management expertise and objectivity. Because the grantor has relinquished rights to the property, the transfer is subject to gift tax; income tax on the income from the trust property is paid either by the trustee for the trust or by the beneficiaries; and the property is not pulled back into the grantor's estate.

Trusts are required to file a federal income tax return if the trust has any taxable income, or if it has gross income of $600 or more for the year. Trusts are referred to as modified conduit entities because they receive a deduction for income that is distributed from the trust and are taxed on income that is retained by the trust. Trust tax rates are very compact. Trusts are taxed at the 35% marginal tax rate when taxable income exceeds $10,450 (in 2007). In comparison, individuals are not taxed at the 35% rate until their taxable income exceeds $349,700 (in 2007), and corporations are not taxed at the 39% rate until taxable income exceeds $100,000.[14] The beneficiary that receives the income from the trust is liable for the tax on the income.

CHAPTER ENDNOTES

1. IRC Sec. 701.
2. IRC Sec. 702(a).
3. IRC Sec. 721(a).
4. IRC Sec. 741.
5. Treas. Reg. §301.7701-3.
6. Treas. Reg. §301.7701-3.
7. IRC Sec. 11(b).
8. IRC Sec. 1032(a).
9. IRC Sec. 351.
10. IRC Sec. 368(c).
11. IRC Sec. 1361(a)(1).
12. IRC Sec. 1363(a).
13. IRC Sec. 1366.
14. IRC Sec. 1; Rev. Proc. 2006-53, 2006-48 IRB 996.

Figure 22.1

COMPARISON OF BUSINESS ENTITIES					
	S CORP	**C CORP**	**PARTNERSHIP**	**LIMITED LIABILITY COMPANY ("LLC")**	**SOLE PROPRIETORSHIP**
Limited Liability	Yes, for all shareholders	Yes, for all shareholders	Generally no; however limited partners have protection from the partnership's debts	Yes, for all members	No
Participation In Management	No restrictions	No restrictions	Generally no restrictions, except participation by limited partners must be restricted in order to preserve limited liability	No restrictions	No; the proprietor is the manager
Qualification	Various eligibility requirements including restrictions on the number and type of shareholders, classes of stock and on the ownership of banks and subsidiaries	No restrictions	A limited partnership usually needs a general partner	No restrictions	No restrictions
Number of Owners	Maximum of 100; members of a family may be treated as one owner	No restrictions	Must have at least 2	No restrictions	One
Classes of Ownership Interests	Only one, but voting and non-voting are permitted	Multiple classes are permitted	Multiple classes are permitted	Multiple classes are permitted	None; only one owner
Check the Box Regulations Effect on Classification	If incorporated under State, Federal or Indian Tribal law it's a corporation	If incorporated under State, Federal or Indian Tribal law it's a corporation	Taxed as partnership, but may elect corporation treatment	Taxed as partnership, but may elect corporation treatment	Not a separate entity
Levels of Income Tax	Generally only one, but some states will tax S corporations as corporations (i.e. double tax will result)	Two	One	One	One
Special Allocations of Income and Loss	No, all allocations are pro rata of stock	Yes, if different classes of stock	Yes	Yes	No
Deductibility of Losses	Shareholders may deduct the corporation's losses only to the extent of their tax basis in their stock which does not include any portion of the corporation's debt	Shareholders may not deduct any of the corporation's losses	Partners may deduct the partnership's losses only to the extent of their tax bases in their partnership interest which includes their allocable share of debt for which they are liable	Members may deduct the LLC's losses only to the extent of their tax bases in their LLC interest which includes their allocable share of LLC debt	Losses are deducted on owners own tax return
Liquidation	Generally, nontaxable at corporate level and taxable at shareholder level through passthrough of corporate tax items	Taxable to both corporation and shareholders	Nontaxable to the extent of a partner's tax basis in his partnership interest	Nontaxable to the extent of a member's tax basis in his LLC interest	Not applicable; business is owner's property

Adapted from *Working with LLCs & FLPs,* 2d Edition by Thomas F. Commito, Copyright 2000, The National Underwriter Company, Cincinnati, OH, pp. 331–332.

Chapter 23

OWNERSHIP OF PROPERTY[1]

In financial planning, it is necessary to know the ways in which property is owned (or titled) and how property is transferred. The way in which property can be transferred can be dependent on the form of ownership. Property transfers involving wills and intestate succession are discussed in Chapter 14.

There are various ways in which property can be owned. In general, property is owned outright, as tenants in common, as joint tenants with rights of survivorship, or as community property. Use of trusts and custodial gifts to minors under UGMA and UTMA are also discussed here.

Outright Ownership

Outright ownership is often as simple as: John owns an automobile, or Mary owns a diamond necklace. John and Mary are generally free to do whatever they want with their property. Of course, if John borrowed money to purchase the automobile, the lender generally has the right to recovery of any outstanding loan upon a transfer of the automobile. In this situation, although John may generally be free to use the automobile as he pleases, John can really transfer only the value of the automobile in excess of the loan.

Life Estate / Remainder

Sometimes outright ownership can be split into a life estate and a remainder. A person with a life estate is generally free to use the property or income from the property for life. The person with the remainder interest receives the property when the person with the life estate dies. For example, Mike owns a house. When Mike dies, Mike leaves the house so that his sister, Sally, can live in the house for her life. Sally has a life estate. When Sally dies, the property will pass to Mike's nephew, Bob. Bob has a remainder interest.

Tenancy in Common

A tenancy in common is a form of co-ownership of property. Tenants in common own an undivided right to possess property. Each tenant is generally free to transfer his interest in the property as he wishes.

Joint Tenancy with Right of Survivorship

Another form of co-ownership of property is a joint tenancy with right of survivorship. Joint tenants also have an undivided right to the enjoyment of property. However, when a joint tenant dies, that person's interest in the property passes to the remaining joint tenant or joint tenants. While a joint tenant is alive, a joint tenant can generally sever the joint tenancy or transfer his interest to another.

For example, Dad leaves a vacation home to his three children, Tom, Ann, and Rita, as joint tenants with right of survivorship. Ann dies first. The vacation home is then owned by Tom and Rita as joint tenants. Tom dies next. Rita succeeds to outright ownership of the vacation home.

Tenancy by the Entirety

In some states, a joint tenancy with right of survivorship between spouses is called a tenancy by the entirety. When one spouse dies, the jointly owned property passes to the surviving spouse. However, while both spouses are alive and married to each other, one spouse cannot terminate a tenancy by the entirety without the consent of the other spouse.

Community Property

Ten states have a form of ownership between spouses called community property. Those states are Alaska, Arizona, California, Idaho, Louisiana, Nevada, New Mexico, Texas, Washington, and Wisconsin.

In a community property state, each spouse owns a one-half interest in property acquired while the spouses are married. Each spouse is generally free to transfer his one-half interest in the property at death as he wishes. However, while both spouses are alive and married to each other, one spouse cannot dispose of the community property without the consent of the other spouse.

Community property can be important even if a couple does not currently live in a community property state. Community property generally remains community property even when the spouses move to a noncommunity property state.

Certain property is noncommunity property even if a couple live in a community property state. Property that a spouse acquired prior to marriage remains the separate property of that spouse. Also, property acquired individually by one spouse by gift or inheritance during marriage is also the separate property of that spouse. Additionally, property acquired by a couple prior to moving to a community property state would generally remain noncommunity property.

Spouses are generally free to make agreements regarding community property. For example, the spouses can agree that what would otherwise be community property is not community property.

Trusts

A trust is a fiduciary relationship in which property is held by one (or more) person(s) for the benefit of one (or more) person(s). The person creating the trust is generally called a settlor, trustor, or grantor. The grantor typically executes a trust document and transfers property to the person who will be responsible for administering the terms of the trust, who is called a trustee. The person for whose benefit the trustee administers the trust is called a beneficiary. The property held in trust is often called the trust corpus or res.

State law controls the creation, operation, and termination of a trust. Common law is generally controlling except to the extent that a state has enacted a statute dealing with a particular aspect of trusts. The trust may generally have any terms except to the extent that a term is illegal or against public policy.

Theoretically, the law of any state with which the trust has contact could apply. Such states could include the state where the grantor resided upon creation of the trust, where the trustee is located or resides, where trust property is located (especially with regard to real estate), or where the beneficiaries reside. The grantor may specify in the trust document the state whose laws are to be applied to the operation and termination of the trust.

Usually, the beneficiaries of the trust are the grantor and/or members of the grantor's family. Having a charity as a beneficiary is also very common.

A trust may provide for management of property, accumulation or distributions of income to beneficiaries, distributions of trust corpus to beneficiaries, withdrawal powers in beneficiaries, and other powers of appointment.

Trusts arising at death (testamentary trusts) are subject to probate at the grantor's death. On the other hand, trusts created during lifetime (inter vivos trusts) are generally not subject to probate.

Trusts created during lifetime are either revocable or irrevocable; a trust created at death is irrevocable. A revocable trust is a trust in which the grantor retains the right to revoke the trust; upon revocation, property in the trust would be returned to the grantor. A trust that is not revocable is irrevocable.

A revocable trust is taxable to the grantor for income tax purposes. The grantor is not treated as making a gift upon transfer of property to a revocable trust; however, a revocable trust is includable in the grantor's estate at death. The grantor of an irrevocable trust generally makes a gift upon transfer of property to an irrevocable trust. Whether the grantor is taxable upon trust income or whether the irrevocable trust is includable in the grantor's estate generally depends on what interests the grantor has in the irrevocable trust.

UGMA / UTMA

The Uniform Gifts to Minors Act (UGMA) and Uniform Transfers to Minors Act (UTMA) provide a way for gifts to be made to children in custodianship. Most states have now adopted the more modern and flexible UTMA.

Under either UGMA or UTMA, property is transferred to a custodian who holds the property for the minor. A custodian can be an adult individual (generally, including the donor), or a custodial entity such as a bank or trust company. Today, almost any kind of property can be transferred under UGMA or UTMA. A separate custodial account must be created for each child.

The minor acquires immediate title to the property held by the custodian. Nevertheless, the custodian controls the property until the age (generally, 18 to 21) that the minor becomes an adult under UGMA or UTMA. The custodian can use the custodial property for the use and benefit of the minor, in the custodian's discretion.

When the minor reaches the age of majority, the property is distributed to the child. Some states permit extension of custodianship after the age of majority is reached. If the child dies, the custodial property passes to the child's estate.

A gift under UTMA or UGMA can avoid certain problems associated with outright gifts to children. A minor who owns property outright is free to do whatever the minor wants with the property, including possibly squandering the property. Also, other people are often hesitant to deal with a minor, because a minor can generally disaffirm contracts while still a minor. Custodianship avoids these problems.

A gift under UTMA or UGMA can also be used instead of a gift in trust for the minor. The custodianship avoids the expenses of a trust. A trust for a minor may be indicated where there is an intent to make a series of gifts to the minor or the amount to be transferred is substantial.

CHAPTER ENDNOTES

1. This chapter is derived from *Estate Planning* and *The Ultimate Trust Resource*, both written by William J. Wagner and published by The National Underwriter Company.

CHAPTER ENDNOTES

Chapter 24

BUSINESS LAW

Law school is a three year program to attain a Juris Doctorate degree. The most basic of business law course in an undergraduate curriculum is usually a three credit hour course for a full semester. But we're going to cover the topic of business law in one brief chapter.

Obviously, this chapter will be very concise and, in effect, will be a glossary of key terms and concepts. The areas to be covered include

- contracts
- torts
- agency
- negotiable instruments
- professional liability
- fiduciary liability
- arbitration and mediation in alternative dispute resolution

CONTRACTS

A contract is an agreement among two or more parties (individuals or entities) consisting of a promise or promises for one or both parties to perform or refrain from performing an identified act or acts. Such agreement is enforceable by a court.

Basic Elements of a Contract

In order for there to be a contact, certain elements must exist.

1. *Agreement* – There must be mutual assent by the parties, evidenced by an offer by one party and some form of acceptance by the other. The mutuality may be manifested formally, in writing, or orally. The action of one party in response to an offer by another may result in an agreement, if the acts were in reliance of the offered promise.

The offer must be a clear, objective proposition that sets forth the material terms of the proposed contract. Such terms include identifying the parties, the subject matter of the agreement, the applicable quantities, and the consideration (price) to be paid for performance.

A valid offer must be distinguished from the following expressions which fall something short of an actual contractual offer

a) a statement of opinion

b) negotiations preceding an offer, including a mere solicitation to a possible agreement

c) a statement of mere intention or desire

d) broad-based advertising, price lists, circulars, etc.

e) offers made under true emotional stress

f) offers made in jest

g) a request for a bid or proposal

h) sham transactions

The material terms of an agreement must be clearly stated in the offer or by reference to a reasonably identifiable outside standard or third party. In addition, the offer must effectively communicate all material terms to the offeree.

An offer may be terminated by

a) actions of the parties, such as a revocation by the offeror or rejection by the offeree

b) the lapse of time, due to the expiration of a specific offer period or, absent a stated period, the passage of a reasonable time for acceptance by the offeree

c) by operation of law, resulting from, for example, death or incapacity of one of the parties, the subject matter of the agreement becoming illegal, or the destruction of the subject matter

An offer is accepted when the offeree clearly demonstrates his agreement to the proffered terms. In order for the acceptance to be effective, the offeree must

a) have knowledge of the terms of the offer

b) demonstrate the willingness and intent to be bound by the agreed terms

c) comply with the conditions of acceptance stated in the offer

Typically an offer is accepted by the offeree making a promise to perform (bilateral contract) or by the offeree performing the requisite acts of the offer (unilateral contract). Silence by the offeree will generally not be considered an acceptance unless

a) there was a similar, prior agreement indicating that such silence is continued acceptance

b) the offeree accepted the benefits provided by the offeror

c) the offeree exercised dominion over the subject matter of the agreement

Generally the acceptance becomes effective

a) in a unilateral contract, when the performance or intended restraint from acting is complete

b) in a bilateral contract, when the offeree provides the requisite promise, typically by delivering a signed contract

2. *Consideration (the proverbial "quid pro quo")* – Consideration is legally sufficient value received for value given. In a typical contract there is at least one promisor (the party who makes a promise to do or refrain from doing something) and at least one promisee (the party who receives a promise). In a unilateral contract there is only one promisor and one promisee. In a bilateral contract, the parties exchange promises, and are thus both promisors and promisees. In a bilateral contract, each promise is independently supported by consideration.

Legally adequate consideration exists when the promisor receives a legal benefit, the promisee experiences a legal detriment, or both. A legal benefit occurs if a promisor receives something (consideration) to which he is not entitled absent the existence of the contract.

A legal detriment occurs if the promisee

a) in a unilateral contract, actually gives up something to which he has a legal right or actually refrains from doing something that he has a legal right to do

b) in a bilateral contract, promises to give up something to which he has a legal right to retain or promises to refrain from doing something that he has a legal right to do

Consideration is provided so long as there is a surrender or receipt of a legal right. It is not necessary that an economic or material loss be incurred by the promisee or benefit received by the promisor.

Certain promises may be enforceable without adequate consideration. Such agreements include

a) charitable pledges and subscriptions

b) a new written promise or reaffirmation of a promise to pay debt otherwise discharged by bankruptcy

c) a new promise to pay debt barred by statute of limitations

d) promissory estoppel or detrimental reliance – applicable in most states – that requires the following:

i. A promise is made to induce a promise to perform a specific act.

ii. The promisor can foresee that promisee will justifiably rely on the promise.

iii. The promisee substantially changes his situation in the expected manner, incurring damage in reasonable reliance of the promise.

iv. It is grossly unfair not to enforce the promise.

3. *Contractual capacity* – The contracting parties must be able to enter into a legally binding agreement.

a) *Minors* – State statutes prescribe the age at which an individual is deemed old enough to enter into a legally binding contract. In most states that age is 18.

Minors may disaffirm a contract while still "under age" and for a reasonable period after attaining majority. However, a minor may be bound by a contract, in some states, if the contract is for life or medical insurance, medical care, educational loans, marriage, transportation by common carrier (bus, train, etc.), or enlistment in a branch of the armed forces.

Other special rules relating to minors and contracts include the following:

i. The transfer of real property cannot be disaffirmed until the minor reaches the age of majority.

ii. While a minor can void a contract, an adult party to the agreement can not. If the minor does void the contract, all parties must make restitution, returning the consideration received.

iii. Contracts for necessities, such as food, shelter, and clothing, not provided by a minor's parent or guardian may be disaffirmed by the minor. However, the provider of the necessities may use quasi contractual concepts to enforce payment for the goods or services.

iv. A contract becomes enforceable if the minor ratifies the agreement upon reaching majority. Such ratification may be expressed (in writing or orally) or implied by the conduct of the minor-turned-adult.

b) *Intoxicated individuals* – A contract is voidable if entered into by someone so intoxicated that he cannot understand the legal consequences of his actions. A contract may be voided while the person is still intoxicated or within a reasonable period thereafter. In such cases, restitution is required and the intoxicated person must pay for necessities that were conveyed. In addition the intoxicated person cannot void the contract if a third party would be injured as a result.

c) *Mental incompetence* – An individual is considered mentally incompetent to enter into a contract if the person's judgment is impaired and he cannot understand the consequences of the transaction. A contract is void if entered into by a person declared legally incompetent by the courts. If the individual has not been adjudicated to be mentally incompetent, the incompetent person may void the contract while he is in fact incompetent or within a reasonable period after regaining his sanity. In addition, a guardian or legal representative of a mentally incompetent person may void a contract entered into by the incompetent individual. Also, reasonable compensation for necessities actually provided to a mentally incompetent person must be paid, even if the contract is disaffirmed.

d) *Certain convicts* (primarily, in some states, those convicted of major felonies) are not considered to have the capacity to enter into contracts.

e) Individuals who are not U.S. citizens who are legally in the country are considered competent. However, *illegal or enemy aliens* have limited contractual capacity.

4. *Legality* – An agreement to perform an act which is illegal or against public policy generally does not constitute an enforceable contract.

5. *Genuineness of assent* – The consent to comply with the terms of the agreement must be genuine, real, and voluntary. Transactions that confront this issue include those involving

a) *Mistake* – A mistake is an error, forgetfulness, or unconscious ignorance of a present or past fact that is material, essential, or significant to the contract. A distinction should be made between a unilateral mistake and a mutual or bilateral mistake.

i. A *unilateral* mistake, involving a mistake by only one party to a contract, is generally not voidable by the mistaken party unless another party to the transaction caused the mistake, knew or should have known of the mistake, and did not rectify the error.

ii. A *mutual* or *bilateral* mistake generally concerns a material fact of which both contracting parties are unaware. Such a mistake would permit either party to void the contract.

b) *Fraudulent misrepresentation* may result from (i) fraud in the execution of a contract or (ii) fraud in the inducement to contract.

i. *Fraud in the execution* occurs when one party is led to believe that an act that he is performing is something other than the execution of a contract. Consequently, the parties' assent to the agreement is not real and there is no legal contract.

ii. *Fraud in the inducement* results when one party induces another to enter into a contractual relationship through a misrepresentation of a material fact. Such contracts are voidable by the induced party.

Fraud may also result from silence or concealment. Although there is no duty to disclose known facts to the other party, there are several exceptions to this general rule. For instance, when there is a confidential or fiduciary relationship between the contracting parties, the party with knowledge must disclose that information to the other party and specific statutes, such as the Truth in Lending Act, require full disclosure of certain relevant facts.

c) *Innocent misrepresentation* occurs when a party makes a misrepresentation without knowing the information is false. In such circumstances, the relying party, if damaged by the misrepresentation, may void the contract.

d) *Undue influence,* which results when one party has control over the other because of a confidential relationship and takes unfair advantage, inducing the other party to enter into a contract. Such a contract would be voidable by the induced party.

e) *Duress* occurs when a party is coerced by wrongful force or threat of force to enter into a contract. The contract is voidable.

6. *Form* – The contractual agreement must be in a form that is prescribed and/or acceptable by law. For example, if transactions involving real estate, the Statute of Frauds requires the agreement be evidenced in writing.

The *Statute of Frauds* requires that certain contracts be made in written form in order for them to be enforceable. Contracts that must be in writing include

a) contracts for sale of real estate interests

b) contracts that cannot be performed within one year

c) collateral or secondary promises to perform in the event an identified primary contractor fails to meet his obligation (e.g., a guarantor)

A writing is deemed sufficient for purposes of the Statue of Frauds so long as it contains the basic, essential terms of the contract.

The *parol evidence rule* generally precludes the admission of oral or other written evidence to change, alter, or contradict a written contract which the parties have stated represents the complete and total terms of the agreement. Parol evidence may, however be admissible to substantiate

a) an acceptable, limited modification of the writing

b) that the contract was void or voidable

c) the meaning of vague or ambiguous terms

d) significant typographical or clerical errors

e) that the writing was incomplete

f) a prior continuing contractual relationship

g) a separate contract with different subject matter

Types of Contracts

There are several criteria that can used to distinguish one category of contract from another. These differentiators include:

1. Method of Assent

   a) *Express* – The parties have stated the terms of the agreement to which they intend to be bound – typically in writing.

   b) *Implied* – The terms of the agreement can reasonably be inferred by the acts of the parties, even if never stated in writing or orally.

   In either case, the agreeing parties must objectively and independently desire to enter into the contract.

2. Nature of the Promise Made

   a) *Bilateral contract* – Both (all) parties to the agreement exchange promises to perform – Mutual promises to do something in the future

   b) *Unilateral contract* – One party makes a promise to another in anticipation of (in exchange for) the performance of some act (or refraining from acting) – No reciprocal promise, just the action

3. Expectation of Compliance with Statutorily Imposed Form

   a) *Formal contract* – Some formal act or documentation required for contract to be enforceable

      i. negotiable instruments

      ii. letters of credit

      iii. contacts under seal or notary

   b) *Informal contract* – Agreement or contract for which no special form is required

4. Stage of Performance of the Contractual Promise

   a) *Executed contract* – All parties have completed their contracted promises

   b) *Executory contract* – Contract has been only partially performed or totally unperformed by all parties

5. Legal Validity and Enforcement

   a) *Valid and enforceable* – All elements of a legal and binding contract are present

   b) *Void* – So-called agreement is not really a contract and has no legal effect

   c) *Voidable* – Some element of the contract is defective or otherwise enables one party to the agreement to avoid a contractual commitment

   d) *Unenforceable* – Contractual promise(s) cannot be verified in a manner sufficient for legal enforcement, or contract fails to meet a formal or procedural requirement

Conditions, Performance and Discharge

A contract *condition* is an event, the occurrence or nonoccurrence of which limits, precludes, changes, causes or terminates a contractual obligation. Common types of conditions include:

1. *Condition precedent* – An even which must occur before performance by the promisor is required. Until all such conditions are met, the promisee cannot legal expect performance by the promisor.

2. *Condition subsequent* – An event which extinguishes an existing contractual commitment.

3. *Concurrent condition* – The performance of one party is conditioned on the parallel performance of the other party.

Conditions arise either (1) expressly (clearly stated by the parties), (2) implied in fact, or (3) implied in law (constructive) – imposed by courts to achieve justice or fairness.

Full, complete performance consistent with the terms of a contract will *discharge* a party from further obligation.

If the *time for performance* is not stated, a "reasonable time period" standard will be applied. If the parties agree that "time is of the essence," they must comply with the stated time. If the time for performance is stated, but not essential, compliance within a few days of the stated date will usually satisfy the contract.

If *partial performance* is accepted, than appropriate payment is due to the performing party. If the partial performance is substantial (only minor or insignificant incomplete aspects remain), and any deviation from the contract terms is not in bad faith, the performing party is discharged but is liable for the failure to fully complete the contract. If the partial performance is less than substantial, there will be a *breach of contract*, resulting in the discharge of the party entitled to receive performance but not the discharge of the party who failed to perform.

A total failure to comply will yield the same treatment to the failing party (no discharge) and the party who does not receive performance (full discharge).

A discharge may occur upon the agreement of the parties. The reasons for an agreement to discharge may be stated in the original contract or may be mutual consent after the contract period has commenced.

A discharge of contractual obligations may also occur by operation of law if

1. There is a material alteration of a written contract without consent.

2. The statue of limitations barring judicial remedies has run.

3. There is a decree of bankruptcy.

4. An unforeseen or intervening event makes performance impossible. Such events include

    a) the subject matter of the contract becomes illegal

    b) the death, incapacity or other serious illness of a party required to perform personal services

    c) the destruction of the subject matter of the contract

    d) anticipated economic results of performance are made impossible as a result of unforeseen, uncontrollable events

    e) a serious and extreme change in conditions making performance impracticable without undue burden (financial or otherwise) on the intended performing party

Typical remedies for breach of contract include

1. *Money damages* – remedies at law

    a) *Compensatory damages* – Compensation for the actual value of the loss or harm

    b) *Consequential or special damages* – Compensation for unforeseeable, remote, indirect, or unexpected harm or loss which does not ordinarily result from such a breach of contract. Consequential damages are not recoverable unless the nonperforming party is made aware of such possible harm.

    c) *Punitive damages* – An extraordinary award by a court granted in order to punish a party for willful or malicious harm caused by the contract breach

    d) *Nominal damages* – an insignificant sum of money acknowledging that the non-performing party did breach the contract, but that the harm or financial injury was minimal

    e) *Liquidated damages* – Formula or amount of damages to be paid as agreed to by the parties and as established in the terms of the contract. Liquidating damages provisions are enforceable unless they are unreasonable, and in effect penalties.

2. *Equitable remedies* – usually consist of

    a) requiring *specific performance* by a breaching party

    b) *recission* – Cancellation or abrogation of the contract

    c) *restitution* – requiring the return of property to it pre-contract condition or return of value

d) *injunctive relief* – An order preventing or restricting a person from doing something

e) *reformation* – Court order correcting an agreement so that it will conform to the intentions of the parties

These remedies are not available where

a) Monetary damages are adequate, determinable, and available.

b) The injured party has acted fraudulently or in bad faith.

c) *laches* - The injured party has unnecessarily delayed in bringing an action against the other party.

TORTS

A tort is a legal wrong by one person against another. It is a violation of a person's rights, usually due to negligence, but it may be the result of a deliberate act.

Tort law is a branch of civil law; the other main branches are property and contract law. Tort law is state law created through the judicial system (common law) or by legislation (statutory law). Many judges and states follow the Second Restatement of Torts as a primary guide to the creation and interpretation of tort law. The Restatement is a publication of the American Law Institute, an organization whose aim is to present an orderly statement of the general law of the United States.

A tort differs from a criminal act, which generally is an intentional violation of another's rights. A tort is subject to civil action and subsequent judgment for damages payable to the person who was wronged. In the case of a crime, the act is subject to criminal prosecution by governing authorities who impose penalties for a person found guilty of the criminal act. A wrongful act may be both a tort and a criminal act, in which case the wrongdoer would be subject to both civil action and criminal prosecution.

A *plaintiff* in a tort action is the alleged wronged party. A *defendant* is the alleged wrongdoer. The plaintiff may sue for *monetary damages* to compensate for the harm done. The plaintiff may also seek injunctive relief, restricting the defendant from continuing the actions which caused the harm.

Among the types of damages an injured party may recover (including both present and future expected losses) are

1. loss of earning capacity
2. reasonable medical expenses
3. pain and suffering

Among the many specific type of torts, the most common include

1. trespass
2. assault
3. battery
4. negligence
5. products liability
6. intentional infliction of emotional distress

Torts fall into three general categories:

1. *Intentional torts* – Wrongs which the defendant knew or should have known would occur through his actions or inactions (e.g., intentionally hitting a person)

2. *Negligent torts* – Occur when the defendant's actions were unreasonably unsafe (e.g., causing an accident by failing to obey traffic rules)

3. *Strict liability torts* – Wrongs which do not depend on the degree of carelessness by the defendant, but are established when a particular action causes damage (e.g., products liability – a liability for making and selling defective products)

Damages, for legal purposes, are the amount of money the law requires to be paid for the breach of some duty or the violation of some right. There are generally two types of damages: *compensatory* (or actual) and *punitive*.

Compensatory damages are intended to compensate the injured party for his loss or injury. Punitive damages are awarded to punish a wrongdoer. For certain types of injuries statutes provide that a successful party receive some multiple of their "actual damages", e.g. treble damages.

AGENCY

An agency relationship occurs when one person (a principal) uses another person (an agent) as a representative in certain transactions or business activities. An agent may bind his principal in a contract with a third party and usually has some degree of independence in his actions.

An agency relationship is distinguishable from an employer-employee relationship under which the employer controls, or has the right to control the employee's actions on his behalf. In addition, employees generally have little if any independent discretion. Employees are most often compensated for time (except commissioned employees) while agents are usually compensated based on results. Employers are required to withhold, remit and pay their share of employee payroll taxes, while principals are not required to do so for their agents.

An agent can also be differentiated from an independent contractor. An independent contractor is generally retained to perform a specific task and is paid upon its completion, while an agent often retains an on-going relationship representing the principal for an identified function or functions, often for an extended period of time. The person who hires an independent contractor usually has very limited if any control over the contractor. In addition, unlike an agent, an independent contractor generally cannot bind the person retaining him to a contract with a third party.

Formation of Agency Relationship

An agency relationship may be formed for any legal purpose. It is a consensual relationship, which often but not always results in a contract. Consideration is not a necessary element of an agency.

General, no formalities are required to create an agency. Unless required by statute or by the Statute of Frauds, a written agency agreement is not necessary. A typical written agency document would be a *power of attorney*.

Since an agent generally represents his principal in contractual relationships, the principal must himself have the legal capacity to enter into contracts. Absent such capacity, the principal could void the contract, but the third party with whom the agent negotiated could not.

An agency agreement (although, as stated above, not always a contract) may be expressed in writing or orally, or implied by the actions of the parties. An agency can be created after the agent has acted for the principal if the principal expressly or by implication ratifies the agent's action on his behalf.

Agent's Duties to the Principal

1. *Duty to perform* – Carryout agreed to functions, etc.

2. *Duty to notify* – Inform the principal of material information relating to the subject of the agency

3. *Duty of loyalty* – Agent cannot compete or use information obtained through the agency relationship for the benefit of others or his own benefit independent of his agency agreement. To put it simply, the agent cannot in any way act in a manner that creates a conflict of interest with the principal.

4. *Duty to account* – Report to the principal with the economic results and other consequences of his actions on behalf of the principal

In the event an agent breaches his duties to the principal, the principal has the right to be indemnified by the agent. Thus, for example, if the principal is required to pay damages to an injured party caused by the agent's tortious act while representing the principal, the principal would be entitled to be recompensed by the agent.

A principal may void an action by an agent on his behalf if the act violates the agent's fiduciary duty to the principal.

Principal's Duties to the Agent

1. The principal must perform in accordance with his contract with an agent.

2. The principal has the duty to compensate, indemnify, and reimburse the agent for his efforts under the terms of the agreement. If no compensation is specified, the principal is obligated to pay expenses, losses and reasonable compensation for the agent's services.

3. The principal has an obligation to cooperate with the agent as the agent acts on his behalf.

The agent's remedies for breach by the principal include indemnification, sue for breach of contract, bring an action for an accounting, or withhold further performance.

Termination of Agency Relationship

An agency relationship may terminate by the parties or by operation of law. The parties may terminate the agency by providing for a specified expiration time in their agreement. Absent a stated time, a reasonableness standard will apply.

An agency will also terminate if the intended purpose is accomplished or if the parties mutually agree to end the relationship. Either party may terminate the agency unilaterally, but may be required to compensate the other who has acted in reliance of the terminating party. An agency relationship may also be terminated for cause.

By operation of law, an agency will terminate upon the death or incapacity of either the agent or principal. Knowledge of the death or incapacity is not required. Bankruptcy of the principal will also terminate the agency, although insolvency does not. Bankruptcy of the agent does not necessarily lead to termination. Impossibility of performance due, for example, to destruction of the subject property, or other unforeseen changes in circumstances will permit a termination of the agency.

If an agency is terminated by a party, notice must be given before the relationship is ended. Notice must also be provided to third parties with whom the agent is dealing on behalf of the principal.

NEGOTIABLE INSTRUMENTS

A negotiable instrument is typically a written document that either provides evidence of financial credit or acts as a substitute for money. If an instrument is negotiable, it would be considered commercial paper, governed by Article 3 of the Uniform Commercial Code (UCC). If it is not negotiable, ordinary contract law applies.

Types of Commercial Paper

1. A *draft* has three parties; the *drawer* (person with funds) who instructs the *drawee* (e.g., bank) to make a payment to a *payee*.

2. A *check* is a special kind of draft that is payable only by a bank as drawee and which is payable upon demand by the payee. The check writer is the drawer.

3. A *promissory note* is an instrument between two parties: the *maker* promises to pay a specific amount to a *payee*. A promissory note may be payable on demand or at a specific date. A certificate of deposit is a form of promissory note in which the bank is the maker and the depositor is the payee.

Negotiation

For an instrument to be negotiable, it must have all of the following elements on the face of the document:

1. must be in writing

2. must be signed by the drawer (draft) or maker (promissory note)

3. must contain an unconditional order or promise to pay

4. must state a set amount of money to be paid

5. must be payable upon demand or at a defined time

6. must be payable to the order of the payee or to the bearer (unless it is a check)

Commercial paper is typically transferred by either (1) negotiation or (2) assignment.

1. *Negotiation* – A person who holds a negotiable instrument is identified as a ***holder***. If the holder meets the requirements of a "holder in due course," he can obtain rights greater than those of the transferor.

   There are two basic methods of negotiating an instrument:

   a) Commercial paper payable "to the order of" a specified person (order paper) is negotiated when endorsed by the transferor and the instrument is delivered to the holder.

   b) "Bearer paper" is negotiated by the mere delivery to the holder. No endorsement is required.

2. *Assignment* – Occurs when a transfer does not meet all of the requirements of a negotiation. In this situation, the assignee can not be a holder in due course and cannot have rights any greater than those of the assignor.

There are several forms of *endorsement* of negotiable instruments:

1. A *blank endorsement* converts order paper into bearer paper by the endorsement signature of the payee/transferor, without identifying a specific transferee.

2. A *special endorsement* identifies a specific person to whom the endorser wants to endorse the instrument (endorsee).

3. A *restrictive endorsement* requires the endorsee to comply with certain requirements, such as "for deposit only."

4. A *qualified endorsement* disclaims the liability normally imposed on the endorser. For example, such a qualification would free the endorser from covering the amount due if the instrument is subsequently dishonored by the drawer/maker.

A *Holder In Due Course* is entitled to payment on a negotiable instrument in spite of defenses otherwise available to the maker or drawer of the instrument. Such enhanced rights are not available to an ordinary holder of a promissory note or an assignee.

In order to be a holder in due course, the holder of the instrument must

1. hold a properly negotiated negotiable instrument

2. give adequate value for the instrument

3. take the instrument in good faith

4. take the instrument without notice that it is already overdue, dishonored, or that a person has a claim to the instrument

The rights of a holder in due course include the following:

1. When a transfer of a negotiable instrument is made to someone who qualifies as a holder in due course, all personal defenses against the holder in due course are stopped. These personal defenses are available against ordinary holders and assignees. One key exception to this rule occurs when the holder in due course takes the instrument subject to the personal defenses applicable to the transferor. The usual Personal defenses include

   a) breach of contract

   b) lack or failure of consideration

   c) prior payment

   d) unauthorized completion

   e) fraud in the inducement

   f) non-delivery

   g) undue influence or duress

   h) mental incapacity

   i) illegality

2. Certain defenses, referred to as *real* or *universal* defenses, may be asserted against any party, including a holder in due course. Such defenses include

   a) forgery

   b) bankruptcy

   c) fraud in the execution

   d) minority incapacity

   e) material alteration of instrument

3. A person who is not himself a holder in due course, but who obtains a negotiable instrument from a holder in due course is called a *holder through a holder in due course.* Such a person obtains all the rights of a holder in due course. Exceptions apply to

   a) *a party who reacquires an instrument* – His status remains as it was originally, and is not enhanced by the intervention of a holder in due course.

   b) *a person who was involved in a fraudulent or illegal act affecting the instrument* – cannot become a holder through a holder in due course.

Warranties on negotiable instruments – There are two types of such warranties:

1. *Contractual liability* – Refers to a liability of any party who signs a negotiable instrument, whether as a maker, drawer, drawee, or endorser.

   a) A maker has primary liability and is thus required to make payment on the note until it is paid or the statute of limitations has run.

   b) No party of a draft or check initially has primary liability since the drawee has only been ordered by the drawer to make payment. However, the drawer has secondary liability and is liable only if the drawee fails to pay.

   c) An endorser of a note or draft has secondary liability and is liable for payment to the holder only if the maker or other primary party fail to make payment

   d) A drawer or endorser can avoid secondary liability by signing or endorsing the instrument "without recourse."

   e) If a certified check is issued, the bank, as drawee, accepts full responsibility for payment, thus relieving the drawer or prior endorsers from liability.

2. *Warranty liability* – Enables the holder to seek payment from secondary parties through a transfer warranty or presentment warranty.

   To recover under a warranty liability, a party does not have to meet conditions of proper presentment, dishonor, or timely notice of dishonor that are required under contractual liability against endorsers.

   A transfer warranty applies whenever a negotiable instrument is transferred, so long as

   i. The transferor has good title.

   ii. All signatures are genuine and authorized.

   iii. The instrument has not been materially altered.

   iv. No party has a good defense against the transferor.

   v. The transferor has no notice of insolvency of the maker, drawer, or acceptor.

   Transfer warranties place the loss of the transaction on the person who dealt face to face with the wrongdoer, who was thus in the best position to prevent the transfer of the forged, stolen, or altered instrument.

Banks and Checks – Banks are not obligated to pay on a check presented more than 6 months after the issue date. However they may, in good faith, make payment and charge the drawer (customer's) account, even if this creates an overdraft of the drawer's account.

Banks are liable to the drawer for damages resulting from the bank wrongfully dishonoring a check. Wrongful dishonor may occur if the bank erroneously believes there are insufficient funds to cover the check. Banks are also liable to the drawer for payment on forged or altered checks, unless the drawer's negligence contributed to the issuance of the bad check.

A written stop payment order on a check is good for six months and is renewable. An oral stop payment order is only good for 14 days. Any stop payment order must be given with sufficient time to provide the bank with reasonable time to act. The bank is liable to the drawer for payment after the effective date of the order, but only if the drawer can prove that the bank's failure to obey the order caused the drawer's loss. If the drawer of the check stops payment, he is still liable to the holder, unless the drawer has a valid defense.

PROFESSIONAL LIABILITY

The concept of professional liability is intended to impose a higher "standard of care" on so-called professionals for their acts which cause harm to others. It is intended to apply to those professions, such as law, medicine, accounting, engineering, architecture, requiring special licensing and a high level of special knowledge and training. In terms of negligence law, "a professional possesses a special form of competence which is not part of the ordinary equipment of the reasonable man, but which is the result of acquiring learning and aptitude developed by special training and experience."

Professional liability insurance is designed to provide insurance coverage for a professional's tangible performance of his duties and cover the "wrongful acts" of the insured, as defined in the insurance policy. This definition is typically narrowed by the requirement that the act be related to the conduct prescribed in the policy. Consequently the insured professional should take care that the policy language adequately describes what the insured is actually doing. Coverage is also limited by other provisions in the policy, such as a clause that sets out the term of the policy and any periods of extension. Most policies also include a "Special Reporting Clause" that requires the insured to report incidents which may give rise to a claim in the future.

Professional liability is recognized as being one of the most difficult kinds of insurance to obtain. The exposures are constantly evolving as a result of the courts' broadening the level of care expected of professionals, contributing to ever increasing defense cost. In addition, juries have continued to award extremely high awards for damages resulting from professional liability.

FIDUCIARY LIABILITY

A fiduciary is someone who agrees to act in the best interest of another person. It is essentially a financial or control relationship, characterized by discretionary control over assets, finances, or actions. Typical fiduciaries include

1. trustees of individual trusts (including irrevocable life insurance trusts)

2. trustees of pension and retirement fund trusts under the Employee Retirement Income Security Act of 1974 (ERISA)

3. corporate directors

4. corporate officers

As compared to a professional, who is held to a high standard of care with respect to the advice provided related to his area of expertise, a fiduciary is held to an even higher standard because of the responsibility and obligation to care for and handle the funds and affairs of the trust beneficiary, employees, shareholders, etc.

A professional, such as an attorney or an accountant, will be held to standards of both a professional and a fiduciary if he is acting as a fiduciary on behalf of his client. Errors in judgment and/or omissions in activity, including inaction, over-action, insufficient action, and wrongful action, may result in significant litigation. Awards can be accompanied by punitive damages and/or more severe civil and criminal sanctions, approaching the dollar magnitude of recent manufacturing product liability awards.

Fiduciary and professional arrangements are governed by written, oral, and implied contracts. Written contracts specify the relationships, obligations, and the actions permitted between the parties. Oral and implied contracts may also contain many significant fiduciary obligations, which bind the parties to common law obligations. In addition, statutes may impose special fiduciary obligations, which can result in potential liabilities. For example, federal law requires that pension fund trustees have a definite fiduciary relationship to invest and protect the funds of employees to whom the funds belong.

With respect to the investment responsibilities of a fiduciary, The Restatement of the Law Third of Trusts (1990) and the Uniform Prudent Investor Act identify the following important principles of prudent investing:

1. *Duty to diversify* – If you decide to forgo the benefits of diversification, you need to have a good reason.

2. *Duty to invest according to a suitable level of risk* – You need to weigh risk and return in the context of the trust's objectives.

3. *Duty to avoid unnecessary expenses* – If you decide to pay higher costs than necessary, you need to have a good reason.

4. *Duty to seek advice when necessary* –You should recognize when you need help, and you must choose an adviser carefully and monitor the adviser's actions.

Liability under ERISA – The passage of the Employee Retirement Income Security Act of 1974 (ERISA) substantially increased the liabilities of fiduciaries in the United States. It also better defined some of the responsibilities and associated liabilities of fiduciaries.

ERISA was created to help protect the interests of pension and employee benefit plan beneficiaries. Under ERISA, an individual (or organization) is deemed a fiduciary if that person (or entity) exercises any discretionary authority or control over the management of any type of employee benefit plan. In particular, any person responsible for the investment, control, or disposition of assets held by the plan would be considered a fiduciary. ERISA broadly defines an "employee benefit plan" as:

> Any one plan, fund or program established or maintained for the purpose of providing to its participants or beneficiaries employee benefits.

Fiduciaries can also be held liable for the acts, errors, and omissions of outside entities that provide administrative and related services. Outside entities representing this exposure include those organizations that service pension and benefit plans: consulting and actuarial consulting firms, law firms, accounting firms, professional administration firms, investment advisers and investment management companies, and the trust departments of financial institutions.

Fiduciary liability insurance is a popular vehicle for the financial protection of fiduciaries, including those responsible for employee benefit plans, against legal liability arising out of their role as fiduciaries. Such insurance coverage can include the cost of defending against claims seeking to establish such liability.

At least two other types of "coverage" are related to fiduciary liability insurance. First, fidelity bonds are required by law (ERISA bonding). This is a form of insurance for dishonesty situations. When dishonest administrators or trustees have financially harmed an employee benefit plan, these bonds may be used, but only for the benefit of the plan and the plan's beneficiaries. This bonding insurance will not protect the trustees themselves from liability claims and is thus completely distinct from fiduciary liability insurance.

The second related coverage is employee benefit liability (EBL) insurance. EBL insurance policies cover many claims arising out of errors or omissions in the administration of a benefit plan, including the failure to enroll an employee in the plan as well as the administration of improper advice as to benefits.

EBL insurance does not cover all situations of fiduciary responsibility, especially those regarding imprudent investment of funds. Fiduciary liability insurance coverage may or may not encompass EBL insurance coverage; the insurer involved, the purchasing entity, and the specific type of fiduciary liability coverage being employed will ultimately determine what scope of coverage is available.

ARBITRATION AND MEDIATION IN ALTERNATIVE DISPUTE RESOLUTION

All the areas of business law discussed in this chapter identify a potential for dispute among parties – persons involved in contracts or other transactions, persons who have a degree of responsibility as fiduciaries for the benefit of others, and to persons who may intentionally engage in undesired activities (such as an automobile accident). Most of the disagreements are easily resolved by "reasonable people" acknowledging their responsibility or reconciling differences in opinion and perhaps negotiating a settlement on their own.

When the parties in conflict cannot resolve their difference by themselves, third party intervention of some form is usually required. The typical forms of such third-party assisted dispute resolution include

1. litigation
2. mediation
3. arbitration

Litigation involves the use of the courts and civil justice system to resolve the legal controversies. It is inevitably expensive, protracted, and somewhat unpredictable. In a business situation, it should be the last resort considered.

In recent years mediation and arbitration have been so clearly identified as preferable to litigation, that the concept of *Alternative Dispute Resolution (ADR)* has become a watchword for their use in cost-effective and efficient resolving business conflicts.

Mediation is a voluntary process in which an impartial person (the mediator) assists with the communications between the parties, promoting reconciliation between the parties that will hopefully lead to a mutually acceptable resolution. The mediator manages the process and facilitates negotiations between the parties. The mediator does not force an agreement or make decisions. The parties participate and negotiate their own agreement, facilitated by the artful mediator.

Mediation can be used in most controversies, such as between merchants and customers, tenants and landlords, employees and employers, as well as complex business disputes.

Mediators are usually attorneys or other seasoned professionals or business persons, and are usually paid a fee for their services. In some cases a mediator knowledgeable in the specific area of dispute is agreed to by the parties, but this is not always necessary or helpful. The attorneys and other advisors of the disputing parties will usually participate in the process, assisting in the communication of their clients' positions.

Arbitration is the submission of a dispute to an impartial person or person (arbitrators) for decision. Like mediation, arbitration is an out-of-court method of dispute resolution. An arbitrator controls the process listens to both sides, but unlike a mediator, an arbitrator will make a decision. Like a trial, only one party will prevail. Unlike a trial, however, appeal right are limited.

"Binding arbitration" is often required under the terms of an agreement as the only means of resolving certain disputes between the parties. Such an agreement will usually identify the means for choosing the arbitrator or arbitration panel (usually three individuals), and the time frame for the arbitration process. Appeal rights are usually extremely limited in such agreed-to binding arbitrations. The arbitrator's award can be reduced to a judgment in a court making it enforceable.

In non-binding arbitration, a decision may become final if all the parties agree to accept it or it may serve to assist a party in evaluating the strength or weakness of his case if pursued in the courts or as a starting point for settlement negotiations.

Chapter 25

MONETARY SETTLEMENT PLANNING

It's amazing how many people actually believe that once they have attained a large sum of money they no longer have a need for financial planning. That's obviously not true, although the direction of the planning needs will typically shift dramatically. Usually the focus of the planning will be on how to invest the funds and manage the cash outflow, that is, the spending. But there are also planning issues and opportunities associated with some of the more common sources of large influxes of cash. In this chapter we will discuss a few of these sources of significant, lump sum funds. Specifically we will cover

- structured settlements
- lottery winnings
- life insurance proceeds and settlements
- lump sum retirement distributions

STRUCTURED SETTLEMENTS

A structured settlement is the payment of money received as payment for a personal injury, workers' compensation under which all or a part of the payment is made in future periodic installments. Whereas the usual form of payment for a personal injury is in the form of a lump sum, *The Periodic Payment Settlement Act of 1982* enacted critical incentives for the use of structured settlements.

Internal Revenue Code (IRC) Section 104(a)(2) provides that the full amount of qualified structured settlement payments is tax-free to the victim/recipient. This is a major advantage over the tax treatment of lump sum payments. Although a lump sum payment for a personal injury is generally tax-free, the income and gains earned on the invested lump sum is subject to regular income tax rules. Consequently, interest (except municipal bond and other exempt interest), dividends, rents, etc. will be subject to ordinary income rates, while long term capital gains would be eligible for preferential capital gains rates.

In addition to the IRC Section 104(a) tax advantages of structured settlements, recipients of structured settlements who are not capable of managing their own funds find the periodic payment feature of a structured settlement appealing. These individuals do not have to worry about making the right decision on investments. They know in advance what they will be receiving every month of the payment period. In addition, the annuity aspects of the settlement provide a certainty of cash flow that many individuals need to manage their expenses. Plus, individuals who are spendthrifts, minors, and others incapable of controlling their spending are protected from spending or losing their entire nest egg from early mistakes.

However, a structured settlement has its disadvantages, which is why you will rarely see individuals accept a structured settlement as full payment for their injury. More often you will see a partial structured settlements combined with a partial lump sum payment, where the lump sum is used to pay off expenses and liabilities (such as legal fees and medical expenses) that have been building during the often protracted period prior to settlement.

But, even beyond these easily identified needs for an immediate infusion of funds, there are other reasons why a large structured settlement is not called for. Many individuals believe they can invest the funds so effectively that they can earn a greater after tax return than the settlement company will provide. This may be particularly the case if the settlement is written during a period of low interest rates, thus reducing the payment amount a settlement company will offer to a recipient. It is also important to many individuals to simply maintain total control over their money and they are not willing to give that up for any tax or other financial benefit.

If the structured settlement provides for payments for a "term certain," what happens if the injured person lives beyond the payment period? He may find himself without resources. But, if the settlement calls for payments only for the life of the injured party, payments will stop at the death of the recipient. Consequently, there would be no funds for the recipient's heirs, no matter how long the recipient lives. This may be important, for example, if the recipient became disabled as a result of the injury and was not able to accumulate funds for a surviving spouse or to fund the education of children.

Consistent with general financial planning concepts, it is always important to keep in mind that circumstances change. While a large structured settlement may have made sense when initially obtained, some time down the road the recipient may find a need for a lump sum of cash that is not available, for example to fund education or for a down payment on a home. This problem can be dealt with through a sale of a structured settlement agreement. In fact, since 2002, the sale of a structured settlement may be federal income tax-free.[1]

To qualify, the law requires a court order for a payment made upon the sale of structured settlement payments. If there is no court order, a tax equal to 40% of the amount of the settlement discount – the difference between the total of the undiscounted future payments and the settlement amount – is imposed on the buyer. This law in effect works in conjunction with state laws that control the process of structured settlement sales.

LOTTERY WINNINGS

Lottery winnings are subject to federal income tax as ordinary income and are usually taxable for state purposes as well. These prizes are also subject to income tax withholding, thus reducing the cash received upon winning.

Lottery winnings of any significant size are usually paid as installments by the awarding state, often over periods as long as 20 to 25 years, further reducing what originally may have seemed to be a jackpot into a disappointing after-tax annuity. For example, a $1,000,000 lottery, payable over 20 years with combined federal and state taxes withheld at an effective 35% rate yields just over $2,800 per month. In addition, it is likely that the taxes withheld are less than the marginal tax rate that would be applied to the winnings when added to other income on the winner's tax return, requiring quarterly estimated tax payments or large tax payments come April 15.

If a lump sum is wanted or needed, it is possible for a lottery winner to sell his annuitized award to one of many companies that specialize in the purchase of long-term lottery awards. Such companies obviously will significantly discount the present value of the future flow they will receive. A court order is often required in order to facilitate such a sale, but most of the annuity purchasers will handle all of the paperwork for the deal.

LIFE INSURANCE PROCEEDS AND SETTLEMENTS

Life insurance proceeds should be separated between (1) death benefits and (2) amounts received pre-death or by surrender of the policy. The areas of difference include

- *Who makes the payment decision?* – The beneficiary of a life insurance death benefit decides what to do with the proceeds from the policy. If the policy is surrendered, the owner of the policy has control over the surrender options. The death beneficiary has no rights.

- *What are the payment options?* – A death benefit may be made in the form of a lump sum or an annuity. Surrender options include lump sum payments, annuities, and/or the conversion of the policy to either a "fully paid" death benefit for life (which would be a reduced death benefit) or for an extended term, which would be the full death benefit for as long a term as the cash value would support, requiring no further premium payments until death. Whereas death benefit annuity payments will generally begin immediately, the annuitization of a pre-death termination of the policy may begin immediately (current annuity) or in the future (deferred annuity).

- *Income tax treatment* – Whereas a death benefit is generally received income tax free, the surrender of a life insurance policy or full or partial withdrawal of policy cash values without the termination of the policy is subject to federal income tax to the extent the cash received exceeds the policy owner's investment in the contract, typically the cumulative premiums paid prior to surrender.

If a death benefit recipient chooses an annuity, the basis in the annuity is the amount of the benefit received. Future payments are allocated between return of basis and taxable over the life of the annuity. If the annuity is for a single life or joint lives, IRS annuity tables are used to determine the amount of each annuity payment that is taxable.

If the policy value is surrendered for an annuity, the payments will also be allocated between return of basis and taxable income, with the premiums paid determining the basis.

- *Estate tax treatment* – If the insured has no "incidents of ownership" in the policy at the time of death, the policy will be excluded from the federal taxable estate. If the insured is the owner, the death benefits are subject to estate taxes. If the policy is surrendered for a lump sum before death, the cash will be an asset of the owner. If the surrender results in the cash value becoming an annuity, the present value of any annuity amounts payable after the owner's death is generally included in the owner's estate.

Life insurance settlements involve the sale of a life insurance policy by the owner in exchange for an amount greater than the cash value of the policy and less than the policy death benefit. There are generally two types of life insurance settlements: (1) viatical settlements and (2) life settlements.

A *viatical settlement* enables someone facing a terminal illness to use the value of the life insurance policy prior to death to assist with the financial burdens of medical care, particularly if there is a loss of income during the final period. Although viatical settlements have been available for a long time, it was not until the AIDS epidemic of the late 1980's that viatication became more common.

The typical benefits of a viatical settlement to a policy owner/insured include

- Relief is provided from life insurance premium costs.
- Settlement income may be tax-free, if certain requirements under the Internal Revenue Code are met.
- Cash is made immediately available to pay accumulating and large medical bills and costs of living.
- Funds may be available to pay for treatment expenses not covered by medical insurance.

The availability of a viatical settlement is based on two major criteria: (1) the specifics of the life insurance policy, and (2) the health condition of the insured.

To qualify, based on industry standards,

- The policy must be at least 2 years old; only non-contestable policies are considered.
- The insurance company (carrier) must have a rating of B+ or better.
- While there is generally no maximum to the size of the policy, the minimum is usually set at $50,000. (Multiple policies aggregating more than $50,000 are generally acceptable.)
- All types of policies will qualify, including term, whole life, universal, variable, joint, and group.
- The policy owner need not be the insured, so long as the owner has an insurable interest.

While the qualifications relating to the insured's health condition are more subjective, the following standards generally permit consideration:

- Life expectancy of the insured must be 7 years or less.
- The terminal illness may include AIDS, heart disease, cancer, Alzheimer's, ALS, or other life threatening disease.
- Although a medical examination may not be required, copies of complete medical records must be provided to verify the insured's health condition.

The Health Insurance Portability and Accountability Act of 1996 (HIPAA) established guidelines that make the proceeds from a viatical settlement federal income tax free. To qualify, the insured must be terminally ill (diagnosed as having a life expectancy of less than 24 months), or chronically ill (permanently and severely disabled by an illness). The state income tax treatment of viatical settlements will vary from state to state.

A *life settlement* creates immediate cash liquidity from a non-performing or seriously underperforming policy, thus allowing the policy owner to convert the investment in an unaffordable or unneeded life insurance policy insuring an individual over age 65, to a productive current asset.

Life settlements are frequently referred to by such terms as Senior Settlements, Lifetime Settlements, or High Net Worth Settlements. They are becoming more frequent as an estate and cash flow planning vehicle for seniors, enabling those old enough to obtain amounts significantly greater than the cash value of the life insurance policies they hold. This includes getting cash even for term insurance policies. The technique is becoming so popular that an active and competitive secondary market for life settlements has been created.

The typical benefits of a life settlement to a policy owner/insured include

- relief from life insurance premium costs
- additional funds to supplement retirement income
- higher cash payout than the cash surrender value
- cash immediately available to pay accumulating and large medical bills and costs of living
- funds to pay for treatment expenses not covered by medical insurance
- alternative funding for long term care (LTC) policies, annuities or other investments

The qualifications for a life settlement will differ far more dramatically from individual to individual than with viatical settlements, primarily because health condition, an essential element to a viatication, is not necessarily a critical factor in a life settlement. General life expectancy criteria for an individual's age group is more typically referred to in a life settlement, adjusted for other factors that would lead to a "rated" premium on the purchase of a life insurance policy. However, whereas a factor leading to a rated premium on a life insurance policy is considered detrimental, the same issue may lead to a higher payment in a life settlement.

To qualify, based on industry standards,

- The policy must be at least 2 years old; only non-contestable policies are considered.
- The insurance company (carrier) must have a rating of B+ or better.
- While there is generally no maximum to the size of the policy, the minimum is usually set at $100,000. (Lower amounts may be considered if the insured has a shortened life expectancy.)
- All types of policies will qualify, including term, whole life, universal, variable, joint, and group.
- The policy owner need not be the insured, so long as the owner has an insurable interest.
- Yearly premiums should generally be less than 5% of the policy's face value.

The industry standard qualifications relating to the insured's health condition generally permit consideration of a policy where

- Life expectancy of the insured senior is 12 years or less.
- There must be a change in health or in table rating since the policy was issued.
- The general target age of the insured is 75 or above.
- Although a medical examination may not be required, copies of complete medical records must be provided to verify the insured's health condition.
- Generally, healthy seniors do not qualify. There must be some type of health issues that limit the insured's life expectancy, even if the health issues are not terminal or chronic (as required in a viatical settlement).

Tax Treatment of Life Settlements

Traditionally, the excess of amounts received on the sale of a life insurance policy over the seller's basis is treated as ordinary income.[2] However, recently some commentators have claimed that amounts received in excess of a policy's cash surrender value (if greater than the seller's basis) will be eligible for capital gain treatment. Note that if the cost basis in the policy is higher than the settlement amount, then there should be no taxable income, but also generally no tax-deductible loss.

LUMP SUM RETIREMENT DISTRIBUTIONS

A participant in a qualified employer retirement plan will often have the opportunity to receive his retirement benefits in a lump sum distribution. The advantages of receiving a lump sum distribution include

- complete control over the investment and use of the funds received (However, the funds received, if not rolled over into an IRA, will be fully and immediately taxable.)

- the possibility of rolling the funds over into an Individual Retirement Account (IRA), thus providing more control over the investment of the retirement funds (within the tax-deferred IRA) and flexibility in the withdrawal of funds (which then become taxable) from the IRA (subject to the minimum distribution requirements generally applicable to all qualified plans)

- the availability of a special 10-year income tax averaging computation for eligible distributions to individuals born before 1936

The alternative to a lump sum distribution from a qualified retirement plan is some form of a deferred distribution, generally in the form of a series of payments or an annuity. The advantages of a deferred payment include

- the deferral of income taxes until funds are actually distributed (available with a rollover to an IRA)

- continued tax-free growth until distribution (available with a rollover to an IRA)

- third party management of investments and cash flow for retirement needs

Obviously, each situation will be unique. Consequently, consideration should be given to at least the following factors in choosing between a lump sum and a deferred payout of retirement benefits, when the choice is available:

- *Age of the participant* (or the participant and beneficiary in the case of a possible joint and survivor annuity option) – This affects the possible number of years of a periodic payout.

- *Health of the participant* (and beneficiary) – This also affects the payout period.

- *Expected investment returns on the funds* – What interest rate is used to compute the annuity and what do you think you can otherwise earn on the funds?

- *Current and future expected income tax rates for the participant* – This involves not only estimating what the participant's income will be each affected year, but, if you are adventurous, also guessing at what changes in the tax law may do to rates in the future.

- *Non-tax aspects* – In particular, what are the participant's needs for the plan funds and other sources of income?

CHAPTER ENDNOTES

1. IRC Sec. 5891.
2. See *Gallun v. Comm.*, 327 F.2d 809 (7th Cir. 1964); *Comm. v. Phillips*, 275 F.2d 33 (4th Cir. 1960).

Part 5:

MAJOR DISCIPLINES

Chapter 26

RISK MANAGEMENT AND INSURANCE

Understanding risk management starts with understanding the two terms:

Risk – The uncertainty of loss. "Pure risk" is the occurrence of some uncertain event that can only result in a loss, such as from a hurricane or fire. "Speculative risk" includes the possibility of gain or loss, such as a stock investment, casino gambling, or playing the lottery.

Management entails a process of planning, organizing, directing, and monitoring.

For personal financial planning purposes, risk can be defined as the uncertainty of financial loss (that is, pure risk – excluding investment loss), and risk management is concerned only with minimizing the risk of such losses.

Risk management is not insurance management, although insurance product does provide a tool in the risk management process.

THE PURPOSE OF RISK MANAGEMENT

The need for an organized approach to deal with risk potentials cannot be overstated. It is important to apply the steps of risk management discussed below, looking to provide consistency as you review all of a client's loss exposures with the goal of reducing the likelihood that something important will be overlooked.

Viewed from other perspectives, the purpose of risk management is to

1. *Conserve assets* – That is, reduce the adverse affects of risk while allowing an individual or business to continue normal activities with as little disruption as possible, without financial hardship.

2. *Balance resources* – Prior to a loss, the planner wants to determine the quantity of resources that will be needed after a possible loss has occurred. In this context, the planner must measure the cost and benefit associated with each risk management technique. The cost is the outlay to utilize the technique, while the benefit is the amount of loss that would be suffered if the outlay were not made.

STEPS IN THE RISK MANAGEMENT PROCESS

The basic steps of the risk management process include the following:

1. identify, analyze, and measure all loss exposures

2. select the technique or combination of techniques to be used to handle each exposure

3. implement the techniques chosen

4. monitor and, as called for, modify the program to obtain optimum results.

Step 1 – Identify, Analyze and Measure

There are four general categories of identifiable possible loss exposure:

1. physical

    a) property - home, auto, personal property

    b) loss of income or profit due to increased expenses

2. financial – liability due to intentional act or negligence of the client or others

3. contractual – loss assumed under a contract or through an association with others

4. human – value of human life

    a) key employee

    b) financial needs associated with an accident, illness, or death

The next phase is to identify the possible causes of a loss, that is, the perils. For example, common causes of property loss include fire, lightening, and flood. Mechanically, insurance, if and to the extent it is an appropriate tool, can manage a particular risk, in two ways.

1. The policy identifies the perils specifically insured.

2. The policy insures all perils except those specifically excluded.

When attempting to measure the loss potential, the factors in determining the amount of the loss include (as appropriate to the nature of the loss)

1. the value of the property

2. the value of assets exposed to liability claims (e.g., as a result of an auto accident) (In particular, you would consider the amount you can afford to lose and the amount of liability insurance that is appropriate. In this context, basic life insurance needs would be analyzed looking to the loss of income, the assets already accumulated, and the financial needs, which must be funded.)

Noteworthy perils, either uninsurable or requiring specific coverage, typically include

1. flood, sewer backup, and surface water runoff

2. earthquake or earth movement

3. war, rebellion, and insurrection

4. nuclear action, radiation, and contamination

5. normal wear and tear, deterioration, contamination, pollution, and damage by domestic animals, vermin or rodents

Step 2 – Select the Risk Management Technique

The common risk management techniques can be classified as

1. *Risk avoidance* – This is typically the least practical method of managing risk. For example, a car will never hit you if you never leave your house, but what kind of a life is that?

2. *Risk control/reduction/prevention* – Risk can often be reduced or controlled by preventive measures. For example

   - regular physical exams

   - keeping smoke detectors and fire extinguishers in key locations in the home

   - maintaining proper legal documentation for business activities and relationships

3. *Risk retention* – Some risks are retained because they cannot be otherwise managed or insured. The most common example of such a risk is war damage. Other risks are retained because the cost of insurance is too high for the benefit received. For example, higher deductibles and co-pay levels have become more prevalent for medical insurance because the cost of such insurance for the lower levels of expenses is simply excessive.

4. *Risk transfer – non-insurance* – Risk transfer techniques do not really reduce or even "transfer" the risk. Instead, they provide for the repayment of loss. Methods of risk transfer include

   - indemnity or hold harmless agreements

   - requiring sub-contractors or contractors to retain responsibility for certain risks

   - requiring lessees to retain certain risk (e.g., car leases).

   Risk sharing is essentially a combination of risk retention and risk transfer.

5. *Insurance* – Except for life insurance, insurance is the one product you purchase that you hope you never enjoy or from which you ever benefit. The purchase of insurance provides the most common method of risk transfer or sharing. The transfer of risk is to the insurance company (for a price) and the risk sharing is in the form of deductibles and co-pays.

While reviewing the specific risk management techniques, be sure to consider the various levels of need for risk management:

- severe – potential to cause demise of a family or business

- important – could cause serious hardship, but not total loss
- optional – exposures that have negligible consequences

Step 3 – Implement the Techniques Chosen

Risk avoidance and reduction are primarily a matter of personal commitment and habit. Being responsible and cautious in everyday activities and endeavors is the crux of minimizing risks that can be, at least in part, controlled. Simple examples include driving within speed limits, proper diet and exercise, and smoke detectors and fire extinguishers.

In evaluating the degree to which to rely on *risk retention and sharing* consideration should be given to the levels of reserves in cash and other liquid assets available and needed to cover loss contingencies. You don't want to be forced to sell assets or incur debt at inappropriate times should a loss occur.

Insurance, the most common technique of risk management, is typically used when there is no other effective way to protect against the risk of significant, if not unrecoverable, loss. The purchase of insurance requires its own analysis of purpose, amount, and type. This is a process that most clients are unprepared to undertake alone. Most financial planners cannot deal with all of the disparate insurance products available for the variety of insurable needs including, but not limited to

- automobile
- homeowner
- umbrella liability
- professional liability
- general business liability
- business interruption
- life (dying too soon)
- superannuation (living too long)
- disability
- medical
- long term care

Step 4 – Monitor the Results

In the financial planning process, there is a continuing need to evaluate the effectiveness of the chosen tools to accomplish the identified goals. Risk management is no different. Change is ever present. Environmental and personal changes may increase or decrease ones risk of loss. For example, as a client accumulates more assets, he has more to lose if sued as a result of a "slip and fall" accident on his front walkway.

The inevitability of changing circumstances and risk of loss leads to the unavoidable conclusion that the risk management techniques in place must also be re-evaluated, and if appropriate, modified or replaced. How frequently should this be done? Clearly when there is a major event that impacts the need for insurance, such as the sale of a business, a review is appropriate. But, regular, periodic reviews are also in order. Yearly routine reviews are probably too frequent. Every three years or so is not out of line. Consider, for example the need to enhance your homeowner's insurance as the value of your house increases, and the appropriateness of increasing shareholder insurance to fund a buy-sell agreement as the value of the business goes up.

GUIDELINES FOR SELECTING AN INSURANCE AGENT

Prior to the age of the Internet market for nearly all products and services, it was nearly impossible to purchase any insurance other than through a license insurance agent or broker. Even today, the vast majority of insurance is obtained through the agent/broker network. How then do you know what to look for in the broker who represents your clients' interests or the company agent you rely on for the best insurance product? Consider working with the person or firm that has

- the appropriate in-depth knowledge of insurance and support resources
- knowledge of which insurance company to use and the access to an acceptable choice of companies
- effective follow-up service for inquiries and claims
- the respect of clients
- clout with insurers and the respect of the claims adjusters

GUIDELINES FOR SELECTING AN INSURANCE COMPANY

In recent years, much has been said and written about the fiscal soundness of many insurance companies. The concern that the insurance company chosen will be able to pay any claims submitted is of course important. But consider all of these factors in deciding which companies fulfill your clients' needs:

- strong financial condition
- appropriate underwriting philosophy
- prompt and fair claims policies and procedures
- prompt and accurate service
- reasonable price, consistent with the quality of service

The insurance industry is so broad and diverse that it is nearly impossible for any consumer to know which companies are best suited for his needs. In addition to the reliance from the insurance agent, individuals can look to reports and guidance from a variety of insurance company rating agencies. These agencies relied on, in part by many insurance brokers, include

- A.M. Best
- Fitch, Inc. (Duff & Phelps)
- Moody's
- Standard & Poor's
- Weiss Research

RISK AND INSURANCE – TERMS AND CONCEPTS

Before proceeding with our explanation of the more common types of insurance, a review of some general insurance terms and concepts is in order:

1. *Indemnity* – An insured shall not be compensated by an insurer in an amount greater than the economic loss. The insured is thus indemnified for the loss, made whole (if the insurance coverage is adequate), but not enriched.

   Indemnity is typically a property and casualty insurance concepts, not applicable to life insurance. But there are a few exceptions to this limitation with property insurance, such as

   - *Replacement cost insurance* – Assuming costs to replace exceed the owners cost to construct or purchase the property, the insured would be enriched.
   - *Insurance coverage valued at a stated amount, regardless of actual value* – This approach is becoming more common in high-end automobile insurance policies that will establish the amount of coverage for the car if totaled, regardless of its actual value just before the accident.
   - *Valued policy laws* – Some states require payment on the limits of the policy if the property is totally destroyed.

2. *Actual cash value* – As it relates to the indemnity principle, the actual cash value of lost or damaged property is the maximum amount that will be paid to indemnify an insured. This amount will usually be less than "replacement cost" as a result of normal depreciation, wear, and tear.

3. *Insurable interest* – For a person to purchase insurance and be able to collect on a claim, there must be something that the policyholder or beneficiary will lose if there is property loss, injury to others (or damage their property), or if the insured dies or becomes disabled due to accident or sickness.

4. *Coinsurance* – A clause in an insurance contract that requires the policyholder to purchase insurance in an amount at least equal to a specific percentage of the value of the property. If the insured complies, the insurer will pay dollar-for-dollar up to the policy limit. If the insured does not comply, the insured's recovery is reduced in proportion to the deficiency. This sort of provision is common in real property insurance policies.

As an example of coinsurance, assume the property damage provisions of a commercial building insurance contract has an 80% coinsurance requirement. The building is worth $1,000,000. A fire occurs causing $200,000 of damage.

- If the owner purchased at least $800,000 property insurance (80% of value), then 100% of the valid claim ($200,000) will be paid.

- If the owner obtains only $600,000 property insurance coverage (60%), only $150,000, or 75% of the loss will be paid by the carrier, representing the pro rata portion of the required coinsurance amount ($600,000/$800,000).

5. *"Other insurance" clause* – Such a provision spells out the way that a loss will be apportioned between that policy and any other insurance the insured has available to cover the same loss. For example, the medical provisions of an automobile policy will, under its provisions, be coordinated with other medical coverage in order to avoid a double up of benefits.

   An "other insurance" clause is a common technique used to implement the indemnity principle. Property insurance policies generally use a pro rata "other insurance" clause to apportion responsibility among multiple coverage providers.

6. *Negligence* – For liability insurance purposes, negligence is typically defined as *the failure to use such care as a reasonably prudent and careful person would use under such circumstances.* When this failure results in injury to another or damage to property, a person determined to be negligent may be found liable for the resulting injury and damage and be legally bound to provide compensation.

7. *Contributory negligence* – This is a form of defense against a claim of negligence. The defendant claims that the plaintiff (injured party) contributed to the loss by acting in a manner that was itself negligent. If it can be shown the loss would not have occurred but for the contributory negligence of the plaintiff, the claim against the defendant may be overcome.

8. *Comparative negligence* – This approach to assigning responsibility for a loss, used by many jurisdictions, is intended to provide a balance between the extremes of strict negligence and contributory negligence. Under this concept, losses must be allocated and apportioned according to the degree to which each party contributed to the injury or damage. The result, typically, is a partial recovery by the plaintiff, not all or nothing.

9. *Assumption of risk* – Participants in certain *activities known to have an inherent element of danger* have, by participating, assumed the risk, relieving other participants or sponsors in the activity of any special duty to protect them.

LIFE INSURANCE – THE BASICS

Life insurance is a unique wealth creation tool that plays a major role in the estate planning process. In evaluating the use of this tool, the following steps are indicated:

1. Determine the *purpose(s)* for which the insurance is needed.

2. Determine the appropriate *amount* of life insurance for each identified need.

3. Determine the proper *type(s)* of life insurance for the identified need(s).

4. Identify the proper *ownership* of the life insurance.

5. Identify the proper *beneficiary* of the life insurance.

Purpose of Life Insurance

Life insurance, as an estate building or estate conversion tool, is often used for the following specific purposes:

- provide for the income needs of a surviving spouse, children, and other dependents

- pay federal and state death taxes and other costs of the estate

- pay outstanding debts

- provide for children's education

- shift wealth from one generation to another in the most cost effective manner possible

- meet "special" financial demands of physically or mentally handicapped or learning-disabled family members (children, parents, siblings, or other dependents)
- benefit a charity
- create an "instant estate"

The following business needs for life insurance may also play a role in the estate planning process:

- fund a buy-sell agreement
- finance a Death Benefit Only (D.B.O.) plan
- provide a basic level of financial security for the families of company employees
- recruit, retain, and reward key employees

Amount of Life Insurance

The starting point in determining the amount of life insurance to have is distinguishing *true needs* from *desires*. For example, creating a financial reserve to fund the future lifestyle needs of a surviving spouse and children (until they are through college and independent) is a need. On the other hand, purchasing life insurance in order to simple enlarge the size of your children's inheritance, beyond what they may actually require, is a desire.

At the beginning of the estate planning process, most clients are not aware of how much cash will be required to settle their estates. In addition, many clients do not understand that a forced sale of a closely held business, real estate interest, or other illiquid asset will generally yield significantly less than could be expected under a planned disposition.

The impact of a liquidity needs analysis can be illustrated graphically using software that will generate a simple, demonstrative flowchart. There are many available software programs that can easily generate an analysis under alternative scenarios, factoring in such variables as projected dates of death and estimated rates of inflation. The financial planner should use judgment and experience in estimating and evaluating the reasonableness of assumptions and variables reflected in the analysis.

In many instances the planner is called upon to review liquidity needs analyses prepared by others whose ultimate aim is to sell products (whether or not appropriate) in order to fund "projected shortfalls." The planner should carefully scrutinize these analyses and the underlying assumptions.

Types of Life Insurance

Despite what many individuals have been led to believe, it is not always best to "buy term life insurance and invest the difference." Certain forms of life insurance are more effective than others to perform specific estate planning goals. For example, if liquidity is not needed until the death of both husband and wife, and there is no viable source for such liquidity except life insurance, a survivorship, or second-to-die policy (typically a cash value policy that does not pay the death benefit until the death of both named insureds) may be most appropriate.

All forms of life insurance consist of three basic elements:

1. *Mortality cost* – The amount of funds required to fund the reserves needed to pay death benefits, as actuarially computed. As you would expect, mortality charges increase every insurance period (e.g., every year) simply because the insured gets older and is closer to his ultimate end.

2. *Administrative costs* – For both mutual and stock companies, the cost of operating the insurance company. For stock companies, the component includes the shareholders' expected profit.

3. *Investment performance* – Both the overall earnings of the insurance company's investments and earnings of the invested cash value of funds ascribed to individual insurance policies are important.

   Investment performance is most critical with insurance policies that are intended to accumulate cash values for the benefit of the insurance owner (reduced premiums) or the beneficiary (higher death benefits). However, even with term insurance, the insurance company's investment performance can affect future premium costs.

The basic types of life insurance include the following:

1. *Term life insurance* is typically the simplest form of life insurance. It provides the beneficiary

only with life insurance protection. There is no built-in savings element (cash value), as with, for example, whole life insurance.

The lowest cost life insurance is usually non-guaranteed, non-renewable term. This most basic policy provides that after each insurance period (usually one year), the insured must re-prove he is healthy enough to be re-insured. In addition, as with any term policy, the premium will increase every period (year) as mortality costs rise.

A yearly renewable term policy will provide the guarantee that the term insurance coverage will be available to the insured, but the guarantee has an associated cost (higher premium). In addition, the annual insurance premium will increase continually due to increasing mortality charges, so long as the policy remains in force.

A term policy for a predetermined period, such as five, ten, or fifteen years, will have a higher annual premium cost than a yearly renewable term policy, but only in the earlier years. In the later years of the multi-year, level premium term, the comparable premiums of yearly renewable term will be higher. The relative total cost of these two policy types will depend on the magnitude of the adjustments the insurance company makes each year to the premium of the annual renewable policy. The fixed multi-period policy usually makes sense where the insured wants the comfort of knowing what the insurance will cost for the entire planned coverage period.

Term insurance is generally most advantageous when the insurance need is limited to an identifiable period of time, especially if that period does not extend beyond fifteen to twenty years. For example, if the only need for the life insurance policy under consideration were to fund the college education needs for a twelve-year-old child, term insurance would usually be most cost effective.

2. *Whole life insurance* is the traditional "cash value" policy with level premium payments designed to remain in force over the entire life of the insured individual. This form of insurance is appropriate for meeting insurance needs the insured will have for his entire life, such as estate liquidity. It generally includes a savings or cash value reserve element. Premiums paid in excess of the mortality and administrative costs of the policy are added to the accumulating cash value of the policy. This cash value earns interest that also accumulates in the policy. It is the accumulation of cash reserves in the earlier years of the policy that enable the policy to retain a level premium over the life of the insured.

   Whole life policies typically have fixed and guaranteed schedules of cash value that can be borrowed against by the policy owner for any reason, or which can be taken in cash upon the surrender of the contract. The level premiums are generally fixed at a specific amount applicable over the entire term of the policy (generally to age 100).

   These policies also provide for guaranteed maximum mortality charges and guaranteed minimum interest (earnings) rates. However, these guarantees, and the planned fixed premiums have a cost. In order to receive the certainties of future cost the policy owner expects from a whole life policy, the basic annual premium will be set at a very high level.

3. *Universal life insurance* (UL) is a form of "cash value" policy with the following variations from traditional whole life:

   - UL provides the policy owner a great deal more flexibility in the payment of insurance premiums. Subject to certain limiting tax rules, premiums can be increased or decreased from year to year, or may even be skipped. The primary concern for the owner is that a sufficient cash value be maintained to cover the future mortality and administrative costs without imposing huge prospective premium requirements.

   - Policyholders may, within limits and subject to the insurance company's insurability standards with respect to increases, change the death benefit levels of the policies.

   - Regulations generally require separate disclosure of administrative expenses, mortality charges and earnings rates for universal life contracts.

- Policyholders have access to the cash value of their policies either through policy loans or direct withdrawals. Whole life policies generally only provide for cash via loans.

- Upon the purchase of a universal policy, a policy owner may choose either a *level* death benefit (Option A or Option I), or an *increasing* death benefit (Option B or Option II). Option A, which is generally the only option available under traditional whole life, provides for a death benefit equal to the *greater of* the face amount of the policy or the cash value as of the date of death. Under Option B (generally not available with a whole life policy), the death benefit is equal to the *sum of* the face amount of the policy and the cash value at the death of the insured.

Example. Assume the face amount of a universal policy is $1,000,000 and the cash value at the death of the insured is $900,000, under Option A the death benefit would be the $1,000,000 face amount of the policy. If the cash value at death is $1,100,000, the death benefit under option A would be the $1,100,000 cash value.

Under Option B, assuming the same $1,000,000 face amount of coverage, with a cash value of $900,000, the death benefit would be $1,900,000 ($1,000,0000 face plus $900,000 cash value). If the cash value at death is $1,100,000, the death benefit would be $2,100,000 ($1,000,0000 face plus $1,100,000 cash value).

To no surprise, the choice of an Option B death benefit has a commensurately higher premium cost. If the policy in effect provides for an increasing death benefit, then there would be a comparable increase in annual mortality charges. However, if you are looking for a simple technique to provide for increasing future insurance needs, without future proof of insurability, an Option B death benefit election should be considered.

Also to no surprise, Option B is only available at the purchase of the policy. While you can choose to level the death benefit and switch from B to A at any time while the policy is in force, a switch from an A election to B is generally not allowed, as that would result in an increase in coverage, and risk to the insurance company, without a showing of qualifying good health.

Consistent with traditional whole life, universal insurance does provide for guaranteed maximum mortality charges and minimum earnings rates. The cash values of universal policies are managed by the insurance company as part of the company's general investment accounts. This means that the funds belong to the insurance company that accounts for them on behalf of the policyholder. Consequently, the cash values of whole life and universal policies are exposed to the other creditors of the insurance company.

4. *Variable life insurance*, like traditional whole life, has a fixed premium and a minimum guaranteed death benefit. However, unlike either whole life or universal life, the risk and reward of investment decisions with straight variable life insurance is more clearly shifted to the policyholder. The cash reserve of a variable policy is maintained in a segregated investment account, and the policyholder, not the insurance company, determines how the reserve funds will be invested. The investment choices are generally in the form of mutual funds, and usually include some variety of equity funds, bond funds, balanced funds, and money market funds. The policyholder has the flexibility to change the mix of investments among the available funds.

   The segregated investment accounts are treated as securities and are subject to SEC regulation. The segregated accounts belong to the policy owner, not the insurance company, and are thus not subject to the risk of the insurer's creditor vulnerability.

   With straight variable, the policy's death benefit will vary with the performance of the investment accounts, but cannot be decreased below the original coverage amount (face) of the policy, so long as the contractual premium payments are maintained.

5. *Variable universal life insurance (VUL)* combines the critical attributes of both variable life and universal life. As with variable contracts, VUL policies provide for flexibility in the payment of premiums and limited flexibility to alter the death benefit. Separate disclosure of administrative expenses, mortality charges, earnings rates and investment expenses are required.

At the time of purchase, the policy owner may choose between a level (Option A) or increasing (Option B) death benefit.

Investments are maintained in separate accounts, regulated by the SEC, and investments are managed by the policy owner, using the available mutual fund options of the policy.

However, unlike the other forms of cash value policy, VUL provides for

- *no guaranteed* minimum cash value
- *no guaranteed* minimum earnings rate
- *no guaranteed* minimum death benefit (although maximum mortality charges are guaranteed)

VUL is popular in circumstances where the policy owner is willing to assume these risks in exchange for the potential of a greater increase in cash value while maintaining the highest level of flexibility and control over the variable policy's components.

6. *Private placement variable life insurance* is a special type of variable (typically VUL) life insurance geared toward the needs and resources of very wealthy individuals. Such policies typically

    - require a large premium (usually $1,000,000 or more)
    - allow the policyholder to choose from among approved money managers (rather than just mutual funds) to manage investments in the policy account
    - charge lower investment management loads than imposed by standard variable policies.

7. *Survivorship life insurance*, also known as second-to-die, joint life, or last survivor life insurance, provides for the payment of death benefits only after both insured individuals have died. Since the insurance company does not have to make a death benefit payment until after the two deaths, survivorship insurance is most frequently used as a tool to provide liquidity to pay estate taxes, or to create an estate for transfer to future generations, when the last of a husband and wife couple dies. Its popularity increased dramatically as a result of the unlimited marital deduction.

    Survivorship life insurance is generally structured as a level premium "cash value" policy (usually whole life, universal, or VUL) covering two lives, but almost any reasonable variation is possible, if appropriate for the client's goals. Such variations might include insurance on more than two lives.

    From a cost perspective, survivorship insurance is typically cheaper than comparable insurance on either of the insured lives. Actuarially this makes sense since no death benefit is paid until after two individuals die. No matter how much older one insured is than the other, and even if the older spouse is seriously ill, there is always a possibility the younger, healthy spouse will die sooner, for example, as a result of an accident.

Ownership of Life Insurance

Typically life insurance is owned by the individual whose life is *insured*. However, under federal estate tax law, if the insured retains any "incidence of ownership," the death benefit proceeds of the life insurance policy will be included in the taxable estate of the insured, whether the insured's estate or someone other than the person or entity is named as the beneficiary of the policy. In order to avoid this undesired estate tax result, a policy on the life of the identified insured is often purchased and owned by the *beneficiary* or some other person.

If the beneficiary of the policy is the insured's surviving spouse, having that spouse also own the policy usually does not have a material estate effect since the proceeds of the policy, if included in the decedent's taxable estate would be eligible for the unlimited marital deduction. However, if for example the insured's children are the intended beneficiaries, ownership by the children or an *irrevocable trust* created for the benefit of the children, would be appropriate owners of the life insurance.

Beneficiary of Life Insurance

While life insurance is intended to provide a lump sum of cash for an identified beneficiary, it is not always the client's intention that all of the cash be made available immediately or all at one time, even if deferred. It may also be the client's goal to make sure the insurance proceeds remain available to provide income for an extended period of time and/or for multiple beneficiaries and generations.

Example. A young executive generally has not had the time to accumulate adequate wealth to provide for all the needs of a surviving spouse and young children. The surviving spouse may need a source of income for the remainder of her life. The family will need enough income and principal to provide for the children until they are self-sufficient and to fund their education. To ensure the funds are properly managed for the identified individuals and period of time, the client might want to consider naming a trust established by his will as the beneficiary of the insurance proceeds. If the client is willing to forego control over the policy during his lifetime, and as a technique to avoid federal estate tax on the insurance proceeds at the latter death of the insured client or his spouse, the client may consider having the policy owned by an intervivos (lifetime) irrevocable trust which is also the beneficiary of the policy. The spouse and children would be the beneficiaries of the trust, receiving distributions in accordance with the client's goals, as set forth in the provisions of the trust.

Basic Tax Implications of Life Insurance

Income Taxes

Generally, life insurance death benefits proceeds are *excludable* from the recipient's gross income for federal and state income tax purposes. However, if prior to death a policy or an interest in a policy has been sold or otherwise transferred for valuable consideration, the death benefit proceeds will be taxable to the recipient/transferee to the extent the insurance proceeds exceed the total of the purchase price for the policy and any additional premiums paid by the transferee/owner (Purchaser's basis in the policy). This is known as the *"transfer for value"* rule.

Example. If Joe purchased a $100,000 policy insuring the life of his brother-in-law, Howard, for $40,000 and paid additional premiums of $5,000 before Howard died, Joe's basis in the policy would be $45,000. Upon receiving the $100,000 upon Howard's death, Joe would have $55,000 of taxable income.

Exceptions to the transfer for value rule are available for a sale or transfer to (1) the insured, (2) a partner of the insured, (3) a partnership in which the insured is a partner, (4) a corporation of which the insured is a shareholder or officer, or (5) if the transferee's basis in the insurance policy is determined, in whole or in part, by the transferor's basis. A slight oversimplification of the exceptions is that if the transfer does not result in a tax basis change, the transfer for value rule will not make the death benefit proceeds taxable to the transferee. If in the previous example, Joe and Howard were business partners, as well as brothers-in-law, the sale of the insurance policy would be exempt from transfer for value rule and Joe would not have taxable income when he received the insurance death benefit.

Generally, transfers between spouses made after July 18, 1984 or transfers which are incident to a divorce, even if for value, are excluded from the transfer for value rule.

Federal Estate and Gift Taxes

The death benefit proceeds of a life insurance policy are generally included in the gross estate of the insured for federal estate tax purposes if

1. the insured's estate is the named beneficiary of the life insurance policy

2. the insured possessed any incidence of ownership in the policy (such as the right to change beneficiaries, surrender the policy, or borrow against the cash value of the policy) at the time of death

3. the insured died within three years following the transfer of his ownership interest in the policy

Gifts of life insurance policies or gifts of premium payments may be subject to the federal gift tax. The value of the gift is based on the fair market value of the insurance policy at the time of the gift of the policy or, in the case of the premium payments, the cash amount of the premium paid.

HEALTH AND MEDICAL INSURANCE

There are two general types of health insurance plans:

1. traditional or indemnity ("fee-for-service")

2. managed care, usually in one of the following form of organization:

   a) Health Maintenance Organization (HMO)

   b) Point of Service (POS)

   c) Preferred Provider Organization (PPO)

The essential expenses usually covered by medical insurance include

- doctor visits
- preventive care
- diagnostic tests
- hospital and extended care
- emergency services
- prescription medications

Other coverage areas include

- family planning, OB-GYN
- maternity and well baby care
- dental care
- vision care
- mental health
- substance abuse
- chronic disease care
- physical therapy

Indemnity medical insurance programs generally provide for a *reimbursement* of the insured medical expenses upon proof of incurring the expense or by *paying the allowed expense directly to the service provider*. Expenses are generally completely covered (subject to deductible and co-pay requirements), no matter what happens.

The major emphasis in an indemnity program is on *patient choice*, patient responsibility, and immediate patient care. These programs provide for more flexibility and typically more comprehensive coverage, but are much more expensive than any managed care program.

Managed care medical insurance focuses on *preventive medicine and lower cost*. The three basic managed care programs have the following key characteristics:

1. A *Health Maintenance Organization (HMO)* charges a set fee for which it provides specified health care during a membership period. The insured must use the HMO's doctors and facilities (with more flexible provisions for emergency or out-of-area needs).

2. A *Point of Service (POS)* program is in effect an option available from some HMO's which permits the participants to use any health care provider, subject to a penalty in the form of the insured paying a higher portion of the total cost than if an "in-network" provider were used.

3. A *Preferred Provider Organization (PPO)* is a health care delivery system that contracts with medical care providers to offer services at discounted fees to the PPO members. Similar to HMOs, instead of reimbursing for expenses incurred, a PPO charges a set fee for which it provides specified health care during the coverage period. Unlike HMOs, however, participants in a PPO typically are allowed to choose between in-network and out-of-network providers, paying a higher cost for out-of-network services.

HOMEOWNER INSURANCE

The purpose of homeowner insurance is to protect homeowner or residential tenant from

1. loss or damage to their property, such as
   - dwelling
   - other structures at the residence
   - personal property
   - loss of use
2. liability claims
   - comprehensive liability coverage
   - medical payments to others

Certain risks should be evaluated independently, either because recent occurrences have made coverage expensive or impossible to obtain, or because the possibility of loss from the risk may vary from situation to situation. Examples of such risks include

- flood – need separate policy
- landslide – may be "bought back" with a rider, if excluded from the basic policy
- earthquake – need separate policy

Other specific risks are almost always excluded unconditionally. Homeowners are expected to handle these issues as normal household "maintenance":

- mold
- rust
- rot
- fungi

There are two basic approaches to insuring property:

1. *"Normal perils"* coverage – Perils not listed are not covered.
2. *"All risks open perils"* coverage – Only perils specifically excluded are not covered. This is typically broader, and more expensive coverage.

Factors that may cause the premium cost of homeowner insurance to vary include:

1. physical damage coverage (typically for at least 80% of the cost to rebuild)
2. amount of coverage (stated as a percentage of coverage on primary dwelling) for
    - other structure (Usually 10%)
    - personal property (Usually 50% for "unscheduled property" plus additional premiums for specifically scheduled (listed) items)
    - loss of use (Usually 20%)
3. deductible for property damages (Generally $250 to $1,000)
4. limit on liability coverage (generally $100,000 (basic) to $500,000) – coordinated with "umbrella liability coverage
5. medical payments to other ($1,000 basic)
6. damage to property of others ($500 basic)

AUTOMOBILE INSURANCE

The basic components of an automobile insurance policy are

- Part A – liability coverage
- Part B – medical payments
- Part C – uninsured (underinsured) motorists
- Part D – damage to the insured's vehicle

Persons generally covered by the policy include

- the named insured and any family member
- any person using the covered vehicle with the insured's permission
- any person or organization for a liability arising out of any covered person's use of the covered vehicle on behalf of the insured person or organization

Automobile liability coverage ((Part A) will often have most or all of the following exclusions:

- any vehicles while they are used to haul property or persons for a fee
- vehicles with fewer than four wheels (separate motorcycle coverage is available)
- bodily injury to employees of the insured
- property rented to, used by, or in the care of the insured (may be an add-on)
- a person who intentionally causes bodily injury or property damage

Liability coverage may be either *single limit* or *split limit*. With single limit coverage, the amount shown in the policy as the maximum limit of liability coverage applies to the total of all bodily injuries and damages from one accident. Split limit coverage provides separate limits to the different coverage elements that may occur in an accident. For example, a split limit of $100,000/$300,000/$100,000 would provide for

- a $100,000 limit for injury to one person
- a $300,000 limit for injuries to all individuals
- a $100,000 limit for property damage in the accident

It is important to tie in these limits of coverage with umbrella liability coverage that may be in place in order to avoid a possible gap or unnecessary duplication of coverage.

Automobile medical payment coverage (Part B) generally covers medical services for the insured, relatives, and anyone else in the insured's vehicle injured in the accident. Part B generally does not cover pedestrians or occupants of other vehicles. Payment is usually prompt, without waiting for a determination of liability. However, such coverage may be subject to an "other insurance" clause, requiring coordination with other medical insurance coverage of the affected individuals.

Under *uninsured motorist (Part C)* coverage, if an insured individual is injured in an accident with an uninsured (or underinsured) motorist, the insured can look to his own insurance carrier to pay him, as if the company were the insurer of the other party (subject to the limits of the injured party's policy). The insured is also covered if injured by a hit-and-run accident when the operator of the other vehicle cannot be identified. While not mandatory, this coverage is at least optional in almost all states.

The coverage for *damage to the insured's property (Part D)* relates to the value of the insured's car. The level of coverage, and the related premium will typically decrease as the vehicle ages and its mileage increases. The coverage applies whether or not the insured is at fault. The covered perils are

- *Collision* – reimburses policyholder for damage to the car sustained by reason of a collision. The premium can be mitigated with a higher deductible.
- *Other than collision (OTC)* – effectively "all-risk" physical damage coverage (everything but excluded items, such as collision, war losses, damage due to wear and tear, road damage to tires, freezing and mechanical or electrical breakdown).

UMBRELLA LIABILITY INSURANCE

Also called *Excess Liability* or *Personal Catastrophe* coverage, umbrella liability insurance provides personal liability coverage protecting individuals and families from large (excess) personal liability claims. The policy supplements the underlying liability coverage provided in homeowner and auto insurance policies. Homeowner and auto liability coverage in effect provide a "deductible" for umbrella coverage.

Obviously, umbrella coverage requires coordination with what must be adequate homeowner and auto coverage in order to avoid any gaps in liability coverage. An umbrella policy of from $3,000,000 to $5,000,000 or more is not unreasonable, particularly in light of recent unprecedented litigation awards. Quite simply, the more you have, the more you have at risk.

TERRORISM AND INSURANCE

Following "9/11", it is no surprise that insurance carriers wanted to exclude from their property and casualty policies all damages resulting from act of terrorism. In order to assure that such risks are insurable, the Terrorism Risk Insurance Act of 2002 was enacted.

The 2002 Act established a temporary Federal Terrorism Insurance Program that provides for a transparent system of shared public and private compensation for insured losses from acts of terrorism. The Act is intended to allow for a transitional period for the private markets to stabilize and "adjust" to the impact of contemporary terrorism on providers and users of commercial insurance.

As a result of the Terrorism Risk Insurance Act, consumers have the right to purchase insurance coverage for losses from "acts of terrorism" that are certified by the Secretary of the Treasury, in concurrence with the Secretary of State and the Attorney General of the United States. For this purpose, an "act of terrorism" is defined as "a violent act dangerous to human life or property…committed by individual(s) acting on behalf of any foreign person or interest as part of an effort to coerce the civilian population of the United States." Under the formula, the United States pays 90% of covered losses exceeding established deductibles (paid by the insurance company).

Chapter 27

INCOME TAX PLANNING

WHY TAXES ARE IMPORTANT TO THE INVESTOR

An investor must consider income taxes (federal, state, and local) as part of the cost of any investment. The objective of financial planning is to maximize the utility of invested capital in order to accomplish the client's financial and personal goals. Consequently, the planner must attempt to minimize the tax element of the investment cost in a manner that is consistent with those goals. An understanding of the basic concepts of the income tax law is therefore essential.

The complexity of the federal income tax law (not to mention the various state and local income tax laws) is almost overwhelming. Specific tax advice should be given only by qualified tax specialists. But planners and clients both must have a working knowledge of (1) the issues involved in the acquisition and disposition of an investment, (2) the issues relating to income and expenses during the period the investment is held, and (3) the federal income tax rate structure. This chapter will focus on these three broad areas and subdivide them as follows:

1. acquisition and disposition issues:
   - (a) basis (including the "at risk" rules),
   - (b) business, energy, and rehabilitation tax credits,
   - (c) timing of reporting gain or loss upon disposition, and
   - (d) character of gain or loss upon disposition;
2. issues relating to income and expenses while the investment is held:
   - (a) "income" defined,
   - (b) character of income or loss,
   - (c) deductible expenses, and
   - (d) timing of recognition of income and expenses;
3. the federal income tax rate structure:
   - (a) income tax rates,
   - (b) the alternative minimum tax ("AMT"), and
   - (c) the "kiddie" tax.

This chapter offers only a primer for a basic understanding of the federal income tax system. For more detailed information on the topic, please consult *The Tools & Techniques of Income Tax Planning* (2nd edition, National Underwriter, 2006).

ACQUISITION AND DISPOSITION OF AN INVESTMENT

Basis

Basis is a key concept to the investor because it is the starting point for determining the amount of gain or loss. It is also the measure of the maximum amount of depreciation or amortization allowable for certain types of assets.

An investor's original basis in a purchased asset is its cost. The cost of property is the amount the investor paid for it in cash or other property. For example, if Bob buys a rental property for $100,000 cash, his original basis in the acquired property is $100,000.

When property other than (or in addition to) cash is used to acquire an investment, and the transaction does not qualify as a tax-free exchange, the cost (basis) of the property acquired is the sum of any cash paid *plus* the fair market value of any property given. For instance, if Bob purchased the rental property for $10,000 cash plus stock of IBM worth $90,000, Bob's original basis in the rental property would be $100,000 (the sum of the $10,000 cash paid plus the $90,000 fair market value of the stock).

Typically, when an investor exchanges one property for another, the market value of the property given up and the market value of the property received will be approximately equal. The fair market value of both properties will, as a practical matter, usually be ascertained by reference to the property whose value is most easily determined. In the example in the previous paragraph, it is easy to determine Bob's basis in the rental property since Bob paid for the property with cash ($10,000) and publicly traded IBM stock ($90,000), the value of which can be easily found.

When property is acquired subject to a mortgage or other debt, the basis of the property is not merely the amount of the investor's equity in the property—the basis is the total of the cash *and* the value of other property paid *plus* the amount of the debt. For example, if Rich buys a $1,000,000 apartment house, paying $250,000 in cash and borrowing the remaining $750,000, his basis in the property is the full $1,000,000.

"At Risk" Rules

An investor's ability to create basis through the use of debt is limited by the "at risk" rules. These rules provide that losses are deductible only to the extent the investor is personally "at risk."

The "at risk" rules limit deductions for borrowing that attempt to be characterized as "at risk" for tax purposes when there is no actual economic risk to the investor. For instance, assume Georgia wants to purchase a $100,000 interest in an oil drilling venture. She intends to invest $20,000 of her own funds while borrowing the $80,000 balance. The bank providing the loan to Georgia has agreed to make a "nonrecourse" loan to her. In other words, the bank will rely solely on the value of the property as its collateral for the debt. In the event Georgia cannot repay the loan, the bank cannot look to Georgia's other assets to cover the unpaid balance. Since the most Georgia can lose on her investment is $20,000 in cash, her deductions will be limited to that $20,000 (plus the amount of income generated from the investment).

The "at risk" rules cover essentially all investment activities except for real estate acquired before 1987. With respect to real estate subject to the "at risk" rules, "qualified nonrecourse financing" is treated as an additional amount at risk. "Qualified" financing is generally defined as borrowings (except convertible debt) from persons or entities actively engaged in the business of lending money (such as banks), and not the former owner of the property. Loans from or guaranteed by a federal, state, or local government agency will also qualify.

Aside from real estate investments, the "at risk" rules apply to the following examples of activities engaged in by an individual for the production of income:

1. holding, producing, or distributing motion picture films or video tapes;
2. farming;
3. exploring for or exploiting oil and gas reserves or geothermal deposits;
4. leasing of depreciable personal property.

An investor is considered at risk to the extent of:

1. cash invested; *plus*
2. the basis of property invested; *plus*
3. amounts borrowed for use in the investment that are secured by the investor's assets (other than the property used in the investment activity); *plus*
4. amounts borrowed to the extent the investor is personally liable for its repayment; *plus*
5. when the investment is made in partnership form:

   (a) the investor-partner's undistributed share of partnership income, *plus*

   (b) the investor-partner's proportionate share of partnership debt, to the extent he is personally liable for its repayment.

An investor is not considered "at risk" with respect to nonrecourse debt (other than qualified nonrecourse financing, see above) used to finance the activity, or to finance the acquisition of property used in the activity, or with respect to any other arrangement for the compensation or reimbursement of any economic loss. For example, if Georgia is able to obtain commercial insurance against the risk that the oil drilling fund will not return her original $20,000 cash investment, she would not even be considered "at risk" on that amount.

Losses limited by the "at risk" provisions are not lost; instead, these amounts may be carried over and deducted in subsequent years (but only if the investor's "at risk" amount is sufficiently increased).

The benefit of previously deducted losses must be recaptured when the investor's "at risk" amount is reduced below zero. For example, assume Tania's loss deductions from her interest in an oil drilling venture total $5,000 through the end of last year. Her basis in the venture at the end of last year (after the deductions) was $1,000. In the current year Tania received $3,000 in cash distributions. That distribution reduces Tania's basis by $3,000 to $2,000.

Since an investor cannot have a negative basis in an investment for tax purposes, Tania must recapture the $2,000 of prior year deductible losses in order to bring her basis up to zero. In addition, Tania will not be able to deduct any losses from the venture in the current year because she has a zero basis.

Property Acquired from a Decedent

Under current law, when an investor dies (in a year *other* than 2010) the beneficiary of his property does not "carry over" the decedent's basis (the rules for property inherited from a decedent dying *in 2010* are explained below). Instead, the basis of property acquired from or passing from a decedent is the fair market value of the property as of the date of (a) the investor's death, or (b) the federal estate tax alternate valuation date if that date (typically six months after the date of death) is elected by the estate's executor. Therefore, if the value of an investment held until death increases from the date of its acquisition, the potential gain (or loss in the case of a decrease in value) is never recognized for income tax purposes. An increase in the property's basis to its federal estate tax value is called a "step-up" in basis.

Note that this "stepped-up basis" is obtained even though no one pays income tax on the intervening appreciation. For example, if an individual had purchased stock that cost $10,000 and that had a fair market value of $50,000 at the time of his death, his beneficiary would receive a $50,000 basis for the stock. The $40,000 appreciation in the value of the stock would never be taxed. If the beneficiary then sold the property for $65,000, his taxable gain would be only $15,000.

The alternate valuation method may be elected by an executor or administrator only if the election will decrease (1) the value of the gross estate and (2) the amount of the federal estate tax imposed. Generally, an election to use the alternate valuation date means that property will be included in the gross estate at its fair market value as of six months after the decedent's death. However, if any property is distributed, sold, exchanged, or otherwise disposed of within six months after the decedent's death, the value of the property at that disposition date becomes the "alternate value."

Example. Assume property was purchased for $10,000 and is worth $50,000 on the date of a widower's death. Assume that his executor sells the asset for $45,000 three months after his death. If the alternate valuation date is elected, the valuation date for this property would be the date of its sale. Its basis becomes $45,000. The estate realizes no tax gain or loss because the $45,000 amount realized on the sale is equal to the property's $45,000 basis.

As a result of the Economic Growth and Tax Relief Reconciliation Act of 2001 (EGTRRA), the "stepped-up basis at death" rules were repealed for property acquired from a decedent *after* December 31, 2009. Note, however, that this repeal is in effect for only one year. (All of the provisions of the 2001 Act are subject to a "sunset" provision that, in effect, revokes the entire Act, including this repeal of stepped-up basis.) For property inherited *during* 2010, special, modified carryover basis rules apply. The recipient of the property will receive a basis equal to the lesser of the adjusted basis in the hands of the decedent or the fair market value of the property as of the date of death. Under these rules, a partial basis step-up is allowed, which is limited to $1,300,000 or $3,000,000 in the case of a surviving spouse. The determination of which assets will receive the step-up is discretionary, to be made by the executor or administrator of the estate.

Property Acquired by Gift

When property is acquired by lifetime gift and there is a gain on the sale by the donee, the general rule is that the property in the hands of the donee has the same basis (subject to an adjustment discussed below) it had in the hands of the donor. This is called a "substituted" or "transferred" or "carryover" basis. The donee of the gift—the new owner—computes his basis by referring to the basis in the hands of the donor. In other words, the donor's basis is "transferred" and "carried over" to the donee so that gain will not escape tax but merely be deferred. The gain remains deferred only until the donee disposes of the property in a taxable transaction.

Example. Assume that Alex purchases stock for $3,000. After it appreciates in value to $9,000, he gives it to Sara. The basis of the stock in Sara's hands for determining gain on a later sale by Sara is still $3,000. Therefore, if she sells it for $10,000, she has a $7,000 gain.

When the donor's basis is used, it is subject to an adjustment for any gift taxes paid on the net appreciation in the value of the gift (but not above the amount of the gift tax paid). For instance, in the example in the paragraph above, if the gift tax were $1,500, the donee's basis would be the $3,000 carryover basis plus $1,000 adjustment, a total of $4,000. The addition to basis is computed according to the following formula:

$$\frac{\text{Net Appreciation in Value of Gift}}{\text{Value of Gift at Transfer}} \times \text{Gift Tax Paid}$$

In our example, the computation would be

$$\frac{\$9{,}000 - \$3{,}000}{\$9{,}000} \times \$1{,}500 = \$3{,}000 \quad \text{Adjustment to Carryover Basis}$$

The basis rule for determining loss on the sale of property acquired by gift is different from the rule for determining the amount of the gain on the sale. For purposes of determining the amount of a loss, the basis of the property in the hands of the donee is the lesser of (a) the donor's basis or (b) the fair market value of the property at the time of the gift. The purpose of this special provision is to prevent investors from gaining a tax benefit by transferring property with a built-in loss to persons who could take advantage of tax losses.

Assume, for instance, that in the example above the value of the stock at the time of the gift was only $1,000. If Alex sold the stock, he would have a capital loss of $2,000 ($3,000 basis – $1,000 amount realized). If Alex had other capital losses of at least $3,000 but no capital gains, the $2,000 loss would be of no immediate tax benefit to him. Were it not for the special provision, Alex might give the stock to his father who had capital gains. If his father were allowed to use Alex's $3,000 basis, his father could sell the stock, take a $2,000 loss, and obtain the tax benefit from the loss that Alex himself could not have used. For this reason, the father, in determining his loss on the sale, must use as his basis the $1,000 fair market value of the property at the time of the gift since that is lower than Alex's $3,000 basis. If Alex's father sold the property for $900, he would only recognize a $100 loss on the sale ($900 proceeds less $1,000 basis). If Alex's father sold the property at a time when it was worth only $1,200 (or any other amount between the $1,000 fair market value at the date of the gift or the $3,000 carryover basis), no gain or loss would be recognized.

General Business Tax Credits

A credit is a dollar-for-dollar reduction in the investor's tax. The business tax credits include the energy, rehabilitation, and low-income tax credits and are designed to encourage investment in certain types of property used in a trade or business, including rental property (and, thus, stimulate economic growth).

The energy credit is a percentage of the taxpayer's qualified investment in energy property and is generally limited to 10%. This category includes solar energy and geothermal property. The rehabilitation credit is available for expenditures incurred to rehabilitate buildings that are certified historic structures or were initially placed in service before 1936. The credit is limited to 10% of qualified rehabilitation expenditures for buildings that are not certified historic structures. Rehabilitation expenditures for buildings that qualify as certified historic structures are eligible for a credit of 20%. Both of the rehabilitation credits apply to residential as well as nonresidential properties. A credit is also available for investment in certain low-income housing.

The energy, rehabilitation, and low-income housing credits are aggregated with certain other credits to form the general business credit. The amount of the general business credit that may offset income taxes in any one year is limited.

The energy and rehabilitation tax credits are not without cost. The investor must reduce his basis for both purposes of computing future depreciation deductions and computing gain or loss upon the sale or other taxable disposition of the asset. The property's basis must be reduced by:

1. 50% of the business energy tax credit, and

2. 100% of the rehabilitation credits.

Upon early disposition of property for which an energy or rehabilitation credit was claimed, and that reduced the investor's tax liability, some or all of the investment credit must be "recaptured," (i.e., reported as an additional tax). Property that is held at least five full years from the date it was placed in service is not subject to recapture. Likewise, early dispositions triggered by the investor's death or by a tax free transfer to a corporation in exchange for its stock will not result in recapture.

If recapture is required, the investor must add to his tax a portion of the credit as indicated in the following table:

If Disposition Occurs Before the End of	Percentage of Investment Credit to be Recaptured
1 Year	100%
2 Years	80%
3 Years	60%
4 Years	40%
5 Years	20%

This recapture has the effect of increasing the investor's basis in the property (which was previously reduced when the credit was claimed). This adjustment to basis is treated as if it were made immediately before the disposition.

However, the low-income housing credit is subject to a 15-year recapture period rather than the 5-year schedule above.

Reporting a Gain or Loss Upon Disposition

The timing of when a gain or loss is reported for tax purposes is critical to the success of the investment. Deferring income until a later year, particularly a year in which the investor is in a lower tax bracket, or accelerating a deduction into a year in which the taxpayer has a great deal of income, can significantly enhance the after-tax return from an investment.

The problems of determining the correct year to report income or take deductions flow from the requirement that income is to be reported on the basis of annual periods. Although there are a few exceptions, as a general rule investors must report income and claim deductions according to annual accounting periods.

Most individuals are "cash basis" taxpayers (i.e., one who reports income as it is received and who takes deductions as expenses are paid) and generally will recognize a gain or loss from the disposition of an asset at the time the transaction is "closed." The mere signing of an agreement to sell does not trigger the recognition of gain or loss. A transaction is not closed until the seller transfers title to the property in exchange for cash or other proceeds.

Installment Sales

The installment sale provisions are particularly important to an investor who has sold an asset for a substantial profit and has received a cash down payment and note from the purchaser for the balance due. Usually these notes are not readily transferable. Without the installment sale rules, the investor would incur a large tax in one year even if he does not have sufficient cash to pay the tax. Installment sales are also indicated when an investor wants to sell property to another party who does not have enough liquid assets to pay for the property in a lump sum at closing.

The basic rules for installment sale reporting include the following:

1. A seller of property can defer as much or as little as desired and payments can be set to fit the seller's financial needs. Even if payments are received in the year of sale, the installment method may still be used for the unpaid balance. For instance, a sale for $1,000,000 will qualify even if $300,000 is received in the year of sale and the remaining $700,000 (plus interest on the unpaid balance) is paid over the next five years.

2. No payment has to be made in the year of sale. For example, the parties could agree that the entire purchase price for payment of a $1,000,000 parcel of land will be paid five years after the sale (with interest being earned on the $1,000,000 during the 5-year period). The only requirement is that at least one payment must be made in a taxable year after the year of sale. This means that an investor should contract to have payments made to him at the time when it is most advantageous (or the least disadvantageous).

3. Installment sale treatment is automatic unless the investor affirmatively elects *not* to have installment treatment apply.

4. The installment note receivable may be independently secured (such as with a letter of credit obtained from a bank) without triggering the recognition of income when the note is secured.

The computation of the gain recognized with each receipt of each cash payment from an installment sale can be illustrated as follows:

Example. Assume an investor purchased land that cost $10,000. Five years later she sells the land for $50,000. Upon closing, she receives $20,000 cash plus a note for the remaining $30,000. The note provides for three annual payments of $10,000 plus interest of 10% on the unpaid balance. The investor's cash received each year is as follows:

	Sale Proceeds	Interest	Total
Year of Sale	$20,000	—	$20,000
First Installment	10,000	$3,000	13,000
Second Installment	10,000	2,000	12,000
Third Installment	10,000	1,000	11,000
Total	$50,000	$6,000	$56,000

Computation of gain – Income is realized in the same proportion that the gross profit (selling price less seller's adjusted basis) bears to the total contract price (amount to be received by the seller). The installment method of reporting is not available for losses. Losses are recognized in full in the year of sale and may be deductible, subject to certain limitations. In addition, upon the sale of certain depreciable property, gain must be recognized in the year of sale to the extent of the "depreciation recapture" amount, even if no cash is received in that year.

This rule results in the following treatment of the components of the proceeds:

A.	Recovery of basis	Tax-free
B.	Gain	Capital gain or ordinary income
C.	Interest	Ordinary income

The amount of each component in any given payment is computed as follows:

$$\text{Recovery of basis} = \frac{\text{Adjusted basis of property sold}}{\text{Total sale proceeds}} \times \text{Amount received (excluding interest)}$$

In the example above the numbers would be as follows:

Year of Sale $\frac{\$10,000}{\$50,000} \times \$20,000 = \$4,000$

First Installment $\frac{\$10,000}{\$50,000} \times \$10,000 = \$2,000$

Second Installment $\frac{\$10,000}{\$50,000} \times \$10,000 = \$2,000$

Third Installment $\frac{\$10,000}{\$50,000} \times \$10,000 = \$2,000$

$$\text{Gain} = \frac{\text{Total sale proceeds less Adjusted basis of property sold}}{\text{Total sale of proceeds}} \times \text{Amount received (excluding interest)}$$

In the example above the numbers would be as follows:

Year of Sale $\frac{\$40,000}{\$50,000} \times \$20,000 = \$16,000$

First Installment $\frac{\$40,000}{\$50,000} \times \$10,000 = \$8,000$

Second Installment $\frac{\$40,000}{\$50,000} \times \$10,000 = \$8,000$

Third Installment $\frac{\$40,000}{\$50,000} \times \$10,000 = \$8,000$

Interest – In this example the interest payable each year was specified in the contract and was, therefore, easily determinable. The amount of the interest income each year is stated in the facts above.

In the event that interest is not specified in the agreement, or the interest rate stated is less than a "test" amount, an interest amount will be "imputed." This means the law will treat the parties as if they had agreed to a minimum rate of interest on the unpaid balance. Since the total cash received will remain unchanged, the effect of imputing an interest element is to reduce the total sales price. For example, if the parties in the transaction above had agreed that the seller would be paid $10,000 in the year of the sale, with four subsequent annual installments of $10,000, it is obvious that the seller is not receiving interest on the unpaid balance—assuming that the sales price is $50,000. The tax law treats the parties as if they had in fact agreed upon a sales price of less than $50,000 together with annual interest on the unpaid balance.

The interest rate that must be used by parties in seller financed transactions is governed by rules relating to the "applicable federal rate" (AFR). The AFRs (which vary, depending on the term of the loan and frequency of payments) are published monthly by the Internal Revenue Service. AFRs are used to set imputed rates of interest on interest free and below-market interest loans, as well as other interest sensitive transactions.

Seller financing of more than $4,800,800 in 2007 (as indexed annually) is subject to an imputed interest rate of 100% of the AFR unless the stated rate is in excess of the AFR. If the seller financing is for less than the indexed amount (where no interest rate is specified or if the specified rate is less than 9% compounded semiannually or a lower AFR), the effective interest rate will be the lesser of 9% compounded semiannually or the AFR.

Several limitations are imposed on the use of the installment sale method of accounting for gain on the sale of property, the most important of which are discussed here. One such limitation is that the installment sale method may not be used for the sale of stock or securities that are traded on an established securities market. A second limitation is that dealers are prohibited from using the installment sale method.

Two special rules apply to certain installment sales of property with a sales price exceeding $150,000:

1. If the aggregate outstanding balance of such sales exceeds $5,000,000 in face value, an interest surcharge is imposed in the year of sale, as well as any subsequent year that the installment obligations are outstanding.

2. If the holder of such an installment obligation pledges the installment receivable as security for a loan, the net proceeds of the secured loan will be treated as a payment received on the installment receivable, thus accelerating the recognition of the income otherwise deferred.

These rules generally apply to *any* non-dealer sales, whether of real or personal property, with exceptions for (1) certain farm property, (2) timeshares and residential lots, and (3) personal use property.

As a final note on installment sales, strict rules govern the use of the installment method for sales between related parties.

Character of Gain or Loss

The effect of having the gain from the sale of property treated as a capital gain rather than ordinary income can be substantial; *net capital gains* are discussed in further detail below. The distinction between capital gains and ordinary income is important. Capital losses can be used only to offset capital gains and a limited amount of ordinary income (no more than $3,000 per year—although unused capital losses may be carried forward and utilized in future years).

The amount of capital gain or loss upon a taxable sale or exchange is determined by computing the difference between the sales price or proceeds received and the investor's tax basis (usually his cost) in the "capital asset." A formula often used for this computation is:

Amount Realized - Adjusted Basis = Gain

Alternatively,

Adjusted Basis - Amount Realized = Loss

In certain situations it may be necessary to treat part of the gain as ordinary income as a result of provisions in the tax law, such as those dealing with original issue discount and depreciation recapture discussed below.

With certain limited exceptions, all securities held by investors are considered capital assets. Most other assets held for investment purposes are also considered capital assets. In general, the following rules apply to the treatment of capital gains and losses:

1. *Net capital gain* (i.e., the excess of long-term capital gains over short-term capital losses) is determined by first separating the long-term capital gains and losses into three tax rate groups. These groups are (a) the 28% group, which generally includes collectibles gain and Section 1202 gain, (b) the 25% group (i.e., Section 1250 gain), and (c) the 15% group consisting of long-term capital gains and losses not falling under (a) or (b). Any net short-term capital losses are then applied to reduce any net gain from the 28% group, 25% group and the 15% group in that order.

2. *Adjusted net capital gain* is net capital gain reduced, but not below zero, by the sum of unrecaptured Section 1250 gain and the 28% rate gain, *plus* ``qualified dividend income" (i.e., dividends received during the taxable year from domestic corporations and certain foreign corporations. The reduced capital gains tax rate (15% or 5% in 2007) applies only to adjusted net capital gain.[1]

3. An investor's capital losses must be used first to offset any capital gains. Investors are allowed to offset net capital losses against ordinary income on a dollar-for-dollar basis—but only to the extent of $3,000 per year ($1,500 in the case of married taxpayers filing separately).

4. Any excess capital losses (from (3), above) may be carried forward indefinitely and used to offset future years' capital gains and up to $3,000 per year of ordinary income.

Holding Period

A capital asset falls into its category of short-term or long-term based upon the time it is held. The calculation of the holding period begins on the day after the property is acquired. The same date in each successive month is considered the first day of a new month. The holding period includes the date on which the property is sold or exchanged. If property is acquired on the last day of a month, the holding period begins on the first day of the following month. The specific holding periods are as follows:

- *Short-term* - held for one year or less.
- *Long-term* - held for more than one year. For assets sold on or after May 6, 2003 and before January 1, 2011, assets in this category are generally taxed at a maximum rate of 15% (5% to the extent of income in the 10% or 15% bracket for tax years 2003 through 2007; and 0% in 2008 through 2010, only). Generally, assets in this category that are sold after December 31, 1997 and before May 6, 2003, are taxed at a maximum rate of 20% (10% to the extent of income in the 10% or 15% brackets). A special transitional rule applies to tax years including May 6, 2003.

  The special rates (18%/8%) that applied to assets held more than five years were repealed under JGTRRA; however, when the rates enacted under JGTRRA (15%/0%) expire at the end of 2010, the 5-year holding period and the 18%/8% rates for qualified 5-year gain will, once again, be effective.
- *Qualified dividend income* – The maximum tax rate on "qualified dividend income" (generally, dividends paid by domestic corporations and certain foreign corporations to shareholders is 15% for taxpayers in the 25% income tax bracket and higher. For taxpayers in the 10% and 15% ordinary income tax rate brackets, the tax rate on qualified dividend income is 5% in 2003 through 2007; the rate for these taxpayers goes all the way down to 0% in 2008 through 2010, only. At the end of 2010, the rates on qualified dividends will return to the pre-JGTRRA levels (i.e., such dividends will, once again, be taxed at ordinary income tax rates).[2]

Special rules apply in the case of gains or losses of:

1. regulated futures contracts;
2. nonequity option contracts;
3. foreign currency contracts;
4. short sales;
5. wash sales;
6. tax straddles;
7. constructive sales; and
8. constructive ownership transactions.

"Tacking" of a holding period is allowed in the case of gifts, tax-free exchanges, and certain other nontaxable exchanges. Tacking means an investor may add the holding period of the prior owner(s) to his own. For instance, if Sara gives Lara stock Sara bought three years ago, Lara's holding period would include the three years Sara held the stock, as well as the period Lara actually holds the stock.

When an asset is acquired through bequest or inheritance, it automatically is treated as though it was held by the recipient for the long-term holding period. This rule applies even if the decedent held the asset for less than one year. For example, assume Sam purchased shares in a mutual fund one month before his death. Sam's heir, Sandi, could sell the shares four months after Sam's death and still obtain long-term treatment on any gain.

Many investors buying stocks, bonds, mutual funds, or other investments have multiple holdings of the same types of assets. It therefore becomes necessary to be able to identify each separate share or unit of a multiple investment so that each share's own basis and holding period can be determined.

If an investor is unable to adequately identify the lot from which securities are sold or transferred, a "FIFO" (first-in, first-out) method must be used. This means that the investor will be deemed to have sold the securities in the order in which they were acquired. In some cases involving mutual fund shares, the investor may be allowed to use an "average basis" method for ascertaining both tax basis and holding period.

INCOME AND EXPENSES WHILE THE INVESTMENT IS HELD

Income Defined

Tax law defines "income" in very broad terms. Income includes "all income from whatever source derived" that is not specifically excluded by a section of the Internal Revenue Code. The implication is that if an item is considered something other than a return of an investor's capital, it will be taxable unless otherwise excluded. The Supreme Court has defined income as "gains received from capital, from labor, or from both combined, provided it be understood to include profit gained through a sale or conversion of capital assets."

Common items realized by an investor that are specifically enumerated by the Internal Revenue Code as income include:

1. gains derived from dealings in property;
2. interest;
3. rents;
4. royalties;
5. dividends;
6. annuities; and
7. income from an interest in an estate or trust.

Note that the tax is levied only on income. The distinction in answering the question of whether an item is income lies between the terms "income" and "capital." An investor may recover, income tax free, his capital investment in an asset. This tax-free recovery of capital concept is inherent in the formula described above for computing gain:

Amount Realized - Adjusted Basis = Gain

Among the very few items common to an investor specifically excluded from income by the Internal Revenue Code are:

1. interest on certain governmental obligations (e.g., many "municipal bonds");
2. certain improvements by the lessee on the lessor's property; and
3. generally, death proceeds received under a life insurance contract.

"Whose income is it?" is an important issue that must be resolved by financial planners. An individual can be taxed on income that he never receives, but which is received by someone else.

Income is taxed to the person who

1. earns it;
2. creates the right to receive it;
3. owns or controls the property that is the source of the income; or
4. controls the right to control who will enjoy the benefit of it.

The tax rule governing income shifting is known as the "assignment of income doctrine." According to this doctrine, although the income itself may be shifted from one individual to another (which may create gift tax problems), the burden of income taxation will not change. The person who earns the income—or owns or controls the source of the income—is deemed to have received it and then passed it on to its actual recipient. For example, if an attorney directs a client to pay his fee to the attorney's mother, or a wealthy investor who owns an office building directs that all tenants pay rent directly to his widowed sister, although the income will be shifted, the tax liability will not.

Although merely assigning income will not shift the burden of taxation, an assignment of an income producing asset will cause the income derived from that asset to be taxed to the assignee. For example, if an individual makes a gift of securities or any other income producing property to his son, income produced by that property after the transfer will be taxed to the son.

To accomplish income shifting tax objectives, the transfer of the property must be made before the income is actually earned and must be (1) complete, (2) bona fide, and (3) the transferor must retain no control over either the property or the income it produces.

Character of Income or Loss

Under current tax law it is necessary to distinguish among:

1. earned income or losses (such as salary, or active business income or losses);

2. "investment" income (such as interest, dividends, royalties, and annuities); and

3. "passive activity" income or losses.

These separate categories of income are important, since an investor may not use passive activity losses (and credits) to offset earned income or investment income. (Losses from active business endeavors may be offset against income from other active businesses, investment income, or passive activity income.) The passive activity loss limitations apply to estates and trusts, personal service corporations, and pass-through entities such as partnerships and S corporations, in generally the manner they apply to individuals. Passive activity losses of closely-held C corporations (where five or fewer shareholders own more than 50% of the stock value) can offset trade or business (earned) income, but not investment income of the corporation.

Disallowed passive activity losses and credits may be carried forward and treated as deductions and credits from passive activities in the next taxable year. Suspended losses from a passive activity are allowed in full when the taxpayer disposes of his entire interest in the passive activity in a fully taxable transaction. Suspended credits may not be claimed in full in the year the taxpayer disposes of the interest in the passive activity. Such credits are carried forward until used to offset tax liability from passive activity income. However, upon a fully taxable disposition of a passive activity, a taxpayer may elect to increase the basis of property immediately before the transaction by an amount equal to the portion of any suspended credit that reduced the basis of the property for the taxable year in which the credit arose.

Passive Activity Defined

In general, the term "passive activity" means any activity that involves the conduct of any trade or business in which the taxpayer has an interest but does not "materially participate."

The definition of passive activity generally includes any rental activity of either real or tangible personal property regardless of whether the individual materially participates. With respect to equipment leasing, short-term rental to certain users (where the lessor provides substantial services) is an active business rather than a passive activity.

In general, "working interests" in oil and gas property held directly or indirectly via a pass-through entity where the investor's liability is not limited (e.g., general partnership) will be treated as an active trade or business, not a passive activity.

Material participation defined – In general, a taxpayer will be treated as materially participating in an activity only if the taxpayer is involved in the operations of the activity on a regular, continuous, and substantial basis. Substantial and bona fide management decision-making by an individual may constitute material participation. For example, if the managerial services are performed on a full-time basis and the success of the business is dependent upon the exercise of business judgment by an individual, such services would constitute material participation. This test applies regardless of whether an individual owns an interest in the activity directly or through a pass-through entity such as a general partnership or an S corporation.

Limited partnership interests are generally treated as not materially participating.

Net investment income defined – Net investment income is not treated as passive activity income and, therefore, cannot be offset by passive activity losses. "Net investment income" means gross income from interest, dividends (other than "qualified dividend income"), annuities, or royalties not derived in the ordinary course of a trade or business, *less*:

> expenses (other than interest) that are clearly and directly allocable to such gross income; *less*
>
> interest expense properly allocable to such gross income; *plus*
>
> gains from the disposition of property generating the interest, dividend, royalty, etc., income; *less*
>
> losses from the disposition of property generating the interest, dividend, royalty, etc. income.

Net investment income includes "qualified dividend income" (generally, dividends paid by domestic corporations and certain foreign corporations to shareholders) only to the extent the taxpayer elects to treat such income as investment income.[3]

Investment income earned within a pass-through entity, such as a partnership or S corporation, retains its character when reported to each investor in the entity, and cannot be used to reduce the passive activity losses that pass through to each investor.

Treatment of former passive activity – If an activity is a former passive activity for any taxable year and has suspended losses or credits from prior years when the activity was passive, the suspended losses may be offset against the current year's income from the activity, and the suspended credits may offset any current year's regular tax liability allocable to that activity. Any remaining suspended losses or credits continue to be treated as derived from a passive activity. Such losses and credits can be used to offset income or tax from that activity in years after it changed from passive to active, as well as income or tax from other passive activities.

Dispositions of an entire interest in a passive activity – Upon the taxable disposition (including abandonment) of an entire interest in a passive activity (or former passive activity), any suspended losses from the activity are no longer treated as passive activity losses and are allowable as a deduction against the taxpayer's income in the following order:

1. income or gain from the passive activity for the taxable year (including any gain recognized on the disposition);
2. net income or gain for the taxable year from all passive activities;
3. any other income or gain.

When an interest in a passive activity is transferred upon the death of the taxpayer, suspended losses may be deducted against income, but only to the extent such losses exceed the amount by which the basis of the interest in the activity is "stepped-up" (see "Property Acquired from a Decedent," above) at the taxpayer's death. For example, assume that Fred has a zero basis in a limited partnership interest just before his death. Fred had a suspended loss in the partnership of $50,000. The value of the interest reflected on his estate tax return is $20,000. Fred's heir to the partnership interest, his son, therefore receives a step up in basis in the property of $20,000. Only $30,000 of the $50,000 suspended losses can be used on Fred's final income tax return.

If an entire interest in a passive activity is disposed of in an installment sale, suspended losses may be deducted each year based on the ratio of the gain recognized each year to the total gain on the sale.

If an interest in a passive activity is disposed of by gift, the basis of the interest to the transferee is increased by the amount of the suspended losses generated from the interest. Such suspended losses added to the transferee's basis are not allowed as a deduction in any taxable year. The increase in basis will, of course, reduce the gain (or possibly increase the loss) from the ultimate taxable sale by the transferee.

Special rules for rental real estate – Where an individual owns an interest in rental real estate in which he actively participates, the individual may deduct up to $25,000 ($12,500 in the case of married taxpayers filing separately) of such losses (which, as previously noted, are passive activity losses) or claim an equivalent amount of credits from the rental activity each year, regardless of the general limitations imposed on passive activities. This $25,000 annual allowance is reduced by 50% of the taxpayer's adjusted gross income (determined without regard to passive activity losses, taxable social security benefits, or IRA deductions) that exceeds $100,000 ($50,000 for married taxpayers filing separately). Consequently, the special $25,000 allowance is fully phased-out for taxpayers with adjusted gross income greater than $150,000 ($75,000 for married taxpayers filing separately).

Any losses in excess of the $25,000, or reduced allowable amount, from rental real estate where there is active participation are carried over as suspended passive activity losses. Such losses may be used in computing the $25,000 allowable amount in subsequent years in which the investor actively participates in the rental real estate activity.

The requirement for "active participation" is less stringent than the test for "material participation" used in distinguishing a passive activity from an active interest in a trade or business. Generally, less personal involvement will be required. However, an individual can never be considered to actively participate in a rental property during a period where neither the individual nor the individual's spouse has at least a 10% interest in the property. Except as provided in regulations, a limited partnership interest in real estate does not qualify as active participation.

In the case of the rehabilitation and low-income housing credits (but not losses), the $25,000 allowance applies on a credit-equivalent basis, regardless of whether the individual actively participates in the rental real estate activity. Even if the interest is in a limited partnership, the credits may be claimed (up to the $25,000 credit equivalent). The phaseout of the credit equivalent for rehabilitation credits, regardless of when the property was placed in service, starts at adjusted gross income of $200,000, rather than $100,000. Similarly, with respect to property placed in service prior to 1990, phaseout of the $25,000 credit equivalent for the low-income housing tax credit starts at adjusted gross income of $200,000, rather than $100,000. With respect to property placed in service after 1989, there is no phaseout of the $25,000 credit equivalent for the low-income housing tax credit. The credit equivalent of the $25,000 allowance is $6,250 for an individual in the 25% tax bracket.

Deductible Expenses

A deduction is permitted for many of the investment expenses incurred by an investor. These expenses fall into two major categories: (1) interest paid on amounts borrowed in order to acquire or hold taxable investments; and (2) other expenses paid in connection with the production of income.

Deductibility of Interest

Subject to some complex rules and limitations, interest paid or accrued within the taxable year on indebtedness may be deductible. Before discussing these limitations, the following general concepts regarding interest should be reviewed:

1. the meaning and significance of the term "indebtedness";

2. whether an item is "interest"; and

3. the effect of one person paying the interest of another's indebtedness.

What is meant by the term "indebtedness"? Indebtedness implies a debtor-creditor relationship. The investor must be unconditionally obligated to pay what he owes while his counterpart, the creditor, must be legally able to demand payment.

The requisites described above are lacking in the case of a gift. If Abe gives a promissory note to his minor daughter, Bea, and, according to the terms of the note, Abe pays Bea interest on the note, the payments will not be deductible. This is because there is no consideration given by the daughter to her father in return for the note. The daughter has no right to enforce payment. In actuality, she has the mere promise of her father to make gifts to her (disguised as interest) in the future.

Perhaps the most common interest deduction denial situation affecting investors is in the case of stock disguised as debt. The importance of the distinction between corporate debt and corporate equity is obvious—interest paid by a corporation on its bonds is deductible, but a dividend paid on its stock is not. Factors weighed by the IRS and the courts in distinguishing between debt and equity include:

1. whether there is a fixed maturity date;

2. whether the amount is payable in any event or is contingent upon corporate profits;

3. whether there is subordination or preference over any other indebtedness;

4. the ratio of debt to equity;

5. whether the debt is convertible to stock; and

6. whether stock and debt are proportionately held by the same individuals.

In essence, these factors are used to answer the question, "Is the investor (the owner of the security) primarily a bona fide creditor, looking for a fixed and reasonably stable and secure rate of return together with a preferential position on his debtor's assets, or is he an entrepreneur accepting the risks of the business in return for the benefits of ownership?"

What is meant by the word "interest"? Interest can be defined as the compensation allowed by law or fixed by the parties for the use of money. No interest deduction is allowed, regardless of the label given to a particular payment, unless the investor has incurred (1) a valid obligation, (2) to pay a fixed or determinable sum of money, (3) in return for the use of money.

The tax law does not stipulate how interest must be computed or paid. Generally, it will be figured as a percentage of the principal sum (e.g., 10% of the amount of the note). Sometimes interest is represented by a "discount." Series EE United States Savings Bonds are a good illustration. An individual might purchase a bond for $500 that will pay $1,000 at maturity. The investor receives no annual interest payments. The difference between what the investor pays for the bond and what he receives when it matures is interest.

It should be noted that many corporate bonds are also issued at a discount. However, although the tax law permits the purchaser of a Series EE bond to defer recognizing income until the bonds mature, the purchaser of corporate bonds issued at a discount must report the interest as income when earned, even though it is not yet received. This annual recognition of income on discount corporate and similar bonds is governed by the original issue discount (OID) rules. Essentially, the OID rules require an investor to determine the amount of the annual discount income he must report, using a constant interest rate (a compound interest method). This results in less income reportable in the early years and greater income in later years.

Interest implies a payment for the use of money. Sometimes mortgages contain penalty clauses if the mortgagor prepays the loan. These penalty payments are for the use of money and are therefore—as payments for the privilege of prepaying mortgage indebtedness—deductible as interest.

"Points" may also be considered interest. Points are premiums in addition to the stated interest rate paid by borrowers to obtain a loan. This additional charge is typically calculated as a percentage of the loan amount (typically 1% to 3%) and is assessed and paid at the inception of the loan. If the fee was paid by the investor as compensation for the use of money, it is interest and therefore deductible. Typically points are deductible ratably over the term of the loan; yet, if certain requirements are met, points can be deductible in the year paid. On the other hand, if all or a part of the charge was for services provided by the lending institution, such as appraisal fees, that portion will not be considered interest.

If one person pays the interest on another person's debt, the deduction will be disallowed; the indebtedness must be that of the individual claiming the interest deduction. If there is a joint and several liability (such as when a husband and wife are joint obligors or comakers of a note), since the obligation to pay the interest extends to each, the entire amount of interest is deductible by whichever co-debtor makes the payment.

Rules Limiting the Deductibility of Interest

Under current law, essentially all the interest expenses of an individual investor (other than interest incurred in the ordinary course of a trade or business in which the individual materially participates) are subject to some limitations. These limitations can be most easily described by the categories to which the debt is properly allocable. These categories include:

1. passive activity interest;
2. investment interest; and
3. personal interest.

Generally, the allocation of interest is based on the use of the proceeds of the underlying debt. Any interest expense properly allocable to a passive activity is added to other passive activity expenses in determining the annual limitation on the deductibility of passive activity losses (discussed above).

"Investment interest" generally includes interest expense paid on indebtedness properly allocable to property held for investment (other than passive activity investments). Investment interest is deductible only to the extent of "net investment income." (Interest expense incurred with respect to rental real estate eligible for the $25,000 passive activity loss exception, discussed above, is not investment interest.) Investment interest generally includes interest expense:

- allocable to the production of "portfolio" income (dividends, interest, royalties, etc.);
- allocable to a trade or business in which the investor does not materially participate, (unless the activity is treated as a passive activity, in which case the interest expense is subject to the passive activity loss limitations); and
- allocable to the portfolio income of a passive activity.

"Net investment income" means the excess of investment income over investment expenses. Investment income includes portfolio income (dividends, interest, royalties, etc.), rents (except from passive activity investments), net short-term capital gains, and ordinary income gains from the sale of investment property (other than passive activity investment property). Investment expenses include expenses (except interest) related to these sources of investment income. The term ``net investment income" includes qualified dividend income (generally, dividends paid by domestic corporations and certain foreign corporations to shareholders) and long-term capital gains only to the extent the taxpayer elects to treat such income as investment income.[4] Annual interest deductions that are disallowed solely due to the investment interest expense limitation rule may be carried over indefinitely and deducted in future years when there is sufficient investment income.

Individuals, estates, and trusts are not allowed to deduct personal interest paid or accrued during the taxable year. Personal interest is defined to include all interest *except*:

1. interest expense incurred or continued in connection with the conduct of a trade or business;

2. investment interest;

3. interest taken into account in computing a taxpayer's income or losses from passive activities;

4. "qualified residence interest";

5. interest on "qualified educational loans" (as discussed below); and

6. interest payable resulting from allowable extensions of payments of estate tax (on the value of reversionary or remainder interests in property).

With respect to mortgage debt incurred after October 13, 1987, interest is deductible on mortgage acquisition indebtedness up to a total of $1 million ($500,000 in the case of married taxpayers filing separately), covering up to two homes. "Acquisition indebtedness" is debt incurred to finance the purchase or improvement of no more than two qualified residences. The amount of acquisition indebtedness upon which the interest deduction is computed must be reduced as principal payments are made and cannot be increased by refinancing unless the additional debt received from the refinancing is used for additional improvements.

In addition to interest on acquisition indebtedness, interest may be deducted on home equity indebtedness of up to $100,000 ($50,000 for married taxpayers filing separately). "Home equity indebtedness" must be secured by the same two qualified residences as the acquisition indebtedness. However, there is no limitation on the use of the home equity indebtedness funds.

Interest on qualified residence debt incurred prior to October 14, 1987 is treated as acquisition indebtedness that is not subject to the $1,000,000 limitation, and is deductible in full. In other words, such amounts are grandfathered under the post-October 14, 1987 rules. However, the amount of pre-October 14, 1987 debt reduces (but not below zero) the amount of the $1,000,000 limitation on acquisition indebtedness incurred after October 13, 1987 (but does not reduce the amount of home equity debt which can be incurred after that date). Any refinancing of pre-October 14, 1987 acquisition indebtedness that extends the term of the debt beyond the original term or exceeds the principal amount of the original debt will no longer qualify under the grandfather provision. However, the interest on a debt with a "balloon" type principal payment requirement is deductible for the term of the first refinancing of such acquisition indebtedness, not to exceed 30 years.

Interest payments due and paid on loans for "qualified educational expenses" are deductible for taxpayers with modified adjusted gross income (MAGI) up to certain limits. "Qualified educational expenses" include tuition, fees, room and board, and related expenses. The maximum deduction is $2,500. No deduction is allowed for an individual who is claimed as a dependent on another taxpayer's return.

If MAGI exceeds certain limits, the deduction for interest on education loans is reduced. For single taxpayers, no deduction may be taken if MAGI is in excess of $65,000 and the amount of the deduction is reduced proportionately if MAGI is between $50,000 and $65,000. For married taxpayers filing jointly, no deduction may be taken if MAGI is in excess of $130,000 and the amount of the deduction is reduced proportionately if MAGI is between $100,000 and $130,000. No such deduction may be taken by married taxpayers filing separately.

Other limitations on the deductibility of interest expense have been in the law for some time. More specifically, interest that would otherwise be deductible cannot be deducted if it is allocable to a class of income wholly exempt from tax. The rationale is that if the income items are entirely excluded from gross income, it is not necessary or appropriate to permit any interest deduction.

Interest on indebtedness incurred to purchase or carry tax-exempt obligations (such as municipal bonds) is not deductible. This rule makes it difficult for an investor borrowing money for investment purposes to deduct interest on those loans if he also holds tax-exempt bonds for investment.

The problem is that the IRS may be able to make a connection between the interest paid on the new loans and the currently existing tax-exempt securities. Likewise, an investor who has financed the purchase of taxable income securities may have difficulty deducting the interest if he later purchases significant amounts of tax-free bonds. It will be presumed that interest was incurred to purchase or carry tax-free indebtedness whenever the investor has outstanding indebtedness that is not directly connected with personal expenditures and is not incurred or continued in connection with the active conduct of a trade or business. This harsh inference may be made by the IRS even though the indebtedness is ostensibly incurred or continued to purchase or carry taxable income investments.

The tax law provides a number of other limitations on the deduction of interest that are of importance to investors. One such restriction is imposed on interest incurred to purchase or carry "market discount bonds" (i.e., bonds purchased after original issue at a price below both its redemption price and its original issue price, because of an increase in the interest rates available on newly issued alternative investments). Such interest is not currently deductible to the extent the investor has deferred the recognition of current income. The interest deduction may be claimed at the time the investor reports the "market discount income," essentially the unreported interest that has accrued on the bond from the date of purchase until the date of disposition.

A similar restriction is imposed on interest expenses incurred in financing noninterest-bearing short-term obligations such as Treasury bills. If the investor acquired the short-term obligation through a loan, the net interest expense is not deductible to the extent of the ratable portion of the bond discount attributable to the current year (the disallowed interest is, however, deductible upon the disposition of the bond). Interest is currently deductible if the investor elects to include the discount as income in the taxable year it is earned.

Deductibility of Investment Expenses Other Than Interest

Many expenses incurred by an investor will be deductible (subject to the 2% floor on miscellaneous itemized deductions) if certain requirements are met. These requirements are that the expenses must be incurred

1. for the production or collection of income;
2. for the management, conservation, or maintenance of property held for the production of income; or
3. in connection with the determination, collection, or refund of any tax.

Additionally, an investor's expenses must be (1) ordinary and necessary, (2) paid or incurred in the taxable year, and (3) expenses rather than capital expenditures. An expense is considered ordinary if it normally occurs or is likely to occur in connection with an investment similar to the one for which an expense deduction is claimed.

Common deductible investment-related expenses include

1. rental expenses of a safe deposit box used to store taxable securities;
2. subscriptions to investment advisory services;
3. investment counsel fees (whether or not the advice is followed);
4. custodian's fees;
5. service charges in connection with a dividend reinvestment plan;
6. service, custodial, and guaranty fees charged by the issuer of mortgage backed pass-through certificates;
7. bookkeeping services;
8. office expenses such as rent, water, telephone, stamps, and stationary incurred in connection with investment activities;
9. secretarial services relating to the management of rental property and investment record keeping;
10. premiums paid for an indemnity bond required for issuance of a new stock certificate to replace lost, stolen, destroyed, or mislaid certificates; and
11. fees incurred for tax advice (including (a) preparation of income tax returns, (b) cost of tax books used in preparing tax returns, (c) tax advice from attorneys and accountants, (d) legal fees for obtaining a Letter Ruling from the IRS, and (e) legal or accounting fees contesting a tax deficiency or claiming a refund—whether or not successfully).

However, deductible investment related expenses of individuals are subject to a limitation. Such expenses are deductible only to the extent they exceed 2% of the taxpayer's "adjusted gross income" (AGI). Thus, for example, if Jon's deductible investment related expenses equal $4,500 in a year in which his AGI is $200,000, his allowable deduction for such expenses is limited to $500 ($4,500 - $4,000 [2% x $200,000]).

Common investment-related expenses that are not deductible (because they are personal in nature or because they are not ordinary and necessary) also include travel to attend shareholders' meetings. An investment related expense need not be essential in order for it to be considered necessary. However, it must be one that the investor reasonably believes is appropriate and helpful. Generally the courts will not question the investor's determination. The standard of what is or is not both ordinary and necessary depends on the situation in the community where the issue arises. If most investors in the same situation would have incurred the same expenditure, the ordinary and necessary tests would be met.

It is essential that an expense be "paid or incurred in the taxable year." This issue is further discussed below in the consideration of "timing of recognition of income and expenses."

To be deductible, an expense must meet one additional major test—it must not be a capital expenditure. If an outlay is an expense, it can be deducted immediately. If an outlay is considered the cost or part of the cost of an asset, it must be "capitalized." This means that the outlay must be added to the investor's basis in the asset. If the asset is depreciable or amortizable, this increased basis will result in additional deductions over the life of the asset. The increased basis may otherwise be used to lower the gain or increase the loss upon a sale or other taxable disposition of the investment.

Common expenditures that are considered capital in nature and are, therefore, not currently deductible include:

1. brokers' commissions and fees in connection with acquiring investments (these are added to the basis of the property);

2. selling expenses (these are offset against selling price in determining capital gains and losses); and

3. expenses to defend, acquire, or perfect title to property (these are added to the basis of the property).

Timing of Recognition of Income and Expenses

Income is reportable in the year that it is received by a cash basis taxpayer. An expense will generally be deductible when it is paid by a cash basis taxpayer. The cash basis method is therefore essentially an "in-and-out of pocket" method of reporting. Items do not have to be received or paid in cash; receipts and payments in property are income and deduction items to the extent of the fair market value of the property.

Income of an accrual basis taxpayer is reportable when it is earned, even if the income is not received until a subsequent year. An expense will generally be deductible by an accrual basis taxpayer when the liability for payment has become fixed and determinable. Most individuals are cash basis taxpayers. The following discussion will focus on the application of the general rules applicable to cash basis investors and four of the major exceptions.

A cash basis investor generally will include interest, royalty, dividend, and other investment income, as well as gains from the sale of investments, in gross income in the year in which cash or other property is received. The following examples illustrate the application of this general rule:

Example. Dividend income is included when the check is received by the shareholder (even if the check is received in a year subsequent to when the dividend was declared or the year when the actual check was issued).

Example. Gain on the sale of property generally, under the installment sale rules, is taxed in the year sales proceeds are received.

A cash basis investor generally will deduct interest and other expenses incurred in connection with his investments, as well as losses from the sale of investments, from gross income in the year in which cash or other property is paid. Thus, interest expense, investment advisory fees, and other deductible expenses are deductible in the year paid. However, losses on the sale of securities generally are deductible on the trade date (even if delivery and receipt of the proceeds occurs in the following year).

The four major exceptions to the general rules governing cash basis investors are

1. the doctrine of "constructive receipt";

2. the "economic benefit" ("cash equivalent") theory;

3. "restricted property" rules; and

4. "prepaid deduction" limitations.

Constructive Receipt

Under the doctrine of "constructive receipt," an item must be included in an investor's gross income even though it is not actually reduced to his possession if it is (1) credited to his account, (2) set apart for him, or (3) otherwise available so that he can obtain it at his own volition without any substantial conditions or restrictions.

The purpose of the doctrine is to prevent an investor from determining at will the year in which he will report income. Without the doctrine of constructive receipt, an investor could postpone the taxability of income until the year in which he chose to reduce the item to his actual possession. For example, a cash basis taxpayer must report interest credited to his bank savings account regardless of whether he withdraws the interest or leaves it on deposit.

Constructive receipt will not apply if the taxpayer's control of the income is restricted in some meaningful manner. For instance, an investor will not be considered to have constructively received money or other property if

1. it is only conditionally credited;
2. it is indefinite in amount;
3. the payor has no funds;
4. the money is available only through the surrender of a valuable right; or
5. receipt is subject to any other substantial limitation or restriction.

The doctrine of constructive receipt is particularly important to individuals whose employers have enhanced their financial security through nonqualified deferred compensation arrangements. For instance, an athlete or a high salaried executive may prefer not to crowd compensation into a high tax bracket year and may want to spread it into later years, particularly if he will be in a lower tax bracket in such later years.

Through an agreement with his employer (entered into before services are performed), an employee can defer a portion of his compensation and therefore the tax on that compensation. Typically the employer will purchase life insurance and/or make certain investments to finance his obligations under the deferred compensation plan. But the employee will be successful in his attempt to defer the tax on the income only if he avoids the doctrine of constructive receipt. If the employee is able to withdraw funds at will, or if funds are irrevocably set aside beyond the claims of the corporation's creditors for the benefit of the employee, the employee's goal of deferring taxation will be thwarted.

Economic Benefit

The economic benefit theory states that when an employee receives from his employer a benefit that is the equivalent of cash, the value of that benefit is currently taxable. The most common example is where an executive receives group term life insurance coverage in excess of the amount excludable from federal income tax. The employee is required to include in income an amount (computed from government tables) that represents the economic benefit he receives when premium payments are paid by his employer.

There is an important difference between the doctrine of constructive receipt and the economic benefit theory. The constructive receipt doctrine requires the inclusion of income when a taxpayer has an unrestricted choice—that is, whether to take or not to take income set apart for him or credited to his account. This theory is concerned with the issue of "when is income realized by the taxpayer?"

Conversely, the economic benefit theory requires income to be included even if the taxpayer cannot "take" the income. Under the economic benefit theory, all that is necessary to trigger taxation is that an employee receive from his employer a benefit that is the equivalent of cash—that is, something with a (1) current, (2) real, and (3) measurable value. The economic benefit theory is concerned with the issue "Has the taxpayer enjoyed a present benefit from his employer capable of measurement and subject to tax?" It relates to the problem of "What is income?"

Restricted Property

Property is often transferred by an employer to an employee in connection with the performance of services. A business may give or sell stock or other property to a key employee but withhold, by separate agreement, significant rights. For example, an employer may transfer stock to an employee but restrict the employee's right to vote the stock or sell it. The idea is that the property rights will be withheld (restricted) by the employer until the employee has performed certain specified services. If the employee fails to achieve his goal or meet the specified requirements, the stock or other property may be forfeited.

Suppose an employer pays a bonus to an executive in the form of company stock. Assume the ownership of this stock is subject to certain restrictions including a provision that if the employee leaves the company within a 5-year period, he will forfeit the stock and will receive no compensation. Such property is appropriately called "restricted stock" or "restricted property."

If an employee is given property with no restrictions, the entire value of the property would constitute current compensation income. For instance, an employee who receives a bonus of 100 shares of his employer's stock currently selling for $200 a share realizes $20,000 of income. But, if certain requirements are met, an employer can compensate an employee in a manner that delays the tax until the employee is given full rights in the property.

The general rules governing restricted property (the so-called "Section 83" rules) provide that transfers of restricted property will be reportable as income in the first tax year in which the employee's rights are (1) not subject to any substantial risk of forfeiture, and (2) transferable free of this risk. In other words, an employee will not be subject to tax on restricted property as long as his rights to that property are forfeitable (subject to a substantial risk of forfeiture) and not transferable by him free of such risk. (This means that if the employee should sell or give the property away, the recipient of the property must also be under a substantial risk that he (the new owner) would forfeit the property if the employee failed to satisfy the conditions necessary to obtain full ownership.)

"Substantial risk of forfeiture" means that rights in transferred property are conditioned, directly or indirectly, upon the future performance (or refraining from performance) of substantial services by any person or upon the occurrence of a condition related to the purpose of the transfer. In addition, there must be a realistic and substantial possibility of forfeiture if the specified condition is not satisfied. The following examples illustrate common situations that probably would *not* be considered substantial restrictions:

1. a consulting contract with a retiring executive that called for only occasional services at the executive's discretion;

2. a requirement that an employee must return the property if he commits a felony; and

3. a "noncompetition provision" (since this is largely within the employee's control).

What happens when the restrictions expire? At the lapse of the restrictions, the employee must include in income the value of the property at that time. Sometimes an employer will remove restrictions in stages so that an employee may "earn out" of the restrictions.

There are two important exceptions to the general rule that the employee becomes taxable on the fair market value of the property (less any amount the employee may have paid for the property) at the time the restrictions lapse. The first of these exceptions is known as the "employee's election." The second exception is the "fair market value rule."

Under the "employee's election," the employee has a "gambler's choice"—he can elect to have the value of the restricted property taxed to him immediately in the year it is received (even though it remains nontransferable or subject to a substantial risk of forfeiture). If an employee makes this election within 30 days of receipt of the property, the general restricted property rules do not apply. Any appreciation in the value of the property is treated as capital gain rather than as compensation. The employee pays no tax at the time the risk of forfeiture expires (and will pay no tax until the property is sold or otherwise disposed of in a taxable exchange). But if the property is later forfeited, no deduction is allowed for the loss.

An employee who makes this election must be willing to pay ordinary income tax on the fair market value of the property in the year he receives the stock or other property. He is gambling that the value of the property will increase considerably before the restrictions lapse (in which case he may be eligible to pay tax on any realized gain as capital gain). He is also gambling that he will not forfeit the stock before he is able to sell or dispose of it without restriction.

The second exception to the strict rule of includability of the fair market value of the property (upon the lapse of restrictions) concerns restrictions that affect value. This exception pertains to value-affecting restrictions that, by their terms, will never lapse. For instance, if the restricted property can be sold only at book value and that restriction, by its terms, will never lapse, that amount will be treated as the property's fair market value.

An employer's compensation deduction will be allowed at the time the employee recognizes income from restricted property. The amount of the deduction will be the same as the amount of income recognized by the employee.

Prepaid Deductions

In certain situations, a cash basis investor can control the year in which he will take deductions. He can, for instance, prepay certain taxes and take the deduction in the year of payment even though the expenses relate to future years. This ability to "time" deductions is limited. For example, multiple years' prepaid rent and insurance premiums cannot be deducted in the year of payment. Deductions generally must be spread over the period covered by the prepayment if the deduction of the prepayment would "materially" distort income.

Special rules apply to the deductibility of interest expense for all taxpayers, whether they use the cash or accrual method of accounting. A cash basis investor must deduct prepaid interest over the period of the loan, to the extent the interest represents the cost of using the borrowed funds during each taxable year in the period. Points paid on an investment loan must be deducted ratably over the term of the loan. An investor on the accrual method of accounting accrues interest ratably over the loan period. This means it must be deducted ratably even if the interest is prepaid.

THE FEDERAL TAX RATE STRUCTURE

Financial planning is so closely tied with minimizing income taxes that it has become necessary for financial planners to have a complete understanding of the federal income tax rate structure. This section of the income tax concepts chapter will briefly explain the current status of the federal income tax rate structure and the workings of what is known as the "kiddie tax."

Income Tax Rates

The income tax rates are applied to a taxpayer's taxable income, which can be defined as the amount of income that remains after a taxpayer subtracts all deductions and exemptions from gross income. For 2007, the income tax rates are 10%, 15%, 25%, 28%, 33%, and 35%.[5] The different rate schedules will apply depending on whether the taxpayer is single, a surviving spouse, married filing separately, married filing jointly, or a head of household. The effect of a taxpayer's tax rate, bracket, and filing status on his income tax liability can be seen below.

The Jobs and Growth Tax Relief Reconciliation Act of 2003 (JGTRRA) accelerated the tax rate reductions scheduled under the Economic Growth and Tax Relief Reconciliation Act of 2001 (EGTRRA). EGTRRA provides for the ``sunset'' or repeal of all provisions after December 31, 2010. As a result, the tax brackets in effect in 2000 are scheduled to resume in 2011. The tax brackets are scheduled to be:

Year	Tax Brackets					
2004 -2010	10.0%	15.0%	25.0%	28.0%	33.0%	35.0%
2011	15.0%		28.0%	31.0%	36.0%	39.6%

For tax years beginning in 2007, income *over* the following amounts is taxed at the marginal tax rate above each column:[6]

	15%	25%	28%	33%	35%
Married Filing Jointly and Surviving Spouses	$15,650	$63,700	$128,500	$195,850	$349,700
Heads of Households	$11,200	$42,650	$110,100	$178,350	$349,700
Single	$7,825	$31,850	$77,100	$160,850	$349,700
Married Filing Separately	$7,825	$31,850	$64,250	$97,925	$174,850
Trusts and Estates	$0	$2,150	$5,000	$7,650	$10,450

With respect to the income levels, above, in the right hand column, please note the following:

15% bracket for married individuals filing jointly – "Marriage penalty" relief. EGTRRA 2001 increased the size of the 15% bracket for married couples filing joint returns to twice the size of the corresponding bracket for unmarried individuals filing single returns, phasing in the increase over four years, beginning in 2005. JGTRRA 2003 accelerated those increases, making the size of the 15% bracket for married individuals filing jointly equal to twice the size of the corresponding bracket for unmarried individuals filing single returns for taxable years beginning in 2003 and 2004. For taxable years beginning after 2004, the applicable percentages were scheduled to revert to those provided under EGTRRA 2001. Under WFTRA 2004, the 15% bracket for married individuals filing jointly is twice the size (200%) of the corresponding bracket for unmarried individuals filing single returns for tax years beginning *after December 31, 2003*. The larger 15% bracket for married individuals filing jointly will "sunset" (expire) for taxable years beginning after December 31, 2010, at which time the tax bracket that was in effect prior to the enactment of EGTRRA 2001 will become effective (i.e., the 15% bracket for single individuals will, once again, be 160% of the 15% bracket for married individuals filing jointly).[7]

Standard deduction for married individuals filing jointly – EGTRRA 2001 increased the basic standard deduction for a married couple filing a joint return, providing for a phase-in of the increase until the basic standard deduction for a married couple filing jointly equaled twice the basic standard deduction for an unmarried individual filing a single return by 2009. JGTRRA 2003 accelerated the phase-in, providing that the basic standard deduction for a married couple filing a joint return equaled twice the standard deduction for an unmarried individual filing a single return for 2003 and 2004, then reverting to the lower, gradually increasing standard deduction amounts provided for under EGTRRA for 2005 through 2009. However, under WFTRA 2004 the standard deduction for married individuals filing jointly (and surviving spouses) is twice the amount (200%) of the standard deduction for unmarried individuals filing single returns for tax years beginning *after December 31, 2003*. The larger standard deduction for married individuals filing jointly will "sunset" (expire) for taxable years beginning after December 31, 2010, at which time the standard deduction in effect prior to the enactment of EGTRRA 2001 will become effective (i.e., the standard deduction for married individuals filing jointly will, once again, be 167% of the standard deduction for single individuals).[8]

For tax years beginning in 2007, the personal and dependency exemption amount is $3,400; however, certain upper income taxpayers are subject to a phaseout of their personal and dependency exemptions. Specifically, the dollar amounts for personal and dependency exemptions of taxpayers with adjusted gross income above certain levels will be reduced by an "applicable percentage." The applicable percentage is two percentage points for every $2,500 (or fraction thereof; $1,250 for married individuals filing separately) by which the taxpayer's adjusted gross income (for 2007) exceeds the following threshold amounts: Married filing jointly (and surviving spouses) – $234,600; Heads of households – $195,500; Single – $156,400; Married filing separately – $117,300. These dollar amounts are indexed for inflation.

In other words, the personal exemption amount for a single taxpayer whose adjusted gross income is $166,401 would be reduced by 10%. If his adjusted gross income were over $278,900, the amount of the personal exemption would be zero, because it is reduced by 100% at that income level for a single person. The reduction of the exemption amount applies to all personal and dependency exemptions claimed by a taxpayer.

An additional limitation phases out some of the itemized deductions of certain taxpayers. This provision reduces the aggregate of most itemized ("below-the-line") deductions dollar-for-dollar by the lesser of (1) 3% of the amount of a taxpayer's adjusted gross income that exceeds $156,400 for 2007 ($78,200 in the case of a married taxpayer filing separately), or (2) 80% of the amount of itemized deductions otherwise allowable for the year. The income amounts at which the limit is imposed are indexed for inflation. The limitation is not applicable to the medical expense deduction, the investment interest deduction, or certain casualty loss deductions, and does not apply to estates and trusts.

The Alternative Minimum Tax ("AMT")

The federal tax law imposes an "alternative minimum tax" (or "AMT") so that individuals with substantial economic income will not be able to avoid a tax liability by using exclusions, deductions, and credits. The AMT attempts to broaden the "taxable income base" to insure that at least some tax liability will be incurred by most investors.

The computation of the alternative minimum tax is extremely complex. The following discussion is designed to cover only the essential elements of the AMT.

The alternative minimum tax is 26% of an investor's "alternative minimum taxable income" (AMTI) not exceeding $175,000 ($87,500 for married taxpayers filing separately) and 28% of AMTI exceeding that amount. Preferential tax rates for long-term capital gains are also used in determining an individual's AMT. Alternative minimum taxable income is computed as follows:

1. taxable income,

   plus or minus,

2. adjustments to taxable income (listed below),

   Plus,

3. the amount of an investor's "preference items" (specified items, described below, on which the investor is receiving preferential tax treatment),

   Minus,

4. in 2007, an exemption up to (a) $45,000 for a married couple filing jointly (or A surviving spouse), (b) $33,750 for a single taxpayer, (c) $22,500 for a married couple filing separately, or (D) $22,500 for an estate or trust return. These exemption amounts were issued as part of the Jobs and Growth and Tax Relief Reconciliation Act of 2003. (The exemption amount is reduced by 25% of the amount by which AMTI exceeds $150,000 for married taxpayers filing jointly, $112,500 for single taxpayers, and $75,000 for married taxpayers filing separately or for an estate or trust return.)

If the tax computed under this formula does not exceed the investor's regular tax, the AMT does not apply. If the computed AMT exceeds the investor's regular tax, the excess of the AMT over the regular tax is added to his tax liability.

The following is a simplified example of the computation of the AMT:

Example. Assume Dr. and Mrs. Ginsburg filed a joint return for 2007. They have two dependent children. Their regular tax was computed to be $27,758.

(1) Their taxable income is	$135,000
(2) Their AMT adjustments to taxable income are	$30,000
(3) Their tax preference items total	$57,000
	$222,000
(4) Their exemption amount is ($45,000 in 2007, less $18,000) (25% of $222,000 less $150,000)	($27,000)
(5) Their alternative minimum taxable income is	$195,000
(6) Their "potential" AMT is	$51,100

The excess of the Ginsburgs' potential AMT ($51,100) over their regular tax ($27,758) is $23,342. This amount becomes their alternative minimum tax liability and is added to their regular tax. They would therefore pay a total tax of $51,100.

The adjustments to taxable income include the following:

1. For property placed in service after 1986, depreciation deductions are adjusted to conform to special rules for the AMT.

2. Mining exploration and development costs, circulation expenditures, and research and development expense deductions must be adjusted to conform to special AMT amortization rules.

3. Gains or losses on the sale of property are adjusted to reflect the special depreciation rules used for AMT purposes.

4. Personal and dependency exemptions are not allowed for purposes of the AMT.

5. Long-term contracts entered into after February 28, 1986 must be accounted for using the percentage-of-completion method for purposes of the AMT.

6. Net operating loss (NOL) deductions are calculated under special AMT rules and cannot offset more than 90% of AMT income. A special provision was added by the Job Creation and Worker Assistance Act of 2002, which allows alternative tax net operating losses generated or taken as carryforwards in 2001 or 2002 to offset up to 100% of AMT income.

7. Certain itemized deductions allowable in computing regular taxable income must be added back in computing AMTI. These itemized deductions include state and local taxes, certain interest and miscellaneous deductions (including reimbursed employee business expenses), to the extent allowable in computing regular taxable income. In addition, the medical expense deduction is subject to a 10% floor under the AMT as compared to a 7.5% of AGI floor used in computing regular taxable income. For purposes of this adjustment item, the phaseout of itemized deductions for certain upper income taxpayers is not taken into account.

8. Upon the exercise of an incentive stock option (ISO), the excess of the fair market value of the option stock over the option exercise price (the "bargain element") is added in computing AMTI in the year of exercise. When the option stock is subsequently sold, the previously computed bargain element amount is subtracted in computing AMTI in the year of sale.

9. Passive activity losses are not allowed in determining AMTI, except to the extent the taxpayer is insolvent.

Items considered "tax preferences" that must be added to AMTI include

1. the excess of accelerated depreciation or ACRS deductions over straight-line depreciation on real property placed in service before 1987 (to the extent not taken into account in computing the adjustment to taxable income discussed above);

2. percentage depletion in excess of cost basis;

3. accelerated depreciation on depreciable personal property placed in service before 1987 that is leased (to the extent not taken into account in computing the adjustment to taxable income discussed above);

4. amortization of certified pollution control facilities;

5. certain excess intangible drilling costs;

6. tax-exempt interest on certain "private activity" (e.g., Industrial Development) bonds issued after August 7, 1986 (with certain limited exceptions); and

7. use of the installment method by dealers in personal property.

In addition, under JGTRRA, an amount equal to 7% of the amount excluded from gross income under IRC Section 1202 is treated as a preference item (the percentage under prior law was 28%).[9]

Alternative Minimum Tax Credit

Individuals are allowed a credit against their regular tax liability in years in which their regular tax exceeds the computed alternative minimum tax. The amount of the credit is based on the amount of alternative minimum tax paid in excess of the regular tax computed. The credit is not available to the extent the prior years' AMT was attributed to excess percentage depletion, tax-exempt interest, or non-AMT itemized deductions.

The credit is limited to the amount necessary to reduce the regular tax to the amount of AMT computed for the year in which the credit is claimed. For example, assume Stanley's computed regular tax for 2007 is $45,000, while his AMT for 2007 is $36,000. Stanley may use up to $9,000 of AMT credits carried over from prior years to reduce the tax he must pay in 2007 from $45,000 to $36,000.

Tax Planning for the AMT

The existence of the alternative minimum tax places a premium on planning techniques. With the availability of the AMT credit, it is less critical to undertake some of the more drastic planning concepts when the taxpayer will be able to use the AMT credit within a year or two after the AMT tax would be due. Here are some planning ideas and considerations:

In order to avoid or minimize the effect of the AMT

1. Determine the maximum amount of deductions or losses that an investor can claim before becoming subject to the AMT. Once an investor reaches the point where the AMT applies, any additional deductions will yield at most a 26% (or 28% as determined by AMTI) tax benefit.

2. An investor can reduce or eliminate tax preference items by:

   (a) electing to capitalize excess intangible drilling costs, mining exploration expenses, and research and experimentation expenses, and amortize them over the permissible AMT periods,

   (b) electing the AMT or straight line methods of computing depreciation, and

   (c) considering an early disposition (in the year of exercise) of stock acquired through the exercise of an Incentive Stock Option.

When it has been determined that the investor will be subject to the AMT

1. The investor should consider deferring current year deductions (which will be of minimal value because of the AMT) and save them for a future year when they will be more valuable, by

   (a) postponing charitable contributions,

   (b) postponing elective medical treatments, and

   (c) delaying making estimated state tax payments.

2. The investor should accelerate ordinary income, since it will be taxed at no greater than the AMT rate. This can be accomplished, for example, by exercising options under an Incentive Stock Option Plan (ISO) and selling the stock within the same year. (This has the double advantage of qualifying the ordinary income from the accelerated sale of the ISO for the maximum AMT tax rate and eliminating the ISO as a tax preference item.)

The "Kiddie Tax" – Unearned Income of Certain Minor Children

A child subject to the "kiddie tax" pays tax at his or her parents' highest marginal rate on the child's unearned income over $1,700 (for 2007) if that tax is higher than the tax the child would otherwise pay on it. The parents can instead elect to include on their own return the child's gross income in excess of $1,700 (for 2007).

A child is subject to the kiddie tax if (1) he or she has not attained age 18 before the close of the tax year, (2) either parent of the child is alive at the end of the tax year, and (3) the child does not file a joint return for the tax year.

Beginning in 2008, SBWOTA 2007 expands the "kiddie tax" rules to apply to children age 18, and children over age 18 but under age 24 who are full-time students—*if* their earned income does not exceed one-half of the amount of their support.

Therefore, SBWOTA 2007 does not change the kiddie tax rules for children who are under age 18. Rather, it expands the kiddie tax to apply where the child:

- turns age 18, or turns age 19-23 if a full-time student, before the close of the tax year;
- has earned income for the tax year that does not exceed one-half of his or her support;
- has more than the inflation-adjusted prescribed amount of unearned income (i.e., $1,700, as further adjusted for inflation for the applicable tax year).

The other factors still apply—that is, the child has at least one living parent at the close of the tax year, and the child does not file a joint return for the tax year.

If the parents have two or more minor children with unearned income to be taxed at the parents' marginal tax rate, all of the children's applicable unearned income will be added together and the tax calculated. The tax is then allocated to each child based on the child's pro rata share of the unearned income.

There are three levels of a minor's unearned income involved in the calculation of the tax on such income (based on 2007 levels):

1. Generally, the first $850 of a minor child's unearned income is exempt from tax because of the child's standard deduction. (The standard deduction of a child claimed as a dependent is limited to the greater of (a) $850 (in 2007) or (b) the sum of $300 and the amount of his earned income, not to exceed the regular standard deduction amount. After the first $850 is used to offset the child's unearned income, any excess is available to offset earned income of the child).
2. The next $850 of unearned income is taxable at the child's bracket.
3. Unearned income in excess of the first $1,700 will be taxed to the child at the appropriate parent's rate.

Computation of the Tax

(A) The amount of tax at the applicable parent's bracket reflected on a child's tax return is computed as follows:

(1) Compute the tax the child would have to pay on earned and unearned income at the child's rates.	$_______
(2) Compute the sum of	
(a) the tax payable if the child had no "net unearned income," plus	$_______
(b) the child's share of the "allocable parental tax."	$_______
Total	$_______

The tax on the unearned income of children subject to the kiddie tax is the greater of (1) or (2).

The term "unearned income" means income from sources other than wages, salaries, professional fees, and other amounts received as compensation for personal services actually rendered.

(B) The net unearned income of a minor child can be computed as follows:

(1) State the total unearned income (or the child's taxable income if lower).	$_______
(2) Calculate the amount not taxable at the parent's bracket — the sum of	
(a) up to $850 (standard deduction amount), plus	
(b) an additional amount which is the greater of (i) $850 or (ii) the allowable deductions directly related to the production of the child's unearned income, assuming the child claims itemized deductions. [This is the amount of unearned income taxable at the child's tax bracket.]	$_______
Total	$_______
(3) Net unearned income is (1) minus (2).	$_______

The $850 amounts used in this computation are for 2007 and are adjusted annually for inflation.

(C) The amount of the tax on net unearned income of all the minor children of an applicable parent is computed as follows:

(1) State the tax that would have been imposed on the parent's taxable income if all the net unearned income of all the parent's children under age 18 were added to the parent's taxable income.	$_______

(2) State the tax that would have been imposed on the parent's taxable income if none of the net unearned income of the parent's children under age 18 were includible. $_______

(3) The allocable tax computed at parent's marginal rate is (1) minus (2). $_______

(D) The tax computed at the parent's marginal tax rate is allocated to a particular child as follows:

(1) State the total allocable tax computed at the parent's marginal rate. $_______

(2) State the child's net unearned income. $_______

(3) State the aggregate net unearned income of all children of the parent under age 18. $_______

(4) Divide (2) by (3). $_______

(5) The child's share of allocable tax computed at the parent's marginal bracket is (4) X (1). $_______

In the case of unmarried parents, the parent whose taxable income is used in computing the tax on the unearned income of the minor child is the custodial parent. In the case of parents who are married but filing separately, the marginal rate of the parent with the greater taxable income will be used in the calculation.

The so-called "kiddie tax" rules apply regardless of the source of the child's assets producing the unearned income. It does not matter whether the child earned the assets producing the income, or received the assets (or funds) as an inheritance or a gift from grandparents or parents.

If a child can be claimed as a dependent on a parent's return, the child may not claim a personal exemption and the child's standard deduction is limited to the greater of (1) $850 or (2) the sum $300 and the child's earned income (up to the maximum of that year's standard deduction (e.g., $5,350 in 2007 for a single taxpayer).

Many parents will be able to elect to include their children's unearned income over $1,700 on their own return, thus avoiding the necessity of filing a return for each child. The election is available if the child has income of more than $850 but less than $8,500, all of which is from interest and dividends. Additionally, there is a tax of $85 or 10% of the income over $850 (whichever is less) for each child to whom the election applies.

CHAPTER ENDNOTES

1. See IRC Sec. 1(h).
2. IRC Sec. 1(h).
3. IRC Sec. 163(d)(4).
4. IRC Sec. 163(d)(4).
5. IRC Sec. 1(i).
6. See Rev. Proc. 2003-85, 2003-49 IRB 1184.
7. IRC Sec. 1(f).
8. IRC Sec. 63(c)(7).
9. IRC Sec. 57(a)(7).

Chapter 28

INVESTMENT PLANNING

WHAT IS IT?

From a client's perspective, investment planning is typically the main reason for consulting with a financial planner. Unfortunately, from a planning perspective, investments are normally the last step of the implementation process – after all of the other planning is complete.

If investment planning leads the other decisions in the financial planning process, the entire plan is set up for failure. Yet, potential clients often come in the door expecting an off-the-cuff, guaranteed investment "pick." Don't fall into the trap! Tell your potential client that if you knew and had access to the best investments (the ones that double every three days and NEVER go down), you would be lying out on the beach of an island in the middle of the ocean that you just purchased – at a bargain price, of course!

Obviously, the goal of investment planning is to achieve an expected rate of return over a specified time period while minimizing the potential for loss. The client must understand what their investments must return in order to meet their goals. Therefore, they need to have a grasp of their current and projected lifestyle as well as their ability to save. Completing a multi-year, multi-scenario cash flow projection with varying assumptions is the best way to fully understand the client's situation and to pass that understanding on to the client.

For more information on the technical aspects of investment planning, see *The Tools and Techniques of Investment Planning*.

THE INVESTMENT PLANNING PROCESS

There are six steps in the investment planning process:

1. *Ascertain the current and projected amount to invest* – The potential investor must first make a conscious decision to save and invest rather than to spend.

2. *Determine the investment time horizon* – Does the investor need to use some portion of the investable assets in the near future? Is the investor buying a house, retiring, sending a child to college? This will help identify the need for shorter-term investments in the portfolio or the ability to invest in longer-term investments that typically will yield a higher expected return.

3. *Coordinate investments with risk tolerance* – In order to achieve a higher rate of return, the investor may need to be willing to accept a higher risk. Risk is simply the volatility of the investments. Volatility has a dramatic impact on an investor's ability to reach his or her goals. The more risk inherent in an investor's portfolio, the greater the potential for gains – but also for losses.

4. *Select the investments* – Based on the information obtained in steps one through three, the planner can now begin the investment selection process. Care should be taken to ensure that the investments truly reflect the investor's needs and risk tolerance.

5. *Evaluate the portfolio's performance* – Investment planning is a dynamic process, just like financial planning. However, outside forces have a material impact on the potential for success. The economy, federal and international governments, taxes, etc. all can change an investment from being suitable at one time to being completely against the investor's needs or philosophy at a different point in time. Compare the portfolio's performance to the appropriate benchmark. For example, a portfolio made up of one-half bonds and one-half equities should not be compared to the S&P 500 Index alone.

6. *Rebalance when necessary* – Rebalancing the portfolio is a process whereby investors are forced to sell high and buy low. If the equities in the 50/50 portfolio were doing well, the portfolio may end up skewed to 65/35 in favor of equities. A rebalancing program would call for the sale of equities (which have done well) and

the purchase of bonds (which have not done as well).

Life Cycle Periods

Each person typically moves through five financial stages throughout his or her life, which are characterized by various issues and objectives that are distinct to each stage. As the financial planner reviews the following descriptions of these various life cycle stages, try to determine which stage best describes the planner's or the client's own situation.

1. *Early career* – age 25-35

    a) often newly married and have young children

    b) establishment of employment patterns for one, or both, spouses

    c) accumulation of income for home purchase

    d) creation of college education funds for children

    e) accumulation of income/assets for starting one's own business

    f) little consideration given to retirement planning, particularly in the early years of this period

2. *Career development* – age 35-50

    a) enhancement of career, upward career mobility, or rapid growth in income from profession or business

    b) accumulation and expenditure of funds for children's college education

    c) integration of employee benefits with investment strategy

    d) employee-benefit coordination between spouses

    e) retirement income planning (financial independence)

    f) purchase of vacation home, travel

    g) beginning of general wealth building beyond basic objectives

    h) geographic relocation

3. *Peak accumulation* – age 50-62 (approximately)

    a) in general, peak of career with possible lessening of work-related activities

    b) period of maximum ability to accumulate wealth for all purposes – these are the years for maximum wealth accumulation in excess of needs for specific objectives

    c) basically a continuation of

    - retirement income planning

    - coordination of benefits from employment with investment strategy; also integration for retirement planning

    - vacation home, travel

    - beginning of some reduced investment risk as portfolio begins to emphasize income production for retirement (particularly near the end of this period)

    - concerns about minimizing income and taxes

4. *Preretirement years* – three to five years prior to planned retirement age

    a) winding down of career and income potential

    b) restructuring of portfolio to reduce risk and enhance income

    c) further tax planning

    d) integration of plan-distribution options with income needs and tax consequences

5. *Retirement*

    a) hoped-for enjoyable life style

    b) adequacy of retirement income

Figure 28.1

INVESTMENT ALLOCATION PERCENTAGES			
	Investment Categories		
Life Cycle Stage	(1) Low risk, secure income-oriented	(2) Medium risk growth type	(3) High risk speculative
Early Career	40 down to 10	60 up to 80	0 up to 30
Development	40 down to 30	50 up to 70	0 up to 20
Peak Accumulation	50 down to 30	40 up to 60	0 up to 15
Preretirement	80 down to 40	20 up to 40	0 up to 10
Retirement	80 down to 60	10 up to 40	0 up to 10

c) preservation of purchasing power

d) new job (paid or volunteer)

Investment Allocation Guidelines

Figure 28.1 provides guidelines for determining appropriate asset allocation percentages to suit the planner's or the client's personal needs. A range of acceptable investment percentages are presented for each life cycle stage and are allocated to the following three broad investment categories: (1) low risk, secure, and income-oriented investments; (2) medium risk, growth-type investments; and (3) high risk, speculative investments. Although there is certainly some overlap between the investment categories, broadly stated, each category includes the following types of investments. Category (1) includes savings accounts, T-bills, money market funds, government bonds, high-grade corporate bonds, participation certificates, and similar types of investments. Category (2) includes municipal bonds, convertible bonds, lower-grade corporate bonds, preferred stocks, high-quality growth stocks, and similar investments. Category (3) includes more speculative growth stocks, most real estate investments, REITs, options, commodities and futures contracts, and similar types of investments. In addition, mutual funds are available that fit within each of these general classes of investments.

Which investment percentage is chosen within each class should now depend on an assessment of risk tolerance and the investment horizon. For example, if the client is 55 years old, considers himself to be in the peak accumulation stage of his financial life cycle, plans to take early retirement at age 62, and considers himself relatively risk-averse, the client should probably invest up to 50% of his portfolio in Class (1), up to 50% in Class (2), and approximately 0% in Class (3).

In contrast, if the client is more risk tolerant and plans to continue working past age 65, the client should probably invest closer to only 10% or 15% in Class (1), between 50% and 60% in Class (2), and perhaps up to 30% in Class (3).

ACTIVE VERSUS PASSIVE MANAGEMENT

The Simple Logic of Active vs. Passive Investing

Exhaustive studies have shown that over the long term, the average actively-managed fund has underperformed its appropriate passive benchmark by about 1.8% per annum on a pre-tax basis (taking taxes into account would increase this figure to approximately 3%). Despite this evidence, the vast majority of individual investors invest in actively-managed funds. Only about 10% of all individual monies are currently invested in passive funds.

If "active" and "passive" management styles are defined in sensible ways, the following must be the case:

1. *Before costs* – The return on the average actively-managed dollar will equal the return on the average passively-managed dollar.

2. *After costs* – The return on the average actively-managed dollar will be less than the return on the average passively-managed dollar

These assertions must hold for any and all time periods. Furthermore, their veracity does not depend on any sophisticated statistical or mathematical analyses or theorems, per se, but only on the laws of simple arithmetic.

This will all be explained rather simply, but first let us define terms, so that no confusion arises over the definitions. First a market must be selected – the stocks in the S&P 500, for example, or a set of "small" stocks. It does not matter which asset class or sector is being analyzed. In fact, the logic applies to the entire world market as a whole, as well as to each and every sector and sub-sector of the world market. Each investor who holds securities from the selected market or asset class must be classified as either active or passive.

Passive investors always buy every security from the market for their portfolios in the same proportion as the securities represent to the total value of the market. In other words, they essentially own an index of the market. Therefore, if security A represents 2% of the value of the securities in the market, a passive investor's portfolio will have 2% of its value invested in A. Equivalently, a passive investment manager will hold the same percentage of the total outstanding amount of each security in the market.

Active investors are other investors who are not passive. Their portfolios will differ from those of the passive investors or managers at some or all times. Active investors or managers usually act on their perceptions of mispricing in the market; because such misperceptions usually change relatively frequently, such investors and managers tend to trade relatively frequently. That is why they are called "active" investors or managers.

Over all periods of time, the market's return will be a weighted average of the returns on the securities within the market. Each passive investor or manager will earn exactly the market return (before transactions costs) since they own all the securities in the same proportions as the market. From this, it follows by simple arithmetic that the return on the average actively-managed dollar must equal the market return. Why? The returns earned by the passive investors plus the returns earned by the active investors must equal the total returns on the market. If the returns earned by the passive investors on the portion of the market they hold equals the returns on the market, the average returns earned by the active investors on their portion of the market must also equal the market return. The market's return must equal a weighted average of the returns on the passive and active segments of the market. If the first two returns are the same, the third must be also. This proves the first assertion by using just simple arithmetic.

To prove the second assertion, simply consider the fact that the costs of actively managing a given number of dollars will exceed those of passive management. Active managers must pay for more research than passive managers, and must pay more for trading, too. Security analysts, brokers, traders, specialists, and other market makers all take a "cut of the action." Because active and passive returns are equal before cost, and because active managers bear greater costs, it must be the case that the average after-cost returns from active management is lower than that from passive management. This proves the second assertion.

Keep in mind – all the assets in a market have to be owned by someone. If everybody owned their proportionate share of the securities of the market, everyone would gain or lose exactly the same percentage as the market gained or lost.[1] If an investor (Robert) decided that he wanted to own 100 more shares of IBM than his proportionate share, then he would have to find someone else (Martin) who thought he could do better owning 100 shares less than his proportionate share. At the end of some specified time period, Robert would either be right or wrong. If Robert were right, his gain on going "long" 100 additional shares of IBM stock would be exactly offset by Martin's loss who went "short" 100 shares of IBM stock relative to his proportionate ownership. Nobody else in the market would be affected in the slightest way by Robert and Martin's active trading. In essence, Robert's active trading is a side bet on the market. Although the market as a whole is not a "zero-sum" game, active trading *is* a "zero-sum" game. Every gain by one market player who does not hold his proportionate share of the assets in the market is exactly and equally offset by losses by other market players who take the opposite position. And, since trading involves more transaction costs than a passive strategy, active management is actually a "negative-sum" game. On average, active traders as a whole must lose relative to passive investors after transaction costs.

Why does this simple logic and arithmetic seem beyond the comprehension of the vast majority of investment professionals and individual investors? Why, for instance, do many investment professionals continue to insist that active management can beat the market indexes?[2]

First, managers who appear to be passive may not be truly passive. For instance, some index fund managers "sample" the market of choice, rather than hold all the securities in market proportions. Some may even charge high enough fees to raise their total costs to equal or exceed those of active managers.

Second, active managers may not fully represent the "non-passive" component of the market in question. Even if one accounts for all the active managers, that may still exclude active holders of securities within the market (e.g., individual investors). Many empirical analyses consider only "professional" or "institutional" active managers. It is, of course, possible for the average professionally or institutionally actively-managed dollar to outperform the average passively-managed dollar, after costs, For this to take place, however, the non-institutional, individual investors must be foolish enough to pay the added costs of the institutions' active management via inferior performance. Another example arises when the active managers hold securities from outside the market in question. For example, returns on equity mutual funds with cash holdings are often compared with returns on an all-equity index or index fund. In such comparisons, the funds are generally beaten badly by the index in up markets, but sometimes exceed index performance in down markets. Yet another example arises when the set of active mangers excludes those who have gone out of business during the period in question. Because such managers are likely to have experienced especially poor returns, the resulting "survivorship bias" will tend to produce results that are better than those obtained by the average actively-managed dollar.

Third, and possibly most important in practice, the summary statistics for active managers may not truly represent the performance of the average actively-managed dollar. To compute the latter, each manager's return should be weighted by the dollars he or she has under management at the beginning of the period. Some comparisons use a simple average of the performance of all managers (large and small); others use the performance of the median active manager. While the results of this kind of comparison are, in principle, unpredictable, certain empirical regularities persist. Perhaps most important, equity fund managers with smaller amounts of money tend to favor stocks with smaller outstanding values. Thus, de facto, an equally weighted average of active manager returns has a bias toward smaller-cap stocks vis-a-vis the market as a whole. As a result, the "average active manager" tends to be beaten badly in periods when small-cap stocks underperform large-cap stocks, but may exceed the market's performance in periods when small-cap stocks do well. In both cases, of course, the average actively-managed dollar will underperform the market, net of costs.

However, the arithmetic does not lie. When properly measured, the average actively-managed dollar must underperform the average passively-managed dollar, net of costs. Any studies that do not support this result must not be measuring properly.

Thus, the *average* actively-managed fund underperforms the average passively-managed fund. That means that over any given period about half of the actively-managed funds outperform the average of actively-managed funds and a somewhat smaller percentage of actively-managed funds are likely to outperform the average of the passively-managed funds. This suggests that one should seek out the actively-managed winners and invest with them, right?

Investing in the Winners Among Actively-Managed Funds

Mutual fund returns are notoriously inconsistent. This makes it difficult to select those funds that will outperform going forward. In 1997, Mark Carhart published a study in the *Journal of Finance* on consistency of mutual fund returns.[3] Over a 31-year period, he ranked each fund annually by total return. He determined that 83% of the top decile funds fell from that position in the following period. He also found that the bottom 10% remained in that bottom decile 46% of the time. Other than those two groups, all other rankings showed no pattern. In other words, investors cannot predict where a fund will rank next period based on its performance this period, except to say that if it ranked in the top 25% it is very unlikely to rank there next period, and if ranked in the bottom 10% it is a flip of the coin whether it will still be there next period or not.

Carhart theorized that many of the worst funds are throttled by high fees and, therefore, cannot gain ground. The high flying funds, on the other hand, are likely to be highly-concentrated and, therefore, annual returns will be volatile. Outperforming funds are also often flooded with new deposits, making those funds more difficult to manage.

Cavanaugh Capital Management also did a similar study, looking at mutual funds ranked in the top 25% for a given year.[4] They tracked actively-managed mutual funds in the large-cap, small/mid-cap, and international arenas and examined how well the funds did the year *after* they landed in the top quartile.

They found, on average, 83% of large cap funds declined in ranking the year after finishing in the top quartile. Close to half (42%) fell into the bottom 50% by rank, on average. Small- and mid-cap mutual funds had performances similar to large-cap funds. In these stock categories, an average of 87% of funds declined in ranking the next period and 48% dropped out of the top half of the rankings. International funds performances were also consistent as with domestic funds. Of the international funds in the top 25% one period, 84% declined in rank the following year, and 45% dropped out of the top half of the rankings.

The conclusion – investors have no way of determining which funds will perform well next year based upon their performance this year and, therefore, may incur significant underperformance risk by selecting actively-managed funds.

These studies looked at year-to-year performances; perhaps some funds show more consistency over longer periods.

The Winter 2001 issue of the *Journal of Private Portfolio Management* contained a study that looked at the odds of active managers outperforming passive managers or index funds.[5] The study looked at all 307 large-cap funds with at least a 10-year history. This methodology creates what is known as "survivorship bias" in favor of active management. Funds that perform poorly typically close because of redemptions by investors, or they are merged out of existence by their sponsor. Thus their performance data disappears.

The returns of the funds were then compared to that of the benchmark S&P 500 Index. Over the most recent 20-year period, the passive strategy outperformed over 93% of all surviving funds. For the most recent 15-year period it outperformed over 99% of all surviving funds. For the most recent 10-, 7-, 5-, and 3-year periods, the passive strategy outperformed at least 95% of all surviving active funds. Finally, for the 61 rolling 5-year periods since the end of World War II, the passive strategy outperformed at least half the active funds 58 times (95%). These results were all computed on a pre-tax basis. Based on historical data, it is quite clear that the results would have been even worse if the returns had been measured on an after-tax basis.

Clearly, on average investors in actively-managed funds were choosing the wrong strategy. Simply accepting market returns would have improved their collective results dramatically.

One example of the fallibility of relying on past success is the findings of William Bernstein.[6] He examined the performance of the top 30 funds for successive five years beginning in 1970, and then compared their performance against that of the S&P 500 Index through 1998. Here is what he found:

- The top 30 funds from 1970 through 1974 went on to underperform the index by 0.99% per year.
- The top 30 funds from 1975 through 1979 went on to underperform the index by 1.89% per year.
- The top 30 funds from 1980 through 1984 went on to underperform by 2.75% per year.
- The top 30 funds from 1985 through 1989 went on to underperform by 1.57% per year.
- The top 30 funds from 1990 through 1994 went on to underperform by 10.9% per year.

Never did the top performers from one 5-year period continue to outperform in the subsequent 5-year period.

Past performance is simply not a good indicator of future performance. However, with so many active funds in play, some are likely to be winners over any given time frame (and must be, if there are any losers). The evidence suggests that despite investors' generally-held perception that skill is what causes the winning result, it appears to be much more likely that the winners are randomly generated and, thus, not likely to be repeated.

The conclusion to draw, once again, is that the prudent strategy – and the one most likely to generate superior returns – is the passive one.

Active management does, however, hold out the hope of outperforming other actively-managed funds and, certainly, passive investing. This hope is what Wall Street and the financial press sell. Unfortunately, the odds of winning the game have proven to be so low that unless one attaches a high value to the entertainment aspect of the effort, then it does not pay to play. When one considers the additional costs of active management (the "vigorish" or "house take" as they call it in the gambling community), investors might be better off investing most of their money passively and then playing Black Jack with the rest of it in Las Vegas or Atlantic City.

The evidence is strong indeed, but note that these studies all examined the big markets, which everyone agrees are quite efficient, so it stands to reason that active managers would have to be quite sharp indeed to outperform passive management. But what about smaller markets that may be less efficient? Active management should be able to outperform passive management in such markets, should it not?

Active Management in Inefficient Markets

The controversial "efficient market hypothesis" concludes that there is no point to fundamental or technical security analysis because all stocks are fairly priced. According to this hypothesis, active buying and selling of stocks adds no value – it just incurs additional transactions costs. Hiring a professional manager is even worse because of the fees required. If markets are efficient, indexing becomes a better alternative. Most investors have come to accept that the big markets are pretty efficient, but what about the smaller markets and/or foreign markets? They cannot be as efficient as the big markets, can they?

Perhaps not. However, for most investors, an "inefficient stock market" (i.e., one with frequent mispricings) makes the case for indexing even stronger. Assuming that in fact stock prices are sometimes wrong, at least in some markets, what does that imply about competition among investors attempting to identify these mispricings?

If the stock market is assumed to be a skill-based game, those with the skill and resources to identify and act on market inefficiencies will probably do well. Consider a dart-throw competition in which one gets a dollar for every dart one puts in the bull's eye. Alternatively, instead of actively participating in the game, one can take the average score of those who do play the game. Passive investing is essentially the same as sitting on the sideline and taking the average score.

In this game, everyone who thinks they have lower than average skills should rationally choose to sit out and let the better players shoot. They would do better by just taking the average of the better half of the dart-throwers. Of course, everyone who believes they are better than average has to realize this is the rational approach for the bottom half in skill, so they must now assess whether they are in the top quarter of the top half in dart-throwing skill. That means that everyone who believes they fall below the top 25% in skill rationally should sit out. But then, of course, the top 25% rationally have to follow the same logic, so that only the top 12.5% actually throw the darts. Ultimately, if everyone behaves rationally, only the best player would eventually shoot and everybody else would get that score as well.

Unfortunately, investors clearly do not see the logic involved in the dart game when it is applied to the markets. In fact, they argue that in the markets where skill may actually be a factor, active participation is the way to go. The logical conclusion is that investors tend to be overconfident in their abilities. However, it is irrefutable that at least half of all active investors would be better off indexing.

As has been demonstrated above, more than half of all active mutual fund managers underperform the market. This is often interpreted as proof of market efficiency. But the fact is that mutual fund managers consistently underperform the market by more than can be accounted for by the extra costs of active management. This in fact is proof that investing is a skill-based game and that active mutual fund managers, as a group, have below-average skills.

In the small-cap arena or in foreign markets, the proportion of active investors outperforming a small-cap index fund or foreign index fund should be even lower, on average, than in the large-cap arena because active investing in small-cap and foreign equities involves higher transaction and research costs. This obvious logic and arithmetic, once again, contradicts conventional wisdom that active managers can do better in the less-efficient small-cap market. However, the percentage of players that mathematically must underperform any given index is dictated by the range of performance outcomes and active management costs, not the informational efficiency of the market that the index tracks.

The above discussion leads us to the question: Which investors or investor groups are most likely to be in the "successful" top group in terms of skills, information, or other competitive advantages? Mutual fund managers, as a group are definitely not in the top group. Two other investing groups, insiders and hedge fund managers, both of which have identifiable competitive advantages, are more likely candidates to be in the top group. And yet there is no empirical evidence suggesting that even these groups can consistently outperform.

So on what possible grounds could virtually any individual investors feel they actually had a competitive advantage or above average skills in the large-cap market, the small-cap market, foreign markets, or any markets? Why play a game in which one's competitors have an advantage, if one can win more often than not

Figure 28.2

MONTHLY STOCK RETURNS (1926 THROUGH 1987)					
	Average Return (%)	**Variation* (%)**	**% of Positive Months**	**% of Months Accounting for 62-Year Cumulative Returns**	**% of Months Accounting for 62-Year Return Above Treasuries**
S&P 500	0.79	5.90	61	6.7	3.5
Small Stocks	0.95	8.89	60	4.0	2.3

* Measures the range around the average return in which two-thirds of the actual returns fell.

by staying out of the active game and taking the average result by investing passively?

Once again, the conclusion is the same, even though the underlying assumptions are quite different. If prices in a market are not efficient and investing is a skill-based game, then low-skilled investors will consistently lose to players with a competitive advantage. If, on the other hand, one assumes that a market is perfectly efficient, then the less-skilled players have the same less-than-even chance of beating the index as everyone else. Market efficiency protects the less-skilled players from routinely making bad investments. There is, however, no such protection in an inefficient market, and so the active investing majority that underperforms the index will tend to be the same every year. The argument for indexing is even stronger for most investors if the stock market is not efficient.

More than half of all active investors, whose only financial justification for being active is beating the index, must fail in that objective each year. The failure rate is as mathematically certain as the forecast that exactly half of the population has IQs under 100 (the median value). Although when it comes to the logic and arithmetic of investing, investors' behavior suggests they may tend to over-represent the bottom half of that distribution.

Tactical Asset Allocation and Market Timing

This question is constantly debated. However, the overwhelming evidence is that even professional market timers cannot consistently outperform the market. Market timing, like all active management strategies, is a "zero-sum" game whereas investing in the market as a whole is a "positive-sum" game, as described above.

The argument is sometimes made that timing reduces risk, since one is invested in cash or T-bills a portion of the time and in the market the rest of the time. Since T-bills are less risky than stocks, the argument goes, the overall risk is lower.

The fallacy here is in failing to account for the risk of missing the big gains in the market. Most of the gains in the market are made during relatively short periods surrounded by long periods of relative stagnation. Figure 28.2 shows monthly stock returns from 1926 through 1987 on S&P 500 and small-cap stocks. All of the return for S&P 500 stocks occurred in just 6.7% of the months; for small-cap stocks, just 4% of the months account for all of the return over this period. Only 3.5% and 2.3%, respectively, of the months accounted for all of the return in excess of T-bills. In other words, if one were invested in the market 96.5% of the time, but one were out for the months of greatest gain, one would have done no better than investing in T-bills.

A similar study of the bull market from 1982 to 1987 gave similar results, based on days, rather than months in the market. This study showed that if one missed just the 40 biggest days, or just 3% of the 1,276 trading days of this bull market, one would have missed 83.7% of the market's 26.3% annual compounded return over the period.

Clearly, the risk of not being in the market when it makes its run is very significant, and conveniently overlooked when the market timers try to sell their concept. The best advice is to invest for the long term and be in the market consistently. No market timer can claim to be accurate over 80% of the time, so timing will inevitably lead to cases where the big market runs are missed.

Figure 28.3

COST OF NOT BEING IN THE MARKET		
Period if Investment	**S&P 500 Annualized Return (%)**	**% of Return Missed**
Entire 1,276 Trading Days	26.3	0.0
Less the 10 Biggest Gains Days	18.3	30.4
Less the 20 Biggest Gain Days	13.1	50.2
Less the 30 Biggest Gain Days	8.5	67.7
Less the 40 Biggest Gain Days	4.3	83.7

University of Michigan Study: Bull Market of 1982-1987
(1,276 trading days ending August 25, 1987)

CHAPTER ENDNOTES

1. Ignore for the moment *how* the market would gain or lose if everyone held their proportionate share of all the securities in the market. If productivity is up, weather has been good, and there have been technological advances, increased earnings and the like, the value of the whole market can and should increase because everyone's perception of value of the future earnings has increased (or vice-versa, if economic and business conditions have worsened).
2. William Sharp, "The Arithmetic of Active Management," *The Financial Analysts' Journal*, Vol. 47, No. 1 (January/February 1991).
3. Carhart, *Journal of Finance* (March 1997).
4. Graff and Dugan, "Fund Returns Are Inconsistent, Making Fund Selection Very Difficult," Cavanaugh Capital Management (April 6, 2001).
5. Swedroe, "The Road Less Traveled – Active vs. Passive – Rank of Index vs. Managed," Buckingham Asset Management.
6. William J. Bernstein, *The Intelligent Asset Allocator* (New York, NY: McGraw Hill, 2000).

Chapter 29

RETIREMENT PLANNING

WHAT IS IT?

The first task in the retirement planning process is to determine the financial needs of retirement in light of Social Security and qualified plan resources, inflation, and the period during which retirement funds are required. The process also includes obtaining information on qualified plan benefits, and recognition of the appropriate role of insurance in retirement planning. Finally, retirement planning involves working with retirement plan distributions and seeing that your client follows certain rules in a timely manner. For more detailed information on retirement planning, see the *Tools & Techniques of Employee Benefit and Retirement Planning*.

THE CURRENT ENVIRONMENT

A larger percentage of the population will live until retirement, and will live longer during retirement, than previous generations. It is more essential than ever that today's baby-boom generation and its successors plan for retirement. This course provides the tools and guidelines required to help you and your clients make sound accumulation and retirement decisions. Some of the factors you and your clients need to understand to successfully plan for wealth accumulation and retirement include the following:

- the magnitude of the financial requirements facing retirees during retirement
- the impact of inflation on retirement
- the effect that financial well-being has on the quality of life
- the planning alternatives that are available for the purpose of developing a plan that leads to financial self-sufficiency

Many current retirees have found that their retirement has fallen short of the "golden years" ideal. Anyone who has been complacent about saving for retirement should be made aware of the financial problems that force retirees to worry about the adequacy of their retirement income or that may make them financially dependent on others. Consider the following:

- Studies indicate that 75% of elderly families cannot afford luxury items because the routine costs of living absorb all their income.
- Even in the most generous employer-sponsored retirement plans, the employer typically only replaces about one-half of a person's salary.
- The combination of an employer-sponsored retirement plan and Social Security almost certainly will not provide adequate funds for maintaining the pre-retirement standard of living during retirement.
- Many people will have to deal with deteriorating health during retirement. Poor health not only creates the problem of increased medical bills, but also entails increases in the purchases of services that retirees were once able to perform for themselves (for example, home maintenance).
- Even at what may appear to be low levels, ongoing inflation during the retirement years will erode the purchasing power of the retiree's income. Inflation has forced many retirees to either work part-time at low wages to replace lost purchasing power, or to liquidate the family home or other financial personal assets to pay bills.

The United States, like most economically developed countries, is concerned about "aging," often known as the *graying of society*. But be careful not to confuse what happens to a whole society, a whole population, with what could happen to your clients as individuals. Population aging refers to what happens when a society has many older people and an increasingly high average age.

The graying of a society can occur in two ways: (1) life expectancy can improve immensely, that is, younger generations can live longer than previous generations so that the average age of the population increases; or (2) an unusually large number of people can be born in one generation, and the normal aging of this group can cause it (for example, the aging baby-boom generation). Both are happening in the United States, but the major factor influencing the graying of America is the aging baby-boomers.

DETERMINING FINANCIAL NEED

In many ways, planning for retirement is like planning for an extended vacation. Unfortunately, unlike vacations, when we rarely if ever just hop in the car and go without any specific destination in mind, many people have no real concept of where they want and need to go, financially, to secure their retirement. Sure, they may be contributing to their company's Section 401(k) plan, expect to receive Social Security, and anticipate that their company's pension plan (if it has one – pensions are increasingly rare) will provide some retirement income, but they generally have no idea whether these resources will be adequate to meet their needs.

The goal of this chapter is to acquaint you with the magnitude of the financial need facing your clients during retirement. It is sobering, to say the least, to explore your client's financial future and discover that pension and Social Security resources may be inadequate and that this problem will be exacerbated year after year by inflation. Other troubling concerns are how to stretch savings over what may amount to be more than a third of life to maintain the lifestyle to which your clients have become accustomed. In this chapter, we will take a hard look at what is needed to support the desired lifestyle throughout retirement. This will generate an analysis of how much one must save in order to reach the desired financial objectives. When you finish this chapter you will have an appreciation for the problem of providing adequate resources for what, with adequate planning, could potentially be the best years of one's life.

Tripod of Economic Security

Traditionally, experts say that retirement security is based upon a three-legged foundation of retirement income sources:

- employer-sponsored retirement plans
- Social Security
- personal savings

This traditional view, though useful, is becoming somewhat incomplete or limited in its description of the sources of retirement income. The Social Security system is facing a crisis and employer-sponsored plans have shifted a great deal more of the responsibility for saving on the individual.

Employer-Sponsored Plans

Pension plans that employers provide vary widely. Even the most generous of pension plans, however, are not geared toward replacing the full income that employees were earning prior to retirement. The trend for employer-sponsored retirement plans has been away from employer-pay-all defined-benefit-plans towards defined-contribution plans and other types of plans where employees pay some or even all of what is being contributed on their behalf.

In addition, very few employer plans provide *cost-of-living adjustments* (COLAs) to pensions once employees are retired. Consider the following:

- Most plans where the employer pension plan provides a monthly retirement benefit based on salary levels and/or years of service (defined benefit plans) are geared toward providing a replacement ratio of between only 40% and 60% of the employee's final-average salary (not the last year's salary, but the average of the last three or five years' salary). In addition, the maximum amount under this type of plan generally will only be paid if an employee has 25 or more years of service with the employer (for an employee whose service is less, the replacement ratio is reduced accordingly). Furthermore, the defined-benefit pension is often reduced for payments to Social Security, and under this situation (known as plan integration), the actual replacement ratio can drop to between 20% and 30% of final-average salary for middle-income employees.

- Plans where retirement money is put into an account for the employee's benefit, such as profit-sharing plans, money-purchase plans, IRC Section 401(k) plans, and tax-sheltered annuity IRC Section 403(b) plans (defined contribution plans), are not protected against pre-retirement inflation. Effectively, defined contribution plans can only provide benefits based on an employee's average earnings over the employee's career, which are virtually always less than the employee's earnings in the final three to five years. This means that the majority of contributions to the account are typically made based on salaries that are lower than the average salary an employee will earn during the employee's participation in the plan. These contributions based on lower "uninflated salaries" tend to limit the accumulation in the plan. Correspondingly, with these types of plans it is unlikely that there will be sufficient resources in the plan at retirement to provide retirement income that represents a significant proportion of one's pre-retirement income.

- Moreover, in defined-contribution-type plans, the responsibility for investing the funds rests primarily with the employee. The company shifts the risk of poor investment performance to the employee. This risk, together with the lack of contributions on behalf of employees who join a defined-contribution plan late in their careers, tends to minimize the effectiveness of a defined-contribution plan as compared to a defined-benefit-type plan.

- Profit-sharing plans may lead to a false sense of security because even though an employee may expect the retirement fund to grow annually, employers can forgo contributions in any given year.

- The increasing trend of employers to sponsor salary-reduction-type plans, such as 401(k)-type plans, TDAs, SIMPLE IRAs, and the like, places even more responsibility upon employees to save for their own retirement. There is a double whammy here. Not only must employees take personal responsibility for a major portion of the contributions made on their behalf through elective deferrals of their own salaries, but also for the level of the employers' contributions. The employers' contribution levels are often tied to the level of the employees' elective deferrals through some sort of contribution matching formula.

- Employers may terminate their retirement plans, leaving employees to continue working without any future employer contributions on their behalf in defined-contribution plans or without further accruals of benefits in defined-benefit plans.

- Most employer plans are not adjusted for inflation after retirement. Even if a plan were permitted to provide initial benefits that are equal to an employee's final salary, and in fact did so, assuming a 4% rate of inflation, after 18 years it would provide only 50% of the purchasing power the employee would need to keep pace with inflation.

So, in summary, in a defined-benefit plan, the employer generally makes all the contributions and assumes all risk and responsibility for investment performance and inflation, since the benefit is generally based upon years of service and some kind of final average salary. Employers who sponsor defined-contribution plans make contributions each year based upon some percentage of an employee's current salary or wage and have no further obligation if investment results do not turn out as anticipated. In addition, since they make contributions based upon current salary and wage levels, they bear no inflation risk for escalating salaries and wages.

In addition, many of the elective-deferral plans do not offer annuities and so most retirees have the responsibility of managing their resources to assure income throughout their retirement without the benefit of a life annuity.[1]

Crisis in Social Security

Social Security is supposed to be a safety net providing a base level of inflation-indexed retirement income based upon a workers earnings history and quarters of qualified earnings. Figure 29.1 shows the levels of pre-retirement income Social Security would replace based upon current promised benefit levels if the workers earned essentially the amounts indicated, in real dollars, over their working careers.

For workers earning about $35,000, increased by inflation throughout their working careers, Social Security, under the current benefit formulas, would provide retirement income equal to about 42% of their pre-retirement income. For workers who essentially just keep pace with the Social Security wage base, the projected benefits are 27% of pre-retirement income. The replacement ratio falls as the worker's income goes up. In every case, however, the Social Security benefit alone would generally be an insufficient retirement income. For the workers earning $35,000, Social Security would replace roughly half of what they will probably need to maintain their

Figure 29.1

SOCIAL SECURITY REPLACEMENT RATIOS					
Current Age	Current Earnings 35,000	50,000	65,000	80,000	110,000
25	45.5%	41.2%	35.1%	31.4%	25.2%
45	43.1%	39.1%	34.0%	30.0%	24.2%
62	36.3%	32.3%	30.1%	27.1%	21.4%
Avg. SS Repl Rate	41.6%	37.5%	33.1%	29.5%	23.6%
% of Earnings Needed	85%	85%	85%	85%	85%
% elsewhere	43.4%	47.5%	51.9%	55.5%	61.4%
$ amount	15,190	23,750	33,735	44,400	67,540

pre-retirement standard-of-living. For workers earning the Social Security wage base, it is projected to replace about one-third of what they need. However, it is not at all clear that the baby boom generation, or later generations of retirees will be able to count on these promised Social Security benefit levels.

Retirees currently eligible for benefits can probably expect to receive their promised level of benefits, unless the cost of living adjustment is reduced. Baby-boomers can expect some decrease in promised benefits after retirement and/or some increase in taxes during their remaining working years.

Benefit reductions for baby-boomers may effectively take many forms:

- direct reductions in Social Security benefit levels
- increased taxation of Social Security benefits
- later normal eligibility ages for Social Security benefits
- income or asset tests for eligibility or Social Security benefit level determinations
- increased taxation on other sources of income, similar to the 15%% excise tax on excess retirement accumulations and distributions of the 1980s and 1990s, or taxation of "tax-free" income from Roth IRAs, municipal bonds, etc.

Baby-boomers will have to try to save more over their remaining working years to have the resources necessary to replace the probable reductions in Social Security benefits. Advise your clients to take maximum advantage of the increased contribution limits and catch-up amounts for elective deferrals in 401(k) plans and the like.

Prospects for the so-called generation-X and younger generations may include

- higher taxes during their working careers
- lower benefits during their retirements
- an effective return on their Social Security contributions that will almost certainly be negative
- a greater responsibility for providing their own resources for their retirement security than the baby-boom generation

Combination Concerns

At this point, it should be apparent that Social Security has its shortcomings and pensions may have their problems–but what about when you put them together? After all, some might say, I have Social Security and both a defined-benefit plan and a defined-contribution plan. The fact is, unfortunately, that in all but the most favorable circumstances (when the pension benefit is adjusted to accurately reflect cost-of-living increases) the combined income from pensions and Social Security will fall short of meeting most people's retirement needs.

One reason for this, as mentioned above, is that even some of the most generous pension plans are often integrated with Social Security. Essentially, this means that the employer-provided pension benefit or contribution is reduced by the Social Security benefit or by employer-provided contributions for Social Security. A second reason for this is, of course, inflation.

Figure 29.2

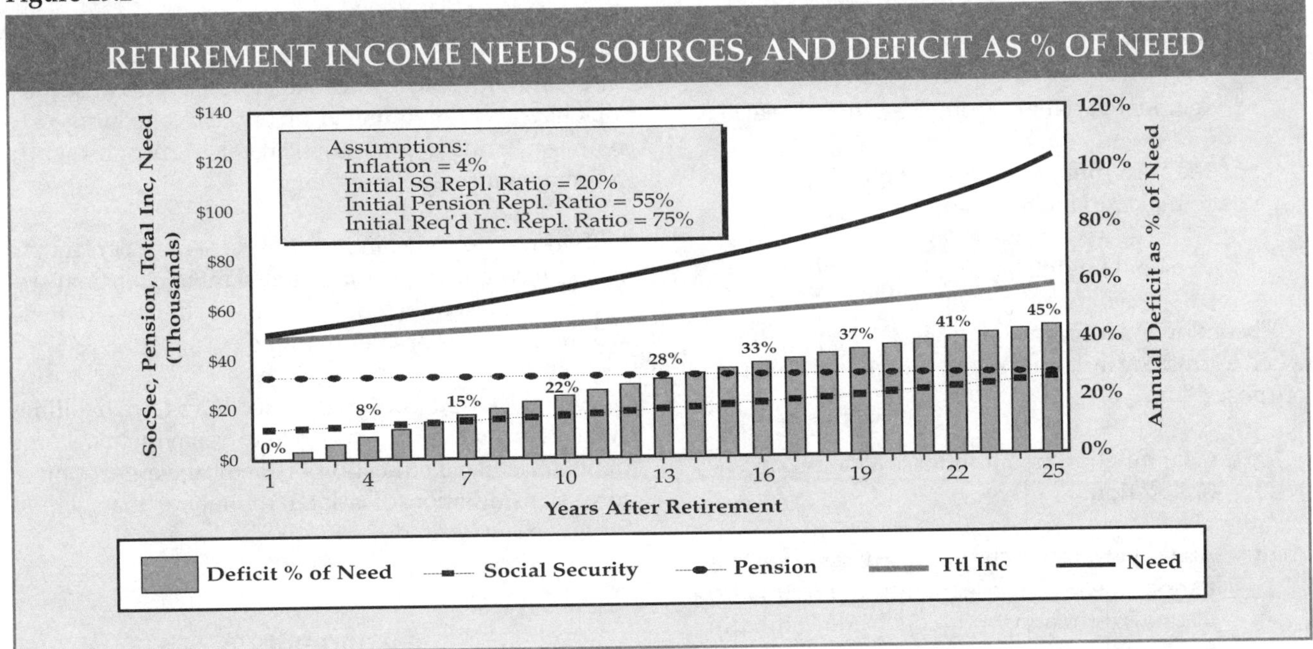

Inflation

Even if pension and Social Security benefits provide a replacement ratio (the amount of final salary that is replaced) that is equal to the amount needed in the first year of retirement, the costs associated with maintaining the standard of living in an inflationary environment will increase each year.

Unquestionably, the biggest threat to economic independence in retirement is inflation. Over the course of the retirement years, inflation will gradually reduce the amount of the retiree's purchasing power. In other words, as the years go by, the price for typical monthly expenditures will increase and retirees will need more income in order to buy the same things. A retiree will have to draw on additional savings in order to meet the monthly bills.

Figure 29.2 shows how the difference between the amount Social Security and a pension plan provides and the amount that is needed to maintain the standard of living grows over time. In this case, it is assumed that (1) Social Security and pension income just equals the required retirement income in the first year of retirement, (2) inflation averages 4% per year, and (3) Social Security keeps pace with inflation, but the pension income is a fixed annual amount. As Figure 29.2 shows, within 10 years the Social Security and pension income will provide only about 75% of the needed income. If the retiree or retiree couple survives for 25 years, the deficit mounts to almost 50% of the need.

Estimating the Inflation Rate

No one can accurately project future inflation rates. Over the period from December 1950 to December 1992 inclusive, the average compound increase in prices was 4.2%. Since 1992, however, it has been under 3% compounded. Many people may be comfortable with projecting a 3%-4% annual increase for long-term estimates of inflation. Others who are more cautious and conservative in their approach may want to choose a higher long-term inflation assumption.

Personalizing the Inflation-Rate Assumption

Inflation affects different goods and services in different ways. In general, the percentage change that the consumer price index measures from one year to the next (inflation) is made up of about 12 different categories of goods and services, which are thought of as the national "market basket" that the "average consumer" buys. But the odds are that *your clients* are not average consumers. Also, retired and older persons as a group are not average consumers either. The point here is that the kinds of things that *retirees* buy may have greater inflation than the overall average consumer price index. This is partially attributable to the fact that retirees typically purchase a higher percentage of services than goods. As a general rule, the prices of services (such as medical expenses) have been growing at a higher rate than goods. It is also important to note that any given individual's personal rate of inflation will vary from the rate of inflation as reported by the CPI because of the following factors:

- regional variations from the national rate
- the overemphasis placed on housing prices used to make up the national rate
- personal buying habits

The following recommendations will help guide you when estimating inflation rates for retirement-planning purposes:

- Gear inflation assumptions to a long-term view of inflation.
- Avoid getting caught up in any one year's inflation rate and, consequently, overestimating or underestimating inflation. Underestimating the actual inflation rate will result in a severe income shortage.

ESTIMATING THE LENGTH OF THE RETIREMENT INCOME NEED

Ideally, everyone would be able to accumulate enough assets so that they could live on the interest alone and never have to liquidate the principal amount. For all but the very rich, this is not a viable strategy. Therefore, in order to provide adequately for the duration of retirement, a planner must make a realistic assessment of the length of the retirement period. This is typically a function of two factors – the expected starting date of retirement and life expectancy.

Expected Starting Date for Retirement

The advent of Social Security in the 1930s created an image that Americans would retire when Social Security benefits began. Until recently, most pension planning tended to support this perception by setting normal retirement age at age 65. Thus, workers and planners almost invariably planned, economically and psychologically, for retirement to begin at age 65.

This assumption may not be wise, however, when you consider that the retirement date for full Social Security benefits will be gradually increased to age 67 between the years 2003-2027 (see chart at page 421). In addition, according to one study, nearly five out of six individuals retire early. As a matter of fact, the average retirement age of American workers is age 62. In some cases, health issues may affect the choice of a retirement date. In other cases, individuals are forced to retire early because their jobs have been eliminated or they are encouraged to retire early under ever-more-prevalent corporate early retirement incentive programs.

Two-wage-earner families introduce another planning factor. A couple may or may not want to coordinate retirement dates. If they do, chances are that one of them will retire earlier or later than the norm.

A final factor to consider is fixed long-term liabilities such as mortgage or major loan repayments. Large debts for college education or medical expenses often force consideration of a later retirement than would otherwise be desired.

Longevity

Clearly, a most critical planning factor is the anticipated length of retirement, which is essentially the number of years the retiree and spouse, if married, can reasonably expect to live. Estimating how long one can expect to live is difficult, since no two people are alike. Even mortality-table data are at best only rough guidelines, even if the statistics accurately represent the mortality of the larger group, since better than half the people of a given age will live beyond the life expectancy for their age.[2]

Research has clearly indicated that longevity is, at least in part, a matter of genetics. Although there is never any assurance that a person will live as long as or longer than older relatives, certainly some guidance can be obtained by looking to the ages at which parents, grandparents, and other close older relatives lived. If family life expectancy reaches into the 80s and beyond, people should be concerned about the adequacy of accumulated funds for the enjoyment of a relatively long retirement. Conversely, in families where most relatives die before the end of their 60s, working family members frequently seek early retirement in order to enjoy some of their accumulated retirement benefits.

A person whose ancestors had widely varied life expectancies may not have any strong personal perception about his or her own life expectancy. Such persons often look to the life expectancy charts promulgated by insurance companies and the federal government. The Department of Health and Human Services Public Health Service creates one such chart.

Figure 29.3

SINGLE MALE AND SINGLE FEMALE LIFE EXPECTANCIES AND SURVIVAL TERMS										
	Male					Female				
Age	LE*	50%	25%	10%	5%	LE	50%	25%	10%	5%
50	26.48	28.1	35.5	40.9	43.8	30.8	32.7	40.3	45.8	48.7
55	22.43	23.6	30.8	36.1	38.9	26.5	28.1	35.5	40.9	43.8
60	18.68	19.5	26.2	31.4	34.1	22.4	23.6	30.8	36.1	38.9
65	15.24	15.7	21.9	26.8	29.5	18.7	19.5	26.2	31.4	34.1
70	12.13	12.2	17.8	22.4	25.0	15.2	15.7	21.9	26.8	29.5
75	9.39	9.3	14.0	18.2	20.6	12.1	12.2	17.8	22.4	25.0

* LE – Life Expectancy

Individual Life Expectancies

Assuming John and Judy represent two people with normal health for their ages (65 and 62, respectively), we can make the following observations. Based upon the 90 CM mortality table,[3] their individual life expectancies are about 15 and 21 years for the husband and wife, respectively. Although life expectancy reflects the average number of additional years a person can expect to live, in general a person has *more* than a 50% chance of living beyond that life expectancy. The median age of death is the age where a person has exactly a 50/50 chance of surviving that long or longer. At their ages, the median numbers of years until death are 15.7 and 22 years, respectively.

Of course, half the people can expect to survive beyond their median ages of death, so it would be unwise to base one's retirement funding plans on median ages of death. As is shown in the survival probabilities section of the table, the 65-year-old husband has a 25% probability (or one chance in four) of surviving almost 22 years to age 86.9 and a 10% chance of surviving almost 27 years to age 91.8. His wife has a 25% chance of surviving almost 28 years to age 90.9 and a 10% chance of surviving about 34 years to age 96.2.

When planning for retirement funding, the critical question is: What level of risk are you willing to bear that you will outlive your income?

For planning guidance, Figure 29.3 presents single male and single female life expectancies and survival terms with survival probabilities of 50%, 25%, 10%, and 5% for ages ranging from 50 to 75.

Special Consideration for Married Couples

For married couples, using whichever spouse's life expectancy is longer will result in underestimating the length of the couple's retirement income needs. The average number of years until the second death of two persons is longer than the individual life expectancy of either person alone. For example, based on the life expectancies for all races in Figure 29.4, the husband of a married couple where each spouse is aged 65 has a life expectancy of about 16.3 years, while the wife has a life expectancy of 19.2 years. However, the average number of years until the second death of a husband and wife who are each aged 65 is about 23.3 years – about four years, or over 21% longer than the wife's life expectancy of 19.2 years. In other words, although each spouse has less than a 50% chance of living an additional 23.3 years, when each life is considered alone, there is a greater-than-even chance that one of the two will live at least an additional 23.3 years. Therefore, joint (second-to-die) life expectancies will generally provide better estimates of the average number of years of retirement income need for married couples.

Joint life expectancies depend on the age and sex of each partner. Figure 29.5 can help to estimate the expected number of years that at least one of a married couple will survive and need retirement income. Keep in mind that this joint life expectancy should be a minimum estimate for the length of the retirement income need. Joint life expectancy is the average number of years until both partners will have died. Slightly more than half of all married couples will have at least one spouse who survives beyond his or her joint life expectancy.

Figure 29.5 shows individual, joint-and-survivor, and first-death life expectancy statistics, as well as survival probabilities, for two lives – a male age 65 and a female age 62. The statistics are based upon the actuarially neutral mortality factors of *Table 90 CM* that the IRS used for valuing life estates, remainders, and annuities for gift and estate tax purposes. Based upon this data, there is a 50% chance that the second death of a married couple, ages 65 and 62 for husband

Figure 29.4

LIFE EXPECTANCY BY AGE, RACE, AND SEX: UNITED STATES 2000									
	All Races			White			Black		
Age	All	Male	Female	All	Male	Female	All	Male	Female
0	76.9	74.1	79.5	77.4	74.8	80.0	71.7	68.2	74.9
1	76.4	73.7	79.0	76.9	74.3	79.4	71.7	68.3	74.9
5	72.5	69.8	75.1	73.0	70.3	75.5	67.9	64.4	71.0
10	67.6	64.9	70.1	68.0	65.4	70.5	63.0	59.5	66.1
15	62.6	59.9	65.2	63.1	60.5	65.6	58.1	54.6	61.2
20	57.8	55.2	60.3	58.3	55.7	60.7	53.3	49.9	56.3
25	53.1	50.6	55.4	53.5	51.1	55.8	48.7	45.5	51.5
30	48.3	45.9	50.6	48.7	46.4	50.9	44.1	41.1	46.8
35	43.6	41.3	45.8	44.0	41.7	46.1	39.6	36.6	42.1
40	38.9	36.7	41.0	39.3	37.1	41.3	35.1	32.3	37.5
45	34.4	32.2	36.3	34.7	32.6	36.6	30.8	28.1	33.1
50	30.0	27.9	31.8	30.2	28.2	32.0	26.8	24.2	28.9
55	25.7	23.8	27.4	25.9	24.0	27.5	23.0	20.7	24.9
60	21.6	19.9	23.1	21.8	20.0	23.2	19.4	17.5	21.0
65	17.9	16.3	19.2	17.9	16.3	19.2	16.2	14.5	17.4
70	14.4	13.0	15.5	14.4	13.0	15.5	13.1	11.7	14.1
75	11.3	10.1	12.1	11.3	10.1	12.1	10.5	9.4	11.2
80	8.6	7.6	9.1	8.5	7.6	9.1	8.2	7.3	8.6
85	6.3	5.6	6.7	6.2	5.5	6.6	6.3	5.7	6.5
90	4.7	4.1	4.8	4.5	4.0	4.7	4.8	4.5	4.8
95	3.5	3.1	3.5	3.3	2.9	3.3	3.7	3.6	3.6
100	2.6	2.4	2.7	2.4	2.2	2.4	2.8	2.9	2.7

National Vital Statistics Reports, Vol. 51, No. 3, December 19, 2002.
Table 11: Life Expectancy by age, race, and sex: Death registration States, 1900-1902 to 1919-21, and United States 1929-31 through 2000.
http://www.cdc.gov/nchs/fastats/lifexpec.htm

and wife, respectively with normal health, will occur in about 23.8 years. However, there is a 25% chance that the second death will not occur for 29.9 years, a 10% chance it will not occur for almost 34.5 years, and a one-in-20 chance that it will not occur for about 37.2 years. In other words, if plans provide enough funds for the joint-and-survivor life expectancy only, half the couples would run out of money about a year early, one in four couples would run out of money about six years too soon, one in 10 couples would run out of money almost 11 years too soon, and one in 20 couples would run out of money about 13-1/2 years before their need expired.

Second-to-Die Probabilities

A common planning fallacy is to assume that using the longer of the individual life expectancies is a good starting point for estimating the period of need during retirement. Certainly the longer life expectancy sets a lower minimum boundary for planning, since there is at least a 50% chance that one partner will survive at least that long, but it completely ignores the joint-life probabilities. So, it will greatly underestimate the likely period of need.

The joint and survivor statistics are more revealing. The average number of years until the second death of a husband and wife, who are ages 65 and 62, respectively, is almost 24 years. This is about three years, or about 14%, longer than the 20.9-year life expectancy of the wife alone. And, once again, this is just the average value, which is less than the median value (50% probability value) of 24.5 years. In other words, out of every 100 couples this age you can expect that 50 of these couples will have at least one partner who survives longer than another 24.5 years. Many of these couples can expect at least one partner to survive considerably beyond even this period.

Figure 29.5

90 CM TABLE LIFE EXPECTANCIES					
If age at end of calendar year is And the sex is				**Person 1** **65** **Male**	**Person 2** **62** **Female**
Individual Statistics					
				Person 1	**Person 2**
Additional **LIFE EXPECTANCY** (years) is				**15.2**	**20.9**
Age at LIFE EXPECTANCY is				80.2	82.9
The probability of living to LIFE EXPECTANCY is				52.0%	53.7%
The probability of surviving the partner is				33.4%	66.6%
The **MEDIAN** age of death for the current age is				**80.7**	**84.0**
Probability of living to MEDIAN age of death				50.0%	50.0%
MEDIAN age of death *less* **LIFE EXPECTANCY** is				**0.5**	**1.1**
Joint and Survivor Statistics					
					Joint
EXPECTED number of years until the **2nd death**					**23.8**
Probability BOTH will LIVE 23.8 more years					8.0%
Probability BOTH will DIE before 23.8 more years					46.3%
Probability AT LEAST ONE will LIVE 23.8 more years					53.7%
Probability AT LEAST ONE will DIE before 23.8 more years					92.0%
MEDIAN years to **2nd death** (50% probability)					**24.5**
				Person 1	**Person 2**
Age if person lives 23.8 more years				**88.8**	**85.8**
Probability of living 23.8 more years				18.4%	43.3%
Probability of living and partner dying in 23.8 years				10.4%	35.4%
Probability of dying and partner living 23.8 years				35.4%	10.4%
Age at **MEDIAN** years to **2nd death** (24.5 Years)				**89.5**	**86.5**
MEDIAN years *less* **EXPECTED** years to **2nd death**				**0.7**	**0.7**
First Death Statistics					
					Joint
EXPECTED number of years until **1st death**					**12.3**
Probability BOTH will LIVE 12.3 more years					50.4%
Probability BOTH will DIE before 12.3 more years					7.6%
Probability AT LEAST ONE will LIVE 12.3 more years					92.4%
Probability AT LEAST ONE will DIE before 12.3 more years					49.6%
MEDIAN years to **1st death** (50% probability)					**12.3**
				Person 1	**Person 2**
Age if person lives 12.3 more years				**77.3**	**74.3**
Probability of living 12.3 more years				63.6%	79.2%
Probability of living and partner dying in 12.3 years				13.2%	28.8%
Probability of dying and partner living 12.3 years				28.8%	13.2%
Age at **MEDIAN** years to **1st death** (12.3 Years)				**77.3**	**74.3**
MEDIAN years *minus* **EXPECTED** years to **1st death**				**0.0**	**0.0**
Survival Probabilities					
With a Probability of ...	**75%**	**50%**	**25%**	**10%**	**5%**
Person 1 will live to age:	*74.2*	*80.7*	*86.9*	*91.8*	*94.5*
Person 2 will live to age:	*75.9*	*83.9*	*90.9*	*96.2*	*99.0*
The # of years until the					
1st death will be at least:	*6.8*	*12.3*	*18.1*	*22.9*	*25.4*
2nd death will be at least:	*18.8*	*24.5*	*29.9*	*34.5*	*37.2*

The survival probabilities at the bottom of Figure 29.5 show that a husband and wife, ages 65 and 62, respectively, have a 25% probability, or a one chance in four, that at least one of them will survive about another 30 years. Out of every 10 couples, we would expect at least one of these couples to have at least one partner who survives almost 35 more years. One in every 20 couples will have one partner who survives over 37 years.

These probabilities will vary as the ages of a retiring couple varies, getting somewhat longer for younger retirement ages and somewhat shorter for older retirement ages. However, for the normal range of retirement ages between about 60 and 70, these probabilities are instructive. In general, it is pretty risky to assume that the retirement income need will not last for at least 30 years beyond retirement, unless specific health conditions or the family's historical longevity patterns clearly indicate otherwise.

The survival probabilities at the bottom of Figure 29.5 show that a husband and wife, ages 65 and 62, respectively, have a 25% probability, or a one chance in four, that at least one of them will survive about another 30 years. Out of every 10 couples, we would expect at least one of these couples to have at least one partner who survives almost 35 more years. One in every 20 couples will have one partner who survives over 37 years.

These probabilities will vary as the ages of a retiring couple varies, getting somewhat longer for younger retirement ages and somewhat shorter for older retirement ages. However, for the normal range of retirement ages between about 60 and 70, these probabilities are instructive. In general, it is pretty risky to assume that the retirement income need will not last for at least 30 years beyond retirement, unless specific health conditions or the family's historical longevity patterns clearly indicate otherwise.

First-to-Die Probabilities

Although a typical retiring couple's retirement income need can be expected to last for at least 30 years, in at least 25% of the cases their real inflation-adjusted income need is not likely to remain level for that entire period. Many factors affect the income need. As people grow older, they generally become less mobile, travel less, and spend less on entertainment. However, their medical expenses and costs for personal help and care generally increase. Which factors will predominate is anybody's guess.

However, one very significant factor is the fact that it is extremely unlikely that *both* partners will survive for 30 years beyond retirement. It is a general rule of thumb that one surviving partner can generally maintain the same standard of living with about two-thirds of the income necessary to support the lifestyle of both partners.

Interestingly, the expected number of years until the first death of two people is *shorter* than the shorter of the two individual life expectancies. In the case of this 65-year-old husband and 62-year-old wife, the expected number of years until the first death is 12.3 years, or almost three years shorter than the husband's 15.2-year remaining life expectancy. So the retirement period that a couple can expect to need full income for each partner is shorter than the period they would expect to need the income for each of them separately.

Even more interestingly, the median (50% probability) number of years until the first death is often even *shorter* than the expected or average number of years until the first death. Just as the median number of years until the *second* death is virtually always *longer* than the average number of years until the *second* death, the median number of years until the *first* death is virtually always *shorter* than the average number of years until the first death (but of lesser magnitude).

The planning implications of these statistics are as follows. The period of time for which one needs to plan to have sufficient retirement income for two people considered together is *less* than the period of time one would need to plan to have that same total income for two people considered separately. However, the period of time beyond the first death for which one needs to plan to have the lesser required survivor income is longer than the greater of the two people's life expectancies.

Even though the median number of years until the first death is generally less than the average number of years, which is itself less than the shorter of the two life expectancies, there remains a significant probability that the first death will occur substantially later than the median number of years. In other words, it would be extremely risky to base one's retirement income security on the assumption that the joint income will be needed only for the median number of years until the first death.

The survival probabilities section of the table is once again informative. Although there is a 50% probability that the joint income will be required for only about 12¼ years, there remains a 25% probability (or one chance in four) that the joint income will be required for over 18 years. There is a one chance in 10 that it will be required for almost 23 years and a 5%, or one-in-20, chance that it will be needed for over 25 years.

Once again, the probabilities vary by the ages of the couple. However, within the normal 60- to 70-year-old range of retirement ages these probabilities are reasonably close to those for the other ages. For younger retirement ages, the number of years until the first death can be expected to occur increases slightly for each probability level. For older retirement ages, the number of years until the first death can be expected to occur decreases slightly.

Planning For Two Separate Income Streams

The basic retirement planning concept is this: When planning for a couple's retirement funding, you can break the planning into two separate income periods or income streams. The first income stream is the amount necessary to meet the survivor-income requirement with the period of need based upon second-death probabilities. The second income stream is the additional income (in addition to the survivor-income provided in the first income stream) required to meet the joint-income need with the period of need based upon first-death probabilities.

Figure 29.6 presents first-to-die and last-to-die statistics based upon the *90 CM Table* mortality factors for male ages ranging from 50 to 75 and female ages five years less, equal to, and five years greater than the male ages as guidance for planning. The table shows first-to-die and last-to-die terms with survival probabilities of 50%, 25%, 10%, and 5%.

Example. John and Mary Dooley are age 45 and 40, respectively, and are hoping to retire when John is age 60. If they have average health and average family mortality histories, based upon Table 90 CM mortality factors they can expect to live for 18.7 years and 26.5 years, respectively, after retirement. However, the expected number of years until they can expect the first of them to die, is only 15.8 years, or almost three years *less* than John's life expectancy of 18.7 years. Conversely, the term of years they can expect until the second of them dies is 29.3 years, or almost three years *more* than Mary's 26.5-year life expectancy. Furthermore, they have about a 10% chance that the first death will not occur for at least 27.3 years, almost a year longer than Mary's own life expectancy of 26.5 years. Similarly, with a 10% chance, the second death may not occur for over 41.1 years. Assuming they do not wish to risk a probability greater than 10% that they will outlive their retirement income, they must plan to have enough capital when they retire to satisfy their joint income needs for at least 27.3 years and the survivor's income needs for another 13.8 years beyond that.

Caution Is Advised

Whether a person is married or single, personal expectations based on family longevity and life-expectancy tables may be helpful in projecting life expectancy, but they may be misleading as well. Consider the following.

- Certain life-expectancy tables may reflect a bias related to the purpose for which they are being marketed. For example, a life-expectancy table used for annuities may tend to overstate life expectancy because insurance company experience shows that people who buy annuities tend to live longer than those who do not buy annuities. Conversely, some insurance tables may tend to underestimate life expectancy because, in some companies' experiences, people who buy large amounts of life insurance tend to live for a period shorter than the norm.

- Life-expectancy tables only provide average life expectancies. But virtually nobody is the "average" person. Even worse, people seem to overlook the fact that even if the tables were uncannily accurate, more than one-half of the people will outlive the projected life expectancy.

- A person's lifestyle and, consequently, health status may vary greatly from that of a person's ancestors. Also, it seems that for every relative a person has who lived well into the relative's nineties, there probably is one who died in the relative's early fifties.

- Higher socioeconomic groups have longer life expectancies.

- Finally, when planning for people who are still years away from retirement, one should account for trends in longevity. Decade by decade since 1990, improvements in longevity ranged from about 2% to 6% fairly uniformly across ages.

Figure 29.6

JOINT FIRST-TO-DIE AND LAST-TO-DIE SURVIVAL TERMS*

Male Age	Female Age	Male LE	Female LE	FD LE	FD 50%	FD 25%	FD 10%	FD 5%	LD LE	LD 50%	LD 25%	LD 10%	LD 5%
	45	26.5	35.2	23.2	23.8	31.2	36.7	39.5	38.6	39.7	45.8	50.9	53.7
50	50	26.5	30.8	21.8	22.3	29.6	35.1	37.9	35.5	36.7	42.2	46.7	49.3
	55	26.5	26.5	20.1	20.4	27.6	33.0	35.8	32.9	34.2	39.5	43.7	46.1
	50	22.4	30.8	19.3	19.6	26.6	31.9	34.7	33.9	34.9	41.0	46.0	48.8
55	55	22.4	26.5	18.1	18.2	25.1	30.4	33.2	30.9	32.0	37.4	41.8	44.4
	60	22.4	22.4	16.5	16.4	23.1	28.4	31.1	28.4	29.5	34.7	38.8	41.2
	55	18.7	26.5	15.8	15.7	22.2	27.3	30.0	29.3	30.2	36.1	41.1	43.9
60	60	18.7	22.4	14.7	14.5	20.8	25.8	28.5	26.4	27.4	32.7	37.0	39.5
	65	18.7	18.7	13.3	12.9	19.0	23.9	26.5	24.1	25.0	30.0	34.1	36.4
	60	15.2	22.4	12.7	12.3	18.1	22.9	25.5	25.0	25.7	31.4	36.3	39.0
65	65	15.2	18.7	11.7	11.2	16.8	21.5	24.0	22.2	23.0	28.0	32.3	34.7
	70	15.2	15.2	10.5	9.9	15.2	19.7	22.1	20.0	20.7	25.4	29.4	31.7
	65	12.1	18.7	9.9	9.3	14.4	18.7	21.1	20.9	21.4	26.9	31.5	34.2
70	70	12.1	15.2	9.1	8.4	13.2	17.4	19.8	18.3	18.9	23.6	27.7	30.1
	75	12.1	12.1	8.1	7.4	11.8	15.7	18.0	16.2	16.8	21.1	24.9	27.1
	70	9.4	15.2	7.6	6.8	11.0	14.8	17.0	17.1	17.4	22.5	27.0	29.5
75	75	9.4	12.1	6.9	6.1	10.0	13.7	15.8	14.7	15.0	19.4	23.2	25.5
	80	9.4	9.4	6.0	5.2	8.8	12.2	14.1	12.8	13.1	17.0	20.6	22.7

Key: LE — Life Expectancy; FD — First to Die; LD — Last to Die

* Survival terms are based upon Table 90 CM mortality factors.

Although there are presumably limits to the potential increases in longevity attributable to improvements in medical technology, nutrition, economic prosperity, and the like, even in the decade between 1990 and 2000, longevity increased again from about 2% to 6% over various age ranges. Even if longevity increases at only 2% per decade over the next forty years, a 25-year-old today could anticipate life expectancy at age 65 to increase about 8.25%, or from the 16.3 years and 19.2 years for males and females, respectively, as shown in *Table US 2000*, to 17.6 years and 20.8 years by the time they reach age 65. If longevity continues to increase for the next four decades at the 3.6% rate shown for 65-year-olds for the decade of the 1990, 25-year-olds today could anticipate that life expectancies for males and females would rise by over 15% to 18.8 years and 22.1 years, respectively, when they reach age 65.

The Length of Retirement

As one can probably gather from the discussion of early retirement age and life expectancy, this is not an exact science. For some people, the retirement life cycle may last longer than their working life cycle. For others the retirement period may be relatively short. In addition to the factors already discussed, personal demographics will factor into the length of retirement. In other words, those persons born later in the baby-boom are more likely to be retired for more years than they worked, whereas those persons born prior to the baby-boom are more likely to work more years than they are retired.

When estimating personal life expectancy, one must be as realistic as possible, and then be conservative. For example, if 30 years is a reasonable estimate of a couple's joint life expectancy, then add five to 10 years to the estimate so that the risk of underestimating the amount needed for retirement is minimized. One thing every person wants to avoid is waking up penniless the morning after the birthday that he or she projected would be his or her last.

Estimating Retirement Income Needs

The type of lifestyle a person can expect during retirement will directly correspond to the person's ability to save for retirement and personal retirement goals.

Keep in mind, people are making choices every day that affect their retirement lifestyles, even though they may have ignored their retirement goals when making the decision. The key to successful retirement planning is to recognize that there are trade-offs: today's lifestyle versus tomorrow's lifestyle. Unfortunately, short-term and immediate-term lifestyle goals often get in the way of successfully securing a comparable retirement lifestyle. Therefore, it is important to prioritize retirement goals so that financial decisions today properly account for both present and future objectives. Factors beyond the retiree's lifestyle may affect retirement planning. In some cases, there are special needs and responsibilities such as care for a dependent parent, spouse, or child; the possibility of early retirement due to health problems, or lack of job satisfaction; or family-business continuation concerns will temper and influence both the priority rankings of retirement objectives and the required funding. Everyone has some control over the retirement lifestyle he or she will enjoy based on the goals set for the future and the financial choices made today in order to achieve them.

OBTAINING INFORMATION ON QUALIFIED PLAN BENEFITS

Information concerning the benefits available from the employer's pension plan can typically be accessed in a variety of ways. If a private employer employs a person, chances are that the employer offers a plan governed by the Employee Retirement Income Security Act of 1974 (ERISA). Fortune 500 companies as well as many small businesses sponsor ERISA plans. If employed in the public sector, such as the federal government or agency, a state government or agency, or a local government, school district, or the like, chances are the employer follows a system, which in some way mirrors the one described below for ERISA plans. Public employers, however, are exempt from ERISA's rules and are apt to provide information in any number of ways. For this reason, employees who work in the public sector should check with their personnel director or benefit adviser to solicit information about the particular plan.

An employee who participates in an ERISA plan must be provided with annual benefit statements, a summary plan description, appropriate tax forms, and access to a plan administrator.

Annual Benefit Statements

The vast majority of ERISA employers offer annual benefit statements as a matter of course. If the employer does not offer an annual benefit statement voluntarily, a person may (and should) request a statement from them. Under the law, the employer is required to honor such requests, (no more than one per year, however). In addition, there are some employers (churches for example) who are exempt from this ERISA requirement. Also, as was stated at the outset, most public employers are exempt from this requirement.

A person can learn a great deal about a retirement benefit from the annual benefit statement. At the very least, these benefit statements must tell all employees their accrued benefit (the benefit earned to date) and vesting status. In addition, these statements frequently contain an estimate of the Social Security benefits the employees will receive, statements concerning any death benefit provided to spouses or beneficiary under the plan, and the value of any contributions that employees have made to the plan.

In order to best understand the accrued benefit, one must be aware of the type of retirement plan by which one is covered.

Defined Contribution Type Plans

If the employer and/or the employee make *contributions to a separate retirement account of the employee*, the plan is some type of defined contribution plan. There are several types of defined contribution plans, including:

- profit-sharing plans
- IRC Section 401(k) plans (also called cash or deferred plans)
- money-purchase plans
- employer stock-ownership plans (generally referred to as ESOPs)
- IRC Section 403(b) plans (also called tax-sheltered annuity plans or tax-deferred annuity plans)
- simplified employee pension plans (also called SEPs)
- salary-reduction simplified employee pension plans (also called SARSEPs)
- stock bonus plans
- thrift plans

- savings plans
- target benefit plans
- cash balance plans
- SIMPLE IRAs
- SIMPLE 401(k) plans

The employer may call the plan by a name different from the ones given above. However, the key is to distinguish whether or not the employer and/or the employee is making contributions to a retirement account. If this is the case, the accrued benefit is the amount that is in the retirement account. This amount will include all contributions made by the employer on the employee's behalf, all contributions the employee has made, and any interest that has been earned on the balance.

In other words, the amount of the accrued benefit is simply the account balance at any given time. It is important to understand that the current value of that account will vary with the account's investment performance and in some cases (when the investments lose money) may be lower when they are actually taken from the funds than when the account was valued for benefit statement purposes.

Defined Benefit Plans

If the employer plan is one that promises a pension benefit at retirement and there is no individual account in the employee's name, then it is a defined benefit plan. A defined benefit plan defines the benefit the employee will receive at retirement, usually based on earnings and years of service. The benefit may be based on the final salary and the amount of years worked for the employer. In these plans, the accrued benefit is the current value of the funds the employee has earned to date that will be used to buy the pension benefit. The plan's actuary determines the value. A couple of factors should be noted when reviewing the benefit statement.

- Is the benefit provided the *current* benefit the employee would receive today if the employee terminated employment, or is it the *projected* benefit the employee will receive at retirement?
- Is the value of the benefit in current dollars or future dollars? Benefits may seem at times to be unreasonably high because they are what the employees will receive 20 or 30 years in the future. Due to inflation, the actual purchasing power of the benefit will be less than it seems. For example, a benefit that will pay $500 a month when at age 67 in the year 2034 is like receiving a $154-a-month benefit in 2004 (assuming a 4% inflation rate).

Vesting

Just because a person has an accrued benefit does not mean that the person will actually receive that benefit. In order to be entitled to the amount of the accrued benefit, the employee must be vested in it. The vesting statement in the annual benefits statement therefore refers to the degree of ownership the employee possesses in the retirement income. Employer plans typically use one of two types of vesting schedules – a graded schedule or a cliff schedule. A graded vesting schedule is a schedule under which the employee becomes gradually vested in the retirement savings over time.

For example, the employee may be 60% vested after completing four years of service with the employer. This means that if the employee left employment at this point, the employee would be entitled to 60% of the accrued benefit.

A cliff vesting schedule is a vesting schedule under which the employee is not entitled to any percentage of the accrued benefit for a specified number of years (typically up to five years) and after which the employee is entitled to 100% of the accrued benefit. For example, an employee of XYZ Company may be entitled to take the entire retirement savings only if the employee holds off changing jobs until the fifth year of employment after becoming fully vested. Conversely, persons leaving XYZ Company after four years would have no savings to take with them when they change jobs.

Summary Plan Descriptions

A second way to analyze pension benefits is to examine the summary plan description (SPD). The summary plan description will contain a wealth of information about the purpose and savings of the plan and the employees' options under the plan, including information about:

- *Early retirement* – Receiving retirement benefits early is allowed under some plans and not under others. If early retirement benefits are a possibility, they may be conditioned on a specific age and/or amount of service; for example, age 55 and 10 years of service. When available, early retirement benefits are generally less than what the employee would otherwise get if the employee retired at the normal retirement age, to account for a longer payout period.

- *Normal retirement age* – In a defined benefit plan, normal retirement age is the age at which payment of retirement benefits begins. Normal retirement age is typically geared to the receipt of full Social Security benefits. Consequently, for those retiring before the year 2003, normal retirement age for receiving full Social Security benefits was age 65. For those retiring after 2002, normal retirement age is delayed because of the increase in the full-payment age for full Social Security benefits. The following table shows the gradual increase of the Social Security retirement age:

Age To Receive Full Social Security Benefits

Year of Birth	Full Retirement Age
1937 or earlier	65
1938	65 and 2 months
1939	65 and 4 months
1940	65 and 6 months
1941	65 and 8 months
1942	65 and 10 months
1943–1954	66
1955	66 and 2 months
1956	66 and 4 months
1957	66 and 6 months
1958	66 and 8 months
1959	66 and 10 months
1960 and later	67

- *Deferred retirement* – The impact of delayed retirement on retirement benefits should be spelled out in the summary plan description. Generally, in a defined contribution plan, employees will continue to receive (or be able to make) contributions to their retirement accounts. In a defined benefit plan, benefits will generally continue to accrue as long as employment continues and the amount of the benefit will probably be increased to reflect the shorter payout period.

- *Payout options available at retirement* – The methods available for paying out retirement savings will be spelled out in the summary plan description. Some plans will offer a lump-sum payment option that provides some interesting planning possibilities; other plans will restrict payment to an annuity format. The type of annuity one chooses will affect the monthly amount of the pension.

- *Potential pitfalls* – The summary plan description should spell out any terms that could result in a participant losing benefits.

- *Claims procedures* – The summary plan description will spell out procedures for presenting claims for pension, health, and life insurance benefits, and remedies for benefits denied under the plan.

Tax Forms

In addition to the annual benefit statement and summary plan description, employees will also be supplied with a variety of retirement-related federal tax forms. Chief among these is Form 1099R. This form is sent whenever a person receives a lump-sum distribution from the retirement plan or whenever a person is receiving annuity payments or periodic payments.

Plan Administrator

In addition to all the written information employees receive about their plans, they also have access to a plan administrator, benefits adviser, or human-resources representative. In some cases, the same person may wear all three hats; in others, a team of experts is available to advise employees.

ROLE OF INSURANCE

In General

Wealth accumulation involves a plan to fund stated objectives over a particular funding timeline. Once sources of accumulation have been identified, planners implicitly *assume* that these sources will be continually available over the funding/accumulation phase. However, losses of human capital or previously accumulated wealth are both subject to the vagaries of life and death.

One of the major implicit sources for accumulation is the current and future earnings of a person through work. But everyone is subject to the risk of premature death or disability. If and when either hazard occurs, it effectively eliminates these sources of funding, and with it, the objectives will fail. Ordinary expenses, such as food, shelter, medicine, mortgage interest and principal, and clothing are generally funded through the current and projected earnings of the individual. Once such earnings are cut off in the case of disability, these expenses will have to be paid from accumulated wealth.

Exceptional expenses for repair or replacement of property and for catastrophic health procedures can likewise represent an unanticipated item that would reduce or eliminate current and future disposable income from which the wealth accumulation objectives were to be funded.

Losses due to a decline in the value of assets also jeopardize the successful implementation of a wealth-accumulation plan. The concept of portfolio insurance is discussed later in this course.

Assessing Risks

The payments of premiums on various insurance coverages impede the wealth-accumulation process by adding additional expense that reduces the net income that is available for investment after necessary expenditures. However, life insurance protects against the loss of income from death during the accumulation phase. Disability income insurance protects against the loss of income from disability during the accumulation phase. Medical insurance protects against substantial medical expenses. Property insurance protects against the loss or replacement cost of damaged or destroyed hard assets. Liability insurance protects against claims against accumulated wealth and earnings resulting from certain legal liabilities.

If probability were the only factor to be taken into account in determining which risks should be insured, very few risks would actually be insured because most risks have a very small probability of occurring. For example, a 35-year-old male about to embark on a wealth accumulation plan may determine that the probability of dying in the current year is less than three in 1,000, hardly anything that should be reasonably anticipated. Similarly, essential hard assets may have a minimal chance of being damaged or partially destroyed, and even less of a chance of being totally destroyed. However small the probability, the insurance principle is *protection against the unexpected* to the extent that the potential loss is large enough to place their other wealth accumulation objectives in jeopardy.

Life Insurance

Some life insurance products have significant accumulation features; others have none. But all have as a basic feature the protection against loss that arises on account of death. Loss can occur both from the cessation of an income stream, as well as any increase in expenses to the family unit. The amount of insurance to protect against this loss is a function of the current value of the unfunded portion of the wealth-accumulation objective.

Disability Income

Overlooked by most advisers is the fact that during a person's working lifetime, the person faces about twice the risk at each age of incurring a serious long-term disability than dying. It is far more likely that the ability to accumulate earnings will be thwarted by disability than by death. Disability is also accompanied by increased expenditures related to the disability. Without the earnings, the family will have to dip into already accumulated wealth to meet current expenses.

Short-term disability will generally not have a significant impact on wealth-accumulation objectives and need not be insured against. Typically, however, advisers recommend that an emergency reserve of about three to six months of income be invested in liquid assets such as money-market funds and bank deposits to meet such relatively short-term needs.

Total or long-term disability is a large enough potential loss to threaten meeting wealth accumulation objectives that it merits insurance protection. Choosing appropriate waiting periods and maximum benefit periods reduces the cost of such protection. The waiting period is the period of time one must be disabled before the benefits begin. The emergency reserve set aside for short-term disabilities can also cover this period. Policyowners may generally elect a maximum benefit period equal to the period until they reach age 65 or until an earlier age if this corresponds to their planned accumulation phase.

Note that most carriers limit the coverage to a percentage of current earnings and virtually all domestic carriers limit the annual benefits to a ceiling of $400,000 or less. For these purposes, the limitations are applied on an aggregate basis of all policies. Excess coverage may be available from foreign insurers.

Medical Insurance

Most persons during the accumulation phase are ineligible for Medicare and Medicaid. Even if a person may qualify for Medicare, the benefits end after a period of time, so true catastrophic coverage is not available. Catastrophic medical coverage is a necessity. However, it is generally wise to avoid insuring small losses that can be more efficiently and cost-effectively self-insured. Choosing a high deductible may reduce the cost for catastrophic medical insurance. Note that most policies have a coinsurance provision that requires the policyholder to pay a portion of such expenses (usually between 20% and 25%) in excess of the deductible. This is generally ameliorated by a stop-loss cap, which limits the expenses subject to sharing borne by the policyholder.

RETIREMENT PLAN DISTRIBUTION PLANNING

Employer retirement plans, such as qualified pension or profit sharing plans or IRC Section 403(b) tax-deferred annuity plans of tax-exempt employers can allow employees to accumulate substantial retirement benefits. Even a middle-level employee may have an account balance of hundreds of thousands of dollars available at retirement or termination of employment. Careful planning is important in order to make the right choices about this plan distribution, not only to get the right result in financial planning for retirement, but also to avoid adverse tax results.

General objectives should be identified first. If an employee does not immediately need the plan distribution for retirement income, a major objective will be to spread the distribution over the longest possible period in order to provide deferral of taxation and to allow the plan account to build up income on a tax-deferred basis. On the other hand, if an employee depends on the plan as a primary source of retirement income, choosing the right options to meet retirement planning needs may be more important than tax-oriented planning, although it is still important to avoid excessive taxation.

What Options Does the Plan Provide?

The first step is to examine plan documents to see what plan distribution options are available. Usually the plan's Summary Plan Description (SPD) explains these in adequate detail. But the underlying plan document may have to be examined to resolve questions. Furthermore, in the event the SPD and plan document provisions differ, the terms of the plan document will govern. By federal law participants in qualified (and certain other) retirement plans must be provided with an SPD and must be allowed to examine the plan document and copy it for a reasonable copying fee.

Not all plans provide the maximum flexibility allowed in distributions under federal law. If the plan provisions are not flexible, the distribution must be designed as well as possible within these limitations. However, plans can be amended to change distribution provisions. If your client is a controlling shareholder or key employee of the employer, it may be possible to change the plan prior to the distribution to provide more favorable results.

Defined Benefit Plan Distribution Provisions

Defined benefit plans must provide a married participant with a *joint and survivor annuity* as the automatic form of benefit. The joint and survivor annuity benefit provides a stated benefit to the participant and spouse while both are living, with a survivor annuity to the nonparticipant spouse. If the nonparticipant spouse dies before the participant spouse, there is generally no further death benefit under this option. The annuity amount for the surviving nonparticipant spouse can be anywhere from 50% up to 100% of the amount payable during the joint lives. Some plans allow a participant to choose an amount of survivor annuity within these limits.

For an unmarried participant, the plan's automatic form of benefit is usually a life annuity – typically monthly payments to the participant for life, with no further payments after the participant's death.

Many plans allow participants to elect to receive some other form of benefit from a list of options in the plan. However, to elect any option that eliminates the benefit for a married participant's spouse, the spouse must consent on a notarized written form. This is not just a legal formality. In consenting to another form of benefit, the spouse gives up property rights in the participant's qualified plan that are guaranteed under federal law. Thus, the spouse should receive something in return for consenting to give up spousal rights. An ill-advised consent, especially where the spouse is not represented by his or her own legal or financial adviser, could be deemed to be an "uninformed consent" at some later time – typically after the participant's death. This could mean the original consent would be nullified by the courts.

Typically plans offer, as an option to the joint and single life annuity, a *period certain* annuity. A period certain annuity provides payments for a specified period of time – usually 10 to 20 years – even if the participant, or the participant and spouse, die before the end of that period. Thus, the period certain annuity provides benefits for the participant's heirs even if the participant (or participant and spouse) die early. Because of this guarantee feature, the annual or monthly payments under a period certain option are less than they would be under an option where payments end at death. A period certain option therefore should be chosen if the participant wants to make sure that his heirs are provided for in case both he and his spouse die shortly after retirement. For example, the participant and spouse might choose this option if they were both in poor health, or if they wanted to make sure that their children (or other heirs) with large financial needs were provided for in the event of their deaths.

Defined benefit plans may allow participants to choose joint annuities with a beneficiary other than a spouse – for example, an annuity for the life of a participant and a son or daughter. Federal tax rules limit the amount of annuity payable to a much younger beneficiary in order to ensure that the participant personally receives at least a minimum portion of the total value of the plan benefit and that plan payments are not unduly deferred beyond the participant's death. (See the minimum distribution rules discussed below, under "Penalty for Distributions Too Late or Not Enough.") Thus, a much younger beneficiary (except for a spouse) generally would not be allowed to receive a 100% survivor annuity benefit.

Defined Contribution Plan Distribution Provisions

Defined contribution plans include profit sharing, 401(k), and money purchase plans. IRC Section 403(b) tax-deferred annuity plans also have distribution provisions similar to defined contribution plans. Defined contribution plans sometimes provide annuity benefits like those in defined benefit plans. In fact, certain kinds of defined contribution plans (e.g., money purchase pension plans) must provide to a married participant a joint and survivor annuity as the automatic form of benefit. Others do not have to meet the joint and survivor requirements as long as the plan provides for the spouse to receive any unpaid nonforfeitable benefit remaining at the death of the participant.

Annuity benefits are computed by converting the participant's account balance in the defined contribution plan into an equivalent annuity. The TIAA/CREF plan for college teachers, for example, is a defined contribution plan that primarily offers annuity options. In some plans the participant can elect to have his account balance used to purchase an annuity from an insurance company. The same considerations in choosing annuity options then apply as have already been discussed.

Defined contribution plans often provide a lump sum distribution option, and sometimes only a lump sum option. Defined contribution plans often also allow the option of taking out periodic distributions over the retirement years, which are not necessarily in the form of an annuity. That is, the participant simply takes out money as it is needed, subject to the minimum distribution requirements discussed later. Lump sum or periodic distribution provisions provide much flexibility in planning.

Tax Implications

For some plan participants, retirement income adequacy is more important than minimizing taxes to the last dollar. Nevertheless, taxes on both the federal and state levels must never be ignored. The planner must consider

1. the direct income tax on the lump sum or periodic distribution
2. penalty taxes
3. estate taxes
4. generation skipping transfer taxes

A qualified plan distribution may be subject to federal, state, and local taxes, in whole or in part. This section will focus only on the federal tax treatment. The federal tax treatment is generally the most significant because federal tax rates are usually higher than state and local rates. Also, many state and local income tax laws provide a full or partial exemption or especially favorable tax treatment for distributions from qualified retirement plans.

Nontaxable and Taxable Amounts

Qualified plans often contain after-tax employee money – that is, contributions that have already been taxed. These amounts generally can be distributed to the employee tax free, although the order in which they are recovered for tax purposes depends on the kind of distribution.

Generally, distributions – whether annuity payments or amounts distributed or withdrawn before any annuity payments begin – are deemed to include both taxable and nontaxable amounts in each payment. In the case of distributions and withdrawals before annuitization, the nontaxable amount will be proportionate to the ratio of total after-tax contributions to the plan account balance. The treatment of annuity payments is explained below.

There is an exception in the case of distributions and withdrawals before annuitization with respect to employee after-tax contributions made before 1987 to certain previously-existing plans. Such amounts will be treated as being paid entirely with non-taxable employee after-tax money until the pre-1987 employee after-tax money has been completely distributed.

Taxable distributions may also be subject to an early withdrawal penalty (see below).

The first step in determining the tax on any distribution is to determine the participant's cost basis in the plan benefit. The participant's cost basis can include

1. the total after-tax contributions made by the employee to a contributory plan

2. the total cost of life insurance reported as taxable income by the participant (the Table 2001 or formerly P.S. 58 costs) if the plan distribution is received under the same contract that provided the life insurance protection (If the plan trustee cashes in the contract before distribution, this cost basis amount is not available. For a person who is now or was self-employed, Table 2001 or formerly P.S. 58 costs are also not available.)

3. any employer contributions previously taxed to the employee – for example, where a nonqualified plan later becomes qualified.

4. certain employer contributions attributable to foreign services performed before 1963

5. amounts paid by the employee in repayment of loans that were treated as distributions

Taxation of Annuity Payments

The annuity rules of IRC Section 72 apply to periodic plan distributions made over more than one taxable year of the employee in a systematic liquidation of the participant's benefit. Amounts distributed are taxable in the year received, except for a proportionate recovery of the cost basis. The method used for recovery of the cost basis depends on the participant's annuity starting date.

If the annuity starting date is after December 31, 1997 and the annuity is payable over two or more lives, the excludable portion of each monthly payment is determined by dividing the employee's cost basis by the number of payments shown in the table below:

If the combined ages of the annuitants are:	Number of Payments
Not more than 110	410
More than 110 but not more than 120	360
More than 120 but not more than 130	310
More than 130 but not more than 140	260
More than 140	210

If (a) the annuity starting date was after November 18, 1996 and before January 1, 1998 and the annuity is payable over two or more lives, *or* (b) the annuity starting date is after November 18, 1996 and the annuity is payable over one life, the excludable portion of each monthly payment is determined by dividing the employee's cost basis by the number of payments shown in the table below:

Age	Number of Payments
Not more than 55	360
More than 55 but not more than 60	310
More than 60 but not more than 65	260
More than 65 but not more than 70	210
More than 70	160

In the case of participants with an annuity starting date after July 1, 1986 and before November 19, 1996, the cost basis is recovered through the calculation of an exclusion ratio that is applied to each payment to determine the nontaxable amount.

The exclusion ratio is:

$$\frac{\text{Investment in the contract}}{\text{Expected return}}$$

Basically, the "investment in the contract" is the participant's cost basis. In the case of a life annuity, the "expected return" is determined by multiplying the total annual payment by the participant's life expectancy. Life expectancies are determined under tables found in Treasury Regulations for IRC Section 72.[4]

Example. Fred Retiree retired in 1995 at age 65 with a pension of $500 per month for his life. Fred's cost basis in the plan was $20,000. Using a life expectancy of 20 years, Fred's exclusion ratio was calculated as follows:

$$\frac{\$20{,}000}{\$120{,}000} = \frac{1}{6}$$

The numerator is Fred's cost basis; the denominator is Fred's annual pension of $6,000 multiplied by his life expectancy. Therefore, 1/6 of each payment Fred receives will be nontaxable. The remainder of each payment is taxable as ordinary income.

Once the exclusion ratio is determined, it continues to apply until the cost basis is fully recovered. Payments made subsequently are taxable in full. If the participant dies before the cost basis is fully recovered, an income tax deduction for the unrecovered basis is allowed on the participant's final return. Special tables are used for joint life expectancies and separate computations may be necessary to determine expected return in some situations, such as where there is a period certain guarantee.

A simplified "safe harbor" method for annuity starting dates after July 1, 1986 and before November 19, 1996 was provided by the IRS.[5] This alternative to the use of the exclusion ratio applied only to payments from a qualified plan or IRC Section 403(b) tax-deferred annuity plan that were to be paid for the life of the employee or the joint lives of the employee and beneficiary. Under this method, the employee's investment in the contract was divided by the number of expected monthly payments set out in the IRS table below. The number of payments was based on the employee's age at the annuity starting date and the same table was used for both single life and joint and survivor annuity payments. The resulting dollar amount was excluded from each payment until the cost basis was fully recovered.

Age	Number of Payments
55 and under	300
55-60	260
61-65	240
66-70	170
71 and over	120

Lump Sum Distributions

A lump sum distribution may be desirable for retirement planning purposes, but the distribution may be large enough to push most of it into the highest tax bracket. In determining the tax on a lump sum distribution, the first step is to calculate the taxable amount of the distribution. The taxable amount consists of (a) the total value of the distribution less (b) after-tax contributions and other items constituting the employee's cost basis. If employer securities are included in the distribution, the net unrealized appreciation of the stock is generally subtracted from the value of a lump sum distribution.

For lump sum distributions received prior to January 1, 2000, limited relief was available under a special, one-time 5-year averaging provision. This election became unavailable for years beginning after 1999; however, the availability of rollovers for plan most distributions provides participants with sufficient flexibility for tax planning needs.

For individuals who attained age 50 before January 1, 1986, lump sum distributions may be treated under a 10-year averaging provision (using 1986 rates and taking into account the prior law zero bracket amount). Generally, the higher the distribution amount, the less likely the taxpayer is to benefit from this special treatment.

Taxation of Death Benefits

In general, the income tax treatment that applies to death benefits paid to beneficiaries is very similar to that of lifetime benefits payable to participants; however, more favorable treatment applies to spouse beneficiaries than to other beneficiaries. Either the annuity rules or the lump sum special tax provisions may be available to the beneficiary receiving a death benefit. However, an additional income tax benefit is available, in that if the death benefit is payable under a life insurance contract held by the qualified plan, the pure insurance amount of the death benefit is excludable from income taxation. The pure insurance amount is the difference between the policy's face amount and its cash value at the date of death. (For decedents dying before August 21, 1996, an additional amount of up to $5,000 was excluded as an employee death benefit.)

Example. Alan Participant, age 62, dies in 2002 before retirement. His beneficiary receives a lump sum death benefit from the plan of $100,000. The $100,000 is the proceeds of a cash value life insurance contract; the contract's cash value at Alan's death was $60,000. Alan reported a total of $10,000 of Table 2001 (formerly P.S. 58) insurance costs on his income tax returns during his lifetime. The taxable amount of the $100,000 distribution to the beneficiary is $100,000 less the following items:

(a) the pure insurance amount of $40,000 ($100,000 less the cash value of $60,000),

(b) Alan's cost basis of $10,000 of Table 2001 (or P.S. 58) costs.

The taxable amount of this benefit is therefore $50,000.

Federal Estate Tax on Distributions

The value of a qualified plan death benefit is subject to inclusion in the decedent's gross estate for federal estate tax purposes. However, only high net worth plan participants will actually be subject to estate tax. First, there is a high minimum tax credit applicable to the estate tax that essentially eliminates estate taxes for gross estates less than $2,000,000 in 2007, increasing to $3,500,000 by 2009. (Note that the estate tax is repealed for 2010 only. The credit for 2011 is scheduled to be $1,000,000.) In addition, the unlimited marital deduction for federal estate tax purposes eliminates federal estate tax upon the death of the first spouse on property transferred to the surviving spouse in a qualifying manner.

In some cases, however, avoiding federal estate tax can be significant. For example, the estate may be relatively large and the participant may be single or unwilling to pay the death benefit to the spouse. Therefore, the marital deduction is not always available. Also, even when the death benefit is payable to a spouse, federal estate tax is not really avoided; a spouse is often about the same age as the decedent, and thus much of the property transferred to the spouse is potentially subject to federal estate tax within a few years at the surviving spouse's death.

Some authorities believe it is possible to design a qualified plan so that death benefits can be excluded from the participant's estate. Here is the rationale: The federal estate tax law provides that all of a decedent's property is includable in the estate unless there is a specific exclusionary provision. Qualified plan death benefits are not subject to any specific exclusion, so they are generally includable. There is, however, a specific provision in the Internal Revenue Code that applies to life insurance: Section 2042 provides that life insurance proceeds are includable in a decedent's estate only if the decedent had incidents of ownership in the insurance policies (or if proceeds are payable to the decedent's estate). An incident of ownership includes the right to designate the beneficiary as well as similar rights under the policy. Some planners have attempted to design qualified plan death benefits using life insurance policies in which the decedent has no incidents of ownership. Some methods for doing this include the use of separate trusts or subtrusts under the plan for holding insurance policies, together with irrevocable beneficiary designations. At this point, the law is not entirely clear on whether these provisions will in fact avoid incidents of ownership. A conservative view is that they will not.

Lump Sum vs. Deferred Payments: The Tradeoffs

Often plan participants have a choice between a single lump sum plan distribution and a series of deferred payments. This requires a choice between competing advantages.

Advantages of a lump sum distribution include

1. the ability to roll over certain distributions
2. 10-year averaging tax treatment (limited to certain distributions to individuals who reached age 50 before 1986)
3. freedom to invest plan proceeds at the participant's – not the plan administrator's – discretion

The contrasting advantages of a deferred payout are

1. deferral of taxes until money is actually distributed (however, such deferral can also be obtained in the case of a rollover)
2. continued sheltering of income on the plan account from taxes while money remains in the plan
3. security of retirement income

There is not one single favored alternative but rather competing advantages. The conclusion depends on many variables – the participant's tax bracket, tax rates, rates of investment return, and the number of years of deferral. A full analysis of these for an individual may be complex. It should certainly be done where very large sums are involved. In other cases, it may be adequate to make a good estimate of the result.

Penalty Taxes

In addition to the regular tax rules, distributions must be planned so that recipients avoid–or at least are not surprised by–two types of tax penalties. These are summarized as follows.

Penalty for Distributions Too Soon

Early distributions from qualified plans, 403(b) tax-deferred annuity plans, IRAs and SEPs are subject to a penalty of 10% of the taxable amount of the distribution, except for distributions:

1. made on or after attainment of age 59½
2. made to the plan participant's beneficiary or estate on or after the participant's death
3. attributable to the participant's disability
4. that are part of a series of substantially equal periodic payments made at least annually over the life or life expectancy of the participant, or of the participant and beneficiary (separation from the employer's service is required, except for IRAs)
5. made following separation from service after attainment of age 55 (not applicable to IRAs)
6. that are certain tax credit ESOP dividend payments, or
7. to the extent of medical expenses deductible for the year under Code Section 213, whether or not actually deducted

In addition, certain distributions made from IRAs for the payment of health insurance premiums by unemployed individuals, and certain distributions used for higher education expenses or first-time home purchases may be exempt from the penalty.[6]

Penalty for Distributions Too Late or Not Enough

1. Distributions from qualified plans, 403(b) tax-deferred annuity plans, IRAs, SEPs, and 457 governmental deferred compensation plans generally must begin by April 1 of the calendar year after the participant attains age 70½. However, a qualified plan participant (other than a 5% owner, as defined for top heavy purposes) who is still working at age 70½ may delay distributions until April 1 of the year following retirement. Distributions from traditional IRAs may not be deferred until retirement under this rule. Roth IRAs are not subject to these rules during the lifetime of the owner.
2. There is an annual *minimum* distribution required; if distribution is less than the minimum, there is a penalty of 50% of the amount that should have been distributed but was not.
3. The minimum initial annual distribution is determined by dividing the participant's account balance (as of the last plan valuation date prior to the year in which distributions must begin) by the participant's life expectancy, as determined under a table set forth in regulations. Unless the participant's beneficiary is a spouse more than 10 years younger than the participant is, the beneficiary's age has no effect on the amount of lifetime distributions.
4. Following the death of the participant, the remaining benefit may generally be distributed over the life expectancy of the beneficiary, determined under tables set forth in the regulations. However, if no designated beneficiary exists (e.g., if the participant named only a charity or his estate as beneficiary), the remaining benefit will have to be distributed under a 5-year rule.

CHAPTER ENDNOTES

1. Of course, retirees can roll balances to an IRA where they can acquire an annuity or to an individual retirement annuity offered by an insurance company, but many are reluctant to do so because they do not want to forfeit their funds in the event they should die early.
2. It is a common misconception that half the people of a given age will die before reaching life expectancy and the other half will live beyond life expectancy; in other words, that there is 50% probability that a person will live to life expectancy or beyond. Life expectancies represent the average age of death for the underlying group. However, since mortality increases with each successive age, the average age of death is not equal to the *median* age of death. The median age of death, which is the age at which exactly 50% of the population of people of a given current age can be expected to have died, is *always* longer than the average age of death or life expectancy. For example, based on 1990 mortality data (IRS Table 90CM), life expectancy for a male age 65 is an additional 15.2 years to age 80.2. However, the age by which exactly half the population of current 65-year-old males can be expected to have died (the median age of death) is 80.7, or almost a half a year longer than the life expectancy.
3. Table 90 CM is an actuarially neutral table based upon 1989-1991data that was previously used to value life, annuity, and remainder interests in trusts for gift and estate tax purposes.
4. Treas. Reg. §1.72-9.
5. Notice 88-118 1988-2 CB 450.
6. See IRC Secs. 72(t)(2)(D)-(F).

Chapter 30

CHARITABLE PLANNING

WHAT IS IT?

Many financial planning clients will show some sort of charitable inclination. However, many will not even broach the subject with their planner; the planner generally needs to mention it first.

Charitable giving is inherently personal. Although it might be nice to think that everyone who has been given much in life believes that they have a duty to return something to those in need, that is frequently not the case. Planners should probe the possibility of a charitable inclination in their clients and be prepared to explain the advantages and disadvantages to a charitable giving strategy within their financial plan.

Clients will tend to be open to charitable planning as a part of their financial plan for one or more of the following reasons:

- the ability to "give back" to the community;
- social benefits, including potential recognition by their peers;
- income (and gift) tax deductions for gifts to charity made during lifetime; or
- estate tax deductions for bequests to charity made at death.

When a charitable intent is identified in the planning process, it is the planner's responsibility to assist in the determination of:

- when the charitable gift should be made;
- whether the client can afford the size of the contemplated contribution;
- the form of the contribution (e.g., direct or through a trust or foundation); and
- the appropriate assets that should be given (e.g., cash, stock, other property).

Although outright gifts of cash (often in the form of a check) are common, an outright gift of cash is not necessarily the most advantageous or convenient type of gift for a donor to make—and in fact, over the long run it may not be the donor's best option. Consideration should be given to non-traditional gifts involving stock or setting up other charitable giving strategies to help the client form a financial planning perspective, as well as helping the client feel good about the gift.

Charitable planning is covered in great detail in *The Tools & Techniques of Charitable Planning* (National Underwriter Company).

OUTRIGHT GIFTS

Most charitable donations are made in the form of outright gifts. In an outright gift, the donor relinquishes total control of either cash or other property. However, the donor can still attach restrictions on how the gift is to be used by the charity. For example, a donation to a university can be limited to the business school or the lacrosse team.

A donor benefits from an outright gift to charity by:

- taking an income (and gift) tax charitable deduction in the year the donation is made (the amount of the deduction is usually equal to the fair market value of the relinquished property); and
- removing the asset(s) from the donor's gross estate by taking an estate tax charitable deduction, and thereby reducing the amount of potential estate tax that would be due upon the donor's death;

Please note that the income tax deduction for charitable contributions is subject to certain limitations. In order to benefit from the deduction in the year of the donation, the donor must have taxable income and itemize deductions. In addition, the donor's deduction for charitable contributions cannot exceed certain percentages of the donor's adjusted gross income.

A donation of highly appreciated property is often a more effective gift than a gift of cash. For example, if a client wishes to give $50,000 to his church, he could write a check for $50,000 on his bank account. While that would certainly please the church, what if he didn't have $50,000 of cash? Perhaps, the client has stock with a fair market value of $50,000. If so, he could consider selling the stock. Let's assume that the client has a basis of $10,000 in that stock. If he sold the stock for $50,000, he would have a taxable capital gain of $40,000 ($50,000 sales price - $40,000 basis) on which he would pay $6,000 of income tax ($40,000 x .15, assuming a 15% federal capital gain tax rate). The client would then have $44,000 ($50,000 sales price - $6,000 tax) to give to the church after taxes. If, instead of selling the stock and giving the cash left after taxes to the church, the client simply gives the stock to the church, he is entitled to a charitable deduction for the fair market value of the stock (or $50,000)—without having to pay the tax on the capital gain. Clearly, from a cash flow and tax perspective, the client is far better off.

Charitable contribution deductions are not allowed for:

- donations to nonqualified organizations, generally one that is not an IRC Section 501(c)(3) tax-exempt organization (a list of qualified charities may be found in IRS Publication 78);
- a contribution to a specific individual;
- the portion of a contribution from which the donor receives, or expects to receive, a benefit;
- the value of the donor's time or services;
- the donor's personal expenses;
- appraisal fees; and
- certain contributions of partial interests in property.

PERCENTAGE LIMITATIONS

The amount of an individual's income tax charitable deduction may be limited to 50%, 30%, or 20% of the donor's adjusted gross income in a given year. The appropriate limit to be applied is dependent on:

- the type of charity;
- whether the gift is made "to" or "for the use of" the charity; and
- the type of property donated.

For a chart summarizing the various deduction limitations, see Figure 30.1.

The percentage limitations are not "stacked"; in other words, each level is reduced by contributions deducted (or carried over) at the next higher level. In general, a donor's charitable deductions must be accounted for in the following order for income tax purposes:

1. gifts subject to the 50% limitation, up to 50% of the donor's AGI;

2. gifts subject to the 30% limitation, up to the *lesser of*:

   a) 30% of the donor's AGI, *or*

   b) the *excess* of:

      (1) 50% of the donor's AGI *over*

      (2) the amount of the allowable contributions made to 50% organizations.

Caution: Contributions of long-term capital gain property to 50% organizations, which ordinarily would be subject to the 30% limitation, must nevertheless be included in the latter amount.

3. Gifts of long-term capital gain property subject to the 30% limitation, up to the *lesser* of:

   a) 30% of the donor's AGI, *or*

   b) the *excess* of

      (1) 50% of the donor's AGI *over*

      (2) the amount of the allowable contributions made to 50% organizations.

4. Contributions subject to the 20% limitation, up to the *lesser* of

   (a) 20% of the donor's AGI, *or*

   (b) the excess of

      (1) 30% of the donor's AGI *over*

      (2) the amount of contributions subject to the 30% limitation, *or*

Figure 30.1

TYPE OF GIFT:	"50 % CHARITIES"	"30 % CHARITIES"
	Public Charities, Private Operating Foundations, Pass-through Private Foundations, Pooled Fund Private Foundations, Certain Supporting Organizations	Private Non-Operating Foundations ("Family Foundations"), Other Qualified Non-50% type Charities (veteran's associations, fraternal groups)
Cash or cash equivalents	Up to 50% of AGI	Up to 30% of AGI
Ordinary income property or short-term capital gain property	Generally, cost basis up to 50% of AGI	Generally, cost basis up to 30% of AGI
Long-term capital gain property	FMV up to 30% of AGI (Under a special election, the taxpayer may choose to deduct the cost basis up to 50% of AGI.)	Generally, cost basis up to 20% of AGI
"Qualified Stock" (long-term capital gain stock with readily ascertainable market quotes)	Not Applicable	FMV up to 20% of AGI (The stock cannot be more than 10% of the value of the corporation's shares.)
Tangible personal property (held long-term)	Related to the charity's use: FMV up to 30% of AGI (or, the cost basis is deductible up to 50% of AGI) Unrelated to Use: Generally, cost basis up to 50% of AGI	Related or Unrelated to the Charity's Use: Generally, cost basis up to 20% AGI
Gifts "for the use of" the charity instead of "to" the charity (e.g., contribution of remainder interest held in trust for benefit of charity)	Up to 30% of AGI	Up to 30% of AGI
• Life insurance premiums paid directly "to" the charity on policies owned by the charity	Up to 50% of AGI	Up to 30% of AGI
• Life insurance premiums paid "to" the life insurance company, or "for the use of" the charity on a policy owned by the charity	Up to 30% of AGI	Up to 30% of AGI

(c) the excess of:

(1) 30% of the donor's AGI *over*

(2) the amount of contributions of long-term capital gain property to 50% organizations to which the 30% limitation applies, *or*

(d) the excess of:

(1) 50% of the donor's AGI *over*

(2) the total of (a) the amount of contributions subject to the 50% limitation, and (b) the amount of contributions subject to the 30% limitation.

Gifts exceeding these limitations may be carried over for up to five years and deducted then, subject to the limitations on deductions in the carryover years. Table 4 from IRS Publication 526, *Charitable Contributions* can be helpful in determining the amount and order of charitable contributions that are deductible as well as the carryover amount, if any.

CHARITABLE BEQUESTS

A charitable bequest is a donation that is made by will, revocable during the life of the donor, and completed only upon the donor's death. A bequest can be made for:

- a specific amount;
- a specific asset; or
- a percentage of the estate.

For estate tax purposes, the donor's estate generally receives a deduction from the gross estate equal to the amount of the bequest. Since there is no tax limitation on the deductible amount of a charitable bequest for estate tax purposes, the estate may deduct the entire value of the bequest.

Charitable bequests come "off the top" for estate tax purposes. If a decedent has a gross estate of $2,500,000, and makes a charitable bequest of $800,000, his estate tax is based upon a taxable estate of $1,700,000 ($2,500,000 - $800,000 charitable deduction). In addition to reducing the amount subject to estate tax, this may also have the effect of reducing the estate tax even more because the $800,000 charitable bequest saves taxes at the highest marginal estate tax rates.

OTHER CHARITABLE GIVING STRATEGIES

There are many types of more sophisticated strategies that planners can recommend to their clients. These advanced strategies are merely introduced below. Please consult *The Tools & Techniques of Charitable Planning* (National Underwriter Company) for more in-depth information.

Charitable Gift Annuity

A charitable gift annuity is a contract entered into between a charity and a donor in which the charity agrees to pay an annuity to the individual donor in return for an amount transferred by the individual to the charity. The charity receives a current gift while the donor is provided with a predictable income stream for the rest of the donor's life. The donor receives a charitable deduction for the excess of the value of the property transferred over the value of the annuity received in return for the property.

Charitable Remainder Trust

A charitable remainder trust (CRT) is a trust that provides for specified payments to one or more individuals (generally, for life or a term of years not to exceed 20), with an irrevocable remainder in the trust property to be paid to or held for a charity. The donor receives a deduction for transferring property to the trust that is calculated based upon a number of factors, such as how long the charity will have to wait to receive what remains in the trust after payments are made to the noncharitable beneficiary(ies) and the interest rate required to value the interest at the time the trust is created.

A CRT may be in the form of a charitable remainder annuity trust (CRAT) or a charitable remainder unitrust (CRUT). A CRAT is one that pays a specified amount to the individual(s) at annual or more frequent intervals. The annual amount must be at least equal to 5%, but not more than 50%, of the initial value of the property transferred to the trust. The value of the charity's remainder interest must also be at least 10% of the initial value of the property transferred to the trust, determined at the time the gift is made.

A CRUT is one that pays a specified percentage of the value of trust assets (valued annually) to the individual(s) at annual or more frequent intervals. Thus, in a CRUT, the payment fluctuates each year with the value of the trust based on the payout percentage established upon the creation of the trust. The annual payout percentage must be at least equal to 5%, but not more than 50%. The value of the charity's remainder interest must also be at least 10% of the initial value of the property transferred to the trust, determined at the time the gift is made.

Charitable Lead Trust

A charitable lead trust (CLT) is the inverse of a CRT. With a CLT, the donor gives the current economic benefit of the trust to the charity (either an annuity or a unitrust interest) for either a term of years or for one or more lives. When the charity's interest ends, either the donor or another person receives the assets remaining in the trust. The donor receives a charitable deduction for the actuarial value of the lead interest given to charity.

Pooled Income Fund

A pooled income fund (PIF) is created by a charity. The donor transfers property to the fund and the donor or a named beneficiary receives an income interest in the fund for life in the form of shares. At the death of the individual, the charity receives the assets remaining from the shares. The donor receives a charitable deduction for the actuarial value of the remainder interest given to charity.

Private Foundations

A private foundation is a charitable organization established by an individual donor or family who wishes to control, as much as possible, the use of their contributions for charitable purposes. Typically, a private foundation is established with a large donation up front. The foundation then passes out smaller pieces of the funds to public charities. They are commonly referred to as family foundations, since the intention of the donor is to have the family share in the responsibility of choosing which charities will receive donations from the foundation.

Donor Advised Funds

For those individuals who want to make a charitable contribution now but do not want to identify the charity just yet or make the investment in a private foundation, a donor advised fund could be a good solution. With a donor advised fund, the donor enters into a written agreement with a sponsoring charity or brokerage to establish an account to benefit the donor's charitable causes. Over time, the donor requests the sponsoring charity or brokerage to make grants to the donor's chosen charities. The charity or brokerage will usually receive a fee for managing the account and providing services.

TOWARDS A ZERO TAXABLE ESTATE

A common estate tax planning technique that has been popular among the wealthy is the charitable bequest of all or part of their estate upon the last to die of the two spouses. The bequest may be made to one or more charities or to the decedents' private foundation. The charitable bequest is deductible for federal estate tax purposes.

If the clients wish to leave other property to their children to replace the amount going to charity, they might create a wealth replacement trust. The wealth replacement trust could be an irrevocable life insurance trust (ILIT) funded by second-to-die life insurance. When the second of the spouses dies, the insurance is paid to the trust and is paid out to the beneficiaries in accordance with the terms of the trust. Structured properly, the life insurance within the ILIT escapes the federal estate tax.

Therefore, the clients get the amount of property they wanted to get to the children without paying any federal estate tax. In addition, their foundation is funded with a large amount of property that the family can manage after their passing.

Example: John and Jane, husband and wife, are 70 years old. They have $25 million, primarily as a result of selling a business within the last two years. They would like the surviving spouse to have the $25 million for life after the other spouse dies. They would also like to leave $5 million to each of their two children (not wanting to "spoil" them) after both spouses are dead and leave the rest to charity. The $10 million net taxable estate will be severely taxed upon the last of John and Jane's death.

Instead, the planner suggests the creation of a $25 million private foundation, after both John and Jane are dead, for their children to manage. The desired estate for the children will be created by $10 million of second-to-die life insurance on John and Jane's lives held in an irrevocable life insurance trust serving as a wealth replacement trust, at a cost of approximately $20,000 per year. John and Jane will not have a taxable estate upon the last of them to die.

CASE STUDIES

CASE STUDIES
Jason and Andrea Dalton

Personal Data

Husband:	Jason Dalton, age 51, Senior Executive for XYZ, Inc.
Wife:	Andrea Dalton, age 48, Homemaker
Children:	Ashley Dalton, age 14 (starting 9th grade)
	Carl Dalton, age 11 (starting 6th grade)
Jason's parents:	Father deceased, Mother, age 77, in nursing home
Andrea's parents:	Mother, age 68, and Father, age 69, in good health

Financial Data

Primary Residence (JTWROS)	$850,000
Mortgage on Primary Residence	($325,000)
Vacation Home (JTWROS)	$350,000
Mortgage on Vacation Home	($125,000)
Cash Accounts (JTWROS)	$80,000
Jason's 401(k)	$400,000
Jason's IRA	$125,000
Andrea's IRA	$17,000
Investment Brokerage Account (JTWROS)	$375,000
XYZ, Inc. Stock (Jason)	$1,300,000
Single Premium Fixed Deferred Annuity (Jason)	$72,000
Cash Value of Life Insurance	$105,000
Jason's automobile	$25,000
Andrea's automobile	$13,000
Ashley's UTMA account (Jason custodian)	$25,000
Carl's UTMA account (Jason custodian)	$17,000

Income/Expense Data

Jason's Salary	$350,000
XYZ Dividends	$52,000
Other Interest & Investment Income	$12,000
Monthly expenses (excluding mortgage and taxes)	$10,000

Other Pertinent Information

- Jason and Andrea have filed for divorce after 16 years of marriage
- Jason and Andrea do *not* live in a community property state
- Jason's cost basis in XYZ stock is $150,000, which he has accumulated over many years
- The Daltons are in a combined federal & state tax bracket of 41%
- The Daltons state that they are very conservative, and their investment account is primarily (80%) fixed-income investments
- Jason's 401(k) account is also allocated to approximately 80% in fixed-income investments; Jason maximizes his 401(k) contribution every year
- Jason has a universal life policy purchased in 1989 with a death benefit of $500,000; Andrea is the beneficiary

- Jason has group term insurance through XYZ with a death benefit of $1,050,000 (3x salary) that is entirely paid for by XYZ; Andrea is the beneficiary
- Andrea has $250,000 of spousal group term life insurance through XYZ; Jason is the beneficiary
- Jason and Andrea are beneficiaries of each other's retirement accounts
- Andrea is the beneficiary of Jason's annuity (where Jason is the owner and annuitant), which has a cost basis of $55,000
- Jason has disability coverage through his employer, providing 60% of monthly income up to $10,000/month; benefits are payable until 65 after a 90-day elimination period; disability is defined as the inability to perform the substantial duties of your regular occupation
- Jason receives adequate medical insurance coverage through XYZ for the family; the Daltons have adequate homeowner's and automobile coverage
- The primary residence mortgage is a 30-year fixed-rate loan, and was originated 6 years ago at 6.75%
- The vacation home mortgage is a 5/1 ARM loan (payable over 30 years), and was originated 2 years ago at 5.25%
- Contributions of $500/month are being made to each of Ashley's and Carl's UTMA accounts
- In the Daltons' state of residence, minors receive full access to UTMA funds at their age 18
- Jason's mother is utilizing her Social Security and survivorship pension income to cover nursing home costs, and will have very little other assets remaining
- Andrea's parents have nearly $1,000,000 in retirement assets that they are spending minimally, which will ultimately be divided between Andrea and her sister

Goals

1. Resolve divorce proceedings in an equitable manner
2. Provide for college education for Ashley and Carl, assuming $12,500/year (in today's dollars) for four years for each of them

Economic Environment

After coming through a recent recession, current inflation, as measured by the CPI, is at 2.0% (however, college costs are inflating at 6%). 90-day T-bill rates are currently 3%. Long-term government bonds are yielding 5.5%. Economic growth is expected to be 4.5% in the coming year, and unemployment is at 4.5%. Interest rates are expected to rise in the near future.

Questions

1. If the Daltons get divorced tomorrow, and in two years, they transfer 50% of Jason's XYZ Stock to Andrea to equalize the post-divorce property, the gift tax consequences will be:

   a) There will be no gift tax consequences due to the unlimited marital deduction for gifts between spouses
   b) There will be no gift tax consequences because the property was transferred as part of the divorce
   c) There will be a fully taxable gift from Jason to Andrea, and Jason will be required to pay gift taxes
   d) There will be a fully taxable gift from Jason to Andrea, but Jason can utilize a portion of his gift tax credit to offset any taxes due

2. The divorce decree states that Jason will be required to pay $5,000/month of alimony to Andrea for 10 years. The tax consequences of the alimony payments are:

   a) Not taxable or deductible by either party
   b) Taxable income to Andrea, not deductible for Jason because alimony is a personal expense
   c) Taxable income to Andrea, and deductible for Jason
   d) Not taxable income to Andrea, but deductible for Jason

3. The divorce decree states that Jason will be required to pay $2,500/month to Andrea for child support until Ashley turns 18 and $1,500/month thereafter until Carl turns 18. The tax consequences of the child support payments are:

   a) Not taxable or deductible by either party
   b) Taxable income to Andrea, not deductible for Jason because child support is a personal expense
   c) Taxable income to Andrea, and deductible for Jason
   d) Not taxable income to Andrea, but deductible for Jason

4. Andrea's divorce attorney stresses the importance of obtaining a Qualified Domestic Relations Order (QDRO) as a part of the divorce proceeds. This is necessary in order to provide for Andrea's share of:

   a) All of Jason's assets
   b) Jason's 401(k) account
   c) Jason's IRA account
   d) Both B and C are true

5. If Andrea's parents were to be killed in a car accident tomorrow, and the divorce is still pending, how would Andrea's inheritance be treated for purposes of the divorce?

   a) Andrea will have to split the assets evenly with Jason, since they were inherited before the divorce was completed
   b) Andrea will not have to split the assets with Jason as long as she retains them in an account titled solely in her name
   c) Andrea would never have to split the assets with Jason, because she inherited them in the first place
   d) Andrea will have to split the assets evenly with Jason, since she did not sign a pre-nuptial agreement to protect them

6. How does the Dalton portfolio compare to their specified risk tolerance? The risk of the Dalton portfolio appears to be:

   a) Consistent with their risk tolerance
   b) Lower than their risk tolerance
   c) Much higher than their risk tolerance
   d) Unable to be determined with the information provided

7. If the cost of college for Ashley is $15,000/year today, how much will a year of college cost her when she matriculates if school expenses are inflating at 6% (to the nearest dollar)?

   a) $18,600
   b) $18,937
   c) $16,883
   d) $17,842

8. If the cost of college for Carl is $15,000/year today, how much will a year of college cost him when he matriculates if school expenses inflate at 6% for the next four years, and then at 5% for the remaining time period (to the nearest dollar)?

   a) $22,554
   b) $21,922
   c) $23,018
   d) $20,878

9. Carl's total taxable income for 2007 was generated solely from his UTMA account, which created $1,400 of interest. Carl's total federal income tax due for 2007 was approximately:

   a) $0
   b) $55
   c) $140
   d) $490

10. Jason decides to invest Ashley's UTMA account assets in a 529 college savings plan. In this situation, when Ashley turns 18:

    a) She will take over full control of the account, because she has reached the age of majority for the UTMA account
    b) Jason will retain control over the account, because he was established as the owner of the 529 plan account
    c) She will be required to immediately recognize all unrealized gains in the account
    d) Both a and c are true

11. The Daltons have decided to send Ashley to a private high school, and need to use $20,000 of their assets to pay the current tuition bill. The tax consequences of taking a $20,000 withdrawal from Jason's annuity for this education expense are:

    a) Recognition of $20,000 of ordinary income, but there is no early withdrawal penalty because this is a qualified education expense
    b) Recognition of $20,000 of ordinary income, and a 10% early withdrawal penalty
    c) Recognition of $17,000 of ordinary income, and a 10% early withdrawal penalty
    d) No recognition of income at all, because this is a qualified education expense

12. If Jason decides to liquidate Ashley's UTMA account now to pay for her private high school expenses, the tax consequences of this sale will be:

    a) Entirely reportable on Jason's tax return, since he is the custodian
    b) Entirely reportable on Ashley's tax return, since the UTMA is for her benefit
    c) Generally, subject to Jason's marginal tax rate because Ashley is a minor
    d) Both b and c

13. The Daltons recently remembered that Ashley's grandmother purchased savings bonds in Ashley's name when she was born, for use for her future college expenses. The tax consequences of the liquidation of these bonds for Ashley's future school expenses will be that they are:

    a) Excluded from income, no matter what, under the bond interest exclusion rules
    b) Included in income, because Jason and Andrea's AGI (adjusted gross income) is so high that they do not qualify for the bond interest exclusion rules
    c) Included in income, because the bonds are titled in Ashley's name, making them ineligible for the bond interest exclusion rules
    d) Excluded from income, as long as Andrea's income in that year remains below the AGI limits

14. If you were to draft a Personal Financial Statement for the Dalton family, the total value of the Jason and Andrea's assets would be:

    a) $3,712,000
    b) $3,754,000
    c) $3,304,000
    d) $3,262,000

15. Jason's maximum 401(k) contribution for 2007 is:

    a) $13,000
    b) $14,000
    c) $16,000
    d) $20,500

16. The Daltons have decided to replace Andrea's automobile with a new vehicle that will cost $30,000 after the trade-in of Andrea's current car. The dealer offers them a choice of 0% financing costs for three years with a balloon payment at the end of three years, or $4,000 off if they make a lump-sum payment now. Any available cash or savings that the Daltons have from these choices will be invested in a 3-year CD at the bank at 4.25%. The Daltons should choose to:

    a) Make a lump-sum payment now at the discounted price, because this way they will have the most savings after 3 years
    b) Select the 3-year 0% financing deal, because this way they will have the most savings after 3 years
    c) Consider the 3-year 0% financing deal with an alternative investment, because of the current interest rate environment
    d) Both a and c are true

17. The Daltons plan to purchase an automobile for Ashley as her future graduation present from high school to head off to college. The car they would like to purchase costs $25,000 today, and they expect its cost will increase at 3% per year. In addition, they can purchase a four-year CD at 4.5%. How much do the Daltons need to set aside in the CD now to have the appropriate dollar amount available to purchase the car in four years (to the nearest dollar)?

    a) $20,964
    b) $22,212
    c) $23,555
    d) $23,595

18. If Jason were to become disabled, his disability insurable benefits would be:

    a) Tax-free
    b) Taxable as ordinary income
    c) Partially taxable and partially tax-free
    d) Unable to be determined from the information provided

19. Assume for this question that the Daltons do not intend to get divorced. The Daltons have stated that they intend to keep their vacation home until retirement, and to make it their permanent residence once they retire. The Daltons have also stated that they are comfortable using a mortgage as 'leverage' to help grow their overall net worth, but would like to be debt-free when they retire in approximately 10 years, even if that means paying off their outstanding balance in a lump sum at that time. In light of this, the Daltons should:

    a) Refinance their mortgage to a 30-year fixed-rate loan
    b) Maintain their current mortgage as is

c) Refinance their mortgage to a 10/1 ARM
d) Pay off their mortgage immediately

20. The Daltons come to visit you for a preliminary free consultation to decide if they would like to hire you as a financial planner. At this meeting, you mention how risky it is to hold such a substantial portion of your net worth in a single stock, although you acknowledged that you did not have any knowledge about this company in particular. Two days after the meeting, Jason contacts you to inform you that he has liquidated all of his company stock, "as you advised." Under the CFP® Code of Ethics, you should:

    a) Not be concerned, because diversifying is always good advice
    b) Not be concerned, because it was only a preliminary consultation and you did not have a signed planning agreement
    c) Be very concerned, because the client may no longer need your services, since he has already received quality investment advice
    d) Be very concerned, because the client acted on advice you gave when you did not have all of the available information

Phillip and Marsha Sanders

Personal Data

Husband:	Phillip Sanders, age 44, disabled
Wife:	Marsha Sanders, age 44, grade-school teacher
Children:	Darlene Sanders, age 17 (starting 12th grade)
	Fred Sanders, age 21 (starting junior year of college)
Phillip's parents:	Both deceased
Marsha's parents:	Mother, age 68, living with Phillip & Marsha, in good health; Father, deceased.

Financial Data

Primary Residence (JTWROS)	$450,000
Mortgage on primary residence	($175,000)
Cash accounts (JTWROS)	$22,000
Phillip's 401(k)	$125,000
Phillip's traditional IRA (no nondeductible contributions)	$105,000
Marsha's 403(b)	$65,000
Mutual fund account (JTWROS)	$44,000
Cash value of life insurance	$2,000
Marsha's automobile	$9,000
Fred's UTMA account (Phillip custodian)	$8,000
Darlene's 529 college savings plan (Phillip owner)	$27,000

Income/Expense Data

Phillip's monthly disability income	$4,000
Marsha's annual salary	$38,000
Interest & investment income	$2,700
Monthly expenses (excluding mortgage and taxes)	$4,500

Other Pertinent Information

- Phillip was in a severe car accident 4 months ago, he has been released back to his home, but is unable to return to his former work as a middle manager for a local firm and is totally disabled
- Phillip has a medical malpractice suit pending against the hospital that treated him; the suit is expected to be settled out of court shortly for $1,250,000
- Phillip and Marsha do *not* live in a community property state
- Phillip and Marsha have simple wills that leave all of their property to the surviving spouse; Phillip and Marsha have power of attorney and health care power of attorney documents that name each other as attorney-in-fact
- The Sanders are in a combined federal & state tax bracket of 20% since the loss of Phillip's income (formerly $80,000/year)
- The Sanders state that they are moderately conservative, and their investment account is primarily (60%) equity investments

- Phillip's 401(k) account is associated with his former employer before he left his job due to the accident
- Marsha's currently contributes $500/month to her 403(b)
- Darlene's 529 plan was originally funded with a $6,000 deposit two years ago.
- Phillip recently acquired a universal life policy last year with a death benefit of $100,000; Marsha is the beneficiary
- Phillip has a term insurance policy with a death benefit of $500,000; Marsha is the beneficiary
- Marsha has a term insurance policy with a death benefit of $300,000; Phillip is the beneficiary
- Phillip and Marsha are beneficiaries of each other's retirement accounts
- Phillip pays for his own disability insurance policy that provides 60% of his former income of $80,000; the policy has a 90-day elimination period and provides benefits until age 65; the policy provides benefits for two years if Phillip is unable to perform the duties of his regular occupation, and after two years provides benefits only if Phillip is unable to perform any occupation that he is reasonably qualified for by education, training, or experience
- Marsha has no disability insurance
- Phillip and Marsha receive adequate medical insurance coverage for the family through Marsha's employment; the Sanders have adequate homeowner's and automobile coverage
- The primary residence mortgage is a 30-year fixed-rate loan, and was refinanced 3 years ago at a 6.25% rate
- Marsha's mother has come to live with the family since Phillip's accident, and her Social Security income generally covers her own expenses; she has little other assets, aside from a $200,000 residence of her own

Goals

1. Manage family finances in the coming months as Phillip's health declines
2. Provide for college education for Darlene and Fred, assuming $15,000/year (in today's dollars) (four years for Darlene, two more years of payments for Fred)

Economic Environment

The economy has been growing strong for several years. Current inflation, as measured by the CPI, is at 3.3% (however, college costs are inflating at 7%). 90-day T-bill rates and money markets are currently 5%. Long-term government bonds are yielding 7.5%. Economic growth was 5.0% last year, and unemployment is at 4.5%. Interest rates are expected to be flat or rising slightly in the near future. Economic growth is expected to slow slightly in the coming years.

Questions

1. If you were to draft a Personal Financial Statement for the Sanders family, the total value of the Phillip and Marsha's assets would be:

   a) $856,000
   b) $822,000
   c) $681,000
   d) $647,000

2. With the settlement of Phillip's lawsuit, some potential tax consequences that Phillip might be concerned about include:

   a) Income tax treatment of the settlement
   b) Deductibility of the fees Phillip will pay to his lawyer
   c) Whether to request the payment in trust or under a structured settlement, rather than outright
   d) All of the above

3. Which of the following education tax benefits is Fred NOT potentially eligible for this year:

   a) Hope Scholarship Credit
   b) Lifetime Learning Credit
   c) Above-the-line Education Deduction
   d) Fred may be potentially eligible for any of the above

4. For financial aid purposes, is there a difference between the treatment of Fred's UTMA account and Darlene's 529 college savings plan?

   a) No, they are both treated as assets of the parents for financial aid calculations
   b) Yes, the UTMA account is an asset of the parents, but the 529 plan is an asset of the child
   c) Yes, the 529 account is an asset of the parents, but the UTMA account is an asset of the child
   d) No, they are both treated as assets of the children for financial aid calculations

5. It has just recently come to Fred's attention that he has a UTMA account in his name. He has decided that he wants to use the funds to buy a new car, despite the fact that Phillip and Marsha intended to use the money for his college expenses. Fred may:

   a) Use the funds however he likes because he is 21
   b) Only use the funds for college, because he is still a college student
   c) Only use the funds for college, because his parents can control the money that they contributed to the account
   d) Use the funds however he likes, once he graduates from college

6. What are the tax consequences of the earnings portion of a withdrawal from Darlene's 529 plan to pay for expenses for Phillip, given that he is both disabled and the owner of the 529 plan?

   a) Tax-free and penalty-free
   b) Tax-free, but subject to a penalty
   c) Taxable, but penalty-free
   d) Taxable and subject to a penalty

7. The Sanders would like to take a withdrawal from Darlene's 529 account to pay for a computer that she will use for school. The tax consequences of the earnings portion of this withdrawal are:

   a) Fully taxable, and no penalties will apply because the funds are being used for a school-related expense
   b) Fully taxable, but a 10% penalty will apply
   c) Fully tax-free, but a 10% penalty will apply
   d) Fully tax-free, and no penalties will apply because the funds are being used for a school-related expense

8. If the Sanders want to improve their ability to qualify for financial aid, which of the following strategies might be appropriate?

   a) Liquidate the mutual fund account to pay down part of the mortgage
   b) Take a withdrawal from Phillip's IRA to pay down part of the mortgage
   c) Both a and b
   d) Neither a nor b

9. Darlene plans to attend a college that costs $15,000/year in today's dollars (payable in a single payment at the start of each school year), with expenses inflating at 6%. How much will Darlene's total college expenditures amount to by the time she graduates (to the nearest dollar)?

   a) $65,619
   b) $69,556
   c) $73,730
   d) $89,630

10. The Sanders owe a semester tuition payment for Fred right now, and another two payments every six months after that – a total of three payments, at $9,000 each. If the Sanders keep Fred's tuition funds invested in a money market (and rates stay level), how much will the Sanders need in the account to cover all of the payments (to the nearest dollar)?

    a) $24,509
    b) $25,704
    c) $26,347
    d) $27,000

11. If the Sanders refinance their mortgage for a 5/1 ARM 30-year loan at 6.25%, and have closing costs of $4,000 which are also refinanced, the monthly total principal and interest payments on the new mortgage will initially be (to the nearest dollar):

    a) $1,078
    b) $1,088
    c) $1,102
    d) $1,113

12. Phillip and Marsha provide $500 to help cover the cost of Marsha's mother's prescription drugs. The tax consequences of these payments for Phillip and Marsha are:

    a) Not deductible, since the payments are not for Phillip or Marsha or their children
    b) Not deductible, because Marsha's mother pays more than half of her own expenses and is not a dependent
    c) Fully deductible as medical expenses, once Phillip has reached the 7.5% threshold for medical expense deductions
    d) Fully deductible as an above-the-line prescription drug deduction for parents

13. Marsha's mother is considering a sale of her residence to live permanently with Phillip and Marsha, after owning and living in the house for the past 20 years until she moved in with the family last month. The house has a cost basis of $50,000. The tax consequences of this sale will be:

    a) $150,000 of long-term capital gains
    b) Tax-deferred as long as she purchases another piece of real estate of equal or greater value
    c) Tax-free, because the sale was necessitated by Phillip's disability
    d) Tax-free, because Marsha's mother has owned and lived in the house for the past two years

14. Phillip would like to move his 401(k) funds to an IRA, since he does not plan to return to work at his employer. He has requested a full distribution of his 401(k) account balance to be sent to him by check. The tax consequences of this distribution are:

    a) Fully tax-free, because Phillip is disabled
    b) Fully tax-deferred and not subject to withholding, because Phillip intends to roll over the proceeds to an IRA within 60 days

c) Fully tax-deferred, but subject to 20% withholding; Phillip will need to make up the 20% to the IRA within 60 days
d) Fully taxable no matter what, because Phillip did not execute this transaction as a trustee-to-trustee transfer

15. Phillip would like to take a withdrawal from his IRA, and would like to know the tax consequences of this transaction.

    a) The withdrawal will be entirely tax-free, because Phillip is disabled
    b) The withdrawal will be entirely taxable, but there will be no early withdrawal penalty because Phillip is disabled
    c) The withdrawal will be entirely taxable, and there will be an early withdrawal penalty because Phillip is not 59½
    d) The withdrawal is not allowed, because Phillip is not 59½

16. Phillip and Marsha want to establish a home equity line of credit to help handle some of the current expenses. The tax consequences of borrowing $50,000 against their house for personal expenses are:

    a) Interest will be fully deductible as mortgage interest, regardless of whether the Sanders are subject to AMT
    b) Interest will be fully deductible for regular tax purposes, but will not be deductible if the Sanders are subject to AMT
    c) Interest will not be deductible, because the Sanders did not borrow the money to acquire or improve their residence
    d) Interest will not be deductible, because borrowing for personal expenses is never deductible

17. If Phillip's health improves to the point where he could get another job in two years for similar pay, even if his health does not allow him to return to his old job, then his disability benefits will:

    a) Cease because he is qualified to obtain such a job
    b) Continue as long as he does not actually get hired for a new job
    c) Cease regardless of his qualifications, because the 2-year payout period has elapsed
    d) Continue because he is not yet age 65

18. The tax treatment of disability insurable benefits from Phillip's disability policy will be:

    a) Tax-free
    b) Taxable as ordinary income
    c) Partially taxable and partially tax-free
    d) Unable to be determined from the information provided

19. Assume that Phillip has recovered to the point where he could probably work part-time at his old office doing some basic work, making approximately 30% of his old income. However, he would prefer not to work at all, and would like to apply for Social Security benefits instead. Is this a reasonable plan of action for Phillips?

    a) No, because Social Security disability benefits are available only if the individual is totally disabled, and Phillip is able to work
    b) No, because Phillip's private disability benefits will make him ineligible for Social Security disability benefits
    c) Yes, because Phillip's private disability and Social Security disability benefits still leave him earning less than his original income
    d) Yes, Phillip can receive Social Security disability benefits as long as he is not actually working again

20. Phillip has actually been feeling remarkably better over the past few weeks, and secretly believes that he could return to work full time right now without too much difficulty. However, his doctor is a personal friend who will continue to certify that Phillip is disabled, and may have been doing so (improperly) already for the past month or two. You should advise Phillip that:

    a) Until the insurance company stops him, he should continue to make claims, because his family really needs the money
    b) His "malingering" behavior is unethical, but is not illegal
    c) If his doctor will certify total disability, he should try to obtain Social Security disability benefits as well
    d) If the insurance company finds out, they will stop his future payments, and may attempt to recover the payments already made as well

James Wilson and Harold Newton

Personal Data

Client 1:	James Wilson, age 37, computer programmer
Client 2:	Harold Newton, age 39, small business owner
Children:	None
James' parents:	Mother, age 62, father, age 61, in good health
Harold's parents:	Mother, age 59, father, age 64, in good health

Financial Data

Primary Residence (Harold)	$300,000
Mortgage on Primary Residence	($155,000)
Bank Checking Account (James)	$7,000
Bank Checking Account (Harold)	$12,000
James' 401(k)	$41,000
Harold's SEP-IRA	$148,000
Trust FBO Harold	$625,000
Mutual fund account (Harold)	$114,000
Harold's automobile	$38,000
James' automobile	$7,000
Jame's credit card	($5,000)

Income/Expense Data

Harold's self-employment income	$235,000
James' income	$62,000
Harold's investment income	$17,000
James' investment income	$200
Joint monthly expenses (excluding mortgage and taxes)	$10,000

Other Pertinent Information

- Harold and James are a same-sex couple and have been together for 7 years; they both live in the house that Harold owns
- Harold has inherited money in a trust from his mother that is intended to be a generation-skipping trust; the trust allows for distributions for health, education, maintenance, or support; most years, Harold has not taken withdrawals from this account; the trust reverts back to Harold's brother at his death if he has no children
- Harold has a will that leaves everything to his parents; Harold has a power-of-attorney and health care power-of-attorney that names his father as attorney-in-fact
- James has no estate documents
- Harold runs a successful consulting practice out of his home
- Harold states that he is fairly aggressive, and his investment account is almost entirely (90%) equity investments
- James contributes $3,000/year to his 401(k), just enough to earn the matching contribution offered by his employer

- Harold contributes $20,000/year to his SEP-IRA
- James and Harold live a fairly extravagant lifestyle of dining out and vacations, funded primarily from Harold's income and assets. However, James still provides the primary support for his basic living needs.
- Neither James nor Harold have any life or disability insurance
- James is the beneficiary of Harold's SEP-IRA
- James' sister is the beneficiary of his 401(k)
- The primary residence mortgage is a 5/1 ARM 30-year loan, and was taken out exactly 2 years ago (Harold has made 24 payments) at a rate of 7.25%
- James is currently paying a 16.99% annual interest rate on his credit card debt

Goals

1. Save for retirement
2. Provide for each other in the event of death

Economic Environment

The economy has been growing strong after rebounding from a recession two years ago. Current inflation, as measured by the CPI, is at 2.9%. 90-day T-bill rates are currently 4.5%. Long-term government bonds are yielding 5.5%. Economic growth was 5.5% last year, and unemployment is at 4.7%. Interest rates are expected to be flat in the near future. Economic growth is expected to slow in the coming years.

Questions

1. Harold has stated that he would like to maximize his retirement contributions while maintaining substantial flexibility in the years that he makes contributions. He anticipates that he will be able to save anywhere from approximately $10,000 to $50,000 per year. Which of the following retirement plans will allow Harold to make the largest total pre-tax contributions?

   a) SEP-IRA
   b) Individual 401(k)
   c) Profit-Sharing Plan
   d) All of the above will have an equivalent maximum contribution with Harold's current income

2. What is the total value of James' assets?

   a) $55,000
   b) $50,000
   c) $48,000
   d) $14,000

3. What filing status can James and Harold use for federal income tax purposes?

   a) Joint, because they have been domestic partners for 7 years
   b) Joint filing separately, because James and Harold are not legally married but are a committed couple
   c) Single (filed separately for each), because James and Harold are not legally married
   d) Head of household (for Harold), because Harold is the primary earner of the household

4. Harold is very concerned he may be subject to alternative minimum tax (AMT). Which of the following strategies are appropriate to recommend to Harold to minimize the likelihood of an AMT liability?

   a) Stop paying state income taxes, because they are an AMT adjustment item
   b) Maximize Harold's home office deductions such as real estate taxes on his Schedule C (to the extent allowable), rather than as itemized deductions on his Schedule A
   c) Avoid purchasing all municipal bonds
   d) All of the above

5. James would like to make payments to Harold to assist with the mortgage, since James has been living in the house with Harold for many years. What are the tax consequences of these payments?

   a) Harold must recognize the payments as rental income
   b) James may deduct a portion of the mortgage interest on his tax return
   c) Both A and B are correct
   d) Neither A nor B are correct

6. If Harold were incapacitated tomorrow, which of the following is true based upon the current situation?

   a) James may legally make medical decisions for Harold, because they have been a domestic couple for 7 years
   b) James may legally manage the financial and administrative affairs for Harold, because they have been a domestic couple for 7 years
   c) Both A and B are true
   d) Neither A nor B are true

7. Harold is very concerned about the reliability of James' automobile, and would like to purchase a new vehicle for James for his birthday in 2007. When James' birthday comes, the couple purchases a vehicle for $25,000 (using Harold's money), and title the car in James' name. Are there any gift tax consequences to this car purchase?

   a) No, the transaction is totally exempt from gift tax
   b) No, because couples that make gifts to each other receive an offsetting deduction, with the result that no gift taxes are due
   c) Yes, Harold will have to recognize at least a $13,000 gift to James, using a small portion of Harold's lifetime gift tax exemption
   d) Yes, Harold will have to recognize at least a $25,000 gift to James, using a small portion of Harold's lifetime gift tax exemption

8. James is concerned about his level of credit card debt, and would like to discuss options to manage this debt. Which of the following strategies might potentially be an appropriate option for James?

   a) Use the cash in the bank account to pay off the credit card debt, and then utilize the credit card as an emergency if he needs cash for a future purchase
   b) Take a loan distribution from the 401(k) to pay off the credit card debt at a favorable rate
   c) Reduce expenses to increase cash flow payments and accelerate the pay-off of the credit card debt
   d) All of the above

9. If James were to pass away in his current situation, his bank account would pass to:

   a) Harold, because they have lived together for 7 years
   b) The state intestacy fund
   c) His living family members, according to the specifications of state law
   d) None of the above

10. James is considering the establishment of a personal computer consulting business out of the home that he shares with Harold. If James sets up a home office, he will be able to deduct:

    a) A portion of real estate taxes as a home office business deduction
    b) His health insurance premiums
    c) A portion of the monthly mortgage payments for the house
    d) All of the above

11. If James were to pass away today, his 401(k) account would be distributed to:

    a) Harold
    b) His sister
    c) It would depend on his state intestacy statute, because James does not have a will
    d) None of the above

12. If James were to become ill, and Harold paid his medical expenses, which of the following is true regarding the tax treatment of Harold's payments?

    a) They are deductible as an above-the-line health expense, because Harold is self-employed
    b) They are deductible as an itemized medical expense deduction subject to a 7.5%-of-AGI floor
    c) Either A or B may apply
    d) Neither A nor B may apply

13. Harold is considering a refinance of his current mortgage, to a 15-year loan at an annual interest rate of 6.25%, rather than his current rate of 7.25%. The total refinance costs are approximately $2,000, and will be capitalized into the new loan balance. The monthly payment of Harold's new mortgage will be (to the nearest dollar):

    a) $1,329
    b) $1,346
    c) 1,415
    d) 1,433

14. If Harold passes away without having any children and the trust balance is distributed outright to his brother, for generation-skipping tax purposes this payment will be considered a:

    a) Direct skip
    b) Taxable distribution
    c) Taxable termination
    d) None of the above

15. What was the original balance of Harold's mortgage (to the nearest thousand)?

    a) $158,000
    b) $160,000
    c) $165,000
    d) None of the above

16. If Harold manages to earn an average annual rate of 9.5% on his SEP-IRA (compounded semi-annually) over the next 21 years, his estimated balance will have grown to (rounded to the nearest thousand):

    a) $995,000
    b) $1,039,000
    c) $6,694,000
    d) None of the above

17. If James chooses to make a monthly payment of $125 on his credit card, instead of the minimum monthly payment of $100, approximately how much faster will he pay off his current credit card balance?

    a) 12 months
    b) 28 months
    c) 32 months
    d) 60 months

18. If Harold manages to earn an average annual rate of 9.5% on his SEP-IRA (compounded annually) over the next 26 years, and continues to make annual contributions of $20,000/year, his estimated balance will have grown to (rounded to the nearest thousand):

    a) $1,567,000
    b) $2,018,000
    c) $3,585,000
    d) None of the above

19. Harold is considering the purchase of a life insurance policy to provide for James in the event that Harold passes away. If Harold were to purchase and own a life insurance policy for $2,000,000 with James as the beneficiary, the potential tax consequences if Harold died in 2007 would be:

    a) A payment of estate taxes on Harold's estate
    b) Taxable income to James for the entire $2,000,000 death benefit
    c) Both A and B are true
    d) Neither A nor B are true

20. James' parents pass away unexpectedly, and leave him a house that they had owned and lived in for more than 30 years. If James sells the house in 10 months, the $50,000 of capital gains on the house over that 10-month period will be:

    a) Taxed as a short-term capital gain, because the house has been held less than one year since the date of death
    b) Taxed as a long-term capital gain, because the house was inherited
    c) Excluded from income, because James' parents owned and lived in the house for at least two of the past five years
    d) None of the above

Janice Peterson

Personal Data

Client:	Janice Peterson, age 49, Accountant
Children:	Carolyn, age 14
Janice's parents:	Mother, age 70, terminally ill; father, deceased

Financial Data

Primary residence (Janice)	$250,000
Mortgage on primary residence	($205,000)
Cash account (Janice)	$6,000
Cash account (Mother)	$1,000
Janice's 401(k)	$153,000
Janice's investment account	$72,000
Janice's automobile	$4,000
Janice's credit card	($13,000)

Income/Expense Data

Janice's income	$135,000
Janice's investment income	$3,500
Family monthly expenses (excluding mortgage and taxes)	$6,000

Other Pertinent Information

- Janice has been a widow for eleven years
- Janice's mother is in a nursing home and is terminally ill, and is expected to live only 2-4 months; she has no remaining assets besides her small bank account, and is currently on Medicaid
- Janice owns a $350,000 term life insurance policy on her mother (it was given to Janice six years ago), and has named herself as beneficiary
- Janice has a will that leaves everything outright to Carolyn, and a power-of-attorney and health care power-of-attorney that names her mother as attorney-in-fact
- Janice's mother has a will that leaves everything to Janice, and a power-of-attorney and health care power-of-attorney that names Janice as attorney-in-fact with no successor
- Janice states that she is extremely conservative, and her investment account is almost entirely (80%) fixed-income investments
- Janice contributes $13,000/year to her 401(k)
- Carolyn is the beneficiary of Janice's 401(k)
- Janice has a $500,000 20-year term life insurance policy that was taken out three years ago; Carolyn is the beneficiary
- Janice has a disability insurance policy paid for by her employer that provides 60% of her income up to $7,000/month; the policy has a 90-day elimination period and provides benefits until age 65; the policy provides benefits if Janice is unable to perform the duties of any occupation for which she is reasonably qualified by education, training, and experience

- The primary residence mortgage is a 3/1 ARM 30-year loan, and was taken out 1 year ago at 4.25%; $75,000 of these proceeds were part of a cash-out refinance that was spent on high quality medical treatment for her mother last year while Janice was fully supporting her mother

- Janice is currently paying an 18.99% annual interest rate on her credit card debt

Goals

1. Provide an adequate quality of life for Janice's mother in her final months

2. Begin developing a college fund for Carolyn

3. Begin planning for future retirement

Economic Environment

The economy has been growing steadily for several years. Current inflation, as measured by the CPI, is at 3.1%. 90-day T-bill/money market rates are currently 4.5%. Long-term government bonds are yielding 6.5%. Economic growth was 3.5% last year, and unemployment is at 4.5%. Interest rates are expected to be flat in the near future. Economic growth is expected to continue to be steady in the coming years.

Questions

1. What is the regular tax treatment of the $75,000 of payments for Janice's mother's medical expenses last year?

   a) Deductible as medical expenses subject to a 7.5%-of-AGI floor on Janice's tax return
   b) Deductible as medical expenses subject to a 10%-of-AGI floor on Janice's tax return
   c) Deductible as medical expenses subject to a 7.5%-of-AGI floor on Janice's mother's tax return
   d) Not deductible at all because Janice's mother did not pay for her own coverage

2. If you were to draft a Personal Financial Statement for Janice, the total value of Janice's assets would be:

   a) $486,000
   b) $485,000
   c) $268,000
   d) $267,000

3. What are the potential concerns of Janice's current estate distribution plan?

   a) Property will be distributed outright to a minor who cannot legally manage assets
   b) Carolyn may not be responsible enough yet to make good spending decisions with such a large amount of assets
   c) Both of the above are issues for concern
   d) None of the above are issues for concern

4. Janice's mother has accumulated substantial expenses under the Medicaid system. When Janice's mother passes away, the state will:

   a) Place a lien against Janice's house to recover Medicaid expenses
   b) Demand payment for Janice's mother's Medicaid costs against the life insurance proceeds
   c) Deny burial rights until Janice's mother's outstanding bills are paid
   d) None of the above

5. When Janice's mother passes away, the tax consequences of the life insurance policy she owns on her mother will be:

   a) $350,000 of income must be recognized by Janice that will be subject to income taxation
   b) The $350,000 death benefit must be included in Janice's mother's estate, where it will be potentially subject to estate taxation
   c) The $350,000 death benefit will be considered a gift from Janice's mother to Janice, and will be potentially subject to gift taxation
   d) None of the above

6. If Janice were to name Carolyn as the beneficiary of the life insurance policy on her mother, and then her mother passed away, the tax consequences would be:

   a) Janice would be subject to gift taxation for a gift to her daughter
   b) Janice's mother would be subject to gift taxation for a gift to her daughter
   c) Janice's mother would be subject to generation-skipping taxes for a gift to her granddaughter
   d) None of the above

7. Janice's 401(k) contribution limit in 2007 is:

   a) $14,000
   b) $15,000
   c) $18,000
   d) $20,500

8. If Janice were to become disabled tomorrow, the benefits of her policy would be:

   a) Fully taxable when paid to Janice
   b) Partially taxable when paid to Janice
   c) Not taxable when paid to Janice
   d) Unable to be determined from the information provided

9. If Janice's minimum monthly payment is $400, then how long will it take to pay off her credit card by making only the minimum monthly payments?

   a) 36 months
   b) 40 months
   c) 46 months
   d) 58 months

10. If Janice has made exactly 12 monthly payments thus far on her current mortgage, then what was the original balance on her mortgage (to the nearest thousand)?

    a) $207,000
    b) $209,000
    c) $210,000
    d) $212,000

11. What is the tax treatment of the interest that Janice pays on the $75,000 of cash-out refinancing?

    a) Fully deductible mortgage debt
    b) Fully deductible mortgage debt, but non-deductible for alternative minimum tax (AMT) purposes
    c) Fully deductible because the proceeds were used for qualified medical purposes
    d) Non-deductible

12. If a financial planner is reviewing Janice's estate documents, items to be concerned about include whether a:

    a) Guardian is named for Carolyn
    b) Successor attorney-in-fact is named after Janice's mother
    c) Personal representative has been named
    d) All of the above

13. Janice would like to begin setting aside money to purchase a car for Carolyn in two years. If Janice is prepared to set aside monthly payments to save $5,000 over the next 24 months, and will be investing these funds in a money market, then she should save (to the nearest dollar):

    a) $195
    b) $199
    c) $202
    d) $208

14. If Carolyn will attend school four years from now, college costs are inflating at 6%, and the current cost of in-state college tuition is $10,000, then the cost of Carolyn's first year of college will be (to the nearest dollar):

    a) $11,800
    b) $11,910
    c) $12,400
    d) $12,625

15. Janice plans to set aside a portion of the proceeds from her mother's life insurance policy for Carolyn's college education, and wants to know how she should save these funds. Janice wants to maximize control over the funds and would like to minimize taxes. Janice plans to contribute $50,000. Consequently, Janice should deposit the funds into a/an:

    a) Taxable account in her own name, ear-marked for Carolyn's education
    b) UTMA account for Carolyn's benefit
    c) 529 college savings plan
    d) Coverdell (Education) Savings account

16. Potential risks for Janice under her current investment strategy for retirement may include:

    a) Inflation/purchasing-power risk
    b) Interest rate risk
    c) Both A and B are true
    d) Neither A nor B are true

17. Strategies for Janice to improve her future ability to retire include:

    a) Reduce monthly spending to allow more cash flow for savings
    b) Pay off high-interest credit card debt as soon as possible
    c) Seek out opportunities to increase income without increasing expenses
    d) All of the above are true

18. If Janice were to deposit $10,000 into an UTMA account in Carolyn's name, the $450 of interest income (in 2007, assuming Carolyn has no other income) would be:

    a) Not subject to tax
    b) Taxed at Carolyn's tax bracket/rates
    c) Taxed at Janice's tax bracket/rates
    d) Taxed at a flat 15% rate

19. Janice is considering the possibility of going into business for herself as a self-employed accountant. If Janice becomes self-employed, she will be able to deduct which of the following business expenses?

    a) One-half of her self-employment taxes
    b) 100% of her medical insurance
    c) Both A and B are deductible
    d) Neither A nor B are deductible

20. Janice has come to you as a financial planner and requested a financial plan. In determining how you should be compensated for this service, with a focus on professional ethics, you should:

    a) Not charge Janice, since she has credit card debt
    b) Only charge Janice a fee, because your recommendations are not valid if you receive a commission
    c) Be paid via commission, because Janice cannot afford to pay a fee
    d) Charge in any way that is fully disclosed, agreed upon by Janice, and is reasonable in relation to the services that you provide

Tom and Sharon Brown

Tom and Sharon Brown are *not* happy with their current investment advisor. They are seeking investment management and financial advisory services from someone they can trust.

You are a registered investment advisor in your home state of Kansas. You have been in business for seven years and work with a select group of 70 clients. You offer financial and investment planning advice for either a percentage of assets under management or hourly fees.

During the initial meeting with the Browns, you gather the following financial information:

Personal Data & Background Information

Primary Contact: Tom Brown
Age: 53
Occupation/Title: Operations Management / VP of Operations

Secondary Contact: Sharon Brown
Age: 56
Occupation: Home Maker

Children: Tom does not have any children of his own. Sharon has three children in college from her previous marriage; Maggie, 18; Shelby, 20; Candy, 22.

Marital Status: Comfortably married for eight years.

Relevant Financial Information

- The Brown's estimated net worth is $3 million. The majority of their financial wealth is allocated among Individual Retirement Accounts, Tom's 401(k) plan, and a taxable investment account.
- Sharon was widowed in her first marriage and the majority of the savings in the taxable account is life insurance proceeds. The account is a joint account and Sharon hopes to use a portion of the savings to help her girls purchase their first home. They have a 529 plan for college expenses.
- Tom has an above average risk tolerance and Sharon leans more toward conservative, low risk investments.

Financial Objectives

- Seek and find a reputable, ethical investment advisor to aid in their wealth accumulation and financial development.
- Both have had undesirable experiences in the past working with other financial planning professionals and seek to understand the regulatory and ethical requirements for financial planners.
- Work with an advisor to help them agree on an investment strategy to preserve their savings for future retirement.

Questions

1. In your first meeting with Tom and Sharon, they are very inquisitive about the compensation of investment advisors. According to the SEC, which of the following are considered forms of compensation?

   a) Receipt of any economic benefit
   b) Single fee charged for advice given on financial outlook
   c) Commission paid on sale of investment and/or insurance product

d) Hourly fee charged reporting and analyzing financial situation
e) All of the above

2. Tom and Sharon are ready to engage your financial planning services; however, they have one concern. Tom is concerned that you are not properly qualified to manage his assets because you are *not* registered with the SEC. What is your best response?

   a) The individual state securities departments collectively assist in the management of the SEC. Therefore SEC regulation is neither permitted nor required if an investment advisor is registered with his or her state.
   b) Registering as an investment advisor in your state is the same as registering with the SEC because many state investment advisor regulations are patterned after the federal Investment Advisor Act of 1940.
   c) Investment advisors with less than $25 million of assets under management are generally prohibited from registering with the SEC.
   d) Investment advisors with less than 100 clients are generally prohibited from registering with the SEC.
   e) All of the above

3. Tom and Sharon have asked you to manage and take custody of their investment accounts. You:

   a) Agree to their request because they have over $1 million in assets; the minimum limit required by law.
   b) Disagree because they don't have over the $5 million in assets; minimum limit required by law.
   c) Agree, and begin to transfer the funds, immediately disclosing the holding location.
   d) Disagree, because investment advisors are not allowed to take custody of their client's investment accounts.

4. Tom and Sharon have asked you to make investment recommendations for their Individual Retirement Accounts. They have agreed to moderate risk, conservative investments that keep up with inflation. Which of the following are suitable recommendations?

   I. Municipal Bonds
   II. Mutual Funds
   III. Corporate Bonds
   IV. Stocks

   a) IV only
   b) I and II
   c) I, III, and IV
   d) II, III and IV
   e) All four are suitable recommendations.

5. You presented an investment policy for Tom and Sharon's accounts. However, Tom insists that you continue his current method of investing. One year later, they realized a 22% loss in their accounts. You should:

   a) Suggest that Tom and Sharon find a new investment advisor
   b) Communicate that you are acting only in the direction given by them
   c) Refund a portion of your fee to compensate for the loss
   d) Split the total loss with Tom and Sharon

6. Tom requests you place a trade to buy 2000 shares of XYZ stock in his account that he has been researching on his own. A month later, after researching the stock yourself, you decide that it would be a great investment for your personal finances. You purchase 5000 shares and disclose the purchase to Tom. Is this ethical?

   a) Yes. It is permissible to place an order in your personal financial account at the same time and/or after the purchase was placed for your client.
   b) Yes. You are protected by the fifteen day waiting period requirement to purchase the same stock as your client.

c) No, because your purchase might make the stock price rise and your client will have a personal gain.
d) No, because you are not allowed to use advice on investment purchases from your clients for personal reasons.

7. Yesterday, Tom was golfing with his best friend, Phil, who is the CEO of ABC company. In conversation, Tom learns that Phil will be announcing next week that ABC company fourth quarter revenue significantly exceeded projections. Tom tells you about the conversation and instructs you to purchase 2000 shares of the stock. What should you do?

   a) Purchase the stock as instructed by your client.
   b) Refuse to purchase the stock and request that Tom no longer engage your services.
   c) Ask Tom to put the request in writing, and then you will place the trade.
   d) Advise Tom to purchase the stock at a later date after the announcement has been made public.

8. Sharon's youngest daughter, Maggie calls you directly. She informs you that Sharon requested she call and obtain the balance of the 529 plan that Sharon uses to pay her yearly education expenses. You should:

   a) Suggest that the Browns set up a meeting in your office to go over the account with Maggie.
   b) Disclose the information over the phone because you represent Tom, Sharon, and their children as clients.
   c) Give Maggie the online account password to check the balance herself.
   d) Request permission directly from Sharon to discuss the account with Maggie.

9. As an investment advisor, you are required by the Investment Advisor Act of 1940 to provide the Browns with information regarding the background and practices of your business. How often are you required to deliver this information?

   a) Only once at the beginning of the advisory relationship.
   b) At the beginning of the relationship, and semi-annually there after.
   c) At the beginning of the relationship, and annually there after.
   d) At the beginning of the relationship, and every time you make an update.

10. Sharon, whom you *never* spoke with following the first client meeting (Tom handles all the financial affairs), calls to inform you that she is filing for divorce. She has asked you to notify her if Tom requests to withdraw funds from the jointly held taxable account. You:

   a) Explain to Sharon that you represent Tom because he is the primary contact on the accounts
   b) Suggest to Sharon that she open a new account and transfer half the account balances
   c) Put a "hold" on the accounts to prevent future withdrawals from either party
   d) Follow the requests made by Sharon within the limits of joint account ownership

Cindy Wilson

Cindy Wilson was referred to you by one of your best clients. She is stressed about her financial situation and is seeking financial advice for the first time. Over the past year, she has incurred several major expenses that she did not expect to pay. Last year, she faced major medical and personal expenses and used her credit cards to cover the majority of these expenses; however, she is now approaching the limits on these cards. She is uncomfortable with her current debt load, and worries that she will not be able to cover future expenses if additional setbacks arise. She would like to know how to best go about restructuring and reducing her debt in the coming year to improve her financial outlook.

Personal Data & Background Information

Cindy Wilson
Age: 32
Health: Excellent
Occupation: Nurse
Marital Status: Divorced
Children: One child, Logan, Age 8

Relevant Financial Information

CINDY WILSON
Estimated Monthly Cash Flow Statement
12/01 through 12/31

Income

Salary[1]	$3,168
Child Support	$450

Expenses

Roth IRA Contribution	$300
Mortgage (PITI)	$892
Car Payment	$316
Food	$220
Utilities	$200
Car Operation (gas, oil, repairs)	$110
Life Insurance	$30
Auto Insurance	$110
Child Care	$310
Clothing	$155
Entertainment	$120
Gifts	$40
Income Taxes	$315
Credit Card Payment	$128
Medical Bill Payment	$120
Student Loan Payment	$120

[1]Works three, twelve hour shifts a week at $22 per hour, 48 weeks per year.

CINDY WILSON
Statement of Financial Position
As of 12/31

Assets

Checking Account	$550
Savings Account	$2,300

Primary Residence	$135,000
Roth IRA	$55,200
Personal Property	$35,000
Car	$15,300
TOTAL ASSETS	**$243,350**

Liabilities

Primary Residence	$92,000
Auto Loan	$16,000
Student Loan	$4,900
Credit Cards	
Discover Card[1]	$3,500
Visa Card[2]	$5,600
Community Medical Center[3]	$1,200
TOTAL LIABILITIES	**$117,300**
NET WORTH	**$126,050**

[1]14.99% APR; minimum monthly payment of $39

[2]18% APR; minimum monthly payment of $89

[3]Remaining medical expenses to be paid; agrees to pay $120 per month until balance is paid. No interest charged.

Client Goals

1. Create a debt reduction plan to pay down credit card balances over a 2-year period
2. Evaluate the most productive way to restructure financial resources to improve financial situation and/or monthly discretionary income
3. Prioritize debt payments to determine which debts she should pay down first
4. Determine whether a home equity loan or line of credit is a good option to consider for help with debt repayment
5. Begin building her savings account to protect her in the future if another financial strain occurs

Questions

1. Cindy is unsure how a financial planner can help her improve her financial situation. In your first meeting, you explain how you will help her using the financial planning process. In order, from start to finish, how will you help Cindy?

   I. Implement and execute plan
   II. Gather data and background information
   III. Develop financial plan
   IV. Establish financial goals
   V. Monitor and measure performance

   a) IV, II, III, I, V
   b) II, IV, III, I, V
   c) III, IV, II, I, V
   d) IV, II, III, V, I

2. How much additional discretionary income does Cindy have remaining at the end of each month that could be applied to medical and credit card payments?

   a) –$318
   b) $132
   c) $248
   d) $380

3. How much could Cindy pay each month if she were to combine her monthly discretionary cash flow with what she is currently paying toward medical bills and credit cards?

   a) $132
   b) $248
   c) $380
   d) $512

4. Which of the following are examples of Cindy's unsecured debt(s)?

   I. Credit Cards
   II. Home Mortgage
   III. Medical Bills
   IV. Student Loan
   V. Car Loan

   a) I, III
   b) II, V
   c) I, III, V
   d) I, III, IV

5. Cindy wants to pay off her VISA card balance within one year from today. To accomplish this goal, what will be her monthly payment, rounded to the nearest dollar, to accomplish this goal?

   a) $89
   b) $320
   c) $505
   d) $513
   e) Not enough information to determine answer

6. Cindy has indicated that she is willing to restructure her income and expenses to devote more income to paying off her credit cards. You have recommended that she increase the amount being paid towards her Discover and VISA cards by the following amounts:

Discover	$100
VISA	$160

   Using the debt to income ratio (with the increased credit card payments), which statement is correct?

   a) Cindy's debt to income ratio is less than 8%; this illustrates that Cindy's financial leverage is less than average if an emergency should arise.
   b) Cindy's debt to income ratio is less than 10%; this illustrates that Cindy's financial leverage is better than average financial leverage if an emergency should arise.
   c) Cindy's debt to income ratio is 25%; this illustrates that Cindy has less than average financial leverage if an emergency should arise.
   d) Cindy's debt to income ratio is 20%; this illustrates that Cindy has better than average financial leverage if an emergency should arise.

7. Cindy is willing to consider using a home equity loan to pay off her credit cards. All of the following are advantages of this strategy EXCEPT:

   a) Cindy could pay less in total interest if amortized over a 5-year period.
   b) The interest could be tax deductible if deductions are itemized on her tax return.
   c) Cindy could improve her debt to income ratio giving her more financial leverage in the future if an emergency should arise.
   d) Cindy is securing her unsecured debt, which gives her more financial leverage when paying the monthly payments.

8. According to your best estimate, how much money would Cindy save per month if she transferred her credit card debt to a home equity loan? She is assuming the home equity loan would be amortized over a five year period with a fixed interest rate of 7%, compared to paying both her credit cards down over a five year period at the current APR.

   a) $45
   b) $40
   c) $35
   d) $20
   e) Not enough information to determine answer

9. Cindy's purse was stolen out of her car. She immediately calls her credit card companies to report the incident, even though no charges were made at the time. Three days later, she notices the following unauthorized transactions were charged.

Discover Card	$344
Visa Card	$28

   How much will Cindy be responsible for paying?

   a) $0
   b) $100
   c) $128
   d) $380

10. If Cindy made a lump sum payment of $1000 from her savings today toward the balance of her VISA card, approximately how much will she save in interest over a 1-year period, if no other payments are made?

    a) $200
    b) $500
    c) $800
    d) $1,100

Jeff and Sharon Williams

Jeff and Sharon Williams have been your clients for five years. They are very happy with your services and you're preparing to conduct their annual financial checkup meeting. During this meeting, you review their goals, update their financial data and review their investment performance.

Personal Data & Background Information

Husband:	Jeff Williams, age 45, Golf Course Manager
Wife:	Sharon Williams, age 45, Teacher
Marital Status:	Happily married for 25 years
Children:	Three Children: Jarrod 24, Brett 18, Susan 16

Client Goals for this Year

Short Term Goals

1. Begin saving to purchase a new SUV for Jeff in five years
2. Review education fund savings to determine the amount that can be withdrawn to pay for Brett's education expenses this year
3. Review loan given to Jarrod to purchase a car
4. Help Susan learn the value of saving a portion of her part-time income for future goals and needs

Long Term Goals

1. Maximize contributions to IRA accounts and employer sponsored retirement accounts to meet retirement needs. Jeff and Sharon would like to retire at age 60.
2. Annually update and review estate planning needs
3. Review savings plan to pay the complete education expenses for all three children

JEFF AND SHARON WILLIAMS
Statement of Financial Position
As of 12/31

ASSETS (Fair Market Value):

Cash

Checking account	$2,200
Money market account	$10,200

Investments

Roth IRA – Sharon	$325,000
Traditional IRA – Jeff	$201,000
Education savings	$70,000
401(k) – Jeff	$506,000
403(b) – Sharon	$105,000
Taxable account	$87,000

Real Estate

Primary residence $307,000

Other Assets

Sharon's auto $12,500
Jeff's auto $5,600
Personal loan[1] as of three years ago 12,000
Personal property $50,000

LIABILITIES:

Mortgage payable – primary residence $250,000
Sharon's auto $4,500

[1]This personal loan was given to Jarrod to purchase a car.

Questions

1. Sharon would like to have $1,000,000 saved in her Roth IRA by the time she retires. If she contributes the current maximum of $4,000 per year at the beginning of each year until retirement, at an average 6% return, will she make her goal?

   a) No, she will be short approximately $152,000 of her goal
   b) No, she will be short approximately $122,000 of her goal
   c) Yes, she will have approximately $152,000 more then her goal
   d) Yes, she will have approximately $122,000 more then her goal

2. Jeff would like to set up an escrow account that produces an after-tax annual return of 4% to make a cash purchase towards a $40,000 car in five years. How much should they save per month to accomplish this goal?

   a) $600
   b) $603
   c) $614
   d) $623

3. Jeff's IRA balance at the beginning of last year was $178,880, after he made his annual contribution. What is Jeff's return on investment rounded to the nearest percent?

   a) -2%
   b) 7%
   c) 9%
   d) 12%
   e) Not enough information to solve

4. Jeff and Sharon gave Jarrod, their oldest son, a loan to purchase a car for $12,000 three years ago. They agreed to an interest rate of 6.5% and monthly payment of $250. What is the balance of the loan today?

   a) $3,255
   b) $3,625
   c) $4,514
   d) $4,668

5. Jeff and Sharon bought 200 shares of growth stock at $55 per share in their taxable account. Today the stock is worth $28,165 with an average annual after tax return of 7.5%. How many years have they owned the stock?

   a) 5
   b) 6
   c) 8
   d) 13
   e) Not enough information

6. Jeff and Sharon are beginning to teach Susan the value of saving a portion of her money from a part-time job. If she saved $100 today at an interest rate of 8%, compounded semi-annually, how many years would it take her to double her money?

   a) 8.8
   b) 12.7
   c) 16.9
   d) 17.6
   e) Not enough information

7. Brett is starting college this year and Jeff and Sharon need to withdraw $10,000 from their education savings at the beginning of each year to pay tuition and books for the next four years. They expect to earn 11% compounded annually on their education savings. What will be the value of the account when Brett graduates?

   a) $32,192
   b) $45,235
   c) $53,987
   d) $59,167

8. Sharon's parents bought the kids a total of 100 shares of aggressive growth stock three years ago at $40 per share. The current value of the stock is $30. The following dividends have been paid on the stock at the end of the year:

   Year 1 $3.45
   Year 2 $4.25
   Year 3 $5.75

   What is the internal rate of return (IRR) earned on this investment?

   a) –3%
   b) -1.3%
   c) 2.3%
   d) 3.07%

Use the following information to answer questions 9-11: Rather then paying rent, Jeff and Sharon want to purchase, with cash, a $95,000 town home for their son Brett to live in while attending college. They expect the home to increase in value at a rate of 5% annually. The opportunity cost for the cash purchase is 7% (discount rate). They believe Brett can find roommates to pay rent toward the purchase that will produce the following net after-tax cash flows:

Year 1 $300
Year 2 $300
Year 3 $400
Year 4 $500

9. What will the value of the home be if sold at the end of the fourth year?

   a) $99,750
   b) $115,473
   c) $124,525
   d) $132,152

10. What is the NPV of the investment at the end of the fourth year?

    a) -$5,656
    b) -$3,962
    c) $2,967
    d) $3,894

11. Is this a good investment for Jeff and Sharon from a purely financial standpoint?

    a) Yes, because the NPV implies that the rate of return on future cash flows is greater then the opportunity cost used to discount future cash flows
    b) No, because the NPV implies that the rate of return on future cash flows is less then the opportunity cost used to discount future cash flows

APPENDICES

Appendix A

PRESENT VALUE OF LUMP SUM

	Interest Rate						
YEARS	3.0%	3.5%	4.0%	4.5%	5.0%	5.5%	6.0%
1	0.9709	0.9662	0.9615	0.9569	0.9524	0.9479	0.9434
2	0.9426	0.9335	0.9246	0.9157	0.9070	0.8985	0.8900
3	0.9151	0.9019	0.8890	0.8763	0.8638	0.8516	0.8396
4	0.8885	0.8714	0.8548	0.8386	0.8227	0.8072	0.7921
5	0.8626	0.8420	0.8219	0.8025	0.7835	0.7651	0.7473
6	0.8375	0.8135	0.7903	0.7679	0.7462	0.7252	0.7050
7	0.8131	0.7860	0.7599	0.7348	0.7107	0.6874	0.6651
8	0.7894	0.7594	0.7307	0.7032	0.6768	0.6516	0.6274
9	0.7664	0.7337	0.7026	0.6729	0.6446	0.6176	0.5919
10	0.7441	0.7089	0.6756	0.6439	0.6139	0.5854	0.5584
11	0.7224	0.6849	0.6496	0.6162	0.5847	0.5549	0.5268
12	0.7014	0.6618	0.6246	0.5897	0.5568	0.5260	0.4970
13	0.6810	0.6394	0.6006	0.5643	0.5303	0.4986	0.4688
14	0.6611	0.6178	0.5775	0.5400	0.5051	0.4726	0.4423
15	0.6419	0.5969	0.5553	0.5167	0.4810	0.4479	0.4173
16	0.6232	0.5767	0.5339	0.4945	0.4581	0.4246	0.3936
17	0.6050	0.5572	0.5134	0.4732	0.4363	0.4024	0.3714
18	0.5874	0.5384	0.4936	0.4528	0.4155	0.3815	0.3503
19	0.5703	0.5202	0.4746	0.4333	0.3957	0.3616	0.3305
20	0.5537	0.5026	0.4564	0.4146	0.3769	0.3427	0.3118
21	0.5375	0.4856	0.4388	0.3968	0.3589	0.3249	0.2942
22	0.5219	0.4692	0.4220	0.3797	0.3418	0.3079	0.2775
23	0.5067	0.4533	0.4057	0.3634	0.3256	0.2919	0.2618
24	0.4919	0.4380	0.3901	0.3477	0.3101	0.2767	0.2470
25	0.4776	0.4231	0.3751	0.3327	0.2953	0.2622	0.2330
26	0.4637	0.4088	0.3607	0.3184	0.2812	0.2486	0.2198
27	0.4502	0.3950	0.3468	0.3047	0.2678	0.2356	0.2074
28	0.4371	0.3817	0.3335	0.2916	0.2551	0.2233	0.1956
29	0.4243	0.3687	0.3207	0.2790	0.2429	0.2117	0.1846
30	0.4120	0.3563	0.3083	0.2670	0.2314	0.2006	0.1741
31	0.4000	0.3442	0.2965	0.2555	0.2204	0.1902	0.1643
32	0.3883	0.3326	0.2851	0.2445	0.2099	0.1803	0.1550
33	0.3770	0.3213	0.2741	0.2340	0.1999	0.1709	0.1462
34	0.3660	0.3105	0.2636	0.2239	0.1904	0.1620	0.1379
35	0.3554	0.3000	0.2534	0.2143	0.1813	0.1535	0.1301
36	0.3450	0.2898	0.2437	0.2050	0.1727	0.1455	0.1227
37	0.3350	0.2800	0.2343	0.1962	0.1644	0.1379	0.1158
38	0.3252	0.2706	0.2253	0.1878	0.1566	0.1307	0.1092
39	0.3158	0.2614	0.2166	0.1797	0.1491	0.1239	0.1031
40	0.3066	0.2526	0.2083	0.1719	0.1420	0.1175	0.0972
41	0.2976	0.2440	0.2003	0.1645	0.1353	0.1113	0.0917
42	0.2890	0.2358	0.1926	0.1574	0.1288	0.1055	0.0865
43	0.2805	0.2278	0.1852	0.1507	0.1227	0.1000	0.0816
44	0.2724	0.2201	0.1780	0.1442	0.1169	0.0948	0.0770
45	0.2644	0.2127	0.1712	0.1380	0.1113	0.0899	0.0727
46	0.2567	0.2055	0.1646	0.1320	0.1060	0.0852	0.0685
47	0.2493	0.1985	0.1583	0.1263	0.1009	0.0807	0.0647
48	0.2420	0.1918	0.1522	0.1209	0.0961	0.0765	0.0610
49	0.2350	0.1853	0.1463	0.1157	0.0916	0.0725	0.0575
50	0.2281	0.1791	0.1407	0.1107	0.0872	0.0688	0.0543

PRESENT VALUE OF LUMP SUM (continued)

	Interest Rate						
YEARS	6.5%	7.0%	7.5%	8.0%	8.5%	9.0%	9.5%
1	0.9390	0.9346	0.9302	0.9259	0.9217	0.9174	0.9132
2	0.8817	0.8734	0.8653	0.8573	0.8495	0.8417	0.8340
3	0.8278	0.8163	0.8050	0.7938	0.7829	0.7722	0.7617
4	0.7773	0.7629	0.7488	0.7350	0.7216	0.7084	0.6956
5	0.7299	0.7130	0.6966	0.6806	0.6650	0.6499	0.6352
6	0.6853	0.6663	0.6480	0.6302	0.6129	0.5963	0.5801
7	0.6435	0.6227	0.6028	0.5835	0.5649	0.5470	0.5298
8	0.6042	0.5820	0.5607	0.5403	0.5207	0.5019	0.4838
9	0.5674	0.5439	0.5216	0.5002	0.4799	0.4604	0.4418
10	0.5327	0.5083	0.4852	0.4632	0.4423	0.4224	0.4035
11	0.5002	0.4751	0.4513	0.4289	0.4076	0.3875	0.3685
12	0.4697	0.4440	0.4199	0.3971	0.3757	0.3555	0.3365
13	0.4410	0.4150	0.3906	0.3677	0.3463	0.3262	0.3073
14	0.4141	0.3878	0.3633	0.3405	0.3191	0.2992	0.2807
15	0.3888	0.3624	0.3380	0.3152	0.2941	0.2745	0.2563
16	0.3651	0.3387	0.3144	0.2919	0.2711	0.2519	0.2341
17	0.3428	0.3166	0.2925	0.2703	0.2499	0.2311	0.2138
18	0.3219	0.2959	0.2720	0.2502	0.2303	0.2120	0.1952
19	0.3022	0.2765	0.2531	0.2317	0.2122	0.1945	0.1783
20	0.2838	0.2584	0.2354	0.2145	0.1956	0.1784	0.1628
21	0.2665	0.2415	0.2190	0.1987	0.1803	0.1637	0.1487
22	0.2502	0.2257	0.2037	0.1839	0.1662	0.1502	0.1358
23	0.2349	0.2109	0.1895	0.1703	0.1531	0.1378	0.1240
24	0.2206	0.1971	0.1763	0.1577	0.1412	0.1264	0.1133
25	0.2071	0.1842	0.1640	0.1460	0.1301	0.1160	0.1034
26	0.1945	0.1722	0.1525	0.1352	0.1199	0.1064	0.0945
27	0.1826	0.1609	0.1419	0.1252	0.1105	0.0976	0.0863
28	0.1715	0.1504	0.1320	0.1159	0.1019	0.0895	0.0788
29	0.1610	0.1406	0.1228	0.1073	0.0939	0.0822	0.0719
30	0.1512	0.1314	0.1142	0.0994	0.0865	0.0754	0.0657
31	0.1420	0.1228	0.1063	0.0920	0.0797	0.0691	0.0600
32	0.1333	0.1147	0.0988	0.0852	0.0735	0.0634	0.0548
33	0.1252	0.1072	0.0919	0.0789	0.0677	0.0582	0.0500
34	0.1175	0.1002	0.0855	0.0730	0.0624	0.0534	0.0457
35	0.1103	0.0937	0.0796	0.0676	0.0575	0.0490	0.0417
36	0.1036	0.0875	0.0740	0.0626	0.0530	0.0449	0.0381
37	0.0973	0.0818	0.0688	0.0580	0.0489	0.0412	0.0348
38	0.0914	0.0765	0.0640	0.0537	0.0450	0.0378	0.0318
39	0.0858	0.0715	0.0596	0.0497	0.0415	0.0347	0.0290
40	0.0805	0.0668	0.0554	0.0460	0.0383	0.0318	0.0265
41	0.0756	0.0624	0.0516	0.0426	0.0353	0.0292	0.0242
42	0.0710	0.0583	0.0480	0.0395	0.0325	0.0268	0.0221
43	0.0667	0.0545	0.0446	0.0365	0.0300	0.0246	0.0202
44	0.0626	0.0509	0.0415	0.0338	0.0276	0.0226	0.0184
45	0.0588	0.0476	0.0386	0.0313	0.0254	0.0207	0.0168
46	0.0552	0.0445	0.0359	0.0290	0.0235	0.0190	0.0154
47	0.0518	0.0416	0.0334	0.0269	0.0216	0.0174	0.0140
48	0.0487	0.0389	0.0311	0.0249	0.0199	0.0160	0.0128
49	0.0457	0.0363	0.0289	0.0230	0.0184	0.0147	0.0117
50	0.0429	0.0339	0.0269	0.0213	0.0169	0.0134	0.0107

PRESENT VALUE OF LUMP SUM (continued)

	Interest Rate						
YEARS	10.0%	10.5%	11.0%	11.5%	12.0%	12.5%	13.0%
1	0.9091	0.9050	0.9009	0.8969	0.8929	0.8889	0.8850
2	0.8264	0.8190	0.8116	0.8044	0.7972	0.7901	0.7831
3	0.7513	0.7412	0.7312	0.7214	0.7118	0.7023	0.6931
4	0.6830	0.6707	0.6587	0.6470	0.6355	0.6243	0.6133
5	0.6209	0.6070	0.5935	0.5803	0.5674	0.5549	0.5428
6	0.5645	0.5493	0.5346	0.5204	0.5066	0.4933	0.4803
7	0.5132	0.4971	0.4817	0.4667	0.4523	0.4385	0.4251
8	0.4665	0.4499	0.4339	0.4186	0.4039	0.3897	0.3762
9	0.4241	0.4071	0.3909	0.3754	0.3606	0.3464	0.3329
10	0.3855	0.3684	0.3522	0.3367	0.3220	0.3079	0.2946
11	0.3505	0.3334	0.3173	0.3020	0.2875	0.2737	0.2607
12	0.3186	0.3018	0.2858	0.2708	0.2567	0.2433	0.2307
13	0.2897	0.2731	0.2575	0.2429	0.2292	0.2163	0.2042
14	0.2633	0.2471	0.2320	0.2178	0.2046	0.1922	0.1807
15	0.2394	0.2236	0.2090	0.1954	0.1827	0.1709	0.1599
16	0.2176	0.2024	0.1883	0.1752	0.1631	0.1519	0.1415
17	0.1978	0.1832	0.1696	0.1572	0.1456	0.1350	0.1252
18	0.1799	0.1658	0.1528	0.1409	0.1300	0.1200	0.1108
19	0.1635	0.1500	0.1377	0.1264	0.1161	0.1067	0.0981
20	0.1486	0.1358	0.1240	0.1134	0.1037	0.0948	0.0868
21	0.1351	0.1229	0.1117	0.1017	0.0926	0.0843	0.0768
22	0.1228	0.1112	0.1007	0.0912	0.0826	0.0749	0.0680
23	0.1117	0.1006	0.0907	0.0818	0.0738	0.0666	0.0601
24	0.1015	0.0911	0.0817	0.0734	0.0659	0.0592	0.0532
25	0.0923	0.0824	0.0736	0.0658	0.0588	0.0526	0.0471
26	0.0839	0.0746	0.0663	0.0590	0.0525	0.0468	0.0417
27	0.0763	0.0675	0.0597	0.0529	0.0469	0.0416	0.0369
28	0.0693	0.0611	0.0538	0.0475	0.0419	0.0370	0.0326
29	0.0630	0.0553	0.0485	0.0426	0.0374	0.0329	0.0289
30	0.0573	0.0500	0.0437	0.0382	0.0334	0.0292	0.0256
31	0.0521	0.0453	0.0394	0.0342	0.0298	0.0260	0.0226
32	0.0474	0.0410	0.0355	0.0307	0.0266	0.0231	0.0200
33	0.0431	0.0371	0.0319	0.0275	0.0238	0.0205	0.0177
34	0.0391	0.0335	0.0288	0.0247	0.0212	0.0182	0.0157
35	0.0356	0.0304	0.0259	0.0222	0.0189	0.0162	0.0139
36	0.0323	0.0275	0.0234	0.0199	0.0169	0.0144	0.0123
37	0.0294	0.0249	0.0210	0.0178	0.0151	0.0128	0.0109
38	0.0267	0.0225	0.0190	0.0160	0.0135	0.0114	0.0096
39	0.0243	0.0204	0.0171	0.0143	0.0120	0.0101	0.0085
40	0.0221	0.0184	0.0154	0.0129	0.0107	0.0090	0.0075
41	0.0201	0.0167	0.0139	0.0115	0.0096	0.0080	0.0067
42	0.0183	0.0151	0.0125	0.0103	0.0086	0.0071	0.0059
43	0.0166	0.0137	0.0112	0.0093	0.0076	0.0063	0.0052
44	0.0151	0.0124	0.0101	0.0083	0.0068	0.0056	0.0046
45	0.0137	0.0112	0.0091	0.0075	0.0061	0.0050	0.0041
46	0.0125	0.0101	0.0082	0.0067	0.0054	0.0044	0.0036
47	0.0113	0.0092	0.0074	0.0060	0.0049	0.0039	0.0032
48	0.0103	0.0083	0.0067	0.0054	0.0043	0.0035	0.0028
49	0.0094	0.0075	0.0060	0.0048	0.0039	0.0031	0.0025
50	0.0085	0.0068	0.0054	0.0043	0.0035	0.0028	0.0022

PRESENT VALUE OF LUMP SUM (continued)

	Interest Rate						
YEARS	14.0%	15.0%	16.0%	17.0%	18.0%	19.0%	20.0%
1	0.8772	0.8696	0.8621	0.8547	0.8475	0.8403	0.8333
2	0.7695	0.7561	0.7432	0.7305	0.7182	0.7062	0.6944
3	0.6750	0.6575	0.6407	0.6244	0.6086	0.5934	0.5787
4	0.5921	0.5718	0.5523	0.5337	0.5158	0.4987	0.4823
5	0.5194	0.4972	0.4761	0.4561	0.4371	0.4190	0.4019
6	0.4556	0.4323	0.4104	0.3898	0.3704	0.3521	0.3349
7	0.3996	0.3759	0.3538	0.3332	0.3139	0.2959	0.2791
8	0.3506	0.3269	0.3050	0.2848	0.2660	0.2487	0.2326
9	0.3075	0.2843	0.2630	0.2434	0.2255	0.2090	0.1938
10	0.2697	0.2472	0.2267	0.2080	0.1911	0.1756	0.1615
11	0.2366	0.2149	0.1954	0.1778	0.1619	0.1476	0.1346
12	0.2076	0.1869	0.1685	0.1520	0.1372	0.1240	0.1122
13	0.1821	0.1625	0.1452	0.1299	0.1163	0.1042	0.0935
14	0.1597	0.1413	0.1252	0.1110	0.0985	0.0876	0.0779
15	0.1401	0.1229	0.1079	0.0949	0.0835	0.0736	0.0649
16	0.1229	0.1069	0.0930	0.0811	0.0708	0.0618	0.0541
17	0.1078	0.0929	0.0802	0.0693	0.0600	0.0520	0.0451
18	0.0946	0.0808	0.0691	0.0592	0.0508	0.0437	0.0376
19	0.0829	0.0703	0.0596	0.0506	0.0431	0.0367	0.0313
20	0.0728	0.0611	0.0514	0.0433	0.0365	0.0308	0.0261
21	0.0638	0.0531	0.0443	0.0370	0.0309	0.0259	0.0217
22	0.0560	0.0462	0.0382	0.0316	0.0262	0.0218	0.0181
23	0.0491	0.0402	0.0329	0.0270	0.0222	0.0183	0.0151
24	0.0431	0.0349	0.0284	0.0231	0.0188	0.0154	0.0126
25	0.0378	0.0304	0.0245	0.0197	0.0160	0.0129	0.0105
26	0.0331	0.0264	0.0211	0.0169	0.0135	0.0109	0.0087
27	0.0291	0.0230	0.0182	0.0144	0.0115	0.0091	0.0073
28	0.0255	0.0200	0.0157	0.0123	0.0097	0.0077	0.0061
29	0.0224	0.0174	0.0135	0.0105	0.0082	0.0064	0.0051
30	0.0196	0.0151	0.0116	0.0090	0.0070	0.0054	0.0042
31	0.0172	0.0131	0.0100	0.0077	0.0059	0.0046	0.0035
32	0.0151	0.0114	0.0087	0.0066	0.0050	0.0038	0.0029
33	0.0132	0.0099	0.0075	0.0056	0.0042	0.0032	0.0024
34	0.0116	0.0086	0.0064	0.0048	0.0036	0.0027	0.0020
35	0.0102	0.0075	0.0055	0.0041	0.0030	0.0023	0.0017
36	0.0089	0.0065	0.0048	0.0035	0.0026	0.0019	0.0014
37	0.0078	0.0057	0.0041	0.0030	0.0022	0.0016	0.0012
38	0.0069	0.0049	0.0036	0.0026	0.0019	0.0013	0.0010
39	0.0060	0.0043	0.0031	0.0022	0.0016	0.0011	0.0008
40	0.0053	0.0037	0.0026	0.0019	0.0013	0.0010	0.0007
41	0.0046	0.0032	0.0023	0.0016	0.0011	0.0008	0.0006
42	0.0041	0.0028	0.0020	0.0014	0.0010	0.0007	0.0005
43	0.0036	0.0025	0.0017	0.0012	0.0008	0.0006	0.0004
44	0.0031	0.0021	0.0015	0.0010	0.0007	0.0005	0.0003
45	0.0027	0.0019	0.0013	0.0009	0.0006	0.0004	0.0003
46	0.0024	0.0016	0.0011	0.0007	0.0005	0.0003	0.0002
47	0.0021	0.0014	0.0009	0.0006	0.0004	0.0003	0.0002
48	0.0019	0.0012	0.0008	0.0005	0.0004	0.0002	0.0002
49	0.0016	0.0011	0.0007	0.0005	0.0003	0.0002	0.0002
50	0.0014	0.0009	0.0006	0.0004	0.0003	0.0002	0.0001

Appendix B

PRESENT VALUE OF ANNUITY DUE

	Interest Rate						
YEARS	3.0%	3.5%	4.0%	4.5%	5.0%	5.5%	6.0%
1	1.0000	1.0000	1.0000	1.0000	1.0000	1.0000	1.0000
2	1.9709	1.9662	1.9615	1.9569	1.9524	1.9479	1.9434
3	2.9135	2.8997	2.8861	2.8727	2.8594	2.8463	2.8334
4	3.8286	3.8016	3.7751	3.7490	3.7232	3.6979	3.6730
5	4.7171	4.6731	4.6299	4.5875	4.5460	4.5052	4.4651
6	5.5797	5.5151	5.4518	5.3900	5.3295	5.2703	5.2124
7	6.4172	6.3286	6.2421	6.1579	6.0757	5.9955	5.9173
8	7.2303	7.1145	7.0021	6.8927	6.7864	6.6830	6.5824
9	8.0197	7.8740	7.7327	7.5959	7.4632	7.3346	7.2098
10	8.7861	8.6077	8.4353	8.2688	8.1078	7.9522	7.8017
11	9.5302	9.3166	9.1109	8.9127	8.7217	8.5376	8.3601
12	10.2526	10.0016	9.7605	9.5289	9.3064	9.0925	8.8869
13	10.9540	10.6633	10.3851	10.1186	9.8633	9.6185	9.3838
14	11.6350	11.3027	10.9856	10.6829	10.3936	10.1171	9.8527
15	12.2961	11.9205	11.5631	11.2228	10.8986	10.5896	10.2950
16	12.9379	12.5174	12.1184	11.7395	11.3797	11.0376	10.7122
17	13.5611	13.0941	12.6523	12.2340	11.8378	11.4622	11.1059
18	14.1661	13.6513	13.1657	12.7072	12.2741	11.8646	11.4773
19	14.7535	14.1897	13.6593	13.1600	12.6896	12.2461	11.8276
20	15.3238	14.7098	14.1339	13.5933	13.0853	12.6077	12.1581
21	15.8775	15.2124	14.5903	14.0079	13.4622	12.9504	12.4699
22	16.4150	15.6980	15.0292	14.4047	13.8212	13.2752	12.7641
23	16.9369	16.1671	15.4511	14.7844	14.1630	13.5832	13.0416
24	17.4436	16.6204	15.8568	15.1478	14.4886	13.8750	13.3034
25	17.9355	17.0584	16.2470	15.4955	14.7986	14.1517	13.5504
26	18.4131	17.4815	16.6221	15.8282	15.0939	14.4139	13.7834
27	18.8768	17.8904	16.9828	16.1466	15.3752	14.6625	14.0032
28	19.3270	18.2854	17.3296	16.4513	15.6430	14.8981	14.2105
29	19.7641	18.6670	17.6631	16.7429	15.8981	15.1214	14.4062
30	20.1885	19.0358	17.9837	17.0219	16.1411	15.3331	14.5907
31	20.6004	19.3920	18.2920	17.2889	16.3725	15.5337	14.7648
32	21.0004	19.7363	18.5885	17.5444	16.5928	15.7239	14.9291
33	21.3888	20.0689	18.8736	17.7889	16.8027	15.9042	15.0840
34	21.7658	20.3902	19.1476	18.0229	17.0025	16.0751	15.2302
35	22.1318	20.7007	19.4112	18.2468	17.1929	16.2370	15.3681
36	22.4872	21.0007	19.6646	18.4610	17.3742	16.3906	15.4982
37	22.8323	21.2905	19.9083	18.6660	17.5469	16.5361	15.6210
38	23.1672	21.5705	20.1426	18.8622	17.7113	16.6740	15.7368
39	23.4925	21.8411	20.3679	19.0500	17.8679	16.8047	15.8460
40	23.8082	22.1025	20.5845	19.2297	18.0170	16.9287	15.9491
41	24.1148	22.3551	20.7928	19.4016	18.1591	17.0461	16.0463
42	24.4124	22.5991	20.9931	19.5661	18.2944	17.1575	16.1380
43	24.7014	22.8349	21.1856	19.7235	18.4232	17.2630	16.2245
44	24.9819	23.0627	21.3708	19.8742	18.5459	17.3630	16.3062
45	25.2543	23.2828	21.5488	20.0184	18.6628	17.4579	16.3832
46	25.5187	23.4955	21.7200	20.1563	18.7741	17.5477	16.4558
47	25.7754	23.7009	21.8847	20.2884	18.8801	17.6329	16.5244
48	26.0247	23.8994	22.0429	20.4147	18.9810	17.7137	16.5890
49	26.2667	24.0912	22.1951	20.5356	19.0772	17.7902	16.6500
50	26.5017	24.2766	22.3415	20.6513	19.1687	17.8628	16.7076

PRESENT VALUE OF ANNUITY DUE (continued)

	Interest Rate						
YEARS	6.5%	7.0%	7.5%	8.0%	8.5%	9.0%	9.5%
1	1.0000	1.0000	1.0000	1.0000	1.0000	1.0000	1.0000
2	1.9390	1.9346	1.9302	1.9259	1.9217	1.9174	1.9132
3	2.8206	2.8080	2.7956	2.7833	2.7711	2.7591	2.7473
4	3.6485	3.6243	3.6005	3.5771	3.5540	3.5313	3.5089
5	4.4258	4.3872	4.3493	4.3121	4.2756	4.2397	4.2045
6	5.1557	5.1002	5.0459	4.9927	4.9406	4.8897	4.8397
7	5.8410	5.7665	5.6938	5.6229	5.5536	5.4859	5.4198
8	6.4845	6.3893	6.2966	6.2064	6.1185	6.0330	5.9496
9	7.0888	6.9713	6.8573	6.7466	6.6392	6.5348	6.4334
10	7.6561	7.5152	7.3789	7.2469	7.1191	6.9952	6.8753
11	8.1888	8.0236	7.8641	7.7101	7.5613	7.4177	7.2788
12	8.6890	8.4987	8.3154	8.1390	7.9690	7.8052	7.6473
13	9.1587	8.9427	8.7353	8.5361	8.3447	8.1607	7.9838
14	9.5997	9.3577	9.1258	8.9038	8.6910	8.4869	8.2912
15	10.0138	9.7455	9.4892	9.2442	9.0101	8.7862	8.5719
16	10.4027	10.1079	9.8271	9.5595	9.3042	9.0607	8.8282
17	10.7678	10.4466	10.1415	9.8514	9.5753	9.3126	9.0623
18	11.1106	10.7632	10.4340	10.1216	9.8252	9.5436	9.2760
19	11.4325	11.0591	10.7060	10.3719	10.0555	9.7556	9.4713
20	11.7347	11.3356	10.9591	10.6036	10.2677	9.9501	9.6496
21	12.0185	11.5940	11.1945	10.8181	10.4633	10.1285	9.8124
22	12.2850	11.8355	11.4135	11.0168	10.6436	10.2922	9.9611
23	12.5352	12.0612	11.6172	11.2007	10.8098	10.4424	10.0969
24	12.7701	12.2722	11.8067	11.3711	10.9629	10.5802	10.2209
25	12.9907	12.4693	11.9830	11.5288	11.1041	10.7066	10.3341
26	13.1979	12.6536	12.1469	11.6748	11.2342	10.8226	10.4376
27	13.3924	12.8258	12.2995	11.8100	11.3541	10.9290	10.5320
28	13.5750	12.9867	12.4414	11.9352	11.4646	11.0266	10.6183
29	13.7465	13.1371	12.5734	12.0511	11.5665	11.1161	10.6971
30	13.9075	13.2777	12.6962	12.1584	11.6603	11.1983	10.7690
31	14.0587	13.4090	12.8104	12.2578	11.7468	11.2737	10.8347
32	14.2006	13.5318	12.9166	12.3498	11.8266	11.3428	10.8947
33	14.3339	13.6466	13.0155	12.4350	11.9001	11.4062	10.9495
34	14.4591	13.7538	13.1074	12.5139	11.9678	11.4644	10.9996
35	14.5766	13.8540	13.1929	12.5869	12.0302	11.5178	11.0453
36	14.6870	13.9477	13.2725	12.6546	12.0878	11.5668	11.0870
37	14.7906	14.0352	13.3465	12.7172	12.1408	11.6118	11.1251
38	14.8879	14.1170	13.4154	12.7752	12.1897	11.6530	11.1599
39	14.9792	14.1935	13.4794	12.8289	12.2347	11.6908	11.1917
40	15.0650	14.2649	13.5390	12.8786	12.2763	11.7255	11.2207
41	15.1455	14.3317	13.5944	12.9246	12.3145	11.7574	11.2472
42	15.2212	14.3941	13.6460	12.9672	12.3498	11.7866	11.2715
43	15.2922	14.4524	13.6939	13.0067	12.3823	11.8134	11.2936
44	15.3588	14.5070	13.7385	13.0432	12.4123	11.8380	11.3138
45	15.4214	14.5579	13.7800	13.0771	12.4399	11.8605	11.3322
46	15.4802	14.6055	13.8186	13.1084	12.4653	11.8812	11.3490
47	15.5354	14.6500	13.8545	13.1374	12.4888	11.9002	11.3644
48	15.5873	14.6916	13.8879	13.1643	12.5104	11.9176	11.3785
49	15.6359	14.7305	13.9190	13.1891	12.5303	11.9336	11.3913
50	15.6816	14.7668	13.9479	13.2122	12.5487	11.9482	11.4030

PRESENT VALUE OF ANNUITY DUE (continued)

	Interest Rate						
YEARS	10.0%	10.5%	11.0%	11.5%	12.0%	12.5%	13.0%
1	1.0000	1.0000	1.0000	1.0000	1.0000	1.0000	1.0000
2	1.9091	1.9050	1.9009	1.8969	1.8929	1.8889	1.8850
3	2.7355	2.7240	2.7125	2.7012	2.6901	2.6790	2.6681
4	3.4869	3.4651	3.4437	3.4226	3.4018	3.3813	3.3612
5	4.1699	4.1359	4.1024	4.0696	4.0373	4.0056	3.9745
6	4.7908	4.7429	4.6959	4.6499	4.6048	4.5606	4.5172
7	5.3553	5.2922	5.2305	5.1703	5.1114	5.0538	4.9975
8	5.8684	5.7893	5.7122	5.6370	5.5638	5.4923	5.4226
9	6.3349	6.2392	6.1461	6.0556	5.9676	5.8820	5.7988
10	6.7590	6.6463	6.5370	6.4311	6.3282	6.2285	6.1317
11	7.1446	7.0148	6.8892	6.7678	6.6502	6.5364	6.4262
12	7.4951	7.3482	7.2065	7.0697	6.9377	6.8102	6.6869
13	7.8137	7.6500	7.4924	7.3406	7.1944	7.0535	6.9176
14	8.1034	7.9230	7.7499	7.5835	7.4235	7.2698	7.1218
15	8.3667	8.1702	7.9819	7.8013	7.6282	7.4620	7.3025
16	8.6061	8.3938	8.1909	7.9967	7.8109	7.6329	7.4624
17	8.8237	8.5962	8.3792	8.1719	7.9740	7.7848	7.6039
18	9.0216	8.7794	8.5488	8.3291	8.1196	7.9198	7.7291
19	9.2014	8.9451	8.7016	8.4700	8.2497	8.0398	7.8399
20	9.3649	9.0952	8.8393	8.5964	8.3658	8.1465	7.9380
21	9.5136	9.2309	8.9633	8.7098	8.4694	8.2414	8.0248
22	9.6487	9.3538	9.0751	8.8115	8.5620	8.3256	8.1016
23	9.7715	9.4649	9.1757	8.9027	8.6446	8.4006	8.1695
24	9.8832	9.5656	9.2664	8.9845	8.7184	8.4672	8.2297
25	9.9847	9.6566	9.3481	9.0578	8.7843	8.5264	8.2829
26	10.0770	9.7390	9.4217	9.1236	8.8431	8.5790	8.3300
27	10.1609	9.8136	9.4881	9.1826	8.8957	8.6258	8.3717
28	10.2372	9.8811	9.5478	9.2355	8.9426	8.6674	8.4086
29	10.3066	9.9422	9.6016	9.2830	8.9844	8.7043	8.4412
30	10.3696	9.9974	9.6501	9.3255	9.0218	8.7372	8.4701
31	10.4269	10.0474	9.6938	9.3637	9.0552	8.7664	8.4957
32	10.4790	10.0927	9.7331	9.3980	9.0850	8.7923	8.5183
33	10.5264	10.1337	9.7686	9.4287	9.1116	8.8154	8.5383
34	10.5694	10.1707	9.8005	9.4562	9.1354	8.8359	8.5560
35	10.6086	10.2043	9.8293	9.4809	9.1566	8.8542	8.5717
36	10.6442	10.2347	9.8552	9.5030	9.1755	8.8704	8.5856
37	10.6765	10.2621	9.8786	9.5229	9.1924	8.8848	8.5979
38	10.7059	10.2870	9.8996	9.5407	9.2075	8.8976	8.6087
39	10.7327	10.3095	9.9186	9.5567	9.2210	8.9089	8.6183
40	10.7570	10.3299	9.9357	9.5710	9.2330	8.9191	8.6268
41	10.7791	10.3483	9.9511	9.5839	9.2438	8.9281	8.6344
42	10.7991	10.3650	9.9649	9.5954	9.2534	8.9361	8.6410
43	10.8174	10.3801	9.9774	9.6058	9.2619	8.9432	8.6469
44	10.8340	10.3937	9.9886	9.6150	9.2696	8.9495	8.6522
45	10.8491	10.4061	9.9988	9.6233	9.2764	8.9551	8.6568
46	10.8628	10.4173	10.0079	9.6308	9.2825	8.9601	8.6609
47	10.8753	10.4274	10.0161	9.6375	9.2880	8.9645	8.6645
48	10.8866	10.4366	10.0235	9.6435	9.2928	8.9685	8.6677
49	10.8969	10.4448	10.0302	9.6489	9.2972	8.9720	8.6705
50	10.9063	10.4524	10.0362	9.6537	9.3010	8.9751	8.6730

PRESENT VALUE OF ANNUITY DUE (continued)

	Interest Rate						
YEARS	14.0%	15.0%	16.0%	17.0%	18.0%	19.0%	20.0%
1	1.0000	1.0000	1.0000	1.0000	1.0000	1.0000	1.0000
2	1.8772	1.8696	1.8621	1.8547	1.8475	1.8403	1.8333
3	2.6467	2.6257	2.6052	2.5852	2.5656	2.5465	2.5278
4	3.3216	3.2832	3.2459	3.2096	3.1743	3.1399	3.1065
5	3.9137	3.8550	3.7982	3.7432	3.6901	3.6386	3.5887
6	4.4331	4.3522	4.2743	4.1993	4.1272	4.0576	3.9906
7	4.8887	4.7845	4.6847	4.5892	4.4976	4.4098	4.3255
8	5.2883	5.1604	5.0386	4.9224	4.8115	4.7057	4.6046
9	5.6389	5.4873	5.3436	5.2072	5.0776	4.9544	4.8372
10	5.9464	5.7716	5.6065	5.4506	5.3030	5.1633	5.0310
11	6.2161	6.0188	5.8332	5.6586	5.4941	5.3389	5.1925
12	6.4527	6.2337	6.0286	5.8364	5.6560	5.4865	5.3271
13	6.6603	6.4206	6.1971	5.9884	5.7932	5.6105	5.4392
14	6.8424	6.5831	6.3423	6.1183	5.9095	5.7147	5.5327
15	7.0021	6.7245	6.4675	6.2293	6.0081	5.8023	5.6106
16	7.1422	6.8474	6.5755	6.3242	6.0916	5.8759	5.6755
17	7.2651	6.9542	6.6685	6.4053	6.1624	5.9377	5.7296
18	7.3729	7.0472	6.7487	6.4746	6.2223	5.9897	5.7746
19	7.4674	7.1280	6.8178	6.5339	6.2732	6.0333	5.8122
20	7.5504	7.1982	6.8775	6.5845	6.3162	6.0700	5.8435
21	7.6231	7.2593	6.9288	6.6278	6.3527	6.1009	5.8696
22	7.6870	7.3125	6.9731	6.6648	6.3837	6.1268	5.8913
23	7.7429	7.3587	7.0113	6.6964	6.4099	6.1486	5.9094
24	7.7921	7.3988	7.0442	6.7234	6.4321	6.1668	5.9245
25	7.8351	7.4338	7.0726	6.7465	6.4509	6.1822	5.9371
26	7.8729	7.4641	7.0971	6.7662	6.4669	6.1951	5.9476
27	7.9061	7.4906	7.1182	6.7831	6.4804	6.2060	5.9563
28	7.9352	7.5135	7.1364	6.7975	6.4919	6.2151	5.9636
29	7.9607	7.5335	7.1520	6.8099	6.5016	6.2228	5.9697
30	7.9830	7.5509	7.1656	6.8204	6.5098	6.2292	5.9747
31	8.0027	7.5660	7.1772	6.8294	6.5168	6.2347	5.9789
32	8.0199	7.5791	7.1872	6.8371	6.5227	6.2392	5.9824
33	8.0350	7.5905	7.1959	6.8437	6.5277	6.2430	5.9854
34	8.0482	7.6005	7.2034	6.8493	6.5320	6.2462	5.9878
35	8.0599	7.6091	7.2098	6.8541	6.5356	6.2489	5.9898
36	8.0700	7.6166	7.2153	6.8582	6.5386	6.2512	5.9915
37	8.0790	7.6231	7.2201	6.8617	6.5412	6.2531	5.9929
38	8.0868	7.6288	7.2242	6.8647	6.5434	6.2547	5.9941
39	8.0937	7.6338	7.2278	6.8673	6.5452	6.2561	5.9951
40	8.0997	7.6380	7.2309	6.8695	6.5468	6.2572	5.9959
41	8.1050	7.6418	7.2335	6.8713	6.5482	6.2582	5.9966
42	8.1097	7.6450	7.2358	6.8729	6.5493	6.2590	5.9972
43	8.1138	7.6478	7.2377	6.8743	6.5502	6.2596	5.9976
44	8.1173	7.6503	7.2394	6.8755	6.5510	6.2602	5.9980
45	8.1205	7.6524	7.2409	6.8765	6.5517	6.2607	5.9984
46	8.1232	7.6543	7.2421	6.8773	6.5523	6.2611	5.9986
47	8.1256	7.6559	7.2432	6.8781	6.5528	6.2614	5.9989
48	8.1277	7.6573	7.2442	6.8787	6.5532	6.2617	5.9991
49	8.1296	7.6585	7.2450	6.8792	6.5536	6.2619	5.9992
50	8.1312	7.6596	7.2457	6.8797	6.5539	6.2621	5.9993

Appendix C

PRESENT VALUE OF ORDINARY ANNUITY

	Interest Rate						
YEARS	**3.0%**	**3.5%**	**4.0%**	**4.5%**	**5.0%**	**5.5%**	**6.0%**
1	0.9709	0.9662	0.9615	0.9569	0.9524	0.9479	0.9434
2	1.9135	1.8997	1.8861	1.8727	1.8594	1.8463	1.8334
3	2.8286	2.8016	2.7751	2.7490	2.7232	2.6979	2.6730
4	3.7171	3.6731	3.6299	3.5875	3.5460	3.5052	3.4651
5	4.5797	4.5151	4.4518	4.3900	4.3295	4.2703	4.2124
6	5.4172	5.3286	5.2421	5.1579	5.0757	4.9955	4.9173
7	6.2303	6.1145	6.0021	5.8927	5.7864	5.6830	5.5824
8	7.0197	6.8740	6.7327	6.5959	6.4632	6.3346	6.2098
9	7.7861	7.6077	7.4353	7.2688	7.1078	6.9522	6.8017
10	8.5302	8.3166	8.1109	7.9127	7.7217	7.5376	7.3601
11	9.2526	9.0016	8.7605	8.5289	8.3064	8.0925	7.8869
12	9.9540	9.6633	9.3851	9.1186	8.8633	8.6185	8.3838
13	10.6350	10.3027	9.9856	9.6829	9.3936	9.1171	8.8527
14	11.2961	10.9205	10.5631	10.2228	9.8986	9.5896	9.2950
15	11.9379	11.5174	11.1184	10.7395	10.3797	10.0376	9.7122
16	12.5611	12.0941	11.6523	11.2340	10.8378	10.4622	10.1059
17	13.1661	12.6513	12.1657	11.7072	11.2741	10.8646	10.4773
18	13.7535	13.1897	12.6593	12.1600	11.6896	11.2461	10.8276
19	14.3238	13.7098	13.1339	12.5933	12.0853	11.6077	11.1581
20	14.8775	14.2124	13.5903	13.0079	12.4622	11.9504	11.4699
21	15.4150	14.6980	14.0292	13.4047	12.8212	12.2752	11.7641
22	15.9369	15.1671	14.4511	13.7844	13.1630	12.5832	12.0416
23	16.4436	15.6204	14.8568	14.1478	13.4886	12.8750	12.3034
24	16.9355	16.0584	15.2470	14.4955	13.7986	13.1517	12.5504
25	17.4131	16.4815	15.6221	14.8282	14.0939	13.4139	12.7834
26	17.8768	16.8904	15.9828	15.1466	14.3752	13.6625	13.0032
27	18.3270	17.2854	16.3296	15.4513	14.6430	13.8981	13.2105
28	18.7641	17.6670	16.6631	15.7429	14.8981	14.1214	13.4062
29	19.1885	18.0358	16.9837	16.0219	15.1411	14.3331	13.5907
30	19.6004	18.3920	17.2920	16.2889	15.3725	14.5337	13.7648
31	20.0004	18.7363	17.5885	16.5444	15.5928	14.7239	13.9291
32	20.3888	19.0689	17.8736	16.7889	15.8027	14.9042	14.0840
33	20.7658	19.3902	18.1476	17.0229	16.0025	15.0751	14.2302
34	21.1318	19.7007	18.4112	17.2468	16.1929	15.2370	14.3681
35	21.4872	20.0007	18.6646	17.4610	16.3742	15.3906	14.4982
36	21.8323	20.2905	18.9083	17.6660	16.5469	15.5361	14.6210
37	22.1672	20.5705	19.1426	17.8622	16.7113	15.6740	14.7368
38	22.4925	20.8411	19.3679	18.0500	16.8679	15.8047	14.8460
39	22.8082	21.1025	19.5845	18.2297	17.0170	15.9287	14.9491
40	23.1148	21.3551	19.7928	18.4016	17.1591	16.0461	15.0463
41	23.4124	21.5991	19.9931	18.5661	17.2944	16.1575	15.1380
42	23.7014	21.8349	20.1856	18.7235	17.4232	16.2630	15.2245
43	23.9819	22.0627	20.3708	18.8742	17.5459	16.3630	15.3062
44	24.2543	22.2828	20.5488	19.0184	17.6628	16.4579	15.3832
45	24.5187	22.4955	20.7200	19.1563	17.7741	16.5477	15.4558
46	24.7754	22.7009	20.8847	19.2884	17.8801	16.6329	15.5244
47	25.0247	22.8994	21.0429	19.4147	17.9810	16.7137	15.5890
48	25.2667	23.0912	21.1951	19.5356	18.0772	16.7902	15.6500
49	25.5017	23.2766	21.3415	19.6513	18.1687	16.8628	15.7076
50	25.7298	23.4556	21.4822	19.7620	18.2559	16.9315	15.7619

PRESENT VALUE OF ORDINARY ANNUITY (continued)

	Interest Rate						
YEARS	6.5%	7.0%	7.5%	8.0%	8.5%	9.0%	9.5%
1	0.9390	0.9346	0.9302	0.9259	0.9217	0.9174	0.9132
2	1.8206	1.8080	1.7956	1.7833	1.7711	1.7591	1.7473
3	2.6485	2.6243	2.6005	2.5771	2.5540	2.5313	2.5089
4	3.4258	3.3872	3.3493	3.3121	3.2756	3.2397	3.2045
5	4.1557	4.1002	4.0459	3.9927	3.9406	3.8897	3.8397
6	4.8410	4.7665	4.6938	4.6229	4.5536	4.4859	4.4198
7	5.4845	5.3893	5.2966	5.2064	5.1185	5.0330	4.9496
8	6.0888	5.9713	5.8573	5.7466	5.6392	5.5348	5.4334
9	6.6561	6.5152	6.3789	6.2469	6.1191	5.9952	5.8753
10	7.1888	7.0236	6.8641	6.7101	6.5613	6.4177	6.2788
11	7.6890	7.4987	7.3154	7.1390	6.9690	6.8052	6.6473
12	8.1587	7.9427	7.7353	7.5361	7.3447	7.1607	6.9838
13	8.5997	8.3577	8.1258	7.9038	7.6910	7.4869	7.2912
14	9.0138	8.7455	8.4892	8.2442	8.0101	7.7862	7.5719
15	9.4027	9.1079	8.8271	8.5595	8.3042	8.0607	7.8282
16	9.7678	9.4466	9.1415	8.8514	8.5753	8.3126	8.0623
17	10.1106	9.7632	9.4340	9.1216	8.8252	8.5436	8.2760
18	10.4325	10.0591	9.7060	9.3719	9.0555	8.7556	8.4713
19	10.7347	10.3356	9.9591	9.6036	9.2677	8.9501	8.6496
20	11.0185	10.5940	10.1945	9.8181	9.4633	9.1285	8.8124
21	11.2850	10.8355	10.4135	10.0168	9.6436	9.2922	8.9611
22	11.5352	11.0612	10.6172	10.2007	9.8098	9.4424	9.0969
23	11.7701	11.2722	10.8067	10.3711	9.9629	9.5802	9.2209
24	11.9907	11.4693	10.9830	10.5288	10.1041	9.7066	9.3341
25	12.1979	11.6536	11.1469	10.6748	10.2342	9.8226	9.4376
26	12.3924	11.8258	11.2995	10.8100	10.3541	9.9290	9.5320
27	12.5750	11.9867	11.4414	10.9352	10.4646	10.0266	9.6183
28	12.7465	12.1371	11.5734	11.0511	10.5665	10.1161	9.6971
29	12.9075	12.2777	11.6962	11.1584	10.6603	10.1983	9.7690
30	13.0587	12.4090	11.8104	11.2578	10.7468	10.2737	9.8347
31	13.2006	12.5318	11.9166	11.3498	10.8266	10.3428	9.8947
32	13.3339	12.6466	12.0155	11.4350	10.9001	10.4062	9.9495
33	13.4591	12.7538	12.1074	11.5139	10.9678	10.4644	9.9996
34	13.5766	12.8540	12.1929	11.5869	11.0302	10.5178	10.0453
35	13.6870	12.9477	12.2725	11.6546	11.0878	10.5668	10.0870
36	13.7906	13.0352	12.3465	11.7172	11.1408	10.6118	10.1251
37	13.8879	13.1170	12.4154	11.7752	11.1897	10.6530	10.1599
38	13.9792	13.1935	12.4794	11.8289	11.2347	10.6908	10.1917
39	14.0650	13.2649	12.5390	11.8786	11.2763	10.7255	10.2207
40	14.1455	13.3317	12.5944	11.9246	11.3145	10.7574	10.2472
41	14.2212	13.3941	12.6460	11.9672	11.3498	10.7866	10.2715
42	14.2922	13.4524	12.6939	12.0067	11.3823	10.8134	10.2936
43	14.3588	13.5070	12.7385	12.0432	11.4123	10.8380	10.3138
44	14.4214	13.5579	12.7800	12.0771	11.4399	10.8605	10.3322
45	14.4802	13.6055	12.8186	12.1084	11.4653	10.8812	10.3490
46	14.5354	13.6500	12.8545	12.1374	11.4888	10.9002	10.3644
47	14.5873	13.6916	12.8879	12.1643	11.5104	10.9176	10.3785
48	14.6359	13.7305	12.9190	12.1891	11.5303	10.9336	10.3913
49	14.6816	13.7668	12.9479	12.2122	11.5487	10.9482	10.4030
50	14.7245	13.8007	12.9748	12.2335	11.5656	10.9617	10.4137

PRESENT VALUE OF ORDINARY ANNUITY (continued)

	Interest Rate						
YEARS	10.0%	10.5%	11.0%	11.5%	12.0%	12.5%	13.0%
1	0.9091	0.9050	0.9009	0.8969	0.8929	0.8889	0.8850
2	1.7355	1.7240	1.7125	1.7012	1.6901	1.6790	1.6681
3	2.4869	2.4651	2.4437	2.4226	2.4018	2.3813	2.3612
4	3.1699	3.1359	3.1024	3.0696	3.0373	3.0056	2.9745
5	3.7908	3.7429	3.6959	3.6499	3.6048	3.5606	3.5172
6	4.3553	4.2922	4.2305	4.1703	4.1114	4.0538	3.9975
7	4.8684	4.7893	4.7122	4.6370	4.5638	4.4923	4.4226
8	5.3349	5.2392	5.1461	5.0556	4.9676	4.8820	4.7988
9	5.7590	5.6463	5.5370	5.4311	5.3282	5.2285	5.1317
10	6.1446	6.0148	5.8892	5.7678	5.6502	5.5364	5.4262
11	6.4951	6.3482	6.2065	6.0697	5.9377	5.8102	5.6869
12	6.8137	6.6500	6.4924	6.3406	6.1944	6.0535	5.9176
13	7.1034	6.9230	6.7499	6.5835	6.4235	6.2698	6.1218
14	7.3667	7.1702	6.9819	6.8013	6.6282	6.4620	6.3025
15	7.6061	7.3938	7.1909	6.9967	6.8109	6.6329	6.4624
16	7.8237	7.5962	7.3792	7.1719	6.9740	6.7848	6.6039
17	8.0216	7.7794	7.5488	7.3291	7.1196	6.9198	6.7291
18	8.2014	7.9451	7.7016	7.4700	7.2497	7.0398	6.8399
19	8.3649	8.0952	7.8393	7.5964	7.3658	7.1465	6.9380
20	8.5136	8.2309	7.9633	7.7098	7.4694	7.2414	7.0248
21	8.6487	8.3538	8.0751	7.8115	7.5620	7.3256	7.1016
22	8.7715	8.4649	8.1757	7.9027	7.6446	7.4006	7.1695
23	8.8832	8.5656	8.2664	7.9845	7.7184	7.4672	7.2297
24	8.9847	8.6566	8.3481	8.0578	7.7843	7.5264	7.2829
25	9.0770	8.7390	8.4217	8.1236	7.8431	7.5790	7.3300
26	9.1609	8.8136	8.4881	8.1826	7.8957	7.6258	7.3717
27	9.2372	8.8811	8.5478	8.2355	7.9426	7.6674	7.4086
28	9.3066	8.9422	8.6016	8.2830	7.9844	7.7043	7.4412
29	9.3696	8.9974	8.6501	8.3255	8.0218	7.7372	7.4701
30	9.4269	9.0474	8.6938	8.3637	8.0552	7.7664	7.4957
31	9.4790	9.0927	8.7331	8.3980	8.0850	7.7923	7.5183
32	9.5264	9.1337	8.7686	8.4287	8.1116	7.8154	7.5383
33	9.5694	9.1707	8.8005	8.4562	8.1354	7.8359	7.5560
34	9.6086	9.2043	8.8293	8.4809	8.1566	7.8542	7.5717
35	9.6442	9.2347	8.8552	8.5030	8.1755	7.8704	7.5856
36	9.6765	9.2621	8.8786	8.5229	8.1924	7.8848	7.5979
37	9.7059	9.2870	8.8996	8.5407	8.2075	7.8976	7.6087
38	9.7327	9.3095	8.9186	8.5567	8.2210	7.9089	7.6183
39	9.7570	9.3299	8.9357	8.5710	8.2330	7.9191	7.6268
40	9.7791	9.3483	8.9511	8.5839	8.2438	7.9281	7.6344
41	9.7991	9.3650	8.9649	8.5954	8.2534	7.9361	7.6410
42	9.8174	9.3801	8.9774	8.6058	8.2619	7.9432	7.6469
43	9.8340	9.3937	8.9886	8.6150	8.2696	7.9495	7.6522
44	9.8491	9.4061	8.9988	8.6233	8.2764	7.9551	7.6568
45	9.8628	9.4173	9.0079	8.6308	8.2825	7.9601	7.6609
46	9.8753	9.4274	9.0161	8.6375	8.2880	7.9645	7.6645
47	9.8866	9.4366	9.0235	8.6435	8.2928	7.9685	7.6677
48	9.8969	9.4448	9.0302	8.6489	8.2972	7.9720	7.6705
49	9.9063	9.4524	9.0362	8.6537	8.3010	7.9751	7.6730
50	9.9148	9.4591	9.0417	8.6580	8.3045	7.9778	7.6752

PRESENT VALUE OF ORDINARY ANNUITY (continued)

	Interest Rate						
YEARS	14.0%	15.0%	16.0%	17.0%	18.0%	19.0%	20.0%
1	0.8772	0.8696	0.8621	0.8547	0.8475	0.8403	0.8333
2	1.6467	1.6257	1.6052	1.5852	1.5656	1.5465	1.5278
3	2.3216	2.2832	2.2459	2.2096	2.1743	2.1399	2.1065
4	2.9137	2.8550	2.7982	2.7432	2.6901	2.6386	2.5887
5	3.4331	3.3522	3.2743	3.1993	3.1272	3.0576	2.9906
6	3.8887	3.7845	3.6847	3.5892	3.4976	3.4098	3.3255
7	4.2883	4.1604	4.0386	3.9224	3.8115	3.7057	3.6046
8	4.6389	4.4873	4.3436	4.2072	4.0776	3.9544	3.8372
9	4.9464	4.7716	4.6065	4.4506	4.3030	4.1633	4.0310
10	5.2161	5.0188	4.8332	4.6586	4.4941	4.3389	4.1925
11	5.4527	5.2337	5.0286	4.8364	4.6560	4.4865	4.3271
12	5.6603	5.4206	5.1971	4.9884	4.7932	4.6105	4.4392
13	5.8424	5.5831	5.3423	5.1183	4.9095	4.7147	4.5327
14	6.0021	5.7245	5.4675	5.2293	5.0081	4.8023	4.6106
15	6.1422	5.8474	5.5755	5.3242	5.0916	4.8759	4.6755
16	6.2651	5.9542	5.6685	5.4053	5.1624	4.9377	4.7296
17	6.3729	6.0472	5.7487	5.4746	5.2223	4.9897	4.7746
18	6.4674	6.1280	5.8178	5.5339	5.2732	5.0333	4.8122
19	6.5504	6.1982	5.8775	5.5845	5.3162	5.0700	4.8435
20	6.6231	6.2593	5.9288	5.6278	5.3527	5.1009	4.8696
21	6.6870	6.3125	5.9731	5.6648	5.3837	5.1268	4.8913
22	6.7429	6.3587	6.0113	5.6964	5.4099	5.1486	4.9094
23	6.7921	6.3988	6.0442	5.7234	5.4321	5.1668	4.9245
24	6.8351	6.4338	6.0726	5.7465	5.4509	5.1822	4.9371
25	6.8729	6.4641	6.0971	5.7662	5.4669	5.1951	4.9476
26	6.9061	6.4906	6.1182	5.7831	5.4804	5.2060	4.9563
27	6.9352	6.5135	6.1364	5.7975	5.4919	5.2151	4.9636
28	6.9607	6.5335	6.1520	5.8099	5.5016	5.2228	4.9697
29	6.9830	6.5509	6.1656	5.8204	5.5098	5.2292	4.9747
30	7.0027	6.5660	6.1772	5.8294	5.5168	5.2347	4.9789
31	7.0199	6.5791	6.1872	5.8371	5.5227	5.2392	4.9824
32	7.0350	6.5905	6.1959	5.8437	5.5277	5.2430	4.9854
33	7.0482	6.6005	6.2034	5.8493	5.5320	5.2462	4.9878
34	7.0599	6.6091	6.2098	5.8541	5.5356	5.2489	4.9898
35	7.0700	6.6166	6.2153	5.8582	5.5386	5.2512	4.9915
36	7.0790	6.6231	6.2201	5.8617	5.5412	5.2531	4.9929
37	7.0868	6.6288	6.2242	5.8647	5.5434	5.2547	4.9941
38	7.0937	6.6338	6.2278	5.8673	5.5452	5.2561	4.9951
39	7.0997	6.6380	6.2309	5.8695	5.5468	5.2572	4.9959
40	7.1050	6.6418	6.2335	5.8713	5.5482	5.2582	4.9966
41	7.1097	6.6450	6.2358	5.8729	5.5493	5.2590	4.9972
42	7.1138	6.6478	6.2377	5.8743	5.5502	5.2596	4.9976
43	7.1173	6.6503	6.2394	5.8755	5.5510	5.2602	4.9980
44	7.1205	6.6524	6.2409	5.8765	5.5517	5.2607	4.9984
45	7.1232	6.6543	6.2421	5.8773	5.5523	5.2611	4.9986
46	7.1256	6.6559	6.2432	5.8781	5.5528	5.2614	4.9989
47	7.1277	6.6573	6.2442	5.8787	5.5532	5.2617	4.9991
48	7.1296	6.6585	6.2450	5.8792	5.5536	5.2619	4.9992
49	7.1312	6.6596	6.2457	5.8797	5.5539	5.2621	4.9993
50	7.1327	6.6605	6.2463	5.8801	5.5541	5.2623	4.9995

Appendix D

FUTURE VALUE OF LUMP SUM

	Interest Rate					
YEARS	3.0%	3.5%	4.0%	4.5%	5.0%	5.5%
1	1.0300	1.0350	1.0400	1.0450	1.0500	1.0550
2	1.0609	1.0712	1.0816	1.0920	1.1025	1.1130
3	1.0927	1.1087	1.1249	1.1412	1.1576	1.1742
4	1.1255	1.1475	1.1699	1.1925	1.2155	1.2388
5	1.1593	1.1877	1.2167	1.2462	1.2763	1.3070
6	1.1941	1.2293	1.2653	1.3023	1.3401	1.3788
7	1.2299	1.2723	1.3159	1.3609	1.4071	1.4547
8	1.2668	1.3168	1.3686	1.4221	1.4775	1.5347
9	1.3048	1.3629	1.4233	1.4861	1.5513	1.6191
10	1.3439	1.4106	1.4802	1.5530	1.6289	1.7081
11	1.3842	1.4600	1.5395	1.6229	1.7103	1.8021
12	1.4258	1.5111	1.6010	1.6959	1.7959	1.9012
13	1.4685	1.5640	1.6651	1.7722	1.8856	2.0058
14	1.5126	1.6187	1.7317	1.8519	1.9799	2.1161
15	1.5580	1.6753	1.8009	1.9353	2.0789	2.2325
16	1.6047	1.7340	1.8730	2.0224	2.1829	2.3553
17	1.6528	1.7947	1.9479	2.1134	2.2920	2.4848
18	1.7024	1.8575	2.0258	2.2085	2.4066	2.6215
19	1.7535	1.9225	2.1068	2.3079	2.5270	2.7656
20	1.8061	1.9898	2.1911	2.4117	2.6533	2.9178
21	1.8603	2.0594	2.2788	2.5202	2.7860	3.0782
22	1.9161	2.1315	2.3699	2.6337	2.9253	3.2475
23	1.9736	2.2061	2.4647	2.7522	3.0715	3.4262
24	2.0328	2.2833	2.5633	2.8760	3.2251	3.6146
25	2.0938	2.3632	2.6658	3.0054	3.3864	3.8134
26	2.1566	2.4460	2.7725	3.1407	3.5557	4.0231
27	2.2213	2.5316	2.8834	3.2820	3.7335	4.2444
28	2.2879	2.6202	2.9987	3.4297	3.9201	4.4778
29	2.3566	2.7119	3.1187	3.5840	4.1161	4.7241
30	2.4273	2.8068	3.2434	3.7453	4.3219	4.9840
31	2.5001	2.9050	3.3731	3.9139	4.5380	5.2581
32	2.5751	3.0067	3.5081	4.0900	4.7649	5.5473
33	2.6523	3.1119	3.6484	4.2740	5.0032	5.8524
34	2.7319	3.2209	3.7943	4.4664	5.2533	6.1742
35	2.8139	3.3336	3.9461	4.6673	5.5160	6.5138
36	2.8983	3.4503	4.1039	4.8774	5.7918	6.8721
37	2.9852	3.5710	4.2681	5.0969	6.0814	7.2501
38	3.0748	3.6960	4.4388	5.3262	6.3855	7.6488
39	3.1670	3.8254	4.6164	5.5659	6.7048	8.0695
40	3.2620	3.9593	4.8010	5.8164	7.0400	8.5133
41	3.3599	4.0978	4.9931	6.0781	7.3920	8.9815
42	3.4607	4.2413	5.1928	6.3516	7.7616	9.4755
43	3.5645	4.3897	5.4005	6.6374	8.1497	9.9967
44	3.6715	4.5433	5.6165	6.9361	8.5572	10.5465
45	3.7816	4.7024	5.8412	7.2482	8.9850	11.1266
46	3.8950	4.8669	6.0748	7.5744	9.4343	11.7385
47	4.0119	5.0373	6.3178	7.9153	9.9060	12.3841
48	4.1323	5.2136	6.5705	8.2715	10.4013	13.0653
49	4.2562	5.3961	6.8333	8.6437	10.9213	13.7838
50	4.3839	5.5849	7.1067	9.0326	11.4674	14.5420

FUTURE VALUE OF LUMP SUM (continued)

	Interest Rate					
YEARS	6.0%	6.5%	7.0%	7.5%	8.0%	8.5%
1	1.0600	1.0650	1.0700	1.0750	1.0800	1.0850
2	1.1236	1.1342	1.1449	1.1556	1.1664	1.1772
3	1.1910	1.2079	1.2250	1.2423	1.2597	1.2773
4	1.2625	1.2865	1.3108	1.3355	1.3605	1.3859
5	1.3382	1.3701	1.4026	1.4356	1.4693	1.5037
6	1.4185	1.4591	1.5007	1.5433	1.5869	1.6315
7	1.5036	1.5540	1.6058	1.6590	1.7138	1.7701
8	1.5938	1.6550	1.7182	1.7835	1.8509	1.9206
9	1.6895	1.7626	1.8385	1.9172	1.9990	2.0839
10	1.7908	1.8771	1.9672	2.0610	2.1589	2.2610
11	1.8983	1.9992	2.1049	2.2156	2.3316	2.4532
12	2.0122	2.1291	2.2522	2.3818	2.5182	2.6617
13	2.1329	2.2675	2.4098	2.5604	2.7196	2.8879
14	2.2609	2.4149	2.5785	2.7524	2.9372	3.1334
15	2.3966	2.5718	2.7590	2.9589	3.1722	3.3997
16	2.5404	2.7390	2.9522	3.1808	3.4259	3.6887
17	2.6928	2.9170	3.1588	3.4194	3.7000	4.0023
18	2.8543	3.1067	3.3799	3.6758	3.9960	4.3425
19	3.0256	3.3086	3.6165	3.9515	4.3157	4.7116
20	3.2071	3.5236	3.8697	4.2479	4.6610	5.1120
21	3.3996	3.7527	4.1406	4.5664	5.0338	5.5466
22	3.6035	3.9966	4.4304	4.9089	5.4365	6.0180
23	3.8197	4.2564	4.7405	5.2771	5.8715	6.5296
24	4.0489	4.5331	5.0724	5.6729	6.3412	7.0846
25	4.2919	4.8277	5.4274	6.0983	6.8485	7.6868
26	4.5494	5.1415	5.8074	6.5557	7.3964	8.3401
27	4.8223	5.4757	6.2139	7.0474	7.9881	9.0490
28	5.1117	5.8316	6.6488	7.5759	8.6271	9.8182
29	5.4184	6.2107	7.1143	8.1441	9.3173	10.6528
30	5.7435	6.6144	7.6123	8.7550	10.0627	11.5583
31	6.0881	7.0443	8.1451	9.4116	10.8677	12.5407
32	6.4534	7.5022	8.7153	10.1174	11.7371	13.6067
33	6.8406	7.9898	9.3253	10.8763	12.6760	14.7632
34	7.2510	8.5092	9.9781	11.6920	13.6901	16.0181
35	7.6861	9.0623	10.6766	12.5689	14.7853	17.3796
36	8.1473	9.6513	11.4239	13.5115	15.9682	18.8569
37	8.6361	10.2786	12.2236	14.5249	17.2456	20.4597
38	9.1543	10.9467	13.0793	15.6143	18.6253	22.1988
39	9.7035	11.6583	13.9948	16.7853	20.1153	24.0857
40	10.2857	12.4161	14.9745	18.0442	21.7245	26.1330
41	10.9029	13.2231	16.0227	19.3976	23.4625	28.3543
42	11.5570	14.0826	17.1443	20.8524	25.3395	30.7644
43	12.2505	14.9980	18.3444	22.4163	27.3666	33.3794
44	12.9855	15.9729	19.6285	24.0975	29.5560	36.2167
45	13.7646	17.0111	21.0025	25.9048	31.9204	39.2951
46	14.5905	18.1168	22.4726	27.8477	34.4741	42.6352
47	15.4659	19.2944	24.0457	29.9363	37.2320	46.2592
48	16.3939	20.5485	25.7289	32.1815	40.2106	50.1912
49	17.3775	21.8842	27.5299	34.5951	43.4274	54.4574
50	18.4202	23.3067	29.4570	37.1897	46.9016	59.0863

FUTURE VALUE OF LUMP SUM (continued)

	Interest Rate					
YEARS	9.0%	9.5%	10.0%	10.5%	11.0%	11.5%
1	1.0900	1.0950	1.1000	1.1050	1.1100	1.1150
2	1.1881	1.1990	1.2100	1.2210	1.2321	1.2432
3	1.2950	1.3129	1.3310	1.3492	1.3676	1.3862
4	1.4116	1.4377	1.4641	1.4909	1.5181	1.5456
5	1.5386	1.5742	1.6105	1.6474	1.6851	1.7234
6	1.6771	1.7238	1.7716	1.8204	1.8704	1.9215
7	1.8280	1.8876	1.9487	2.0116	2.0762	2.1425
8	1.9926	2.0669	2.1436	2.2228	2.3045	2.3889
9	2.1719	2.2632	2.3579	2.4562	2.5580	2.6636
10	2.3674	2.4782	2.5937	2.7141	2.8394	2.9699
11	2.5804	2.7137	2.8531	2.9991	3.1518	3.3115
12	2.8127	2.9715	3.1384	3.3140	3.4985	3.6923
13	3.0658	3.2537	3.4523	3.6619	3.8833	4.1169
14	3.3417	3.5629	3.7975	4.0464	4.3104	4.5904
15	3.6425	3.9013	4.1772	4.4713	4.7846	5.1183
16	3.9703	4.2719	4.5950	4.9408	5.3109	5.7069
17	4.3276	4.6778	5.0545	5.4596	5.8951	6.3632
18	4.7171	5.1222	5.5599	6.0328	6.5436	7.0949
19	5.1417	5.6088	6.1159	6.6663	7.2633	7.9108
20	5.6044	6.1416	6.7275	7.3662	8.0623	8.8206
21	6.1088	6.7251	7.4002	8.1397	8.9492	9.8350
22	6.6586	7.3639	8.1403	8.9944	9.9336	10.9660
23	7.2579	8.0635	8.9543	9.9388	11.0263	12.2271
24	7.9111	8.8296	9.8497	10.9823	12.2392	13.6332
25	8.6231	9.6684	10.8347	12.1355	13.5855	15.2010
26	9.3992	10.5869	11.9182	13.4097	15.0799	16.9491
27	10.2451	11.5926	13.1100	14.8177	16.7386	18.8982
28	11.1671	12.6939	14.4210	16.3736	18.5799	21.0715
29	12.1722	13.8998	15.8631	18.0928	20.6237	23.4948
30	13.2677	15.2203	17.4494	19.9926	22.8923	26.1967
31	14.4618	16.6662	19.1943	22.0918	25.4104	29.2093
32	15.7633	18.2495	21.1138	24.4114	28.2056	32.5683
33	17.1820	19.9832	23.2252	26.9746	31.3082	36.3137
34	18.7284	21.8816	25.5477	29.8069	34.7521	40.4898
35	20.4140	23.9604	28.1024	32.9367	38.5749	45.1461
36	22.2512	26.2366	30.9127	36.3950	42.8181	50.3379
37	24.2538	28.7291	34.0039	40.2165	47.5281	56.1268
38	26.4367	31.4584	37.4043	44.4392	52.7562	62.5814
39	28.8160	34.4469	41.1448	49.1054	58.5593	69.7782
40	31.4094	37.7194	45.2593	54.2614	65.0009	77.8027
41	34.2363	41.3027	49.7852	59.9589	72.1510	86.7500
42	37.3175	45.2265	54.7637	66.2545	80.0876	96.7263
43	40.6761	49.5230	60.2401	73.2113	88.8972	107.8498
44	44.3370	54.2277	66.2641	80.8985	98.6759	120.2525
45	48.3273	59.3793	72.8905	89.3928	109.5302	134.0816
46	52.6767	65.0204	80.1795	98.7790	121.5786	149.5009
47	57.4176	71.1973	88.1975	109.1508	134.9522	166.6935
48	62.5852	77.9611	97.0172	120.6117	149.7970	185.8633
49	68.2179	85.3674	106.7190	133.2759	166.2746	207.2376
50	74.3575	93.4773	117.3909	147.2699	184.5648	231.0699

FUTURE VALUE OF LUMP SUM (continued)

	Interest Rate					
YEARS	12.0%	12.5%	13.0%	13.5%	14.0%	14.5%
1	1.1200	1.1250	1.1300	1.1350	1.1400	1.1450
2	1.2544	1.2656	1.2769	1.2882	1.2996	1.3110
3	1.4049	1.4238	1.4429	1.4621	1.4815	1.5011
4	1.5735	1.6018	1.6305	1.6595	1.6890	1.7188
5	1.7623	1.8020	1.8424	1.8836	1.9254	1.9680
6	1.9738	2.0273	2.0820	2.1378	2.1950	2.2534
7	2.2107	2.2807	2.3526	2.4264	2.5023	2.5801
8	2.4760	2.5658	2.6584	2.7540	2.8526	2.9542
9	2.7731	2.8865	3.0040	3.1258	3.2519	3.3826
10	3.1058	3.2473	3.3946	3.5478	3.7072	3.8731
11	3.4785	3.6532	3.8359	4.0267	4.2262	4.4347
12	3.8960	4.1099	4.3345	4.5704	4.8179	5.0777
13	4.3635	4.6236	4.8980	5.1874	5.4924	5.8140
14	4.8871	5.2016	5.5348	5.8877	6.2613	6.6570
15	5.4736	5.8518	6.2543	6.6825	7.1379	7.6222
16	6.1304	6.5833	7.0673	7.5846	8.1372	8.7275
17	6.8660	7.4062	7.9861	8.6085	9.2765	9.9929
18	7.6900	8.3319	9.0243	9.7707	10.5752	11.4419
19	8.6128	9.3734	10.1974	11.0897	12.0557	13.1010
20	9.6463	10.5451	11.5231	12.5869	13.7435	15.0006
21	10.8038	11.8632	13.0211	14.2861	15.6676	17.1757
22	12.1003	13.3461	14.7138	16.2147	17.8610	19.6662
23	13.5523	15.0144	16.6266	18.4037	20.3616	22.5178
24	15.1786	16.8912	18.7881	20.8882	23.2122	25.7829
25	17.0001	19.0026	21.2305	23.7081	26.4619	29.5214
26	19.0401	21.3779	23.9905	26.9087	30.1666	33.8020
27	21.3249	24.0502	27.1093	30.5414	34.3899	38.7033
28	23.8839	27.0564	30.6335	34.6644	39.2045	44.3153
29	26.7499	30.4385	34.6158	39.3441	44.6931	50.7410
30	29.9599	34.2433	39.1159	44.6556	50.9502	58.0985
31	33.5551	38.5237	44.2010	50.6841	58.0832	66.5227
32	37.5817	43.3392	49.9471	57.5264	66.2148	76.1685
33	42.0915	48.7566	56.4402	65.2925	75.4849	87.2130
34	47.1425	54.8512	63.7774	74.1070	86.0528	99.8588
35	52.7996	61.7075	72.0685	84.1115	98.1002	114.3384
36	59.1356	69.4210	81.4374	95.4665	111.8342	130.9174
37	66.2318	78.0986	92.0243	108.3545	127.4910	149.9005
38	74.1797	87.8609	103.9874	122.9823	145.3397	171.6360
39	83.0812	98.8436	117.5058	139.5850	165.6873	196.5233
40	93.0510	111.1990	132.7816	158.4289	188.8835	225.0191
41	104.2171	125.0989	150.0432	179.8168	215.3272	257.6469
42	116.7231	140.7362	169.5488	204.0921	245.4730	295.0057
43	130.7299	158.3283	191.5901	231.6445	279.8392	337.7816
44	146.4175	178.1193	216.4968	262.9165	319.0167	386.7599
45	163.9876	200.3842	244.6414	298.4103	363.6791	442.8401
46	183.6661	225.4322	276.4448	338.6957	414.5941	507.0519
47	205.7061	253.6113	312.3826	384.4196	472.6373	580.5744
48	230.3908	285.3127	352.9923	436.3162	538.8065	664.7577
49	258.0377	320.9768	398.8813	495.2189	614.2395	761.1475
50	289.0022	361.0989	450.7359	562.0735	700.2330	871.5139

FUTURE VALUE OF LUMP SUM (continued)

	Interest Rate					
YEARS	15.0%	16.0%	17.0%	18.0%	19.0%	20.0%
1	1.1500	1.1600	1.1700	1.1800	1.1900	1.2000
2	1.3225	1.3456	1.3689	1.3924	1.4161	1.4400
3	1.5209	1.5609	1.6016	1.6430	1.6852	1.7280
4	1.7490	1.8106	1.8739	1.9388	2.0053	2.0736
5	2.0114	2.1003	2.1924	2.2878	2.3864	2.4883
6	2.3131	2.4364	2.5652	2.6996	2.8398	2.9860
7	2.6600	2.8262	3.0012	3.1855	3.3793	3.5832
8	3.0590	3.2784	3.5115	3.7589	4.0214	4.2998
9	3.5179	3.8030	4.1084	4.4355	4.7854	5.1598
10	4.0456	4.4114	4.8068	5.2338	5.6947	6.1917
11	4.6524	5.1173	5.6240	6.1759	6.7767	7.4301
12	5.3503	5.9360	6.5801	7.2876	8.0642	8.9161
13	6.1528	6.8858	7.6987	8.5994	9.5964	10.6993
14	7.0757	7.9875	9.0075	10.1472	11.4198	12.8392
15	8.1371	9.2655	10.5387	11.9737	13.5895	15.4070
16	9.3576	10.7480	12.3303	14.1290	16.1715	18.4884
17	10.7613	12.4677	14.4265	16.6722	19.2441	22.1861
18	12.3755	14.4625	16.8790	19.6733	22.9005	26.6233
19	14.2318	16.7765	19.7484	23.2144	27.2516	31.9480
20	16.3665	19.4608	23.1056	27.3930	32.4294	38.3376
21	18.8215	22.5745	27.0336	32.3238	38.5910	46.0051
22	21.6447	26.1864	31.6293	38.1421	45.9233	55.2061
23	24.8915	30.3762	37.0062	45.0076	54.6487	66.2474
24	28.6252	35.2364	43.2973	53.1090	65.0320	79.4968
25	32.9190	40.8742	50.6578	62.6686	77.3881	95.3962
26	37.8568	47.4141	59.2697	73.9490	92.0918	114.4755
27	43.5353	55.0004	69.3455	87.2598	109.5893	137.3706
28	50.0656	63.8004	81.1342	102.9666	130.4112	164.8447
29	57.5755	74.0085	94.9271	121.5005	155.1893	197.8136
30	66.2118	85.8499	111.0647	143.3706	184.6753	237.3763
31	76.1435	99.5859	129.9456	169.1774	219.7636	284.8516
32	87.5651	115.5196	152.0364	199.6293	261.5187	341.8219
33	100.6998	134.0027	177.8826	235.5625	311.2073	410.1863
34	115.8048	155.4432	208.1226	277.9638	370.3366	492.2235
35	133.1755	180.3141	243.5035	327.9973	440.7006	590.6682
36	153.1519	209.1643	284.8991	387.0368	524.4337	708.8019
37	176.1246	242.6306	333.3319	456.7034	624.0761	850.5622
38	202.5433	281.4515	389.9983	538.9100	742.6506	1020.6747
39	232.9248	326.4838	456.2980	635.9139	883.7542	1224.8096
40	267.8635	378.7212	533.8687	750.3783	1051.6675	1469.7716
41	308.0431	439.3165	624.6264	885.4464	1251.4843	1763.7259
42	354.2495	509.6072	730.8129	1044.8268	1489.2664	2116.4711
43	407.3870	591.1443	855.0511	1232.8956	1772.2270	2539.7653
44	468.4950	685.7274	1000.4098	1454.8168	2108.9501	3047.7183
45	538.7693	795.4438	1170.4794	1716.6839	2509.6506	3657.2620
46	619.5847	922.7148	1369.4609	2025.6870	2986.4842	4388.7144
47	712.5224	1070.3492	1602.2693	2390.3106	3553.9162	5266.4573
48	819.4007	1241.6051	1874.6550	2820.5665	4229.1603	6319.7487
49	942.3108	1440.2619	2193.3464	3328.2685	5032.7008	7583.6985
50	1083.6574	1670.7038	2566.2153	3927.3569	5988.9139	9100.4382

Appendix E

FUTURE VALUE OF ANNUITY DUE

	Interest Rate					
YEARS	3.0%	3.5%	4.0%	4.5%	5.0%	5.5%
1	1.0300	1.0350	1.0400	1.0450	1.0500	1.0550
2	2.0909	2.1062	2.1216	2.1370	2.1525	2.1680
3	3.1836	3.2149	3.2465	3.2782	3.3101	3.3423
4	4.3091	4.3625	4.4163	4.4707	4.5256	4.5811
5	5.4684	5.5502	5.6330	5.7169	5.8019	5.8881
6	6.6625	6.7794	6.8983	7.0192	7.1420	7.2669
7	7.8923	8.0517	8.2142	8.3800	8.5491	8.7216
8	9.1591	9.3685	9.5828	9.8021	10.0266	10.2563
9	10.4639	10.7314	11.0061	11.2882	11.5779	11.8754
10	11.8078	12.1420	12.4864	12.8412	13.2068	13.5835
11	13.1920	13.6020	14.0258	14.4640	14.9171	15.3856
12	14.6178	15.1130	15.6268	16.1599	16.7130	17.2868
13	16.0863	16.6770	17.2919	17.9321	18.5986	19.2926
14	17.5989	18.2957	19.0236	19.7841	20.5786	21.4087
15	19.1569	19.9710	20.8245	21.7193	22.6575	23.6411
16	20.7616	21.7050	22.6975	23.7417	24.8404	25.9964
17	22.4144	23.4997	24.6454	25.8551	27.1324	28.4812
18	24.1169	25.3572	26.6712	28.0636	29.5390	31.1027
19	25.8704	27.2797	28.7781	30.3714	32.0660	33.8683
20	27.6765	29.2695	30.9692	32.7831	34.7193	36.7861
21	29.5368	31.3289	33.2480	35.3034	37.5052	39.8643
22	31.4529	33.4604	35.6179	37.9370	40.4305	43.1118
23	33.4265	35.6665	38.0826	40.6892	43.5020	46.5380
24	35.4593	37.9499	40.6459	43.5652	46.7271	50.1526
25	37.5530	40.3131	43.3117	46.5706	50.1135	53.9660
26	39.7096	42.7591	46.0842	49.7113	53.6691	57.9891
27	41.9309	45.2906	48.9676	52.9933	57.4026	62.2335
28	44.2189	47.9108	51.9663	56.4230	61.3227	66.7114
29	46.5754	50.6227	55.0849	60.0071	65.4388	71.4355
30	49.0027	53.4295	58.3283	63.7524	69.7608	76.4194
31	51.5028	56.3345	61.7015	67.6662	74.2988	81.6775
32	54.0778	59.3412	65.2095	71.7562	79.0638	87.2248
33	56.7302	62.4532	68.8579	76.0303	84.0670	93.0771
34	59.4621	65.6740	72.6522	80.4966	89.3203	99.2514
35	62.2759	69.0076	76.5983	85.1640	94.8363	105.7652
36	65.1742	72.4579	80.7022	90.0413	100.6281	112.6373
37	68.1594	76.0289	84.9703	95.1382	106.7095	119.8873
38	71.2342	79.7249	89.4091	100.4644	113.0950	127.5361
39	74.4013	83.5503	94.0255	106.0303	119.7998	135.6056
40	77.6633	87.5095	98.8265	111.8467	126.8398	144.1189
41	81.0232	91.6074	103.8196	117.9248	134.2318	153.1005
42	84.4839	95.8486	109.0124	124.2764	141.9933	162.5760
43	88.0484	100.2383	114.4129	130.9138	150.1430	172.5727
44	91.7199	104.7817	120.0294	137.8500	158.7002	183.1192
45	95.5015	109.4840	125.8706	145.0982	167.6852	194.2457
46	99.3965	114.3510	131.9454	152.6726	177.1194	205.9842
47	103.4084	119.3883	138.2632	160.5879	187.0254	218.3684
48	107.5406	124.6018	144.8337	168.8594	197.4267	231.4336
49	111.7969	129.9979	151.6671	177.5030	208.3480	245.2175
50	116.1808	135.5828	158.7738	186.5357	219.8154	259.7594

FUTURE VALUE OF ANNUITY DUE (continued)

	Interest Rate					
YEARS	6.0%	6.5%	7.0%	7.5%	8.0%	8.5%
1	1.0600	1.0650	1.0700	1.0750	1.0800	1.0850
2	2.1836	2.1992	2.2149	2.2306	2.2464	2.2622
3	3.3746	3.4072	3.4399	3.4729	3.5061	3.5395
4	4.6371	4.6936	4.7507	4.8084	4.8666	4.9254
5	5.9753	6.0637	6.1533	6.2440	6.3359	6.4290
6	7.3938	7.5229	7.6540	7.7873	7.9228	8.0605
7	8.8975	9.0769	9.2598	9.4464	9.6366	9.8306
8	10.4913	10.7319	10.9780	11.2298	11.4876	11.7512
9	12.1808	12.4944	12.8164	13.1471	13.4866	13.8351
10	13.9716	14.3716	14.7836	15.2081	15.6455	16.0961
11	15.8699	16.3707	16.8885	17.4237	17.9771	18.5492
12	17.8821	18.4998	19.1406	19.8055	20.4953	21.2109
13	20.0151	20.7673	21.5505	22.3659	23.2149	24.0989
14	22.2760	23.1822	24.1290	25.1184	26.1521	27.2323
15	24.6725	25.7540	26.8881	28.0772	29.3243	30.6320
16	27.2129	28.4930	29.8402	31.2580	32.7502	34.3207
17	29.9057	31.4101	32.9990	34.6774	36.4502	38.3230
18	32.7600	34.5167	36.3790	38.3532	40.4463	42.6654
19	35.7856	37.8253	39.9955	42.3047	44.7620	47.3770
20	38.9927	41.3490	43.8652	46.5525	49.4229	52.4891
21	42.3923	45.1016	48.0057	51.1190	54.4568	58.0356
22	45.9958	49.0982	52.4361	56.0279	59.8933	64.0537
23	49.8156	53.3546	57.1767	61.3050	65.7648	70.5832
24	53.8645	57.8877	62.2490	66.9779	72.1059	77.6678
25	58.1564	62.7154	67.6765	73.0762	78.9544	85.3546
26	62.7058	67.8569	73.4838	79.6319	86.3508	93.6947
27	67.5281	73.3326	79.6977	86.6793	94.3388	102.7437
28	72.6398	79.1642	86.3465	94.2553	102.9659	112.5620
29	78.0582	85.3749	93.4608	102.3994	112.2832	123.2147
30	83.8017	91.9892	101.0730	111.1544	122.3459	134.7730
31	89.8898	99.0335	109.2182	120.5659	133.2135	147.3137
32	96.3432	106.5357	117.9334	130.6834	144.9506	160.9203
33	103.1838	114.5255	127.2588	141.5596	157.6267	175.6836
34	110.4348	123.0347	137.2369	153.2516	171.3168	191.7017
35	118.1209	132.0969	147.9135	165.8205	186.1021	209.0813
36	126.2681	141.7482	159.3374	179.3320	202.0703	227.9382
37	134.9042	152.0269	171.5610	193.8569	219.3159	248.3980
38	144.0585	162.9736	184.6403	209.4712	237.9412	270.5968
39	153.7620	174.6319	198.6351	226.2565	258.0565	294.6825
40	164.0477	187.0480	213.6096	244.3008	279.7810	320.8156
41	174.9505	200.2711	229.6322	263.6983	303.2435	349.1699
42	186.5076	214.3537	246.7765	284.5507	328.5830	379.9343
43	198.7580	229.3517	265.1209	306.9670	355.9496	413.3137
44	211.7435	245.3246	284.7493	331.0645	385.5056	449.5304
45	225.5081	262.3357	305.7518	356.9694	417.4261	488.8255
46	240.0986	280.4525	328.2244	384.8171	451.9002	531.4606
47	255.5645	299.7469	352.2701	414.7533	489.1322	577.7198
48	271.9584	320.2955	377.9990	446.9348	529.3427	627.9110
49	289.3359	342.1797	405.5289	481.5299	572.7702	682.3684
50	307.7561	365.4864	434.9860	518.7197	619.6718	741.4547

FUTURE VALUE OF ANNUITY DUE (continued)

	Interest Rate					
YEARS	9.0%	9.5%	10.0%	10.5%	11.0%	11.5%
1	1.0900	1.0950	1.1000	1.1050	1.1100	1.1150
2	2.2781	2.2940	2.3100	2.3260	2.3421	2.3582
3	3.5731	3.6070	3.6410	3.6753	3.7097	3.7444
4	4.9847	5.0446	5.1051	5.1662	5.2278	5.2900
5	6.5233	6.6189	6.7156	6.8136	6.9129	7.0134
6	8.2004	8.3426	8.4872	8.6340	8.7833	8.9349
7	10.0285	10.2302	10.4359	10.6456	10.8594	11.0774
8	12.0210	12.2971	12.5795	12.8684	13.1640	13.4663
9	14.1929	14.5603	14.9374	15.3246	15.7220	16.1300
10	16.5603	17.0385	17.5312	18.0387	18.5614	19.0999
11	19.1407	19.7522	20.3843	21.0377	21.7132	22.4114
12	21.9534	22.7236	23.5227	24.3517	25.2116	26.1037
13	25.0192	25.9774	26.9750	28.0136	29.0949	30.2207
14	28.3609	29.5402	30.7725	32.0600	33.4054	34.8110
15	32.0034	33.4416	34.9497	36.5313	38.1899	39.9293
16	35.9737	37.7135	39.5447	41.4721	43.5008	45.6362
17	40.3013	42.3913	44.5992	46.9317	49.3959	51.9993
18	45.0185	47.5135	50.1591	52.9645	55.9395	59.0942
19	50.1601	53.1222	56.2750	59.6308	63.2028	67.0051
20	55.7645	59.2638	63.0025	66.9970	71.2651	75.8257
21	61.8733	65.9889	70.4027	75.1367	80.2143	85.6606
22	68.5319	73.3529	78.5430	84.1311	90.1479	96.6266
23	75.7898	81.4164	87.4973	94.0699	101.1742	108.8536
24	83.7009	90.2459	97.3471	105.0522	113.4133	122.4868
25	92.3240	99.9143	108.1818	117.1877	126.9988	137.6878
26	101.7231	110.5012	120.0999	130.5974	142.0786	154.6369
27	111.9682	122.0938	133.2099	145.4151	158.8173	173.5351
28	123.1354	134.7877	147.6309	161.7887	177.3972	194.6067
29	135.3075	148.6875	163.4940	179.8815	198.0209	218.1014
30	148.5752	163.9078	180.9434	199.8741	220.9132	244.2981
31	163.0370	180.5741	200.1378	221.9658	246.3236	273.5074
32	178.8003	198.8236	221.2515	246.3772	274.5292	306.0757
33	195.9823	218.8068	244.4767	273.3518	305.8374	342.3895
34	214.7108	240.6885	270.0244	303.1588	340.5896	382.8792
35	235.1247	264.6489	298.1268	336.0955	379.1644	428.0254
36	257.3759	290.8855	329.0395	372.4905	421.9825	478.3633
37	281.6298	319.6147	363.0434	412.7070	469.5106	534.4900
38	308.0665	351.0731	400.4478	457.1462	522.2667	597.0714
39	336.8824	385.5200	441.5926	506.2516	580.8261	666.8496
40	368.2919	423.2394	486.8518	560.5130	645.8269	744.6523
41	402.5281	464.5421	536.6370	620.4719	717.9779	831.4023
42	439.8457	509.7686	591.4007	686.7264	798.0655	928.1286
43	480.5218	559.2917	651.6408	759.9377	886.9627	1035.9784
44	524.8587	613.5194	717.9048	840.8361	985.6386	1156.2309
45	573.1860	672.8987	790.7953	930.2289	1095.1688	1290.3125
46	625.8628	737.9191	870.9749	1029.0080	1216.7474	1439.8134
47	683.2804	809.1164	959.1723	1138.1588	1351.6996	1606.5069
48	745.8656	887.0775	1056.1896	1258.7705	1501.4965	1792.3702
49	814.0836	972.4448	1162.9085	1392.0464	1667.7712	1999.6078
50	888.4411	1065.9221	1280.2994	1539.3162	1852.3360	2230.6777

FUTURE VALUE OF ANNUITY DUE (continued)

	Interest Rate					
YEARS	12.0%	12.5%	13.0%	13.5%	14.0%	14.5%
1	1.1200	1.1250	1.1300	1.1350	1.1400	1.1450
2	2.3744	2.3906	2.4069	2.4232	2.4396	2.4560
3	3.7793	3.8145	3.8498	3.8854	3.9211	3.9571
4	5.3528	5.4163	5.4803	5.5449	5.6101	5.6759
5	7.1152	7.2183	7.3227	7.4284	7.5355	7.6439
6	9.0890	9.2456	9.4047	9.5663	9.7305	9.8973
7	11.2997	11.5263	11.7573	11.9927	12.2328	12.4774
8	13.7757	14.0921	14.4157	14.7468	15.0853	15.4317
9	16.5487	16.9786	17.4197	17.8726	18.3373	18.8142
10	19.6546	20.2259	20.8143	21.4204	22.0445	22.6873
11	23.1331	23.8791	24.6502	25.4471	26.2707	27.1220
12	27.0291	27.9890	28.9847	30.0175	31.0887	32.1997
13	31.3926	32.6126	33.8827	35.2048	36.5811	38.0136
14	36.2797	37.8142	39.4175	41.0925	42.8424	44.6706
15	41.7533	43.6660	45.6717	47.7750	49.9804	52.2928
16	47.8837	50.2493	52.7391	55.3596	58.1176	61.0203
17	54.7497	57.6554	60.7251	63.9681	67.3941	71.0132
18	62.4397	65.9873	69.7494	73.7388	77.9692	82.4551
19	71.0524	75.3608	79.9468	84.8286	90.0249	95.5561
20	80.6987	85.9058	91.4699	97.4154	103.7684	110.5568
21	91.5026	97.7691	104.4910	111.7015	119.4360	127.7325
22	103.6029	111.1152	119.2048	127.9162	137.2970	147.3987
23	117.1552	126.1296	135.8315	146.3199	157.6586	169.9165
24	132.3339	143.0208	154.6196	167.2081	180.8708	195.6994
25	149.3339	162.0234	175.8501	190.9162	207.3327	225.2208
26	168.3740	183.4013	199.8406	217.8248	237.4993	259.0228
27	189.6989	207.4515	226.9499	248.3662	271.8892	297.7262
28	213.5828	234.5079	257.5834	283.0306	311.0937	342.0415
29	240.3327	264.9464	292.1992	322.3748	355.7868	392.7825
30	270.2926	299.1897	331.3151	367.0303	406.7370	450.8809
31	303.8477	337.7135	375.5161	417.7144	464.8202	517.4037
32	341.4294	381.0526	425.4632	475.2409	531.0350	593.5722
33	383.5210	429.8092	481.9034	540.5334	606.5199	680.7852
34	430.6635	484.6604	545.6808	614.6404	692.5727	780.6440
35	483.4631	546.3679	617.7493	698.7519	790.6729	894.9824
36	542.5987	615.7889	699.1867	794.2184	902.5071	1025.8998
37	608.8305	693.8875	791.2110	902.5729	1029.9981	1175.8003
38	683.0102	781.7485	895.1984	1025.5552	1175.3378	1347.4363
39	766.0914	880.5920	1012.7042	1165.1401	1341.0251	1543.9596
40	859.1424	991.7910	1145.4858	1323.5691	1529.9086	1768.9788
41	963.3595	1116.8899	1295.5289	1503.3859	1745.2358	2026.6257
42	1080.0826	1257.6262	1465.0777	1707.4780	1990.7088	2321.6314
43	1210.8125	1415.9544	1656.6678	1939.1225	2270.5481	2659.4129
44	1357.2300	1594.0737	1873.1646	2202.0391	2589.5648	3046.1728
45	1521.2176	1794.4579	2117.8060	2500.4493	2953.2439	3489.0129
46	1704.8838	2019.8902	2394.2508	2839.1450	3367.8380	3996.0648
47	1910.5898	2273.5015	2706.6334	3223.5646	3840.4753	4576.6391
48	2140.9806	2558.8141	3059.6258	3659.8808	4379.2819	5241.3968
49	2399.0182	2879.7909	3458.5071	4155.0997	4993.5213	6002.5444
50	2688.0204	3240.8898	3909.2430	4717.1731	5693.7543	6874.0583

FUTURE VALUE OF ANNUITY DUE (continued)

	Interest Rate					
YEARS	15.0%	16.0%	17.0%	18.0%	19.0%	20.0%
1	1.1500	1.1600	1.1700	1.1800	1.1900	1.2000
2	2.4725	2.5056	2.5389	2.5724	2.6061	2.6400
3	3.9934	4.0665	4.1405	4.2154	4.2913	4.3680
4	5.7424	5.8771	6.0144	6.1542	6.2966	6.4416
5	7.7537	7.9775	8.2068	8.4420	8.6830	8.9299
6	10.0668	10.4139	10.7720	11.1415	11.5227	11.9159
7	12.7268	13.2401	13.7733	14.3270	14.9020	15.4991
8	15.7858	16.5185	17.2847	18.0859	18.9234	19.7989
9	19.3037	20.3215	21.3931	22.5213	23.7089	24.9587
10	23.3493	24.7329	26.1999	27.7551	29.4035	31.1504
11	28.0017	29.8502	31.8239	33.9311	36.1802	38.5805
12	33.3519	35.7862	38.4040	41.2187	44.2445	47.4966
13	39.5047	42.6720	46.1027	49.8180	53.8409	58.1959
14	46.5804	50.6595	55.1101	59.9653	65.2607	71.0351
15	54.7175	59.9250	65.6488	71.9390	78.8502	86.4421
16	64.0751	70.6730	77.9792	86.0680	95.0218	104.9306
17	74.8364	83.1407	92.4056	102.7403	114.2659	127.1167
18	87.2118	97.6032	109.2846	122.4135	137.1664	153.7400
19	101.4436	114.3797	129.0329	145.6280	164.4180	185.6880
20	117.8101	133.8405	152.1385	173.0210	196.8474	224.0256
21	136.6316	156.4150	179.1721	205.3448	235.4385	270.0307
22	158.2764	182.6014	210.8013	243.4868	281.3618	325.2369
23	183.1678	212.9776	247.8076	288.4945	336.0105	391.4842
24	211.7930	248.2140	291.1049	341.6035	401.0425	470.9811
25	244.7120	289.0883	341.7627	404.2721	478.4306	566.3773
26	282.5688	336.5024	401.0323	478.2211	570.5224	680.8528
27	326.1041	391.5028	470.3778	565.4809	680.1116	818.2233
28	376.1697	455.3032	551.5121	668.4475	810.5228	983.0680
29	433.7451	529.3117	646.4391	789.9480	965.7122	1180.8816
30	499.9569	615.1616	757.5038	933.3186	1150.3875	1418.2579
31	576.1005	714.7475	887.4494	1102.4960	1370.1511	1703.1095
32	663.6655	830.2671	1039.4858	1302.1253	1631.6698	2044.9314
33	764.3654	964.2698	1217.3684	1537.6878	1942.8771	2455.1176
34	880.1702	1119.7130	1425.4910	1815.6516	2313.2137	2947.3411
35	1013.3457	1300.0270	1668.9945	2143.6489	2753.9143	3538.0094
36	1166.4975	1509.1914	1953.8936	2530.6857	3278.3481	4246.8112
37	1342.6222	1751.8220	2287.2255	2987.3891	3902.4242	5097.3735
38	1545.1655	2033.2735	2677.2238	3526.2992	4645.0748	6118.0482
39	1778.0903	2359.7572	3133.5218	4162.2130	5528.8290	7342.8578
40	2045.9539	2738.4784	3667.3906	4912.5914	6580.4965	8812.6294
41	2353.9969	3177.7949	4292.0169	5798.0378	7831.9808	10576.3553
42	2708.2465	3687.4021	5022.8298	6842.8646	9321.2472	12692.8263
43	3115.6334	4278.5465	5877.8809	8075.7603	11093.4741	15232.5916
44	3584.1285	4964.2739	6878.2907	9530.5771	13202.4242	18280.3099
45	4122.8977	5759.7177	8048.7701	11247.2610	15712.0748	21937.5719
46	4742.4824	6682.4326	9418.2310	13272.9480	18698.5590	26326.2863
47	5455.0047	7752.7818	11020.5002	15663.2586	22252.4753	31592.7436
48	6274.4055	8994.3869	12895.1553	18483.8251	26481.6356	37912.4923
49	7216.7163	10434.6488	15088.5017	21812.0937	31514.3363	45496.1908
50	8300.3737	12105.3526	17654.7170	25739.4505	37503.2502	54596.6289

Appendix F

FUTURE VALUE OF ORDINARY ANNUITY

	Interest Rate					
YEARS	3.0%	3.5%	4.0%	4.5%	5.0%	5.5%
1	1.0000	1.0000	1.0000	1.0000	1.0000	1.0000
2	2.0300	2.0350	2.0400	2.0450	2.0500	2.0550
3	3.0909	3.1062	3.1216	3.1370	3.1525	3.1680
4	4.1836	4.2149	4.2465	4.2782	4.3101	4.3423
5	5.3091	5.3625	5.4163	5.4707	5.5256	5.5811
6	6.4684	6.5502	6.6330	6.7169	6.8019	6.8881
7	7.6625	7.7794	7.8983	8.0192	8.1420	8.2669
8	8.8923	9.0517	9.2142	9.3800	9.5491	9.7216
9	10.1591	10.3685	10.5828	10.8021	11.0266	11.2563
10	11.4639	11.7314	12.0061	12.2882	12.5779	12.8754
11	12.8078	13.1420	13.4864	13.8412	14.2068	14.5835
12	14.1920	14.6020	15.0258	15.4640	15.9171	16.3856
13	15.6178	16.1130	16.6268	17.1599	17.7130	18.2868
14	17.0863	17.6770	18.2919	18.9321	19.5986	20.2926
15	18.5989	19.2957	20.0236	20.7841	21.5786	22.4087
16	20.1569	20.9710	21.8245	22.7193	23.6575	24.6411
17	21.7616	22.7050	23.6975	24.7417	25.8404	26.9964
18	23.4144	24.4997	25.6454	26.8551	28.1324	29.4812
19	25.1169	26.3572	27.6712	29.0636	30.5390	32.1027
20	26.8704	28.2797	29.7781	31.3714	33.0660	34.8683
21	28.6765	30.2695	31.9692	33.7831	35.7193	37.7861
22	30.5368	32.3289	34.2480	36.3034	38.5052	40.8643
23	32.4529	34.4604	36.6179	38.9370	41.4305	44.1118
24	34.4265	36.6665	39.0826	41.6892	44.5020	47.5380
25	36.4593	38.9499	41.6459	44.5652	47.7271	51.1526
26	38.5530	41.3131	44.3117	47.5706	51.1135	54.9660
27	40.7096	43.7591	47.0842	50.7113	54.6691	58.9891
28	42.9309	46.2906	49.9676	53.9933	58.4026	63.2335
29	45.2189	48.9108	52.9663	57.4230	62.3227	67.7114
30	47.5754	51.6227	56.0849	61.0071	66.4388	72.4355
31	50.0027	54.4295	59.3283	64.7524	70.7608	77.4194
32	52.5028	57.3345	62.7015	68.6662	75.2988	82.6775
33	55.0778	60.3412	66.2095	72.7562	80.0638	88.2248
34	57.7302	63.4532	69.8579	77.0303	85.0670	94.0771
35	60.4621	66.6740	73.6522	81.4966	90.3203	100.2514
36	63.2759	70.0076	77.5983	86.1640	95.8363	106.7652
37	66.1742	73.4579	81.7022	91.0413	101.6281	113.6373
38	69.1594	77.0289	85.9703	96.1382	107.7095	120.8873
39	72.2342	80.7249	90.4091	101.4644	114.0950	128.5361
40	75.4013	84.5503	95.0255	107.0303	120.7998	136.6056
41	78.6633	88.5095	99.8265	112.8467	127.8398	145.1189
42	82.0232	92.6074	104.8196	118.9248	135.2318	154.1005
43	85.4839	96.8486	110.0124	125.2764	142.9933	163.5760
44	89.0484	101.2383	115.4129	131.9138	151.1430	173.5727
45	92.7199	105.7817	121.0294	138.8500	159.7002	184.1192
46	96.5015	110.4840	126.8706	146.0982	168.6852	195.2457
47	100.3965	115.3510	132.9454	153.6726	178.1194	206.9842
48	104.4084	120.3883	139.2632	161.5879	188.0254	219.3684
49	108.5406	125.6018	145.8337	169.8594	198.4267	232.4336
50	112.7969	130.9979	152.6671	178.5030	209.3480	246.2175

FUTURE VALUE OF ORDINARY ANNUITY (continued)

	Interest Rate					
YEARS	6.0%	6.5%	7.0%	7.5%	8.0%	8.5%
1	1.0000	1.0000	1.0000	1.0000	1.0000	1.0000
2	2.0600	2.0650	2.0700	2.0750	2.0800	2.0850
3	3.1836	3.1992	3.2149	3.2306	3.2464	3.2622
4	4.3746	4.4072	4.4399	4.4729	4.5061	4.5395
5	5.6371	5.6936	5.7507	5.8084	5.8666	5.9254
6	6.9753	7.0637	7.1533	7.2440	7.3359	7.4290
7	8.3938	8.5229	8.6540	8.7873	8.9228	9.0605
8	9.8975	10.0769	10.2598	10.4464	10.6366	10.8306
9	11.4913	11.7319	11.9780	12.2298	12.4876	12.7512
10	13.1808	13.4944	13.8164	14.1471	14.4866	14.8351
11	14.9716	15.3716	15.7836	16.2081	16.6455	17.0961
12	16.8699	17.3707	17.8885	18.4237	18.9771	19.5492
13	18.8821	19.4998	20.1406	20.8055	21.4953	22.2109
14	21.0151	21.7673	22.5505	23.3659	24.2149	25.0989
15	23.2760	24.1822	25.1290	26.1184	27.1521	28.2323
16	25.6725	26.7540	27.8881	29.0772	30.3243	31.6320
17	28.2129	29.4930	30.8402	32.2580	33.7502	35.3207
18	30.9057	32.4101	33.9990	35.6774	37.4502	39.3230
19	33.7600	35.5167	37.3790	39.3532	41.4463	43.6654
20	36.7856	38.8253	40.9955	43.3047	45.7620	48.3770
21	39.9927	42.3490	44.8652	47.5525	50.4229	53.4891
22	43.3923	46.1016	49.0057	52.1190	55.4568	59.0356
23	46.9958	50.0982	53.4361	57.0279	60.8933	65.0537
24	50.8156	54.3546	58.1767	62.3050	66.7648	71.5832
25	54.8645	58.8877	63.2490	67.9779	73.1059	78.6678
26	59.1564	63.7154	68.6765	74.0762	79.9544	86.3546
27	63.7058	68.8569	74.4838	80.6319	87.3508	94.6947
28	68.5281	74.3326	80.6977	87.6793	95.3388	103.7437
29	73.6398	80.1642	87.3465	95.2553	103.9659	113.5620
30	79.0582	86.3749	94.4608	103.3994	113.2832	124.2147
31	84.8017	92.9892	102.0730	112.1544	123.3459	135.7730
32	90.8898	100.0335	110.2182	121.5659	134.2135	148.3137
33	97.3432	107.5357	118.9334	131.6834	145.9506	161.9203
34	104.1838	115.5255	128.2588	142.5596	158.6267	176.6836
35	111.4348	124.0347	138.2369	154.2516	172.3168	192.7017
36	119.1209	133.0969	148.9135	166.8205	187.1021	210.0813
37	127.2681	142.7482	160.3374	180.3320	203.0703	228.9382
38	135.9042	153.0269	172.5610	194.8569	220.3159	249.3980
39	145.0585	163.9736	185.6403	210.4712	238.9412	271.5968
40	154.7620	175.6319	199.6351	227.2565	259.0565	295.6825
41	165.0477	188.0480	214.6096	245.3008	280.7810	321.8156
42	175.9505	201.2711	230.6322	264.6983	304.2435	350.1699
43	187.5076	215.3537	247.7765	285.5507	329.5830	380.9343
44	199.7580	230.3517	266.1209	307.9670	356.9496	414.3137
45	212.7435	246.3246	285.7493	332.0645	386.5056	450.5304
46	226.5081	263.3357	306.7518	357.9694	418.4261	489.8255
47	241.0986	281.4525	329.2244	385.8171	452.9002	532.4606
48	256.5645	300.7469	353.2701	415.7533	490.1322	578.7198
49	272.9584	321.2955	378.9990	447.9348	530.3427	628.9110
50	290.3359	343.1797	406.5289	482.5299	573.7702	683.3684

FUTURE VALUE OF ORDINARY ANNUITY (continued)

	Interest Rate					
YEARS	9.0%	9.5%	10.0%	10.5%	11.0%	11.5%
1	1.0000	1.0000	1.0000	1.0000	1.0000	1.0000
2	2.0900	2.0950	2.1000	2.1050	2.1100	2.1150
3	3.2781	3.2940	3.3100	3.3260	3.3421	3.3582
4	4.5731	4.6070	4.6410	4.6753	4.7097	4.7444
5	5.9847	6.0446	6.1051	6.1662	6.2278	6.2900
6	7.5233	7.6189	7.7156	7.8136	7.9129	8.0134
7	9.2004	9.3426	9.4872	9.6340	9.7833	9.9349
8	11.0285	11.2302	11.4359	11.6456	11.8594	12.0774
9	13.0210	13.2971	13.5795	13.8684	14.1640	14.4663
10	15.1929	15.5603	15.9374	16.3246	16.7220	17.1300
11	17.5603	18.0385	18.5312	19.0387	19.5614	20.0999
12	20.1407	20.7522	21.3843	22.0377	22.7132	23.4114
13	22.9534	23.7236	24.5227	25.3517	26.2116	27.1037
14	26.0192	26.9774	27.9750	29.0136	30.0949	31.2207
15	29.3609	30.5402	31.7725	33.0600	34.4054	35.8110
16	33.0034	34.4416	35.9497	37.5313	39.1899	40.9293
17	36.9737	38.7135	40.5447	42.4721	44.5008	46.6362
18	41.3013	43.3913	45.5992	47.9317	50.3959	52.9993
19	46.0185	48.5135	51.1591	53.9645	56.9395	60.0942
20	51.1601	54.1222	57.2750	60.6308	64.2028	68.0051
21	56.7645	60.2638	64.0025	67.9970	72.2651	76.8257
22	62.8733	66.9889	71.4027	76.1367	81.2143	86.6606
23	69.5319	74.3529	79.5430	85.1311	91.1479	97.6266
24	76.7898	82.4164	88.4973	95.0699	102.1742	109.8536
25	84.7009	91.2459	98.3471	106.0522	114.4133	123.4868
26	93.3240	100.9143	109.1818	118.1877	127.9988	138.6878
27	102.7231	111.5012	121.0999	131.5974	143.0786	155.6369
28	112.9682	123.0938	134.2099	146.4151	159.8173	174.5351
29	124.1354	135.7877	148.6309	162.7887	178.3972	195.6067
30	136.3075	149.6875	164.4940	180.8815	199.0209	219.1014
31	149.5752	164.9078	181.9434	200.8741	221.9132	245.2981
32	164.0370	181.5741	201.1378	222.9658	247.3236	274.5074
33	179.8003	199.8236	222.2515	247.3772	275.5292	307.0757
34	196.9823	219.8068	245.4767	274.3518	306.8374	343.3895
35	215.7108	241.6885	271.0244	304.1588	341.5896	383.8792
36	236.1247	265.6489	299.1268	337.0955	380.1644	429.0254
37	258.3759	291.8855	330.0395	373.4905	422.9825	479.3633
38	282.6298	320.6147	364.0434	413.7070	470.5106	535.4900
39	309.0665	352.0731	401.4478	458.1462	523.2667	598.0714
40	337.8824	386.5200	442.5926	507.2516	581.8261	667.8496
41	369.2919	424.2394	487.8518	561.5130	646.8269	745.6523
42	403.5281	465.5421	537.6370	621.4719	718.9779	832.4023
43	440.8457	510.7686	592.4007	687.7264	799.0655	929.1286
44	481.5218	560.2917	652.6408	760.9377	887.9627	1036.9784
45	525.8587	614.5194	718.9048	841.8361	986.6386	1157.2309
46	574.1860	673.8987	791.7953	931.2289	1096.1688	1291.3125
47	626.8628	738.9191	871.9749	1030.0080	1217.7474	1440.8134
48	684.2804	810.1164	960.1723	1139.1588	1352.6996	1607.5069
49	746.8656	888.0775	1057.1896	1259.7705	1502.4965	1793.3702
50	815.0836	973.4448	1163.9085	1393.0464	1668.7712	2000.6078

FUTURE VALUE OF ORDINARY ANNUITY (continued)

	Interest Rate					
YEARS	12.0%	12.5%	13.0%	13.5%	14.0%	14.5%
1	1.0000	1.0000	1.0000	1.0000	1.0000	1.0000
2	2.1200	2.1250	2.1300	2.1350	2.1400	2.1450
3	3.3744	3.3906	3.4069	3.4232	3.4396	3.4560
4	4.7793	4.8145	4.8498	4.8854	4.9211	4.9571
5	6.3528	6.4163	6.4803	6.5449	6.6101	6.6759
6	8.1152	8.2183	8.3227	8.4284	8.5355	8.6439
7	10.0890	10.2456	10.4047	10.5663	10.7305	10.8973
8	12.2997	12.5263	12.7573	12.9927	13.2328	13.4774
9	14.7757	15.0921	15.4157	15.7468	16.0853	16.4317
10	17.5487	17.9786	18.4197	18.8726	19.3373	19.8142
11	20.6546	21.2259	21.8143	22.4204	23.0445	23.6873
12	24.1331	24.8791	25.6502	26.4471	27.2707	28.1220
13	28.0291	28.9890	29.9847	31.0175	32.0887	33.1997
14	32.3926	33.6126	34.8827	36.2048	37.5811	39.0136
15	37.2797	38.8142	40.4175	42.0925	43.8424	45.6706
16	42.7533	44.6660	46.6717	48.7750	50.9804	53.2928
17	48.8837	51.2493	53.7391	56.3596	59.1176	62.0203
18	55.7497	58.6554	61.7251	64.9681	68.3941	72.0132
19	63.4397	66.9873	70.7494	74.7388	78.9692	83.4551
20	72.0524	76.3608	80.9468	85.8286	91.0249	96.5561
21	81.6987	86.9058	92.4699	98.4154	104.7684	111.5568
22	92.5026	98.7691	105.4910	112.7015	120.4360	128.7325
23	104.6029	112.1152	120.2048	128.9162	138.2970	148.3987
24	118.1552	127.1296	136.8315	147.3199	158.6586	170.9165
25	133.3339	144.0208	155.6196	168.2081	181.8708	196.6994
26	150.3339	163.0234	176.8501	191.9162	208.3327	226.2208
27	169.3740	184.4013	200.8406	218.8248	238.4993	260.0228
28	190.6989	208.4515	227.9499	249.3662	272.8892	298.7262
29	214.5828	235.5079	258.5834	284.0306	312.0937	343.0415
30	241.3327	265.9464	293.1992	323.3748	356.7868	393.7825
31	271.2926	300.1897	332.3151	368.0303	407.7370	451.8809
32	304.8477	338.7135	376.5161	418.7144	465.8202	518.4037
33	342.4294	382.0526	426.4632	476.2409	532.0350	594.5722
34	384.5210	430.8092	482.9034	541.5334	607.5199	681.7852
35	431.6635	485.6604	546.6808	615.6404	693.5727	781.6440
36	484.4631	547.3679	618.7493	699.7519	791.6729	895.9824
37	543.5987	616.7889	700.1867	795.2184	903.5071	1026.8998
38	609.8305	694.8875	792.2110	903.5729	1030.9981	1176.8003
39	684.0102	782.7485	896.1984	1026.5552	1176.3378	1348.4363
40	767.0914	881.5920	1013.7042	1166.1401	1342.0251	1544.9596
41	860.1424	992.7910	1146.4858	1324.5691	1530.9086	1769.9788
42	964.3595	1117.8899	1296.5289	1504.3859	1746.2358	2027.6257
43	1081.0826	1258.6262	1466.0777	1708.4780	1991.7088	2322.6314
44	1211.8125	1416.9544	1657.6678	1940.1225	2271.5481	2660.4129
45	1358.2300	1595.0737	1874.1646	2203.0391	2590.5648	3047.1728
46	1522.2176	1795.4579	2118.8060	2501.4493	2954.2439	3490.0129
47	1705.8838	2020.8902	2395.2508	2840.1450	3368.8380	3997.0648
48	1911.5898	2274.5015	2707.6334	3224.5646	3841.4753	4577.6391
49	2141.9806	2559.8141	3060.6258	3660.8808	4380.2819	5242.3968
50	2400.0182	2880.7909	3459.5071	4156.0997	4994.5213	6003.5444

FUTURE VALUE OF ORDINARY ANNUITY (continued)

	Interest Rate					
YEARS	15.0%	16.0%	17.0%	18.0%	19.0%	20.0%
1	1.0000	1.0000	1.0000	1.0000	1.0000	1.0000
2	2.1500	2.1600	2.1700	2.1800	2.1900	2.2000
3	3.4725	3.5056	3.5389	3.5724	3.6061	3.6400
4	4.9934	5.0665	5.1405	5.2154	5.2913	5.3680
5	6.7424	6.8771	7.0144	7.1542	7.2966	7.4416
6	8.7537	8.9775	9.2068	9.4420	9.6830	9.9299
7	11.0668	11.4139	11.7720	12.1415	12.5227	12.9159
8	13.7268	14.2401	14.7733	15.3270	15.9020	16.4991
9	16.7858	17.5185	18.2847	19.0859	19.9234	20.7989
10	20.3037	21.3215	22.3931	23.5213	24.7089	25.9587
11	24.3493	25.7329	27.1999	28.7551	30.4035	32.1504
12	29.0017	30.8502	32.8239	34.9311	37.1802	39.5805
13	34.3519	36.7862	39.4040	42.2187	45.2445	48.4966
14	40.5047	43.6720	47.1027	50.8180	54.8409	59.1959
15	47.5804	51.6595	56.1101	60.9653	66.2607	72.0351
16	55.7175	60.9250	66.6488	72.9390	79.8502	87.4421
17	65.0751	71.6730	78.9792	87.0680	96.0218	105.9306
18	75.8364	84.1407	93.4056	103.7403	115.2659	128.1167
19	88.2118	98.6032	110.2846	123.4135	138.1664	154.7400
20	102.4436	115.3797	130.0329	146.6280	165.4180	186.6880
21	118.8101	134.8405	153.1385	174.0210	197.8474	225.0256
22	137.6316	157.4150	180.1721	206.3448	236.4385	271.0307
23	159.2764	183.6014	211.8013	244.4868	282.3618	326.2369
24	184.1678	213.9776	248.8076	289.4945	337.0105	392.4842
25	212.7930	249.2140	292.1049	342.6035	402.0425	471.9811
26	245.7120	290.0883	342.7627	405.2721	479.4306	567.3773
27	283.5688	337.5024	402.0323	479.2211	571.5224	681.8528
28	327.1041	392.5028	471.3778	566.4809	681.1116	819.2233
29	377.1697	456.3032	552.5121	669.4475	811.5228	984.0680
30	434.7451	530.3117	647.4391	790.9480	966.7122	1181.8816
31	500.9569	616.1616	758.5038	934.3186	1151.3875	1419.2579
32	577.1005	715.7475	888.4494	1103.4960	1371.1511	1704.1095
33	664.6655	831.2671	1040.4858	1303.1253	1632.6698	2045.9314
34	765.3654	965.2698	1218.3684	1538.6878	1943.8771	2456.1176
35	881.1702	1120.7130	1426.4910	1816.6516	2314.2137	2948.3411
36	1014.3457	1301.0270	1669.9945	2144.6489	2754.9143	3539.0094
37	1167.4975	1510.1914	1954.8936	2531.6857	3279.3481	4247.8112
38	1343.6222	1752.8220	2288.2255	2988.3891	3903.4242	5098.3735
39	1546.1655	2034.2735	2678.2238	3527.2992	4646.0748	6119.0482
40	1779.0903	2360.7572	3134.5218	4163.2130	5529.8290	7343.8578
41	2046.9539	2739.4784	3668.3906	4913.5914	6581.4965	8813.6294
42	2354.9969	3178.7949	4293.0169	5799.0378	7832.9808	10577.3553
43	2709.2465	3688.4021	5023.8298	6843.8646	9322.2472	12693.8263
44	3116.6334	4279.5465	5878.8809	8076.7603	11094.4741	15233.5916
45	3585.1285	4965.2739	6879.2907	9531.5771	13203.4242	18281.3099
46	4123.8977	5760.7177	8049.7701	11248.2610	15713.0748	21938.5719
47	4743.4824	6683.4326	9419.2310	13273.9480	18699.5590	26327.2863
48	5456.0047	7753.7818	11021.5002	15664.2586	22253.4753	31593.7436
49	6275.4055	8995.3869	12896.1553	18484.8251	26482.6356	37913.4923
50	7217.7163	10435.6488	15089.5017	21813.0937	31515.3363	45497.1908

Appendix G

TAX EXEMPT EQUIVALENTS

	Tax Rate								
TAX EXEMPT YIELDS	15%	16%	17%	18%	19%	20%	21%	22%	23%
3.00	3.53	3.57	3.61	3.66	3.70	3.75	3.80	3.85	3.90
3.25	3.82	3.87	3.92	3.96	4.01	4.06	4.11	4.17	4.22
3.50	4.12	4.17	4.22	4.27	4.32	4.38	4.43	4.49	4.55
3.75	4.41	4.46	4.52	4.57	4.63	4.69	4.75	4.81	4.87
4.00	4.71	4.76	4.82	4.88	4.94	5.00	5.06	5.13	5.19
4.25	5.00	5.06	5.12	5.18	5.25	5.31	5.38	5.45	5.52
4.50	5.29	5.36	5.42	5.49	5.56	5.63	5.70	5.77	5.84
4.75	5.59	5.65	5.72	5.79	5.86	5.94	6.01	6.09	6.17
5.00	5.88	5.95	6.02	6.10	6.17	6.25	6.33	6.41	6.49
5.25	6.18	6.25	6.33	6.40	6.48	6.56	6.65	6.73	6.82
5.50	6.47	6.55	6.63	6.71	6.79	6.88	6.96	7.05	7.14
5.75	6.76	6.85	6.93	7.01	7.10	7.19	7.28	7.37	7.47
6.00	7.06	7.14	7.23	7.32	7.41	7.50	7.59	7.69	7.79
6.25	7.35	7.44	7.53	7.62	7.72	7.81	7.91	8.01	8.12
6.50	7.65	7.74	7.83	7.93	8.02	8.13	8.23	8.33	8.44
6.75	7.94	8.04	8.13	8.23	8.33	8.44	8.54	8.65	8.77
7.00	8.24	8.33	8.43	8.54	8.64	8.75	8.86	8.97	9.09
7.25	8.53	8.63	8.73	8.84	8.95	9.06	9.18	9.29	9.42
7.50	8.82	8.93	9.04	9.15	9.26	9.38	9.49	9.62	9.74
7.75	9.12	9.23	9.34	9.45	9.57	9.69	9.81	9.94	10.06
8.00	9.41	9.52	9.64	9.76	9.88	10.00	10.13	10.26	10.39
8.25	9.71	9.82	9.94	10.06	10.19	10.31	10.44	10.58	10.71
8.50	10.00	10.12	10.24	10.37	10.49	10.63	10.76	10.90	11.04
8.75	10.29	10.42	10.54	10.67	10.80	10.94	11.08	11.22	11.36
9.00	10.59	10.71	10.84	10.98	11.11	11.25	11.39	11.54	11.69
9.25	10.88	11.01	11.14	11.28	11.42	11.56	11.71	11.86	12.01
9.50	11.18	11.31	11.45	11.59	11.73	11.88	12.03	12.18	12.34
9.75	11.47	11.61	11.75	11.89	12.04	12.19	12.34	12.50	12.66
10.00	11.76	11.90	12.05	12.20	12.35	12.50	12.66	12.82	12.99
10.25	12.06	12.20	12.35	12.50	12.65	12.81	12.97	13.14	13.31
10.50	12.35	12.50	12.65	12.80	12.96	13.13	13.29	13.46	13.64
10.75	12.65	12.80	12.95	13.11	13.27	13.44	13.61	13.78	13.96
11.00	12.94	13.10	13.25	13.41	13.58	13.75	13.92	14.10	14.29
11.25	13.24	13.39	13.55	13.72	13.89	14.06	14.24	14.42	14.61
11.50	13.53	13.69	13.86	14.02	14.20	14.38	14.56	14.74	14.94
11.75	13.82	13.99	14.16	14.33	14.51	14.69	14.87	15.06	15.26
12.00	14.12	14.29	14.46	14.63	14.81	15.00	15.19	15.38	15.58
12.25	14.41	14.58	14.76	14.94	15.12	15.31	15.51	15.71	15.91
12.50	14.71	14.88	15.06	15.24	15.43	15.63	15.82	16.03	16.23
12.75	15.00	15.18	15.36	15.55	15.74	15.94	16.14	16.35	16.56
13.00	15.29	15.48	15.66	15.85	16.05	16.25	16.46	16.67	16.88
13.25	15.59	15.77	15.96	16.16	16.36	16.56	16.77	16.99	17.21
13.50	15.88	16.07	16.27	16.46	16.67	16.88	17.09	17.31	17.53
13.75	16.18	16.37	16.57	16.77	16.98	17.19	17.41	17.63	17.86
14.00	16.47	16.67	16.87	17.07	17.28	17.50	17.72	17.95	18.18
14.25	16.76	16.96	17.17	17.38	17.59	17.81	18.04	18.27	18.51
14.50	17.06	17.26	17.47	17.68	17.90	18.13	18.35	18.59	18.83
14.75	17.35	17.56	17.77	17.99	18.21	18.44	18.67	18.91	19.16
15.00	17.65	17.86	18.07	18.29	18.52	18.75	18.99	19.23	19.48

TAX EXEMPT EQUIVALENTS (continued)

TAX EXEMPT YIELDS	Tax Rate 24%	25%	26%	27%	28%	29%	30%	31%	32%
3.00	3.95	4.00	4.05	4.11	4.17	4.23	4.29	4.35	4.41
3.25	4.28	4.33	4.39	4.45	4.51	4.58	4.64	4.71	4.78
3.50	4.61	4.67	4.73	4.79	4.86	4.93	5.00	5.07	5.15
3.75	4.93	5.00	5.07	5.14	5.21	5.28	5.36	5.43	5.51
4.00	5.26	5.33	5.41	5.48	5.56	5.63	5.71	5.80	5.88
4.25	5.59	5.67	5.74	5.82	5.90	5.99	6.07	6.16	6.25
4.50	5.92	6.00	6.08	6.16	6.25	6.34	6.43	6.52	6.62
4.75	6.25	6.33	6.42	6.51	6.60	6.69	6.79	6.88	6.99
5.00	6.58	6.67	6.76	6.85	6.94	7.04	7.14	7.25	7.35
5.25	6.91	7.00	7.09	7.19	7.29	7.39	7.50	7.61	7.72
5.50	7.24	7.33	7.43	7.53	7.64	7.75	7.86	7.97	8.09
5.75	7.57	7.67	7.77	7.88	7.99	8.10	8.21	8.33	8.46
6.00	7.89	8.00	8.11	8.22	8.33	8.45	8.57	8.70	8.82
6.25	8.22	8.33	8.45	8.56	8.68	8.80	8.93	9.06	9.19
6.50	8.55	8.67	8.78	8.90	9.03	9.15	9.29	9.42	9.56
6.75	8.88	9.00	9.12	9.25	9.38	9.51	9.64	9.78	9.93
7.00	9.21	9.33	9.46	9.59	9.72	9.86	10.00	10.14	10.29
7.25	9.54	9.67	9.80	9.93	10.07	10.21	10.36	10.51	10.66
7.50	9.87	10.00	10.14	10.27	10.42	10.56	10.71	10.87	11.03
7.75	10.20	10.33	10.47	10.62	10.76	10.92	11.07	11.23	11.40
8.00	10.53	10.67	10.81	10.96	11.11	11.27	11.43	11.59	11.76
8.25	10.86	11.00	11.15	11.30	11.46	11.62	11.79	11.96	12.13
8.50	11.18	11.33	11.49	11.64	11.81	11.97	12.14	12.32	12.50
8.75	11.51	11.67	11.82	11.99	12.15	12.32	12.50	12.68	12.87
9.00	11.84	12.00	12.16	12.33	12.50	12.68	12.86	13.04	13.24
9.25	12.17	12.33	12.50	12.67	12.85	13.03	13.21	13.41	13.60
9.50	12.50	12.67	12.84	13.01	13.19	13.38	13.57	13.77	13.97
9.75	12.83	13.00	13.18	13.36	13.54	13.73	13.93	14.13	14.34
10.00	13.16	13.33	13.51	13.70	13.89	14.08	14.29	14.49	14.71
10.25	13.49	13.67	13.85	14.04	14.24	14.44	14.64	14.86	15.07
10.50	13.82	14.00	14.19	14.38	14.58	14.79	15.00	15.22	15.44
10.75	14.14	14.33	14.53	14.73	14.93	15.14	15.36	15.58	15.81
11.00	14.47	14.67	14.86	15.07	15.28	15.49	15.71	15.94	16.18
11.25	14.80	15.00	15.20	15.41	15.63	15.85	16.07	16.30	16.54
11.50	15.13	15.33	15.54	15.75	15.97	16.20	16.43	16.67	16.91
11.75	15.46	15.67	15.88	16.10	16.32	16.55	16.79	17.03	17.28
12.00	15.79	16.00	16.22	16.44	16.67	16.90	17.14	17.39	17.65
12.25	16.12	16.33	16.55	16.78	17.01	17.25	17.50	17.75	18.01
12.50	16.45	16.67	16.89	17.12	17.36	17.61	17.86	18.12	18.38
12.75	16.78	17.00	17.23	17.47	17.71	17.96	18.21	18.48	18.75
13.00	17.11	17.33	17.57	17.81	18.06	18.31	18.57	18.84	19.12
13.25	17.43	17.67	17.91	18.15	18.40	18.66	18.93	19.20	19.49
13.50	17.76	18.00	18.24	18.49	18.75	19.01	19.29	19.57	19.85
13.75	18.09	18.33	18.58	18.84	19.10	19.37	19.64	19.93	20.22
14.00	18.42	18.67	18.92	19.18	19.44	19.72	20.00	20.29	20.59
14.25	18.75	19.00	19.26	19.52	19.79	20.07	20.36	20.65	20.96
14.50	19.08	19.33	19.59	19.86	20.14	20.42	20.71	21.01	21.32
14.75	19.41	19.67	19.93	20.21	20.49	20.77	21.07	21.38	21.69
15.00	19.74	20.00	20.27	20.55	20.83	21.13	21.43	21.74	22.06

TAX EXEMPT EQUIVALENTS (continued)

TAX EXEMPT YIELDS	Tax Rate 33%	34%	35%	36%	37%	38%	39%	40%	41%
3.00	4.48	4.55	4.62	4.69	4.76	4.84	4.92	5.00	5.08
3.25	4.85	4.92	5.00	5.08	5.16	5.24	5.33	5.42	5.51
3.50	5.22	5.30	5.38	5.47	5.56	5.65	5.74	5.83	5.93
3.75	5.60	5.68	5.77	5.86	5.95	6.05	6.15	6.25	6.36
4.00	5.97	6.06	6.15	6.25	6.35	6.45	6.56	6.67	6.78
4.25	6.34	6.44	6.54	6.64	6.75	6.85	6.97	7.08	7.20
4.50	6.72	6.82	6.92	7.03	7.14	7.26	7.38	7.50	7.63
4.75	7.09	7.20	7.31	7.42	7.54	7.66	7.79	7.92	8.05
5.00	7.46	7.58	7.69	7.81	7.94	8.06	8.20	8.33	8.47
5.25	7.84	7.95	8.08	8.20	8.33	8.47	8.61	8.75	8.90
5.50	8.21	8.33	8.46	8.59	8.73	8.87	9.02	9.17	9.32
5.75	8.58	8.71	8.85	8.98	9.13	9.27	9.43	9.58	9.75
6.00	8.96	9.09	9.23	9.38	9.52	9.68	9.84	10.00	10.17
6.25	9.33	9.47	9.62	9.77	9.92	10.08	10.25	10.42	10.59
6.50	9.70	9.85	10.00	10.16	10.32	10.48	10.66	10.83	11.02
6.75	10.07	10.23	10.38	10.55	10.71	10.89	11.07	11.25	11.44
7.00	10.45	10.61	10.77	10.94	11.11	11.29	11.48	11.67	11.86
7.25	10.82	10.98	11.15	11.33	11.51	11.69	11.89	12.08	12.29
7.50	11.19	11.36	11.54	11.72	11.90	12.10	12.30	12.50	12.71
7.75	11.57	11.74	11.92	12.11	12.30	12.50	12.70	12.92	13.14
8.00	11.94	12.12	12.31	12.50	12.70	12.90	13.11	13.33	13.56
8.25	12.31	12.50	12.69	12.89	13.10	13.31	13.52	13.75	13.98
8.50	12.69	12.88	13.08	13.28	13.49	13.71	13.93	14.17	14.41
8.75	13.06	13.26	13.46	13.67	13.89	14.11	14.34	14.58	14.83
9.00	13.43	13.64	13.85	14.06	14.29	14.52	14.75	15.00	15.25
9.25	13.81	14.02	14.23	14.45	14.68	14.92	15.16	15.42	15.68
9.50	14.18	14.39	14.62	14.84	15.08	15.32	15.57	15.83	16.10
9.75	14.55	14.77	15.00	15.23	15.48	15.73	15.98	16.25	16.53
10.00	14.93	15.15	15.38	15.63	15.87	16.13	16.39	16.67	16.95
10.25	15.30	15.53	15.77	16.02	16.27	16.53	16.80	17.08	17.37
10.50	15.67	15.91	16.15	16.41	16.67	16.94	17.21	17.50	17.80
10.75	16.04	16.29	16.54	16.80	17.06	17.34	17.62	17.92	18.22
11.00	16.42	16.67	16.92	17.19	17.46	17.74	18.03	18.33	18.64
11.25	16.79	17.05	17.31	17.58	17.86	18.15	18.44	18.75	19.07
11.50	17.16	17.42	17.69	17.97	18.25	18.55	18.85	19.17	19.49
11.75	17.54	17.80	18.08	18.36	18.65	18.95	19.26	19.58	19.92
12.00	17.91	18.18	18.46	18.75	19.05	19.35	19.67	20.00	20.34
12.25	18.28	18.56	18.85	19.14	19.44	19.76	20.08	20.42	20.76
12.50	18.66	18.94	19.23	19.53	19.84	20.16	20.49	20.83	21.19
12.75	19.03	19.32	19.62	19.92	20.24	20.56	20.90	21.25	21.61
13.00	19.40	19.70	20.00	20.31	20.63	20.97	21.31	21.67	22.03
13.25	19.78	20.08	20.38	20.70	21.03	21.37	21.72	22.08	22.46
13.50	20.15	20.45	20.77	21.09	21.43	21.77	22.13	22.50	22.88
13.75	20.52	20.83	21.15	21.48	21.83	22.18	22.54	22.92	23.31
14.00	20.90	21.21	21.54	21.88	22.22	22.58	22.95	23.33	23.73
14.25	21.27	21.59	21.92	22.27	22.62	22.98	23.36	23.75	24.15
14.50	21.64	21.97	22.31	22.66	23.02	23.39	23.77	24.17	24.58
14.75	22.01	22.35	22.69	23.05	23.41	23.79	24.18	24.58	25.00
15.00	22.39	22.73	23.08	23.44	23.81	24.19	24.59	25.00	25.42

TAX EXEMPT EQUIVALENTS (continued)

	Tax Rate								
TAX EXEMPT YIELDS	42%	43%	44%	45%	46%	47%	48%	49%	50%
3.00	5.17	5.26	5.36	5.45	5.56	5.66	5.77	5.88	6.00
3.25	5.60	5.70	5.80	5.91	6.02	6.13	6.25	6.37	6.50
3.50	6.03	6.14	6.25	6.36	6.48	6.60	6.73	6.86	7.00
3.75	6.47	6.58	6.70	6.82	6.94	7.08	7.21	7.35	7.50
4.00	6.90	7.02	7.14	7.27	7.41	7.55	7.69	7.84	8.00
4.25	7.33	7.46	7.59	7.73	7.87	8.02	8.17	8.33	8.50
4.50	7.76	7.89	8.04	8.18	8.33	8.49	8.65	8.82	9.00
4.75	8.19	8.33	8.48	8.64	8.80	8.96	9.13	9.31	9.50
5.00	8.62	8.77	8.93	9.09	9.26	9.43	9.62	9.80	10.00
5.25	9.05	9.21	9.38	9.55	9.72	9.91	10.10	10.29	10.50
5.50	9.48	9.65	9.82	10.00	10.19	10.38	10.58	10.78	11.00
5.75	9.91	10.09	10.27	10.45	10.65	10.85	11.06	11.27	11.50
6.00	10.34	10.53	10.71	10.91	11.11	11.32	11.54	11.76	12.00
6.25	10.78	10.96	11.16	11.36	11.57	11.79	12.02	12.25	12.50
6.50	11.21	11.40	11.61	11.82	12.04	12.26	12.50	12.75	13.00
6.75	11.64	11.84	12.05	12.27	12.50	12.74	12.98	13.24	13.50
7.00	12.07	12.28	12.50	12.73	12.96	13.21	13.46	13.73	14.00
7.25	12.50	12.72	12.95	13.18	13.43	13.68	13.94	14.22	14.50
7.50	12.93	13.16	13.39	13.64	13.89	14.15	14.42	14.71	15.00
7.75	13.36	13.60	13.84	14.09	14.35	14.62	14.90	15.20	15.50
8.00	13.79	14.04	14.29	14.55	14.81	15.09	15.38	15.69	16.00
8.25	14.22	14.47	14.73	15.00	15.28	15.57	15.87	16.18	16.50
8.50	14.66	14.91	15.18	15.45	15.74	16.04	16.35	16.67	17.00
8.75	15.09	15.35	15.63	15.91	16.20	16.51	16.83	17.16	17.50
9.00	15.52	15.79	16.07	16.36	16.67	16.98	17.31	17.65	18.00
9.25	15.95	16.23	16.52	16.82	17.13	17.45	17.79	18.14	18.50
9.50	16.38	16.67	16.96	17.27	17.59	17.92	18.27	18.63	19.00
9.75	16.81	17.11	17.41	17.73	18.06	18.40	18.75	19.12	19.50
10.00	17.24	17.54	17.86	18.18	18.52	18.87	19.23	19.61	20.00
10.25	17.67	17.98	18.30	18.64	18.98	19.34	19.71	20.10	20.50
10.50	18.10	18.42	18.75	19.09	19.44	19.81	20.19	20.59	21.00
10.75	18.53	18.86	19.20	19.55	19.91	20.28	20.67	21.08	21.50
11.00	18.97	19.30	19.64	20.00	20.37	20.75	21.15	21.57	22.00
11.25	19.40	19.74	20.09	20.45	20.83	21.23	21.63	22.06	22.50
11.50	19.83	20.18	20.54	20.91	21.30	21.70	22.12	22.55	23.00
11.75	20.26	20.61	20.98	21.36	21.76	22.17	22.60	23.04	23.50
12.00	20.69	21.05	21.43	21.82	22.22	22.64	23.08	23.53	24.00
12.25	21.12	21.49	21.88	22.27	22.69	23.11	23.56	24.02	24.50
12.50	21.55	21.93	22.32	22.73	23.15	23.58	24.04	24.51	25.00
12.75	21.98	22.37	22.77	23.18	23.61	24.06	24.52	25.00	25.50
13.00	22.41	22.81	23.21	23.64	24.07	24.53	25.00	25.49	26.00
13.25	22.84	23.25	23.66	24.09	24.54	25.00	25.48	25.98	26.50
13.50	23.28	23.68	24.11	24.55	25.00	25.47	25.96	26.47	27.00
13.75	23.71	24.12	24.55	25.00	25.46	25.94	26.44	26.96	27.50
14.00	24.14	24.56	25.00	25.45	25.93	26.42	26.92	27.45	28.00
14.25	24.57	25.00	25.45	25.91	26.39	26.89	27.40	27.94	28.50
14.50	25.00	25.44	25.89	26.36	26.85	27.36	27.88	28.43	29.00
14.75	25.43	25.88	26.34	26.82	27.31	27.83	28.37	28.92	29.50
15.00	25.86	26.32	26.79	27.27	27.78	28.30	28.85	29.41	30.00

Appendix H

USEFUL FINANCIAL WEB SITES

AMERICAN DEPOSITARY RECEIPTS
www.adr.com

AUTOMOBILES
www.autos.msn.com

BETTER BUSINESS BUREAU
www.bbb.org

BONDS
www.bondsonline.com
www.convertbond.com
www.investinginbonds.com
www.publicdebt.treas.gov

BROKERS (ON-LINE)
www.tdameritrade.com
www.etrade.com
www.schwab.com

CHARITABLE GIVING
www.bigwriteoff.com
www.charitywatch.org
www.leimberg.com
www.leimbergservices.com
www.pgdc.com
www.taxwisegiving.com

CHARTING (STOCKS)
www.bigcharts.marketwatch.com
www.stockcharts.com

COLLEGE FUNDING
www.collegesavings.org
www.savingforcollege.com

COMMON STOCKS
www.bloomberg.com
www.bulldogresearch.com
http://finance.yahoo.com
www.fool.com
www.starmine.com
www.stocktrak.com

DIVIDENDS
www.dripinvestor.com

DIVORCE INFORMATION
www.divorcesource.com
www.equalityinmarriage.org

EARNINGS REPORTS
www.bestcalls.com
www.earningswhispers.com

ECONOMIC INFORMATION (GENERAL)
www.census.gov
www.ceoexpress.com
www.economy.com/dismal
www.economy.com
www.economy.com/freelunch/default.asp

EMPLOYEE BENEFITS
www.benefitslink.com
www.ebri.org

ESTATE PLANNING
www.estateplanninglinks.com
www.leimberg.com
www.ria.thomson.com/estore/detail.aspx?ID=ETPL
www.trustsandestates.com

FINANCIAL PLANNING
www.financial-planning.com
www.investmentadvisor.com
www.investmentnews.com
www.fpanet.org/journal
www.moneycentral.msn.com

FOREIGN EXCHANGE (CURRENCY)
www.forexnews.com
www.oanda.com

GOVERNMENT DATA
www.congress.gov
www.federalreserve.gov
www.fedstats.gov

INDIVIDUAL RETIREMENT ACCOUNTS (IRAs)
www.irahelp.com

INSIDER TRADING
www.quicken.com/investments/insider
www.hoovers.com

INSURANCE
www.insurance.com
www.insurancenewsnet.com
www.insweb.com

INTEREST RATES
www.bankrate.com
www.money-rates.com

INTERNAL REVENUE SERVICE (IRS)
www.irs.gov
www.irs.gov/formspubs

INVESTING (GENERAL)
www.aaii.com
www.bloomberg.com
www.hoovers.com
www.invest-faq.com
www.investorwords.com
www.IPOfinancial.com
www.ipolockup.com
www.marketguide.com
www.multexinvestor.com
www.riskgrades.com
www.siliconinvestor.com
www.standardpoor.com

INVESTMENT CLUBS
www.iclub.com

MAGAZINES (FINANCIAL)
www.businessweek.com
www.businessweek.com/investor
www.forbes.com
www.fortune.com
www.fsb.com
www.money.cnn.com

MEDICARE
www.medicare.gov

MORTGAGE DATA
www.eloan.com
www.freddiemac.com
www.lendingtree.com

MUTUAL FUNDS
www.ici.org
www.mfea.com
www.morningstar.com

NEWSPAPERS (FINANCIAL)
www.ft.com
www.wsj.com

NEWSPAPERS (GENERAL)
www.iht.com
www.investors.com
www.nytimes.com
www.publist.com

OPTIONS
www.cboe.com
www.optionscentral.com
www.888options.com

PENSIONS
www.dol.gov/dol/topic/retirement
www.ebri.org
www.pbgc.gov/search
www.plansponsor.com

RETIREMENT PLANNING
www.aarp.org

SECURITIES REGULATION
www.sec.gov

SOCIAL SECURITY
www.medicare.gov
www.ssa.gov
www.ssa.gov/mystatement

STOCK EXCHANGES
www.amex.com
www.nasdaq.com
www.nyse.com
www.nysedata.com/OpenBook

TAXES
www.eftps.gov

U. S. TREASURY
www.treasurydirect.gov

INDEX

A

B

C

D

L

M

N

O

P

Q

R

S

T